Simon Ingram was b[...] published journalist, he [...] the *Independent* and the E[...] [...]itor of *Trail* magazine for nine years and is a contributor to the Country Diary, the *Guardian's* century-old natural history column. He is the author of *Between the Sunset and the Sea* (2015) and lives in Stamford, Lincolnshire.

Praise for *The Black Ridge*:

'Thrilling'   *Guardian*

'Delicious ... Evokes the weather and the rocks and the people of the Skye I know better than anything else I've encountered.'   Neil Gaiman

'The depth of research is extensive, yet his writing is so poetic that the pages fly by.'   Rosie Morton, *Scottish Field*

'A hillwalker's paean to the Cuillin that blends scenery, folklore and wonder ... The Skye Cuillin has obviously captured Simon Ingram's heart and that fact resounds from every page ... [*The Black Ridge*] will undoubtedly become a classic narrative of this scenically magnificent, legend-rich and geologically unique part of Scotland.'

Cameron McNeish, *The Herald*

'[Ingram's] Cuillin journey makes riveting reading ... It's unputdown-able.'   Maggie Fergusson, *Spectator*

Praise for Simon Ingram's *Between the Sunset and the Sea*:

'Wonderful'   Clare Balding

'This is the work of a polymath mountain-lover with a backpack-sized curiosity and the stamina to take notes when most of us would be gasping for breath. It's not just painstakingly researched, it's also well written ... An intrepid, original book'   *The Times*

'A welcome and refreshing addition to the increasingly crowded field of New Nature Writing. Warm, poetic and humane yet shivery with the vertiginous thrill and allure that mountains cast over some of us.'

Stuart Maconie

'Almost Tolkienian in delivery ... *Between the Sunset and the Sea* turns mountain climbs into a form of poetry.'   BBC *Countryfile*

'Rich, thought-provoking and lyrical'   *Scotland Outdoors*

'Accessible and refreshing ... Written in an engaging style that quickly takes the reader into its confidence. The endearing confession of an authentic mountain addict.'   *Country Walking*

'Makes for an engrossing read ... A book of considerable depth, full of fascinating and well-researched detail'   *Walk* magazine

THE BLACK RIDGE

Amongst the Cuillin of Skye

SIMON INGRAM

WILLIAM COLLINS

William Collins
An imprint of HarperCollins*Publishers*
1 London Bridge Street
London SE1 9GF

WilliamCollinsBooks.com

HarperCollins*Publishers*
1st Floor, Watermarque Building, Ringsend Road
Dublin 4, Ireland

First published in Great Britain by William Collins in 2021

This William Collins paperback edition published in 2022

2023 2025 2024 2022

2 4 6 8 10 9 7 5 3 1

Excerpts from 'An t-Eilean [The Island]' (page 14) and 'An Cuilithionn [The Cuillin]'
(pages 22, 285 and 487), from *An Cuilithionn 1939: The Cuillin 1939 and Unpublished Poems* by
Sorley Maclean are reprinted by kind permission of Carcanet Press, Manchester, UK
Excerpt from 'The Cuillin Hills' (page 487), from *Selected Poems* by Andrew Young is reprinted
by kind permission of Carcanet Press, Manchester, UK

All photographs © Simon Ingram
Illustration credits:
Page 124 Eye sketch of the Cuillin as drawn by James Forbes
Page 142 'Loch Coruisk, Skye' (1831) by Joseph Mallord William Turner
Page 142 Samuel Johnson, as painted by Sir Joshua Reynolds, Everett Collection, Shutterstock
Page 168 maps reproduced from the National Library of Scotland under the creative commons license

The author would like to acknowledge the inspirational wood engravings of Paul L. Kershaw, as
photographed in the image on page 8 and the artwork of Alastair Niven, in the image on page 338
Simon Ingram asserts the moral right to be identified as the author of this work
in accordance with the Copyright, Designs and Patents Act 1988

A catalogue record for this book is available from the British Library

ISBN 978-0-00-822626-8

Typeset in Vendetta by Palimpsest Book Production Ltd, Falkirk, Stirlingshire
Printed and Bound in the UK using 100% Renewable Electricity at CPI Group (UK) Ltd

MIX
Paper from
responsible sources

FSC™ C007454

For Rachel, Evelyn and Eliott.

May you find the joy and wonder in the world that I have found in you.

The Cuillin /*An Culthionn*
    from
kjølen (Norse) – rocky height
    or
Cúchulainn (Gaelic) – legendary warrior
    or
Cuil Fhinn (Gaelic) – hiding place of Fingal (Finn MacCool/
    Fionn mac Cumhaill)
    or
cuilionn (Gaelic) – sea holly
    or
coolin (Welsh) – worthless

Nobody knows for sure where the name comes from; Go,
then choose one you like.

Contents

First Sight   1

PART ONE – ASCENT

Introduction   9

1   Fire   35

2   Rock   71

3   Blood   109

4   Ice   125

5   Mist   143

6   Labyrinth   169

PART TWO – TRAVERSE

7   Gap   203

8   Night   233

9   Summit   257

10   Pinnacle   299

11   Edge   339

12   Tower   367

13   Executioner   407

PART THREE – DESCENT

14   Shadow   443

15   Treasure   481

16   End   509

Last Look   535

Acknowledgements   539

Bibliography   543

Index   547

First Sight

You are standing in the sky. Beneath your feet is a circle of rock, broken and agleam with rain. That's all you see. The rest is just whips of fine-grained cloud, riding a wind that comes from everywhere. Ahead, you sense space: a coldness, where the ground drops away into an abyss you can't look into, but is just there, looking back.

It's a mountaintop. It could be anywhere in the world, but it's not; it's this one, right here. Beyond that cloud is whatever you came for. Why you're here, in this wild place. It took days of travel. Hours of walking. A night, somewhere back there. The cycle of sunset and sunrise completing the detachment from the world you know best, and a reacquaintance with one you know less, but whose simplicity you crave. Then this climb into the sky, and here you are. Looking for something. Something just there, beyond the cloud.

Your mind tries to reach beyond, scripting visions onto the dead flat before you. Your other senses grasp. They find smells, and tastes. The marine sting of salt. The salt of sweat. Rain running over your lips, making them itch and curl. The warm fog of your own body, the heat of hard work. Your neutered sight is like a box around you, and makes even distant sounds feel close and crisp. The call of a storm petrel, echoing off a thousand walls. Here and there off in the grey, the wind finds a gully or crack, catching your ear like murmurs from the corner of a dark room. But the loudest sounds are you. Your breath, your heartbeat fat in your ears, the thin crackle of rain on your jacket.

d then the scene changes. The cloud begins to draw back, revealing
es. Shadows at first, a glimmer of dark, an angle, the impression of
something, real or imagined. Something colossal, immovable. Ancient. Of
the earth.

Then you see it: a mountain ridge, high above and wrapped around you.
Earth, raised up, cracked and twisted, in discord, striking the sky as a line
of unruly barbs. You have to raise your head to see the top, and turn it to
see its edges. First sight: that visual handshake.

A wilderness of rock. Your eyes set forth into it, and become lost
among its shapes. Your mind follows, wandering the fishbone ridges,
the skull-eye caves, deep lines and the high, sharp peaks. A lake, far
below, down in cold shadow, its waters still as a photograph. The sea,
on the edges of it all.

It's time-worn, this thing – but not by any measure the living can relate
to. The humans that have seen it have seen it the same, other than the fine
details. You look upon this landscape, this sink of history, of memory, in
this time, now. From every time upon everyone, it has looked impassively
back. Glistened by rain. Clad in white. Scorched by sun. Overhung by stars
and black as night, or slid between infinities of richest colour, a borderline
between the sunset and the sea.

The cloud cracks. Narrow light falls on the mountain, in bursts of gold.
They chase over the ridge in stripes of brilliance, leaping vertical rock,
vaulting dark gullies and buttresses, moving with the sky's organic drift
over savage ground, like bright ribbons on the wind.

This is the landscape of fable. You've always known it: that malevolent
rampart, those dark materials, the ceaseless boil of cloud over mountain,
terrible and alluring, a smile of broken teeth. It's a signature of danger, or
adventure, or wonder, all three.

What are you looking for in there? Are you a mountaineer, tracing the
walls and ribs and sinks of the mountainside for the way that is the easiest,
or hardest? Perhaps you are the painter, letting the lines of the landscape
and the shadowplay take fantastical forms in your mind. The writer, the
thinker, the seeker of existential answers. Perhaps you're just anyone, looking
for escape. For a complication your life lacks. A simplicity you crave. Perhaps
you are lost. Perhaps this is the place that finds you. Keeps you.

These mountains are a state of mind in minds through the centuries. But they are also a place, on this island. Here, a climb into the sky finds the horizon is a black ridge, explored only by clouds, wild souls and uncanny dreams.

PART ONE

ASCENT

The varied earth, the moving heaven
The rapid waste of roving sea
The fountain-pregnant mountains riven
To shapes of wildest anarchy
By secret fire and midnight storms
That wander round their windy cones.
Of subtle life, the countless forms
Of living things, and wondrous tones.

'Chorus', Alfred, Lord Tennyson, 1830

Introduction

Sgùrr Hain, Isle of Skye
Winter

Up the mountain, I saw nothing. My knees fell to the slope, rain battering into my hood, eyes struggling to see out. Above, the gully opened to the skyline in a gate of cloud. Somewhere up in the murk was the thing that had brought me here. A stupid thing. But one that even now, in this, I still wanted to find.

More wind roared down the gully, pressing long-soaked, long-warmthless clothing against skin and making me gasp. With cold hands I pulled the map from my pocket. Breathing hard, I looked through rain-beaded eyelashes at contours through the mad lens of wet on the plastic case. Hopeless. But I knew where I was, more or less. The place I was standing in, the place I wanted to be and the terrain I'd covered since waking up all occupied a chunk of the map no bigger than my thumb – an area thick with hugger-mugger contours and crag-scrawl. My position was halfway up a scratch in the lines, beyond which a flattening signified the ridge linking the mountain of Sgùrr Hain with the neighbouring peak of Sgùrr na Stri. Neither summit reached higher than five hundred metres, yet neither summit could see a thing. I didn't like the noise the wind was making as it crashed around the crags above, or the clip at which the cloud was moving, or the boundlessness with which the rain was falling – every drop further swelling the cataracts I'd have to re-cross to get out of here. I didn't like the way the sea, grey and impassive at my back, was looking at me. Just now, I didn't like anything about this place.

It was very far from what I'd hoped for, my dreams of crystalline views and mountains fat and white usurped by this worn-looking, February-dead imposter landscape. The few glimpses through rips in the sky had revealed mountains streaked with rotten bones of snow. It felt rangy and dangerous out here, the sort of Scottish winter nobody looks forward to and most avoid. The whole landscape seemed composed of water in various states of being: water in the air, water on the rock, water running. Before I'd even started climbing, I'd crossed four streams vomiting meltwater, felt its sick, strong heave against my boots. When climbing mountains, you could expect to fall to your death or perhaps get hypothermia. You don't expect to drown.

What was I doing here? I didn't need to be here. There was no need, but there was a reason. A reason why I had travelled five hundred miles to the Isle of Skye, one of the edgiest outposts of Britain – then walked into the island's own edgiest outpost. A reason to cross rivers, spend a cold and very lonely night out in a bothy, then climb up this pathless peak in the middle of winter. Though as reasons go it was an odd one, and one that to me was starting to stack up to a mistake. I was here to find the place where somebody died.

Everything is different on Skye. Even when you arrive on the island, as I did, over that bowed whalebone of bridge from the mainland in the darkness of a winter night, you still sense a shift in the landscape and a change in the air; a kind of atmospheric fidget from wherever you are to somewhere else entirely.

Naturally, I'm not alone in thinking this. Better writers than me have tried to evoke Skye, and we'll encounter a few as we go. These are the musings of the painters and the poets, the scientists and the fugitives, the warring clansmen, the Vikings, the itinerants, the explorers, the artisan wanderers who have, however briefly, felt this island pass beneath them. Then there are the people who were born here, the people who came for a summer and never left, and the travellers of today. Nature's voice, too: the rocks, the lochs, the wind and the sea. The magic, the light, and the magic light of a million Instagram images. And the legends and the myths that here seem to sit just beyond your sight. The living, and the dead. They're all part of Skye.

The drama of this island has tattooed itself on a thousand years of travellers. But ask any one of them to describe Skye in specific terms and you trigger a mess of contradictions, confusions and superlatives.

The island is big, but spindly. Mountainous and many-moored, yet defined by coastline. Its edges of cut-in lochs, pinnacled bays and forbidding, columnar cliffs with their confetti of birds feels like the torn edge of the world. Skye's moody landscapes can have the most angelic moments of clarity – the sort that make you feel you have slipped into a heavenly dimension of theatrical light and scenery. Other times you can feel you are braving a tempest whilst wrapped in a binbag. This place has a singular identity, but its history is defined and continues to be dominated by off-comers and outgoers. It's an island and yet, because of that bridge, it joins the mainland. It's a place defined by its distant horizons – but also by the mountains that break them.

What is certain is that Skye affects you somehow. The funny thing about the many literary renderings of the island throughout history is that they generally divide into scenic orgasms in prose, or are passionately bleak. Almost all, though, have a tinge of twilight around the edges – a certain sinister turn to the words, no matter how prosaic the subject.

Take the *Ordnance Gazetteer of Scotland*'s description of Skye's geographical form, published in the 1880s. It begins cheerfully by describing the island as 'part of the body of a huge whale, the tail lying to the south-east next to the mainland, and the body stretching away to the north-west', before darkening: 'but it is a whale that has suffered from the onslaughts of the ocean, for the outline of the sides, instead of being smooth and regular ... is everywhere cut into.' It's gruesomely accurate.

By the time Skye had become familiar enough to draw tourists, occasionally these intimidating dispatches became awesomely depressing. Henry Thomas Cockburn of Bonaly – better known as Lord Cockburn – painted a miserable portrait of Skye from Corry, near Broadford, in his diary of 6 September 1841:

The cold, cheerless rocks, the treeless desolation, the perpetual tendency of the clouds to rest, as if it were their home, on the tops of the hills ... the utter want of natural verdure, the grey, benty colour of the always

..ched pasture, the absence of villages and of all human appearance
these things mark Skye as the asylum of dreariness.

If weather be Cockburn's culprit, it's worth noting that by the numbers
Skye's weather is actually no worse than on the mainland; it actually beats
some other parts of the west coast in sunshine hours. It's just that the high
ground here tends to hold cloud more noticeably than other, lower-lying,
islands, hence its famously evocative nickname: the Gaelic *Eilean a' Cheò*,
Isle of Mist – or more romantically, the Misty Isle.

It may not just be a whimsical name, either. The Norse, who controlled
the island for several centuries, referred to Skye in their sagas as *Skíð*, *Skýey*,
Skuy or *Skuyö* – the latter two meaning 'cloud' and 'mist', respectively. Some
have suggested that the island could be named after its folk, who are known
as *Sgiathanach* – a word probably of Gaelic origin, with *skia* (shield) or *skian*
(sword) paired with *neach*, meaning people, suggesting a place seemingly
predisposed to combat – a fitting description given its tumultuous history
and no small amount of blood-spill.

It has also been claimed that Skye might even be named after a mythological character named Skiach or Scáthach, 'a goddess or mortal – no one knows
which – but undoubtedly a great warrior'. According to Otta Swire, a celebrated
scholar of the island's folklore, 'some say she took her name from a Gaelic
name for Skye, others that Skye took its name from her.' Skiach is said to
have trained warriors in the island's mountains. But we'll get to that.

The island's shape may have some claim to the name too. The Latin *Scetis*
– 'split', probably – appeared to vaguely correspond with Skye's location in
the *Ravenna Cosmography*, a kind of early Roman gazetteer of place names
that appeared in around 700 CE, and probably based on a map made by
Ptolemy some six hundred years earlier. The Norwegian linguist Arne Kruse
sees the Norse word *Skio* as an audible imitation of the Old Irish name for
Skye, *Sci* or *Sceth* – and noticed that Roman, Norse and Irish terms all
derived from the same origin. The split theory 'most likely', he wrote, refers
'to the long inlets in the western part of the island'.

Despite this, a name for the island that answers today as Skye was
conspicuously absent from one of the first printed maps specifically of
Scotland, which emerged around 1560. On this map – the Regno di Scotia

– the Hebrides are jumbled up off the west coast, as if swept together like stray leaves. Locations are wildly approximate, but a few are recognisably named: Iona, Mvla, Isla and Levissa for Iona, Mull, Islay and Lewis. Skye is there, but whoever made this map – possibly an Italian named Paolo Forlani – tellingly seemed not to realise its many limbs comprised a single land mass. He divided it up, making islands of its peninsulas as if visualising the aftermath of a great geological scissoring, and it was not until Abraham Ortelius's impressively resplendent *Scotiae tabula* of 1580 that the name 'Skye' first appeared, spelled just as it is today.

Timothy Pont, one of the earliest travellers and mapmakers to depict Skye in detail, produced a map of the 'Yle of Skie' for Joan Blaeu's 1654 *Atlas of Scotland*. Pont probably drew his map much earlier – in around 1590 – and it's a dramatic thing: a squabble of peninsulas dangling south off a narrow spine, from which a muscular, straight-raked headland strikes northwest at an almost perfect right angle. It's just an impression of the island's true architecture – but even by the standards of the time, accurate enough to suggest just how confounding its geography is.

Nomenclature took a bit of a backward step after that, with the comprehensively titled *New mapp of Scotland or North Britain with considerable improvements according to the newest observations*, produced by Tho Bowles of London in 1731. The mapmaker's big idea was to fill in any gaps between place names with helpful geographical descriptions; Skye is now *Skiei*, and 'in this island is found aggt chrystal and marble and Herrings are taken in all the bays.'

Skye's name could also have arisen from its likeness to a butterfly, a crustacean or, most famously, a bird. *Scetis* in the *Ravenna Cosmography* could also have derived from the Celtic *skitis*, meaning 'winged' – thought to refer to the peninsulas of land outstretched from a meaty, mountain-muscled midriff like a striking eagle, according to Jim Crumley in *The Heart of Skye*, with 'its wing tips at Duntulm and Waternish Head, its head bearing down in Kyleakin and Kylerea, its talons slung loosely below Point of Sleat'. This led to the Gaelic *An t-Eilean Sgitheanach* – often translated as the 'winged isle,' with *sgiath* meaning 'wing' in Gaelic. It takes some seeing, but the tumultuous sweep of the island and its swirl of peninsulas do correspond to something in a kind of mid-air flail. Donald Munro, High Dean of the

Isles, made the observation in 1549: 'This Ile is callit Ellan Skiannach in Irish, that is to say in Inglish the *wyngit Ile*, be reason it has mony wyngis and pointis lyand furth fra it.' Timothy Pont, too, refers to parts of Skye as 'wings' in the description of the island credited to him in Blaeu's *Atlas of Scotland*, where he notes: 'The promontories are stretched into the sea like wings for which it is called by some writers ... as *skia* in the old language signifies a wing.' Less poetic is the blunt yet beckoning – and anonymous – description of Skye recorded in Macfarlane's *Geographical Collections* from the 18th century: 'It is great and big ... ther ar mountaynes in it.'

More recent comparisons include Malcolm Slesser's salty analogy of Skye's form as 'a lobster's claw ready to snap at the fish bone of Harris and Lewis', in his 1923 SMC guide, *The Island of Skye*. Meanwhile Sorley Maclean, a Scottish Gaelic poet deeply associated with Skye, clearly thought the 'winged isle' theory had legs when he wrote:

> Great beautiful bird of Scotland,
> Your supremely beautiful wings bent
> About many-nooked Loch Bracadale,
> Your beautiful wings prostrate on the sea
> From the Wild Stallion to the Aird of Sleat
> Your joyous wings spread
> About Loch Snizort and the world ...

Maclean chose to name this poem simply 'An t-Eilean' ('The Island'), which, to many, is the only name that Skye needs, standing sharp through the blizzard of evocations and descriptions.

But perhaps another rather newer term cuts through them, not to evoke form or append name, but to conjure feel – a single word never intended for, but uncannily suited to Skye: *Xenotopia*. This was quipped by landscape writer Robert Macfarlane, from the Latin *xenos* and *topia*. Translated literally, it means 'stranger-place'. I love that, because this *is* Skye. Stranger than other places, and a stranger itself. There it sits, a place of extremes, of infinite circular conflict – of people against people, people against weather, weather against rock, rock against people. A place of migration and immigration and emigration, where storms trail and strafe across the land much like its transient dwellers and the strangers who come to the island, over the centuries and in numbers. All drawn to this tempestuous edgeland by – well, by *something*.

The village of Elgol roughens the tip of the Strathaird peninsula like a barnacle-pile. A cluster of boxy white crofts and a few newer developments – almost all of them of the woody Scandinavian eco-home ilk – Elgol is the end of the road in every sense. But where wheels can't go, your feet can.

The previous afternoon I had arrived in the village beneath a sky that was a ragged patchwork of white and grey, stitched with threads of sun. The air was a soup of salt and that metallic nautical smell that pervades any coastal settlement as I locked the car, swung my pack on, and looked for the finger post inscribed with my night's destination.

The way to Camasunary Bay from Elgol follows the coast along a path that is in places overgrown, squelchy and precarious. Progress was slow, but aside from the brevity of daylight at this time of year I felt in no rush; bothy nights in winter are long and cold, and it wouldn't have done to arrive too early. The Atlantic filled everything to my left, a sheet of hammered iron except at the shore, where it melted to foam. Often the path rose above lichen-blackened cliffs to a height that twitched the stomach and knees; beneath lay grey rocks and the occasional bright disturbance of washed-up rubbish – a buoy, yellow polystyrene, a coil of blue or orange plastic fishing rope.

The land had been turned brown by winter. On the hillsides to my right, crags broke the surface in dark, wet wounds. Ahead, along the line made between coast and sea, stood a great mass of cloud, and a shadow. I had seen many pictures of this place, all wide angles and spacious vistas. Now I was here, everything felt compressed, bristling and dirty, a place of water smells and creeping cold. It was like walking through a rinse cycle.

The path dropped to a storm beach, then climbed some cliffs through a haggle of arthritic rowan and thorns. Another drop, the path rounded a final corner and, two hours after leaving Elgol in the straining light of late afternoon, I arrived at the opening of Camasunary Bay. Here, Loch Scavaig bites its salty teeth into the land and a huge glen spills into the sea.

Immediately ahead stood a robust building of corrugated metal over clapboard over stone: the bothy. Shelter from the deteriorating weather, and my home for the night. It looked so close to the water that a stiff tide might envelop it. It also looked strong enough to cope.

The door swung heavily open on new hinges to a porch. Someone had dragged a piece of driftwood just inside, presumably with the intention of burning it – and had left it there on finding that a fireplace was one thing this bothy didn't have. My heart sank slightly at this, but given the circumstances it was a minor gripe.

For such a wild place, it's perhaps unexpected that Camasunary Bay has three buildings, spaced sentinel-like across the coastal plain. This new bothy, which a plaque inside the door tells visitors was built by the Royal Engineers in 2016, is one; the bothy it replaced, a squat crofter's cottage on the opposite side of the bay, the second; and finally the lodge, a little-occupied dwelling on the sandy croft the bay was named after: *Camas Fhionnairigh*, bay of the fair, or the beautiful, or the white shieling. I doubted any had anyone in them tonight.

Skyeman Alexander Nicolson – a man whom we will get to know rather well – once remarked that the lack of a hotel or some other convenience here, given the exemplary location, was a missed opportunity:

> Here undoubtedly is the place where, where in Switzerland would be ...
> a Grand Hotel et Pension de Camasunary. It is not well to disturb the
> sacred solitude of nature's great scenes. But we should be reasonable,
> and if people will go, and ought to go, to go to see such places it would
> be better that they should be able to do so with some degree of comfort.

Nicolson's vision, rather happily, never came to pass. Some writers record that for a time there was a temperance retreat in the bay – a remote place for 'reclaiming drunkards', as Charles Weld delicately wrote in 1860, 'where it is to be presumed the total abstinence system can be enforced with complete success'. But however rustic, there is still comfort to be found here where there might easily have been none. The three buildings have enabled each other, too; the lodge's owner paid for the new bothy to be built when he decided to reclaim the old one, a charitable act indeed, given how welcome a free shelter with a firm roof is in this sea-lashed corner of Skye. I was certainly thankful.

My boots squeaked on the floor as outside turned to inside. It was big, for a bothy: two rooms, one with a table, one with a double deck of conjoined bunks, and both with a window onto the sea, spilling milky light over the floor. I walked through to the sleeping room, swung off my bags and shoved the load onto the bench, my movements filling the building with sudden noise and ringing echoes. I wondered how long it had lain silent before my interruption.

The bothy logbook stood open on a shelf half full of spent tea-lights and marked with multiple burns. I'd slept in maybe twenty of these shelters over the years, and it was always fun to look in this special book: to leaf through damp-puckered pages full of the thoughts of the intrepid, the relieved, the transient, the knackered. Like Skye in microcosm, everyone who passed this way had a story and most recorded it too, as if compelled to mark the occasion. The last entry was from three days earlier: a walker attempting the Skye Trail who sheltered here awhile from the rain before continuing on. The last overnighter had been weeks back. I noticed the doodles of one entry matched the style of a rather self-centred piece of graffiti on the door between the two rooms, which someone had thought an appropriate canvas to draw a figure sporting a Mohican and a kilt, and wielding a woodcutter's axe. I didn't know which was harder to fathom: that someone with such limited artistic skill would decide an interior door of this bothy was a suitable place to express themselves, or that the same person happened to arrive with a thick marker pen.

I began to unload night things: stove, mat, sleeping bag. Dry, warm clothes were dug out of their waterproof bags; heavy, wet clothes strung up in the thin hope they might dry a little. I pulled out something to read and a miniature electric lantern I had taken to carrying, suddenly both grateful for it and slightly fearful that it might fail. In the absence of a fire it would be dark in here, and these places didn't exactly have plug points. The lodge, five hundred metres away, looked empty, which meant this lantern and my headtorch would be the only source of illumination for miles in a sixteen-hour night.

The light began to silver, then grey, then die. I debated turning the lantern on but instead pulled on my wet jacket and went outside in search of a stream, clutching a waterproof bag turned inside out to collect water. The landscape was now almost monochrome – grey beach, sea, hillsides and cloud. The mountains that I knew peered down on Camasunary were masked, including the one I'd come here to climb: Sgùrr Hain, which stood just over a mile away to the north-west. It could have been twenty.

In a gloomy mood I trudged across the beach to search for fresh water. The white lodge was there, vacant and darkening, losing contrast in the falling dark. Choking the spaces between the rocks were more bits of plastic: bottles, boxes, floats, rope, morasses of polystyrene, one plastered with faded Japanese text – all of it chucked up onto this comparatively microscopic bite of beach. God knows how much else was out there. Scanning the fading ground for the line of a stream, I found a filthy outlet and started to trudge inland to where it wasn't clogged by something unpleasant. Eventually I found enough of a clean flow to fill a couple of litres, and I turned with my suddenly heavy burden back towards the bothy.

It was nearing complete darkness when I reached the building and sloughed in, immediately cranking up my little lantern to ease the atmosphere of the isolation. Minutes later my stove was rolling a boil, I layered clothing for the night, the windows fogged, and the room filled with the smells of pasta and cheese sauce. I ate, poured a mug of hot chocolate, and soon was zipped into my sleeping bag with a book of Sorley Maclean's poems, the frugal glow from the lantern casting mad shadows on the wall with every rustle. The sea's breathing was now joined by a snuffling wind and, later, the slow static of rain on the corrugated roof, getting louder as the night thickened.

When my eyes could no longer focus on the words I let them close, leaving the lantern on for some comfort. I thought about my journey over the last couple of days – from home and everything and everyone there, along thrumming roads through teeming cities, motorway services withering to ancient Highland petrol stations and isolated inns, over the bridge, then to here – a place completely cut off, in little more than twenty-four hours. Civilisation had tapered to a single point, and there I was. It wasn't a bad feeling, or a particularly good one. It's just rare these days to feel quite so alone.

Deep in the night I wandered out of the bothy door for a pee to find, after the shock of total dark had passed, that a thick sea mist had crept up to the shore. It was weird, just hanging on the water, like a wall of ghosts, halting where it met the land. At my back, the cloud had lifted slightly and after a long stare, I fancied I could see the shadows of mountains beyond. It was cold, and an occasional half-snow was in the air, disappearing where it reached the ground. The silence was total. I stood there until I shivered, then retreated inside.

Sleep was fitful, my ears awake for the skittering of mouse claws on wood – that paranoia of something racing along the sleeping platform towards me. And this being a bothy, there was always the possibility of someone shambling in during the night, although given the weather and the lean season it seemed unlikely. And, rather thankfully, so it proved.

The next morning, after a brief lull just after dawn, the weather deteriorated once again. I stripped out everything from my pack I didn't need – sleeping gear, stove, little lantern – piled it all in a corner of the bothy, and struck off along the clattery beach towards where I presumed Sgùrr Hain began.

And so, a few hours later, this was it and here I was, at the sharp end of this strange little quest. Halfway up an obscure mountain on the Isle of Skye, looking for the place where someone I never knew presumably took one last look at something, then – for whatever reason – died.

The gully opened out to a wide shoulder. Before me oily rocks poked out of grass, stretching towards a flat grey. That wasn't the sky, I thought. That was a drop, and a smothered view. Dropping a bright waterproof bag on the ground and spearing it with a walking pole to mark the top of the gully, I struck out along the grass on a bearing the map confirmed was vaguely the right direction. Moments later, pacing my distance and squinting at every little boulder that emerged from the mist ahead, I spotted something. As I moved towards it, its shape crisped into a squat, black arrowhead pointing at the sky. I'd found it.

It was a hefty thing, but somehow smaller than I'd imagined. With nothing beside it to lend a sense of scale, the photograph I'd seen made it look magisterial: a proud triangle of gabbro rocks. Perhaps it was the absence of any view that diminished it somehow, yet here it was: Captain Maryon's Monument. It stood a little taller than me, wet-black, moated by a filthy puddle. A tiny mountain peak, named after a man. I removed my gloves to touch it, to feel the teeth of the rock bite my skin. This was no cairn, no simple pile of stones: this thing had been crafted, shaped. A hell of a task out here. And where was the plaque? I thought for a moment it had been taken away but then I found it, oddly tucked on a corner near the ground, apologetically, like a signature:

> Erected in memory of Staff Captain
> A. J. Maryon G. H. Q. India Command
> who met his death here in July 1946.
> He lay on this spot for nearly two
> years and now rests in Portree.
> This cairn was built by his friend
> Myles Morrison ex Staff Captain R. E.
> who served with him in the 1939–45 War.

What a strange pilgrimage. I stood there in the pissing rain, feeling it crawling between the seams of my clothing, feeling the February cold beginning to squeeze. Leaning against the cairn and staring into the cloud, I was satisfied to have reached this place, yet in the grip of a strange and increasingly overstretched anticlimax: standing in the sky, with nothing but my imaginings to paint a scene around me, and a memory locked wordlessly into this stone.

I can't really tell you why Captain Maryon's story both captivated and haunted me. I think mostly it was because it offered more questions than answers. It was enigmatic, oddly truncated, unlikely, dream-like, dark – a Skye story to its bones.

His full name was Arthur James Maryon, and he was thirty-seven years old, which, I note now – with nothing more than passing relatability – is my age as I write this. His address was, appropriately, Pinnacle Hill in Bexleyheath. He had served with the 5th Mahratta Light Infantry during the Second World War. His name appeared on the war memorial at Brookwood Cemetery in Surrey – notable in itself as he died after the war, but before 1947, the year that the Commonwealth War Graves Commission considered the end of wartime service.

I include these strange details as really they are the only details. Aside from these skeletal facts and this enduring, meticulously made monolith on Skye, Maryon is a ghost. We can't know how he died, if he meant to die, or why. We just know that he died *here* – on an obscure spot offering little to explain his passing. You could argue mountaineering is inexplicable in general, but Maryon wasn't mountaineering when he met his end. Looking around the spot where I stood, the only way you could die from external causes here was if you killed yourself with something brought with you, got hit by lightning or a meteorite, or jumped from an aeroplane and landed here. Which suggested either a sudden, terminal physical ailment – possible, even at his age – exposure, or suicide, we'll never know which. And another part of his story added another layer of mystique.

We know that Maryon left the Sligachan Hotel on or around 8 July 1946 and that his body wasn't discovered until 1 July 1948. This was the thing that had caught me, put a terrible vision to the tale: as stated on the plaque, his body had lain here, in the open on this spot, for almost exactly two years. This idea – of a body just lying here – seemed to me so awful and odd. How wild must a place be to allow him to remain unfound for so long, particularly as the presence of a monument to his memory suggested that someone had probably missed him, and conceivably went out looking for him? What kind of place was this?

Well, that's the thing. This isn't just any spot. It was what this monument was looking at, the view it owned, that joined our stories together. I knew what lay behind that cloud, that wall of murk to the west. The view it gives is the only tangible reason to climb this obscure, rough-skinned rise amidst an arena of much grander objectives. Maryon's monument might have brought me to this spot; but there was no question that what drew this unfortunate soul here was the same thing that brought me to Skye. Purely by being here, Maryon must have been a man with a fascination for grand and savage places.

I stood there and thought of Maryon, whoever he was. Thought of him going from living to dead, from a person to a thing, a body, wasting to hard edges, forming to the ground, becoming part of the mountain. I thought of this because of some lines the poet Sorley Maclean wrote, lines in a book which I'd read by dim light in the bothy last night, and which was now saturating in my rucksack.

Who is this, who is this in the night of the spirit?
It is only the naked ghost of a heart
a spectre going alone in thought,
a skeleton naked of flesh on the mountain.

Who is this, who is this in the night of the heart?
It is the thing that is not reached,
the ghost seen by the soul
A Cuillin rising over the sea.

Through a thinning in the murky sky ahead, something moved. The cloud shifted over an object, sharp and dark and big, and for a second I saw it. Three spires, descending from high above and to the right, like barbs on a monster's back. It was just a glimpse – and barely that. But it was enough to tell me that behind the wall of battleship grey it was there after all. The crooked black ridge of mountains that cuts this island in two: the Cuillin.

I first became aware of something fearful and remarkable on the Isle of Skye when I was a teenager. I'd bought an anthology of mountain writing from a charity shop, and on the back of the dust jacket there was a full-page print of what looked like a woodcut. The woodcut, or engraving, or whatever it was, held a darkly lucid vision – all hard angles and scorched textures in stark black and white. From a distance it looked like a bombed-out cathedral, cloud rising around it like smoke. In it a figure, with their back to the viewer and on a skyline in the top right, was negotiating a ledge over a huge, white drop. To the left of the image was a ridge-crest, rising from the cloud below, all weird and twisted in form. It reared to a distinctive fin of rock, then fell again into cloud. In the background rose a triangular peak, a continuation of the same ridge. Beyond, yet another.

I stared at this picture for a long time. Everything about it gripped and rattled me: the textures, the aesthetic of the landscape it depicted, even the purposeful-looking swing of the figure's arm as they rounded the skyline obstacle. A thing, an objective, and a human on an adventure.

Was this a real place? It had to be, but there were no accompanying words. I had to hunt for the credit on the back inner flap of the jacket, which stated it was by an artist named Paul L. Kershaw and showed 'Collie's Ledge, The Cuillin, Isle of Skye'. That was in Scotland; I knew *that*. But scenes from high in the British mountains were to me then, as they are to most now, a mystery-in-ignorance – and a spectacular surprise when, or if ever, encountered.

Frustratingly, there was nothing in the book about Skye, or the Cuillin ridge, or Collie – whoever or whatever that was. It was a book that collected a whole host of grand musings about the Himalayas, the Victorian conquest of the Alps, the Romantics and their ecstasies about the Lake District. The image on the back cover was an incongruous fragment of something entirely different, something that grabbed my attention yet didn't seem to comfortably fit the broader picture – grafted onto the whole like a geographical exclamation mark.

In many ways, this is in keeping with the Cuillin in general. In terms of the British mountainscape, the place does not fit at all. It's completely out of kilter with everything, in terms of its geology, its architecture, its visual smack – everything. Britain's mountains are weathered and noble, all different, certainly, but cut from at least similar basic stock. The Cuillin ridge is not. Its mountains are steeper, harder, stranger. Wilder. Sharper. Angrier. Most British mountains delivered their gravitas with a kind of dramatic dignity. The Cuillin – and I use the singular, as the ridge is a collective of peaks – looks as if it has sailed in from some terror-place on ragged sails, taking anchor off the west coast and peering into Scotland's interior like a demon at the window. From every angle, the Cuillin was an environment with a complexity and an atmosphere unlike any other I knew of. And this was before I even knew it at all.

'The first sight of them leaves you speechless,' wrote W. Kenneth Richmond in *Climber's Testament*. 'You have heard so much about them, imagined so much, studied them in photographs, and here they are at last – larger than life and out-leaping your wildest expectations.' I started to appreciate this more directly when my own explorations of Britain's mountains took me into Scotland, and within sight of the Cuillin ridge itself. There it was off the coast of Torridon, Applecross, the Isle of Rum, from the coast at Mallaig, its barbs peeping out shockingly behind benign headlands and low-rise peninsulas, astonishing to think of its angles and jags, those ruinous masts and turrets, as a permanent fixture and not some transient, drifting freak. It didn't look real.

The Cuillin ridge occupied a different compass point each time I saw it but was always a strange, disjointed presence. I once camped on the beach at Redpoint, a remote limb of beach on Scotland's north-west coast, facing the hulk of Skye across the Minch, with Raasay and Rona layered in the shelter of its silhouette. From there I sat on the sand and looked across at the island, watched the sky redden, the land blacken and the lighthouses on the headlands begin to wink, a fog slowly building from the water. In many ways this became my conception of Skye, too: a dark otherland, that *xenotopia*, its existence transient between snatches of windblown mists. Then at night, the twinkle of lighthouses, the breath of the sea and, flattened by dusk into silhouette, those beckoning, frightening mountains.

And the Cuillin ridge *is* frightening. Frightening at a basal, molecular level. It is the mountain concept in its purest form: no nobility, no masquerade of fearsomeness that fails when you scratch it. Here is a land-scape imagined by a mind brooding on dark metaphorical fictions: impassable, obstinate, steep, the place where the bad things are. I challenge you to look at the Cuillin ridge and not feel it stroke your more suggestible side.

And on the ground this plays out beneath your feet. For the mountain walker, the Cuillin presents a challenge so far in excess of anything else in the British Isles, it is very nearly off limits. The closest you can get elsewhere approximating the traverse of the entire ridge – the end-to-end enchainment of all the major peaks in the range, and the gold medal achievement here-abouts – is still several leagues short of what is actually required in terms of skill, stamina and constitution.

These were the last of Britain's mountains to be climbed. Most high points in Scotland and elsewhere in Britain took their names from ancient, generic or apocryphal sources – animals, objects, tributes of resemblance, references to colour or occasionally legend. The Cuillin's peaks were named after the people who climbed them. 'The only mountains in Scotland to be named after men,' wrote the writer and mountaineer Ben Humble. 'Hoary names they have. And never were there men more worthy.' Named for people who had to be first drawn to this place. To these mountains.

And it is here, at the place where Captain Maryon's Monument stands, that you can appreciate the tableau of the Cuillin from the centre of its maw: sea, loch, sky and, linking all with its ragged lines, the Black Cuillin ridge itself, curled in an arc of skyward-pointing barbs around this much smaller, human-made one. Within a head-sweep from the monument, within these dark mountains rent in rock and layered in tiers, lies a grand tale.

And yet it was a loch that arguably started it all. Far below me and my perch in the sky, down there through the murk, lay Loch Coruisk. When early travellers came to Skye in the 18th century, it was word of this extra-ordinary citadel lake, hidden from all eyes but the intrepid, that they took back. On their trail came the artists, who would attempt to capture visions of it with all the enraptured melodrama of the Romantic age. Here was the lake that prompted tangible terror in Sir Walter Scott, whose evocations of Skye in *The Lord of the Isles* were almost elementally malevolent in nature. Scott's Corriskin was a 'dread lake',

> With its dark ledge of barren stone
> Seems that primeval earthquake's sway
> Hath rent a strange and sheltered way
> Through the rude bosom of the hill,
> And that each naked precipice,
> Sable ravine, and dark abyss
> Tells of the outrage still.

The focus on the lake could be because, before the Romantics, mountains were either ignored or actively hated by early travellers, who equated them with the wastelands of the subverted afterlife. Dante's chosen metaphor for hell was a mountain; and sharp, arid peaks like the Cuillin were damnation's chosen set-dressing from the Classical age all the way to Tolkien's Mordor. The Romantics channelled this repulsion into exultation – Joseph Addison's 'agreeable horror' – after which mountains became quite the thing to provoke rapture in everything from poetry to art to philosophy.

But at a time when nature's more rugged scenes were exaggerated, dark-ened, corralled into artificial symmetry and pre-ordained compositions, here was a landscape that defied embellishment. Separated from the claws of the Atlantic by a sinew-bridge of land, this deeply tucked-away loch prompted feelings of unease from first sight.

Even Lord Cockburn, he of the 'asylum of dreariness', was stunned into reverence by Coruisk:

> The dark pinnacles, the silence, deepened rather than diminished by the sound of a solitary stream – above all, the solitude – inspired a feeling of awe rather than solemnity. No mind can resist this impression . . . there is nothing except the little loch, towered over by the high and grisly forms of these storm-defying and man-despising mountains.

Man-despising. At a time when home-bred explorers were extending their reach to the far corners of the world in search of ever-more ambitious objectives – Alps, Caucasus, Andes, Himalaya – here was a tight fist of virgin ground, terrifyingly tempting in form, located just off the Scottish coast. So formidable was these mountains' challenge that it is almost certain that every summit on the mainland – as well as many in the Alps – was climbed before the first mountaineering feet trod on a Cuillin peak to make the last of the British first ascents.

When the mountaineers did begin to explore the Cuillin they found a lethal dichotomy, a thing by turns seductive and abrasive: a labyrinth of blackened rock that built from the sea in a complex series of hollows and ribs, sharpening, dividing, reaching ever-higher angles of intense pitch and form to terminate in a slinking and bucking crest seven miles in length, never lower than 2,500 feet and in some places little wider than a human foot. And every dispatch from this place was so consistently perturbed, conjuring up a landscape fearfully singular amongst the British hills. When walking in the Lake District or the Brecon Beacons you were strolling with the angels; on the Cuillin you were dancing with the devil.

Whatever your take, the Cuillin of Skye provokes a reaction. Mine was to ignore it. Not out of disinterest, you must understand – but because I identified the ridge as rather throwing a spanner in the works of my personal exploration of the British mountains. These peaks were scarier, altogether trickier than anything else I was likely to encounter. So I snubbed the ridge, pretended it wasn't there, and remained in a state of geographical dismissal. And being on an island, it *is* ignorable. Because it's separate, somehow.

But as years became decades of exploring the Lake District, North Wales, every corner of the Highlands and other parts of Skye itself, the Cuillin's mysterious grin seemed to gain a glimmer, like the untouched chamber in a ransacked tomb. Life changed, I got older, got married, had children. And for the very best of reasons, my priorities switched, and I felt my time in the mountains slipping into the mist. I'd done well: Britain's high places had sculpted my life and given me some of my most vivid memories. But still, there was the Cuillin ridge.

Skye's strange, sharp peaks haunted me. I could live without climbing up onto the ridge, live without saying I'd taken on the toughest mountain journey in Britain and survived. Of course I could. But then there's nothing about the fascination with mountains that's justifiable. And little by little, the range sunk its hooks into me, like it had done before to so many others, and my own Skye story began. The more I read, the more I realised that I was simply one of a long line of travellers whose eyes had been drawn by the island and seduced by its peculiar atmospheres.

The idea that here was a place, a range of mountains, of which I had no experience whatsoever, began to stir me – a mid-life mountain crisis, if you like. This would be a brand-new adventure, an opportunity to get to know these mountains better than any others I knew, to understand where they came from, who explored them, the boots they had felt, the ghosts they kept, the secrets they held. And I could finally step onto that ridge, and maybe even make the journey across it – the *traverse* of the Cuillin! – and pin its ragged rosette on my own mountain life. Quite unexpectedly, the mountains I had been avoiding for most of my life were about to have my entire focus.

Of the ridge itself I knew only the sharpest edges of detail. I knew that the Cuillin as a range was a kind of perfect storm of everything that can challenge and endanger you in the British mountains, all augmented with the natural exaggeration of mystique. That you could die of fright at the drops. Of drowning in the rain. Of thirst from the dryness. Of hypothermia, or hyperthermia. That the ridge was harder, steeper, longer, scarier than anything else in Britain – not just by a bit, but by a lot. That the rock was so sharp it tore skin and equipment to pieces in days, and was filled with enough metal to render a compass useless. And if your compass did work, the map was so complex that it too was almost useless once you were in the heights.

To climb the Cuillin you need things you don't need on everyday British mountains. Water is scarce. Rain is frequent, as is cloud, wind and brisk shifts between them. The slopes are damagingly steep. Ropes are needed here, not solely to tackle rock climbs but just to make your way around. To get to the summits. There's nowhere else in Britain where you need a rope just to get to the *summits*. And – uniquely – unless you were particularly competent, you needed a *guide* on the Cuillin. An actual human, enlisted to keep you safe, and help you get what you came for.

I knew experienced people who had tried to traverse the ridge three, four, five times and failed. Bad weather. Running out of time. Running out of water. Loss of motivation due to exhaustion. Loss of confidence due to fear. Injury, equipment failure, bad decision-making – this was a place that tested everything you had. What this mountain range represented at its simplest level was an almost perfect obstacle. Put succinctly by a friend of mine, traversing the entire ridge in one continuous push – the grand prize for any would-be Cuillin assailant – is like 'running a marathon, and being terrified for every second'. In other words, I sort of knew the headlines, even though I didn't really know the Cuillin, or Skye, at all. But this was all about to change.

I reached the car in Elgol almost exactly twenty-four hours after I'd left it. My clothes hung off me like wet towels and it was a relief to get them off, even in air filled deep with chill. I jumped behind the wheel in my thermals, started the engine and cranked up the heater, and the car was soon a moving box of steam. Mobile phone reception returned in Broadford, and I made my way in collapsing weather back to a far-tucked village called Portnalong, where a room, dry clothes and a bar were waiting.

I'd found the Taigh Ailean Hotel a few days before I arrived on Skye, amidst the slow realisation that most of the big seasonal places whose names I knew were closed for the winter. A modest white building on the shore of Loch Harport, it was run by an English couple, Katie and Johnny

Heron, who had moved there some years earlier. Bearded and with a chip practical manner, Johnny had come to Skye on a whim and bought the ho – which translates as 'Alan's House', and was built on the site of an old croft, as is everything else in Portnalong – there and then. Katie, a former teacher with a dark bob, bookish spectacles and a refined English delivery that gave her the air of an intellectual on a bohemian kick, or vice versa, moved here without having even seen the building. Neither had ever run a hotel before, but their story wasn't strange. Not for Skye.

A shower, a change and a drink in the inn's 'Munros Bar' later, Johnny and Katie had rather unexpectedly piled me into their truck and driven the three miles through navy, sleety darkness to the neighbouring settlement of Carbost. A grid of hilly streets and low-rise buildings, this village over-looks Loch Harport, the curved inlet that burrows into Skye from the west. If central Skye were a clock face, the loch would sit at around eight.

To the off-comer, Carbost is known primarily for three things: the Talisker distillery, the Oyster Shed and the Old Inn. In summer all are packed with tourists; in the Old Inn in February, deep into the off season and the long nights, you tend only to find locals. People forget that Skye isn't just a place people come to: it's a *real* place. And in the winter, in places like Skye, places like the Old Inn become important beacons in the dark.

Johnny had explained that while both were full in high season, in February there wasn't enough trade to support both the Taigh Ailean's bar and the Old Inn, so they supported each other on alternate days, which I thought was nice. Inside a low room lit by fairy lights and the glow of a wood burner were a panelled bar, stone walls and a decently oiled bunch of patrons, all talking in the familiar way that suggested they probably met up most nights. Everyone seemed to know everyone else. I noticed Scottish accents and just as many English ones, among which was Johnny's.

'We did wonder,' he said, 'what it would be like moving here. Whether we would get stick, being off-comers or whatever. But so many people who now live on Skye are from elsewhere. Everyone is an immigrant somewhere down the line, whether it's from Harris, the mainland, England, or another place altogether.'

I asked about the human history – the clans, the old rivalries that had punctuated Skye's history with infamous blood-soaked battles, as if mirroring the brutal landscape and climate. Johnny shook his head dismissively and indicated the bar. 'So there you are, a MacLeod,' he said, indicating a big man dressed in ghillie tweeds sitting towards the corner making talk with the barman, 'and a MacDonald.' He pointed to a tall, lean figure who had just stooped in from the adjacent room. 'That's Farquhar. Hell of a fiddle player.' Johnny took a drink, wagged his head, then continued. 'It's sometimes there a bit . . . but in banter. Pool and football, shinty. That sort of thing.'

People came, people left, and the inn remained at a sociable simmer, the air of easy, instant familiarity I found immediately likeable. More Skye stories. The film star who had been at the Oyster Shed that week. The landlord taking issue over the boundary of his neighbour's croft. More Skye accents – Brummie, East Midlands, Swedish, Scottish – all glued together by certain affectations tossed in: 'see', 'ah', 'och', 'wee'.

At one point I found myself alone and increasingly curious about a series of canvasses I'd noticed dotted around the inn's walls. Some were large, some tiny, and all clearly by the same artist: stark white, made of tight agitations of black scrawl building to form the shapes of mountains. Shapes of the Cuillin.

A man I'd seen behind the bar wearing a padded gilet was busy collecting glasses.

'Who's the artist?' I asked, indicating the paintings.

The man had a shaved head and looked about forty. 'Those?' he said, as he looked slowly around at the canvasses, as if noticing them for the first time. 'That'd be me.'

'Really?'

'Aye.' He offered his hand. 'Ali. I run the place.'

I asked him if he climbed in the Cuillin. He said he used to, but not since he lost some friends up there, not long ago. He looked at his pictures in a slightly de-focused way, and for a minute looked like he might cry.

'It's a way to stay close. Just parking up and walking from the roadside, getting some frustration out. This one over here,' he said, taking me to a small canvas on the opposite wall. On it was a triangular-shaped peak cleaved by a black gash. I recognised the mountain, but couldn't remember the name of it. I didn't have to. 'Sgùrr an Fheadain,' he said, the Gaelic sliding from his lips, half words, half air. The knots of ink were intense, layered on thickly, vivid on the white. 'I was angry when I did this one. I can see it in the lines.' He coughed a chuckle. 'They're good for it, the Cuillin, you know ... they're harsh. The darkness. The dread.'

That word again. But I understood. When it came to the Cuillin ridge, dread ran deep in me. Ever since I saw its barbs scraping above the headland from Mallaig, something settled in my gut and began to chew. Because somewhere inside me was the same remote, irrational pull that anyone who has flirted with mountain climbing can identify with. I climb mountains, but I'm no climber. I hate heights and avoid risks. But mountains had me, in a way that wasn't ever going to slacken. And I knew that one day I'd need to take a closer look at the Cuillin ridge. That one day I'd find myself pulling on my boots, taking a deep breath, and limbering up for the hardest, nastiest mountains in the land. Because if you love the British mountains, sooner or later, the Cuillin calls. Don't ask me why; it's just the way it is.

Not long after returning to Skye I was chatting with an old friend, Thomas Lyle, who knew the Cuillin well. Spend twenty years in mountain rescue, as Lyle had, and tales of horror and confusion on the ridge find their way to you like cold, grasping fingers. I told him about my night in the bothy at Camasunary, and of standing there, where Maryon had lain all those years ago, in that place. I held back on some of my queerer thoughts about the island and its ridge, but I needn't have, because quite out of nowhere he said, 'That's the thing about Skye. That darkness.'

'You mean the colour of the rock?'

'No.' He shook his head. 'That's not what I mean at all.'

I waited, then he continued. 'I'll say this about being up there on the ridge – it's magnificent. But it's the most sinister place in the British mountains I've ever been.'

'Can you be more specific?'

'Not really. It's just a feeling. Get up into the Cuillin and you'll either absolutely fall in love with the place or you won't ever want to go there again. But it will get you.' He gave me a look. 'One way or the other.'

This, I would become increasingly aware, was the thing about the Cuillin. It had 'got' many people. All the people who had fallen under its weird,

cryptic spell. I wanted to understand *why* it got them – people like Walter
Scott, Sorley Maclean, Captain Maryon, all the way to people like Ali and
his unfortunate friends – and now, seemingly, me. Mountains everywhere
inspire; some mountains possess. And slowly, this strange island's mountains had possessed me.

So on returning home, I did what I thought would get me there. I
blocked out two weeks in the diary later in the year – one to explore at
leisure, and another to attempt a traverse from one end of the ridge to the
other. And then I began my journey through its past, collecting maps and
scraps and the beginnings of a book collection that would slowly take over
a room of my house. I began to think about choosing a guide, to get excited
at the thought of exploring something new, having a mountain project on
the horizon, and – being on the other side of the mid-thirties hump –
eager to feel physical and youthful while my best walking trousers still
fitted me. What I didn't realise was that this frivolous decision would cast
a tall and strange shadow over me, not for a couple of weeks, or a few
months. For five years I would stalk these mountains and, in their peculiar
way, they would stalk me. Here was a place stacked with more interest,
history and dark fascination than a mountain range of its modest proportions had any right to. The Cuillin was filled to the brim with memories,
with a voice that spoke only to the eyes, and the feet.

I'll warn you now, this is not going to be a smooth ride. Attempting to
traverse the ridge's story is a little like trying to traverse the ridge itself –
you can approach it with the best of intentions, but your chosen quarry
might have other ideas. The ridge does not lend itself well to any kind of
chronological approach. Names and tales and characters will pop into view
and disappear from time to time before their appropriate moments, but
that's OK. We'll get to know the important ones when we meet them up
on the ridge. We'll go down spurs, into shadowy valleys, spend a night lost
in the mist and endure the odd moment of thrill – but that's all part of
what the Cuillin ridge is about. It's a warren, a shapeshifter, an enigma, a
chimera, a confounder of all who appraise it. It twists and turns, bucks and
soars, falls and breaks, lightens and darkens – and so does its story. Its
history and the names of those who made it are inscribed on the map of
the Cuillin, stitched into its fabric, etched into its slopes, echoing in its

shadows. And this place in turn has left a piece of itself on those it has captured along the way: a change in gaze, a stiffening of hairs, a scratch on the memory.

This is the story of Skye's black ridge. It is also the story of the journey that others – travellers, scientists, artists, mountaineers, perhaps you, and now me – have made towards it. From that first spy of those dark sails over the sea, onward into its shadow, up to its heights, and under the spell of its frightening magic.

1

Fire

Cars stood silent in a five-deep rank, facing the coast. Then came an eruption of ignitions from the left-hand corner, and people were snuffing out cigarettes and climbing back into cars. Steadily, the rank began transferring itself line by line onto the flatbed of an ungainly-looking boat. Soon everyone was on the move again into the stairwells of a tall, thin passenger compartment on one side of the boat, and up to the blustery top deck to look about.

I was expecting the Mallaig to Armadale crossing to be either quaint or quietly tired, an obsolete way of getting to Skye, trading on old habits and nostalgia. It was, hearteningly, neither. Amongst those on the deck of the rattly and industrial MV *Loch Leven* were selfie-taking travellers, backpackers, motorcycle tourers in shiny black leather peering around the deck like upright sea lions, and a good few quietly unshowy passengers I took to be locals. All of whom, for whatever reason, had chosen to approach Skye this evening as it is, by how it was: as an island, and by boat.

A thick rumble and a cough of diesel smoke and the boat moved off. The rusting tangle of Mallaig compressed to a stripe beneath a hill-ramped coast to the stern, and the Sound of Sleat opened to the bow. The sinking sun was lighting everything gold. Ahead, a green tree line of sharp-crowned conifers gave every impression of capping just another low-lying, woody peninsula. Normally this horizon would harbour a second layer of sharper, taller teeth. But not today: the Cuillin ridge was being coy. It was there, somewhere, behind the cloud – uneasily uncertain in size and position, like an unseen shark beneath the waves.

So come on now. What is it about the Cuillin ridge? This black, scary spiky thing, this fairy-tale fantasy of a mountain range, that has inspired so many? You're holding, for instance, a whole book about what is ostensibly a very large piece of rock, and not even a particularly venerable or verdant one at that. I can't, at this juncture, tell you how many pages it's earned in this particular volume as we're only on number 36. But I'd say there were thousands of pages even I could write about this mountain range, although that is probably insufficient because this place just has *something* about it. But what?

For the time being let's ignore the mountaineering aspect of it – the statistics, the technicalities, the terrible struggle of getting across it – and let's just focus on the ridge as an object, as a ridiculous, jagged, geological organism. Allegorise it if you want: fearful objective *X*, the obnoxious *terra incognita* of our own personal existence, the thing that grabs your senses and stamps itself on them like a proprietorial branding iron. We all have our own Cuillin: it just so happens that in this case, our Cuillin is *the* Cuillin.

The first thing you notice as being remarkable about the ridge is that it's there at all. It's quite a shock. If the noble lines of the rest of the horizon suggest a patient at rest, the Cuillin ridge is the moment they got a bit flustered – hard jags, excited steeps and the sort of drops to make you swoon. It just looks so *different* to everything else. That's reason number one. Reason number two is quite simply because of where it is. Were the Cuillin ridge on the mainland, perhaps surrounded by other less singular presences, its power to infatuate might be less potent. It's a moot point because of course it isn't on the mainland. It's on Skye. And quite apart from everything else, Skye's an island – self-contained, other, adrift. And islands always feel like an adventure, don't you think?

These days, if you're approaching Skye from the south, catching the boat replaces the last hour of your mainland road journey. As it drops you on a different, more remote part of the island there's little in it, logistically. But I was determined to make this trip by boat. Because once upon a time, you had to.

This was the way Skye was accessed by all, prior to the controversial opening of the 570-metre bridge at Kyle of Lochalsh in 1995. The bridge linked south-east Skye with the mainland and, in the eyes of many, emasculated it, robbing the island of its island status. Author and climber W. H. Murray's lament in 1977 that a bridge would make Skye 'just another peninsula' was, if a little dismissive, effectively true. But anyone expecting more of the same beyond the bridge is in for a fright. With over twenty years of hindsight, the idea that having a physical link to the mainland could somehow diminish the island's charisma seems as thin as the bridge itself. But back then, perhaps not so much. Then, the island had to set its schedules by the ferries, which in turn had to set theirs by the storms. Isolation wasn't uncommon. But bridge or no bridge, there is still nothing like Skye. And in really bad weather they shut the bridge, too – meaning that in its wildest throes, this place becomes a physical island once again.

So that was why I was going by boat. I was also interested in making landfall on a different part of the island. Armadale sits on the southern edge of Skye, in a natural portage sheltered by little islands and an easterly aspect. Forty-five minutes after leaving Mallaig I was sitting in my car again as the boat drew in to port, eyes fixed on the horizon obscured by the drawn-up ramp, watching the tops of the shoreline trees slowly mingle with the array of antennae that signalled our arrival at the shore. The ramp came down, and here was Armadale, a tight knot of galleries and a café, with a woody, beckoning place at their back.

Suddenly engines were revving, vehicles were waved off the boat, and after a few seconds of bouncy excitement I was alone, accelerating up a quiet coast road, with the sea to the right reflecting a sky going pink.

Aside from the air of occasion any journey by sea engenders, I didn't really think arriving by boat to Skye would feel novel. But it did. Perhaps it was the clearing weather, the clean Hebridean air blasting through the windows, or simply being here – with exciting days ahead. It put me in an intensely good mood. Now all I had to do was dump the car, find somewhere to camp, then wait for the mountain range I had come for to emerge from hiding. And I had just the place in mind.

I said earlier that there is nowhere like Skye. This sounds like something you might read in a tourist brochure, but I really mean it. Here you will find a jumble of singular landscapes not only dramatically different to the mainland, but dramatically different to each other. Each occupies one of a rather neatly separate arrangement of peninsulas wheeling out from a central hub as if a bunch of landscapes that just didn't fit had been lashed together into a kind of pontoon and set adrift. And to top it off, there was the other-worldly battlement of the black ridge itself. Find somewhere else where you can feel so completely in a different place with the slightest of geographical relocation and I'll buy it for you.

Consider its form and this starts to make some sort of sense. Look at Skye on a map and it entirely lacks the geographical restraint of its neigh-bouring islands. There's heart-shaped Rum, thumb-shaped Arran, Coll and Tiree demure twins, Harris and Lewis sprawling, conjoined ones. But Skye is outstretched, tensed, fingers spread, legs split, back arched — every kink in its shore, every peninsula, every upward grasp of its mountains speaks of rigour.

Peter Bicknell, a mountaineering scholar who would become an early record holder for the Cuillin traverse, described it well: 'The map of Skye is for me the most exciting map in the world, with its fantastic coastline, its outlandish Norse names — Trotternish, Vaternish, Talisker, Snizort — and its contour lines hugging the coast till in the Coolin, in the words of Montague, they "begin to sing together, like the biblical stars".'

Measuring around fifty miles on its longest axis and twenty-five at its widest, the landmass itself is a relatively burly but hardly colossal 639 square miles — considerably less than the Lake District — yet has a coastline that runs to 456 miles. And unlike many others of its size, this squirrely edge with its maritime atmosphere and bendy, bandy roads ensures there are few places where you can forget you're on an island. Nowhere on Skye is more than five miles from the sea.

So let's take a journey on imaginary wings across that map, following my course and leaving the mainland for the island north-west across the water. First you will meet Sleat, a peninsula shaped like a south-westerly-pointing spear along the edge of which I was now driving into the evening. This forms the southern edge of Skye, looking back to the rest of Scotland across the narrow sound that bears its name. Further north-east up the coast, there's an attempt at an ill-fitting dovetail with the mainland at Kyle of Lochalsh, where you'll find the bridge. But continue north-west from

Armadale, away from the mainland and into the island's sway, and you soon cross Sleat's woody, low-lying terrain, with its lighthouses and loch-spattered moors, before again meeting a coast, where the sea lochs of Eishort and Slapin cut the peaks of an 'M' into the island's still-narrow midriff.

You now enter the airspace over another peninsula – Strathaird – to the end of which Elgol clings. Things are starting to get rougher down there now; hills are growing beneath you, pathless and gentle but with sudden edges and drops. From these you can see the drama building ahead, as you cross Loch Scavaig and enter the realm of the Cuillin. The two contrasting ranges that comprise this region – the serrated ridge of the Black Cuillin and the lumpier Red Hills (called the Red Cuillin by some) – form the studded belt-line of Skye around which its other peninsulas seem to splay. The Cuillin divides two sides of the island.

Soaring over the mountains and continuing north-west, you find Minginish, a backwater in the north-western shadow of the Cuillin. This is less a peninsula than an almost-severed appendage, nearly cut from Skye by the fjord-like Loch Eynort to the south, and the similarly intrepid Loch Harport to the north. Skye is full of these limbs of the sea punched deep into the land, placing you near the blue wink of water, or within clawing distance of its mists, at so many points on the island. Following the natural curve of the land we turn north, travelling first across the interior of the island – a raised inland moor scattered with plantation forest, strikingly open and big-skied after the jostled contours of the Cuillin. Here streams run and lakes lie amongst shallow glens and hill lochs in an area today almost devoid of settlement.

Continuing north, we reach the sea again, where the great bite of Loch Snizort nearly cleaves the island into two. Hover above the shore here and first look left, and you'll spy a duo of peninsulas fanning out into the Sea of the Hebrides: Waternish and Duirinish, with Loch Dunvegan and nebulous Loch Bracadale lapping their wriggling coastlines. Duirinish is green farmland, Highland cattle and coastal cliffs; Waternish similar but more austere and rumpled, with the odd pagodas of MacLeod's Tables snaring your eye. To your right, the peculiar knuckles-and-spikes of the Storr gateway the Trotternish, a huge, north-striking peninsula. As its spine it has a stepped, green-felted ridgeline that culminates in the Quiraing, a collapsed castle of ruinous steeples and green keeps, beyond which Skye makes its spectacular last gasp at the sentinel-like cliffs of Rubha Hunish.

As has often been said, whoever created the world was showing off when they made Skye. And the reasons for this huge variation in form and feel start, rather literally, at ground level. Or to be more accurate, quite a long way beneath it.

The sun had set by the time I reached Broadford and once again turned for Elgol. The road slung through a reedy slack holding Loch Cill Chriosd, named for the ruined church standing above it. As I passed, the loch's waters caught pink skies and the outline of Blàbheinn (often shortened to the incorrect but catchy Blaven). This burly sentry of the Cuillin ridge was blackening in the light, its spires gathering a cloak of pale cloud.

My plan to be on the hill before full dark wasn't going well. By the time I reached the head of Loch Slapin at Torrin the light was dying fast. No moon had risen, and a night without a moon or streetlights of any kind is a dark night indeed in a place like Skye. As the road glimpsed the coast and headed south along the sharpening Strathaird peninsula the scattered lights of boats and the occasional house ahead became disparate beacons as the island fell under the wing of the night.

Then, a few hundred metres short of my destination, my headlights caught something unexpected on the skyline of the road ahead. I slowed, then stopped. Lit against the deep navy sky was a wall of Highland cattle, their breath steaming in the cooling air.

Laugh if you like at these shaggy brown creatures with the hippy fringe and enormous handlebar horns – you can buy toy ones in the gift shops – but the Highland cow is an imposing animal. A couple of them were lying down and the rest just stood there. All were monumentally indifferent to my car. One was a calf.

I didn't really know what to do here. I'd have googled it if I'd had a phone signal, but that had long vanished. I'd read about Highland cattle, but was struggling to remember what. I was sure they were definitely either very good natured or very aggressive. I did know that cows were, in general, rather underrated as a danger – something it didn't seem a good idea to test alone on a dark island out of signal. So I just sat there, car idling, considering the best course of action when faced with the modern equivalent of a triceratops herd blocking a single-track road.

I was probably being daft. Had there been any locals around they'd probably have just strode up and shoo'd them with a tut and maybe a ruffle of their hair. But there was nobody around at all. I ventured a couple of timid toots on the horn and crawled the car forward towards them, again without any useful reaction. Eventually, feeling unjustly – not to mention bizarrely – thwarted, I reversed down the road to a pull-in several hundred metres back. Fifteen minutes later I was pushing west up a pathless hillside, cursing the cows, myself and the dark – but determined to get to where I wanted to be, if only to see if my hunch was right.

Stand anywhere high in the Northwest Highlands or the Hebrides on a clear day with an uninterrupted view, and you'll see the Cuillin ridge. It's like a speedbump in any sweep of eyes across the horizon, from any angle – eyes slow to a stop on its dark bristles for some absorbed scrutiny, even if just for a moment. But despite this, it's hard to find a place where you can see it *all*. And so, for several weeks before leaving for Skye I had been searching maps for the ultimate viewpoint of the Cuillin ridge. The saddle between Sgùrr na Stri and Sgùrr Hain – where Captain Maryon had met his mysterious fate – was the most popular to square up to the ridge at close quarters. But my glimpse through the clouds in the winter felt *too* close; you didn't get the full picture, the full combination of mountain range, loch, coastline and sea that built such a spectacular piece of landscape. I wanted something more panoramic where I could take the whole thing in, in context. I'd looked at maps, photographs, compared elevations, imagined sightlines. And the reason I was slogging up this stubbornly raked slope above Elgol on this particular evening was that I was pretty sure I'd found it.

The hill was called Ben Cleat. It was barely anything: 277 metres high, dumpy and pretty featureless other than some crags to the north and west. But the map confirmed there was nothing higher between Ben Cleat and the view I wanted, which meant that come morning, the prospect should really be quite something. I'd not found any pictures or descriptions as to whether this was likely to be the case, so tonight I was putting my money where my map said it was.

Climbing a hill on good, rocky ground in darkness cut by the light of a big moon is one of the best things you can do. Climbing grass on a black night wearing a headtorch isn't. The only thing you can see is the area lit by the spotlight attached to your head, which means you need to keep your head pointing at your feet to see where you're putting them. It's not easy to walk this way on steep ground. By the time I'd fallen over twice I tried switching off the light to see if my eyes would adjust to the dark, but it really was *dark*; were it not for the crouched lights of Elgol tilting away to my back, it would have been like wearing a shroud. But slowly I pushed upwards, the angle beneath my feet began to slacken, and eventually I sensed the rise ahead of me give way to a starless, misty sky. Elgol's cluster of light had vanished behind the hill; ahead of me was just dark. I switched off my torch and stood, breathing hard, and let my eyes grope for light. Somewhere in that darkness was the sea, the coastline, distant islands. And the ridge. Switching on my torch again, I pulled out my compass and found the approximate direction. It must be there, right in front of me, like a taunting hand in a black room.

Right or wrong, I was tired, it was late and I needed to get my tent up. Sludging around the lumpy top, I started scouring the ground for a flat patch. Every levelling I found seemed to have a lump of cowpat on it, which sent my mind back to the Highland cattle on the road; I hoped there wasn't a herd up here, too. Eventually I found a human-sized patch that was relatively dry and shit-free, and, with a final check of the compass, threw down my pack and pulled out my tent.

When the walking and the heavy breathing and the tent-pitching stops, wild camping in a remote place like this affords a preternaturally deep silence. This can be disconcerting, or at least take some getting used to. After the constant noise of the drive, the packing, the walk, the unpacking and the breathless nylon rustling of pitching camp, as I tightened the last guy of my tent near the summit of Ben Cleat, that silence fell. Chilly now, I listened. A soft but insistent booming sound: the sea impacting the shore, far below but close-sounding. Distant, weak tweet noises: birds. And that was it. It's an uneasy feeling to the noise-accustomed sometimes, this silence in wild places. I began to become nervy of hearing something I didn't like the sound of out in the dark and the quiet, so I busied myself getting into my tent, oddly grateful for the noise.

A thin cloud had started to hug the ground as I climbed inside, took a last look north-west and zipped up the tent. It was a wretched, soggy camp on bad ground. The dawn might be an anticlimax; I might not get what I came for. Skye's weather loved to scupper a well-laid plan; it had foiled mine in February; maybe it would foil me again now. The forecast was for rain and cloud tomorrow. As I zipped myself up tight I prayed it would be wrong.

Approaching a subject like the Cuillin, with so many threads of history and natural curiosity so intertwined, it's rather difficult to know where to start. Charles Weld, writing in 1860, said of the ridge:

> You cannot fail to be struck by the remarkable form and character of the rocks. Do not, I pray you, think of visiting . . . without making yourself, to some degree, acquainted with the geological features of those mountains. You are not only in the presence of some of the most sublime scenery in this varied world, but also of wonderful phenomena.

Unusually for Weld, this was good advice. It's a rather involved tale, but as it took the earth four-and-a-half billion years and an awful lot of effort to get here I'm sure we can spare a few pages. So let's start at the beginning of the journey that led to the moment that the Cuillin ridge exploded into existence, then consider the melting, seeping, scraping, sculpting, cracking, and breaking that made the thing that today you put your hands on: the rock.

That rock. Whether you realise it or not, all your reasons for coming here, every stick that stokes your fascination with the Cuillin ultimately begins with the rock they call gabbro. In the right circles, the mere mention of its name stirs a sort of lustful exhale. Its coarse grains are like cells packed with DNA, setting the blueprint for everything the Cuillin grew to be, of every kink and profile, of all that defines it as unique. It gives it its height, its character, its grip, its feel – and also its danger. And the most remarkable thing about it is, it's very young rock. Until ridiculously recently, it wasn't there at all.

Of course we're talking geologically recently, not recently in the sense that an elderly relative might remember a Hebridean skyline un-menaced by the Cuillin. And this is a long haul: the ancestral foundations of Scotland stretch back almost as far as recorded geological time. This foundation is Lewisian gneiss, a silvery, wrinkled, three-billion-year-old rock that you can still find in abundance in the northern Highlands, and slivered into Skye on Sleat and Strathaird, the oldest rock rubbing up against the newest in the Cuillin, a scamp at just sixty million years old. Superficially this may be unremarkable to most. But consider the time scales between these two neighbouring types of rock and things start getting increasingly remarkable. If Lewisian gneiss has been around for an hour, the Cuillin ridge has occupied just seventy-two seconds of Scotland's geological history. This means that while the gneiss pre-dates most life on earth, the Cuillin is younger than most species that have ever existed. And here on this island, they sit side by side.

That there were creatures vaguely resembling modern-day birds, reptiles and mammals on earth long before this mountain range came to be is, to me at least, incredible. However much we conceive of mountains as being memory sinks of shelly fossils and the product of great expanses of time and extremes of pressure, it still seems surreal that entire massifs could be younger than the recognisable lifeforms of the past. But more significant is the point on the timeline where the formation of the Cuillin ridge stands, the theatrical eulogy of two intertwined curtain calls – the last of our mountain ranges to be built, and the final flamboyant bow of British volcanism.

Before this, rather a lot happened to the landmass upon which Scotland currently sits. Geology is a difficult thing to get your head around. Most people simply haven't got the patience to try to understand it and give up rapidly and hopelessly – rather like you might give up rapidly and hopelessly when trying to levitate a pint glass with your mind. I don't mean this unkindly, just that there's a lot of complexity to unpick, and as a science we still really aren't anywhere near breaking the back of it.

A fitting case in point, Britain's geology is *incredibly* complicated. Scotland in particular has the most varied geology of anywhere of comparable size on the planet, and resembles a sort of rocky scrapheap. That's hardly surprising, considering the journey the country had been on by the time it reached its current position in the North Atlantic. For a time prior to this, most of Scotland was part of an archipelago off the coast of a supercontinent called Laurentia, which included what would become modern-day Greenland and North America. This archipelago was shoved forcefully into an intimacy with England and Wales, having spent an eternity with at least an ocean between them. En route, Scotland had travelled the Southern Hemisphere, drifted by the South Pole, with occupants and environments dressed for the appropriate latitude it was moving through at the time. In *Scotland: The Creation of Its Natural Landscape*, Alan McKirdy and Roger Crofts paint a rather festive picture of this 'voyage', describing Scotland as 'drifting across the surface of the planet like a great ark, constructed of rock rather than wood, and driven not by the tides and the winds but by the movement of plates on the earth's surface', and carrying a 'varied cargo of plants and animals'.

This cargo has resulted in fossils from wildly different environments existing in close proximity within different strata of Scottish rock. These souvenirs of a life long passed are like fading tattoos, discreetly covered up as lifestyles evolve – a fern from when Scotland was tropical and jungly, a crinoid sea lily from when it was the seafloor of a tropical lagoon, footprints from when it was the hunting ground of dinosaurs. But here's the thing: they're not in the correct temporal order, and for a long time nobody looking at these traces could fathom what on earth was going on.

Understanding how these rocks came to become so mangled and out of sequence – old rocks on top of young, vastly different ages rubbing up side by side and the odd peculiar anomaly – is perhaps the hardest part of all this to get your head around. I did a geology degree and I'm really not sure, despite thousands of pounds of academic investment, that I came out of those woodstain-foetid lecture rooms any the wiser. But in the years since I've got more of a grasp of the topic, and not from impenetrable geological maps, academic textbooks or interpretation graphics. It's largely thanks to my daughter and her Play-Doh.

Let me explain. The things that had always stumped me were the maps. Maps are the key to everything – a cipher to a place, a subject, a way of thinking. And geological maps are magnificent works of intense colour and detail. Like all maps, they show surface features – the exposed outcrops of a particular rock type in a particular place. We all now know that rocks are represented in layers over millions of years, and each layer is a capsule of the environment at that particular time – sandy river delta, volcanic land-scape, shelly seabed and so on. Given such a process, you would expect the surface layer of rock to be a product of the most recent environment, give or take older anomalies exposed by the whittlings of erosion. But rather than being uniform, these geological maps were chaotic, full of speckles and slashes of wildly contrasting rocks from different ages and origins. I understood that this was a visualisation of what was going on at the surface but I had no idea how to reconcile it with what was going on under the ground, let alone figure out how it came to be that way.

One day I was watching my little daughter playing with Play-Doh of various colours. She was rolling each out in strips – red, yellow, blue – and building them up in layers. Sandwiches and cakes, she said. Then she started slicing them up. After that she lost interest and pottered off to do something else, and I was left at the table. I picked up one of the sandwiches of Play-Doh and began folding it and rolling it around in my fingers, after which the neat coloured layers took on a pretty, mixed-up, marbling look, where the different colours had joined and fused. I remember thinking it looked a little like a geological map.

It was actually a near-perfect miniature of a geological map – and not just that, a miniature of geological *process*. Geology is pressure and time, on a giant scale. That's the reason old rocks end up on top of new ones, and how layers become fragmented, mangled and chaotic – anywhere that has been geologically lively enough to produce mountains or cliffs or valleys has had its rocks squashed, rolled, squeezed and folded over the aeons in pretty much the same way I'd been messing with that Play-Doh. Continental collisions, uplift, fracturing, folding, pressure – all done with my fingers, on a scale the size of a coaster.

But in a world without geological maps or Play-Doh, the under-standing of even the basic processes that led to the formation of the Cuillin ridge didn't long pre-date its first explorers. Back then – the middle of the 18th century – science was philosophy, and religion the text of reason. Jacquetta Hawkes, in her articulate chronology of Britain, *A Land*, summed up the argument between science and faith over the ever-moving, shifting earth:

It is the endless problem of philosophers; either they give process, energy its due and neglect its formal limitations, or they look only at forms and forget the irresistible power of change.

Prior to the period, most thinkers – religious, philosophical or otherwise – still believed the world had only been around since one lively week ending at the curiously precise time of 6 p.m. on 22 October 4004 BC. This was the figure offered in 1650 by the Archbishop James Ussher, an Irishman whose interpretive work on the Old Testament reckoned this to be when that God cleared away the last of his decorating sheets (or whatever He did at the end of such a task) and presumably collapsed on the sofa with a large drink. The 'Ussher chronology' became the foundation of what we now call New World Creationism. In the face of this, any opposing idea was nothing short of heresy, and in the eyes of many threatened to unbalance the entire foundations of the Bible. But still, the ideas came, though to start with they were somewhat accommodating in their attitude towards religion. A surge in this period of (slightly) more secular thinking north of the border was to become known as the Scottish Enlightenment, but further afield in Europe there were other theories being presented to explain the earth's origins that required no almighty Creator.

One was catastrophism, which sidestepped any theological quagmires by suggesting the earth had been shaped by a series of sudden and disfiguring eruptions, storms and deluges, such as Noah's Old Testament flood, that had bashed and scalded the surface of the planet into its current form. This was initially proposed by controversial French scientist Georges-Louis Leclerc, better known as the Comte de Buffon, who challenged Ussher's dating of the earth by claiming the planet was at least 75,000 years old and possibly (and why not?) created by a comet colliding with the sun. Although pressure from the theology department at the Sorbonne in Paris forced him to publicly retract his ideas as he'd sailed into waters a little too choppy for their liking, Buffon continued to promote his theory in many of his subsequent works.

The man who developed Buffon's ideas and popularised catastrophism was another Frenchman, Georges Cuvier. A Lutheran scientist, Cuvier's keenness to investigate the earth's origins was to make sense of the bones he was digging out of geological strata, which were far too large and strange to come from any recently living animal. The word 'fossil' had been used since the Middle Ages to describe anything that came from the ground; it's where the term 'fossil fuel' originated. But with the growing understanding of how long the processes of the earth took to do just about anything, certain uncomfortable truths were beginning to rise to the surface, along with the curious bones and petrified trees emerging from ever-deeper excavations.

Put simply, this hard evidence of clearly ancient processes at work meant Creationism as described in the Bible was looking increasingly shaky – and a lot of powerful institutions didn't like this idea at all. As Buffon had found, even during the so-called Enlightenment, God was still very much an influence on philosophers and scientists trying to forge a kind of nervous truce between science and religion. Even Isaac Newton spent considerable time attempting to determine the age of the earth, not from the ground beneath his feet but from scriptures. As Alexander Pope wrote in *An Essay on Man* in 1733:

> All are but parts of one stupendous whole,
> Whose body Nature is, and God the soul

The idea of catastrophism supported Cuvier's own theory of extinction events – 'revolutions' – that had re-shaped the earth, and it neatly explained why long-dead creatures had ended up buried in a layer of rubbly rock and sediment, although his reasoning fell short of explaining why the bones themselves had started to turn to stone. Cuvier had a particular knack for drawing deft conclusions from skeletal remains, and his relentless examination of every interesting item clawed from quarries or lurking misidentified in museum stores led to him being known internationally as a good man to present with anything peculiar found in the ground. Cuvier had already suggested a 'world previous to ours', where giant mammals walked the earth; his inspections of what he judged to be the remains of a very large reptile – notably a jaw and tooth unearthed in Stonesfield near Oxford – led him to observe that mammal bones were found near the surface, and reptile bones in older, deeper deposits devoid of mammalian traces.

From this Cuvier made two uncanny observations: first, that rock layers and the march of time were linked; second, that the older remains came from a world dominated by land and sea reptiles, not mammals. While most of Cuvier's own practical work was on ancient elephants and sloths – and despite the word not being coined for some years after his death in 1832 – his name will forever be bound to the Latin for 'terrible lizard': *dinosaur*.

Another popular theory of the day was Neptunism, put forward by German scientist and miner Abraham Gottlob Werner. Central to this hypothesis was the sea being the chief agent in the sifting and layering of the materials that made up a geological stratum. Werner's theory was quite outlandish even by the standards of the age; his notion was that the earth was initially entirely made of water thick with suspended sediments, which over time settled and compacted into a core, then formed continents consisting first of granite (the oldest and hardest), then newer material near the surface, which contained fossils.

Neptunism's elemental and theoretical foe was Plutonism – a term that would eventually have particular relevance in any discussion of Skye and the Cuillin. Also called Vulcanism, this school claimed the earth's form was largely a result of volcanic eruptions and outpourings of lava. Given its associations in religious literature with hell, the idea of a fiery underworld was a hit with the more theologically inclined, and was first proposed by the Italian abbot Anton Moro, who had studied Italy's volcanic islands. The two theories did heated battle in a colourful array of arenas throughout the late 18th century – principally in scientific and religious halls, but occasionally in literature too. Even Goethe visited the argument in *Faust*, where the play's eponymous scholar condemns the demon Mephistopheles's belief in Plutonism 'as a tale of seething madness'.

The arguments between Plutonism and Neptunism, and later catastrophism, eventually led to something approaching a single theory comprising elements of all three. Neptunism – were you to ignore the world of water, and the idea that granite was made from suspended stodge – roughly describes the process of sedimentation, which creates sandstone, limestone, shales and other fossil-rich rock. Plutonism – if taken as being pressure, heat and its associated explosions and seepages – forms the core of the planet, and in tandem with transient sedimentation has reworked much of its surface. And every now and again, catastrophism in one of its many forms has stepped in to shake things up: floods, earthquakes, landslides, and the occasional stinker of an asteroid.

Which brings us back to Scotland, and the interesting man who drew all of this together in the most timely way. Geology as a science was born in the country, and the first person who had a serious go at it – that is to say, attempted to explain the creation of the world without instrumental use of the word 'God' – was a Scottish academic named James Hutton.

Born in 1726 in Edinburgh, Hutton started his career in law, before indulging a curiosity for chemistry (and fleeing the responsibilities of an illegitimate child) by moving to France and taking a degree in medicine. Returning first to London in 1750 as a qualified doctor, he resumed his chemical tinkering and, in correspondence with his Edinburgh friend James Davie, stumbled upon a lucrative enterprise that created *sal ammoniac* from soot, a mineral used in the production of everything from stained-glass windows to crispy bread. The resulting chemical works in Edinburgh removed at a stroke the need to import the substance at great expense from the Middle East, and secured Hutton and Davie a comfortable income for life. A spell as a property magnate and an agricultural landlord followed, largely on a farm he had inherited from his father near Berwick – and so began the phase of his life that history would remember.

During his time as a landowner, Hutton began to cultivate an interest in what was at the time called natural philosophy but would come to be known as geological science. Pottering about on his farm, with an inquiring mind and the spare time to indulge it, Hutton wrote to his friend Sir John Hall of becoming 'very fond of studying the surface of the earth ... looking with anxious curiosity into every pit or ditch or bed of a river.' Hutton consumed works on all the contemporary theories, and soon came to believe that the earth was *extremely* ancient, based on his canny deduction that soil derived from weathered rock. For this to occur, he noted, new rock must be being produced from below at a rate that was almost incomprehensibly slow. Moving back to Edinburgh in 1768, Hutton travelled widely to gather further evidence for his theory, first documenting the dramatic features of England's south coast, then undertaking an exhaustive tour of Scotland.

Of particular interest to Hutton on this tour was the distribution and occurrence of rock types, particularly granite, and basalt – the dark rock the Germans called *schwartzstein*, Swedes *trap* and Scots *whinstone* – the origins of which were in fierce dispute between Plutonists and Neptunists. Hutton was ostensibly a Plutonist, in that he appreciated the logic of rocks having a volcanic origin. Much of his later work and his examinations of basalt moving 'in a serpentine manner' through other types of rock leaned more towards the volcanic origin than the watery one.

But following his extensive fieldwork across Britain, Hutton's mind was working harder on the bigger picture. All this came to a climax when Hutton chartered a boat with the chemist Sir John Hall, and mathematician and diarist John Playfair, to observe the structure of the sea cliffs on the east coast of Scotland. Hutton studied a sequence of strata at Siccar Point where one series of ancient – we now know, 435 million years ancient – sedimentary graywacke rock, folded and distorted by much pressure and time, was directly overlaid by a fresher, clearly much newer rock in a quite different orientation. That there was a clear inconsistency, a missing puzzle piece, suggested that the foundation rock had been laid in quite different conditions to the surface rocks, and that the material between the two unrelated layers – some 65 million years' worth – had been weathered away.

Siccar Point would turn out to be the eureka example of a series of such boundaries, albeit inconclusive ones, that Hutton identified across Scotland: one near Jedburgh, one on the Isle of Arran and another in Teviotdale. They became known by the generic term of 'Hutton's Unconformity' – a name given not to one specific location but to a type of outcrop displaying this kind of anomaly. The word 'unconformity' related to a peculiarly disjointed geological sequence, although the key to Hutton's conclusions wasn't the rock that was there, but the rock that wasn't. Rather like a cloth pulled deftly from beneath a laid table, or lines deleted from a paragraph, this juxtaposition of rocks that were different in every way to each other – their conditions of creation, composition, angle of repose and the small matter of the time it took to build, then erode away that missing intervening layer – lengthened the world's geological timescales by an almost unfathomable extent. As Hutton's biographer, John Playfair, wrote:

> We felt necessarily carried back to a time when the schistus on which
> we stood was yet at the bottom of the sea, and when the sandstone
> before us was only beginning to be deposited . . . The mind seemed to
> grow giddy by looking so far into the abyss of time.

The abyss, it would seem, looked back. Hutton's influential 'Theory of
the Earth', published in 1788, was a masterwork of diplomatic reasoning,
acknowledging most of the major ideas of the time yet making far more
sense than any of them on their own. He called his theory 'Uniformitarianism',
a reference to its central idea that the same processes that shaped and
continue to shape the earth have been consistently the same, are ongoing
and everywhere, constantly recycling and repeating before our very eyes –
just rather too slowly to appreciate. This idea of a cycle, in which soil and
weathered rock are washed into the sea, compacted into rock, forced through
the crust by heat to the surface then eroded back down into soil and sediment, was a direct affront not only to biblical interpretation of the earth's
origin and Ussher's somewhat brisker timescales, but to most other theories
doing the rounds at the time. Hutton's paper contained a memorable expression of what became known in geology as 'deep time': the idea that the
earth's age stretched far, far further back into the past than anyone could
imagine. Hutton stated simply: 'We see no vestige of a beginning, no prospect of an end.'

Interestingly, though, Hutton was not an atheist. He identified as a deist,
in that while he didn't follow a specific religion, he considered – insisted
on, in fact – the existence of an omnipotent consciousness in the formation
of the planet and its machinations. 'This globe,' he stated in 'Theory of the
Earth', 'is evidently made for man . . . [it] is a habitable world, and on its
fitness for this purpose, our sense of mission in its formation must depend.'
His idea of the planet as cyclical and infinitely recycling was, however, starkly
at odds with the Christian idea of a unidirectional and human-witnessed
history of the earth, in which the planet was made, was sculpted by disas-
ters and would one day end forever. From our current perspective, this
difference may seem trivial – but at the time it was anything but. Hutton's
seemingly casual blending of natural processes with the will of a higher
consciousness was quite alien to many of his contemporaries, particularly

in Europe, and much of his writing reads more like philosophy than geology. He asked us to consider the earth as 'not merely . . . a machine' but as 'an organised body . . . in which necessary decay of the machine is naturally repaired'.

Essentially the theological position boiled down to efficient management: the Christians believed the world had to be maintained by a deity who liked to get rather ruthlessly hands-on at times to keep things habitable. Hutton's deity designed the world and its processes so well to start with that the world rather nicely maintained itself.

The scientific community responded largely negatively to Hutton's theory of total, gradual destruction and infinite rebuilding – not least because of his knack for impenetrable phrasing, which made the finer points of his argument almost impossible to grasp. Chief amongst his detractors was a group known as the Wernerians, followers of the Neptunist theory of Abraham Gottlob Werner. Hutton had gone to some lengths to assert that land appearing above the ocean was the result of the seafloor being elevated by the action of churning heat within the earth, contradicting the Wernerian belief that it came from the waters receding and exposing towering sediments on the seabed. He did so with the reasonable observation that nobody could explain where the receding seas went, nor where the material required to build the land materialised from.

But Hutton's assertion that the hard, crystalline rocks of Arran and the granite he had sought so doggedly across the Highlands was of volcanic origin, rather than the sedimentary origin its appearance so readily suggested, met with near-universal opposition. Mineralogists were quite content with the idea that cooling rock formed powdery, glassy rocks, but not the warty, granular granites and gabbros. The Wernerians could suggest convincingly that the grains were *deposited*, while Hutton could not demonstrate that heat could forge and fuse them, despite his observations that the spitting, readily observable volcanoes found around the world were clearly the cooling valves of the earth. This derailed him, and his theory failed to connect with many in the scientific establishment, even his Enlightenment contemporaries. Richard Kirwan, an outspoken Irish chemist who opposed Huttonian theory, wrote in 1793 that while aspects of the Wernerian theory 'escape our reason', the effect of Hutton's conclusions was to actively contradict much of the accepted wisdom of the day. They were just, it would seem, a step too far.

Hutton's response to challenges to his theory, as you might expect of one so evidently fastidious, was simply to gather ever-increasing amounts of evidence. As his theory turned out to be correct, this evidence was not in short supply. The two volumes of highly detailed work that followed in 1795, also called *Theory of the Earth*, were if anything diluted by rather too much of it, augmented by Hutton's wanderings down obscure corridors of thickety language that tested the engagement of even his most attentive readers. The books' impact was not quite, as posterity has proven, as resonant as they deserved. Rachel Laudan dryly summed this up in *From Mineralogy to Geology: The Foundations of Modern Science*: 'Numerous reasons have been advanced to explain this, including his bad prose style, his unorthodox theory of erosion, his equally unorthodox theory of heat and most generally his theology.' Put more pithily by Bill Bryson in *A Short History of Nearly Everything*, Hutton's sprawling but impenetrable masterwork ranks as 'maybe the least read important book in science'.

Painted in later life by Sir Henry Raeburn, Hutton is portrayed as a solemn figure with a high hairline, a sallow expression and a hawkish nose. One visitor to Hutton's Edinburgh residence once remarked that the place was 'so full of fossils and chemical apparatus that there is hardly room to sit down', and accordingly, in the portrait Hutton is sitting at a desk cluttered with rocks, a shell and, quill at the ready, what appears to be a voluminous manuscript. After his death in 1797, a string of friends, successors and well-wishers played pass-the-parcel for many decades with the unbound heft of his third volume of geological theorising. First port of call for the manuscript was Hutton's friend and biographer John Playfair, who would produce an admired illustrated retrospective of Hutton in 1802. Scientist Lord John Webb Seymour was the next custodian, who drew on some of the work for his own research and declared the manuscript 'nearly ready for the press' in 1814. When Seymour died, the work found its way into the hands of geologist Leonard Horner, who entrusted it to the Geological Society of Edinburgh, founded in 1834. By the time Horner passed it into the society's archive it was 1856. It remained there until 1899.

The man who finally put a full stop of sorts on the work of James Hutton was Sir Archibald Geikie, a man whose love affair with the Hebrides left a legacy of books and acts that would make his name important in the history of not only geology, but the Cuillin too. Geikie wrestled Volume III of *Theory of the Earth* into print in the last year of the 19th century, and in his preface he gives a fine summary of how far the stock Hutton's theory had risen in the century since his death: 'It is a source of deep gratification to me to have been permitted to render a service to the memory of the Father of Modern Geology,' he wrote, using the title commonly applied upon Hutton, then as now. 'I fain hope that the present long-delayed publication of his third volume may be the means of directing renewed attention to his immortal work . . . which must ever remain one of the great landmarks in the onward march of science.'

You may well wonder what all of this has to do with the Cuillin ridge. To this I offer two reasons: first, to understand the origin of these mountains – as with knowing the background to a work of art – helps you appreciate them to the full. There is no other mountain range in Britain with a geology that lays down its terms of passage across it quite so starkly. If you do not understand the rock, you cannot truly know the ridge. The second is that the early investigators of the Cuillin ridge – the proto-mountaineers, scientists and 'curiosity men' – were people like Hutton, as important to the growth of geological knowledge as they were to the initial explorations of this particular mountain range.

It would be under the auspices of scientific discovery that the early geologists would investigate the Cuillin ridge and climb its peaks. And the Cuillin would later return the favour to science by providing the field ground for research that would deepen the understanding of how our planet works. Not bad for a fairly compact mountain range on a Hebridean island.

At 3 a.m. I needed a wee, and after some personal deliberation I pulled myself out of my tent. The wind had dropped and the night was thick. I looked east for light, and saw only a slightly brighter stripe of grey beyond the black knuckles of the mainland across the Sound of Sleat. The sky seemed cloudy and starless, which didn't give me much hope for a glorious dawn. But I could just see the outline of a sharp mountain to the north-west, which after

the previous evening's groping around in the dark I took as proof that I was
at least camping in the right place to get a view. Noticing the heavy dew on
the flysheet of my tent and yelping as a good deal of it skittered down my
neck as I climbed back in, I closed my eyes and fell into a shallow dose,
waking at intervals, as if worrying about an early appointment.

During one of these stirrings I poked my head out and looked in the
direction of the mountain I'd seen. There it was, the end of the ridge, the
darkest of three shades of grey in the weak pre-dawn: grey rock against grey
sky, grasped by grey wadding – cloud, and lots of it. Disappointed but
clearly now off-duty in my vigil for anything spectacular riding over the
horizon come daybreak, I fell heavily asleep.

I awoke to the tent burning with light and warmth. Without thinking,
I opened a hole in the zipper of the tent door, my eyes searching through
for my visual compass: that grey peak that signalled the position of the
ridge. Only it wasn't grey. Its topmost ramparts were gold and glowing
against a sky of sharp blue. I dived for my boots.

How deep do you want to go with the origins of the Cuillin itself? Geology
from here can go one of two ways. When I started my research into the
ridge I trawled through all the geological papers I could find, convinced I
needed every last detail as to how this extraordinary mountain range came
to be – what built it, why it was so different and what made it look the way
it looked. The more I read, the more I realised that this was the archetypal
scientific rabbit hole – enticing at first, engaging for a while, then prone to
break off into a bewildering maze-warren with many spurs, dead ends and
unexplored alleyways leading into catacombs of obscure and perhaps irrel-
evant facts. And of course, the occasional chamber full of the arguing
scientists who dug it.

James Hutton's notion of the endless building and weathering of the
earth is the literal groundwork. In *A Land*, Jacquetta Hawkes evocatively
slides this science into poetry, likening the building and breaking of mountains to breathing:

> The bosom of the landscape lifts and falls
> With its own leaden tide

Isn't that nice? Far more resonant than pages and pages of detail that read, for example, like this:

In this chapter we have to describe certain ultrabasic rocks, and rocks bordering on the ultrabasic in composition, which are younger than the laccolitic bodies of plutonic peridotites, and since the differences are petrographical as well as geological, separate descriptions are necessary.

You grasp my point. Happily, we don't need to be that technical here, but if the above leaves you salivating for more, there's plenty out there if you want it; see the bibliography if you want to go looking. You well might, too, as some of the most important mountaineering in the Cuillin was done by geologists with a theory in their nostrils. To that end, there are a few more things you need to know about how the ridge itself came to be, but I'm going to do my best to make it as painless as possible.

Scotland and England celebrated their geological union around 410 million years ago, when an ocean that dwarfed the present-day Atlantic – known to interested trilobites as the Iapetus – completed its closure along a line just to the north and roughly parallel to Hadrian's Wall in an intersection known as the Iapetus Suture. Still affiliated with other land masses (Scotland with North America, England with what would become continental Europe), the two impacted like crashing container ships, crumpling up a mountain range quite possibly as high as the present-day Himalaya, but long since worn down to the stubs of the present-day Highlands and Southern Uplands. The cracking and pressure-fracturing of the crust gave birth to volcanoes, the remnants of which can be found in the Lake District, the West Highlands and the Cairngorms, mangled amongst other much older rock.

This was the first significant event in the building of the landscape we know today, the joining of our land and the knitting together of the patchwork that makes up these modest isles. If you've ever wondered why Britain's landscape is so varied over such a small area, that's why. The second significant event was the opening of the North Atlantic, which had as much of an effect on the shaping of the planet as it sounds.

The concept of continental drift – the manner in which the great landmasses of the planet fragment and move around their watery world, like scale on the surface of a stewed cup of tea – was way beyond James Hutton's imagining. But it does share much with his theory, not least the idea of an eternal churn of renewal. The brief moment in geological time after the Iapetus Ocean closed and Scotland and England got friendly was a period of widespread affection amongst the continents. At this point they were all holding hands together in one unfathomably large landmass called Pangaea. This lay adrift in Panthalassa, one unfathomably large ocean. Many envision Pangaea to be continental Year One, the maternal whole from which everything else split, but this isn't so. Continents had been colliding with each other for billions of years already – it just so happened that at this point they all collided together. Pangaea formed around 335 million years ago and began to break apart some 175 million years ago. It had happened before, and it will happen again. Rebuild, recycle. Breathe in, breathe out. During the early stages of Pangaea's break-up, North America, Greenland and Europe sat as one great landmass made up of three distinct parts: Laurentia, Baltica and Avalonia.

Like much of geological theory, the understanding of the processes involved in this is pretty recent; there are Beatles records that pre-date anything approaching a clear view of how this most colossal of geological events works. That said, the idea that the continents were at one point attached to each other was nothing new; the evidence was, to put it mildly, eyeballing us from even the earliest days of cartography – or at least the 1600s, when maps began to take shape in a way we would recognise today. Even now, give any jigsaw-loving six-year-old a map of the world and they're likely to suggest South America and Africa might cuddle together rather neatly, as indeed they once did. Evidence for this wasn't in short supply, either. Rock outcrops along the coasts of present-day Namibia and Nigeria link up as neatly with those in Brazil and Argentina as a French stick torn in two, while across Scandinavia, Scotland, Ireland, Greenland and the eastern United States lie fragments of an ancient mountain range – the Caledonides – that were clearly all formed in the same period and once stood together as one single belt. Bits of the Scottish Highlands, the Appalachians of the eastern United States and the Scandinavian Caledonides (the latter still bearing the name of this once great range) may have all developed regional accents and physical characteristics in the 500 million years since their separation, but once upon a time they were rather harder to distinguish.

Fossils had also been found on opposing coasts that bore too uncanny a resemblance to each other to have developed in isolation on continents separated by oceans. The clear implication was that these creatures – notably proto-dinosaur reptiles called mesosaurs– once walked together on common ground before it was torn asunder and cast adrift. The more romantic might imagine two affectionate reptiles called mesosaurs – let's call them Steve and Eve – staring at each other helplessly from the shores of continents separating like steamer ships, forever to be parted with an ocean between them. Obviously, Steve and Eve were dead millions of years before their forceful scissoring, rather like words in a printed sentence, that once lay together on a piece of paper long since ripped and scattered.

So scientists knew that the continents were once joined and had since drifted apart; what they couldn't figure out was *how* it was happening. The answer came from a curious man named Harry Hammond Hess. The commander of a lively attack transport in the Pacific during the Second World War and a Princeton lecturer in geology back home, Hess kept his sonar equipment running day and night whilst criss-crossing the ocean. He was ostensibly looking for enemy submarines, but with the diverting benefit of also mapping the sea floor. His readings revealed much about the sub-oceanic landscape – principally that it was made up of vast, flat and deeply uninteresting basins. These were, however, occasionally interrupted by strange flat-topped seamounts Hess named 'guyots', and the odd colossal undersea mountain range. Hess also found that the inverse of these ranges – deep trenches descending to awesome depths of six miles or more – could be found near several oceanic edges.

Continuing his research after the end of the war, Hess's 1962 paper 'History of Ocean Basins', despite being one of those pieces of geological work that is almost impossible for the casual reader to understand, was evidently impossible for learned geologists to put down. Even to citizen scientists, it contained a few statements of particular clarity that would have seismic repercussions down the decades. 'The mid-ocean ridges are the largest topographical features on the earth,' he writes, before quoting some facts stating that the ridges were typically almost precisely in the centre of the ocean, and that they had been found to have unusually high heat flow along their length.

What Hess didn't know then was that the ridges were *seriously* huge, and contiguous – a 50,000-mile network of ranges that wrapped the planet like the rough stitching on a baseball. Hess's eventual hypothesis was that the crustal plates of the earth, whose boundaries were marked by these mountain ranges and trenches, were moving on top of a kettle of hot, stodgy mantle. These plates were kept churning around by convection currents and the rotation of the planet – an engine room known as a geo-dynamo. The reason the planet didn't crack and spill its contents was that fresh crust was being produced on the seabed and those submarine mountain ranges were in fact gigantic, scabbed cracks where the mantle was forcing itself through onto the seabed. Sure enough, these mid-ocean ridges each had a valley in their centre, deep inside which mantle was emerging to form new crust, pushing the plates apart as it went. This rate is thought to vary from the speed that fingernails grow (about 4cm per year) to the speed that hair grows (around 16cm per year).

This also explained why the seafloor was so devoid of ancient sediments – as Hess put it, the average oceanic bed is 'swept clean' of everything every 300 to 400 million years. He also suggested that the reason the earth isn't just getting bigger and bigger, as it would with a constant production of new crust, was that on the opposite side of the ocean it was being dragged back into the mantle and melting at the same rate it was being produced. The whole thing was rather like a series of conveyor belts – one side rising, one side falling – and the whole lot in motion all the time. 'The continents do not plow through oceanic crust impelled by unknown forces,' he wrote. 'Rather they ride passively on mantle material as it comes to the surface at the crest of the ridge and then moves laterally away from it.' The guyots, he deduced, were volcanic islands that had risen from the sea at the mid-ocean ridge, then were eroded below sea level as the conveyor belt moved them away from it.

This describes most of what Hess's colleague Robert Dietz snappily called 'seafloor spreading', all apart from final conclusive proof, which is too interesting not to include and just an extraordinary piece of science in itself – not least because of its ironic relevance to the Cuillin ridge.

Whether or not you habitually carry a compass around in your pocket, you'll be aware that its needle points north from everywhere on earth (the obvious exception being the North Pole, which is the only point on earth where every direction is south, and is presumably rather a cruel place to take a compass). But did you ever wonder *why* the north is the north and the south is the south? After all, there is no such thing as north and south in space. The short answer is that the planet is only polarised this way *at the moment*. The earth's magnetism flips on a relatively speedy basis, geologically speaking. North has become south and vice versa on average every 200,000 years. What this does to life on earth isn't known. Barring a certain amount of cartographical chaos it's unlikely to be much, although one paper on the subject suggested that animals reliant on magnetism for direction-finding such as pigeons and whales might need to 'develop different means of navigation', but stopped short of suggesting options. We do, however, know what it does to the rocks.

Molten rock, such as that erupted from the seafloor, contains a relatively high volume of magnesium and iron. As the new crust cools from lava to rock, the metallic elements of the rock are bestowed alignment with the polarity of the earth at that time. Called 'natural remnant magnetism', this permanent polarisation of rocks had been noticed earlier in the century, and is a kind of manufacturing stamp that records the position of the poles at the moment the rocks were formed. Big deal, right? But combined with the theory that new crust was being rolled out from the mid-ocean ridge on that conveyor belt production line over millions of years – and we know that the earth's magnetic field flips every few hundred *thousand* years – here was a very interesting test for Hess's theory of seafloor spreading. If correct, the oceanic floor should capture all of the earth's magnetic reversals over millions of years, reading back to the mid-ocean ridge like a very slow but very extensive geological log.

Frederick Vine and Drummond Matthews were the scientists who deduced this – the former studying under the latter at Cambridge University in the 1960s. The magnetism of seafloor rocks had been mapped as early as the 1950s, when magnetometers – dragged behind ships hunting enemy submarines, and bankrolled by an increasingly paranoid military – identified both the polarity produced by seafloor rocks and the fact that it alternated over distance. In a 1966 paper, Vine, Matthews and a Canadian scientist named Lawrence Morley pulled together mapping data from around the oceans and discovered something extraordinary. The alternating polarity of the seafloor rocks formed stripes of varying thickness, extending in parallel from mid-oceanic ridges. Imagining rock polarised negatively as white and positively as black, the results looked rather like a barcode. The clincher was that the barcode of polarity was *precisely* replicated on the opposing side of the mid-oceanic ridge, demonstrating at a stroke that not only was the seafloor spreading, it was spreading from the mid-oceanic ridge at exactly the same rate on either side. The bonus was a neat geological record of when the earth's poles had flipped across hundreds of millions of years. This – along with further excellent work by scientists Tanya Atwater, Marie Tharp and Lynn Sykes – cemented the theory of plate tectonics. And our understanding of how our world works took a giant leap out of darkness. It also explains why compasses can never be fully trusted on the Cuillin ridge.

You may have grasped that Skye's rocks could be described with a level of complexity that would easily fill this book ('Just *this* book?' I hear the geologists cry), but all you really need to know from this foundation is that Skye's geology falls into three contrasting groups. For simplicity let's call out these groups in order of age: the bedrock, the volcanic lavas and the volcanic ruin.

As mentioned earlier, there are some very old rocks on Skye, in the southeast of the island facing the mainland – the ancient Lewisian gneiss formed deep in the earth's crust billions of years ago. Periods of uplift brought this to the surface and exposed it, and exposed it remains, long since mangled into a dramatic swirly, silvery mess and thrusted out of sequence in a narrow band on the coast of Sleat. Then came the sediments, what would become known as the Torridonian sandstone. Today this towers in the mountains of Wester Ross, formed from grit dropped by great rivers in a hot, desertlike landscape a billion years ago, when the creatures that would eventually become dinosaurs were yet to stride out of the sea.

When the dinosaurs did emerge, they left their mark on Skye. The north of the island (though not an island at all in the dinosaurs' day) is Scotland's richest ground for dinosaur discovery, and one of international importance

– with bones, marine skeletons, fossils and other traces of animals moving around in the Jurassic period, about 165 million years ago. Most famous are the beaches around Staffin, where long-necked diplodocus-like creatures left circular prints in the fresh sand of a lagoon, preserved soon after by a cap of grittier sediment washed in by storms, perhaps. There is also an extraordinarily vivid three-toed impression – the sort of shape you imagine when you think of a dinosaur footprint – made by a toothy carnivore similar to a tyrannosaur on the beach at An Corran. It is extraordinary that not just the same island but the same *beach* also saw what was until very recently the smallest dinosaur footprint ever found (1.78cm) and the first evidence, very much later on, of Mesolithic humans on Skye well over 100 million years later. I'm telling you, this is an interesting place.

Dinosaur remains are a miraculous find anywhere – the scientific equivalent of finding a diamond mine in your garden. They are rare in Scotland, as in most very old, geologically pulverised countries. Yet Skye, now bestowed with corny nicknames such as the 'Jurassic Isle' and 'Scotland's dinosaur stamping ground', seems rich in them. Both the presence of footprints in the original rock they were made in – as opposed to traces in displaced boulders or deposits – and much later remains suggest the need for a stable geology. But Skye's geology, as is evident by what happened next, is anything but stable – yet there on the Staffin peninsula we have a little pocket of dinosaur activity of extraordinary quality. Why? No one really knows.

What I found interesting was learning that Skye was not born from the sea. Despite the volcanism that defined its most dramatic features, it wasn't like Surtsey or Stromboli or one of those other islands that spit steam as they climb from the water. The presence of these ancient rocks and signs of life betrays the slightly disappointing fact that Skye's status as an island is actually quite incidental, probably due to a glacier bulldozing out the land that attached it to the mainland as little as two million years ago. I'd always imagined the place as a kind of Hebridean Iceland – a volcanic alien related to Britain's mainland by proximity alone. But that it isn't only makes what follows so much stranger.

The scientific term for what gave rise to Skye's defining period of geological activity is the North Atlantic Igneous Province – a surge of localised

volcanic activity thought to have caused the break-up of the supercontinent
of Pangaea and the opening of the modern oceans. Little is known for sure
about this, but we do know that beneath the earth's crust is the mantle: a
2,800-kilometre deep reservoir of rock and metal at varying degrees of
temperature and sludginess. Contrary to what many people imagine, the
earth doesn't suddenly become molten, glowing liquid if you break the
surface like an eggshell. Most of the mantle rock beneath the crust – in the
zone known as the asthenosphere – despite being pretty viscous in geological terms, in human terms is pretty rigid. It is also, however, prone to
inconsistencies in temperature. Like an uneven dough bake, the areas of
hotter mantle cause localised melting of rock to occur, enabling more fluidic,
high-temperature molten material to gather. These isolated zones of
increased heat and more mobile rock are called 'mantle plumes'. And the
places where they meet the earth's solid crust and begin to warm it up, crack
it and eat through it are called 'hotspots'.

One such hotspot began to localise under the North Atlantic, roughly
between where Greenland and Iceland now sit. At the time the land was
joined as part of the supercontinent of Pangaea. The hotspot caused the
mantle to thin, and the crust to stretch and weaken. Eventually the plates
began to tear, Pangaea started to break apart and the North Atlantic slowly
opened. Great wellings of magma formed in an arc, in areas of the crust
underpinning what is today Northern Ireland and the Hebrides. Huge
reservoirs of molten rock – plutonic complexes – formed beneath land
covered in forests, river valleys and gentle hills. This activity centralised into
a handful of volcanic centres, like armies quietly gathering: these were under
the Isle of Arran, Blackstones Bank at the entrance to the Sea of the Hebrides,
Mull, the Ardnamurchan Peninsula, Rum and Skye. Then, around 60 million
years ago, the cracks began to open.

The first eruptions would have been dramatic, their contact with water
causing violent explosions. Basaltic magma spat aloft, and droplets fell as
ragged glass. Then the lava began to flow. This was flood basalt, so-called
because it usually only occurs on the ocean floor and has a suffocating,
swamping quality. Flood basalts are found on Iceland, where today we find
an authentic idea of what the scene must have been like. Lava spewed
fountain-like from great cracks, smothering everything, destroying

everything. Within hundreds of years, it killed the landscape. It burned forests, choked rivers and lagoons, filled valleys, and built a smoking grey desert known as the Thulean plateau. As the Atlantic began to open, the plateau broke messily apart, leaving caps of thick basalt lava atop every fragment of the dividing landmass – from the Faroes to Greenland, to Skye and the rest of the Hebrides. Many of these had magma chambers beneath them, which periodically reignited and built into huge, sometimes explosive volcanoes as the plates continued to rift and the ocean widened. The volcanism didn't all come at once; sediments between the flows indicate long periods of dormancy, and a return to less scalding conditions before the lava began anew. Ash deposits at the base of some of these flows suggest explosive starts, but mainly the lavas seeped quickly and gently, much in the manner of any domestic uncorking: the flow that follows the pop.

As an aside, the lively central point of this same activity today is Iceland – a country literally torn in two by the mid-Atlantic Ridge. Little more than an elevated portion of this subterranean mountain range, Iceland's odd qualification as a country that is being eroded at its shores at precisely the same rate as it is being built in its centre has given rise to the notably youthful complexion of its rock; nothing on the island is more than 16 million years old. The still-present mantle plume creates a situation that might unnerve anyone who spends a considerable amount of time there. Visualisations of the plume in cross section depict it as a kind of distended stomach of magma, red and potent, with the tiny scab of Iceland as its cracked, weeping plug.

The name for the landscape that smothered the North Atlantic Igneous Province was *trap*. Some writers have characterised the geography of the Hebrides as being divided into the 'gneiss islands' and the 'trap islands' – meaning the Outer and Inner groups respectively. It's simplified somewhat, but broadly true. *Trap* is named after *trappa*, Swedish for 'stairs'. You can find the word in India, at the Deccan Traps – probably the most frighteningly awesome volcanic landscape on earth, and a powerful reminder that the planet could kill us at any moment should it wish.

Any visitor to Skye today will understand the 'stairs' analogy in a variety of landmarks. Most of central and northern Skye is considered 'trap', usually expressed as huge, felty-green plateaux such as those found between Portree and Dunvegan. The green is down to the fecundity that good, basalt soil promotes, so where you see it underfoot, you're probably on the basalt lava flow. Occasionally these lava flows formed hills with stepped sides and flat tops, such as MacLeod's Tables on the Duirnish Peninsula. Sometimes they would make columnar jointed flows – those distinctive, stepped basalt columns that look too uncannily hexagonal to be true. The columns are created by a pattern of slow cooling, contracting and jointing of the lava, resulting in the astonishing visual features of the Giant's Causeway in Northern Ireland, Fingal's Cave on the Isle of Staffa, and Kilt Rock at Staffin, Skye – and many more in Iceland, and beyond. They were all formed by the same process at around the same time. They aren't always six-sided, either – but this shape is common enough to make you wonder, why hexagons? Again, no one really knows for sure.

Go to Trotternish, and here you have more steps. The peninsula is defined by a twenty-mile array of green moleskin ramps, climbing to over 700 metres in parts. It's a place, like so many on Skye, that straddles a balance between the fearsome and the fetching – more so when you understand that this entire ridge is a huge series of landslides. Once again, here is a Skye feature that is the most dramatic of its type anywhere in Britain, quite different to the landscapes around it. When the lava flowed, like oil poured over layered sponge it smothered the softer, crumblier sediments of limestone and sandstone laid down in the Jurassic – the same material the dinosaurs of Staffin padded around on. Gravity plus lava flows several hundred metres thick on top of weak sediments is a bad mix – like stepping heavily on a ham sandwich – and the sediments duly gave way to the pretty chaos that now defines the peninsula. Where the debris has fallen to earth the landscape has taken on a dramatic air, with all manner of steeples, gaunt pinnacles, rock-mazes and bouldery warrens. More teeth here – the Quiraing, the Old Man of Storr, both weird and savage, both icons of Skye, both seasoned stand-ins for mythical landscapes in everything from science fiction films to computer games. And then we come to the last howl of Skye's volcanism, its youngest, brashest rock and its most enduring legacy: the black ridge itself.

Over a million and a half years, give or take, Skye's volcanism intensified and moved. From fissures in the north-west, activity consolidated around a single focus in what is today the island's south-east. The lava flows and explosions built a great shield volcano, beneath which lay a huge magma chamber. Imagine this chamber as a funnel, with the pipe of the funnel shoved deep into the earth, feeding basalt magma upwards into a cone-shaped reservoir 20 kilometres wide. Then imagine this huge sink of magma sitting under the surface, its contents squeezing up through cracks, bursting forth at the surface and building a huge volcanic dome.

The volcano that stood in southern Skye probably wasn't beautiful. Beautiful volcanoes tend to be stratovolcanoes, like Fuji or Rainier. The Skye volcano was what's called a basaltic shield volcano, which are almost always sprawling, lumpy edifices, like a big pile of clothes. Big it was, certainly; perhaps two miles high, with long, cindery slopes spreading ten miles wide or more. You can see such volcanoes today in Hawaii, Iceland's Skjalbreiður and the Piton de la Fournaise on Réunion Island – a mountain that Brian Upton in *Volcanoes and the Making of Scotland* identifies as being a likely modern approximation of the Skye volcano.

As well as being big it was also productive, oozing a staggering amount of lava over its active cycle. It has been suggested that it held magma in the structure of the volcano itself, which erupted then refilled from its lower chamber, rather like a toilet cistern feeding off the mains. The caldera rim would have built and collapsed countless times over its eruptive cycle, climbing to the greatest height and steepness gravitationally possible then falling in on itself. As the volcano gained height, the magma was unable to hydraulically reach the height of the main vent and burst from the sides of the volcano. The shield itself was gradually eroded down, then built again and so on. Rise, fall. Breathe in, breathe out.

Eventually, as new seafloor began to convey Skye away from the mantle plume, its source of fuel began to peter out, and – around 55 million years ago – the volcano fell quiet. This was the silencing of what is now called the British Tertiary Volcanic Province, and the last volcanism our isles would know between then and now. No longer compelled to the surface by inexhaustible convection currents from below, the magma chamber began to cool, congeal, solidify and crack. Without the urgency of a magma feed, this cooling took a while. Where the hot molten basalt sat against crustal rock, melting occurred and granite magma was created. These granite plutons crystallised into huge masses of rough, pink rock that would later form into what we now call Skye's Red Hills. The slow cooling of the main magma chamber of basalt deep within the volcano produced a coarse-grained, dark rock that was little-jointed and very hard: the gabbro of the Black Cuillin.

The lavas eroded away. The surface of the earth fell, as weathering and time took their toll. The great volcano collapsed. And gradually, the hard rock of the magma chamber was exposed. This rock was never erupted: it is lava that solidified where it sat, like curdling milk. Today that rock is amongst the barest in the Hebrides. Steep and arid, little soil sits on it, not much grows. And the most dramatic piece of it stands atop southern Skye like a strange, thorned crown.

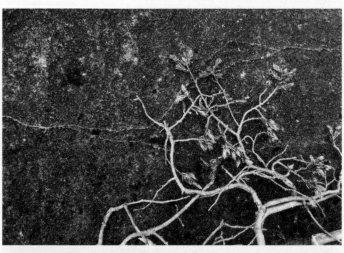

2

Rock

I sat in a crouch near the summit of Ben Cleat, feeling the sun warm my back and watching my shadow slowly shorten towards me across the dewy grass. I was probably grinning. In front of me lay the Cuillin ridge – the whole monstrous, gorgeous thing. A calm sea wrapped its edge, beyond which islands seemed to drift aloft in the morning haze. As the light descended further onto the mountains its brilliance intensified, lifting the scene into a complex of a billion shadows and angles, spreading and deepening and bristling across it.

It was almost overwhelming sitting there, looking at it all. There are some places you can touch that themselves touch the past – like a landscape caught in limbo between two times. The Cuillin ridge is one such place. I wasn't at touching distance, not yet. But as I gazed at the ridge as a whole, imagining its formation and trying to see it actually happening, it seemed it would only take a nudge to slip behind the present. In *The Misty Isle of Skye* (1905), J. A. MacCulloch – never one to knowingly underwrite – said of the ridge:

> All is sheer rock, black, wrinkled, chaotic, torn and shattered into every conceivable shape. You seem to stand in nature's primeval workshop; here are the very bones of the old earth.

Look at the Cuillin ridge today and you're not looking at the collapsed rim of an old volcano. Your mind tries to form the ridge into what it thinks it is, so you see an angle here, a crater there, part of a caldera arc in the distance. But this thing isn't the crumbly shield of ash and lava flow. This is the chamber that fed it. You're looking at its engine. Its guts.

And *that* rock, which has come to define the Cuillin ridge's personality and singularity. 'Here you have the great simplicities of nature – a single ridge, a wall of rock, the sea, nothing more,' wrote J. Hubert Walker of the ridge in his love letter to Scotland, *On Hills of the North* (1948). 'And yet of such substance is that rock, such its colour and texture, that instantly it reflects the moods of the ever-changing weather born of that surrounding sea.'

We should probably talk about colour – this book is called *The Black Ridge*, after all – as the colour is down to the rock, too. The range is most generally called the Black Cuillin. There are many versions of the second word, but 'black' is pretty unambiguous. Yet pick up a piece of it, and you might find it's not black. In the case of the gabbro, it's a kind of pitted, ashy grey or sandy brown, or sometimes dusted with rust when there's iron. It's sharp-grained like shark skin, not light like pumice, nor a weight-sink like Lewisian gneiss; it feels no lighter nor heavier than it looks like it should. It may be very much darker and there are times on the ridge when it seems almost pale. But its unchanging, immutable attributes are that it's very hard, very rough and very sharp. The less heralded but very much present basalt component of the Cuillin is more 'blocky', more slippery and finer-grained – lacking the adhesive properties of gabbro and fracturing in sharp lines, like porcelain. It can be smooth enough to shimmer, unlike the matte, rough gabbro. Similarly, though, basalt's appearance also reflects its conditions, ranging in colour from rouge to charcoal. Indeed, despite their contrasting qualities, the two geological ingredients can appear so similar it can be hard to see the join.

But collectively, the rock's colour is deceptive. Like clear ice that bends and absorbs light and turns blue in glacial masses, the whole takes on a darker, cindery pall when baked into a mountain range, lending the whole a decidedly dark aesthetic. Though, as with much else on Skye, this is by no means a constant.

'I cannot think of the Cuillin as black,' wrote Ben Humble in *The Cuillin of Skye*. 'Light grey, steel blue, rose-flushed in dawn, tipped blood-red in the evening sun. Yet it cannot be denied that they are more normally sombre and black, which gave rise to the legend that no vegetation grows amongst them.'

John Buchan, the celebrated Scottish writer, was another soul the Cuillin 'got'. Descriptions of the ridge found their way into some of his novels, with an edge that suggests he had seen in it far more than simply a setting. Here's a couple of lines from *Mr Standfast*:

I made out ugly precipices, and glens which lost themselves in primeval blackness. When the sun caught them – for it was a gleamy day – it brought out no colours, only degrees of shade. No mountains I had ever seen ... ever looked so unearthly and uncanny.

And so there is maybe a perception at play, a certain atmospheric suggestion. Someone tells you it was formed by a volcano, so in your mind you envision something burnt and charred – an image hardly contradicted by what your eyes then see. Next, those severe shapes take root in your recollections in that barbaric colour. It becomes an atmospheric memory, a landscape theatric. 'Like Glencoe, to realise one's dreams, it has to be viewed under louring skies,' wrote Ernest A. Baker, 'with a cloud of gloom on the dark frontlet of the Cuillin.'

Many have tried to rationalise this prod of a suggestion. The following, for instance:

The colour ... ranges, with varying conditions of moisture and light, through every tone of purple; deepening to a velvety black in glimpses caught through a wrack of mist or brightening to burnished copper under the level-rays of a cloudless sunrise.

Such is the effect of this place that even those committed to a dispassionate presentation of the facts are spurred into orgasms of hyperbole; that passage there is found in a *scientific* paper, Alfred Harker's seductively titled 'The Tertiary Igneous Rocks of Skye'.

'Altogether the hills here have a strange weird look,' wrote Alexander Smith of the 'Cuchuillins' in *A Summer in Skye* – an atmospheric and eccentric mid-19th-century work by the Edinburgh poet and essayist, and the most successful book on Skye ever published:

> I was in continual presence of bouldered hillside sloping away upward to some invisible peak, overhanging wall of wet-black precipice, far-off serrated ridge that cuts the sky like a saw ... Each is as closely seamed with lines as a man of a hundred, and these myriad reticulations are picked out with a pallid grey green.

And from poetical to painterly: 'To paint the Coolins successfully, some knowledge of geological formation is essential,' noted Alasdair Alpin MacGregor. 'There you get colourings that are to be found nowhere else in the world.' Oddly, he chooses the 'green of the screes' as his example – a colour not immediately associated with screes anywhere, let alone the Cuillin. But whatever its colour, ultimately it's all down to the Cuillin's rock: that remarkable recipe of gabbro and basalt. It built the range, gave it its quality – but not its shape. And this is perhaps even more uncanny than its colour.

From a distance the whole thing just flattens into silhouette, an unswerving battlement with a frill of dangerous-looking peaks as ramparts. Though the particulars of this silhouette vary with direction, the ridge always appears treacherous. This is what your eyes tell you when they trace from one end to the other in that peculiarly human way of scrutinising the possibility of movement across terrain. When people with mountaineering on their mind mention the word 'traverse', you picture a straight line from here to there, like a bridge or a tensioned tightrope. But the thing is, the ridge is not straight. There isn't a single straight line in the entire range. And nothing straightforward, either.

Now I was getting a good look – my first ever in totally clear weather – at the entire ridge from my south-eastern eyrie on Ben Cleat, I was actually looking into the embrace of a great arc, albeit from a slightly askew viewpoint. Tracing that ragged skyline from left to right, my eyes were making a curving traverse, tracking over the same ground my body would soon have to negotiate. From this distance it was impossible to appreciate the subtleties or the scale. But watching the morning sunlight creeping over every crease in the ridge like a searchlight, I could at least begin to get familiar with what I was in for.

Here, the ridge begins from the left as a great apron of rock with its hem spread in the Atlantic. This apron, smooth and broad with the tiniest lip of cliff where it meets the water, gathers quickly and steeply, rising from the waters into a taper, stitched with a band of crags halfway up and cut by a deep scar, climbing to a peak the shape and sharpness of a rose thorn. It looks like a tough climb, and it probably is: there are no hoisted starts, no cheeky nibbles at the task of climbing into the Cuillin. You start at the sea and climb every metre of whatever height your summit lies above you – in the case of this first peak, 895 metres. Because it's shoved out towards you, from here this looks like the highest major peak in the range. But it isn't, it's the lowest: Gars-bheinn.

The summit ridge of Gars-bheinn is like one horn of a pair, a crescent swooping north to the next – Sgùrr a' Choire Bhig. Next comes the Munro of Sgùrr nan Eag, blocked from my line of sight, somewhere in the shadows behind Gars-bheinn. Instead, here my eye fell on a long tapering rib, lit by the sun and descending off the main ridge to the right, into the centre of the ridge's embrace and the shadowy recess I knew held the fabled Loch Coruisk – from here more than ever the Cuillin's secretive central keep. This spur could only be the Dubhs Ridge, one of many subsidiary limbs that descend off the ridge's spine like draped wings. This one, containing the tops of Sgùrr Dubh Beag and Sgùrr Dubh Mòr, rose to an unseen summit where it met the main ridge: Sgùrr Dubh an Da Bheinn.

Here the main ridge begins to arc right, climbing to a great pyramidal peak rent into two at its highest reaches, as if split by an axe. At this point the Cuillin turns to face north, marking the move with a sudden buck of its spine, the highest point on Skye and the Hebrides: Sgùrr Alasdair. Across the split gap lies the lower twin, Sgùrr Thearlaich – then, after another chasm, the ridge rises again in a raised fist, its line of knuckles square to the sky: Sgùrr MhicChoinnich, and the Coireachan Ruadha Crags, with the mythical Collie's Ledge hidden somewhere in amongst them.

Then somewhere north of the bulk of Sgùrr Alasdair and the long crags of Sgùrr MhicChoinnich lies perhaps the most sought-after summit on the ridge, and its infamously prominent final twenty metres – Sgùrr Dearg and its rocky topknot: the Inaccessible Pinnacle.

Next, a deep slack: the Bealach Coire na Banachdich, one of the few civilised crossing points of the ridge between the two remote worlds of Coruisk and Glen Brittle, a pass well known to mountain rescue personnel; then the great dome of crags comprising its namesake with the Ordnance Survey's extra vowel, Sgùrr na Banachdaich. Here the ridge's pulse quickens again, with the pinnacled summits of Sgùrr Thormaid and Sgùrr a' Ghreadaidh, before falling to a pass in the ridge, An Dorus, 'the door'. Then the ridge bears north-west. Sgùrr a' Mhadaidh, a charred-looking spire and just one of four tops, then another drop that emphasises the sharp prominence of Bidein Druim nan Rahm, two needle-nose pincers aloft from the ridge, and one of the most striking of the Cuillin's features from this – and indeed, either – side. An extraordinarily long spur then exits the ridge towards you here: the Druim nan Ramh, running almost all the way from the seaward outflow of Loch Coruisk to the crest of the Cuillin. A few steps of the crest later and Bruach na Frithe strikes a level, high-looking platform, before the tilted stack of Am Bàsteir and the Bàsteir Tooth protrude from the ridge, like weird obelisks. All that remains, a final climax, is Sgùrr nan Gillean – a gorgeous curve of ridge up to a nail-sharp point, then subsequently, descending, several more on its shoulder: one, two, three.

In silhouette, robbed of detail, it would be almost perfect – like a bristly 'M' stretched near-straight by its outer limbs. At one end, the wild Atlantic. At the other, the glissade down into the unseen Glen Sligachan, beyond the ridge's serrated, sweeping tail. And there it ends.

Perhaps you found the previous paragraphs a breeze to read. I didn't find them a breeze to write. These names, while atmospheric as the Gaelic mountain names are always, are lost on me. This is said with no prejudice, just ignorance. To me, give or take a few rudimentary generics, they are just alien words, and what they speak means little. Just as I wouldn't expect to pick up a book written in Norwegian and fully appreciate the subtleties embedded in its language, I could never expect to run my eyes across a line of Gaelic mountain names and nod sagely in recognition of their meaning. And something is lost there, for me. Because presumably when you name a mountain, you don't name it lightly.

But while their spellings have varied wildly in the relatively short time they have been appointed to the features of the Cuillin, with one or two ambiguous exceptions their meanings have not. So while the local names must and will be preserved at all costs, consider too what the Gaelic speaks in English – for these are the keys to doorways leading deep into much of this range's intrigue.

So when the map says: Gars-bheinn, Sgùrr a' Choire Bhig, Sgùrr nan Eag, Sgùrr Dubh an Da Bheinn, Sgùrr Alasdair, Sgùrr Thearlaich, Sgùrr MhicChoinnich, Sgùrr Dearg, Sgùrr na Banachdaich, Sgùrr Thormaid, Sgùrr a' Ghreadaidh, Sgùrr a' Mhadaidh, Bidein Druim nan Ramh, An Caisteal, Sgùrr na h-Uamha, Bruach na Frithe, Sgùrr a' Fionn Choire, Am Bàsteir and Sgùrr nan Gillean . . .

. . . let yourself hear: *Echoing Mountain, Peak of the Little Corrie, Notched Peak, Black Peak of the Two Mountains, Alexander's Peak, Charles's Peak, MacKenzie's Peak, Red Peak, Smallpox Peak, Norman's Peak, Peak of the Thrashings, Peak of the Wolf, Pinnacle of the Ridge of Oars, The Castle, Peak of the Cave, Slope of the Forest, Peak of the Fine Corrie, The Executioner and the Peak of the Gullies.*

These are just the *major* peaks, you understand. Countless more christenings drape the Cuillin ridge, all inscribing a story that stretches back to the days people first looked upon it, right up to relatively recent times. Their nuances doubtless hold nameless secrets still. As said, they are the only mountains in Scotland named after the people who climbed them.

As I sat there on Ben Cleat, watching cloud begin to form amongst the hollows and snare the peaks like wool on razor wire, that was what I could see. I knew that in amongst this were untold numbers of impediments and lengthy pauses for thought – gaps, drops, gullies, ledges, pinnacles, crests, scree runs, towers – all lost to the eye at this distance. Not to mention the ridges descending off the main crest like chutes, spurs that led to dead-end precipices, the serpentine arcs and jags of the way across, and countless tucked-away hollows and corries.

Out of context with anything immediately relatable to human size – a building or roads, say – it's very hard to get a grip on exactly how big the ridge really is. In *Over the Sea to Skye* (1926), Alasdair Alpin MacGregor addressed this when he wrote, 'To get a proper idea of the strength and magnitude of the Cuillin peaks, they ought to be viewed from a comparatively low eminence . . . [or] there is a tendency to lose that sense of proportion.' He continued:

It is only when a sheep or deer is detected on the hillside that one to whom this chaos, this place before time, is unfamiliar receives any real indication of the stupendousness of these mountain masses, and of the unbelievable distances that must be traversed to reach them.

This is perhaps a little melodramatic, but certainly hits on a point. Perhaps it's the sea, perhaps it's the low-lying nature of much of their surroundings, but the Cuillin ridge looks *massive*.

In terms of height, the ridge tops out at just shy of a kilometre above sea level, and given that the sea is omnipresent from most aspects of the Cuillin – and the ridge is generally a thing of a very precipitous nature – it really does look it. A kilometre high is three of London's Shard stacked on top of each other with a bit to spare, ten Big Bens, 384 staircases made of 4,953 domestic stairs, or thereabouts. This height is maintained with an odd consistency. Almost all of the ridge's major peaks inhabit a narrow band of elevation between 920 and 990 metres, with none of the passes and gaps between them dipping below 760 metres, making the Cuillin particularly sustained, and particularly high. Once you're up, you stay up.

This would be good news, were it not for the complexity of the ground that's up there with you. Seven miles long, the whole thing is a mountaineering obstacle course. Were you to fall off the highest peak and make an uninterrupted free-fall to the waves, it would take the average-sized human around fourteen shrill seconds to complete the journey. It would almost certainly be your last: by the time you hit the water, you'd have reached around 120mph. But enough scaremongering, as there's nowhere on the ridge where could such an unimpeded fall to sea level is possible. And even if you were to fall from such a height on the ridge, the rock would tear you to pieces long before you got anywhere near it. While pondering that happy fact, I packed up my belongings and began to stroll back down to the road in the morning light.

After my night on Ben Cleat I'd reinstalled myself in Portnalong at the Taigh Ailean, where, between the inevitable downpours, I could cosily work my way through a considerable pile of books in the name of research. This had started innocently, as merely a way to familiarise myself with the ridge before setting foot on it in the name of polite enquiry. It had, however, developed into a fascination of rather larger proportions as the Cuillin's literary rabbit hole deepened.

Soon after I'd arrived, Katie Heron had seen me hefting a large box from the boot of my car up the stairs. 'Excuse me,' she said, 'but oh my God, *what* is that?'

'Skye books. Research.' I made a conspiratorial noise and tapped the box.

'You're turning that room into a library,' she said, peering over her glasses at me, then looking slightly askance, as if processing the idea. 'Which, I suppose, is fine.'

We shared a nod, then I waited until she'd gone into the kitchen before heading to the car to get the second box.

Skye has had a lot of words written about it – too many, really. This is perhaps a dangerous statement to commit to print in yet another rather large book concerning Skye, except (and I say this with the confidence of a man who carries two boxes of written material about this island around in his car) these accounts are mostly from the distant past, and – guide-books aside – fall generally into three categories.

First, the Climbing Endeavour, most likely appearing in old volumes of the *Scottish Mountaineering Club Journal* or occasionally in the *Alpine Journal*, full of occasionally brilliant but usually grandiose discourse about a Great Adventure, fraught with weather and conditions and difficulty and gear and questionable holds and redoubtable companions addressed only by their last names. These are typically great fun, not least because the writers seem to inhabit some kind of P. G. Wodehouse parallel universe, full of chipper old socks braving inadequate lodgings, sharing ropes, ruminating over whether things will 'go' or not, and watching Hastings – there's *always* a Hastings – overcoming some kind of dangerous obstacle or being a good-enough sport to fall to their death without taking the pipe tobacco with them. (This last point is of course an exaggeration – none of these chaps would be silly enough to trust the *entire* supply of pipe tobacco to one person.)

Second, the Scientific Dissection, usually geological or botanical, but occasionally bleeding over into cultural disseminations and critiques, and often published as papers in journals or books with words like 'Discussions' or 'Observations' or 'Analysis' in the title.

And last, there's the beloved Bemused Journal, usually produced by dandyish mainlander travellers, a mystifying frequency of clergymen, or else financially endowed youngsters on some sort of Grand Tour of the Highlands on the hunt for their artistic eureka.

Outside of these there have been a number of novels set on the island that have used the Cuillin as a kind of backdrop to everything from family crises to international espionage. And, naturally, the mountains have given birth to some fine poetry – written both by Skye natives and visitors.

The real interest, I was beginning to find, lay in the dispatches from Skye that started out as one or the other of these but ended up falling somewhere in between – written by people who had been affected by this place, turned by its magic and its darkness, and felt the need to share this somehow, however inappropriate the context. You could detect this deeper incision of the island into its observer by a kind of developing frown in their vocabulary. Like the way one addict can identify another, or poker players learn to spot tells, when it came to an interest that went beyond the superficial, I was beginning to recognise the signs. People who brought unexpected words into descriptions, who lingered on feelings or failed to explain themselves convincingly – these were the ones I was really interested in, the people whom the Cuillin had *got*.

I would spend a lot of time over the next few days driving from place to place, looking at the ridge from different angles, trying to combine these views into an understanding of the ridge's form and how it all fitted together, and on the whole failing miserably. It's a difficult thing to visually pin down, but an endlessly fascinating one.

Some views of the Cuillin mask its position beside the sea, robbing it of a huge part of its identity. This is a maritime ridge, and everything about it, on its south side at least, is about the interplay between sea and mountain. Stand on Ben Cleat and consider the way the sea creeps into the shadow of the ridge in Loch Scavaig, and flirts with the shore at Camasunary Bay, and it's striking how much character the ridge absorbs from the water.

But look at the ridge from the east, and the view most people encounter is the angle on the Cuillin from Sligachan, home to the famous hotel. However pleasing, this provides by far the weakest impression of the ridge.

Sligachan means 'place of shells', in reference to its proximity to the tidal Loch Sligachan, which by virtue of its mainland-facing aspect has none of the oceanic character of the west. From here you look at the Cuillin ridge obliquely – a bit like looking at the London Eye end-on, or the Taj Mahal from the back. That the full extent of the ridge is hidden doesn't mean it's a disappointing view, and it has certainly had its share of admirers. Alasdair Alpin MacGregor praised the prospect from Sligachan grandly, stating:

> It is hard to believe that the Coolins and the obnoxious, perfume-smelling loafing places of the modern city ... could possibly be within ten thousand miles of one another – so wild, so remote, so terrifying are the Alps of Skye.

It's ironic, then, that this view – dominated as it is by close-at-hand Sgùrr nan Gillean – does away with that mountain's most striking feature. Pinnacle Ridge, which gives the vision of the Cuillin its dramatic flourish from so many distant perspectives, is eclipsed against the bulk of the mountain from here, rendering the peak deceptively plain from this famous rallying point for mountaineer and tourist. Appreciate how small the mountain and its pinnacles are when looking at the ridge from other angles and you appreciate how little of the ridge you're seeing from Sligachan.

Sligachan does, however, provide a view of the peculiar Bàsteir Tooth, that unsettling tilt of rock that gives this otherwise undramatic skyline of mountains a striking signature – and reminds you that what you're looking at is a truly singular British mountain range. Not that this fact is lost on anyone who wanders a little beyond the roadside. W. A. Poucher, the mid-20th-century photographer and guidebook writer, nailed the treachery of this shape-shifting nature in *The Magic of Skye* when he wrote that Glen Sligachan

> should be the first walk undertaken by the initiate because the glen deeply penetrates the fastness of the group ... the stern ruggedness of the mountains is gradually unfolded and this closer contact with them will act as a deterrent for any rash expedition that may have been contemplated after viewing them only from afar.

Change position again, this time to Carbost – around 8 on Skye's central-ised clock face. Now you're on the other side of the Cuillin, the side that somehow feels like the back, as it doesn't seem to rise directly from the sea and there are no lochs or deep glens extending into its sway. Here the ridge is less opulently barbed and more muscular. The spikes shorten to teeth, the angles between them become hard, and the ridge transforms from gothic to brutalist. In the early morning the sun rises behind the ridge, which becomes a screen against the eastern sky. But as the day unfolds and the sun sidles over the crest, its light drops onto the layers of the Cuillin and its shadowplay reveals the complexity hidden in the dark. Late afternoon reveals this side of the ridge to be almost symmetrical, built from gigantic pyramidal buttresses. And again, you find yourself looking *into* something.

My first thought when I saw the Cuillin from Carbost fully clear of cloud remains the one my mind keeps seeing: it looks like a bat. Great, triangular wings of bony shoulders and lean sinews either side of a sharp, nasty little head. It's this angle that begins to grow and tower and twist as you make your way out of Carbost onto the high bluff above Loch Harport, then to the Trien junction that marks the spur into Glen Brittle.

The thing is, no matter which angle you look at it from, it really couldn't be anything other than the Cuillin ridge. It's a testimony to its unique aesthetic, its scribble against the sky. Part of this is down to a set of recurring aesthetic riffs that you notice – if you stare at it for long enough from enough different viewpoints – form a composition that is quite unmistakable.

This is unique amongst British mountain ranges. Sure, it wouldn't take much for someone to identify a Lakeland or Snowdonian mountain scene; both have their own way of playing with light and shade and colour that marks them out. But for a single mountain range to be so *instantly* identi-fiable – even at close quarters – is quite something, especially considering the Cuillin ridge is just one of a handful of mountain ranges on this island. Part of this comes from its geology: that rock, and its dark and austere character. But the rock is merely the cell that builds the thing: it's the thing it makes that grabs and holds the gaze, the product of those recurrent motifs, that Cuillin DNA. And this shouts loud, given that rock is the single instru-ment of expression the ridge has to work with. There are no forests climbing the flanks, no notable shimmer of vegetation; from bottom to top it's almost entirely naked rock. And all of it climbs towards the first and most obvious of the Cuillin's motifs: those peaks are *sharp*.

'They present indeed a unique fragment of Alpine scenery among the mountain-groups of Britain,' wrote Alfred Harker in his 1901 geological dissection of Skye, continuing:

> The spiry summits and acute, deeply notched ridges are all the more striking when seen across a foreground of basaltic plateaux, or contrasted in the same view with the rounded outlines of the granite hills.

The aspect from Drynoch is a fine place from which to appreciate this – whereas looking south from the hill of Cnoc Carnach on the Trotternish peninsula places gabbro Black Cuillin and granite Red Hills next to each other – throwing their respective contrast into quite literally sharp relief. The Cuillin's pointiness is down to the gabbro, and its extraordinary resistance to weathering; but in combination with this you have the ridge's relative youth. They are our youngest mountains, yet to be blunted by the heavy sanding block of time. The rock's response to this sanding block is different; granite you would describe as 'smooth weathering', in that it responds with contours and sweeps, as a sculpture might. The gabbro is 'rough weathering', in so far as it fractures and tears sharp in protest.

Which leads us on to another of those visual motifs. This is what you might call the cloven hoof: a triangular peak or buttress bisected by the cut of a long, straight gully. The geological reason for this is the weathering of a softer rock from within the gabbro, eaten out like grouting from between tiles by water and frost-cracking. These features, more often than not, once contained a dyke – the name given to a stream of raw basalt magma injected along solidified vertical fissures. Dykes spread from a volcanic centre, as W. H. Murray put it in *The Islands of Western Scotland*, in a crack-like pattern 'exactly as in glass shattered by a bullethole'. Cooling quickly into fine-grained dolerite and basalt, these dykes (the collective term for which is rather enjoyably a 'swarm') were softer than the surrounding gabbro, and when vertical, as frequently was the case, had gravity against them. They were, then, relatively quick to succumb to the rigours of time.

You see this elegantly demonstrated from the Carbost side of the ridge by its central feature, the triangular Sgùrr an Fheadain, almost cleaved in two by Waterpipe Gully – a particularly notable example given it is the backdrop to the Fairy Pools, number one on Skye's scenic bucket list for every selfie-snapping sightseer. A near-identical feature slices Sgùrr na Stri in two, and also on the colossal Blàbheinn, and in countless lesser-known locations throughout the Cuillin complex.

Dykes, with their generally thicker horizontal equivalents, sills, their bulbous relatives laccoliths, and the much more extensive intrusions known as cone sheets, have done much to shape the schematic of the Cuillin. The easiest, crudest way to think of these generally basaltic features are as skinny, vertical pipes (dykes) skinny horizontal slabs (sills), lens-shaped lumps (laccoliths) and diagonally inclined planes (cone sheets) cutting through the ridge.

Cone sheets, like dykes, are formed when basaltic magma squeezes up into fissures in a solidifying volcanic complex. Like the radial cracks around that bullet hole, they form directly above the hardening, collapsing chamber – metre-thin concentric sheets in the shape of an upturned funnel with the open end facing the sky. This gives them a highly distinctive shape and pitch across an area such as the Cuillin. Simply, all angles of the cone sheets tilt towards an apex beneath a rough, nondescript bump north-east of Loch Coruisk called Meall Dearg. This is the point generally considered to have been the centre of the Cuillin magma chamber – an unassuming hub that marks the location around which the entire system once revolved, a relic altar forming the centrepiece of a great geological ruin.

These invasions of molten rock that forced their way, boiling and viscous, into the fractures in the gabbro today form part of its structure – running through it like shrapnel, and over it like scars.

The exciting bit is how the cone sheets and dykes strike the ridge. This not only has both a huge visual effect on the Cuillin; it also determines how easy the ridge is to negotiate. Think about that funnel shape of cone sheets radiating upwards from just above Coruisk, and the ridge's position in an arc around its west flank, and you'll appreciate why a cone sheet running through the ridge does so diagonally. Imagine flinging a very big, very sharp frisbee from Coruisk towards the ridge – and instead of soaring above it into the sky, it embeds itself into it on ascent, sticking half in one side, half out of the other. On the Glen Brittle side it's pointing towards the sky, where it breaks the surface of the ridge as a convenient, purchase-friendly ledge. On the Coruisk side, the opposite edge of the same frisbee will be inclined towards the ground, presenting a scary, tilting slip towards a precipice. Imagine that on a huge scale and you have the Cuillin's cone sheets. The place where this geological feature has a real effect on passage across the ridge can be observed – and very much experienced – is between the summit of Sgùrr Dearg and Sgùrr a' Ghreadaidh, where an exposed cone sheet makes up the actual crest of the ridge. Here the ridge's deck is tilted like that of a listing ship: the western side steep but forming rough terraces where the cone sheet breaks the ridge in an upward incline, and the eastern side dipping perilously away towards Coruisk, where the sheet emerges pointing down.

More visually apparent are the effects of dykes. Where the dykes have weathered on the crest, deep gaps appear between tusk-like gabbro pinnacles, as if someone has cut a notch by drawing a wire to and fro across the ridge. You find the word 'trap' in a lot of early accounts of encountering dykes in the Cuillin, too. This is generally a term applied to basalt more than other erupted rock. 'Slippery trap' is a term that was frequently applied, presumably with a rueful smirk, to the basalt sections of the ridge, which catches out unwary feet by being soap-slick versus the gabbro's much-celebrated adhesion. Often marking the position of a dyke or cone sheet, this change often happens without warning underfoot, with attention necessary to spot the difference. There is even a feature called the Trap Staircase on Sgùrr Sgumain – a large dyke that, as observed by J. H. B. Bell, 'cuts through the gabbro wall like an overhanging piece of ornamental masonry'.

There are more of these visual signatures, but I will end for now with steepness. The steepness of the Cuillin is extraordinary not because of the extreme angle, which reaches up to 35° and 40° in many areas of the ridge and almost 50° on outlying Sgùrr na Stri and Druim nan Ramh, on slopes nearly half a kilometre in length. It's extraordinary because the mountains manage to hold this angle without breaking under gravity into actual precipices. This shows how structurally strong the gabbro is; more like iron than rock. This steepness doesn't stop when weathering takes its toll, either.

Due to its high frictional quality, the screes the gabbro makes sit at a steeper angle than most, prickly rock on prickly rock holding everything together and aloft like geological Velcro. In places the scree's pitch looks truly precarious, such as the Great Stone Shoot on Sgùrr Alasdair.

It also explains one of the reasons why the Cuillin slopes are so nakedly rocky: they are too steep to hold much vegetation, to retain rich soil or carry water for anything other than a brief and lively moment as it finds the path of least resistance to the sea. Gravity pulls everything down but the ridge itself.

And yet, beneath all this there are valleys of the most extraordinary beauty and depth, some holding lochans, many rich in vegetation and colour that is all the more striking given the sharp and austere backdrop. Here are all the hallmarks of an alpine environment, shrunken down to fractional scale. Same severe lines, same sculpted valleys ribbed with arêtes, same busted-tooth silhouette. The one thing the Cuillin ridge lacks these days – other than absolute elevation, and this is probably why – is the thing that made the place look this wild in the first place. The one thing capable of taming the gabbro: ice. Lots and lots of ice.

Portnalong isn't the absolute easiest base for the Cuillin ridge, but I liked it. It felt like an agreeable adjunct, a place where real people lived and worked, in houses spaced apart from each other on their own little patch. The village was settled after the First World War by families of crofters, fishermen and weavers from over-populated Lewis and Harris, in the hope that a livelihood would be easier to forge on Skye. The local produce of throws, scarves and clothing became known as the 'famous Port-na-Skye' tweed. Each family was given a croft and a smallholding of between fifteen and twenty acres, three cows and the share of a sprawling sheep pasture; many descendants of these Hebridean off-comers were still here. I could understand why. The village spreads thinly high on the banks above water that is half loch, half sea. The sea mists gather at the mouth of Loch Harport on cool, clear mornings, making it look like the end of the world lies at the end of Skye – and beyond it led to a bright, grey, beautiful nothing. In early mornings white-tailed eagles strafe the waters. In the evenings stars fill a sky thousands of light years deep. This is the sort of place you get to like very quickly.

I liked the ridge from here, too. Close enough to be a presence, a dark wall in the morning, gilded in the evening. But not oppressive or dominant: just one of many things in the view, its shadow grasping at you. And for me, it was time to start exploring it, and making my way to the place that, in my mind at least, was the ridge's beginning: in the west, at the end of Glen Brittle, where the Cuillin climbs from the water.

In the journals of early travellers to Skye, you'll often encounter the idea that there are really only two centres from which to mount any exploration into the Cuillin: Sligachan and Glenbrittle, at more or less opposing ends of the ridge (unlike the valley in which it lies, the settlement of Glenbrittle is spelled as one word). Sligachan, beneath Sgùrr nan Gillean in the north, has the famous hotel, with mountaineering history soaked into its walls along with centuries of pipe smoke. And there is Glenbrittle, a dim but warm ember of scattered farmhouses and crofts at the end of its glen, opening out onto the loch that christens them both. But there are in fact several places where you can access the Black Cuillin – Elgol being one, Coire na Creiche another, Torrin another still – and many other striking points that land you in its midst, however circuitously.

You can't knock the proximity and convenience of lower Glenbrittle and Sligachan to the ridge's terminal points, though, and both were worth a look for their part in the history of the Cuillin's exploration.

I'd decided to do the Cuillin traverse, as that seemed the best (and most ballsy) way to see it all. But I hadn't decided exactly how I was going to tackle it, other than I'd elected to do it from south to north: beginning with Gars-bheinn and ending with the pinnacled climax of Sgùrr nan Gillean. It's often done the other way around for various practical reasons we'll come to – but I was running off pure psychology. To me, a meal and a bed in a celebrated inn felt more like an ending to work towards than a beginning to start from. Plus, before I began the serious stuff, I wanted to make a symbolic little pilgrimage. I wanted to splash the sea onto my boots, then follow a stream up into the sway of the Cuillin, up from the beach, up to a high valley or *corrie*. Up there was something I really wanted to see – or, more specifically, touch.

Well over a century ago, in the first lively years of Cuillin exploration, Glenbrittle was a deep-cut and far-flung outpost. Locals ran knockabout hostelries and small facilities catered for climbers, and the valley served as loose hub for mountain rescue teams. It would seem little has changed. There's now a campsite right on the beach. There's a hostel, making use of a fine old house. There's a car park, a farmhouse, a shop-cum-cafe-cum-still-essential-telephone (mobiles are useless down here), and a permanent mountain rescue base. And there, set back from the road, with a presence as grand as the Aiguilles above Chamonix, is the ridge.

On this particular morning I found myself driving down the glen, scattering sheep, wipers raking painfully across a windscreen indecisively speckled with rain. You drive past half of the ridge when you drive down Glen Brittle – the closest you can get to a roadside safari of it – and on a clear day it is breathtakingly close, all crags and high-tucked valleys and acres of naked rock, bursting out of the lowland greenery of the glen like claws piercing silk. Unfortunately, it was not a clear day. The ridge might not have been there at all were it not for its shadow behind the cloud.

Glen Brittle, however, was buried in a strange, ethereally bright fog. Ever wondered why it's always breezy on beaches? It's because air moving over cold water suddenly finds warm land, and rushes to meet it, like a draught finding an open doorway. The Hebridean microclimate notwithstanding, large tracts of water do strange things to moisture, and this mist – hugging the waters of Loch Brittle and spilling onto the road – was such a thing, the sort that makes you pull over and just stare. I slid the car into a parking space and looked down at the wide, pebble-speckled beach. The tide was low, leaving great slicks of water on the sand. Two people were walking a wiry dog, thin silhouettes against the mist, inverted in the water at their feet like a mirage, while gulls pecked around. The road between the bright sea and the dim, cloud-shrouded mountains behind me felt like a strange junction of existential plains. And then the rain started, and my thoughts abruptly changed direction – as everyone's do on Skye sooner or later – to the weather.

There are some quite good jokes about Skye weather. Two of my favourites:

Traveller: 'Does it always rain here?'
Local: 'Of course not – it snows sometimes.'

Traveller: 'Excuse me, little boy, but does the sun ever come out?'

Little boy: 'I don't know, I'm only six.'

… and so on. Both are nonsense: the furtive sun is everywhere and nowhere all the time, making up for its absence with frequently staggering lightshows. And snow rarely sticks around long, if it falls at all in the mild and salty climate. Amongst mountain climbers, however, the weather – wind and rain, usually – is the most frequently cited culprit for fractured plans on the Cuillin, and when those plans are the culmination of months of anticipation, weeks of planning and a drive of many, many hours, they do tend to vocalise the sting a bit more than they usually might. But the weather on Skye actually isn't *bad* – not compared with the rest of the west coast, anyway – it's just very unpredictable. And it changes very quickly, and very often.

There's a great scene in H. V. Morton's *In Search of Scotland* of an exchange at a hotel that could easily be the Sligachan in the closing years of the 19th century. A group of enthusiasts of various local distractions – a salmon fisherman, an artist, a mountaineer and a deer stalker – are crowded around a barometer. 'Going up, damn it,' says the salmon fisherman. 'Need rain, heaps of it. No water in the river.' The artist, however, expresses her delight that she might at last 'get Loch Coruisk in ideal light . . . that blue, you know?' The deer stalker replies simply, 'Going up! That's the stuff.' And the mountaineer, who clumps into the room wearing 'dubbined boots embroidered with crab-like nails', chips in: 'I'm afraid it's going to be misty, but as long as the rain holds off . . .' Then, as Morton writes:

Just as the gallant company is about to spread itself over the mountainside, the weather does exactly what the barometer said it wouldn't do – but at least somebody is sure to be delighted.

This, it seems, is essentially a faithful encapsulation of the Skye climate: don't plan for the weather, because the weather doesn't plan itself. According to C. F. Gordon Cumming's *In the Hebrides* (1883):

One thing I will say for Skye weather: whatever it does, it does in thorough earnest. I went there intending to remain a week; but it was four months before I left its hospitable shores, and during all that time we had either drenching rain or broiling heat in about equal parts.'

Even Charles Dickens alludes to Skye's vague weather in a piece for *Household Words* in 1852, describing the island as 'a hilly, rocky, misty sort of place with pasture ground and potato fields'. It was not his finest moment.

That whimsical name, *Eilean a' Cheo*, the 'Isle of Mist', seems the one most intrinsically associated with the weather – though not everybody thinks it appropriate. 'The *Isle of Mist*, how much more thrilling than the Isle of Skye! But why it should be called so, I do not know. Rain there is plenty, but scarcely any mist,' wrote the travelling clergyman J.A. MacCulloch, who nevertheless called his book *The Misty Isle of Skye*. He goes on to make the interesting if not entirely convincing point that in the days when the name was first given to 'this green isle of the west, the whole of the land was covered in forest', and that this more fecund landscape was more conducive to mist than modern Skye. His real point, though – or certainly the one, as a scholar of Celtic mythology, he more enthusiastically exploited – was the dual meaning of the word 'mist'.

The name implies something remote, secret, impenetrable ... and I should like my readers to believe the island has these qualities. The island is indeed full of mystery: the mystery of nature's charm and beauty, and the spell of a weird story.

It is undeniable that the hills shift character with even subtle fidgets of their microclimate. 'The mountains seem to play their own variations in mood on the prevalent theme provided by the weather,' wrote J. Hubert Walker in *On Hills of the North*.

On a black day of storm and rain and hail, they are indeed terrible; on a dark day of lifeless mist they may seem malevolent or merely indifferent; on a sunny day of life and light they seem almost to sing.

Walker goes on to describe days of climbs cut short by weather of frightening indecision, of cloudbursts and gales and sunshine, before making the brave attempt to package his advice for negotiating Skye's climate in a single rather excellent sentence:

> So of the weather in the Cuillin, I would sum up by saying: if it is not obviously bad, it is probably strangely beautiful.

Inevitably the weather has made its mark on many more accounts of Skye, though with occasionally – if dubiously – beneficial results. Alasdair Alpin MacGregor describes feeling so anxious at being lost in the mist on an excursion from Sligachan to Coruisk, during which he had 'been up to the hips in quagmires and pools and streams more than once', that he was 'obliged to complete the entire detour without a single halt ... to drink I did not require to pause, because the rains were running over my lips much faster than I could consume of them'. There are similarly extreme accounts at the other end of the scale, of climbers being high in the arid Cuillin in conditions so hot and dry that the rock burned their hands while they gasped for water.

The meteorological reason for all this contrariness is that the sky above Scotland is essentially a dogfight between the volatile weather systems of the Atlantic meeting the more stable systems of the continent – a bit like a much larger version of that windy beach. This leads to both the swiftness of the changes in weather, and the restless and bewitching interplay between clouds, crisp northern light and rain. Skye, like many of its neighbouring Hebrides, exhibits all three of the ingredients a place requires to be climatically volatile: it's mountainous, coastal and – like the rest of the western British coastline – mild.

People mention the 'Gulf Stream' when trying to explain the peculiar conservatism of the British climate, but what they really mean is the North Atlantic Drift – the name of the extension of the warm tidal current that's squirted out of the tropical latitudes of the Gulf of Mexico with enough momentum to cross the Atlantic and run up the edge of the west coast like a warm radiator. This relatively balmy sea means the adjoining land experiences winter temperatures that are warm – at least in comparison to coastal regions of a similar latitude that lack the influence of a current like ours. In Skye's case, a handy comparison lies directly across the Atlantic.

Kikiktaksoak Island off the coast of Northern Labrador in Canada – a place that even *sounds* like its name was first said through chattering teeth – is of similar size, coastal aspect and latitude to Skye, but enjoys a February temperature average of around -15°C. In the same month, Skye's average sea-level temperature hovers around freezing but rarely dips below it. The thawing effect of the sea, and the way it slips its warm limbs deep into the island, give Skye both a remarkably effective natural thermostat and a rather nice heating system. The island's temperature fluctuates remarkably little year-round. Sea-level Skye is hardly ever blisteringly hot, and its roads are rarely blocked with snow.

If that sounds curiously amenable for an island notorious for its weather, don't forget the rain. This falls year-round, but mainly in the winter – where, despite the joke, it does typically fall as water, not snow. Between December and March, southern Skye gets around 180mm of precipitation a month, with a yearly total of around 1,800mm – which, while well over double Britain's national average of 880mm, actually isn't quite up there with the worst. If we were to consider precipitation a nuisance, Skye's is about as bad as Fort William, very much worse than Keswick but considerably better than Betws y Coed.

It rains on Skye a lot more than on low-lying Shetland, Uist and Lewis – where locals have described storms quite literally racing over their heads only to be dramatically punctured on the sharp peaks of the Cuillin. On average it's almost twice as wet as Manchester and around three times as wet as London, but surprisingly only a third wetter than Cornwall and South Devon, which get a much better press for their weather. But it does depend where on Skye you are. And as anyone on the island will tell you, in the local vernacular there's a big difference between a 'shower' and 'rain'. A 'shower' can be over in a minute, or an hour, or a few hours – and often be interrupted with the glassiest, most brilliant sunshine and an abundance of rainbows. 'Rain', however, can last an entire summer. In 2009 it rained on the island for forty-eight days straight. Skye-based journalist Neil Stephen, writing in the *Guardian*, said the period was the wettest spell on the island since 1861. 'As all locals know,' he wrote rather dryly, 'summer ends in the Highlands when the English school holidays begin.' What he was referring to is the tendency of Skye to be at its most unappealing in the months when most people are likely to visit – the months of July and August – which no doubt contributes to its bad reputation. During these months the wind lessens, clouds of midges make for the skin of anyone foolish enough to expose it, and heavy clouds stuttering with lightning press down on the often busy island.

May and June are considered the best times to be on Skye if you have mountains in mind. Periods of high pressure, cool conditions keeping the midges out of the air and long daylight hours (in June, it rarely gets fully dark) make it the smartest bet. At the other end of summer, September has much to recommend it – although darker nights and more unsettled conditions make it a rather riskier date for the diary.

All of this is slightly redundant for the hillwalker, though, as the reliability of anything on Skye stops the second you start increasing your altitude. Put mountains in most places and – like a rock placed in a stream – they will disrupt the behaviour of the local weather. Place a huge kilometre-high ridge on an island that is already something of a battleground for climatic systems, and things are going to get rough. Then there's temperature. In dry air, temperature decreases with altitude – about 10°C for every thousand metres. In typically moist air such as Skye's, this is closer to 5 degrees, but still means that you could stand on the beach at Glenbrittle in a comparatively roasting 9°C and look up at a summit considerably closer to freezing.

Despite this, snow rarely lingers long on the Cuillin. After winter cold snaps, the tops are often silvered with a dusting, and you'll find a dump in the high northern corries, where the air is height-chilled, the peaks throw cold shadows over the snow and the few lochans within freeze. But the vertiginous slopes, combined with the warming, maritime effect of the sea, means that thick snow is uncommon on the ridge. That's not to say it doesn't happen; it just usually doesn't stay for long.

The next and probably most serious factor is wind. We've already seen how wind-speed picks up where land meets the sea; add a mountain into the mix and not only is that air increasing in speed, it's rising in height. A rule of thumb is that winds from the north and east are dry, and winds from the south and west are damp. Most of Skye's wind comes from the south, but the strongest wind comes from the south-west, arriving unimpeded across the sea and slamming into the slopes of the Cuillin, where it races up the ramp of the mountains and rapidly cools. This causes air particles carried in the wind to cool with it, which condense into cloud. So in anything other than stone-still air – and when was the last time you had that at the seaside? – there's more than likely to be cloud hanging off those peaks. So there really is more to the nickname 'the Misty Isle' than mystique.

Mystique and weather do flow together, though. Aside from jokes and incessant grumbles, the weather has been such an intrinsic part of the experience of the island it has developed its own mythology of superstition. A text in the 8th-century collection of legal tracts, the *Senchus Mór*, carries with it this verse:

> From the East blows the Purple Wind,
> From the South the White,
> From the North the Black
> And from the West the Pale.

The Scottish naturalist Seton Gordon referred to this in *The Charm of Skye* (1929), noting that:

> the black wind is usually the bearer of clear air and rare visibility . . . it is usually on nights of north wind that the aurora is seen. When reddish rays appeared and gave place to others of darker hue, it was believed that bad weather, which would last for some time, was approaching.

More eccentric forecasting comes courtesy of Martin Martin, the Skye man responsible for one of the earliest accounts of the Hebrides and their ways. 'Women observe that their breasts contract to a lesser bulk when the wind blows from the north,' he wrote in 1774, 'and that then they yield less milk than when it blows from any other quarter; and they make the like observation in other creatures that give milk.' Apparently smell was a good indicator, too. 'When the sea yields a kind of pleasant and sweet scent,' he wrote, 'it is a sure presage of fair weather to ensue.'

Shrunken breasts and fragrant seas aside, another uncanny meteorological tendency of the Hebrides is to be the weather yin to the mainland's yang. There's a local tradition that if you can see the hills of the mainland clearly from the islands, bad weather is on the way – and this counter-intuitive forecast often holds true. Likewise, a bad forecast for the mainland often means good weather on the islands, and vice versa.

Put all of this in a practical setting and you can appreciate why Skye weather has such a distressing effect on the mountaineer. Hang about anywhere and you're going to get wet at some point. The higher you climb, the colder you'll get and the more likely the rain will turn to snow. You're also more likely to encounter disorienting mists, wind strong enough to cut you in half and – if you're lucky enough to get a warm day – you're wandering around on rock so full of metal, you can never rule out the chance of a lightning strike. You should never suspect a mountain range of malev-olence, of course, but it's easy to feel that the Cuillin perhaps hates you just a little bit.

However, as with most things of dreadful reputation, the reality is rarely as bad as you fear. Those who spend significant time amongst the Cuillin begin to realise that nothing – good or bad – does what it's supposed to. The mountaineer Charles Pilkington once wrote, with one imagines a pen damp with irony if nothing else:

> My personal experience of Skye weather is that it is the driest place in the British Isles, for I have been there three times, spending at least ten days on each occasion, and have had [a total of] only four hours of rain.

He does admit that his brother experienced a slightly different Skye on one of their visits, when it rained for three weeks straight: 'a wee bit moist', he allowed.

Gordon Stainforth, who once spent 150 days photographing the ridge for his fine illustrated book *The Cuillin: Great Mountain Ridge of Skye*, noted that the ridge was completely clear of cloud for 71 days, and was rarely obscured by it for more than four in a row. 'And this,' he wrote, 'included a summer which was regarded as unusually bad even by the locals.'

So you really cannot predict or define the weather here. To twist that tired old expression about bad weather and inappropriate clothing, on Skye there is no such thing as weather at all – there are only 'conditions'. And as usual for such places, the best plan for anyone in meteorological distress is: 'If conditions are bad, wait a minute.'

Glenbrittle today remains a backwater, and is even quieter than it was fifty years ago. The people of this little place have for generations acted as a kind of collective mother hen to anyone venturing up onto, or staggering back off, the Cuillin. Back in the late 1800s and early 1900s, when climbing was really getting going down here, Glenbrittle seemed commendably domestic and was held in the deepest esteem by all who fell into its embrace. Here there was always a splendid meal and a warm bed in some firelit cottage, with an oiling of whisky to take the chill from the bones. In those days there was a post office from which to send dispatches. Planes carrying wealthy travellers and upper-crust mountaineers would regularly land here on a makeshift strip, reducing the journey from Renfrew from twelve hours by train, boat and rough-shod road to ninety minutes – until the Glen Brittle road became so rutted the service was withdrawn. A van from the Carbost grocery would brave this notorious track twice a week, but even before this wily climbers stocked their Glen Brittle camps by ordering food packages by mail that *just* fell within the weight limit of the postal service.

Now the hub of the place was clearly the campsite and its shop, which appeared to be the only place to get anything in Glen Brittle other than wet. I was beginning to become thoroughly endowed with this last commodity as, increasingly hunched, I walked the long path between the scattering of tents, their nylon flysheets crackling with the gathering downpour, towards the shop – a corrugated and faintly agricultural-looking building nestled where the campsite met the slopes of the Cuillin.

As I approached I saw a large dog standing near the doorway, its fur slick with rain, looking out with its mouth agape. When it saw me approaching its mouth snapped shut in sudden and keen interest. It looked like the sort of dog that might waggle up to you and make a slobbery fuss, but alas no. As I walked in it launched itself at me, with the sort of singularity of purpose that makes you leap out of your skin and cover your crotch.

'Aaaa!'

As I jumped back, a hand reached out and snared the dog by the collar, and a tall man with a dark beard and a wetsuit hanging around his hips hauled the creature inside, its claws scraping on the floor.

'Barry, shoosh. Don't mind him, he's mostly mouth.'

'Mostly?'

'Well, he does like to guard things.'

'Against customers?' I said as I edged inside, the dog still rumbling at his side.

The man shook his head. 'Och, no, we're just camping.' He pointed at the floor, and the dog followed his finger and, with a final, magnanimous grumble, lay down. 'Someone walked past the tent yesterday and he gave him a right telling off. Practically chased him halfway up into the corrie.' He chuckled at this, before indicating a man with coils of blond hair walking out from a storeroom. 'Anyway. That's your man there if you're looking for help.'

The shop was unexpectedly swish, all wood and chrome, and a big step up from your usual hole-in-the-wall campsite shop. One wall was racked with essentials for campers like midge nets, gas and food, another was packed with locally hewn souvenirs, while a spacious seating area and a wood-burning stove gave the place a decidedly Scandinavian feel. Up on the wall was a map of the Cuillin, with annotations taped on indicating the time it would take to reach certain accessible valleys and what kind of walk it was.

I gave Barry – which, by the way, is a daft name for a dog – a wide berth and walked to the counter, where the man with the hair was drying his hands on a tea towel. 'What can I get for you?' he said in a bright English accent. I looked above him at the wall-mounted menu and saw with interest that the coffee was branded 'The Cuillin Coffee Co – Est 2015' with a stylised two-tone illustration of Sgùrr nan Gillean as its logo.

I ordered a Cuillin Americano and we made small talk about the weather, which he said couldn't be that bad as 'there weren't any tents in the sea.' He grinned, did some slamming things with the coffee machine, then said good-naturedly, 'You know, it's only really tourists who talk about the weather here. Stay for long enough and it just becomes a thing in the background.' He gave me the coffee and I told him what I was looking for: a waterfall named the Demon Shower.

He frowned. 'The Demon Shower? Can't say it rings a bell.' He relayed my question to the man with the dog, both of whom looked up.

'Don't recognise the name,' he replied. 'But there's a few waterfalls just down the coast there. And you can see the big one from the beach.'

If you want to follow nature's path from the very bottom of a mountain, follow the water. Streams are nature's pathways, with waterfalls their most spectacular stretch. And I couldn't think of a more organic way to start investigating the Cuillin ridge than from the point where the waters that drain from it most resplendently meet the sea. It's like climbing up a thrown rope. Of course, how this translated on the ground was for me to discover – but a tempting starting point had, with a bit of research, appeared with very little bidding. The Demon Shower, as it had been christened by someone at some point, was the culmination of the Allt Coire Làgan and the Allt na Buaile Duibhe, which combined to enter Loch Brittle in a spectacular cascade of water. *Allt* meant 'stream' – I made a mental note to look up what *buaile duibhe* meant later on.

I left the cafe and, after the briefest rise following the path towards Coire Làgan, following a very few hooded walkers with rain-slick covers over their daysacks, peeled right and began to follow the coast, immediately on a slightly rougher, less-trodden path and immediately alone. The way crossed angled grass as it traversed back towards the loch, which entered the land as a deep bite. As I moved further away from Glenbrittle I could start to appreciate its context: a broad stripe of yellow beach where the glen opened to the water. On either side the land rose: on the far side the stepped, shelf-like peninsula that sat between Loch Brittle and Loch Eynort, topped by An Cruachan at 435 metres, the whole covered in felty green skin ribbed with shadow. Then, on this side, the Cuillin: dark and burly, rising to over twice that. The dividing line between the lava plateau and the gabbro core, split by Glen Brittle, right there to see, lying between the rest of Skye and the most extraordinary mountain range in Britain. The newest, roughest, hardest, sharpest, scariest one – and the one that nobody can seem to spell the same way twice.

Euilvelimi. Cuilluelum. Cullaelum. Cuchullin. Cuchuillin. Cuthallia. Quillin. Cuilfhionn. Cullin. Cullins. Coolin. Coolins. An Cuilthionn or An Cuiltheann. You find all of these, and no doubt a few more, dotted throughout the ridge's written history. Never has there been a mountain range with such an indecisive christening; often you find it not only spelled differently, but expressed as plural and singular in the same piece of writing.

Even the earliest accounts suggest a local ambiguity as regards the range's name. Thomas Pennant, in 1772, was unwilling to restrict himself to commit to any fewer than three names, describing it as the 'mountains of Cuchuillin, Cullin or Quillin, which reach to the sea'. How fitting that a mountain range of such complexity, such fidgety moods and confounding structure should – in true outlaw fashion – have a name just as impossible to pin down. An endlessly bastardised mongrel of Norse and Gaelic, it feels as if there has been a secret competition amongst those who have made the Cuillin their business to discover and commit to print every conceivable variation of the word.

The reason for this isn't hard to appreciate. First, in the days when maps were vague or non-existent and the only reference points were verbal, people tended to write what they *heard* – which, depending on who the speaker was, could have a myriad of interpretations on the page. These would more often than not be by an English hand, interpreting a Skye tongue – so it's not at all surprising that misheard or often resplendently miswritten names, complete with articulations of burr and spittle, made it through to publication: picture English travellers hearing Gaelic voices, on an island heavily influenced by Norse nomenclature, and you can appreciate there are as many ways to pronounce a word that sounds like 'Cuillin' as there are to write it.

Even today, the first syllable of 'Cuillin' can either begin with a soft 'ch' or a hard 'k' in the same place – followed by a gruff 'uh' or tuneful 'oo'. The second and final syllable can either be said as 'in', 'un' or just breathed out of existence in that wonderful Highland way, like a sigh.

The first map of Skye to feature any kind of vaguely recognisable annotation married to a vaguely recognisable landscape was published in Joan Blaeu's *Atlas of Scotland* of 1654, although drawn much earlier by Timothy Pont. On it, as you might expect for its age, the mountain groups are slightly confused and their names indecisive; here we have a range indicated as 'Klammaig Hils or Glanock,' most likely meaning Glamaig and the Red

Hills, and a more significant range named the 'Culluelun or Gulluin hils'. It's probably the first appearance of what would eventually become the Cuillin on a map.

Today we're told the correct way to spell it is *Cuillin*, because that is the word the Ordnance Survey uses on its maps – and as a yardstick of consistency it's better than most. But even the normally redoubtable OS makes a *faux pas* by calling the ridge the 'Cuillin Hills'; the suffix is unnecessary, for the same reason you wouldn't say the Himalaya *mountains* or the Andes *range*, for example. The Cuillin of Skye is singular, although there are many occasions where the plural sounds far more natural. And just to complicate things, within the Black Cuillin you have the Cuillin ridge but also the Cuillin outliers of Sgùrr na Stri, Sgùrr Hain, Blàbheinn and Clach Glas. So it's a singular term to describe a collective group, of which the ridge is the key component. Does it matter? Not really. What's far more evocative – and elusive – is the murky origins of the word itself.

Perhaps if we could demystify the origin of the term, or discover the source of the thinking behind it, it would clear the spelling up a little. But if anything this makes things even more mysterious and ambiguous, because not only are the many different versions of *Cuillin* misspelled, many of them *mean* different things. And as nobody knows whether the origin of the word lies in Irish Gaelic, Scottish Gaelic, Welsh, Norse or Pictish – and there are cases to be made for all of them – and whether it's a tribute to a person or character, it's rather hard to know upon which derivation to hang your assumptions.

To complicate things even further, what you also have in the words Cuillin, Coulin and Coolin – and also Cuchuillin, Cuchullin and Chuchulain – is a homophone: a word that, while meaning different things and being variously spelled, sounds the same or at least similar, particularly when the variable inflections of accent, dialect and even language are factored in. Which sadly means that whatever was meant when the name was first uttered, the chances are it has been miscommunicated or misheard dozens of times since.

The aforementioned H. V. Morton – he of the colourful weather-themed dining room exchange – said of 'The Coolin', that they fascinate and thrill me . . . you look up at their incredible, fantastical summits, so still and yet so weirdly alive. You feel that someday these heights will shout together and announce the end of the world. But was ever a mighty spectacle cursed with such a piffling name? It is like the sound of a small lawn being mown.

He then goes on to concede that the Gaelic '*A Chuilionn* looks better, as does the modified *Cuillin*'.

A good place to start then, out of appropriate respect if nothing else, is Scots Gaelic – as close to a native language as Skye has. The modern Gaelic for the ridge is *An Cuilthionn*, and it has also gone by *An Cuilionn* and *An Cuiltheann*.

There is no direct translation; that would be too easy. Bearing in mind that Highlanders usually named their landscape features for a regional eccentricity, in terms of the words that vaguely resemble the modern Gaelic name we have either *cuilionn-mara*, the sea-holly, or simply holly – *cuilionn* – which is certainly apt, both for the resemblance of the peaks to the sharp edges of holly leaves, and the range as a whole to a spiky wreath. It has even been suggested that this analogy works on a macro level, and that the prickliness of the rock underhand contributed to the name. So far, so good, but as Peter Drummond points out in his excellent *Scottish Hill Names*, Gaelic mountains relating to trees or other types of flora typically do not come from a resemblance in appearance, but on account of the prevalence of a species growing there. And while Seton Gordon, Skye's most reliable botanical observer, does make note of a 'stunted holly tree' at the mouth of Coire Làgan – the Cuillin has never been particularly known for holly to the extent that might inspire a name.

There's another theory that the word *Cuillin* means 'worthless', which seems unlikely, as the derivation is from an obscure Welsh word. The only thing preventing this being discounted out of hand is that the idea was apparently suggested by Colin Phillip, a climber, painter and Cuillin scholar in the early 20th century.

Shifting dialect into Irish Gaelic, a visual resemblance of the word is to the *chuilfhionn*, or coulin: a traditional long hairstyle popular with Irish men in the 15th century. The style was outlawed when land across the Irish Sea was seized by the British crown, triggering a systematic prohibition of all things traditionally Irish. Again, it doesn't seem all that likely.

Irish mythological heroes – Gaelic heroes, we should say – do feature fairly highly when it comes to naming the landscape. One of these was Fingal, or Fhionn, and a popular idea about the origin of the word *Cuillin* was that the mountains were the *Cuil Fhionn*, the 'nook' or 'niche' or hiding place of Fingal, the Irish warrior king. Warriors and the Cuillin are something of a theme, which we'll touch on later, but it's generally accepted that the mythological heirs to the name *Cuillin* are thought to be later alignments to a more ancient name. Mountaineer and Gaelic aficionado Alexander Nicolson – a qualified commentator indeed, as we shall see – held the view that the name was historically A' Chuilionn or the Coolin, and that 'they were never known until very recent times as the Cuchullin Hills, [and] only to the makers of guidebooks, who thought it grander than the other.'

Another possible Irish derivation is the drearily functional *cuilleann*, which means 'very steep slope', but traditionally the name is only added to settlements at the foot of mountains, not in them – for instance at Kilcullen, County Kildare.

If we're playing the game of finding other place names with sympathetic spellings, *Coulin* was used by some influential early climbers, William Naismith amongst them. It's certainly audibly similar to *Cuillin* and *Coolin*, and is a name that pops up on other Highland maps – particularly in Torridon, from where Skye and the ridge are clearly visible. Here you have a Loch Coulin, a Coulin Forest and a Coulin Pass, in a landscape also dominated by sharp and impressive mountains. But this name is actually a *name* – specifically Anglo-Saxon and of great vintage, dating from before the Norman Conquest and often belonging to landed families in possession of large estates. It's thought to derive from the name Nicholas, as this was commonly shortened to Colin. To link this to the Skye Cuillin won't really stand up to scrutiny, first because of its unlikely provenance and second because the idea of the most dramatic mountain range in the British Isles being called 'Colin' is just far too much to bear.

Another possibility seems to be my theory alone – always a bad start – but to be fair, it's no more tenuous than the rest. And while it may seem a little obscure, *most* mountain names are obscure and are often hung on the thinnest resemblances and associations. Remember, before the mid-18th century, the names of the local high places (and presumably the care with which they were named) probably ranked somewhere between which variety of swede to grow on the vegetable patch and where you were going to get your frock-coat mended on the give-a-shit scale. Mountains were not then the subject of much-agonised christening, and there's no reason to think the Cuillin was any different.

Anyway, I came across it when I investigated the word *Coolin* – and found that was also the name given to an Irish air, an orchestral composition of considerable vintage, possibly as early as the 13th century. An alternative, arcane spelling of this tune is *Coolun*, which is thought to have meant long locks of fair hair – not the first time a long hairstyle has come into this discussion – as well as evidently having an association with something of beauty. The second meaning is an obvious one to link, but the first struck me as at least vaguely likely. I challenge you to look at the great runs of strikingly pale scree cascading off the Cuillin in pale, intertwining braids and not see at least something in this idea. Enough to inspire the name of a mountain range? Probably not. But then something grand and enduring can be derived from the smallest thing.

Interestingly, the alternative meaning of the song name 'Coolin' is 'The Lady of the Desert'. And the Irish Gaelic spelling of this is *An Chúileann* – certainly visually similar to one Scots Gaelic name for the Cuillin: *An Cuiltheann*.

And then, of course, Skye's place etymology is drenched in Norse. The most likely candidates for the name *Cuillin* from Scandinavia are *kjolen*, meaning 'rock height' or 'ridge', or *kjollen*, which is thought to refer to the sweeping keel of a boat, such as on a Viking longship. This chimes with the Druim nan Ramh, or the 'Ridge of Oars', a lateral spur descending from the middle of the Cuillin ridge as if from a boat. In most respects this seems to convincingly tick the boxes in terms of pronunciation, provenance and visual similarity; there is even a mountain range along the Norway/Sweden border bearing the name *Kjolen*. A pretty likely fit, then – except for one thing. Why would *kjolen* suffer so badly in translation next to so many other nicely intact Old Norse names on the Skye map?

Mountain aficionados may also raise a smug hand here and point out that however singular the range, the word *Cuillin* isn't unique to Skye's black ridge, nor even unique to Skye. But this is, so to speak, a red herring. On Skye there are the Red Cuillin, but this name – applied to the fine but rather lumpier granite mountains of Glamaig, Marsco and their outliers – is rather a misnomer. 'Red Hills' was first coined by geologist John MacCulloch, with 'Cuillin' added at some point by mapmakers as a kind of local generic to distinguish the two neighbouring mountain groups from each other. Presumably this was just in case the dramatic visual contrast, geological make-up and clear physical separation of the ranges was insufficient. Their Gaelic name is *na Beanntan Dearga* – simply, the Red Hills, which is as it should be. Climb to their summits and you will appreciate that these peaks, whilst of similar origin and fine places, are built from a very different blueprint. Were you to climb one and look beyond Skye's shores to the south-west, however, you will see the other rather more convincing bearer of the name *Cuillin* – the range that impressively knuckles the neighbouring Isle of Rum.

There are many physical similarities between the Cuillin of Skye and the Cuillin of Rum. Both comprise dark, volcanic rock collected into steep peaks and arranged in corrie-chewed ridges. Rum's mountains are, however, lower and much less numerous than their counterparts looming across the stretch of water Archibald Geikie pleasingly christened 'The Cuchullin Sound' on his geological map of 1876.

But here's the thing: despite being widely used today, it is not known when the *mountains* of Rum became the *Cuillin* of Rum. The nomenclature is widely accepted, and appears in all the guides. But no historical Ordnance Survey maps record the name 'Cuillin' on Rum, and they still don't. Rum's history is deeply ancient but shadowy, and the island spent much of its modern life as a private shooting estate under eccentric stewardship, only opening up to tourists in the latter half of the 20th century. We'll probably never know when the mountains first took on the name Cuillin, or if they were named in tandem with Skye's range, anecdotally amongst locals or as a kind of tribute later on. The view of Skye's Cuillin is inescapable when looking north-east from Rum, and it wouldn't take a huge amount of imagination to tie up the two ranges' visual connection by bestowing a common name.

Rum's mountains were indisputably named by the Norse, however. Despite some British Admiralty charts of the 18th century resorting to practical naming for the purposes of navigation (one from 1794 makes the nasty Anglo-Gaelic *faux pas* of labelling one of the peaks Benmore Hill, literally Big Hill Hill), Rum's mountains carry unmolested Norse names: Ainshival, Hallival, Trollabhal, Barkeval. As Peter Drummond notes, the Norse tended to name mountains with a certain functionality, usually reflective of their most striking attributes. Such is the similarity between the Cuillin of Rum and of Skye that the name of *kjolen*, 'rocky height', given to both is convincing enough, particularly when you consider the importance of these mountain ranges as seafaring compasses. As the Vikings didn't use maps, we are left to wonder about the specifics. But here's something worth considering: the individual peaks of Rum have stand-alone Norse names – whereas the ones on the Cuillin ridge are mostly Gaelic. And however they were spelled, since their first appearances on the map the Cuillin has been singular – *the* Cuillin. Later corruptions turned it into all manner of plurals, from the Cuchuillins to the Coolin Hills – but the accepted proper term indicates the ridge as one single feature. Could it therefore be that the Norse considered and named this sustained, high battlement as one great mountain – the *Kjolen* – and gave separate christenings to the less linear, more spaced-out peaks on Rum? It's not a perfect theory, but it makes sense. And for the little it's worth, it's the one I'd stake my shirt on.

So the meaning of the word *Cuillin* has been suggested as signifying anything from someone's name and their place of hiding, to a visual resemblance, to a haircut, a plant, a cruel assessment of their agricultural value, a Viking boat – and a certain mythological hero whom we are yet to meet. And after all that, the most likely meaning is a word that means 'rocky ridge.' This, at the end of our perilously pedantic pathway, comes as something of an anticlimax, no?

But remember: in the end, nobody will ever know for sure if any of the theories are right, and nobody knows if any of them are wrong. It's a matter for the beholder to absorb, then decide for themselves, which I think is rather nice. But of the name, make no mistake: the Black Cuillin of Skye is the only true Cuillin there is.

There's a fork in the road in the story of the ridge just here. Were we being chronologically faithful, now would be the time to talk about glaciation – but I'm going to save that excitement for a little later. For now, let's talk about another invasion. One that came from the sea – and left a legacy that lives and breathes on Skye to this day.

3

Blood

The south-west corner of Skye in which we find ourselves is, as it happens, a fine place to understand the beginnings of the history of the humans that have inhabited – and still inhabit – this island. Skye's history of wayfarers goes back a very long way. The island has been defined by travellers and off-comers, as most islands generally are. And as it was, so it remains.

The oldest traces of the first humans to make Skye their home – or at least a base for hunting – lie close to Staffin's dinosaur prints, on An Corran beach at the northern end of the island. In 2015 a 'shell midden' of charred hazelnut shells, interspersed with tooled stones and bone fragments that may have been worked by hands like our own, was discovered on this north-eastern edge of Skye. The nutshells were radiocarbon dated to almost 9,000 years ago – a period representing the very earliest evidence of post-glacial human activity in Britain. This places people on this beach in the period scientists call the Mesolithic, and the rest of us call the Middle Stone Age. An earlier dig at An Corran ('rocky point' in Gaelic) also yielded evidence of later, rude structures suggesting a history of continuous transient occupation here in the centuries since – animal bones from the Neolithic, or New Stone Age; copper pins from the Iron Age; and a rock structure from the medieval period.

Most informative are the human bones found at An Corran. Thirty-eight bones and seven teeth were discovered here, which archaeologists later interpreted as belonging to at least five individuals: an adult over 40, another around 35, a teenager and two children. The eldest adult had osteoporosis.

Other bones excavated here gave insight into what walked with them, fed them and clothed them: elk, bear, wild boar. They probably had fires in a cave beneath low, sheltered cliffs where they boiled molluscs and nuts; they carried spears with heads of flint; and they dressed in fur and leather, perhaps making primitive trinkets from bone.

However counter-intuitive it is to imagine wild Hebridean islands as being settling-places for the earliest peoples, they were actually perfect. Here were fertile volcanic soils, long and abundant coastlines offering rich fishing grounds and bounteous produce such as kelp, with the influence of the sea keeping temperatures away from the extremes of the mainland.

Evidence of a similar type and vintage has been found in Applecross, over the Inner Sound between Skye and Scotland's west coast, suggesting these Stone Age people used primitive boats to cross stretches of water. Although not much evidence of boats of this age has been found, there is little doubt they existed. It has even been suggested that the boats were sturdy enough to ferry livestock from distances even further away from the mainland than Skye. Boats are in fact the only explanation for these animals' ancient presence there.

Not far from where I was exploring now above Loch Brittle lies another site of ancient humans on Skye, this time beneath the shadow of the Cuillin. Climb a short distance up from Glen Brittle – perhaps past the Allt na Buaile Duibhe mentioned earlier, which I later discovered means 'stream of the black settlement'; that name alone speaks volumes – and you will see a peninsula rolling in a rough taper to the south-west, shaped like a worked flint. At its end the flint has a drilled eyelet – a loch that catches the after-noon light. This is the point of Rubha an Dùnain. And there is nowhere on Skye that tells such a story of the island's human history than this now uninhabited prow of land.

The peninsula isn't easy to reach for people who avoid toilsome walking. It stretches 6 kilometres from the road, out to nowhere. But to stand here not only grants you a rare view of the Cuillin, it enables you to perch on the topmost tier of Skye's human history from the very beginning to almost the present day. And from this peninsula, you can also look out from Skye back into its past.

Rubha an Dùnain points away from Skye towards the islands of Soay,

Rum, Canna, the Outer Hebrides and beyond. But look at it from the seaward side with the Cuillin beyond, and here instead is an inviting alighting point to passing boats, a jetty of land amenably extended. It's important to think of Rubha an Dùnain from this direction, because Skye, while close to the mainland on its south-eastern edge, has always been defined by those inbound from the sea. The water presented fewer challenges and hardships than the land, and the great ridge of the Cuillin – while an insurmountable obstacle for those travelling cross-country – was evidently a useful sighting point for early seafarers.

The first people at Rubha an Dùnain were perhaps just like those at Staffin, who from evidence gathered here and on the facing shores of Rum were possibly seasonal itinerants, collecting supplies and material for tools. But burial cairns still stand here from 5,000 years ago, and here too is a chambered walk-through tomb, once a great mound of stones with cavities beneath, long since grown over with grass and dating from a similar time. This suggests occupation here was somewhat less fleeting than as an outpost for hunter-gatherers, and perhaps was the first permanent occupation on Skye. It's unclear whether people were being buried here before they were spending lives here, but there are scattered roundhouse ruins and evidence of enclosures, suggesting that by the Bronze Age at least, people were farming and subsisting on Skye, at the end of this peninsula in the shadow of the Cuillin.

At the tip of Rubha an Dùnain a great wall still stands, some three metres tall and in places four metres wide at its base. Built of robust stones, the wall is thought to date from the Iron Age, and to have sheltered a smelting pit and basic forge, but was subsequently fortified to cut off the end of the peninsula and form some sort of watchtower. Here we sense a change in the nature of the stones, from functional to defensive – and an indicator of the long period of more troubled times on Skye that would inform much of its later history.

Round fortifications of Iron Age vintage also gave Skye a word found in the bedrock of names still on the map: the broch, also known as a *dun*. Typically built on headlands and places of prominence or visibility, they were often sites where castles would eventually stand, inheriting the names of the earlier structures. Hence Dunvegan, Duntulm, Dunscaith. And Rubha an Dùnain.

The Iron Age ushered in a period known as the Dark Ages. These times are so-called not because there was anything particularly eerie about them, but because they've yielded lean historical detail – over a period of five hundred years or so either side of the birth of Christ. Here we find the Picts – probably the most romanticised and mysterious early residents of Scotland – whose serpentine designs on standing stones bewitch with their ancient mystique, mainly because we know so little about them. The Latin term 'pictus', *painted*, was given by the terrified Romans who encountered them on their steady conquest north, although the name might have come from some Iron Age peoples obscurely referring to themselves as *Pritani*. One writer describes the Picts as possibly the greatest mystery of ancient Europe, given that nobody has any idea where they came from. Either way, they are frequently cited as Scotland's first 'race', insofar as they formed a loose collection of regional tribes or kingdoms that viciously opposed the entry of Romans into Scotland, and eventually united under one king and one nation: Pictland.

The consensus about this doubtless varied people is that they were clever, tenacious, skilled in art and formidable in battle. They were matrilineal, passing bloodlines through the female side of the family, with a tradition of oral storytelling but no written language; the many carved stones they left could be anything from markers of tribal territory to religious offerings, or even a rudimentary form of communication. Pictish relics in the west of Scotland are rare, and Skye is no exception; the most notable of three Pictish stones found on the island is the 'Tall Stone', the Clach Ard, near Portree. It hasn't stood there long; it was found propping up the door of a cottage in around 1880, and its original location prior to that is unknown.

What is known is that around the 5th century CE a huge migration of Irish Scoti – from *scottia*, meaning 'raider' – came to the west coast and isles from over the sea to the west. Unlike England, Ireland had remained beyond the frontier of the Roman Empire but was short of cultivable land. With England in the grip of the Roman withdrawal, the Scoti made for the wild lands and islands of the country that would later bear their name. Not for the last time, the raiders would become settlers. Colonising the west, from Dunadd in Argyllshire and further up the west coast, the off-comers would create an overkingdom that spanned from the facing tip of Northern

Ireland across the sea, with Skye its northern edge. Under the rule of King Fergus the Great, this kingdom was known as Dal Riata.

What was now established was a cultural divide of two opposing kingdoms cutting Scotland in half: the Picts to the east and the north, the Scoti on the west and in the isles, with the Grampian mountains forming a natural divide between the two.

Relations were not harmonious between the two kingdoms, to say the least. The intricate annoyances and tensions of the kindreds and kingdoms are too complicated to describe (read any of it and you'll understand the inspirations behind *Game of Thrones*, put it that way), and there were many attempts to invade the other's territory. Then in the sixth century, an enormous complication arrived: Christianity.

Imagine you're on the tip of Rubha an Dùnain, and gazing out over the little loch there to the sea. Perhaps walk to the old wall and look south-south-west. If you haven't got your compass – and *tsk* if you haven't – look at the channel between Rum and Eigg, that is to say the mountainous island ahead of you and the one that looks like an upturned boat to its left. If it's very clear you may see a distant island on the horizon between them. That's Mull. And off the coast of Mull is Iona. The year is now 563, and a small wood and leather boat with thirteen men aboard is making its way towards that island's southern shore.

The story of the man who would become St Columba is quite remarkable, but as ever with such things, it's difficult to know how much to believe. He was born near what is modern Donegal in 521, and was reputedly the great-great-grandson of Ireland's King Niall. Roman Catholicism had recently arrived there, and Columba (he was known in life as Colum Cille, or 'church dove', but we'll call him Columba for simplicity) was one of the most scholarly students of the faith.

Columba didn't leave Ireland in the best circumstances. A dispute with his mentor Finnian of Clonard over the right to keep a clutch of facsimile scriptures caused an escalating series of arguments that reached the king, and, rather astonishingly, escalated further into a war in which three thousand people were killed. The fallout caused Columba to be vilified and – understandably, one might say – for his conscience to fall into turmoil. In an act of clemency, Columba was allowed to enter self-imposed exile, during which, on the clearly incisive advice of a hermit, he left Ireland with the aim of converting as many to Christianity as had perished in battle on his account – to 'save' the souls he had lost, if you like. In 563, with twelve disciples, Columba sailed for the Hebrides. His aim was to stop his journey when no longer in sight of Ireland. This he finally achieved when he alighted on the tiny island of Iona, off the coast of Mull and some thirty miles south of Skye – deep in the kingdom of Dal Riata.

Having been given Iona by Dal Riata's king, Columba set about establishing a monastery on the island, which would later become the centre of Christianity in the Highlands. As a bringer of literacy and enlightenment, he was venerated wherever he travelled. He was seen as a diplomat between the regional tribes, but also between the kingdom of Dal Riata and the Picts, into whose territory he led missionary expeditions to win followers and improve relations between the kingdoms. As a result his presence was considered something of a coup, with the king of Dal Riata hoping he could help win power from the Picts.

By establishing an important monastery on Iona, Columba is often cited as the missionary who brought Christianity to what became Scotland – but he was by no means the first to try. St Ninian, a Briton, consecrated a church in Wigtownshire in 397 and may have made it as far as Orkney; and both St Mungo and St Serf were active in the area of modern-day Glasgow at around the same time Columba was making his way to the Hebrides. But it's St Columba who was most effective at winning the acceptance of the rural people, not least because he was a warrior himself and, when it came to his calling – according to historian Robert Gunn – '[he] wasn't opposed to conversion at sword point'.

Some of the more colourful stories about St Columba come from his travels into Pictish lands. One recounts how he arrived at the fort of the Pict's King Brude at Inverness, who refused the missionaries entry. Columba made the sign of the cross at the barred gates, which swung open as if by magic, and the king converted on the spot. Another concerns Columba coming upon a group of Picts who were burying a man killed by a vicious water creature while swimming in a river. Columba sent a follower – the admirably devout Luigne moccu Min – into the water to tempt the creature, which reappeared, only to be stopped 'as if pulled back by ropes' when

Columba made the sign of the cross and shooed it away. This naturally impressed the bystanding Picts, who saw it as a miracle. The geographical significance of the event near a certain infamous body of water, which was described in Adomnán's hagiography of Columba, hasn't been lost on enthusiasts of Scottish folklore: 565 is considered the date of the first appearance of the Loch Ness monster.

Columba made two visits to Skye, lending his name to a rock (from which he is said to have preached) and a small island on a bend in the River Snizort in 585. Upon this small isle would later be built an abbey and a cathedral with an 80-foot transept that would become one of the island's most venerated sites – and would establish Skye as the most important Christian centre in the Hebrides. Columba and his successors put their name elsewhere on Skye; anywhere with 'Kil' in the title refers to a place of worship or burial, and these are often suffixed with a name. Hence we have Kildonan (named for St Donan), Kilmartin (Martin) and Kiltaraglen (Talorgan).

A word you might come across from around this time of rampant religious conversion is 'pagan'. This is one of the more confusing (and misused) words deployed to describe the belief system of the time. In Columba's day, 'pagan' was simply a word Christian converts used to denote rural people, into which category you would put the Picts, the ordinary citizens of Dal Riata and anyone else whose beliefs lay outside the dominant faith. Pagans are often depicted as earth-worshipping, magic-dabbling people fond of sacrifice, and there is certainly truth in this, along with their belief in deities and demons associated with life-giving vessels, such as wells and places of harvest. But what this usually describes in this country is Celtic polytheism, strains of which are scattered in the early history of the Dal Riata people – the people who would become known as the Gaels.

While we're at it, let's quickly clear that one up now too. What do we mean when we say Gaelic and what do we mean when we say Celtic? You'll hear the two terms interchanged seemingly freely, so it's probably best we consider the reason why.

Take Mexico, the United States, Argentina, Peru and Canada – all different, individual countries but which, along with others, comprise the geographical unit we call the Americas. Small, divergent fragments of an encompassing whole, in this case a geographical group. Now imagine that instead of a geographical group it's an ancestral group. We'll call it Celtic. And from that ancestral group, there emerge a couple of principal units – like North America and South America, to continue our continental analogy, only these units are called Goidelic and Brythonic. Just as their continental equivalents divide into countries, these further divide into languages and dialects: Brythonic into Welsh, Cornish and Breton, and Goidelic into Manx, Irish and Scottish Gaelic.

The Celts as a cultural unit were first lumped together before the advent of Christianity as comprising people with similar habits and appearance. Geographically they are thought to trace a common origin to the Hallstatt region of Austria in around 600 BCE, then migrating north and west into France and Spain, followed by Britain and Ireland as the centuries passed. With the Roman conquest, the Celtic presence in continental Europe was quashed, pushed north and marginalised, eventually finding its last stronghold in the distant wild places of Britain: Ireland, the Isle of Man, Wales, northern Scotland and the Hebrides. In these places, far from Roman influence, the Celts evolved their own distinct identities and dialects. These endure to this day with varying degrees of vigour.

Scottish Gaels are the outpost of Celtic culture particular to Scotland. It also makes sense of the old but accurate dictum 'all Gaels are Celts, but not all Celts are Gaels.' Think of it like that, and you already know more than most people.

The Picts were, as we've mentioned, an anomaly, but the two cultures would intermingle, with the term 'Gaelic' increasingly denoting geography and language, rather than a particular gene pool. This gradual unification – the Kingdom of Alba, as it became – would be a result of Columba's spread of Christianity and the seeds of faith he sowed, which would bloom into a solidarity of sorts. Until, that is, the arrival of a common foe from the north would leave an everlasting mark on Skye.

Before we leave the tip of Rubha an Dùnain, let's take a walk to the south-eastern tip of Lochan na h-Àirde. Here a narrow 'S' of a watercourse about 100 metres long and maybe three or four metres wide links the loch with the sea. This location caused a bit of a stir in 2011 when some tell-tale timbers thought to date from around 1100 CE were found on the bed of the loch. If you were to study scholarly descriptions of the site, you might come across phrases such as 'stone-lined channel with associated noosts, ca. Medieval period, Norwegian expansion zone'. Were you to look at the news reports, you might find something a little more enticing. This is no natural waterway; somebody built it. The channel was a canal, and the loch was no mere ornament. It was a Viking shipyard.

One thing I noticed when I first came to Skye, and notice still, is that it doesn't feel like Scotland. It feels like Skye. It's its own place, but feels the touch of other lands, near and far. Of these, the most robust comes from the north-east, from Scandinavia. To this day, Skye carries the wild north-lands in its tapestry of people, nomenclature and landscape in a far more concentrated way than anywhere else in the Hebrides. Skye's Scandinavian heritage runs through it like strange, foreign bones – diverging the island's cultural identity from that of Scotland, and fortifying its own. In the words of Alexander Smith, 'with a Norse murmur the blue Lochs come running in . . . the sea rovers come no longer in their dark galleys, but hill and dale wear ancient names that sigh to the Norway pine.' That's lovely, isn't it? Wistful, atmospheric, romantic – peculiar emotions for one of the most savage interludes in Scottish history. And that's saying something.

Say the word 'Viking' and you picture the image we've all been brought up with: cunning, bloodthirsty, all-conquering Scandinavians, inbound on ships made of wood intent on pillage and conquest. I'd love to say this was all a myth, but essentially that's the size of it. The first Norsemen to set foot on Skye were essentially pirates: strong-minded chieftains who had broken stride with the kings of Norway and set off to find their own territory. The Hebrides, including Dal Riata-ruled Skye, with their sheltered bays, fertile soils and livestock, made ideal bases from which to dominate, resupply and then attack the Norwegian coast, with the date of these early raids put as early as 794 CE.

With initial local unrest soon quelled, the arriving Norse enslaved the Gaels, and a century later their foothold on Skye was sufficiently established for more settlers, loyal to the separatist raiders, to start arriving across the North Sea in large numbers and begin launching ever-more ambitious attacks on their homeland. Predictably, this was met with bloody retribution from Norway, who launched sea attacks on the Hebrides. We don't really know what happened to the natives. But crude images found scratched on stones from the west coast, and the historical record's suggestion of a discontinuity of language and culture – but the continuation of genetics – suggest a fairly grim situation. The natives were probably either killed, enslaved for labour or as child-bearing vessels, or forced to flee for the mainland. As time passed and memory faded, a new identity began to emerge – along with the continuation of the war between the Norse-held separatists and the land from which they came.

The Gaels, caught amongst the pointy bits between these rascal settlers and the full force of their sovereign land, were inclined to form an uneasy truce with their unwelcome masters. After many long-distance skirmishes, a more official sovereignty eventually fell over the region, as the Hebrides entered the stewardship of Norwegian magnates. These, unlike their separatist forebears, did recognise the rule of the Norwegian kings.

Soon some of the islands of the Hebrides were so misaligned from the mainland they were known as *Inse Gall* ('Islands of the Foreigners'). On Skye and elsewhere, the aspirate Gaelic words were replaced with the harder alveolar 'l's and 'o's of Norse, and their spiky spellings. Here emerge the words Eishort, Minginish, Trotternish, Toravaig and more.

We've mentioned that the mountains are an interesting anomaly: the Cuillin's peaks have Gaelic names, by and large. Because the Norse off-comers didn't use maps – none that have been found, anyway – travellers were known to have their own names for landmarks that were useful for navigation. But as the Norwegian scholar Arne Kruse points out,

> names used by fishermen whilst fishing typically never leave the narrow context within which they exist . . . and they hardly ever influence the names that people living next to the mountains have for the mountains. Consequently, they will, as a rule, never appear on a map.

This could lend weight to the idea that *Cuillin* came from an orally imparted *kjolen*, as if referring to a single mountain. This could also be the reason why most individual names for Skye's mountains came much later.

Today many of the place names on Skye are intermingled between the three: Gaelic, Norse and English, and represent a unique fusion of worlds.

Much like, these days, the people. Intermarriage in the coming centuries built the foundations of a new people, the Gallgaels, *gall* for 'foreigner', otherwise known as Norse-Gaels. Strong and robust genetic traits began to fortify populations closer in kin to Norway, 800 miles across a wild sea, than the majority of the British land just across the Sound of Sleat. The Gaels of Dal Riata had tenacity and guile; the Norse, ingenuity and fortitude. Contrary to the popular myth, neither side in this period introduced the modified MC1R gene into the mix: both Gaels and Norse already had red hair.

Beyond this wild and disputed territory, the rest of Scotland had become a kingdom under Alexander III – and it wanted the Hebrides back. A period of advance and retreat followed, with brutal ethnic cleansing taking the place of diplomacy when it failed to tempt the ruling Norse magnates to defect to Scotland. The Norse were finally cut down during a regrouping on the west coast at the Battle of Largs in 1263. The 59-year-old King of Norway, Haakon IV Haakonsson – known to history as Haco – sailed to assist Olave the Black, mooring a fleet of Norwegian ships at modern-day Kyleakin on Skye before sailing south to Largs in Ayrshire, in attack. A storm blew in; their ships were wrecked, and limped back north, defeated, to overwinter on the Orkneys. Haco died there on 16 October that year, and as far as Norse rule in the Hebrides went, that was that. The Norse never again ruled Skye – though, of course, they never really left. Many of the people they became carry this questionable historical interlude with a certain pride. Attend the festival held at Largs each year and you'll find yourself amongst a majority of enthusiastically celebrating Vikings, not Gaels.

In 1266 the Treaty of Perth was passed. Skye became part of Scotland, officially – and rather romantically – the Territory of the Lords of the Isles. The departure of the Vikings didn't lead to harmony, however – just another era of ever more complicated squabbling with the arrival of the clan system on Skye.

Clans had been around elsewhere in the wilder outposts of Scotland for over a thousand years. They had their origins in the tribes that once collected the Highland denizens together into groups of both geographical and familial loyalty. The system was based around a landowner – a chief – whose property was managed by subcontractors called tacksmen, who leased the land to individual tenant families to work and subsist from. These groups of people would have an implicit arrangement of loyalty: if you belonged to a clan, you were expected to defend its interests from incoming threats until your head left your body, a not unheard-of outcome. Skirmishes were legendary, with one early observer of the society, the Greek traveller Strabo, writing in 7 BCE of the proto-clan tribes' blend of volatility and loyalty. 'The whole race is war-mad', he wrote.

> On account of their trait of simplicity and straightforwardness they easily come together in great numbers, because they always share in the vexation of those of their neighbours whom they think wronged.

By the time of the Treaty of Perth, the Hebrides were effectively autonomous – not Norse, nor Scottish, but something in between. It's here the name MacDonald becomes significant. The first Lordship of the Isles after the departure of Norse rule fell to Aonghus Mór mac Domhnaill (Angus Mor MacDonald) – 'Mac' meaning 'son'. Rather like an unruly but logistically coveted suburb of a city, successive Scottish kings attempted to bring the Isles to heel in the late 13th century, with the isles duly resisting – and even attempting to extend their sway to the mainland.

And so as the nature of the structures around Rubha an Dùnain mingled and evolved from Viking toehold to clan stronghold, so did the people who built them. The little loch was used as an overwintering portage for long-ships and later the birlinn galleys, a place where they were repaired and perhaps even built: agile longships with sweeping, symmetrical seed-pod hulls, just like you'd imagine.

The behaviour of the clans towards each other, particularly on an island such as Skye, was unremittingly peculiar and unimaginably vicious. Look at a clan map of Scotland and you see their names stamped across territories, like stickers on property. Taking territory from another clan was a coup. Marrying off the daughters of one clan to another, however, was seen as a victory and often functioned as a peace offering; yet the clans frequently stole castles from each other, tore each other apart on the battlefield, and found new and strange ways to punish one other and those caught between.

The Cuillin witnessed it all: the mountains and corries frequently ran with the blood of the clans, and some of the most notable skirmishes made their way into landmarks. Sgùrr na Stri, near Captain Maryon's monument, is commonly translated as 'Peak of Strife' – but it is more properly called 'Peak of Contention', for its possession was a point of particular dispute between the MacLeod and MacKinnon clans. In 1730 the two chiefs met on Sgùrr na Stri and agreed a 'march', or divide, between their two lands. After the accord was agreed, the rather horrible means of ensuring the locals were aware of precisely where the boundary lay was to procure a middleman – a boy from the adjacent isle of Soay – and thrash him almost to death on the site of the new boundary. This was justified with the odd logic that at least one person would never forget the exact spot, and presumably could be consulted on the matter at any point henceforth. Why on earth they didn't just erect a marker stone is a question worth asking, and perhaps is symbolic of the curious brutality of the time. It also gives a more robust case for the name 'Peak of Strife'.

Other Skye clans included the MacAskill, Nicolson, Martin, MacQueen, MacInnes, MacArthur and Macpherson, but it is the MacLeods and MacDonalds that were the most vehemently opposed, and their names ring loudest in these corries of the Cuillin. The mountains were the scenes of some of their worst, and final, fights, most notably in Coire na Creiche – where in 1601 they fought the last clan battle of Skye.

The famous Bloody Stone in Harta Corrie is a haunting place even without the aura of bloodshed that makes it notorious and allegedly gave it its name following a battle there. In the interests of appreciating this vicious interlude in Skye's history, on a spare morning of drizzle I'd taken a walk up Glen Sligachan, flat-floored and broad, between the Cuillin and Marsco, to look for the Bloody Stone. The river climbs into a stream, and ends like a grasping hand high in Lota Corrie, in the rafters of the ridge. You could imagine the glen and its river would be idyllic under blue skies, with the deepenings in the meanders of the river sharply blue-clear, like tropical plunge pools. But the northern end of the black ridge looms, and on a murky day feels claustrophobic – and the cloud and rain do the rest. The stone itself probably fell from the ridge; it's high and sits uneasy, like a collapsed house. Saplings sprout from it. Moss thickens its ledges. It looks alive, like a rock shouldn't.

But you stare because of the stories of its dead. The MacLeods and MacDonalds fought here in the corrie, it's said, and corpses were piled high around the stone, mainly the vanquished MacLeods. It's a recent suggestion; early lowland travellers made note of the stone as the site where an injured traveller reputedly expired, but there's little doubt of the tale today. A sink of memory above all of this, the ridge stands silent and says nothing.

Still following? We'll close our excursion into history where we started, on the peninsula's end at Rubha an Dùnain, where scattered blocks and some foundations mark the site of the Clan MacAskill's seat. A great house once stood here and people used these stones to mount horses. The MacAskills were in the service of the MacLeods to keep watch on the seaways, which perhaps explains the remote location of the property. Now, like so much of rural Skye, it's vacant – here a circle has come full, from some of the earliest occupiers of Skye to the moment when so much of it ceased with the onset of the Clearances. But that, of course, is another story.

A mild squall began to chop the air as I started back along the peninsula to look for my waterfall. The track held on to my boots in places, but the relentless rhythm of the walking was soothing. Soon I came to a stream pulsing with power, and I knew I had found a vein of something sizeable. I followed the water first down to the shores of Loch Brittle, where big slabs of rock slid into the sea, a slimy black line marking the divide where they met. I walked to the water and let it wash over my hands. I touched the rock. It was sharply knotted, like a coral. I looked closer, close enough to smell the seawater, and saw that what I took for the rough texture was actually a skin of tiny barnacles, blackened with algae. Life that had become part of the rock.

An apostrophe of black in the water around a hundred metres offshore caught my eye. I looked at it long and hard before I realised it was the head of a seal, looking back. I stood there, where Skye met the sea, for about ten minutes, enjoying the feeling of being where the mountains began and the ocean ended, and vice versa. I let the sea splash up, wetting my boots, and took gulps of the air. Sea level. I would get no lower than this. From here the way was up.

The stream raced down the rocks from above, where it had cut a channel and smoothed its way. The rock was slippy, and as I climbed the stream grew into a torrent. The Demon Shower, if that is indeed what it was called, was a voluminous waterfall around twenty metres high occupying a damp, green hollow. It was a little watery world in there, and impressive – elemental power trapped in a capsule valley of its own making. I walked as close as I could, until I could feel the spray scathing from it, and the roar of the water, inexhaustibly rushing from the mountains above. When I stood back I felt the nibble of midges where the air was still. The walls of this little gorge were steep, but heavily vegetated. Backtracking to a part of the stream I could cross, I climbed up and took hold of some greenery which I used to haul myself up onto what seemed to be a sheep track. Then, on the open, pathless hillside, I started to climb.

4

Ice

Above the waterfall, the stream raced towards it through a plateau of boggy grass and heather in balled sprigs. Ahead, the ridge was hidden by cloud – all but its lower spurs, poking out like feet from beneath a curtain. Above they betrayed a murky depression, where the mountains gave way to the high valley: Coire Làgan. I followed the water up towards it.

Isn't it remarkable how streams just keep flowing? Even after days with no significant rain, or snowmelt, or huge lakes above with seemingly inexhaustible volumes, the way thousands of gallons a second can race down a mountain day and night and not run dry is something that will always amaze me. Stand under the Demon Shower and consider the mass of water coursing past, and it's difficult to fathom.

Water rarely lingers in the Cuillin, except in the air. Springs are hard to find up there, occurring only in a few spots on the ridge, and all but a couple are unreliable during dry spells. Thirst is a common complaint in the Cuillin. But after rain, water runs *off* it in great torrents, skittering random paths over chaotic rock surfaces, inscribing cameo streams in unlikely places, or else it finds cracks, runnels and grooves, invades them and scratches them deeper and deeper, scarring the surface into damp channels that sit forever in foetid shadow. Then in winter it freezes and expands and bursts the rock, and the Cuillin gains a fresh scar. And so on and on.

Other than runoff, the main source for this water is mountain lochs. The streams that flow out of the Cuillin run from a very few of these, cupped in the palms of shadowed corries. I read somewhere that some lakes might still contain the water of melted glaciers. I wondered if that was true, or simply a romantic idea. Could water remain in a lake for thousands of years? What would it be like to make a cup of tea with *that*? It seemed unlikely. But up here, you could almost believe it. You could almost believe that the lake is bottomless and there's a monster living in it that roars in Gaelic. You could almost believe anything.

The waterway beside me narrowed and narrowed as I climbed. I'd hoped it went all the way up into the corrie, but soon it began to intermittently disappear amongst the scrub, until all that remained was the odd black crack in the grass and a faint trickle from within. I looked at the map, then looked up at the mountains, still inscrutable behind cloud. I was going into that, through that veil. Up, into Coire Làgan.

If the Cuillin ridge is Britain's monument to volcanism, the corries beneath it are its temples to glaciation. As high and dramatic as the ridges fly, the corries plunge deep – sometimes fertile and comely, often black and shadow-cold. They face every aspect, give every peak its shape and arm the ridge with vertiginous drops on all sides. Warren-like and deep-dug, these hollows are as intrinsic to the character of these mountains as they were essential to their making. At their most basic, they are the gates to the ridge; spend any time on the tops, and you will have either walked up, or be looking down on, a corrie. Both the corries and the ridge represent extraordinary examples of their respective landforms – but neither would exist without the other, and so corries must be considered as much a part of the Cuillin ridge as the crest itself. After all, they were formed by the same process.

It's one of nature's most beautiful ironies that something as seemingly permanent and stubborn as a mountain can be completely reconfigured, shattered, shaped and even levelled by a force as fleeting and physically indecisive as water. The two seem so opposing, so counter to each other – so perhaps it's fitting that some sort of attrition should occur. But this *is* a place of extremes: light and dark, wet and dry, high and low, yin and yang. But we have, in the final shaping of the Cuillin to date, a war of elements even more symbolic. That these mountains born of molten heat would be all but torn down by their elemental opposite: ice.

Of course, when you look at it more scientifically, the decks are levelled.

As we've seen, mountains are far from permanent in the earth's grand scheme, and water – even before it takes the form of a glacier – is the single most powerful natural force on the planet. Given sufficient time and a steady flow, the smallest of streams could carve a mountain in two, or cut a canyon a mile deep.

Fifty million years ago Scotland's volcanic activity ceased for the last time, and Skye was left a strange and vacant landscape. A long period of weathering followed, during which almost all of the volcano's basalt shield was scraped away, exposing the great gabbro magma core. For millions of years Skye – much like the rest of Scotland – was sub-tropical, home to abundant scaly, then hairy, life. As the aeons passed, the continents moved torturously into their present positions. And then, not so very long ago, something strange happened: the world started to get colder.

This period, which lasted from around two million years ago to a little less than 12,000 years ago, has been named by scientists as the Pleistocene epoch; the rest of us know it as the Ice Age.

You might expect that it must have taken rather more than a few years of unseasonably bristly temperatures to trigger a period that saw almost a third of the planet covered by ice sheets. This included most of North America, the top half of Russia, both poles, most of the world's major mountain ranges, all of Scandinavia, Ireland and everything in Britain north of the Bristol Channel. This was serious ice, too – many sheets were two miles thick, containing so much water that the surface of the sea dropped by 100 metres globally. Were you around (and the first creatures that conceivably could pass for you after a very rough night were making their way out of Africa around this very time) at the glacial maximum, you could have walked in a straight line from Svalbard to south-west Ireland without getting your feet wet – though they would most certainly have gotten cold. Average temperatures at the edges of the ice sheets were a balmy -6°C, with much of the rest of the surrounding country struggling to get above freezing. Over time the temperatures warmed then cooled, with glaciers retreating and advancing accordingly – but the average remained low enough to allow ice sheets to remain continuously throughout this period. From a deep time standpoint, we are still in this period. We are still in an ice age.

Our rapid and unnatural emergence from this period of cold, sped along enthusiastically by our own activities, is what we call climate change. But what led to the cooling of the planet still isn't fully understood. The most popular theory is that a change in pitch of the earth's axial tilt around the sun, called 'orbital forcing' – like a wobbling top – created just enough shade and diminished the sun's influence to cause the few degrees drop necessary to promote the beginnings of glaciers, which in turn became ice sheets and began the planet's self-perpetuating descent into the mother of all cold snaps. This is essentially nothing more than a magnification of the process that leads to seasons, that is to say the way that the sun strikes certain parts of the planet for certain amounts of time at certain times of the year. The earth's fragile balance, with its tolerable heat and cold, means that it doesn't take much to shift us towards one or the other – and not a lot more than that to wipe us out altogether.

When it comes to the Cuillin, have no doubt: its entire appearance is down to glaciation. That this is the most complicated structure of corries and ridgelines anywhere in Britain is obvious; the degree by which it is so is quite extraordinary. You'll hear it called 'the closest to the Alps we have', or rather discourteously, 'Britain's only genuine mountain range'. What people mean when they say this – and they are mountaineers and geologists, by and large – is that the Cuillin ridge feels like the European Alps in miniature. The Alps are similarly barbed and similarly steep and similarly challenging to climb. The two look similar because of what the ice has done to them. The Alps are complex in geology, comprising piles of rock of all different ages thrust up like a rucked pastry, but glaciers still loll from their high valleys, steepening their ridgelines and shattering their crests, keeping the wounds open and their profile sharp. The ice may be gone from the Cuillin, but its tough, relatively homogeneous rock gives it a raggy and raw look, as if the ice were scratching it out only yesterday.

This newly minted cragginess, tempered with its relative accessibility, made the Cuillin a case study of particular importance to the very earliest musings concerning glaciers and their legacy. And most of these insights centre on the Cuillin's corries – the shadowy lows to the ridge's soaring highs. Like Coire Làgan, the one I was walking into now.

High corries like Coire Làgan are actually *cirques* – hanging depressions high in mountains carved out by ice making a chair for itself. When these glaciers went, they left spaces, some the size of sports halls, others the size of towns. In places named by the Welsh they are *cwms*; in Northern England the word is generally 'dale'; in Scotland they are *corries*.

There are more than seventy named corries on Skye, typically prefixed with the Gaelic 'coire', which should be pronounced kor-*ai* – and not *choir* like the singing collective, or *kor-a*, like the stuff bristly doormats are made of. Some of Skye's corries are barren and possess an atmosphere of dread; some are filled with a lake, or meadow, or waterfall. Some beetle with people; some hardly see a soul. And some of the Cuillin's corries changed our understanding of the way the world was built.

The corrie whose lip I was about to crest isn't Skye's biggest, nor necessarily the prettiest. Shaped like a dented cauldron tucked into the rafters beneath the highest peak of the Cuillin ridge, it is through Coire Làgan that most people make their ascent onto the ridge's crest – and the valley so many look dizzyingly down on whilst tackling some of its most famous reaches. But today I had another reason for being up here.

I was excited. You'll have to excuse me, but after all this waiting and wondering, I was about to explore the Cuillin ridge for the first time – to climb up into it, get hold of it and just be there, in amongst it. It's a funny thing common to anyone who likes to travel, at home or abroad. To spend months or years sitting at home imagining a place, wondering what it's going to be like, how it's going to smell, what it's going to *feel* like. And then when you finally get there, taking a moment to just stop and say to yourself: 'I'm on Skye, walking up into the Cuillin ridge. I'm doing that.' Everything I had been reading, all the things I'd learned – this was that place, here, under my boots.

By this point in our journey it won't surprise you that the idea that there once existed ancient and sprawling tracts of ice, and that these were responsible for sculpting the great mountain ranges of the world – and a good deal more besides – took a while to catch on in the early 19th century. And this despite the fact there were plenty of glaciers still chewing at mountains in places quite in vogue for the deep-thinking traveller. This was most resplendently evident in the Alps, where the Grand Tour was still a popular rite of passage for young people of a certain standing, who nonetheless failed to presume these same processes were once hard at work in the now ice-free mountains of their homeland.

As it happened it did turn out to be continental Europe, and Scandinavia, that produced the first speculative ideas that glaciers may have been more prevalent in times past than they are today. But when the idea was finally mooted, the existence of glaciers in Scotland was far from a popular one. Don't forget, this was the time of catastrophism, where most people heartily believed the world was shaped by biblical floods and the wrath of God, so such ideas were the realm of dangerous radicals – though with Hutton's Uniformitarianism theories gathering a respectable following, the doors of enlightenment were slowly creaking open.

These were given another hearty kick in 1824 by the Norwegian Jens Ensmark, who, with his canny ability to join visual dots, speculated that the glaciers he saw hanging from the topmost reaches of his chilly local mountains were once much longer and thicker, and may even have actually *carved* the fjords of western Norway rather than simply clogged their throats. A few years later, in 1830, the German–Swiss geologist Jean de Charpentier came to much the same conclusion when he suggested that the strange boulders and moraine formations of the high alpine grasslands of Switzerland were put there by glaciers that had long since melted. But he stopped short of speculating about exactly what caused them to be there in the first place or, indeed, why they disappeared.

The first person to really dig out glacial theory – and the first to assert that Britain, too, had once been home to glaciation – was a Swiss scientist named Louis Agassiz. Initially sceptical of de Charpentier, in 1840 Agassiz suggested that throughout its recent history, the earth had moved between periods of cooling – ice ages – and warming, and that the sculpted corries and steep-sided valleys of the Highlands had been scooped by glaciers long since vanished by the simple act of melting. His investigations in Switzerland concluded that its glaciers had once been much greater in extent, as evidenced by polishing of the bedrock and the 'striations,' or scratched lines, gouged into them. These lay parallel to the orientation of the valley, indicating movement along it much like the marks left by a table dragged across a wood floor.

Agassiz made many perceptive observations, and he hypothesised that glaciers didn't just inhabit high cirques or long, elevated valleys, but once smothered entire regions like thick blankets, which he called 'nappes'. He swiftly became the toast of the scientific community, and visited the Scottish Highlands in 1840 with an English geologist named William Buckland. Their idea was that the gradual violence of glacial action left ancient scars – and Agassiz and Buckland set out to find them. As an aside, Buckland was himself something of a scientific catch; it was he who described the very first dinosaur, which he named *Megalosaurus*, or 'great lizard', in 1824. Remarkably, a year earlier, he had also stumbled upon the remains of Britain's oldest specimen of what could be described as a modern human in a cave in Paviland, South Wales. He also had a tendency to lecture on horseback and do fieldwork in an academic gown, and he chose to broaden his knowledge of zoology by *eating* as many specimens as he could, culminating in his rather off-brief consumption of the preserved heart of Louis XIV.

Eccentricities aside, Buckland was a creationist, and believed that what he had noticed whilst investigating the Highlands – deposits of boulders, large amounts of gravelly debris and strangely polished rocks – were the result of the biblical floods. Upon hearing Agassiz's theory, Buckland travelled to the Alps and, upon noticing similar features in areas of heavy glaciation, invited the now celebrated scientist back to Britain to cast his eye over the Highlands.

The first area to be identified as showing evidence of glacial action was a ridge of moraine debris near Nithdale in Dumfries. This were soon followed by the deduction that the puzzling 'parallel roads of Glen Roy' – horizontal terraces running as straight as rails across the hillsides high above the Lochaber glen, a feature that had confounded observers for decades – were the watermarks of an ancient, ice-dammed loch. 'The parallel roads of Glen Roy are intimately connected with this former occurrence of glaciers, and have been caused by a glacier from Ben Nevis,' Agassiz confidently stated in a letter of 1840, adding that 'the existence of glaciers in Scotland at early periods can no longer be doubted.'

Agassiz never visited Skye, nor as far as we can tell did Buckland. But even before these formidable brains took to the Highlands in search of ice, another – the first of the true explorers of Skye's mountains – was already hard at work drawing similar conclusions in the depths of the Cuillin.

James David Forbes is a book in himself, albeit a very long and not entirely happy one. His claim to fame on Skye takes two strident forms: one as *the* pioneering mountaineer of the range. The other was as the first scientist to bring the ridge to the forensic forefront of one of geology's most contentious theories, just as Skye was becoming a popular tourist destination.

Born in 1809 into a devoutly Christian noble family in Aberdeenshire, Forbes's mother died when he was eighteen months old. One of six children, he also lost a brother and his father before reaching adulthood, his increasing isolation something to which his biographers have attributed his rather aloof and dogged nature. Forbes's grandfather, Sir William, had been an authority on finance who advised the British prime minister – and young James, whose principal education was at home, seemed pre-destined for a well-heeled career in law.

Forbes's early scientific studies were therefore carried out in heretical secret and in anonymous correspondence with the leading figures of the day. In his letters he signed his name with the Greek symbol for 'alpha' until the death of his father, whereupon he abandoned law as a vocation and threw himself vociferously into the field then still known as 'natural philosophy'. By the age of seventeen Forbes was conducting geological observations on Mount Vesuvius, and two years later he turned these studies into an eight-part series for the *Edinburgh Philosophical Journal*. Recommended for the Fellowship of the Royal Society of Edinburgh at twenty, he was forced to wait until the minimum age of twenty-one before his acceptance, soon becoming Professor of Natural Philosophy at the University of Edinburgh at the remarkably youthful age of twenty-three. So far, so precocious. But what made Forbes different was that he was *tough*.

This is all the more remarkable considering that Forbes had been a sickly child, with a precarious general state of health at best. Periods of astonishing relentlessness were counterbalanced by a tendency to plunge into the periods of illness that would define much of his later life, but what he accomplished in his most active years – between 1826 and 1843 – was extraordinary indeed. Described by a friend as 'dignified and commanding [of] presence… wielded by a will of rare strength, purity and elevation', Forbes was lantern-jawed with deep-set eyes and, painted in later life, a rakish comb-over.

By the time he first arrived on Skye in 1836 he was already an accomplished traveller and mountain adventurer, having walked between Lake Geneva and Lake Como in 1832, in addition to youthful tours in Italy. What contrasted Forbes immediately with his contemporaries was that he wasn't afraid to actually get up into the Cuillin, nor was he prepared to accept the many rumours about the ridge – specifically the increasingly persistent claims that the mountains were unassailable, a provocative word to a mountaineer.

The source of much of this talk, and the only scientist to have made what could be called a serious attempt at demystifying the Cuillin before Forbes, was John MacCulloch – who had provided the first real scientific descriptions of the ridge in his epic two-volume work *Description of the Western Isles of Scotland* (1819). Now, you can say many good things about MacCulloch's work. A field surgeon by training (he was responsible for coining the word 'malaria'), MacCulloch's book was certainly extensive and ambitious, given that he was attempting a detailed discourse on a subject very much in its infancy on a scale never before considered, let alone attempted.

MacCulloch's extensive surveys throughout the country would result in the first geological map of Scotland. On what he called 'Sky', he succeeded in identifying the major rock groups on the island, divided them into 'trap' for the basalt and 'hypersthene' for the gabbro, and went some way to identifying patterns of their occurrence, amongst much else.

So far, so good. But when it came to deductions requiring more intrepid fieldwork, MacCulloch becomes rather vague, smothering his sentences with assertions of the impossibility of further observations. And my, what sentences. MacCulloch was no fan of vivid economy, and his descriptions of Skye run on and on, despite being – as MacCulloch himself defensively asserted – little more than a summary. 'Those who may follow me will find a great deal that is not here described,' he wrote, 'although little that has not been examined.'

But as Forbes revealed with the slightest of his own exploratory scratchings on Skye, this wasn't entirely accurate. MacCulloch's observations were quite possibly conducted with either his nose against the rock – entirely possible, considering the toilsome detail – or else at such a distance to require a squint and a telescope. Ultimately, though, it seems that the

Cuillin's 'thoroughly inaccessible nature', as he put it, disagreed with both his powers of drawing scientific conclusions and his stomach for bolder investigations.

One very astute observation, though, was that the

roughness of the surface of this rock is scarcely less remarkable than its nakedness – being comparable to nothing more properly than to a coarse rasp; in consequence of which it is easy to walk or run over those steep declivities which would otherwise be impracticable.

This is the first recorded endorsement of the Cuillin's legendary adhesion to interested feet.

MacCulloch's biggest failure on Skye, and among his greatest contrasts with James Forbes, was that he never managed to put this to the test. Forbes seized upon this with ill-concealed glee:

In the months of April, May and June the traveller will certainly find many favourable opportunities for ascending the Cuchullin Hills, which Dr MacCulloch assures us he attempted no less than 'SEVEN TIMES in five successive summers'

He added, 'Such a want of success seems incredible if the Doctor had been at all serious in his intention,' before needling that MacCulloch's favourite method of studying geology was from a boat.

Bitchy undertones aside, Forbes's 1845 paper 'Notes on the Topography and Geology of the Cuchuillin Hills and the Traces of Ancient Glaciers which They Present' is a strikingly observed piece of work that he submitted to the Royal Society of Edinburgh as a description of 'the least known portion of a yet little-known island in our own country'. And so it was. While others had merely looked up into the heights of the Cuillin, Forbes was the first to actually grapple with them. He was also the first to compare the Cuillin to the greater ranges on distant continents, claiming their 'fantastic outlines, in certain positions, may vie with any in the whole world', and memorably see a resemblance of part of the range with M. Élie de Beaumont's description of the 'Montagne de la

Grave [sic] in the Alps', as resembling 'a gigantic nutcracker, menacing heaven with its open jaws'.

Forbes's paper reads like a much-waited-for dispatch from Mars, all delivered in the professional, matter-of-fact manner of a man whose science means business, and for whom business means science. Aside from the adventurous stuff – which we'll get to – Forbes's most modern idea comes in the conclusion to his paper. Remarking upon the huge boulders guarding the gates of Coruisk, 'angular transported blocks being found isolated in the most curious and seemingly unnatural positions', Forbes uses in his description a new alpine term, *blocs perches* – 'perched boulders' – dropped by a melted glacier like boats cast up a mountain by a wave. He refers to de Charpentier's glacial theory, before stating that the Cuillin represented the 'exact appearance of a tract of country invaded by a glacier that has since retreated, but left unmistakeable land-marks [on] its former domain'. Forbes goes on to note that the evidence of glaciation is by no means confined to the area around Coruisk, and that it is 'reproduced in the wild corries on almost all sides of the Cuchullins'. He notices the contrast between the 'cloven mountains' and spiry, serrated outlines of the summits and the rounded, moulded surfaces of the rock in the valley 'smoothed and shaven in their forms ... parallel to the length of the valley', adding that 'the surfaces in question are quite like the surfaces ground down by art.'

He had hit upon something here that subsequent researchers would come back to again and again: sharp, ice-shattered summits and smooth, ice-ground valleys. Brutalised above, crafted and sculpted below. Moreover, he had found evidence on the ground. Forbes had found the artist's signature. And it was this that I wanted to find.

An hour after leaving the waterfall I entered the high valley of Coire Làgan. Behind the cloud that masked the ridge I was beginning to sense fantastic impressions. Moving constantly, the cloud drained into the space between buttresses and spurs like a sheet drawn over furniture, showing the shape of what was beyond but never really showing *it*: that broken rim of rock crest I knew from pictures lay above. Below was a tapestry of smooth rock plates, moistened by veins of waterfalls, with that finger-hammered look of wet pottery clay.

The path underfoot had gone from a cutting through hillside to a slinking crack through rock, catching little stones in its corners and disappearing beneath big, plate-like slabs. This was my way into the corrie. Up there lay a lake – a miniature, eye-socket lake – from which the highest peaks of the ridge shot upwards in a single throw. If Coruisk was the inner citadel of the Cuillin, this valley was the western high keep – and while today I was clearly not going to get a view, I couldn't wait to explore it.

The way ahead tilted upwards at a boulder of cindery rock, and I started up it. The surface underfoot wasn't as slick as it looked from afar. It held one of my feet, then the other, at an angle that caused me to grin. I touched it. It hurt a little. *That* rock. This was the gabbro effect – the gravity-defying, confidence-giving grip, so tantalising to early climbers with its promise of the impossible. The next boulder I walked up, despite the steep angle. I took my hands off the rock and stood, leaning forward to compensate, as if into a wind, and used the grip of the rock to hold my boots. In my first few upward steps on Cuillin gabbro I could appreciate at once the possibilities and the potential perils of this stuff. You step without a thought, and you move without a care – as if the rock might catch you if you fell.

I kept going. The scenery began to inflate, the terrain becoming entirely rocky. I could feel the air of elevation. I was now into the cloud and visibility had dropped to a few dozen metres – enough to see a few details of the surroundings and give a little context, but not enough; on a clear day from here the views were knockout. Today I was going to have to imagine it all.

At least I wouldn't have to imagine the lake. My map told me I was close to it – a couple of hundred metres – but the climb just kept going. The water cascading down the rocks, staining them dark, had to be coming from that lake. It was teasing. I wanted to see the lake appear, to see the rocks give way to the calm, dead flat of water.

I didn't need to go into Coire Làgan to look for traces of glaciers; the whole Cuillin ridge is evidence enough. Before its glaciation, it's likely that the broader topography of Skye looked generally fairly similar to today, with one key difference: it wasn't an island. It is likely the sound separating Skye from the mainland was gouged during an early onset of ice, probably around two and a half million years ago.

Scientists now think that the Cuillin experienced only two major phases of glaciation, both during the last ice age. It's possible that the ridge was glaciated at earlier periods, but since the evidence of previous ice is usually quite literally swept away by the next, we will probably never know. What's clear, however, is that the glaciation of the Cuillin was quite unique compared with the rest of Scotland. Coruisk was scooped out so heavily under a huge icecap that parts of the corrie floor beneath the lake lie 38 metres below sea level, emphasising the valley's unsettlingly sunken aspect. In 1894, noting that the arrangement of the Cuillin's glacier-cut valleys didn't quite fit the formula exhibited by the rest of the west coast, geologist Archibald Geikie hit upon the idea that the Cuillin had its own independent icecap, feeding glaciers advancing down the corries to the sea like splayed fingers from a palm. This sheet of ice was sufficiently robust to maintain independence from the main ice sheet spilling off the west coast. Then in 1901 Alfred Harker suggested that the dramatically steep headwalls on either side of the Cuillin ridge and the sharpness of the crest running between them was due to the ice eroding the corries on each side so heavily that they came close to intersecting, 'leaving only narrow arêtes and triangular, slightly concave-faced pyramids'. He also suggested that the greater number and more developed nature of the corries to the north and north-east of the ridge were due to the glaciers chewing away at these aspects for longer than on the opposing side. The reason? They spent more time in the shade. A logical but insightful idea: that the eventual form of a mountain range could be influenced by the shadows it throws. So here we have an explanation for the steepness of the corrie walls, the narrowness of the crest and the geometry of the ridge – and all down to a substance ghost-like in geological transience, despite an awesome legacy rent in stone.

In the rather simpler, possibly exasperated words of Dr Simon Wellings – a geologist with whom I had struck up a correspondence whilst trying to make sense of all of this – 'the Cuillin stick up because of their hard gabbro. But they are craggy because of the glaciers.' This, he explained, was down to a process called 'plucking' – ice freezing into the crevices of rock then ripping the rocks from the mountain, leaving a raw, wounded surface, much like skin left on a frozen metal pipe, were you foolish enough to grasp it. Generations of weathering and freeze-thaw have emphasised this, which, along with the tough rock and its relative youth, gave the ridge its rebelliously lacerating appearance. When did the ice go? It's a good question. Generally the consensus is around 12,500 years ago, but the fits and starts of the planet's climate are cyclical and endless, and no doubt at some point in the future the Scottish mountains will again feel the cold and wounding touch of glacial ice.

Simon had then dropped an interesting theory into the mix. 'Did you know,' he went on, 'that they think there were glaciers in the Cairngorms in the 1700s?'

I didn't. 'Really?'

He told me that recent evidence showed that several small but active glaciers were quietly at work in the depths of the landlocked Cairngorms as late as the 1700s – nearly 12,000 years later than the last ice was thought to have left.

It's not inconceivable because on the whole, it really doesn't take much to start a glacier. An average drop of a few degrees that lingers enough for snow to consolidate in a deep, shadowy corrie can be all that's needed to lay the foundations. Most of the time the north-western climate doesn't allow a glacier to get a toehold, but once it does it can become self-perpetuating – like a cartoon snowball rolled down a hill, gathering mass and becoming unstoppable. And counter-intuitively, it isn't especially the cold winters that cause it, but particularly cool summers: summers that would allow the snow to lie unmelted in shadowy Scottish corries, year after year. It's thought that even today, an average temperature drop of just 1.5°C and an increase in precipitation of 10 per cent over a period of a decade would be enough to reignite glaciation in the loftier areas of Scotland.

The last time this happened was during a period in Britain's history known as the 'Little Ice Age'. With a trigger point of around 1250 – possibly caused by the sun-stifling ash cloud of a huge Indonesian volcanic eruption – three 'climatic minimums', low points in a cycle of cooling, have since been identified as beginning in 1650, 1770 and 1850. During these periods lakes and rivers, including the Thames, froze; disease from malnutrition increased, along with vioent crime; and a confused society lashed out at potential causes, even reinstating witchcraft trials in the hope of curbing supernatural influences on the climate.

And sure enough, as I later confirmed in a paper published in *The Holocene* journal, the period saw the reinstatement of small glaciers in the Scottish Highlands. All it took for this to happen was that fall in mean annual temperature of 1.5°C. Exactly how the authors proved this theory is a canny illustration of just how far glacial science has come, as Simon Wellings explained: 'They look inside the quartz crystals of rocks that have been broken when the glaciers came through. Inside is an element called beryllium, which when exposed, reacts to the cosmic rays that hit the planet constantly, and produces beryllium-10. So by measuring the amount of beryllium-10 in the quartz they can work out how long it's been exposed to the cosmic rays, and therefore when the rock was broken, and therefore when the glacier broke it.'

'You're kidding.'

'Nope. It's called cosmogenic beryllium-10 dating,' he said, before adding, I think for the purposes of amusement but you're never sure with geologists, 'It's super-cool science.'

Perhaps you skipped through all of that or lost track along the way. But if you take anything away from the period that crafted the range into how it looks today, that gave it its bristles and its complexity and its obstacles, make it this: a passage written by the Scottish naturalist John Muir, which sums up the whole enterprise rather nicely:

> ... glaciers, back in their white solitudes ... exerting their tremendous energies in silence and darkness. Outspread, spirit-like, they brood above their predestined landscapes, work on unwearied through immeasurable ages, until, in the fullness of time, the mountains and valleys are brought forth, channels furrowed for rivers, basins made for lakes ... then they shrink and vanish like summer clouds.

I stood in the corrie head at the edge of the lake. In front of me the waters of Lochan Coire Làgan were still and grey. The lochan is small – around 100 metres across at its widest – and shaped like a rough-hewn arrowhead, but I couldn't appreciate that. From my point of view I could have been standing on the shore of an ocean. The far waters of the lake disappeared into the cloud, the two greys mingling and concealing all distance beyond. I half expected to hear the clang of a nautical bell or see the eerie sweep of a lighthouse. But it was awesomely silent.

Mountains are uncanny places; they have a disquieting intensity, yet bring a strangely elemental familiarity that's very exciting. It doesn't take much for this to unnerve. Above me in the cloud, I could hear the tinkle of little rocks, up in the hard angles of the mountains I couldn't see but I knew were there. Perhaps they were shifting about in the Great Stone Shoot, which lay just there, beyond the murk. But I could *feel* it, that unknown knowing, as anyone would feel with something huge and invisible towering over them. Above me on all sides were some of the great summits of the Cuillin ridge, leaning in, peering down, displacing the air. All I could see was a few feet of rock beneath my feet, the lake in front of them, and a few boulders, out in the water near the shore.

It was suddenly cold. The moisture from the mist was being caught as beads of water on my woollen top. I set my bag down, pulled out my jacket and put it on, the scraping sounds of the nylon loud and thin in the silence. I felt self-conscious about making noise; I don't know whom I was worried about disturbing. It seemed so removed from the cheerfulness of the Glenbrittle campsite cafe with its Cuillin Coffee and dog named Barry and its general gentle bustle. And this, just an hour or so's walk up the corrie; a world away. It was probably the weather, the waning light of the afternoon, the distant tug of hunger. No grass, no plants poking out from between rocks, no birdsong, no splashes from fish in the loch. No life, except me. When I moved, the sound was tinny and sharp. I clicked my fingers and it was like the mist itself gave an echo back. I'd read that this little lochan in Coire Làgan had at its heart a declivity that plunges deep for a body of water its size. Seen from the peaks invisibly above it, it gives the lochan a dark centre, like the pupil of an eye.

Walking up into the Cuillin was, in all respects, walking into a very different place. All of those dripping descriptions from Skye's literature, all the melodrama and querulous evoking; I suppose this feeling was what got them, and – up here in Coire Làgan – was beginning to get me. I half expected to round a boulder and meet a ghost.

In a way, I *was* looking for signs of a ghost. Cautiously, I circled the lake, my eyes at my feet. And here they were, right under them. In fact, like details emerging in a dark room, they were everywhere. Lines. Tens of thousands of perfectly parallel lines with the texture of a vinyl record, running over the moulded boulders of the corrie, following gravity's path.

Glaciologists call them striae – striations – and they show the actual marks made by the last glacier as it scraped along the rock. These grooves were made by stones, tiny bits of debris, pressed between the ice and the bedrock and dragged with such force that they left their impressions in it, like fingernail scrapes. Every now and again I'd cross a deeper one, where a bigger or harder stone had been crushed into the rock on its agonising, gravitational drag of aeons. As it descended, more snow and more ice piled against the corrie headwall, scratching pieces of it off as it went, pushing the glacier down the valley. Building ice at its head, losing it at its foot. Down at the end of the glacier – in the case of Coruisk and Sligachan, hanging into the sea, but to the west probably ending in the river-cut Glen Brittle – ice sheared off and melted, its flow further smoothing the rocks around it. A perfect equilibrium: the glacier machines, cutting the valleys and sharpening the mountains with their slow, heavy scrape. And here I was, right in the engine room.

I stayed in the silence of the corrie for a long time. I thought these markings an extraordinary thing to touch – a bridge between the distant past and right now, like discovering the footprints of some long-extinct animal and placing your own foot inside.

Following in footsteps, it seems, is a theme on Skye. When James Forbes was up here in this corrie, tracing the lines and scratching his head, he was only the latest and most intrepid of a line of travellers from all types of backgrounds to come to Skye and to capture their thoughts in a work of sorts. Forbes's happened to concern the geology, but understanding the scientific processes underpinning such a dramatic landscape was in 1836 a comparatively recent motive for journeying to this wild Hebridean island. And by this point, Skye had become quite the destination already.

5

Mist

I

Dear Reader, if you have sensed in the journey so far a certain keenness in your narrator to reflect on previous words written about Skye, permit me to assure you that it is all done in the affectionate interests of continuing a long and lively tradition. Even in the most impenetrable of the early literature associated with the island you can sense its writer retracing the steps of the preceding one, clutching a copy of their work, reinterpreting its more lingering points like a centuries-long chain of Gaelic whispers. And it was one of these works in particular that drew interested eyes from all quarters of the artistic and literary world to the wilds of Scotland, and set in motion the chain of travellers who would put Skye on the map. And in a strange and dog-legged sort of way, it would make them look at the landscape in a whole new light.

An early description of what we now recognise as Skye comes from a priest called Donald Monro in 1549. Written in Scots, his description of this 'roughe and hard land,' whilst preoccupied with churches and castles, includes a reference to the 'maney grate hills, principally Euilvelimi and Glannock'. The Cuillin presumably, and perhaps Glamaig. One of the first evocations of Skye by an outsider, Timothy Pont in the early 17th century, gives a lively skip over the island he called 'Sky'. His account is amusingly varied to the modern eye, merging observations of the temperament and skills of the people – 'for the most part . . . strong and nimble, of a good complexion, lives verie long' – the fertility of the ground and, despite not being able to speak or understand Gaelic, local tradition and superstition. He also manages a bit about the climate: 'the Isle is blest with good and temperate Air ... though sometymes foggy and the hills often surrounded with mist, so that they can barely be discerned.' The misty isle, indeed.

After Pont – and almost certainly thumbing a copy of his work – came Martin Martin. A Skyeman born the slightly fancier Martainn MacGille-Mhartainn on Trotternish, Martin's *A Description of the Western Isles of Scotland* (1703) was an idiosyncratically observed voyage intended to record and preserve the customs of the Hebrides, and perhaps along the way redefine the perception of Highlanders as being uncultured ruffians in the eyes of the wider world. It's harsh but possibly true to say that in this he failed. His long descriptions of the peculiarities of medical practices, dietary customs, illness and cultural eccentricities reinforced what he might have been hoping to dispel, with many passages suggestive of what at the time might be perceived as witchcraft.

And it is as earthy ruffians that the islanders were most certainly viewed – even by their lowland countrymen in the cities of the south. This perception was hardly helped by the divisions caused by the rebellions of the 18th century, the often anarchic allegiances of the clans and the competing claims to the throne that culminated in the Battle of Culloden. And Skye's place in all of this would reach a zenith of sorts when a certain young fugitive arrived on its shores.

It's telling that Skye's greatest claim to historical fame – the one remembered with a kind of dewy-eyed pride for centuries afterwards – is its complicity in what was technically an act of treason: the island's connection to the escape of Charles Edward Louis John Casimir Silvester Severino Maria Stuart – better known to history as Bonnie Prince Charlie, or the tediously persistent 'Young Pretender'. The story of Stuart's supposed right to the throne of England, Wales and Scotland is appallingly complicated and I'll spare you the details, mainly because I don't fully understand them myself, other than to say that once upon a time, there were Stuart monarchs on the throne of Scotland. And then there were the Hanoverian monarchs of England. And somewhere in the middle, a kingdom uniting Scotland, Ireland, Wales and England was formed. Along the way there had been a few, how shall we say, hiccups – the English Civil War, the execution of

Charles I, a revolution and the nation's brief but lively spell as a republic – but order was restored when Queen Anne, a Stuart, became the first monarch of the brand new Kingdom of Great Britain in 1707. Unfortunately for the royal line of the Stuarts, Queen Anne died without a living heir. So, after a complicated succession route – all to do with religion, of course – the throne of the now rather grand nation passed to a Protestant Hanoverian monarch, George I, in 1714.

Meanwhile, Anne's Catholic relatives – who, since King James II of England's exile during the Glorious Revolution in 1688, had been busy marrying themselves into European aristocracy – were enjoying a florid life on the continent. Dismayed at the chain of events across the Channel, the now late king's family began agitating from afar, calling for revolution amongst Catholic quarters in loyal Scotland to restore his family line to the throne. These Catholics were in many cases Highlanders, Islanders and others on the edges of society. The term given to those sympathetic to James's cause utilised the word *Jacobus*, the Latin for James. History knows them as the Jacobites.

The cause was led by the former king's son, James Stuart. Despite leading failed uprisings in 1708 and 1715, James – the 'Old Pretender' – had little success, but a stiff will. By 1745 the sharp end of the action had passed to his son Charles, who landed on the shores of Eriskay in the Outer Hebrides on 23 July in command of a French battalion. His intention: to lead a Jacobite insurgency to retake the now muscular throne of Great Britain.

Charles – which, multiple appellations aside, was the name he was known by – was not trying to take the throne for himself, but for his father. He was initially quite successful, winning the surrender of Edinburgh and Carlisle, and leading an army of 6,000 as far south as Derbyshire. He was then forced back north under the advice of his council, who assured him that support was waning with every southward step, and that government retaliation was imminent. It was – and culminated bloodily in the Battle of Culloden outside Inverness on 16 April 1746: the last great pitched battle on British soil.

It was a disaster. The Jacobites were outgunned and outnumbered in every imaginable sense. The fighting lasted barely an hour, and resulted in the deaths of around 2,000 Jacobites, versus just 300 on the British front.

The whole affair highlighted Charles's fatal lack of battle nous, and was the final blow to the Jacobite cause – with its followers swiftly becoming hunted, marginalised outlaws, pushed to the wildest western fringes of the land.

Skye's involvement in all this came while Charles was fleeing the fallout of Culloden. Making his way cross-country as a sort of illicit celebrity, the 'Bonnie Prince' was living rough, subsisting on the hospitality of Jacobite sympathisers. His circuitous route around the Highlands to evade capture – and run back to France – led him to the Outer Hebrides, and eventually to Skye.

Bonnie and young he may have been, but if this conjures up a picture of a perfumed, doe-eyed tyke carried on the cloud of familial entitlement . . . well, you'd be right. Most images of the Italian-raised prince portray him precisely thus, with one writer describing him in autumn 1745 as being a 'slender young Man, about five feet ten inches high, of a ruddy complexion, high-nosed, large rolling brown eyes, a long visage: his chin was pointed and Mouth small . . . his Hair was red, but at that Time he wore a pale Peruke.'

He was assisted in his flight by a young woman he had met named Flora MacDonald. Justifiably ubiquitous in all of Skye's stories concerning the entire affair, Flora MacDonald was clearly an extremely principled and brave woman – and took enormous personal risks to aid Charles's flight. The two met on South Uist, where Flora was compelled to help the fleeing aristocrat, despite both her stepfather and fiancé being involved in the hunt for him.

It was not, it must be said, a dignified escape. Disguising Charles in frumpy maid's clothes and rechristening him Betty Burke, she used her stepfather's military connections to acquire a rowboat in which Flora, her two 'servants' – one particularly quiet, tall and shifty – and six boatmen spirited across the Minch from the isle of Benbecula to Kilmuir on Skye on 28 June 1746. Flora arranged for Charles to spend the night in Kingsburgh House, from where he travelled overland in the dark from Portree to Elgol across some of the roughest ground on the island. This was no trivial journey: in some places he was bogged down to the waist. Ben Humble notes in *The Cuillin of Skye*: 'Let anyone who doubts Prince Charlie's powers as a Hillman follow that route over the hills through the night.' Along the way – I love this – he was apparently told by one of his stewards in hushed and hopefully withering tones to defrock his womanly attire, as he was more conspicuous with it on. He was then transferred to Raasay, from where he was spirited away back to the mainland, and eventually France. He left Flora a locket with his likeness, but never saw her again.

That was essentially the size of it for Charles and Skye. Charles promptly returned to the continent and into obscurity. He achieves a certain kudos for his ability to evade capture and overcome the terrain without complaint, often at a pace that amazed his envoys – though his speed was presumably a consequence of the ransom on his head.

But essentially it is Flora MacDonald whom Skye reveres – despite the niggling detail that the much-romanticised heroine was actually from South Uist. Her life following the adventures of 1746 would be eventful: after Charles's escape, she was arrested and briefly interred in the Tower of London. Emigrating to North Carolina in 1774, she became caught up in the American Civil War and forced into hiding. Journeying back to Scotland, her ship was attacked by the French, with Flora sustaining a wound in the arm after refusing to take refuge below deck. Returning to Skye to pass her latter years, she would die on the island in 1790, wrapped, according to her wishes, in the bedsheet Bonnie Prince Charlie had slept in.

It seems that the principal role Skye played in the tale, other than the acts of its adopted heroine, was that the islanders did not betray him – not even for a £30,000 reward offered by the authorities. This honour-over-avarice stance is perhaps the source of the pride, felt by some about Charles's otherwise rather embarrassing and cowardly escape: that no matter how doomed the rebellion, how swift and harsh the assured fallout, Charles was not turned in by the countrymen who harboured him. It also, of course, inspired a song by Sir Harold Boulton:

> Speed Bonny Boat like a Bird on the Wing,
> Onward the sailors cry,
> Carry the lad that's born to be king,
> Over the Sea to Skye.

Sentiment aside, the Battle of Culloden and the failure of Charles's coup unfortunately resulted in far more than just defeat. The Highlanders who had supported the Jacobite cause were now the enemy of the Crown, which – in the manner of many especially vengeful victors – set about vilifying every aspect of their culture. Plaid was outlawed; Gaelic shunned. Anything emblematic of the Highlands was considered deviant and shameful.

The mountains and islands of the west and their enclaves of 'barbarous miscreants' with their strange Gaelic tongue were seen as the dark places of the country, long overdue for subjugation. But less than fifty years after Culloden the Highland landscape would witness a juxtaposition of cultures when it became a gravitational point for the Romantics. They came seeking the ultimate domestic expression of what the philosopher Joseph Addison had famously coined the 'agreeable kind of horror', which kick-started the appreciation of such rude and rugged places. This led to the sudden about-face of the public perception of Britain's wild and wasted landscapes, the uplands and heaths, these becoming the substitute for the Grand Tour when things began to get dicey on the continent.

Similarly, the Highlanders and their society evolved, seemingly overnight, from being a barbarous and backward vexation of a culture to one with a suddenly cherishable mythology, earthy poetry and music that seemed to speak the very voice of the mountains. This thickly atmospheric stage was referenced and revered by the likes of Blake, Voltaire, Goethe and Napoleon, of all people – and all at once the Hebrides was *the* place to be. And with this sudden shift, Skye began a journey from being an obscure outpost of troubled stewardship, embattled clans and weather as scary as its denizens to enjoying a veneration that continues to this day.

So the obvious question is, exactly what was it that turned the tide? For this, we have to thank two things: the first was a famous 63-year-old hypochondriac who arrived on Skye shortly before 1 p.m. on 2 September 1773. The second – and this is where it starts getting strange – was the deception he came here to expose.

II

The thing about Dr Samuel Johnson was that, in well-heeled 18th-century society – to use modern parlance – he was kind of a big deal. The presence of the 'good doctor' (a curiously enduring title, given that his doctorate was honorary) anywhere at all was evidently worth noting – let alone on a windswept Hebridean island. A poet, essayist, dictionary compiler, philanthropist and committed Tory, Johnson was without doubt one of the most distinguished travellers to set foot on Skye – give or take the odd saint, Norse king or fleeing prince. But what he lacked in title he certainly made up for in personal eccentricities.

Physically, he certainly must have been quite something to behold. Tall, lumpy-featured and usually depicted resplendent with a wig, Johnson's litany of maladies and idiosyncrasies is arresting both in nature and quantity. As relayed by many of his contemporaries and biographers, Johnson was prone to an array of uncontrollable physical gesticulations, vocalised grunts, clucks and whistles – barks, even – that would startle those close by. A fellow essayist, Fanny Burney, said of Johnson:

> His mouth is almost constantly opening and shutting as if he were chewing. He has a strange method of frequently twirling his fingers and twisting his hands. His body is in continual agitation seesawing up and down; his feet are never a moment quiet; and in short, his whole person is in continuous motion.

Johnson also had the habit of extending his limbs systematically, 'with a full cup of tea in his hand, in every direction, often to the great annoyance of the person who sat next to him, indeed to the imminent danger of their cloathes'.

Another compulsion was to touch every lamppost he walked by whilst on foot in London, and, if ever he missed one, to suspend all conversation to return and make contact with it. Added to this – and may I just say, the poor man – he had weak eyesight, was afraid of bones, partially deaf and plagued by depression, insomnia and a distracting fear of sudden death. He was suffering symptoms that today we might ascribe to obsessive–compulsive disorder, and Tourette's syndrome.

It is heartening that despite being beleaguered with then little-understood afflictions, Johnson was undoubtedly revered, which – in the frequently cruel society of the 18th century – says something of the man's achievements. 'He was to the last a convulsionary ...' remarked Thomas Tyers in a *Biographical Sketch of Samuel Johnson*. 'His gestures ... in the street attracted the notice of many, stare of the vulgar, but the compassion of the better sort.' If nothing else this makes it understandable why the ninety-four-day journey this ageing and couched man of letters had planned – an uncomfortable voyage that on several occasions put him even more in fear of his life, and doubtless rattled his London-softened bones – attracted considerable interest.

Skye was an intrinsic part of his trip, and it was after Johnson's visit that the travellers really came flooding in. Many seemed eager to simply follow the trail left by the great man, often drawing parallels with his journey in awe-breathed prose ('*He* stood here! *He* saw that!') and travelling to locations that caught his pen, as if following in the footsteps of a prophet.

Which is all quite odd, as Johnson's account of the island wasn't exactly the work of a man in thrall to his surroundings. Taken merely as a travelogue, he did little if anything to endear Skye to the wider world other than to suggest it was a place probably best avoided. Accompanied by thirty-two-year-old James Boswell, a well-connected Edinburgh societal dandy who had made the much older Johnson's acquaintance a decade earlier, the two formed the quintessential mismatched and occasionally bickering duo – strapping, tolerant Boswell and the puffing, withering Johnson – as they made their progress across the Highlands, and eventually to Skye.

They stayed on the island for a month, much of it pinned down by bad weather, moving from one humbled host to another in a touring spectacle of wit, erudite presence and general greatness (or something) that drew spectators from all around. Johnson's journal of the trip was eloquent – given his reputation and standing, it would be a scandal if it weren't – and demonstrated his brilliance of observation and love of minutiae. He made many well-crafted comments concerning clothing, food, agricultural practices and the mannerisms of the locals that sometimes border on the profound. But is it exciting? 'Viewed as a whole . . . it is a very trashy, lumbering, dull performance, unworthy of Johnson's inordinate reputation,' wrote one critic, 'but, nevertheless, occasionally relieved by lucid intervals . . . of uncommon interest and power.'

It is really Boswell we have to thank for his rather lighter complimentary account of the same journey, published the year after Johnson's. In addition to the considerable advantage of having Johnson as his principal subject, Boswell is the livelier narrator, his book much more of a romp than Johnson's cultural ramble. For the Skye segment he dances a Highland jig on the summit of Dun Caan on Raasay, drinks bowls of punch until 5 a.m. in the now ruined house of Coire-chat-achan at the feet of Beinn na Caillich, and in Portree describes an improbably flirty encounter between Johnson and the heroine of Bonnie Prince Charlie's flight herself, Flora MacDonald. While Johnson gives little more than a reverent sentence to this 'woman of middle stature, soft features, gentle manners and elegant presence', Boswell suggests some sort of a *frisson* between the two, as well as mentioning that Johnson slept in the very bed the unfortunate Charles occupied whilst on the run almost thirty years earlier.

Flora aside, Johnson's account of Skye is notable for making little mention whatsoever of the Cuillin or indeed any of the island's hills, or much of its landscape. Not unusually for the time, Johnson seemed quite unresponsive to it, remarking when asked how he liked the Highlands, 'Who can like the Highlands? I love the people better than the country.'

He managed to fall over, provide an accurate observation on the discrepancy between the 'Skye mile' and the typical mile ('the computation of Sky has no connection whatsoever with real distance') and the memorable and much-quoted slight: 'A walk upon ploughed fields in England is a dance upon carpets, compared to the toilsome drudgery of wandering in Skie.' He does admit, 'Here are mountains that I should once have climbed, but to climb steeps is now very laborious, and to descend them dangerous,' but all in all he seems singularly unmoved by the scenery. Clearly this was not Johnson's primary interest, but it is still an odd omission, given the Cuillin was and remains Skye's most striking visual feature. Perhaps it was due to the bad weather; more likely it was because the brooding nature of the landscape, the mystical charm of the Gaels and their mountains were either unknown or unappreciated irritants to most who travelled here.

Or at least, they had been until very recently.

Which brings me back to that *deception*. It would be remiss not to mention the preoccupation that was one of the reasons Samuel Johnson – an academic and literary critic – decided to conduct this improbable tour of the Western Isles. It was his investigation of a phenomenon that was the key catalyst in the change in perception of the Highlanders and their culture during a period that has since become known as the Celtic revival. More specifically, a successful work of recent literature that Johnson was determined to expose as a fraud: the product of a farmer's son from Kingussie whose 'translation' of an ancient Gaelic manuscript had become an international sensation. This man's name was James Macpherson, but the work was then and would forever more be associated with its mystical, ancient narrator – once described reverently as the 'Homer of the north': Ossian.

The story of the Ossianic poems – the saga of the saga – is the stuff of bad fiction. But it's impossible to overstate the influence it had on the perception of the landscape in which the poems were set. After studying divinity at the University of Edinburgh, Macpherson, who had been born 24 years earlier in Inverness-shire in the shadow of the Cairngorms, set off to travel the West Highlands and Islands. Along the way he reportedly acquired a series of extremely venerable manuscripts written in an archaic form of Scots-Irish Gaelic known as Erse. With a fondness for the language and the ability to speak it – though not well – Macpherson, informed there was no market for Gaelic poems, set about translating them into resplendent English, publishing the first collection as *Fragments of Ancient Poetry, Collected in the Highlands of Scotland, and Translated from the Gaelic or Erse language* in 1760.

A year later, encouraged by his impressed associates, Macpherson once again returned to the West Highlands, alighting on Skye, the Uists and Benbecula in search of further ancient literary ephemera. This time he returned having made a significant discovery: the complete manuscript of an epic based upon the life of a Scottish warrior king from the 3rd century CE, as recounted in old age by his son, Ossian.

The story goes that Ossian had been a legendary warrior himself who, though now blind and stooped, wrote a series of poems fuelled by the fantastical exploits of the warriors of old, including his father the king, in the West Highlands, the Hebrides and what is today Northern Ireland, as well as the stormy waters in between. Once again, Macpherson set to translating the work, publishing the first of the series in December of the same year. Not one to buck the trend of comprehensive titles, it was called *Fingal, an Ancient Epic Poem in Six Books, together with Several Other Poems composed by Ossian, the Son of Fingal, translated from the Gaelic Language*. But most people today know it simply by the name of the king at its centre: Fingal.

The work was a sensation. An intoxication of wild seas, warriors, magic and earthy ways set against a backdrop of the murky and mystical north, here was a cultural offering that rivalled the Norse sagas for atmosphere, the Greek epics for heroics and the works of Shakespeare for tragedy – and all of it taking place in a landscape that had been all but ignored for its aesthetic and cultural merit. That it arrived on the cusp of the Romantic movement is indisputable, that it may have been instrumental in that movement gathering steam has been widely suggested, and the work certainly caused an appropriate stir at the right time.

Macpherson, however, attracted considerable suspicion from the critics. First there was the question of the tales' provenance. This was raised immediately on publication, when the Irish literary establishment accused Macpherson of appropriating their own legends for Scotland's literary gain and his own financial enrichment. All understandable, given that the character of Fingal is clearly based on Fionn mac Cumhaill – more commonly known as Finn MacCool – a warrior figure in Irish mythology. Best known from a series of poetic accounts, or 'cycles', preserved in medieval texts from around the 11th or 12th century, much of what's known as the Fenian Cycle is credited to Oisín, Fionn mac Cumhaill's son, considered the greatest poet of ancient Ireland. You naturally grasp the critics' point.

The parallels are repeated in many other situations and characters throughout Macpherson's work to an extent that makes it embarrassing to suggest the material did not have a common source. But Macpherson refuted allegations of reimagining pilfered ideas and maintained the material was entirely genuine, claiming that he pieced together the work not just from manuscripts but from word-of-mouth folk tales told to him by a number of Gaelic speakers. It was therefore reasonable, given the shared Gaelic heritage and the seaward proximity of western Scotland and Northern Ireland, that the legends and figures from both regions would be similar.

The Skye connection here is intriguing. In 1760 James Macpherson is known to have met Alexander Macpherson (no relation), a blacksmith in Portree famous for his redoubtable memory and a talent for reciting oral poetry. According to Norman Macdonald and Cailean Maclean in *The Great Book of Skye*, Macpherson spent four days and nights with the blacksmith, recording a variety of poems and reputedly leaving with an item known as the Leabhar Dearg – the Red Book – a Gaelic manuscript heirloom that contained fragments of the story of Fingal. James Macpherson, it seemed, promised return of the manuscript, but took it and was never seen again in Portree. So it would appear that – however scurrilous the method, which perhaps accounted for his reluctance to be terribly specific about his sources – Macpherson's story checked out.

Unfortunately the controversy didn't end there. Macpherson was at no point able to produce any of the ancient manuscripts he claimed to have seen, though he did indicate where a fragment of a venerable Fingal manuscript was to be found – and maintained his defence that much of the material was transcribed from oral accounts. There were also similarities detected between the poems and certain aspects of not only Irish but English literature; Ossian's Address to the Sun in Carthon, for example, being likened to Satan's Address to the Sun in Milton's *Paradise Lost*.

Enter Samuel Johnson. It's unclear why the whole affair hit such a nerve with him; it could have been either Macpherson's cheek in attempting to hoodwink the public or the literary quality of the poetry, as he held equal scorn for both. Uncomfortably, Boswell was something of a fan, having met Macpherson on several occasions and once described him as 'a man of great genius and an honest Scotch highlander.' But Johnson became absorbed in exposing Macpherson as a heretic. The whole business became rather unseemly from both quarters; Johnson seized every opportunity to publicly insult Macpherson, calling him variously a liar and a fraud, and his work a forgery and 'as gross an imposition as ever the world was troubled with'. A particularly acidic retort came upon being asked if he really believed any man today could write such poetry, to which he replied: 'Yes. Many men. Many women. And many children.'

Unfortunately Johnson's eagerness to denounce Macpherson was sometimes *too* eager. His assertion that there were no manuscripts in Gaelic – what he termed the 'rude speech of a barbarous people' – more than a century old exposed not only his anti-Scottish bigotry but his ignorance, as the Advocate's Library in Edinburgh contained manuscripts three times that age.

Macpherson, for his part, remained steadfast but irritable when questioned on the work's origins, with one observer remarking, 'The absurd pride of Macpherson, who scorns, as he pretends, to satisfy anyone who doubts his veracity, has tended much to confirm this general scepticism.'

Macpherson's retrospectively rather enjoyable war of words with Johnson has become a model of the squabble-by-correspondence. It began when Johnson published this damning paragraph in his *Journey to the Western Isles of Scotland*:

> I believe [the Ossianic poems] never existed in any other form than that which we have seen. The editor, or author, never could shew the original; nor can it be shewn by any other; to revenge reasonable incredulity, by refusing evidence, is a degree of insolence, with which the world is not yet acquainted; and stubborn audacity is the last refuge of guilt.

Macpherson was furious. Initially attempting to halt the publication of Johnson's book, he then demanded that apologetic pieces of paper be inserted into the published copies denouncing the passage. When both of these civil avenues failed, he challenged Johnson to a duel. Johnson – hardly surprising, given what we know about his physical maladies – refused. Macpherson then sent a final letter to Johnson, now sadly lost, in which he reputedly lambasted his foe for protecting a 'liar and traducer' behind a shield of age and infirmity. Johnson replied in withering style:

MR. JAMES MACPHERSON.

I RECEIVED your foolish and impudent letter. Any violence offered me I shall do my best to repel; and what I cannot do for myself, the law shall do for me. I hope I shall never be deterred from detecting what I think a cheat, by the menaces of a ruffian.

What would you have me retract? I thought your book an imposture; I think it an imposture still. For this opinion I have given my reasons to the publick, which I here dare you to refute. Your rage I defy. Your abilities, since your Homer, are not so formidable; and what I hear of your morals inclines me to pay regard not to what you shall say, but to what you shall prove.

You may print this if you will.

SAM. Johnson

It was, one might say fortunately, their final correspondence. Such was the digging that went on to attempt to settle the matter, a committee was established – spurred by the author Hugh Blair and the philosopher and historian David Hume, and chaired by lawyer Henry Mackenzie – to 'leave no hinge or loop to hang doubt on' as regards the authenticity of the Ossianic poems. This involved a kind of questionnaire to be dispatched in the hand of investigators to far-flung corners of the Highlands and Islands asking – and I'm clearly paraphrasing here – if anyone fitting the description of Macpherson had ever come calling, quill in hand; if any ancient poetic manuscripts were likely to have been lurking in drawers or under beds in the recent past; if anyone knew of the characters involved in the saga, knew of anyone else who knew of them, or had sat around a fire reciting them at any point; and if there was anything anywhere written in comparable Gaelic to which an alignment could be made with the published work.

The results – somewhat surprisingly – tentatively upheld the work. According to the report, the local awareness of Fingal and his world was as 'strong as the belief in any ancient fact whatsoever', and the figure of blind Ossian – *Ossian dall*, as he was known – was as familiar an evocation of emasculated strength as the Bible's Samson. The characters were stalwarts of Gaelic mythology, and held many similarities to characters observed in stories the world over, starting with the Ancient Greeks and their warriors, gods, rites of passage and shrivelled foes.

The report of the committee concluded that while Macpherson hadn't been entirely straight with the public concerning the poems' heritage, he clearly hadn't made it all up either. Macpherson in his process was inclined to 'add what he conceived to be dignity and delicacy . . . by changing what he considered too simple or too rude for modern ear and elevating what, in his opinion, was below the standard of good poetry'. To what extent Macpherson had taken liberties with the source material – or made mistakes with his etymology or translations – was to remain forever unclear, given that many of the storytellers Macpherson met were dead by the time of the report. But the work was hailed, for exactly the same reason, as an 'original whole, of much more beauty, and with much fewer blemishes, than the committee believe it now possible for any person, or combination of persons, to obtain'.

Given such lengthy scrutiny, it was inevitable that the poems of Ossian would subsequently have a tang of scandal about them, regardless of the evident ingenuity that went into their making. One commentator on the affair in 1805 prophesised Ossian 'is likely to share the fate of Shakespeare, that is . . . to be loaded and oppressed by heavy commentators until his immortal spirit groan beneath vast heaps of perishable matter'. The comparison is a canny one, as Shakespeare was no stranger to reimagining familiar characters around well-furrowed storylines himself. The art was, as is critical here, all in the telling.

In any case, the criticism did little to halt the popularity or influence of the Ossianic poems. Praise for Macpherson's 'discovery' arrived on his doorstep from all over the world, and continued for decades. Thomas Jefferson announced Ossian as 'the greatest poet that ever existed'. The celebrated Italian scholar Melchiorre Cesarotti wrote to Macpherson to congratulate him on what he termed his 'valuable discovery of a new poetic realm and the treasures you have bestowed upon the literary world', before announcing his intention to translate them into Italian:

> Your rocks covered with leafy oak and fog, your tempestuous skies, your rumbling creeks . . . your prairies woven entirely with thistle. [In Ossian] Scotland has given us a Homer who does not chatter on . . . but I need not praise Ossian to the man who has been able to render its qualities with so much strength and precision.

More than that, the poems have been cited as being a key source of national identity and cultural pride in the difficult years following the Battle of Culloden, when the Highlands were raw from the failure of their rebellion and their absorption into the United Kingdom. Soon after that, as a national property of considerable stock, the poems gave the entire union a stirring odyssey of courage from which to draw strength as the Napoleonic Wars erupted in Europe and threatened to spill onto British soil. With palpable irony, Napoleon himself is said to have carried a copy of the poems with him, once stating: 'I like Ossian for the same reason that I like to hear the whisper of the wind and the waves of the sea'.

In Germany the poems were universally venerated, quoted by Goethe and set to music by Schubert and later by Brahms; in France they were satirised by Voltaire. Wordsworth, however, claimed to have had Macpherson's number from the get-go, recounting in his preamble to the *Lyrical Ballads* that:

> Having had the good fortune to be born and reared in a mountainous country ... from my very childhood I have felt the falsehood ... imposed upon the world under the name of Ossian. I knew the imagery was spurious ... from the lips of a phantom ... begotten by the snug embrace of an impudent Highlander under a cloud of tradition.

But this did not stop him from reverently referencing Ossian with his own 'Glen Almain; Or, the Narrow Glen' in a manner that hardly feels like a jab at a literary heretic.

Even Queen Victoria tossed in a barbed comment when, whilst travelling through Glen Coe, she spied the so-called 'Ossian's Cave', high above the valley: 'One cannot imagine how anyone could live there, as they pretend that Ossian did.'

You find reference to Ossian and his associations all over the Highlands: more caves, a loch, rocks, a grave and any number of human creations, from concert halls to travel companies. For reasons many probably couldn't define if asked, his very name carries whispers of the Highlands and the Gaels with it. It's understandably a source of discomfort that the crowning literary glory of an ancient culture still sits uneasily – but whatever their source, the Ossianic poems are still rightly revered as works that capture the stew of folklore and the atmosphere of the Highlands with concentrated heft. Macpherson created an ark of folklore that would be otherwise lost – and along the way set a steer that would influence our interpretation of Gaelic culture and the landscape from which it was born.

The point of all of this is simply that, upon publishing the Ossianic poems when he did and *how* he did it, Macpherson caused a stir that prompted people in faraway wingback chairs to ask a question they had never thought to ask: is that what Scotland's Highlands and its people were *like*?

In *The Scenery of Scotland*, Archibald Geikie refers to the Ossianic poems in a remarkably evocative passage:

The local truth of the descriptions and allusions is altogether remarkable – the golden sunsets over the western ocean, the surge of the breakers on the dark rocks of the iron-bound shore … the scattered boulders and lonely cairns, the rapid chase of sunshine and shadow as the clouds are driven over firth and fell, the deepening gloom of the gathering storm when the gale howls down the glens, tearing the rain-sheet into long, swiftly following shreds like troops of dimly-seen ghosts. These features are depicted with such simple truth that, whatever may be the value we are disposed to set upon the poetry, we must admit that in Scotland it could only have been born … and that it is genuine of the soil.

And these are the words of a geologist.

By the time naturalist Thomas Pennant wrote his own much-quoted account of his journey in 1769 the secret was thoroughly out – he was surprised to find the more accessible areas of the Highlands 'inonde with southern visitors', keen to feel the romance of Macpherson's poetry with their own grasping eyes. Two years later, the crowd was joined by Johnson and Boswell. Countless others then came looking for what Johnson saw, and – as more and more were exposed to what lay amongst the mists – Skye began to speak its own truth. The Highlands and the Hebrides were resolutely on the travellers' map, and to this day, there they remain.

As the years went by, it seems Macpherson was eventually forgiven by the literati – though perhaps not in his own lifetime. He remained cantankerous and unapologetic to the last. After a brief spell in Florida as advisor to its governor – a critic suggested he 'travel amongst the Chickasaws and Cherokees, in order to tame and civilize him' – he returned to Britain a rich landowner, only to be embroiled into an ugly scene concerning the crofters he cleared off his estates to make way for sheep. 'MacOssian', as he was sarcastically nicknamed, died in 1796. In a final swipe at Samuel Johnson and the other 'men of letters' to whom he was always a fraud, Macpherson was interred just feet away in the hallowed churchyard of Westminster Abbey. Many consider his place there deserved; others believe he bought his way in. Either way, to this day – like sleeping dogs, or not – there he, and his critics, lie.

Without Macpherson and Ossian, our view of the Highlands might be quite different. Incidentally, it's Ossian we have to thank for establishing the name *Eilean a' Cheo* – the Isle of Mist – and specifically the name of one of the characters, which will ring familiar to anyone who has been paying attention. He was based upon a formidable Irish warrior, whose travels across the sea and his battles and grapples on a distant island became legendary. His name was CúChulainn, but Macpherson's name for him was Cuthulinn. Most refer to him today as an intertwined mix of the two: Cuchullin. And we'll get to how this mythological character may or may not have become a name of a certain mountain range a little later on.

III

While the Ossianic poems created the palette of the broader scene, and Johnson and Boswell's accounts filled in some character detail, it was the apparently inescapable figure of John MacCulloch, the geologist, who forms the last in this little chain of travellers destined to evoke Skye's darker and more dramatic environments – and ink in a very specific location on Skye's tourist map. For all the criticism he received from other quarters, not least James Forbes, MacCulloch's most enduring offering to Skye's literary story is memorable indeed.

It's contained in a letter he wrote to his lifelong friend Sir Walter Scott, the 'Bard of the Highlands', in 1814, which contains the first literary description of what was soon to become Skye's most secretive and darkly romanticised place. In the coming years it would draw travellers from all over the world to experience it – not least Scott himself, who would impart it palpably to the masses in *The Lord of the Isles*.

Along with a group of Skye boatmen, MacCulloch had landed on the shores of Loch Scavaig, intent on investigating the nearby geology. A local informant had assured him he 'would find rocks enough . . . [the place is] as far from bonny as possible,' and MacCulloch was enraptured with the idea of a finding a location seething with rocky drama and claiming that immortal first glimpse (aside from a few local sorts who evidently didn't count). 'I should at least see scenery which, as it appeared to have been utterly neglected by the only two persons who had ever opened their eyes on it, would crown me with the laurels of a discoverer,' he wrote, scenery 'embodying all sorts of impossible rocks into all sorts of impossible shapes'.

But it was what lay beyond the head of Loch Scavaig that snared his attention – a valley that 'burst on my view and, in a moment, obliterated . . . all the valleys that have ever left their traces on the table of my brain'. This was, of course, the dark sanctuary of Coruisk – the deep-cut, deep-dark lake beneath the Cuillin's clawed rampart. MacCulloch wrote that he felt he'd been 'transported by some magician into the wilds of some Arabian tale'.

There's a little more to John MacCulloch's journey into Coruisk's shadows than hyperbole – I'm saving that – but Scott followed suit, on a tour of the region that same year, and published *The Lord of the Isles* in 1815. He had been assured by MacCulloch that only a handful of people knew of the location – but after publication of this poem, that would change and quickly:

> For all is rocks at random thrown,
> Black waves, bare crags, and banks of stone,
> As if here were denied
> The summer sun, the spring's sweet dew,
> That clothe with many a varied hue
> The bleakest mountain-side.

The Lord of the Isles would be hailed as Scott's last great poem, and even one that spared the West Highlands and Islands from ruin – notably by the painter William Daniell, who in 1818 wrote in a letter to the poet asserting that he had 'rescued [the region] from obscurity'.

And so, duly, the travellers came. Boat trips braved the wild waters of Loch Scavaig to land tourists at Loch Coruisk – and in some cases *only* Loch Coruisk. After the publication of *Lord of the Isles*, in 1831 J. M. W. Turner painted *Loch Coruisk* in swirling, furious strokes, simultaneously showing little of the valley's topographical form but everything of its atmosphere. It was, Turner reputedly said, the grandest scene he had ever beheld. Alfred, Lord Tennyson would visit, and note of the Cuillin's storms, 'countless forms' and 'wondrous tones'. This pocket of concentrated wildness with such power to inspire would become a kind of otherworldly offshore tourist attraction – Ossian's world, where the 'oohs' and 'aahs' and clicks of well-heeled shoes would echo around a valley entirely at odds with the world of their wearers.

And they couldn't get enough of it. According to Katherine Haldane Grenier in the fascinating *Tourism and Identity in Scotland, 1770–1914*:

Nearly every nineteenth-century description of lochs Scavaig and Coruisk, whether in a guidebook or personal account, owed something to MacCulloch and Scott ... this rendition of the Highland landscape permeated popular culture to such a degree that it became difficult to see Skye in any other way.

The new breed of dandy traveller to Skye was not universally appreciated by island folk. It wasn't long before tracts appeared that venomously lambasted the privileged class of 'curiosity men' reaching Skye shores, seemingly for the purpose of using the scenery to exercise their melodrama muscles while poking fun at the locals and their quaint ways. The target was, fittingly enough, John MacCulloch. This was because as well as his exhaustive analysis of the geology of the region, he also found time to produce his own sensitive assessment of its denizens in a further *four* volumes, with the title *The Highlands and Western Isles of Scotland, Descriptions of Their Scenery and Antiquities, with an Account of the Political History and Ancient Manners, and of the Origin, Language, Agriculture, Economy, Present Condition of the People Founded on a Series of Annual Journeys Between the Years 1811 and 1821 and forming a Universal Guide to That Country*. It was these volumes that comprised the letters to Sir Walter Scott, and it was this work that got MacCulloch – and anyone resembling him in the years to follow – into rather hot water.

MacCulloch was reputedly a troubled soul; but in any case he was certainly a misanthrope, and his descriptions of the 'coast-dwelling Celts' he encountered on his travels (and frequently availed of hospitality) were often used as objects upon which to aim his surly commentary. He ridiculed them, condemned them 'as being slovenly and prone to procrastination', not to mention his peculiar assertion that he never saw 'a culinary vegetable of any kind' during his entire time in the Highlands. Unsurprisingly, none of this went down well with the locals.

A critique of his work by one James Browne was published in 1825, entitled *A Critical Examination of Dr Macculloch's Work on the Highlands and*

Western Isles of Scotland. It ran to 300 extraordinary, rage-spitting pages, spectacularly setting MacCulloch up as an example of the emerging class of feudally inclined traveller 'miserably qualified for the task' of deconstructing a culture about which they had no meaningful frame of reference. The vicious introductory comments were aimed squarely at the new breed of Skye 'tourist', and – if for nothing more than for their excellently withering writing – are worth quoting at length:

> Acquainted with a state of society and manners different from, and, in some respects, diametrically opposite to that which they went to explore ... profoundly ignorant of the language of the people, and more deeply read in the volumes of men than in the great book of Nature, plodding antiquaries, crazy sentimentalists, silly view-hunters, cockney literati, and, worst of all, impudent 'Stone Doctors' armed with their hammers, have successively invaded the unconquered mountains of Caledonia, to share the hospitality of the simple hearted natives, and to export, for the edification of the crowd, dry descriptions of cairns, castles, vitrified forts, and parallel roads or the mawkish rhodomontade of drivelling deliration, or paltry and pitiful views of scenery worthy of the pencil of Salvator himself, or gossiping mendacious anecdotes of the cunning, selfishness, extortion, filth, indolence, and barbarism of a race who never closed their doors against the stranger till his treachery and ingratitude taught them to regard him with suspicion and distrust.

The book makes reference to Ossian, and uses MacCulloch's fondness for referencing the work as further testament to his degeneracy. In a chapter entitled, rather splendidly, 'Specimen of Nonsense', MacCulloch's work is assessed as having 'literary character ... as contemptible as the spirit in which they are written is malignant.'

In a rather more straightforward personal attack on MacCulloch, so angered was 'Old' Lachlan MacKinnon in Coire-chat-achan that he had a series of chamber pots commissioned and distributed amongst his friends, each with a portrait of MacCulloch's face occupying a strategic area of the inner base.

The locals' irritation with the 'stone doctors' treating their lands as scientific curiosities is perhaps best conveyed by one apocryphal anecdote. It concerns the ghillie who, when tasked to carry a sackload of rock specimens over miles of rough ground back to their geologist's hostelry, dumped the painstakingly collected specimens immediately after taking leave of their sight, only to replace them with a similar weight of rock from outside the hotel door. Another fine story from a slightly later time is found in Archibald Geikie's *Highland Reminiscences*, in which he describes being noticed as a young geologist on Skye in the mid-1800s by a bemused group of crofters, who had taken to calling him Gille na Clach – 'lad of the stones.' Upon being accosted by one who enquired what was in his bag, Geikie had replied he had stones. 'Stones!' came the reply from the crofter, who had then with amusement asked what he was going to be doing with the stones. Geikie told him he intended to take them 'south and look at them all very carefully'.

'Lookin' at stones! Well, well!' the crofter replied. 'And have ye no stones in your *ain* countrie?'

Amidst all of this, James Forbes occupies a transcendent role. While he undoubtedly arrived on Skye as one of these 'stone doctors', he left, however inadvertently, as something quite different, the first of an entirely new breed of traveller. The pivotal point was described in a single line in his 1845 paper:

On my first visit to Skye [in 1836], I succeeded in reaching the summit (then deemed inaccessible) which passes for the highest of the Cuchullin hills.

He is talking about Sgùrr nan Gillean – the northern end-stop of the ridge above Sligachan, and not in fact the highest summit, though due to its shapely appearance and prominence, widely thought so at the time.

It was almost certainly the first of the major summits of the ridge to permit an outsider. In the company of an 'active forester' named Duncan MacIntyre, whom Forbes had enlisted to guide him from the inn at Sligachan to Coruisk, his mountaineering ears twitched when his guide told him he had attempted Sgùrr nan Gillean 'repeatedly without success, both by himself and also with other people who had engaged him for the purpose'.

MacIntyre, an interesting character of whom more anon, then suggested a route different to those he had already attempted on this complex and much-pinnacled peak – and on 7 July, in Forbes's words, 'We succeeded in reaching the top.' Forbes erected a flag and a small cairn, and guesstimated the height at 3,000 feet. He then made these observations:

> The extreme roughness of the rock [rendered] the ascent safe, where, with any other formations, it might have been considerably perilous. Indeed, I have never seen a rock so adapted for clambering.

Forbes had arrived a geological tourist, and left as Skye's first true mountaineer-adventurer – and the Cuillin ridge's first true explorer. He would return to the Cuillin in the following years, walk around the ridge, intersect it 'from various directions', and climb Sgùrr nan Gillean again, as well as making the supposed first ascent of Bruach na Frithe, both with MacIntyre. Then, as a final gift, like all true explorers fresh from an unknown realm, he left us a map.

High in Coire Làgan I ate some supplies I'd bought from the campsite shop and sat, watching the mist mither the water. Gradually I felt the moisture begin to cling to my clothes and hair, and when I felt a shiver, decided that the murk was there to stay and it was probably time to make a move. I regretted not seeing the view from the corrie – but I was glad I had seen and stood in the corrie itself.

Just as Coire Làgan breaks into descent towards Glenbrittle there's a black pinnacle. It stands by the side of the path just a little way up the hillside to give vantage, sentry-like. I saw it on the way up, high to the left, mithered by cloud. On the way down I saw it again, clearer, and walked off the path up to it.

It was maybe ten metres high, a kinked triangle like a witch's hat. It might have fallen here; this seemed likely, given it stood where a glacier had passed. I touched it. It was made of gabbro, a refugee, out of time and place, from higher up the ridge. Fractures ran around it, gave it joints. Holds. I circled the pinnacle, slid my hands across it, felt the sting of it. And let my eyes test its cracks.

I'd approached it because I thought it might be climbable. I knew that mountain objectives that often look impossible from afar often show a more amenable nature up close. It seemed that the reverse was true here. This little pinnacle, amusing as it looked from the path, now seemed daunting.

I put both hands on the rock and took hold of it. I felt cold moisture on my fingers, and they hurt as my weight transferred from the ground to my hands, pressing them into the abrasive gabbro. One leg up, then the other, planted on the steep rock, where they held me uncomfortably, while my hands hunted for the next crack-rung above. Even this small step up changed perspective. Suddenly there was a little air beneath me, and my instincts turned to falling, and what that would be like from here. Just a few feet. Not a few thousand. Far enough to hurt, that's all. I found a crack for my right hand and pulled up on it. Three points of contact at all times – there was a rule I remembered. I wondered if the normal principles for scrambling worked in the Cuillin, a place where everything else seemed to be different. Pulling my body away from the rock, I took another step up, bringing my left leg higher. Now, even with this tiny increase, I was high enough to break something. A leg, an arm. A neck, if I was unlucky. My face was against the rock. It smelled murky, and felt like a coarse file. A scrape against it would strip the skin from my face. This was what the ridge above and around me was made of. The Black Cuillin in miniature, to which I was clinging by fingers, and friction.

I had nowhere to go. My right hand was secure, but I couldn't find anywhere for my left. My boot scratched for a hold, and failed. Straining, I hung on for a second, contemplating a dive for a higher crack, but then relented, and with a slow scraping of nylon half stepped, half slid down to the first hold, then jumped heavily down to the hillside.

I'd hoped for better results from my first Cuillin climb. It was just a little pointy rock in Coire Làgan – but even that was enough to tell me that between now and anything else I hoped to do in the darkening world of rock-rafters high above me, I wasn't quite ready yet.

But I had time. I had the summer to prepare. To let the midges subside, along with the crowds and rain and soupy heat and storms of July and August. September would be cooler. Quieter. And it would allow me a few months to get ready to tackle the ridge itself; ready physically, and perhaps psychologically too. But before leaving Skye this time I had somewhere to be. I needed to have one of the more important conversations concerning my dealings with the Cuillin ridge – with the person who was going to keep me alive up there. Tomorrow morning I was going to meet my guide.

6

Labyrinth

In the archives of the British Film Institute in London there's an excerpt from a film shot in 1916. Unassuming under the title 'Identifier 62271: British Sports and Pastimes, Series 5', it's a little over three minutes long and, though silent, has the scratchy aesthetic and opulent title cards that make you imagine a plinky-plonk piano soundtrack as you watch. A kind lady at the Institute's library had sent me an email containing a link to watch it online, so that night I sat on the bed in my room at the Taigh Ailean and, as the rain fell outside in the dark, loaded it up. After the title card 'Climbing', I watched the century-old footage crackle to life on my computer screen and let out a little cry of delight.

There, unmistakeable and unchanged from a century earlier, was the very pinnacle – the bent witch's hat in Coire Làgan – I had been attempting to climb that afternoon. For a second it was like our times were touching, until I checked the date and realised that whilst this footage was being filmed, men were dying in the trenches of the Western Front, which suddenly made it not the same at all. Everyone I was watching in these pictures lived in a world without mobile phones, nylon, television, commercial planes, the Rolling Stones. George Mallory was alive and climbing hard. Edmund Hillary hadn't been born. Skye was still an island in every sense. But the pinnacle looked just the same. I love that about mountains; they are, in our terms at least, pretty timeless things. They stay still while human history churns around them, indifferent to our occasional intrepid splashes into their heights.

Anyway. Here on screen, separated in time by a hundred years but otherwise no different, a man of evidently impressive age is making short work of this pinnacle. He wears a flat cap that throws his face into shadow, except for a fluffy white beard. His clothes hang slack – a pale felt coat, plus fours – and nailed boots on his feet. Across his body he has a coil of hemp rope he isn't using for anything other than to look the part – this climb is all about friction, and confidence. But it's the way he moves.

Sometimes the movement in these old films is a kind of creaky haste that makes everyone in them look like over-wound clockwork toys, but this one looked real. You see the concentration, feel every hesitation, every strain, somehow hear every scratch and scrabble. His boots, the nails visibly shiny, slip on the rock, but the man defies the yank of gravity, using his knees and elbows, shifting his weight, stretching arms and splaying spry legs, moving up the rock as if his joints were magnetised to it. It's neither dignified nor fluid – climbing isn't, generally – but clutching, weighted, dogged. He reaches the top, and the film cuts away, rather unexpectedly, to skating.

And with that, we enter the world of mountaineering – a field in which the Cuillin ridge stands as the British Isles' precarious apex. I should say at this point, just in case you haven't gathered by now, I'm no rock climber. I reach the tops of mountains using my legs, occasionally my hands, but rarely ropes and ideally never nerves. I used to be a little more intrepid, but then I became a dad. This had, in me, triggered a recalibration of instincts as regards self-protection – not for selfish reasons, but purely because a couple of little people actually need me around now. But that aside, I've never been a thrill seeker when it comes to heights on mountains – just someone who likes the thrill of a mountain, by being at height. There's a difference.

Rock climbing for the sake of rock climbing – for the chewing of the obstacle, rather than the reward of the summit – is quite different to what you might call hillwalking or even mountaineering. They might occupy a similarly rocky theatre of action, but one is much more focused on the detail, placing a huge amount of emphasis on a small amount of progress. Climbing is less a leisurely appreciation of your wider surroundings than a high-stakes grapple with them at close quarters. It's a bit like the difference between sailing a boat and riding a surfboard: you're both in the sea, obeying its rules and having fun – but that's about the only thing you've got in common.

That's not to say that the two pursuits don't share intriguing parallel lines. Climbing is brimming with a richly philosophical and occasionally nihilistic culture: you just need to look hard to find it packaged in a way that permits normal people like you and me to appreciate it.

The best book I've read about rock climbing is the mystifyingly obscure *Native Stones* by David Craig. It's a slim volume that drifts over the major emotions of rock climbing and somehow fuses memoir, poetry and philosophy into a reasoned testament of intent. Here it is the physical action that counts as much as the scene:

> It all happens at a pace that can be remembered: as deliberately as a work of art shaping under your pen ... as lengthily as a night when one dream dissolves into the next and none of them are forgotten ... the brilliant minutes ... as though a flare had exploded and shown you the features of your earth as you had never seen them before.

With these words in your ear, watch the old man in this old film, or grapple with any rock yourself, and the act of climbing becomes almost profound.

This is a pretty arcane bit of footage, and would be of little note were it not that it contains – as far as mountaineering in the Cuillin goes – a little bit of historic gold. The man on the rock is probably the most well-known climber in the history of the Cuillin. He's one of the men with a mountain in this range named after him: John MacKenzie.

MacKenzie was in his sixtieth year when the footage was shot in 1916. Born down the coast from Sligachan in Sconser in 1856, he was one of four brothers – the others being Murdo, Donald and Archie. All would become guides, taking tourists, have-a-go deer stalkers and eventually mountaineers into the hills around Sligachan. John is often said to have had the middle name 'Morton', though it was most likely just an alias – a name to write in the Sligachan Hotel's fishing book to disguise the fact he was a local and avoid rubbing tourists' noses in the peat with his prodigious catch record. Evidently, the name stuck so well that many knew him simply as 'Morton' in later life, with Murdo being known as 'Myles' for presumably similar reasons.

MacKenzie remains the most famous of the Skye climbers. Through his long life he would become 'the only guide of Swiss quality Britain had ever produced', according to the obituary written by the man with whom he is always associated: an eccentric and brilliant English scientist and mountaineer named John Collie – known to all by his middle name, Norman. Collie had come to Skye in his twenties to fish, spied some climbers high on Sgùrr nan Gillean and was instantly – if you'll pardon the term – hooked. Having never so much as felt a climbing rope in his hands, he enlisted the help of a knowledgeable ghillie at the Sligachan Hotel – John MacKenzie. And so, the legend goes, began a friendship and climbing partnership that would last half a century.

Much has been written about Collie and MacKenzie and their contribution to the story of mountaineering in the Cuillin. It's wholly deserved. But despite what you're led to believe, their partnership isn't the whole story of Cuillin mountaineering. It's not even close.

You could be forgiven for thinking otherwise, though – and there are those who certainly see the pair as epitomising the exploration of the Cuillin. If you want to see evidence of this you need only visit Sligachan and peer into Seamas' Bar, the cavernous establishment attached to the main hotel. During the time I was visiting Skye for this book, it housed a semi-permanent installation entitled 'Heroes of the Cuillin'. This wasn't just a display but a fundraising exercise, complete with donations box, to gather funds for lifesize bronze statues of Collie and MacKenzie. These would be sited on a prominent knoll just to the east of the hotel, where the two of them would gaze down Glen Sligachan towards Sgùrr nan Gillean. Accompanying the display was a miniature of the sculptures, designed by local artist Steve Tinney, with the pair standing on the back wall of the room like a couple of fancy, watchful gnomes. This was evidently an advanced and long-standing appeal: by the time this book is published, it's quite possible the bronzes will be there, feeling the rain, in Glen Sligachan.

Now I want to say right here that anything that celebrates the heritage of this place gets my vote. The two figures will certainly be a striking addition to the landscape around Sligachan and will inspire people to learn about the characters depicted, and the mountains. And however unnecessary a statue is to engender this amidst such natural grandeur, jolly good show.

But something about them rang awkwardly with me. Collie is standing behind, dashing and stately, pipe in hand. MacKenzie is diminutive, sitting stoutly, beard-jutted, legs dangling off the sculpture's prow, like a kind of wily leprechaun. The work wasn't *overtly* hierarchical, though it sort of felt it. It might well have been faithful to the last hair (the statues had received the blessing of both Collie and MacKenzie's few surviving relations), but for some reason I just didn't connect with it. Maybe it was that the bronze needed to make the life-sized sculptures was going to cost around £120,000 – which is a lot, considering the relative cost of, say, mountain rescue equipment or a community centre. Maybe it was that word 'Heroes', which you might more rightly apply to an aid worker, paramedic or some altruistically courageous figure. Or maybe it was simply because I hadn't gotten to know its subjects well enough yet to know if they'd have approved. These famous explorers of the Cuillin: heroes, even. A visionary English chemist, and the first and greatest mountain guide in Scotland, said the legend. But was the legend true?

The problem was this word 'first'. MacKenzie was a fine guide, quite possibly the perfect exponent of the craft – but he wasn't the first. And any suggestion that he was, and that the story starts with him, erases a very important part of the history of the Cuillin. But we'll get to that. First of all, I had the small matter of finding the person who would unlock the Cuillin for *me*. Like Collie, who arrived on Skye clueless but enthralled in 1886, I needed a MacKenzie of my own.

There's no doubt that the Cuillin ridge presents a different order of severity to anything on the British mainland. The mountaineer Frank Smythe, when qualifying his description of the Cuillin as Britain's only 'genuine' mountain range, wrote 'genuine in the sense that, unlike other British hills, they cannot be walked up but must be climbed.' Sure, there are harder climbs and short sections on mountains that demand similar levels of skill and nerve – but these are in brief, isolated chunks generally on walls and spurs, or buttresses exploited purely for their sport. The Cuillin ridge presents the unique challenge of a mountain range whose entire crest is almost completely off limits to the casual walker or 'daunderer' – an appealing old Scots term – to anyone who can't deal with incredibly complex, threatening terrain and sheer, sustained 'exposure' (constant and terrifying drops to you and me), who is unable to judge the weather or doesn't know their way around a rope.

And this isn't just for rock climbing or traversing between the peaks; this is simply to get to their *summits*. Actually tackling the whole thing involves another level of difficulty and commitment altogether, requiring luck with the weather, speed, stamina, and a degree of mountain fitness and steadiness that can stomach almost constant danger for the entire length – which, if everything goes well, will take the average mountaineer who doesn't like to rush two days with an overnight bivouac on the ridge.

Notice the use of the word 'mountaineer' here: this is not walking. This is walking, and scrambling, and a fair bit of climbing and abseiling – with the associated technical demands of ropes and harnesses and karabiners and knots and all the rest. These things take time to do safely. And time is something anyone traversing the Cuillin ridge is seriously short of. You're also likely to be short of water, so you'll need to carry that. And if you're spending the night up there, you'll be carrying everything else too, unless you have the foresight to stash it up there first. Some forfeit the night out, opting instead for nimble speed, and might manage it in a fiercely long day of sixteen hours or more. And that's if they don't get swallowed by mist, lost, run out of daylight or energy, or food, or nerve. Most don't make it at all. Only about a third of those who set off on the traverse succeed.

So that's how hard the Cuillin ridge is. But to the matter of exactly how *hard* the Cuillin ridge is. What you have to remember when reading, say, excerpts from the *Scottish Mountaineering Club Journal* or the *Alpine Journal* from the late 19th century is that – unlike much of the mountain literature of the day, which were personal takes on locations already known – most of the early accounts of the Cuillin were of the *first ever* explorations of some of these peaks. When climbers did cotton on to Skye, it became very fashionable, very quickly – giving the Cuillin the interesting merit of being simultaneously the least explored, most dangerous and most popular mountain range in the British Isles.

It is generally accepted that none of the dicier Cuillin summits – with the arguable exception of one – were climbed before Victorian times, with the last not yielding until the 20th century. This means that many of the highest summits in the Alps had been reached by the time the Cuillin ridge was being explored in earnest. This could be because the first travellers' descriptions that filtered back from Skye had one common motif repeated again and again – they were considered impossible to climb.

The first explicit articulation of this came, inevitably, from the pen of the geologist John MacCulloch, following his explorations of Skye. He wrote that 'the upper peaks are mere rocks, and with acclivities so steep and smooth as to render all access as impossible.' But as so snipingly pointed out by James Forbes, MacCulloch generally preferred to explore mountains with his eyes, and considered any ascent that could not be made on horse-back an inconvenience of the very highest degree, so he was perhaps not the best judge.

Forbes, of course, showed such thinking to be false. After his ascent of Sgùrr nan Gillean in 1836, mountaineers began to earnestly prowl the Cuillin and the tables rather dramatically turned, with the most common comment in later decades being the *ease* by which difficult positions could be obtained, given the remarkable friction of the gabbro. The more intrepid of the early travellers on the peaks couldn't believe their luck to find such an alluring range of mountains possessing rock whose adhesive properties some climbers said enabled them to defy the principles of gravity. As Forbes would note, this was a place that seemed *designed* for climbing.

The enthusiasm with which this was publicised was perhaps a little premature – there are plenty of crumbly bits in the Cuillin, and several of the highest summits are composed of the altogether rather sketchier basalt – but there were plenty eager to test the theory. But its legendary adhesive-ness aside, the traverse of the Cuillin – hell, anything on the Cuillin – still represents an intimidating objective. So even for experienced mountain folk, the first question worth asking is whether they have the right stuff to attempt the ridge at all.

W. A. Poucher, writing in 1949, offers a marvellously logical definition of the required ability as 'anyone who has been roaming the mountains for years ... who has learned to distinguish between the possible and impos-sible according to his powers'. But even Poucher, who by this time was well known for his own impressively limpet-like powers in the mountains, concedes that with the Cuillin you cannot simply leave cautionary advice at that.

'Beset with perils are the serried ranks of mountains comprising the Coolins,' wrote Alasdair Alpin MacGregor in *Over the Sea to Skye*. MacGregor certainly appeared to consider the Cuillin hazardous, albeit in that rather genteel sort of way that does make you wonder how high his yardstick for hardship stood. A brief cautionary sermon suggests that 'even those familiar with these mountains should observe certain maxims . . . after a good drenching, the next easiest thing to get in the Coolins is a sprained ankle or a dislocated thigh'. He continues: 'Into the heart of the Coolins no one should venture without a haversack containing food: you never know how many hours you might be delayed waiting for the mists to clear,' before adding the lax instruction that 'no one need carry water to the Coolins, for even in the hottest summer, its burns are never dry.' He doesn't make any reference to the location of these burns, which in itself is telling as in the high Cuillin there are few, but he does give a useful warning to the traveller who takes the isolation of the Cuillin lightly: 'A needle in a haystack and a human being lost in the Coolins are in very much the same position.'

Being lost seems a preoccupation of MacGregor's when he speaks of the Cuillin, for he was not a mountaineer, merely a 'hill-wanderer', and clearly one in possession of a decent sense of gallows humour:

> If you feel you must collapse, it is a mistake to do so until you have arrived at the side of a track or footpath, where, if you are lucky, you may be discovered eventually in a state of semi-decomposition. Better to be found dead by the side of a track in the Coolins than not found at all!

I sensed shades here of Captain Maryon. Perhaps the most uncompromising rundown of the hazards presented to the walker by the Cuillin comes from Malcolm Slesser, who, by the time he updated the Scottish Mountaineering Club guide *The Island of Skye* in 1975, he knew of enough people who had come thoroughly unstuck on or around the ridge for trends of misadventure to emerge. Under the heading 'Some common causes for difficulty', his list makes for sobering reading:

Failure to judge the length of time required for expedition; unduly slow or incompetent companion. Illness: sprained ankle. Unexpectedly difficult ground. Mist: darkness: snowstorm: loss of way. High wind (especially on ridges). Extreme cold: frostbite. Members of the party becoming separated. Deep soft snow. Deep hard snow. Avalanches, walking over cornices. Ice glazed rocks or paths. Sudden spates, rendering burns uncrossable or only safely crossable with a rope. The compass is extremely unreliable in the Cuillin owning to the magnetic nature of the rock ... violent and variable readings, foot by foot.

Seton Gordon, a much-loved natural historian who made his home on Skye, was a frequent and intrepid explorer of the Cuillin. He was rather more equivocal in his assessment of the hazards: 'Mist is the danger on the Cuillin, [it] curtaindrops within five minutes, and in mist it is easy to lose one's way and find oneself on the brink of one of the many precipices,' though he also adds that the mountains should be avoided in strong winds as 'their ridges are so narrow.'

This speed of meteorological change was another thing that marked the Cuillin out as unique. You did things in a different way here. And another of these differences was that you didn't tackle the Cuillin ridge without a guide.

Finding the right mountain guide is hugely important, for reasons that go far beyond the merely functional. The relationship between a guide and their charge is deceptively complex from both points of view. First off, there's the issue of trust. You both begin as strangers, then you place your life in their hands in the most literal sense. Meanwhile, your guide is tasked with keeping you safe in an environment that is potentially anything but – regardless of the fact that you might be a complete liability and entirely capable of endangering them, too.

Then there's the issue of spending time with this person in one of the more intense places to get to know someone else: the mountains. In the mountains you walk together, eat together, talk, sleep, brave bad weather, enjoy good weather, make decisions and get exhausted together – in short, you're in at the deep end alongside whoever you're up there with. This often crafts a dynamic that *only* works in the mountains, as that's the one thing you have in common. I have a friend I only see for mountain trips, and even up there we barely talk beyond discussing the essentials. But it's a dynamic we both enjoy. No effort, no pressure, no forced conversation, no awkwardness, no filling of silence with inane chit-chat. Just the simplicity of escape from every other thing, into the fucking mountains. It's brilliant.

Conversely, if the person you're with turns out to be disagreeable, it doesn't for one second escape your attention. And again, this works both ways, for guide and client.

But guiding isn't just about safety and competence. I have a friend whom I'll call Rob, seeing as that's his name. He's incredibly qualified and redoubtably trustworthy, and every year he makes a pilgrimage to Skye with the express reason of crossing the ridge, most of the time with a brace of very lucky clients in tow. If I just wanted someone to take me across it and keep me alive, he would be the choice. But here was the thing: he wasn't a local. He lived and worked in North Wales and went to Skye as a visitor, albeit a seasoned one. This wasn't his backyard, the place where he was immersed day in, day out in all seasons. And for reasons I couldn't really articulate, I wanted someone who was.

The guiding culture in the Cuillin is interesting, not least because in Britain, it is really the only one. You'll often hear the ridge compared to the Alps, or described as 'alpine' – which is often put down to their rocky, arête-heavy topography, and the rather more cautious manner in which they need to be approached. There are really only two or maybe three routes on the mainland which might warrant the term: the formidable Tower Ridge on Ben Nevis being the only obvious one of comparable screech, despite being far shorter and rather more linear in nature. There's this, some bits and pieces in the north-west Highlands and Glen Coe, and a few shorter raggedy outings in North Wales and the Lake District that might for a brief moment or two adopt the smell or recruit the skills of a route you might describe as being alpine. That is to say, the sort of airy place where the boundary between hillwalking and climbing has been elevated into the middle ground of mountaineering. But compared with the long, complex branches of the Cuillin, these are mere splinters. The fact is that once into its most characteristic ground, the black ridge of Skye is closer to the Alps in feel than it is to its own country.

Also, traversing the Cuillin ridge leans far more onto alpine philosophies than elsewhere. Once you're up onto the ridge crest, the object is to stay up on it and remain as faithful to its course as you can, surmounting impediments as they present themselves. The reason for doing this is sporting rather than logical – you run a hurdle race *for* the hurdles, otherwise you would just run around them – but with rather greater consequences should you misjudge it.

In contrast to the Alps, on the Cuillin ridge there are several points where you can escape to the safety of the valley – which is why 'motivation' is often cited as key to success. But it would be wrong to say that the ease to quit is the reason the Cuillin ridge traverse is one of the most failed-on routes in the world. And after all, something has to *make* you quit.

The most fragile truces between success and failure rely on what you could call the three Ws: weight, water and weather. The *weight* you carry, and the effect it has on your manoeuvrability, centre of gravity, speed and stamina could make the difference. *Water* is a perennial problem, being hard to come by without a costly diversion, heavy to carry in useful quantities and critical for motivation: thirst is a powerful lure back down to the valley, and dehydration the enemy of sound judgement. And yet if there is too much water, in the form of rain, snow, ice or cloud, which with wind collect into W number three, *weather*, it can scupper you just as comprehensively. So success rests on a collision of environmental good fortune, physical strength, mental commitment, stripped-back preparedness and organisation. Then there is the silent fourth W: *will*. Anything compromising the first three weakens the last.

And so as an objective, the Cuillin ridge presents an anomaly to the walker. In the church of what you might call the mountain faith, hillwalking and the act of tackling an alpine route occupy quite different pews. Hand a coiled rope to most British hillwalkers and, given its redundancy for reaching the top of almost all of our mountains, they'll look at it as if it's about to rear up and bite them in the neck.

As a result, Skye's mountain guides are different to their colleagues on the mainland. And this is not some contrivance to enrich the local economy or a tribute to the tradition of keeping naïve tourists alive on Skye, although both are happy benefits. Elsewhere in Britain you can hire someone to take you out for a day in the hills, but there is no other place where, unless you're particularly seasoned, your safety is most definitely at stake if you don't.

Nor would it do to simply acquire a guide from Chamonix or Zermatt and invite them onto the Cuillin ridge and expect them to be inherently conversant with the challenge. The Alps, despite their complications of avalanche, glacier travel and altitude that all gnaw at the brain, don't enjoy the wonderful and swift unpredictability of a North Atlantic coastal climate or a cold that's wet rather than dry. Sudden mists, gales that blow in from nowhere, rainstorms that turn into hail in the middle of summer, and the ever-present possibility that you're in a quite different place to where you think you are make this mountain range uniquely testing to guide. Not harder necessarily, nor even objectively more dangerous – just a bit more, well, *disobedient*.

It's for this reason that many guides who operate in these hills eschew the generic term 'mountain guide' and its associated trappings, favouring instead the more specific 'Cuillin guide'. They're being neither self-effacing nor snobby. They're simply identifying their special knack when it comes to managing the quirks and ticks of this particular creature. It's like being invited to take a tour of a cage filled with angry big cats with either a 'mammal wrangler' or a 'lion whisperer'. I know which I'd choose.

When John MacKenzie was described by Norman Collie as the 'only guide of Swiss calibre Britain has ever produced', he didn't mean that he was especially well made, punctual or habitually neutral in times of war. Guides in the Swiss mountains were hunters and shepherds, hard men who relied on the mountains for their income and therefore knew the way they behaved, and the idiosyncrasies of their moods and terrain, confident that where the animals went, people could too. Mountaineers recruited them because they brought a redoubtable local angle to the table.

And so it was with the early guides on Skye; they were shepherds. In leading stalking and fishing parties, they were required to know the terrain of their patch intimately. They weren't hired for their deft ropework or knowledge of an Italian hitch; they were hired for their instinct on terrain they knew like the lines on their face. Mountaineers brought the technical proficiency and the ambition; guides brought the tenacity and the instinct. And together, across the world and through the ages, this dynamic endured:

a mutually beneficial partnership that reached its zenith on a mountain summit, and its success when safely back home.

The unfortunate thing in my own instance was I *didn't* have the technical proficiency or the knowledge of an Italian hitch. All I was bringing to this particular party was desire, and a good deal of apprehension. But these days, thankfully, Cuillin guides are, like most mountain guides, rather more well-rounded in all levels of mountaineering skill. They are climbers, because they have to be. And so for these reasons amongst many others, even experienced hillwalkers should hire a Cuillin guide. It will make the endeavour much more rewarding, and dramatically increases your chances of accomplishing it – and surviving it.

Doing the ridge traverse without a guide never even occurred to me; in truth, I was rather looking forward to it, if only to recreate the dynamic I'd been reading so much about. I knew that guiding had modernised since the time of most of my books and century-old papers. And yet I couldn't shake the image, which had arisen completely without my consent and was rooted in some romantic corner of my brain, of my guide being some ghillie from a local farm with a mile-high stare and a stoic, unshakeable manner. They would have a beard, and so therefore would probably be a man. They would have a name like Angus or Mac or Hamish, say 'wee' a lot, carry whisky, and know the ridge so well they didn't need a map. And of course – though I'm willing to allow that this particular detail might have been stretching things somewhat – they would wear a kilt.

Now I had to find that person. So naturally, I asked around amongst knowledgeable pals for recommendations. I received a hearty few of these, some contacts of contacts, a few half-known names, most with caveats or involving compromises. But it wasn't until I talked to my friend Andrew, who with a group of mixed experience had been guided up the Cuillin's notorious Inaccessible Pinnacle the previous summer, that I heard the kind of noises I was listening for.

'You need to hire this guy,' he said without hesitation. 'He's good.'

With that I listed my criteria, hoping to see him nod with increasing affirmation. Instead I received an expression that began blank and ended up as a frown.

'Jesus. No, none of that. You'll be asking me if he wears a kilt next.'

'Is he from Skye?'

'No, I don't think he is. But you know, a lot of people on Skye aren't from Skye.'

This wasn't going well at all. 'Is he even Scottish?'

Andrew – himself Glaswegian – frowned again. 'I'm not sure. He was pretty vague about that.'

'So why him?'

He thought about this for a minute. 'You know, on the day we did the In Pinn we were hungover as *fuck*. And he marched us up there like we were in the army. Then when we got up, all these guides were making their clients even more nervous with all these high fives and pep talks. We had none of that. He just got on with it.' He paused again, before chuckling. 'Ask him about the European Death Knot...'

'Excellent. Well, I'm glad I asked.'

'The thing is,' he continued, 'you don't really *want* any of that bonhomie stuff. That's for tourists. There was this one moment when we were having a breather high on the ridge and we'd maybe let our guard down a little. Eating and joking. And he just looks round and he sees this, and says without even thinking, "Andy – face the drop. Never turn your back on it." We talked some more – mainly me asking questions, Andrew answering patiently.

In the end he convinced me that it was at least worth a conversation, so I emailed Skye Adventure – the company Google returned when I typed the guy's name – and set up a meeting.

A week later I was back on the island, staying in Portnalong at the Taigh Ailean. I mentioned who I was meeting the next morning to Katie. Mid-swig on a glass of something she began nodding. 'Mmm.'

'You know him?'

'Mmm.' Another swig. 'He's good.'

She didn't offer a huge amount more, but she seemed quite sure. And so it was with curiosity – and a little nervousness considering that at the very least my success on the ridge, not to mention my life, would depend entirely on this person – that I walked up the stairs to the Café Arriba in Portree to meet Matt Barratt.

Portree is agreeable, albeit in that rusty-round-the-edges sort of way common to many port towns that are still actually ports. Named 'Port Re', 'Re' as in *regis* – for the occasion when King James sailed into its harbour and declared it 'fine' – the town is Skye's de facto capital. It's nestled in the crook of a to-die-for natural inlet facing away from the Atlantic, and positioned more or less halfway up the island. It has a handsome water-front painted in chirpy pastel colours with the air of a working town, having somehow avoided becoming a total sacrificial lamb to tourism. You do find the shops where you can buy scratchy tweed cushions and post-cards and paintings, but there's also a Co-op with aisles labelled in Gaelic, a Boots where you can buy batteries and blister plasters, and at least as many pubs where you're likely to get a pint of Tennant's hurled at you as ones where you'll end up sharing a table with the kind of tourist that wears a beret and a turtleneck. I liked Portree a lot.

It was raining when I found the cafe – steamy-windowed, on the first floor of a building the colour of raw salmon overlooking the harbour – and climbed the stairs. A very tall man with deep-set eyes and wild hair stood in its doorway and looked down at me as I did. He said my first name as a question, a short pair of syllables in a soft voice. Then he held out a hand. The moment of truth.

Now, climbers – like most devotees of most physical pastimes, have in my experience a certain set of visual cues that betray their vocation. That way rugby players have shoulders that swallow their necks, swimmers are triangular and horsey people dress like time travellers. With climbers, it's the hands. Climbers almost always have hands like lobster claws – huge, strong and with nails that curve timidly in on the fingertips from years of forced attrition with cracks, sills and faces. Veins run like cables up their forearms. In the case of individuals over the age of thirty, their faces are tanned and crease-lined, particularly round the eyes, from upward, sunward squinting on the sort of ground where sunglasses would fall to their deaths. In their world, sunglasses are for posers anyway.

Sometimes they walk with a stoop, either spry like a teenager or stiff, as if burdened. Joints are absent-mindedly rubbed and massaged when in repose – a knee, an ankle, a shoulder – where premature wear or an old injury niggles. Little fuss is made about sartorial concerns, which lean more towards practical than pretty. Trousers hang slack and unrestrictive. Tops and caps advertise gear brands, and typically carry some form of battle scar – a modification, a tidied tear, a patch of gaffer tape or paint splash or peeling logo. Shoes are weary, with scuffs at the toe and signs of endless soakings. Everything – clothes, body, outlook, has lived – and possibly only just. The climber vibe is utilitarian and roughened, but with a seasoned swagger. Kind of a cross between a rock star and a builder.

When considering employing a guide – a professional climber, effectively – their appearance and manner are in my view just as important as any CV. I'm not sure I'd feel comfortable trusting my objective – and life – to someone who looked like they spent most of their time at a desk, acted too confident or not confident enough, or mentioned the pub too many times. Maybe this is unfairly judgemental, but hey, it's my life on the end of their rope.

And so here was Matt Barratt. And he was not quite what I expected. His hands checked out – fingers disproportionately chunky, no dodgy rings. He was wiry and unshaven, with piercing eyes and a coils of unruly hair, and could have been anything between thirty and fifty. But this guy didn't stoop. In fact, he stood so straight that at times he looked like he might fall backwards. As I followed him into the cafe, he kind of sailed around the tables like a galleon navigating icebergs. He greeted the staff with a hip-level wave, sat down, aristocratically folded one leg over the other and ordered a mug of Earl Grey, which he then sipped delicately, an appraising look on his face.

'So,' he said.

'So,' I said back. I fell on the obvious topic. 'This rain. You must watch the weather like a hawk in your job.'

He took another sip of his tea and nodded. 'Ah. And the decorators.'

'The decorators?'

'House painters. You see them loading their gear in first thing, when the weather's set. Doing jobs while they can. Good to keep an eye on.' He pointed out the window. 'On Skye you have the outdoor jobs and the indoor jobs like everywhere else. It's just that the weather influences the outdoor jobs here more than in most other places.'

'Huh,' I said. 'Never thought of it like that.'

'There you go.'

During the course of our getting-to-know-you chat, I learned a few things about Matt Barratt. His answer of, 'Oh, all over' when I asked him when he was from was eventually pinned down to Germany, where he was born. He then grew up moving around military bases until finding a career in the outdoors, training as an instructor and resolutely climbing the ranks to gain his Winter Mountaineering and Climbing Instructor. Along the way he'd been on expeditions all over the world in various capacities and worked with vulnerable youngsters experiencing the outdoors in Applecross, where he'd 'enjoyed the shift pattern – a month on, followed by three weeks off'. From there he'd spied Skye across the water, where he eventually formed a company – Skye Adventure – with his friends and fellow instructors John Smith and Sarah Sutton. He'd been on the island just shy of ten years. He said he liked it for its frontier mentality, at which point he'd grinned mysteriously. Then he said, 'In contrast to my last job, this job is great. In this job everyone *wants* to be up there.'

He was quiet, thought before he spoke, then did so in short, economical bursts – as if between held breaths – with an accent seemingly made up of spare parts. This I was beginning to recognise as the signature of long-term Skye off-comers: not Scottish, not English, not Irish – but bits of all of those, with something else thrown in too. Like Skye itself, and everyone in it.

Talk turned to the Cuillin. He described his early adventures on the ridge as 'putting the time in, getting to know it. The first couple of years there's a lot of time consulting the map, leaving people for a moment while you frantically try to work out where you are. It's really the best way.' He smiled, eyes down. 'You've got to get lost on the ridge to really get to know it.'

Matt seemed practical and knowledgeable. Steady. He delivered cautionary remarks as if he wanted to make me aware of the realities, not put me off. I didn't get the sense I was ever going to have to worry about getting a word in – but the more we spoke, the more I couldn't really imagine this guy making a mistake or panicking. He just didn't seem the panicking type, and I liked that.

'So,' he said again. 'Cuillin traverse. South to north. Over two days?'
I nodded.

'September? I would say, don't leave it too late. Shorter daylight, can get a bit windy.'

'What would be a good place to bivvy out?' I asked.

He wagged his head, as if this was a question that depended on too many factors to discuss just now. 'Depends. The way the ridge is put together means there are different aspects and shelters depending on the direction of the weather. And the weather on the northern ridge and the southern ridge can often be very different all at once.'

He asked me what sort of experience I had, and I told him. As a hillwalker I was solid. And I really was. I loved the mountains, and spent as much time in them as I could. It's just that lately, it hadn't really been much. After reeling off the highlights of my mountain life – magnifying the few truly scary things I had been hauled up with the use of ropes, naturally – I began to delicately list the things that were worrying me, to see if they worried him.

'If I'm honest, I'm a little out of shape.'

'OK.'

'And I haven't done much roped climbing recently. Not for a few years.' I paused. Matt dipped his teabag.

'And I have a slight problem with heights. Well, really bad exposure, you know? I get a little skittish.' I employed the appropriate climbing term. '*Gripped*.'

'OK.'

'But I'm guessing I'll be on a rope for 90 per cent of the time anyway.' I saw his eyes move to the table. 'Right?'

He paused, then frowned. 'Well, you know, you've got to move quite quickly over complicated terrain. It's difficult to do that with a rope on.'

'So what, like fifty–fifty?'

He wobbled his head again. 'Mmm. Maybe ten–ninety.'

'*Ninety* per cent unroped?'

'Give or take. It all depends on the client.'

I could almost hear a *thunk* as the landscape of this endeavour changed shape in my head.

'In any case, we'll see.' He sat back. 'I'll help you achieve what you want to achieve, but in the end we'll have to make judgements as we go. To increase the chances of success. You'll be in safe hands. But you know, it's important to accept that there's some danger in being up there. That there's risk.' He smiled. 'Otherwise you'll be terrified for most of the time.'

I let this sink in for a second. I was about to disagree, to tell him that didn't make sense. Then I realised it made perfect sense; of course it did.

I then asked him the question I'd been worrying about. 'Is there anything I can do to prepare myself for this?'

'Get out there. Onto scrambling ground, a climbing wall if not. Work on your movement skills.'

'And that's good preparation?'

'All helps.'

'What's the most important thing?'

'Motivation.' He smiled. 'When it comes to the full traverse, you need to really want to do it.'

'I really want to do it.' I paused, and then said again, 'I *do* really want to do it.'

A beat. 'OK, then.' Matt nodded and stood up, teetering slightly as he stretched. 'You should try the Coca-Cola cake.' He tapped the table, shook my hand, threw another low wave to the cafe staff and sailed out. I found out later that at some point, somehow, he'd paid the bill – Coca-Cola cake and all. And for many reasons, not least this, I knew I'd found my guide.

James Forbes was, as far as we know, the first outsider to climb one of the spikier Cuillin peaks. But he was there for the science, regardless of the accompanying enjoyment. The honour of being the first *tourist* to plant feet on the ridge for frivolous reasons actually pre-dates Forbes's ascent of Sgùrr nan Gillean by a year – and gives us an excellent picture of the man who would become, fairly undisputedly, the first of the Cuillin guides.

The tourist in question was a clergyman named Charles Lesingham Smith, whose account of a 'most arduous task' during a day out in the Cuillin represents the first snapshot of an individual straying up into these daunting mountains with nothing more worthy than adventure in mind. Published as a relatively slim volume – slim by the excessive standards of the day, that is – *Excursions Through the Highlands and Isles of Scotland in 1835 and 1836* is the most insightful of the many early accounts written by well-heeled lowland twits at large in the Highlands. Lesingham Smith was in many respects a greatest hits album of the typical traveller of his time: an enthusiast of the sublime, preoccupied with 'Fingalians' and frequently name-checking Ossian, he was a lecturer in mathematics at Christ's College, Cambridge, as well as a priest and sometime poet. His most enduring legacy was not to be his verse – and given that the volume that appeared later in his life featured such works as 'To the Snowdrop', 'My Mother's Sentiments' and 'Sent with a Present of Seaweed to Some Children', let's all thank God for that. Instead, it would be one quietly significant day on Skye, 5 September 1835, the day he decided to strike for Coruisk on foot in the company of a forester we've already met: Duncan MacIntyre, the ghillie who would, a year later, lead James Forbes to the summit of Sgùrr nan Gillean.

The previous day, Lesingham Smith had already tried to reach Coruisk by boat. As he later recounted, that escapade was dominated by a sort of stand-off between the traveller and his boat crew. Having been told the wind was too strong, our Cambridge scholar – clearly a better judge of Hebridean tempests than a group of Skye sailors – reassured the men that the wind equated to 'only a capful' and that they should put to sea precisely as planned. Having fortified their commitment with the promise of 'a pound and a bottle of whisky', Lesingham Smith and crew set off across Loch Scavaig towards Coruisk, the traveller quickly discovering amidst the drenching white horses and mad tossing of the 'cockleshell' boat that there *might* have been some substance in the note of caution raised back on dry land. 'Every moment the men found their task more arduous and, I suppose, more dangerous,' he gallantly allowed. 'The one who spoke a little English asked me if I wished to put back; I said, "Certainly not", for I was sure there was no real danger.'

Changing tack, the head boatman attempted to persuade his charge that the walk back from Coruisk through Glen Sligachan to the inn would be perilous in the inevitable darkness, to yet more assertions of confidence from Lesingham Smith. The boat did eventually turn back, on the insistence of the boatman that they would run ashore – and with the wind now in their sails rather than against the bow, covered the distance they had taken half an hour to gain in 'two or three minutes'. Lesingham Smith manages to emerge from this appearing magnanimous, again insisting that he 'did not think there was any danger, but only suspected the men of wishing to get more money or whisky', despite then describing what was clearly a storm blowing in soon after their arrival back at Elgol. Tossing the men a few shillings for 'their labour and fright', he turns for Sligachan. So there we have a measure of the man who, the day after, left the hotel with MacIntyre and headed down the glen – this time intending to reach Coruisk by foot.

Little is known about Duncan MacIntyre, even though he was the first real guide of any sort mentioned in the considerable literature of the Cuillin. Lesingham Smith depicts him as a man with an adventurous streak to rival his own. 'I set out with the forester who, from having employed fifteen years in preserving the red deer amongst these glens, is acquainted with every stone in them,' he wrote. Part-way down the glen the pair were beset by rain and took shelter in Harta Corrie – 'Harticory' – under a 'great stone that had fallen from the rocks above', quite possibly the fabled Bloody Stone. Here MacIntyre took the chance to tell Lesingham Smith about the Cuillin. 'Though there is seldom snow, the storms are awful ... the gusts of wind so violent as to take up large stones. [MacIntyre] has often heard one of these hurricanes coming down the hollow, and has been obliged to lie flat down until it has passed over him.' The guide then spoke of the deer and their presence on the high slopes around the glens, given their delight in 'clean ground ... ground on which no animal whatever is to be seen or scented'.

The pair proceeded, reaching a rise from which Lesingham Smith finally clapped eyes on Coruisk. MacIntyre said, 'We have been just two hours and a half in coming this journey, which takes most gentlemen at least five.' The forester mentioned a shepherd who had told him of a possible short cut over the 'rocks just above ... and that it was much shorter than to go all the way round as we came', and MacIntyre indulged Lesingham Smith in a little more flattery: 'I'll just tell you the truth, I've never been over myself, and I've never liked to propose it to anyone I've brought here; but you are a light gentleman, and if you like we'll try.'

At this point Lesingham Smith's journal begins to read like satire. 'This is a very weighty proposition,' he wrote, 'for to scale these rocks is no trifle ... we'll take our dinner first, then hold a council of war.' There follows a description of mutton ham and biscuits and a robust amount of whisky, after which Lesingham Smith said, 'If you are for the rocks, I am ready to start.'

MacIntyre points out a give in the skyline he once chased some deer up, clearly favouring their choice of route. 'We'll maybe have to "angle round" a bit, but we've a long day before us.'

With a bit of forensics on a modern map it's clear the stretch of ground the men were negotiating was almost certainly the approach to the Druim nan Ramh, the 'ridge of oars', a rough spur descending south-east from the Cuillin into the eastern glen that glides down into Glen Sligachan. The severity of the route they took is unclear from Lesingham Smith's description but it sounds tremendous, with MacIntyre suggesting at one point that 'one step may send us all the way back' and another 'where we were obliged to crawl on our hands and knees . . . [up a] cleft in the bare rock just like a chimney', as well as stretches where 'the one was obliged to push the other up; and he in turn pulled up the first.' It does certainly sound, to use the modern term, very much like scrambling – particularly when you consider Lesingham Smith's assertion that 'a single false step would have hurled us to destruction . . .' and that 'the first man might loosen some stone that might sweep down the hindmost.' However, when taken with the observations that Lesingham Smith's 'umbrella...became a sad nuisance' and that the forester's two dogs were not only present but 'constantly in the way', you do start to wonder just how dangerous this escapade was.

It should be mentioned that Lesingham Smith was hardly a casual tourist: he'd been on several excursions in the Alps and had already climbed Ben Nevis twice, amongst much else. Either the terrain was particularly taxing or he was in a dramatic mood, but regardless, the two eventually 'stepped forth proudly and joyously upon the very topmost crag!' Upon reaching their high point, they evidently enjoyed a fine view. Here we have a feel of the scene that greeted them, one of 'unparalleled sublimity and grandeur . . . a faint description, faint and feeble indeed compared with the original, which defies alike the representative power of epithet, metaphor, and language itself'. MacIntyre then told Lesingham Smith that 'nothing but a shepherd or a red deer has ever been here before us . . . take my word for that.'

According to Lesingham Smith, his guide proceeded to give an impromptu and beautifully turned account of the varieties of contemporary traveller:

> I often think in my own mind that it is very strange you noblemen should come to see these wild hills of ours, and our noblemen should go to London to ruin themselves; but you've the best of it, Sir, for you gain health and strength, and our lords lose both that and fortune, too.

Whether he actually said this or not, what we find in MacIntyre is a person well acquainted with the terrain, in tune with its nature and possessed of a field-gained practical knowledge of how to negotiate it. We also have someone observant of his charge and their capabilities, clearly keen for them to achieve a goal they believe is within their physical and mental grasp – and happy to be gently pushy with it. See how MacIntyre, in spotting the potential for an escapade outside of his usual pedestrian fare, emboldens the clearly capable Lesingham Smith to accompany him, to the gratification of both. In short, in MacIntyre we have the blueprint for a Cuillin guide of today.

What I especially like is Lesingham Smith's description of MacIntyre's attire and effects. 'He wore a sailor's jacket, and carried a stout staff in his hand; and a telescope in a leathern case swinging round his shoulders.' An idiosyncratic, vaguely piratical get-up, tailored to his personal needs: another hallmark of the modern guide.

Lesingham Smith didn't reach a summit, he didn't even attempt a summit, and if we're being pedantic he was never actually on the main Cuillin crest itself. What makes his account noteworthy is that although this might not have been the first time anyone actually went up onto the ridge for fun, Lesingham Smith's is the first description of anyone doing so.

Over a decade earlier, a team of Ordnance Survey surveyors, under the command of Colonel Thomas Colby, had been on the ridge proper – and not just a spur like Lesingham Smith, MacIntyre and his dogs. They'd been there for work, trying to climb Sgùrr nan Gillean as part of the gruelling trigonometrical survey of Scotland. They were defeated not far from the summit by the 'gendarme', a fearsome – and since collapsed – pinnacle of rock blocking progress up the west ridge at a height of around 850 metres.

Colby was a piece of work by anyone's standards, as you might expect for a man charged with the task of officially mapping Scotland's toughest terrain. When he was younger a pistol had blown his hand off, but he remained a committed field man nevertheless, and in 1819 he and his band of surveyors headed for the Cuillin.

Ian R. Mitchell, in the excellent *Scotland's Mountains Before the Mountaineers*, makes the interesting point that the surveyors had their sights on the grand prize, Sgùrr nan Gillean – and therefore anything less would be considered and recorded as a failure. If they had got as far as the 'gendarme' on the mountain's west ridge, not only were they in the thick of the Cuillin's crest, it's possible – though deeply unlikely – they had already summitted, say, Am Bàsteir and thought it merely a lesser top of the ultimate goal. If so, it would make the OS surveyors the first party to make any real progress on the Cuillin's spikier bits. But this seems improbable, as anyone competent enough to climb Am Bàsteir would have had little difficulty finding an alternative way up Sgùrr nan Gillean. Unfortunately, Colby's notebooks were destroyed in a fire in 1841, so the question appears unresolvable.

We'll certainly never know details of whether the ridge was explored by any adventurous locals in the years prior to what you might call the 'learned lowland invasion' of the early 1800s, but it's rather unlikely that it took a generation of pen-wielding, Samuel Johnson-stalking travellers to open native Skye eyes to the possibility of adventurous exploration on their own turf. The idea that *nobody* – not clansman, nor farmer, nor curious youngster egged on by a sibling or traveller looking to cross the most obvious barrier on the island – went up there just to have a look, cut a corner or spy on an enemy is almost ludicrous. Mountaintops make great lookouts, and are the perfect place from which to spot livestock, predict weather and – dare I say it – enjoy the sort of view that surely had some kind of stirring effect on the observer before such a thing became fashionable.

Sadly, particularly since the people who would have made these explorations were likely to have been either unable or disinclined to record their exploits, all we have is a history of sorts written by the often rather self-aggrandising, well-heeled off-comers, who – by corralling the locals – claimed that this discovery, or that ascent, or the spying of this view, or the probing of that valley, touched *their* eyes and feet before all others. In his writings,

John MacCulloch frequently depicted himself as brave in the eyes of his guides, as did Lesingham Smith and plenty more of their ilk. In the earliest accounts these locals were usually cast in the role of bemused sidemen, charged with the well-being of a paying guest and often, if not actually poked fun at, then described with a kind of passive, down-the-nose prejudice.

It's also quite easy to imagine these early guides deliberately downplaying their own knowledge of the terrain so as to give their guests the satisfaction of feeling intrepid and pioneering, thereby bringing them back for more – much to the benefit of their own livelihood and the local economy. Interestingly Samuel Johnson himself, in the preamble to his *Tour of the Hebrides* – whilst describing the societal discord between the Lowlanders and the Highlanders – described the latter in a richly ambiguous analogy as:

> the *mountaineers* . . . not easily conquered, because they must be entered
> by narrow ways, exposed to every power of mischief from those that
> occupy the heights . . . and have an agility in climbing and descending
> distinct from strength or courage.

He was of course using figures of speech. But these are rather uncanny, given that those he was describing were in general considered ignorant of or indifferent to the mountains. For such language to be employed in 1785 makes it almost certain the Gaels were easily conversant with their high places before the tourists came along. 'Fowling,' as Martin Martin called it, was being practised by the St Kilda hunters – and plenty of others – to snatch eggs and gannet chicks for the traditional, seasonal Hebridean food *guga* since at least 1549, when Donald Monro wrote about it. Climbing Hebridean sea cliffs was about as daring and hazardous an activity you could imagine – and like any such endeavour, engendered a certain pride and prowess amongst those who undertook it.

So in all likelihood, they climbed to the tops of their mountains too. We know that when the Cuillin satellite of Beinn na Caillich was climbed in 1772 by Thomas Pennant – hailed by many as the first ascent – the mountain already had a large cairn and a robust mythology attached to it. And when the Ordnance Survey arrived to survey the island in 1819, they found that many of the mountains – including a number on the Cuillin ridge – were already familiar enough to have acquired names. If it needed spelling out any clearer that the mountain people of old had at least a fleeting acquaintance with their hills, take the old Gaelic proverb *anail a' Ghaidheil am mullach:* 'The Gael's rest [is] the summit.'

Then there was the old shepherd's saying, *Air a' chreig* – 'On the rock'. Sheep got stranded *air a' chreig*, and in such cases there were certain people who would go for it. Who were those people? Along with the guga fowlers, were these shepherds Scotland's first mountaineers, the shepherds who would later become guides? When it comes to the Cuillin, we will probably never know for sure. What we do know is the name of the man who was so excited about his day in the mountains to write it down: Lesingham Smith, with MacIntyre the first facilitator. And all this over twenty years before John MacKenzie was even born.

Lesingham Smith would continue his tour of Scotland, Ossian in his eyes and umbrella in his hand. MacIntyre, of course, would cement his status as Skye's first guide by leading James Forbes to the summit of Sgùrr nan Gillean a year later. And a decade after that, Forbes drew his map of the Cuillin.

Truly, maps are fascinating things. They are a window onto how someone sees a place. They translate the most strongly perceived elements into order and form in a way that is at once informative and deeply personal. No two maps are alike – and in the days before satellites and aerial photos, were purely down to observations and interpretation from the ground. If you ever have a spare afternoon, try to make one – even of a familiar area. It's an insightful exercise, and if nothing else will remind you that without your gadgets you're forced to consider your surroundings on a whole new, rather more challenging level.

The first maps that were produced depicting the Cuillin ridge were duly absorbing. The most striking of all of these – indeed, the most striking still – was an early admiralty map entitled *A general chart of the west coast and Western Islands of Scotland,* produced in 1755 by one Murdoch Mackenzie. As indicated by the title, the map shows the entire sweep of Scotland and the Hebrides, from the tip of Kintyre to the northern limit of Lewis with pretty commendable accuracy. Skye sits almost in the middle – and central in that, in the correct position, is a weird, incongruous black area of artistic shading. It looks like a raven's wing.

This rendering of both the Cuillin's position and, weirdly, its character is extraordinarily unsubtle, made all the more notable by the fact that there are no other significant mountains marked on the map, indeed hardly any other details of any kind. The motive for this is unclear – either the ridge served some sort of critical navigational function or the sight of the ridge made enough of an impression on the cartographer for him to ignore the mountains of Rum, of Lewis and Harris, Arran, Mull, and the entire west coast of Scotland, but render the Cuillin not only singularly, but scarily.

The first Ordnance Survey map of the ridge in 1882 was heavily criticised by mountaineers; whilst impressive to look at, it contained several fairly major errors. The inaccuracies weren't *that* bad and fairly forgivable given that not all of the peaks had been named and some still hadn't been climbed by the time the first six-inch sheet was published. Considering the general uselessness of the mountains for anything agricultural or military, the labour required for keeping a few climbers adequately located was hardly justification for life-threatening effort on the part of the surveyors. Against this backdrop, it's respectable that they tried at all.

These errors from the normally infallible Ordnance Survey were a bit unfortunate, though – and not just for reasons of navigational fidelity. As Seton Gordon writes in *The Charm of Skye* (1929), a great and wild pass between Sgùrr na Banachdaich and Sgùrr Dearg had 'long been known as An Dorus Mòr – in English, the Great Door'. It's an apt name for this most logical crossing point between Glen Brittle and Coruisk. He then states how curious it was that An Dorus Mòr had been positioned wrongly on the maps of the time, where it appears much further north as the pass between Sgùrr a' Ghreadaidh and Sgùrr a' Mhadaidh, where there was a fine but rather smaller and less accessible weakness in the ridge crest. He then adds sadly: 'It is only right that the error should be mentioned before the true position has been forgotten.' Despite Gordon's efforts, his plea was in vain – it *was* forgotten, and An Dorus Mòr remains misplaced to this day, its old location rechristened as the rather less romantic Bealach Coire na Banachdich.

The irony is that, up on the ridge crest, a map may not even do you all that much good. Look at it on a map and the Cuillin is bewildering. Perhaps attempting to atone for its first sheet, the Ordnance Survey's current interpretation of the ridge undermines itself with the detail of what it's trying to convey. It's frantic as a result, a messy stamp of merging contours, the chaotic black scrawl of crag upon crag, ridges swirling like the arms of galaxies and banners of Gaelic in every conceivable orientation, making it quite impossible to tell crest from dip, summit from buttress, main ridge from perilous offshoot. You have to admire the dedication of the cartographers – but the result of their labour is a fitting reflection of the chaos of the ridge itself.

Charles Pilkington, who in Sgúrr Thearlaich, would have one of the Cuillin's peaks named after him, rather unkindly described the earlier map of the ridge as harbouring the most 'magnificent and complicated system of mistakes … unequalled in the British Isles'. It's therefore inevitable that the mountaineers would end up making their own maps of the ridge, all based upon James Forbes's map of the Cuillin.

The 'eye sketch', as Forbes called it with that modesty of scientists, is wonderfully expressive and commendably accurate. He has got the correct shape of the ridge, and notes everywhere the signs of the geological phenomena he was investigating, with the 'conspicuous glacier markings' inscribed like fingerprints at the head of several corries. Forbes's map was a labour of time and patience, in which he was assisted by Louis Albert Necker – a 'foreign member' of the Royal Society of Edinburgh and the inventor of the famous Necker cube illusion – who provided a barometer and readings from Portree to help guesstimate the heights of the island's summits.

Look at Forbes's map and you immediately gather a sense of the relative dimensions of the ridge and its most significant features. What you can also appreciate is its mad, oddly organic, form. Depicted from above, its main crest is a fractured C-shape, the two sides joined like rough sutures, its many offshoots splayed from the crest in a weird marriage of symmetry and chaos, like a broken cobweb. Mountain ranges don't usually look like this. Later maps, such as that of J. Hubert Walker in 1948, give the ridge almost animal features, the ridgelines augmented with plate-like scales, like a crocodile's spine. Look at it for long enough and you start to lose your sense of the ridge. It ceases to be the image it projects from afar of being something you just totter along from one end to the other, and starts to assert itself as it really is: a kilometre-high puzzle. The Cuillin is part obstacle course, part labyrinth – a labyrinth that instead of walls has drops. And it was into this that I would soon, finally, be going.

PART TWO

TRAVERSE

We move in space,
at once aware
of solid rock
and empty air.
'On a Mountain Ridge', D. J. F., 1984

7

Gap

I
Tryfan, North Wales
Summer

The gap is small. You could step it without a thought, were it not for the worry of somehow tumbling messily into this small chasm and banging your head, breaking your back or dislocating your arm. It would hurt. Hurt a lot. Then, oh, there's the awful drop to the right. The long and awful drop. Spy a car on the road down there – slow from here, like a jet plane seen from the ground – and resist the spin that starts to take your head, resist the need to crouch, grasp your boots and breathe quickly. And then someone says, 'Jump'.

Hesitation. Doubt. Clenching fear. And yet the gap is small. There is *no reason* this should be hard. This is entirely psychological – rooted in the very basic impulse of the brain to recognise danger and alarm the body – ironically, the very thing likely to cause a damagingly jerky wobble or a hesitant step.

A voice from below. 'Mate, you don't have to.'

'I want to.' This should be easy. 'There isn't any reason why not.'

A pause from below. Then: 'There really isn't any reason why, either.'

I'm standing on an irregular six-foot pillar of rock, about the size of a coffee table. It's polished like one too: the edges look like they've been bevelled, and the whole thing has a nasty tilt that makes it feel just a little too precarious. Facing it across a three-foot gap is another pillar: smaller, thinner, leaning a little more drunkenly. The pair are called Adam and Eve, and make up the very top of the mountain called Tryfan. Both stand on a precipice. From my perch, it looks like I would fall straight off it if I slipped. An absolute certainty of death. And for what? To say I've done this jump. This jump that people like to do, because they can. Because it's there. Just another variation on climbing the mountain, beating the clock, facing the foe. To become, in the strident words of mountaineer Lionel Terray, a conquistador of the useless.

I was in Snowdonia, making what I felt was the best preparation for what lay ahead, just weeks away now, on Skye. Snowdonia's ridges are sharp and mean, a quality that, while not exactly a facsimile of the Cuillin, was at least useful for deadening nerves, hardening stamina, and building that shy and fickle ally to the scrambler: confidence.

The voice at the base of the pillar belonged to Jim Provost, my old mountain pal, whom I'd joined in North Wales to climb this 3,000-foot mountain, one which had been on his personal bucket list for some time. The six of you who bought my first book might remember Jim, an ex-RAF jet pilot who'd seen the British mountains from a rather more fast-paced seat than most of us will ever enjoy, and was now exploring them at a sedate fashion more befitting – as I liked to remind him – his advancing age.

Jim's fascination with Tryfan is not unusual for those who happen to catch it in their view at any point, as there's no more arresting mountain in Wales and England. Its sides ripple in and out, like the ribs of the starving; its ridges run crenellated and steep, its form is triangular, brutal, scaly, prehistoric. Unlike many British mountains, Tryfan is steep from every angle, and in sharp discord amongst its rather less ballistic neighbours – and all the better for it.

It's a hypnotic siren call, more so when you discover the peak is not as difficult as it appears. It's less terror-fest than engaging clamber, more like a compliant climbing frame than an impregnable mountain. It's huge fun, and engenders a feeling of can-do confidence on its blades of slate not unlike what I'd heard about the Cuillin ridge's Velcro-like gabbro. When you think you can do something, you'll be surprised by how much you can do.

Jim had expressed his urge to climb Tryfan pretty much every time our conversation turned to mountains, which was whenever we talked. He'd found himself at the foot of it several times and had thought better of going up – at which point he'd send me a text message informing me that he had 'almost climbed Tryfan again.' I was glad we'd climbed it together. But now we were up here, watching the cloud drift on and off the summit, there was the matter of that final, pointless step. The twin pillars of Adam and Eve, visible even from the road, perched atop Tryfan's silhouette like a rifle sight. That final step, or leap, of faith. Making it is said to grant you the 'freedom of Tryfan', whatever that means. Perhaps, I thought, the freedom never to have to do it again.

I'd waited for a moment when the summit was quiet – itself an achievement in this part of North Wales – then took hold of the larger pillar by a ledge halfway up the corner and hoisted myself clumsily up, all hard rock on knees and elbows. Jim stood at the bottom, arms folded, squinting up. I stood gingerly to my full height, feeling the sense of exposure around me gather and the nerves in my legs start to buzz. Suddenly every breath of wind, every movement of my body, seemed exaggerated and potentially unbalancing. Even Jim's voice made me jump a little.

'All right?'

'Just gathering myself. Make sure you take a picture.'

He moved to the place where everyone takes the shot, the one where the space between the pillars appears the widest. I looked ahead to the other pillar. Landing was the thing. What if it was more tilted than it looked? What if it was slippy from the polish of countless boots landing on the same six-inch square? What if all these thoughts reasserted themselves just as I stepped, and I hesitated and stumbled? There was no reason why this should be hard. Just like playing on tree trunks in the park with my daughter. My son. My wife. And this pointless, dangerous leap.

'You don't have to,' Jim said again.

I stepped. It was a jumpy step, not a leap. I didn't like the feel of the other pillar's pitch, but it was grippy and its top slightly sunken, and held my boot. I didn't look at the drop on the other side; I just breathed out, and looked down at Jim. Thumbs up.

My heart was thundering. I felt relief, elation, the tingle of thrill.

And then, small, but there – the smallest tincture of confidence amongst the adrenaline. I turned, and jumped back.

I've seen pictures of braver or stupider people than me doing the jump between Adam and Eve with every shade of visual confidence. That was the funny thing: the pictures of people leaping Adam and Eve were always identical in composition and viewpoint. The only thing different was the body language of the person making the leap – the betrayal of awkwardness, of fear, of reflexive fright. Or conversely, the look of someone completely at ease with something inherently life-threatening, or their own ability to ignore their surroundings and just focus on the surmountable yet sensational obstacle at hand. There's something interesting in that. It's the difference between people for whom a traverse of the Cuillin ridge, say, is a challenge that is purely physical, and people like me, who have a whole other battle to fight.

Jim – for all his many splendid qualities – is not a man I would turn to for empathy. Or sympathy. Or, necessarily, tact. In many respects this is what makes him the perfect companion: no humouring, no posturing, no bullshit. Qualities like that are excellent safety features in the mountains. I'd challenged Jim to do the leap after me, but he shook his head, without the slightest question. 'Nothing to prove,' he said. I considered arguing, but there was no point with Jim.

'So, the Cuillin.' He left this hanging in the air, a crease in his face.

'You don't fancy it?'

He shook his head, frown lines deepening like tightening wires. By the time he started to talk, his expression looked truly haunted. 'Why? Seems a bit daft.'

I shrugged. 'Same reason we're up here, I suppose. You get it.'

'To a point.' Jim started to shake his head again. 'But you're scared of heights.'

'I'm not scared of heights.' I emphasised the point: 'I'm not *scared* of heights. I just need to get used to them. It can take a while. That's perfectly normal.'

'Taken you a good long while.'

'It's normal,' I said again.

He shrugged, dropping the subject. 'Well. Rather you than me. One thing, though, if you're going to do this. Can I have your trousers?'

'My what?'

'When they find you, can I have your trousers?' His eyes were on my legwear, appraising it like chops at a butcher's. Jim was always in the butcher's. 'I had a pair like that, and I've just worn them out. Use them for gardening now.' He frowned again. 'Though I suppose it depends what state they're in.'

'Well, I'll leave instructions in the pocket, shall I? If salvageable for gardening, send to Jim.'

He shrugged again. 'No sense in waste.'

That was another thing about Jim. I was never really sure when he was joking.

Gallows humour is a defence strategy for people who play rough with mountains. Through my time as a journalist for an outdoor magazine I'd met pretty much everyone who was anyone in the world of occupational mountaineering. All of them had begun their high-climbing careers just like younger versions of Jim and me, teaming up with like-minded mates, and heading off to kill ever more dangerous sharks, so to speak. Sooner or later most had witnessed terrible things happen to people close to them. But they still carried on – it was what they did. As a result, most of these characters, and characters they almost always are, had to develop a view of the world that was calibrated rather differently in order to survive.

Certain stories over the years stuck with me. There was the mountaineer who described a delicate conversation with his wife, the mother of his three children, about his decision to join a pal on an expedition to the notoriously dangerous Annapurna in Nepal, a mountain with a 30 per cent chance of death on a summit attempt. Not a chance of failure, you understand: chance of *death*. The conversation had, rather predictably, turned into an argument. The following day he received news that his prospective climbing partner had been killed on another mountain. 'I remember thinking, you *bastard*,' he told me. 'Why couldn't you have died a day earlier? It would have saved me that argument.'

Another story from this world came courtesy of a Highland mountain rescue team that was based in an old church. One particular call-out concerned a casualty who, suffering exhaustion and mild exposure, fell asleep during a rescue and was brought in to the base to rest under the eyes of the team. Naturally the rescuers – spotting a potential jape – positioned the slumbering casualty beneath the opulent stained-glass window still in situ in the church. Due to uncontrollable giggles amongst the protagonists I never did hear the story of the casualty's reaction when they opened their eyes to what was, to all appearances, their funeral.

In amongst the real danger – particularly in the Russian roulette stakes of high-altitude mountaineering – you can perhaps forgive the development of a slightly dark sense of humour. You probably find it in the ranks of every edgy occupation, from soldiers to pathologists – but it's curious when you find it in a hobby. In many ways it's a good thing: a sign you are aware of the risks inherent in what you're doing and comfortable enough about them to joke. Resign yourself to the risk, and at least you can focus on avoiding it. This was a concept I was beginning to grapple with as regards the Cuillin ridge. As Matt Barratt had said, 'You've got to accept there's danger in being up there. Otherwise you'll be terrified.'

As we have by now well established, the Cuillin ridge is not like other British mountain ranges. Not in form, in build, not to look at or to understand – and not to climb. It's far more cryptic. Playing heavily on my mind during the summer before my traverse attempt, and particularly the day on Tryfan, was that most basic of worries. Could I *do* this? Was I even physically – or more pressingly, mentally – equipped for the hardest, most demanding mountain expedition in the British Isles?

And this it most certainly is, without any question at all. 'To know the Cuillin is to love them,' wrote. J. Hubert Walker in *On Hills of the North*, 'and to know them fully you have to get in among them, grapple with them and feel that good rough rock under your hands and feet.' Unfortunately, the Cuillin's uniqueness was precisely what made it so difficult to prepare for: there was no real equivalent.

Trying to discover how hard the ridge was on a level I could relate to became a near-mania. Every time I went to the hills in the company of someone who had some kind of form with the Cuillin, I would request casual measures of comparison with practically every piece of terrain, interrogating them about relative steepness, difficulty and exposure. The response was generally either a hollow chuckle, a head shake or some ambiguous dismissal. So then I changed tack and started asking direct questions instead. Fairly quickly I learned not to ask rock climbers. One such exchange – several, on reflection – went broadly like this:

'You've done the Cuillin ridge, haven't you? What's it like?'

'Oh, wonderful. So easy. The gabbro is like Velcro. Even in the wet. Just glorious.'

'Really? So a walker like me could do it?'

'Oh, no. Not you.'

'Why?'

'It's just really hard. The basalt is like soap when it gets wet. Wet, slippy soap. Lethal. Just lethal.'

It soon became clear that nobody was going to be able to give me any truly practical advice, except perhaps Matt – whom by now I had booked for three days in mid-September to be my Cuillin guide for my traverse. September is the Gaelic 'month of peace', they say. I was hoping it was true. Either way, as the days began to chill, the leaves turned gold and the date I'd circled on the calendar came ever closer, like the climax of some strange pregnancy – I stopped asking questions. Either way, I was about to find out precisely what the Cuillin ridge was like.

II
Elgol, Skye
Autumn

The weather was electric. Gulls hung on the wind, and amongst the nautical paraphernalia of Elgol's tiny harbour, every flag and strap strained on its rail beneath a sky chaotic with cloud. I stood at the end of the slipway, adjusting to the weight of a rucksack into which I had packed my life for the following two days. Ahead, over the water, the Cuillin ridge was four seasons in one view: a maelstrom of sunlit edges, deep shadow, the softening glow of rain and the brilliant arc of a rainbow beyond steely waters speckled with white chop.

Elgol's sight of the Cuillin is famous. Its rocky beach and cheerful jetty are a pilgrimage point for landscape photographers, brought to this distant and wild place to capture the same view as generations of landscape photographers before them – and for whom Elgol is quite intrepid enough.

It's a special place, though, and it's from here – for centuries – that tourists have left the comfort of civilisation to experience the Cuillin's elemental bristle, headed for Coruisk across Loch Scavaig, easels in tow, notebooks in hand and magnificent dread on their minds.

I'd met Matt in Glen Brittle just after ten o'clock that morning. He'd emerged stiffly from his van in grey, clearly well-favoured mountain gear wearing a baseball cap and a wary half-smile.

'And how are we feeling?' he asked.

'All set, I think.'

Adopting a stern countenance for a second, Matt eyed my rucksack and ran through a questioning checklist of what was in it. Bivvy bag. Sleeping bag. Something to lie on. Warm jacket. Extra warm jacket. Head torch. Extra head torch. Hat. Gloves. Extra gloves. I'd nodded with growing hesitancy as he went down the list.

'Because it's going to be cold. Could be very cold.'

I nodded. He continued.

'Food for today, boil in the bag meal for tonight, breakfast for tomorrow, food for tomorrow?'

'Yes and yes.'

'And water. Three litres' carrying capacity? And enough water to get you through today?'

I nodded affirmatives. I'd panicked earlier over the extra water carrier, stuffing an empty two-litre Highland Spring bottle into my bag in lieu of something more rugged; I knew it was there because when I walked I heard a muffled plastic crackle from within my rucksack. Matt checked off his own list of kit – including the rope and an assortment of metal tackle strung out like a fisherman's catch – and handed me a nylon harness. As he did so, he looked sideways past me and frowned. 'Is that your helmet?'

I followed his eyes to a white dome hanging from my rucksack. 'That looks like a very old helmet,' he said. 'How old is it?'

Both of us were frowning at it now.

'Eight years? Ten?' I said. 'It's never been clonked.'

'Where's it been kept? Cupboard? Garage? Shed?'

I looked at my feet. 'Shed.'

He nodded and turned back to his van. A moment later he handed me a zippier-looking blue model.

New helmet strapped to my rucksack and rucksacks loaded, we'd left my car in the glen as a failsafe and I found myself again travelling the long road to Elgol, this time as a passenger and not minding one bit. Passing Sligachan and following the coast for Broadford, we took the turn for Elgol. Civilisation thinned, the ground opened, and we entered that gorgeous coastal landscape of lochs and inlets, the occasional roofless church, and mountains gathering around us. I'd driven this road in winter, spring and now autumn, and felt almost familiar with it. The feeling landed hard when once again a herd, indeed probably the same herd, of Highland cattle filled the road – a huge wall of hair and horns blocking the single track. Keeping my previous failure to navigate this same impasse in the spring to myself, I looked at Matt, who had slowed to a crawl, but not a stop.

'What do we do?'

'They'll take the hint.'

The van inched forward until the front half of the van was lodged in what was essentially a hairy cul-de-sac. I looked questioningly at him.

'They'll move,' he said.

And sure enough, as Matt eased the van delicately forward, one by one they dispersed passively onto the verges. As we passed I noticed a tiny Morgan sports car tucked into a layby driving the other way, the driver watching us with an expression somewhere between paralysed terror and gratitude. Matt smiled but said nothing.

It's a long drive to Elgol, but worth it simply for the novelty of starting from the sea, and the bonus of nipping a few leg miles out of the approach. But the boat was really the only option for me. It turned the approach to the Cuillin from a trudge into an adventure. This view felt like the beginning of the ridge – and a boat was the most elegant, historic and direct start to the expedition across it, right from the water itself. Centuries of fascination. And it all started with a journey into this view.

But the stately sway of a sailboat or the chug of a tourist ferry was not quite what greeted us at the end of Elgol's slipway this particular September morning. Our voyage looked to be rather more exciting, and an awful lot brisker, aboard an orange RIB driven by a young man with an expression aslosh with adrenaline. He turned the boat against the slipway and helped us in.

'You climbing?' he asked.

'Traversing,' Matt replied. 'Night up on the ridge tonight.'

'Awesome.' The RIB pilot bounced his eyebrows. 'So as it's just you, are you happy to just get over there nice and quick?' he said as we loaded on, the scratch of boots on the concrete slipway turning to the thick squeak of wet rubber underfoot. Matt nodded an affirmative as he slid into the front row of vinyl-and-chrome seats. 'I take it you've had the comprehensive safety briefing?'

Matt nodded and tapped his lifejacket. 'Pull the red toggle?'

'Pull the red toggle.' Another grin. 'Right!' His arm went down on the throttle, the engine opened to a roar and the boat surged into the waters of Loch Scavaig, pointing straight towards the Cuillin. This was it. We were on our way.

The boat sped across the loch like a stone skipped across concrete. Every time it made contact with the water a hard, vibrating concussion went through the seats, accompanied by a blast of spray and the terrific noise of wind and motor. Either side of the raised nose of the boat I could see the peaks of the Cuillin ratcheting up in height ahead. It felt like we were speeding into something's mouth.

The four-mile crossing took just a few minutes. To the right a flurry of now familiar peaks paraded past – Ben Cleat, the soaring fin of Blàbheinn, Camasunary Bay with its white farmstead, and the knuckled, cleaved mass of Sgùrr na Stri.

As we approached, the pilot slowed. The towering Gars-bheinn, the most south-easterly peak and the start of the ridge, transformed with proximity from a long, sheer slope into a looming series of platforms, terraces and slabs. Then we were underneath it, and it was just a mass of rock and shadow with no top in sight. The engine was cut and around the delicate fidget of the water an awesome, thick silence gathered. The driver, perhaps sensing it too, let the boat drift a little longer than necessary, steering its momentum between islets, into the calm inlet beneath Gars-bheinn which I later saw on the map was named Loch na Cuilce,

'Loch of the Reeds'. Part of me hoped it meant 'Loch of the Silence', as the quiet was quite uncanny and three-dimensional. After the maelstrom of the crossing, it was so peaceful I could hear my own heartbeat. It was working hard.

'I'll push the nose onto those slabs and you can climb out,' said the pilot, and with a guttural chug from beneath the boat, followed by the scratch of Kevlar and rubber on rough rock, Matt was off and I was handing him the rucksacks. We were now suddenly looking at the sea, from the land. The boat drifted out, the driver waved us off with a 'Best of luck' and a grin before easing the boat out between the barnacled islets, then opening up back out into Loch Scavaig. Silence settled again. As I watched the boat disappear I felt a gnaw of apprehension. We were now on our own in one of the most remote places in Britain, about to tackle its hardest mountain climb.

It was cool in the shadow. Cindery boulders leaned over us, single pieces of rock towering high and peering in with dark weight. Above us I saw a patch of blue sky, the sun lighting grass and rock on the slope above. Matt fiddled with his jacket and extended a walking pole, leaning back against it in repose, like a dandy on a cane, and looking out at the loch. Hardly Duncan MacIntyre's idiosyncratic attire, with his staff and his sailing jacket and his telescope, but not far off in spirit. A single stick. A baseball cap with a hood pulled over the top, low-cut, grippy-looking shoes instead of boots – all good gear, used hard. And a strange pair of bright orange gloves. Fearing for a moment they were marigolds and I'd made some sort of awful character misjudgement, I looked closer; they looked like the sort of prickled-rubber gloves someone might wear on a building site, or for gardening. I asked, and Matt looked at them thoughtfully. 'Super tough, waterproof. Good Cuillin gloves,' he said. '£2.80 a pair. No sense trashing something more expensive on this rock.' I looked at my own gloves, which were, alas, a lot more expensive. The leather palm and fancy bits on the fingers seemed suddenly frail and inadequate.

We stood in silence for a few more moments. A few splashes in the water from fish. The thin piping call of a rotund black bird strafing the surface on frantic wings. Just over there was Coruisk. Nearby, unseen, must be the famous Coruisk Memorial Hut, a little stone building adrift in a place with no roads and few paths, where climbers sleep. You find the hut mentioned in many mountain stories. Mainly mountain rescue stories.

Before I could focus too hard on this last point, Matt spoke. 'All ready?' He pointed his stick above us. 'So. Bit of a sloggy climb now to a nice, lovely, level grassy platform. Then a bit more of a sloggy climb again to the summit.' I caught enough of a smile to suggest he was underplaying the word 'bit'. But then he was off, slowly moving up the rock slabs, which were covered in grass, drainage water and a kind of black slime in shadowed corners. They were slippy. The Cuillin wasn't supposed to be slippy. Pulling my rucksack on and staggering slightly under its weight, I followed gingerly, foal-like on skittery legs, whilst adjusting to my new centre of gravity. It had been a while since I'd carried a bag this heavy. Matt half turned back to me. 'Oh, and we're at the height of slippy black slime season. So be careful.'

On we went, gathering a little height on steep grass, then a little more, then emerging into the sunshine on the lower slopes of Gars-bheinn proper. Above lay a 680-vertical-metre climb to the eastern shoulder – and the start of the Cuillin ridge. We were on our way up.

Imagine, if you will, equipping a small child with a large piece of paper and a box of crayons, and asking them to draw a mountain scene. Then beneath it, some sea. Then an island in it. A lake. An island in that. A sandy beach. A forest. Moor. Grassy hills. Spire-like peaks. This done, ask them to draw in this scene every kind of weather that comes to mind. Big, fluffy clouds. The mist of rain. Blue sky, white sky, sky the colour of coal. Bursts of brilliant sunshine. Mountains disappearing beneath drapes of mist. Choppy lines everywhere to suggest all of it scudding around on a lively engine of wind. And then, just to gild it – because children's minds are the purest window onto idealism, and bless them for that – there will somewhere unfurl the technicolour crescent of a rainbow.

I stood there, six hundred metres above the surface of Loch Scavaig on the shoulder of Gars-bheinn, and I saw this. All of it, in half a head-turn. And it was *beautiful*. I don't want to sound too gushy, but it was one of those rare scenes, the sort where you just can't quite believe the reality of the place, that it even existed, and moreover, that right now you are *standing here in it*: a confluence of landscapes and conditions tossed together in a cauldron, filled up with pure air and light, and swirled together into a glorious, Hebridean-flavoured stew.

After all this time, it had come together electrifyingly right at the moment of truth. Not only was I on the first steps of the Cuillin ridge traverse, I could *see* the Cuillin ridge, the thing I was about to walk along – two circumstances by no means mutually inclusive. But on top of that, here was everything else that made this landscape and its environment so unique, so bewitching, as if I were in something whose edge I couldn't see past. I can't explain it. It was a magnificent vindication of expectation – like meeting my hero and being really, really impressed.

From high on Gars-bheinn's shoulder, the ridge's form could be seen at close quarters. If the northern end of the ridge was all about pinnacles, the southern end was all about sweeps above black corries and nautical vistas: the crest a kind of craggy plank astride the two. That's how it looked from afar and I was pleased to see that, above, it seemed as below. Climbing in a curve ahead, the ridge sliced the scene in two. To the left, the flank of the mountain fell in an unbroken slope precipitously to the sea. There were the small isles, lined up in a trio along the horizon: Eigg an upturned rowboat, Canna distant and adrift, both flanking Rum, muscular and mountain-bristled, in shadowy anchor on a painfully bright sea. The whole was a tapestry of shadow, scaly silver and steel. Where the sun broke the cloud, it threw scalding puddles of light on its surface.

Then, the dark side of the ridge, to our right, went steeply down into the cauldron around which the Cuillin curved in a chipped rim. Gars-bheinn doesn't look directly down on Loch Coruisk; the mountain forms the spine from which a series of ridges descends towards this infamous lake, its waters caught in glimpses between them. These ridges – unnamed – are gapped by an abyssal northerly corrie, Coire a' Chruidh, the name meaning 'Corrie of the Cattle'. I recalled seeing a painting depicting cattle at the head of Loch Coruisk just beneath that corrie. I'd thought the cattle a fanciful addition. Perhaps not.

Beyond it, its entirety masked by the surrounding spurs, my first views of Coruisk's fabled waters were already confounding the hyperbolic descriptions I'd read of it. Scott's 'dread lake', this place so legendarily blackened by prose looked positively beckoning. A burst of light was catching its northern shoreline, and illuminating the island that stood in its centre, as if spot-lit. So much for it never being touched by the sun.

The mountains didn't disappoint on the ominous front, though. All around the loch the peaks of the central and northern Cuillin ridge, including the fanciful tilt of the Bàsteir Tooth and the spired Sgùrr nan Gillean, were black with shadow. But as menacing as these were – particularly as I knew they lay ahead – I couldn't wipe the smile from my face. The whole scene was awash with transient sun, the softening of showers, and then – just as we crested the shoulder of Gars-bheinn – a rainbow burst across the huge ribbed wedge of Blàbheinn.

So many things can get between you and a moment like this: schedule, distance, time, weather that doesn't cooperate, sea conditions that bar passage. Then once in a while you negotiate the hurdles, you get where you want to be against what feels like all the odds, and everything falls into place and burns an image onto your memory that you will never forget. For me, this was that moment. For that moment, everything was as perfect as I could imagine.

'Gars-bheinn,' said Matt by way of congratulations, as we arrived on the rough, broad nub of the summit – and the first of our Cuillin peaks. He said it *gar-ven*. 'Not even a Munro. Not worth the effort. Clearly.' Matt leaned on his stick and observed the view – that incredible view – with a smirk. 'It's always quiet at this end. This section of the ridge, from Gars-bheinn to Sgùrr nan Eag ... the only people you see up here are people attempting the traverse. You start to realise,' he looked about him, 'that away from the Inaccessible Pinnacle, and those who just want to bag Munros, this is a very quiet mountain range.'

Not that it matters, but Gars-bheinn is 895 metres high, according to the Ordnance Survey. It was ludicrous to think of this fine, shapely peak being ignored simply because it didn't merit the Munro list. Nothing about the situation of this peak underwhelmed. There was no ugly trig pillar, no worn paths, nothing to suggest this wasn't just a bouldery nub like any other, rather than the southern terminus of the greatest ridge traverse in the land. Just an airy position, a pleasing maritime kiss to the air and a view powerful enough to melt your brain.

The summit had a rough circle of stones, maybe four or five rows deep: a bivvy ring. We'd passed a couple more on the shoulder. Traversers making the walk-in from Glen Brittle often sleep here, gathering height and hunkering down in these circles, ready for the big push across the whole ridge at first light. The direct start with the boat had bought us several more hours of daylight, which meant several more hours of walking along the ridge into the evening. In conditions like this, I couldn't think of anything better.

'Oh, this is typical,' Matt said. He was being sarcastic, but not very. I knew that we were lucky, but I didn't get the sense this level of meteoro-logical spectacle was anything unusual to behold up here. Nor did I expect it to necessarily last. Matt watched with an expression of easy contentment as I took it all in. I'd noticed he'd had his hood up and his waterproof zipped since we'd left the boat, while I'd reorganised my clothing at least twice in the same period. Eventually, with a tiny shared nod, he moved off from the summit, one stick in his right hand, sure-footedly and deliber-ately. I followed.

The southern end of the ridge is like a turned shoulder to the sun. Walking the crest between Gars-bheinn and Sgùrr nan Eag, we were walking the join between sunshine and shadow, light and dark. To our right, the deep shadow of the corries. To the left, slopes warm with sun. As I followed Matt, I looked for somewhere I could stand with a foot in each; there was nowhere without falling rightwards into oblivion, so I resisted.

If you define ridge traversing as the enchainment of summits, we were about to forge our first link. This section drapes like a slack rope between Gars-bheinn and the neighbouring peak of Sgùrr a' Choire Bhig. This is another 'nothing' peak, if you want to believe the numbers. At 875 metres, or 2,877 feet, it still isn't a Munro ß– if Christ the Redeemer were on the summit it would be, but he's not, and so the summit remains damned. Or blessed, so mercifully does it miss the traffic of those trying to tick off the 282 Scottish 3,000-foot summits that make up that idiosyncratic list. Being of insufficient vertical separation from its neighbours (it's a ridge, after all), it also isn't on the more elevationally pedantic Corbett register of lower summits. But really that whole thing is a bit meaningless. Especially when you get up here and see what you're missing.

When it comes to ridge walking, things move rather more quickly once you're up. One of the first things to occur to me – initially tentatively, then with rather more concern as we began to move along the broad but rocky sweep up to the prominent knot of rock that marked the next summit – was something that was as disconcerting as it was surprising. Something that contradicted an expectation I had kind of taken for granted.

'Matt?'

'Ah?'

'Is it supposed to be slippy?'

He turned and looked at my feet. 'Nice small steps. The more uncertain you are, the smaller those steps should be.'

'But is it *supposed* to be slippy? I thought the thing with the Cuillin was you couldn't fall off it because the rock was so grippy?'

'Who told you that?'

I mumbled something about reading it somewhere. Actually, I had read it everywhere.

'Oh, you can still fall off it. The gabbro mainly comes later. This bit is basalt, some of the summits too. Basalt is slippy.' He sniffed. 'If you do fall, try to fall to the left. Then you might survive.'

Other things were surprising me too. The ever-dramatic Romantic imagination liked to characterise this range as desolate and, that most antiseptic of all words, *sterile*. Some of the most famous words written about the Cuillin spoke of this concentrated hostility to life. 'The prospect to the west was desolation itself,' wrote Thomas Pennant. 'Vegetation, there was little or none,' Walter Scott recorded in his diary, on the visit that would yield *The Lord of the Isles*, in which he ground in his point with the lines:

> Above, around, below
> Nor tree, nor shrub, nor plant, nor flower,
> Nor aught of vegetative power
> The weary eye may ken.

Lord Cockburn was eager to point out Scott's inaccuracy when he was confronted with Coruisk's 'vegetable life', as he called it, having collected a dozen or so wild flowers. 'Scott won't admit to either mosses or heathbells. This may be fair enough in a fancy piece, but it is bad in a portrait,' he wrote in 1841. 'Such exaggerations are unnecessary for this place. Enough of a stern sterility and of calm defiance remains ... the scene would have been the same had man not existed.'

A favourite of the hyperbolics, Charles Weld, writing much later in 1860, uses the word 'sterile' or 'sterility' no fewer than three times in as many paragraphs – in the same three somehow also finding space for such cheerless adjectives as 'solemn', 'grim', 'dark', 'gloomy' (twice), 'torn', 'furrowed', 'savage', 'waste', 'treeless' and 'storm-vexed'. And this was one of his *less* melodramatic passages.

You get the idea. The Cuillin presented a scene that people so badly *wanted* to be fearsome and oppressive – if only to authenticate their reasons for being there, and heighten the feeling of awesome dread, that 'agreeable horror' that they had journeyed to this remote place to somehow imbibe.

There's some interesting behaviour being exhibited here – a sort of desire to disengage from the comfort and emerging luxuries of civilised life to scratch some other, basic itch. Almost as if we were reconnecting with something that is now, in the age of constant connection, perhaps obvious – but even then was a preoccupation, despite dispatches warning of horror and dread. Katharine Haldane Grenier, in *Tourism and Identity in Scotland, 1770–1914*, discusses the reactions of Victorians to Coruisk as being akin to atmospheric Chinese whispers: with one hysterical description influencing the reactions of the next observer. She refers to a traveller in 1820 'so affected by the sombre atmosphere of the loch that he feared he was growing suicidal, and hastened to turn back'. She writes:

> The source of the terror inspired by these lochs was the complete lack of human associations. The Cuillins often seemed to be not only untouched by humanity, but untouchable. People who ventured there were overpowered.

Almost inevitably the reality was slightly more amenable to life – which was apparent no matter how hard one strained not to see it. A great illustration of this comes courtesy of Turner who, when he painted his own swirling vision of the loch, inadvertently disproved the claim that the valley was bereft of vegetation in a way that may well have saved his life. The tale has it that when Turner slipped whilst searching for a stance from which to paint, it was a luckily grasped sprig of turf that saved him from falling and breaking his neck.

In our first few hundred metres on the ridge I almost stepped on a newt – the first newt I had ever come across, anywhere – a streak of pale green in the grass at my feet which, on closer inspection, yielded a perfect little face amidst the smeary salamander-like outline. Matt pointed out to me roseroot, cloudberry, blaeberry. This place wasn't sterile at all. It was green. At this time of year it positively glowed with life. Intimidating and severe the Cuillin was: lifeless it was not. Certainly not here.

'I saw a stoat just under the summit of Blàbheinn once,' Matt said, when I asked him about what life he'd observed up here. 'In winter it's easier to spot signs of passage; you see a lot of prints. I've seen fox tracks right up on the crest. And then there are the ravens.' And as we walked steadily and slowly towards the slack curve of the ridge leading to Sgùrr na Coire Bhig, I listened as Matt told me about the Cuillin ravens.

It's tempting to think of the Cuillin as the domain of the eagle, the wild crags beneath its majestic, powerful wings. And there are both kinds of Scottish eagle here: golden and white-tailed, or sea eagle. But they don't own this ridge, either emblematically or in reality. The black ridge belongs to the black birds: the corvids. Ravens, hoodie crows, rooks – the death birds, the bone-pickers. They're spattered around it like gothic confetti, their pronk-like calls taunting the corrie headwalls, the only soundtrack in these mountains beyond the water, the rain and the wind.

Matt told me there were a number of spots further along the ridge where guides would bring up clients from the corries below, eager to tick off the Munro summits on either side of a bealach, or pass. As was common, they would leave their rucksacks in a pile at the pass, then nip up to the summit unburdened. For a time, upon return they would frequently find their sacks gaping open, their contents strewn around or missing. The ravens, it seemed, had learned how to undo the buckles, zips and fasteners, and had taken to rummaging through them while their owners were at large on the nearby summits.

Now the raven is a smart bird. We're talking chimpanzee and dolphin levels of intelligence; they've been known to push rocks down on people getting too close to their nests, or – with truly unfathomable slyness – play dead beside a carcass to imply poisoning, thus sending an elemental signal to scare off less conniving scavengers. They're big too: the biggest walk as tall as a spaniel sits. Collectively they're a 'conspiracy' or 'unkindness' of ravens, an underhand incarnation of the famous 'murder' of crows, and anyone in the region of the Cuillin during this spate of rucksack desecration might understand why. Their combination of strength and cleverness added up to a pretty determined Highland robber, and in pursuit of food the ravens pulled out and cast aside anything separating them from it. The resulting mess was often greeted with dismay as well as confusion – and occasionally suspicion.

'I once got accused of going through someone's sack,' Matt told me, as we proceeded easily along the ridgeline towards the summit of Sgùrr a' Choire Bhig. 'Probably with good reason. All her shiny things were cast about all over the mountain. She wasn't all that interested in hearing about ravens.' So chronic was the problem that guides began putting rocks on top of the rucksacks, weighing them down to dissuade the ravens from investigating. The method was a successful deterrent, and the pillaging stopped. 'Word must have spread amongst the ravens that the sacks were off-limits. So they forgot about them. Now word has spread amongst the guides, and we've stopped putting rocks on them.' Matt said. 'A lovely circle of inter-species feedback.'

After its cataclysmic birth, when life did come to the Cuillin it was – like everything else up here – unlike anywhere else. The island's rich basalt soil gave the northern end of the island its green shimmer and its potential for cultivation, but the Cuillin, despite its austere appearance from afar, still had life. It was just more selective in the kind of life it had. Seton Gordon once described finding 'in a single rock crack . . . at the same time wild hyacinth, primrose, tormentil, sea campion and seathrift mingling their blossoms', whilst also noticing nearby meadowsweet, honeysuckle and blackberry. Gordon also mentions finding the alpine flowers 'moss campion, cushion pink, rose root, starry saxifrage and milkwort' against the waters of Loch Coir' a' Ghrunnda, not too far from us just now. Gordon's observations in the Cuillin depict the place as a kind of frugally attended but tenacious Eden, and as a naturalist his view is perhaps more persuasive than a clutch of gasping, drama-craving travellers seeking to pour scenic salt into expectant wounds.

In his writings about Skye he describes encountering a hare on Sgùrr Dearg, 'her ears laid back . . . she looked surprised and miserable as she hurried . . . to her shelter amongst the rocks below.' In the gloom on the same mountain after sunset he saw the flowers of the sparse but vivid vegetation 'assume new tints . . . the violets were glowing purple . . . the small buds of the moss campion were afire'. One peak – the aforementioned Blàbheinn – is an outlier of the main ridge but an outstanding example of the characteristics of its rock and feel, as is its precipitous annexe Clach Glas; in all but Blàbheinn's standalone nature, it's worthy of inclusion in any discussion of the Cuillin. I mention it now because, in the face of such accusations of sterility, it's interesting that a possible meaning of its ambiguous name – if derived from the Gaelic *blàth bheinn* – means 'hill of the bloom'.

Today the Cuillin – with Blàbheinn, Clach Glas and everything in between – is classed as a National Scenic Area. The somewhat peculiar, if pleasing, definition of this credits the landscape as being exemplary of that 'popularly associated with Scotland, and that for which it is renowned'. The Cuillin is also a Special Protection Area, and a Site of Special Scientific Interest – and not just for the singular nature of its geology but for its biological assets too. In the citation these assets are listed as flood-plain fen, open water transition fen, alkaline fen, blanket bog, subalpine dry heath, tall herb ledge, upland birch woodland, bryophyte assemblage and vascular plant assemblage. I don't pretend to know what much of that means, exactly. But once again: does this sound like a sterile landscape?

The really special Cuillin plant, though – and perhaps the one whose fragile presence says the most about this mountain range – is the fiercely rare alpine rock-cress, *Arabis alpina*. This delicate and pretty flower, with white petals arranged around a yellow carpel and leaves with serrated edges, is a member of the mustard family. It's only found in two colonies on shady ledges high in one corrie of the Cuillin, and carries with it the sort of mystique that makes a certain breed of Tracheophyta-loving botanist positively clammy with excitement. It can take years to get a toehold and flower, preferring habitats that are unremittingly harsh – which perhaps explains its presence in the Cuillin. But the interesting thing is that the Cuillin is the *only* place it's found in Britain. Here's a plant that is widespread across the European Alps, the Atlas and Rift mountains of North Africa, the Himalaya and the high peaks of the Rockies. And the only British location worthy of it is the Cuillin. I love that.

Matt and I stopped in a broad grassy slack for a snack. As I unclipped my helmet from my rucksack it fell and began rolling on the angled ground. I managed to stop it just before it developed into a terminal tumble, and in instinctively moving quickly to grab it I almost started one of my own. Everything is so steep here; even on fairly innocuous-looking grassy slopes, drop something and it's unlikely to stop. That's a good lesson to learn quickly.

I looked at Matt, busy arranging intricate ingredients on a pitta from a container in his lap. If he'd seen my near-blunder, he didn't let on. Instead, he pointed ahead without looking up and said, 'Rubha an Dùnain down there. See the little pocket of forest?'

I looked down to where that long prow of land waded out into the sea, spying the Viking shipyard lochan at the end, and – with sudden recognition – remembered looking back at the ridge from down there months before. I followed the peninsula's left shore down to a furry little nook, near where it met the island proper far below. Here, caught in the sun, was a canopy of trees, covering an escarpment leading down to the sea, quite hidden from view to anyone not looking from an elevated position.

'A lovely patch of old woodland just there,' Matt said. 'You don't get much of that on Skye.'

I looked and let my gaze move across the channel to the dark, low-lying island just offshore. The sun was caught in the kilometre-wide water, lighting it like smelt. Matt saw my attention shift and, indicating the hourglass-shaped island, said, 'Do you know much about Soay?'

'Not much.'

'Do you know about Gavin Maxwell?'

'The otter guy? The naturalist?'

Matt frowned. 'You haven't heard about when he owned Soay, then.'

I shook my head. Matt started to re-pack his food and tighten his straps. 'Well,' he stood up. 'I'll save that for later. We'd best be getting a move on.' He stopped and looked at me. 'I think also perhaps we should put our helmets on now. Harder to drop it when it's on your head.'

We wandered on, steady but with purpose, once again finding a rhythm, as if slowly transforming from walkers to something, well . . . a little different. Our headwear seemed a good barometer of this: first caps, then caps and hoods, now helmets. Tomorrow would add ropes and harnesses to the mix. But this afternoon was just outstandingly scenic, exhilarating walking in a tremendous position, on the silent southern crest of the Cuillin ridge. I was surprised how much I was enjoying being here, and without the slightest trepidation. Maybe this was all an illusion. Maybe the Cuillin ridge was all bark: visually intimidating from afar but amenable at close quarters, as is often the way with mountains. All those broken-glass edges and pointed summits ahead, maybe they all just laid out accommodating ramps and ladders of rock, inflating from perilous-looking, footstool-sized high points from a distance, to the sort of summits you can have a picnic on when you actually get up there. Maybe this was going to be easier than I thought.

This gave me cheer as I walked. Despite knowing, deep down, that this *had* to be the soft end – that I was simply being eased in.

The ridge's bucks and falls began to intensify as we walked. Looking ahead to upcoming stretches, the fall to the right was steepening, with one section near vertical, cut with dark, downward scores, like an upturned comb. The way to the left remained a slope rather than a drop.

Matt noticed I was skirting slightly, as was my habit, to the gentler side, just enough to allow the rise of the ground on my right to block the impact of the drop.

'You can cut under there. But you'll be missing the true terror of the Cuillin,' Matt said. 'Which is why we're up here. Don't forget that.'

I looked questioningly at him, and he looked back down, grinning slightly.

'We're up here to scare ourselves. Otherwise we're just bagging peaks. *Crest is best.*'

'Crest is best?'

'That's right.' He indicated the way with a bladed hand. 'The rock is sound, you're not on scree. And navigation is easier. You might not be happy about it. But at least you're more likely to know where you are.'

Things broadened for a moment as we surmounted the minor top of Sgùrr a' Choire Bhig. Then, just before kinking leftwards and up towards the summit of Sgùrr nan Eag, the ridge crest flattened, where the ground was level enough for boulders to lie. As Matt went, I saw him incline his stick to the ground and call back a single word: 'Gabbro'.

I caught up with him and he pointed his stick at the join; a place where the rock underfoot changed, in adhesive terms at least, from bad to good. It didn't look much, just a vague shift, like a tidemark from dark to slightly darker dark, more apparent when standing back. I scratched my foot on both sides. Subtle; only a bit more bite on the gabbro. But I could imagine it was enough to make the difference. 'Don't take it for granted,' Matt said, as he carried on along the ridge. I noticed, purely by the change in the brilliance of his blue helmet, that in the space of time we'd been looking down at the ground the light had shifted completely. The spires of the central ridge ahead of us had lost their gilding, and were now soot black, the clouds above hammered with dark patches. No weather; just conditions. And conditions were changing.

The story of the discovery of *Arabis alpina* in the Cuillin contains rather more casual interest than most articles usually found in the *Journal of Botany*. The story appeared in the 1887 volume, a colossus of a publication written in a kind of Latin-heavy style that makes even the geological discourses mentioned in earlier chapters read like *Thomas the Tank Engine*. Here, alongside articles with such ominous titles as 'Notes on Pondweeds' and 'Remarks on the Nomenclature of the Eighth Edition of the *London Catalogue*', lies a slender entry by one H. C. Hart, which, quite incidentally, carries with it a little piece of mountaineering history.

Henry Chichester Hart was an Irish mountaineer and a member of the Alpine Club. He was also a botanist, and apparently on his honeymoon when he made the discovery that, as rather ambitiously recorded later in another botanical publication, 'would make him famous'. It did not make him famous, alas – at least not outside of botanical circles – but even in the equally parochial world of 19th-century mountaineering it's fair to say that Hart ranks as one of the most overlooked characters of his day, despite a small but diverting degree of infamy. We'll return to him in Chapter 11, but for now it was his chance discovery in Coire na Creiche – or more specifically, the chance footnote his discovery sprouted – that is of particular interest.

'These mountains are almost uniformly naked rock and very steep with dangerous cliffs and corries,' he wrote. 'So steep and bare there is exceedingly little soil or foothold for vegetation.' Nevertheless, Hart lists seven observed species of alpine plant – including the Alpine lady's mantle, dwarf saw-wort and starry saxifrage. And then he made an important find. 'To my great surprise ... [here was] a plant with which I was already familiar from my travels in Greenland,' he wrote, adding, 'I felt a rare pleasure in climbing these peaks, but I little thought such a prize was waiting for me.'

Arabis alpina was a fine discovery, but it's what Hart was doing up there in the first place – carrying with him an aneroid barometer, a comparatively recent invention – that would make his recording of the alpine rock-cress perhaps the second most important discovery of his day in the Cuillin. By way of illustrating the scene he noted the following, and you'll notice Hart's phonetic spelling of the peaks: 'The summits and ridges are in many parts over 3,000 feet.' And then he says: 'I measured Scur Alister by the aneroid to be 3,260 feet above the sea, and I believe it to be higher than Scurna Gillean, which has generally been considered the highest.'

He had just correctly specified the highest point of the Cuillin. And as Matt and I began our approach to the summit of Sgùrr nan Eag, this mountain swooned into view ahead. A pair of burly triangles, one much higher, separated by a dramatic cleft – the signature of the highest ground on Skye.

The walk between Loch Scavaig and Sgùrr Nan Eag was the most exhilarating, elemental, *alive* three hours in the mountains I have ever had. Nothing horrible happened. Everything went to plan. But it was just so immersive. It was steep and a slip would carry consequence, but the drops were never too frightening. The line was purity itself. This was the joy in mountain walking, of ridge walking – of being high, vertiginously so, but free to stride over ground broad enough to meander on, your head up, and just enjoy. Pure, perfect perspective. And as aesthetically astonishing as I could imagine any walk could be.

What I couldn't fathom was why most people chose to miss this bit out. Stopping and looking back at Gars-bheinn – from here an arc of shadowed ridgeline slung high to a rocky apex, with long drops either side filled with sea – I was struck by how fine this mountain looked. People only think of it as being the scrappy southern end of a ridge with far greater aesthetic merit elsewhere. But looking at it in isolation, with the whole ridge at your back and just this peak to admire as if it stands alone, it's worth its own fame. A sign, if any were needed, that there's a hell of a lot of mountain packed into this ridge.

Sgùrr nan Eag's name means 'Peak of the Notches'. I wasn't sure exactly why – I'd thought maybe it had something to do with the gullies that scratched its east face – but as we began to climb up the ash-coloured rock towards its rounded summit I got my first real wobble of adrenaline. 'Bit of care here,' Matt said, as he slowly walked up a steep, fractured pillar of gabbro. As I got close, I saw that it was a bridge crossing a gap around six feet wide. The slab was sturdy and pitched, but I could see by the way Matt stepped that it perhaps presented, shall we say, a moment of thought. As I followed, I saw the fall beneath, down steep walls to the floor of the corrie, into space and air, the security of the ridge momentarily dropping away, and the all too familiar bubble of nerves in my knees and my stomach. By reflex I crossed it on my hands and knees, hoping I'd be across before Matt saw. But he did, of course, and we shared a look – mine possibly apologetic, his bemused. 'It's OK,' he said. 'The more points of contact the better. The Cuillin doesn't care.'

We reached the summit of Sgùrr nan Eag soon after. A ten-foot cairn – 'biggest cairn in the Cuillin', as Matt noted – gave it considerably more occasion than the relatively unadorned but far more aesthetically pleasing top of Gars-bheinn. As we stood beside it and took a moment to rehydrate, I felt the cold prickle of rain hitting the right side of my face. Not much, but enough to remind us of the clip of the sun and a subtle elemental nudge that we were still some way from where we were going to spend the night

– though where that might be was still, quite literally, up in the air. Matt had his phone out and was loading up the weather forecast, his eye swivelling from it to the sky and back. 'The wind has changed a little,' he said.

The north ridge of Sgùrr nan Eag drops down to a pass. These pinched openings across the spine of the ridge – the dips between the vertebrae, if you like – are called *bealachs*. As they are strategically important for escape off the ridge to the valley, and historically for getting from one side of the ridge to the other, most have names – sometimes relating to the peaks they separate, sometimes the corries. This one was the Bealach a' Garbh-choire, taking its name from the rocky 'v' that opened out to the right. Garbh-Choire means 'wild corrie', and it fits: looking down into it to the south-west, it was a long way to anywhere where there were people. Through veils of silvery rain I caught sight of Blàbhein, the sea-grey of Loch Scavaig, a few faint and very distant lights coming on in the horizon murk marking Elgol beyond, and the gunmetal streak far below, interrupted by spurs descending from the ridge, of Loch Coruisk. Beneath the heavy, rain-filled sky there was a touch of rose in the darkening east.

Here the ridge crest kicked to the right, the prospect to Sgùrr Alasdair opened ahead, and the cauldron of Coir a' Ghrunnda below to the left. This high, broad corrie holds a lake with a squirrely edge, surrounded by steep scree – except where it opened, like a spout, to Glen Brittle far below. Coruisk aside, this is the Cuillin's biggest corrie loch, and one of only a few. In good light it has a pale, green halo and a dark centre, almost phosphorescent, like a petrol spill. Skye's fairy tales say the colour is caused by the green garments of the lady sprites, who wash their clothes in it at dawn. Tonight the edge was like tin and the centre like iron, its texture enlivened by a quickening rain. Above it, the line of mountains was losing its detail, contrast seeping out of the landscape.

Matt stopped and turned to me. 'You know, everyone always says finding water on the Cuillin is difficult. But,' he used his pole to lift up a saucer-sized piece of rock at his feet to reveal a perfect little pool of clear water, 'you can always find a cupful here.' I made an impressed noise, and meant it. 'My little party trick,' he said, flipping the lid shut. We didn't need water yet, so it seemed somehow rude to take it.

The rain got heavier, shimmering in the air. I fiddled with my hood, pulling it over the top of my helmet, not liking the big, draughty gaps this caused. Matt's hood had been up all afternoon. Rain billowed in on a suddenly noticeable wind and, with progress slow on the intricate ground and failing light, I felt a shiver dash down my back. The atmosphere of the place had shifted as if a switch had been flicked.

Here suddenly were tall rocks, crags high above us, a strange labyrinth amongst the gathering cloud and dark. A tower loomed ahead, fittingly called Caisteal a' Garbh-coire – 'The Castle' of its eponymous corrie – around which we traversed, in doing so moving from one side of the crest to the other. As we tracked around it I noticed the rain-darkened rocks on this side were of a strange texture, covered in walnut-sized pits and ridges, like the surface of a sea sponge.

We continued, the murk thickening, the rain thickening and ceaseless. 'So, probably time for a judgement call,' Matt said. He had stopped beneath a small overhang that offered perhaps a few inches of shelter and was looking at me with a kind of earnest but slightly hangdog stoop. Standing close, I could hear the rain hitting his nylon as well as mine, with a sound like bacon sizzling. Everywhere was the sound of water. Water hitting rock, water trickling down rock, trickling down us.

'I'm thinking a bivvy out in this would be pretty depressing,' Matt said. 'Like this place,' he indicated one of several more human-built rock rings around us with his stick. This was clearly a popular spot. 'Five-star location. But no roof. And no water supply, other than what's falling on it. Forecast says it might get better,' but his tone suggested this was by no means a guarantee. 'Unfortunate luck. And we've got to think about tomorrow. Grade 3 scrambling for breakfast, after a night of no sleep . . .' Then he paused. 'Or there's a cave.'

I nodded, slightly apprehensively. I could see the piles of mountain over Matt's shoulder that made up Sgùrr Alasdair and Sgùrr Sgumain, tomorrow morning's first objectives. You can load your pack up with the best waterproof gear and fill your mind with intrepid intentions; but get up here, and the prospect of a night exposed in the wet and cold loses its novelty like heat leaving a warm body. And come sunrise, steep, nasty mountains and tiredness aren't the best bedfellows. But a cave! This seemed like the ideal compromise. An easy decision. I didn't even know why we were discussing it.

I said, 'Cave?'

Matt didn't move, a dark expression on his face. 'Caves have disadvantages.'

I looked at him. He turned his eyes up at the sky and bobbed his head. 'They drip. Even after the rain stops.'

I had stopped listening. 'For a roof, I'll take drips over this.'

He paused, then nodded, as if conceding to a hard-haggled deal. 'Cave, then?'

I nodded back. 'Cave.'

8

Night

There was once a great Irish warrior, the son of a king. He fell in love with a girl named Emer, but her father thought him unworthy. Prove your valour first, he said. Travel across the ocean to Dunscaith, on Skye. There, a queen named Scáthach trained the greatest heroes of all. So the warrior crossed the sea in a trio of great strides, alighting on Skye with the third. To reach this so-called 'school for heroes' he had to pass through the Plain of Ill Luck, with its lacerating grasses. Then through the Perilous Glen, filled with vicious creatures.

Finally he had to cross the Bridge of the Cliff, a great battlement that had 'two low ends, and a mid-space high'. So treacherous was this that only the bravest could cross it. Stand on one end, and the other end would rise vertically and throw you back. The warrior attempted the traverse three times and failed. Eventually he grew mad and leaped recklessly at the bridge, vaulting the centre and landing on the ground beyond. Impressed by what she saw, Scáthach tested the warrior by fighting him night and day. Unable to vanquish him – or he, her – Scáthach presented him with a barbed spear infused with magic and forged by the 'little people' who lived deep in the mountains across which they'd fought. In honour of his strength, she named the island's greatest mountains after him. His name was Cúchulainn.

The story of Cúchulainn and Scáthach is told with endless variations. In some the Bridge of the Cliff *is* the Cuillin; in others his valedictory, barbed weapon is forged *from* the Cuillin. Cúchulainn himself is described either as being simply a tall and powerful hot-tempered man, or as a giant with seven pupils in each eye, seven fingers and toes on each hand and foot, whose shout is so loud it could kill. Thomas Pennant makes reference to 'Quillin, prodigious mountain of Cuichuillin . . . like its hero, stood like a hill that catches the clouds of heaven', of the view from Beinn na Caillich – referring to the ridge as a single peak and further knotting up those incestuous names.

Whatever his name and origin, Cúchulainn drifts like mist in folklore between the Ulster Cycle, Manx legend and the Ossianic sagas. Invariably he meets a tragic end, of which there are too many versions to go into, but this guy is a tortured and troubled hero if ever there was one. Then there is his mentor-foe: another pleasing consistency is that Scáthach is often called *Skiach*, which is an old word for Skye itself. One took their name from the other, it seems. No source suggests which.

The legend of Cúchulainn as being the true root of the word 'Cuillin' is dismissed with curious keenness these days, the association having been promoted when the Ossianic sagas rose to popularity, then discarded when they fell into murky disrepute. But personally, I like the connection. There are a lot of appropriate motifs in there: the spiky weapon, the tricky Bridge of the Cliff, the challenging and dangerous terrain, the general magical aura of both story and mountain range. The names entwine across history almost interchangeably. Indeed, in the absence of a definite alternative, why not? And frankly, as night falls on the Cuillin, just about anything is believable. You'd believe the rock itself had eyes that opened.

High on the southern ridge, in the rain, Matt and I edged around the top of Loch Coir' a' Ghrunnda in light spinning the last of the day's thread. Then the damnedest thing happened. The rain lessened and the air began to glow – first an intense orange, followed by pink. The water smeared over every rock caught a little of the light and – just for a few minutes – oppressive turned to ethereal, the sun dropped below the cloud somewhere unseen and lit the world in a final sideways fire.

It continued to glow as we traversed the top of Loch Coir' a' Ghrunnda. Clouds were darkening behind the twin pyramids of Sgùrr Sgumain and Sgùrr Alasdair above, picking out against the sky the peculiar pinnacles that seemed to make the slope to the latter's summit bristle. I tried to appoint scale to them with my eyes, but with nothing human on the flat black of the mountain I couldn't tell if these little splinter-silhouettes on the ridge were a foot tall, or as big as a house. To me they looked like figures, watching from the ridge line. It was an eerie thought.

Night on any mountain can be beautiful. It can transform the world before you into soft tones, hard contrasts and be so transcendent in its beauty you question – particularly on a mountain range like the Cuillin – how it is that people don't speak of this time, in these places, as one of the world's wonders. Then you question how it is that you have somehow managed to get it all to yourself. Seeing this kind of a scene in a picture is one thing. In reality, when you feel the ebbing warmth of sunset on your face, the first grasps of chill, and feel the landscape wrapped around you, occupying every direction, it is something else. This is the siren song of the mountain – the reason you do it. It is *intensely* sensory, a realignment of your own personal barometer for spectacle.

And then, by degrees but swiftly, it begins to get dark. And something else starts to kick in – something that, no matter how you try, you cannot reason your way beyond. A kind of slow, primal panic. The feeling that you are somewhere you shouldn't be, and as far as coping with it is concerned, things are about to get a whole lot more challenging.

Nightfall in the Cuillin brings all this, and an additional conundrum for the traverser. Doing the ridge in a day, even with the seemingly endless hours of summer, is a tall order on every level. It is possible: common, even, when all the intricacies of the traverse have been rehearsed and the weather plays ball. The ridge itself is a little more than seven miles from first to last peak, but unless you have the use of a helicopter – or the ability to shorten the walk in by boat, as we did – there is considerable distance to cover at each end to add to the mileage. The full traverse, from Glen Brittle to Sligachan – or vice versa – clocks in at almost double that, whichever corners you cut. And these aren't normal miles, remember: they are Skye miles of both types. Four of the exhilarating kind, around three of the terrifying, technical kind, and around eight more of the stodgy ones of near imperceptible progress.

So to do the entire ridge in a day is an undertaking beyond what most are capable of in a manner they might enjoy – and beyond what nearly all of us would want. Which means stopping for the night is a necessary evil, despite the difficulty concerning decent shelter, water and the need to carry all your stuff.

And stop you must. The Cuillin forces you to conform to the circadian principles of day and night rather more stringently than other mountain ranges. It can be quite jolly to go for a walk after sunset in the Cairngorms, or climb Scafell Pike under a full moon with crisp snow underfoot. But the Cuillin doesn't offer such leisure to the wise. Given that this landscape more or less has it in for you by day, this is not the kind of place to move around at night – however temptingly surreal the shadows it casts about it beneath a full moon. It would be like putting a blindfold on and stumbling through a glass-blower's workshop, arms outstretched, and hoping nothing bad will happen. The complexity of the ridge is such that purely navigating by map in the dark is almost impossible, unless you happened to be blessed with a lunar spotlight, good knowledge of every duck and dive of the crest and a judgement for negotiating technical ground that isn't clouded with the inevitable fatigue of a demanding day already. I had only been walking for six hours with plenty of stops, and I was ready for rest. So given all of these factors, the idea of just pressing on into the darkness hours is a plan of action reserved for a very few highly experienced, extremely fit – or deeply unclever – individuals. When the lights go out in the Cuillin, the second the ground becomes indistinct at your feet you would be well advised to stop, cling on and hunker down. This is the time the ridge returns to nature, and becomes a whittle-blade for folklore in the crofts below; and sensible climbers would do well to be tucked up.

Loch Coir' a' Ghrunnda had gained a delicate kiss of mist. It was raining again, and I saw Matt throw down his rucksack onto a green patch about as big as a living-room rug in the scree ahead and bend down. It was a spring – a little oasis in the rock desert. And our water source for tonight, and tomorrow.

I watched as he pulled out a bottle and plunged it into a gap by his feet, where across a mane of brilliant green moss I saw the flash of running water. He took a deep drink then plunged it back, then moved so I could do the same. After the afternoon's walk the water tasted sumptuously clean and cold. I filled up my bottles and followed Matt as he started out up the grey scree slope. Above him the crags of Sgùrr Alasdair and Sgùrr Sgumain were darkening, the cloud above them a stern bronze. And below them, I saw where we were going: the triangular gape of the Sgumain Cave, high above the floor of the corrie, a hole in the face of the mountain. I was tired – surprisingly so. This last slope was going to be hard. And that cave looked – well, precarious.

Midway up the slope Matt stopped and pointed upwards towards the crest. Maybe fifty metres above us, framed in my hood, was a spiked outcrop with a V-shaped groove in the rock buttress – like a pair of open pliars – through which I could see the deepening grey of the eastern sky.

'TD Gap,' he said.

The TD Gap! The TD Gap was famous, a bite in the ridge between Sgùrr Thearlaich (T) and Sgùrr Dubh (D) an Da Bheinn, described rather well by Malcolm Slesser's SMC guidebook as 'one of the main ridge's principal traps'. An earlier guidebook had dryly advised that 'a party of tourists should not all descend to the gap at the same time, in case they might have to remain there permanently.' By tourists, read climbers. Tourists don't attempt the TD gap.

I'd wanted to try the Gap, indeed had somehow expected it to come a little later. But there it was, appearing at a rather inconvenient hour and condition. I'd always pictured it in my head as something unavoidable, a chasm in a skinny crest with huge drops on either side. Yet looking up at it, from the broad scree fan of a corrie, it wasn't at all what I was expecting. I was expecting something much more ... well, frightening. Granted, we were looking at it from below, which does have the habit of hiding an obstacle's true scale. But now I could see that it was avoidable in a way I hadn't quite imagined. Not knowing exactly how to articulate this, I looked at Matt. 'What's it like?'

'You don't go anywhere near it in the wet,' he said darkly. 'That's all you need to know about that.'

I peered back up at the gap in the gloom, suddenly reminded of Tryfan, although it was completely different. The TD Gap didn't look small. And on Tryfan, you're in the air, in space. This place was claustrophobic, leering, like some ruined remnant in a bombed city. It felt intimidating without seeming malevolent – though I fancied that if the light dropped much more, or the clouds continued their fall over the summit ridge of Sgùrr Alasdair, or the rain fell with just a little more commitment, I might have to revise that last bit. This place had a power, a presence. Standing in the gloom amidst walls of steep, glistening rock, beneath the pincer of the TD Gap, above the dimming waters of Loch Coir' a' Ghrunnda, with the darkness of the sea beyond and Sgùrr Alasdair watching regally over it all, I felt like I was in the hall of the mountain gods.

I had never really appreciated this 'darkness', as people kept calling it. It was why I wanted to spend the night up here, to see whether this brought out the more sinister side of the Cuillin a little more. Plus, to *not* spend the night up here would be to deprive yourself of an intrinsic part of the experience: the ridge bivouac. You can't really say you've experienced every shade of the Cuillin until you've spent the night on it. Because night unsettles the feelings kept calm by daylight. It takes away all the comfort – then lets the monsters loose in your mind.

So for better or worse, as Matt's voice rang down from halfway up the scree ramp leading to the cave, ringy and metallic against the rocks around us, I was about to find out. 'Nearly there,' he shouted. 'Don't delay. Your evening of uncomfortable sleeping and dubious food awaits.'

The Sgumain Cave looked, to my eyes at least, very accommodating. I'd been expecting an overhang beneath jostled crags. But this was a little cavern, perhaps as big as a theatre box, with a huge triangular opening at the front that tapered, wedge-like, to a pointed recess in the mountain. Its spacious, fairly flat floor was cleared of rocks, giving room enough for four, maybe, while its walls were ragged with sharp corners of rock, as was the opening. Standing at the back and looking out gave the novel and disquieting impression of sitting in the mouth of a huge, toothy shark. The sky was drained of colour now, and cloud was scudding across it as the light was seeping away, but I could still make out the hooky shapes of Sgùrr nan Eag, Gars-bheinn beyond it and the sea beyond that. At the bottom of the scree-slope tongue below the entrance, Loch Coir a' Ghrunnda looked like a smelter's spill. Hell of a view. Hell of a position, too. I loved it. Ask a ten-year-old to picture sleeping in a cave dug into the face of a mountain, and the scene inside the Sgumain Cave would be it.

'This place is amazing,' I said.

'At least we're nice and late,' Matt said, as he busied himself with extracting comforts from his pack. 'Nothing worse than being in here for thirteen hours.'

'Why? Don't you like caves? Ghosts? Cave spiders?'

He unrolled his bivvy bag. I noticed his sleeping bag was already inside it.

'Caves drip,' he said again, inflating a sleeping mat and shoving it inside. 'You'll see.'

Bits of the cave were indeed damp, I'd noticed that much. I looked up at the cave roof. It looked oily, and I registered the occasional 'thwock' of water hitting the nylon of my rucksack. But it didn't look torrential.

Surrounded by cold-radiating rock except for the opening, our lack of movement meant we were turning chilly. We were wet, if not exactly wet through – and the temperature was falling with the light. Removing waterproofs, Matt threw on a padded down jacket and a hat, his wiry frame suddenly huge against the mouth of the cave. Sounds were magnified in the close confines of the cave. A tinny clank, the crackle of plastic, the slosh of water and then the stove was on, the low hiss of burning gas promising warmth was on the way. Soon the cave was filling with steam, caught in the white light of our head torches.

I set my little lantern on a ledge at the back, piled the bottles of water in the corner and joined Matt at the mouth of the cave. Just inside the opening some previous occupants had built a little rock windbreak about the height of an ankle – something that couldn't possibly serve any functional use but did at least mark a notional boundary between inside and outside.

Matt straightened, as if struck by a thought, and looked out of the cave entrance. 'I have a stash not far from here. A tarp, a tent flysheet . . . a few bits that might help. You'll be OK for a minute? Make a campfire if you like. I'm sure some of these rocks will burn.'

With that he was out of the cave, traversing the slope to the right, the bob of his headlamp fading. I heard the clink of his steps on the scree, then heard them more faintly, then he was gone. For a minute all was quiet. Then I heard the clinking steps again, along with the crackle of nylon.

It's quite a thing, settling down for the night somewhere wild like this – whether it's camping, occupying a bothy or, as in this case, hunkering down in a cave. It's a feeling that whispers to your tired body a hymn of relief and excitement, as if the act of finding and carving out a little crook of comfort in a place where there is none is quite the most satisfying thing in the world. It's a suggestion of something ancient – a sense of belonging outside. It's far more covetable and joyous to find any little comfort in a wild place than even more comfort in an already comfortable place – leaving home for a weekend at a posh hotel, for example. It's something baked in to our genetics at ingredients level: the desire to achieve shelter, to get warm, get fed, hunker down and let the melee outside do its worst. Anyway, it's a good feeling – particularly in a place like the Cuillin. Until you remember you've forgotten the whisky.

This lacking, I offered Matt food, as he did me. I took the peanuts he passed my way but he declined the crisps. 'I've already tricked you into eating my bag a bit lighter,' he said. 'You should eat your own food.'

The mountains outside blackened, and then a strengthening silvery light began to gleam through the clouds. Inching out of the cave mouth, I turned off my torch and let the detail of the corrie and the peaks emerge, zipping up my down jacket against the cold and jamming my hands under my arms. As the light gathered, detail within the dark shapes of the mountains began to show as the moon reflected off every slick, skyward-facing surface. They were shimmering, as if scattered with fragments of a broken mirror. It was beautiful.

'Wow.'

'Just a shave off full,' Matt said, squinting up at the sky, arms tightly folded. 'A moonlight ascent of Sgùrr Alasdair would be almost tempting,' he added, poking his head out of the cave mouth, 'if coming down off it wasn't such a terrifying prospect.' There was something in his voice that wasn't as dismissive as his words. We watched for a while as we ate our food – dehydrated pasta and chicken tikka – the sort of rattly meal you pour hot water over and let it inflate for ten minutes into something resembling food. It tasted great.

We had a hot chocolate, then finally turned off the stove. Matt had covered the floor with a tent flysheet, onto which we'd thrown down our bivvy bags, packed with mats and warm sleeping bags. A steel peg hammered into the roof by a previous occupant acted as a hook, onto which Matt hung the bagged-up remainders of the food. Seeing my look, he said, 'Mice. They'll chew into your pack if they're hungry enough.'

The cloud had slowly thickened while we ate and drank, and when I was rehydrated enough to answer a final call of nature I carefully moved out of the cave a little way along the slope, the scree steep beneath my feet. Behind me, the dim glow of my lantern made the cave mouth look like a golden hole in the mountain. All else was darkness, and silence. I looked back along the ridge towards Gars-bheinn and thought again of the view of the ridge from Ben Cleat above Elgol – that magnificent sweep of peaks – and pictured myself in amongst it, maybe a third of the way along. Our sleeping bags were laid out at over 800 metres tonight. We were probably the highest people on Skye – the highest in the Hebrides maybe. Since stepping off the boat, we hadn't seen a soul.

But just as I had this thought my eye was caught by a single pinprick of light, high in the darkness of the ridge to the south. It was on the slope beneath the summit of Sgùrr nan Eag – just a tiny electric dot, static in position but swivelling this way and that, like a headtorch on someone's head. Perhaps we weren't alone after all; someone was up there, probably bivvying in one of the shelter rings we'd passed that afternoon. Suddenly I had a crude human scale for the ridge, revealed by the dark. As I finished my ablutions and turned to go back to the cave, I wondered if he, or she, or they could see us, and our cave, peering out of Sgùrr Sguman like a tiny, dim eye in the mountain. That thought in mind, I climbed into my sleeping bag and waited for warmth to flow into my body. And, hopefully, sleep.

Back in the early days, those caught out by darkness on the ridge would often attempt to descend into Glenbrittle from the high corries of Ghrunnda, Làgan or Banachdich. Earlier still, Skye was notorious for its lack of good hostelry. 'It would be well for the tourist in Skye,' wrote the ever-tetchy Charles Weld in 1860,

> [if] his Lordship [Lord MacDonald, the local laird] would provide good inns for visitors to his romantic island. With the exception of those at Portree and Broadford, all the other inns in Skye are sorry taverns, where you must be prepared to rough it in bed and board.

But with the arrival of the mountaineers, and following the development of the Sligachan Hotel, there arose a clutch of havens in Glenbrittle too – formal and informal – that were always ready to receive often wretched but deeply grateful guests. Mary Campbell's Cuillin Cottage became something of a climbers' institution. Agnes Chisholm, postmistress at Glenbrittle, ran a peerlessly organised operation from her home, and was said to position members of her family on the slopes of the glen after sundown to watch for movement high on the ridge. This might have been for mother-hen reasons, or perhaps something more practical. 'On an open peat fire she could cook a more than welcome three-course dinner, which seemed to be miraculously ready however late we came,' one climber wrote after her death in 1952.

Ernest A. Baker – a man whose prose is difficult to read without affecting a sort of shrill toot – complained in 1923's *The Highlands with a Rope and Rucksack* of 'Skye's most elusive quarry: a bed' and that in a Skye village '[there is] no middle class. There is the mansion, as it is called in the Highlands ... and there is the poor man's house, which is a byre; nothing in between.' He recounts a few stories of nights spent in the shadow of the Cuillin being routinely fleeced, invaded by ducks, beleaguered by midges and beset with puzzlement as to where their hosts would sleep, given Baker's party invariably occupied every square inch in whatever 'queer place' they found themselves. He also mentions the Greek legend related by the Roman satirical writers Juvenal and Persius. According to the story, anyone who passed a night on the summit of the twin-topped peak Mount Parnassus acquired the genius of a poet. It's a curiously transferrable legend, often associated with Cadair Idris in Wales, and at some point it became attached to the Cuillin too.

Many have certainly enjoyed the opportunity to test the theory. Most bivvy out; as far as caves went, Matt told me he knew of four on the ridge: the Sgumain Cave we were occupying now, a cave near Sgùrr Dearg that was 'a horrible tunnel ... you have to sleep head to foot, which means one of you is sleeping right into the mountain,' another beneath An Caisteal, and one on Sgùrr Ghreadaidh.

There were other caves or 'howffs', natural hollows or human-sized tucks, in the corries. Ben Humble, in *The Cuillin of Skye*, describes spending a night in a cave – 'more a slit in the rock' – near Loch Scavaig, into which he and two companions bundled miserably, finding stones for a windbreak at the entrance, heather for bedding and driftwood for a fire. In an odd twist that indicates the date – it was 1946 – Humble notes that the firewood came from 'the relics of torpedoed and mined ships that litter the shores of the island', much like our modern-day plastic crap.

Other writers deliberately sought a wild night on the ridge for its atmosphere and sensory novelty. Seton Gordon wrote widely on the bird and plant life of the Highlands, but it was Skye that finally got him. He lived for fifty years on the island until his death in 1977, aged an impressive ninety-one. In 1929 he wrote one of the very finest books about the island, *The Charm of Skye*, his prose seamlessly alternating between folklore and fact.

Here we join him spending a summer night in a hollow of stones on Sgùrr Dearg, beneath the Inaccessible Pinnacle. From this eyrie he watched the lighthouses springing to life on the headlands around him as the sun finally sank in the west towards midnight. 'In its last rays Sgùrr nan Gillean glowed richly,' he wrote, 'but in the corries the fingers of night were already resting.' With a sense of ancient and benevolent spirits around him, he describes being completely at comfort as the mists and midsummer twilight bathed the ridge, his observations of nature mingling fiction and mythology without breaking step. 'No one who has seen a summer sunset from the Cuillin can fail to sense the nearness of things spiritual,' he writes. Gordon invokes the 'half-forgotten Celtic Gods . . . the *Daoine Sithe*, the Spirit of the Hills . . . all these are more closely joined . . . than the affairs of everyday life.'

He too saw a strange light on the ridge, 'a tiny flash . . . burning for an instant upon the flank of Sgùrr na Banachdaich'. Speculating that for a moment one of the *Sithe* had momentarily opened the door of an underground dwelling, 'a few minutes later a long lane of light extended eastwards from that hilltop, and floated in the sky like some glowing banner.' He deduced that the light was probably from the distant lighthouse on Hyskeir, somehow queered by the mist, but he remained unsure, the illumination perhaps coming from some quite different place, or plane, altogether.

At midnight the 'northern sky burned as if afire', but a couple of hours later the wind gathered near the summit, bringing with it mists, fingers of

vapour, 'low, dark and moving at speed' across the afterglow. Gordon
returned to his shelter. Emerging at intervals, he saw cloud pressing in on
Sgùrr Alasdair, breaking over its summit and flowing down the Great Stone
Shoot. Hastily, he began to descend in the thickening mist, chastened but
alive with the memory of the sunset.

To Gordon the hills were not to be feared. He spoke of them fondly and
saw them as kindly, even wise. But to most lowland dwellers, mountains
have been demonised since ancient times, and the dread outlines and shadowed recesses of the Cuillin have triggered more than their share of ominous
responses in their beholders – particularly when darkness falls. And if the
people of Skye didn't regard the ridge as sinister or in some way possessed
when the mountains remained a distant backdrop, they certainly did when
they began to look closer.

One of the first travellers to document the jumpy reactions of locals to
the Cuillin – and to employ them to assist in his explorations of its sombre
inner reaches, and one in particular – was a man we've met several times
already. It was 1814, and in the company of a group of local boatmen, John
MacCulloch was about to discover Loch Coruisk.

For all his deficiencies as a mountaineer and opacity as a geologist,
MacCulloch's flair as a travel writer was considerable. He may have been
pompous and culturally ignorant – many of Skye's earliest travellers sadly
were – but he could certainly capture a scene. Despite a preamble full of
MacCulloch's usual bluster, after laying eyes on the waters of Loch Coruisk
you quickly get the sense that the party's superstitions about the valley and
its lake ran as black and as deep as its water. It was a calm day, the water
'glassy and dark', the mountains seeming 'to approach each other and
exclude the day ... the valley thus seems lost in a sort of perpetual twilight.'
To MacCulloch's eyes the Cuillin, claustrophobically encircling the lake, was
a shadowed wall filled with 'mysterious darkness', but it's his description
of the loch and its surroundings that stuck. Here was a place

> where mortal foot had scarce ever trod ... Not a billow curled on the
> shore of the black lake ... not even a bird was to be seen, no fish dimpled
> the water, not a bee nor a fly was on the wing. It appeared as if all living
> beings had abandoned this spot to the spirit of solitude.

It's interesting that MacCulloch never mentions the valley's beauty or 'sublimity'. Immediately – and with no literary precedent – his words are ominous and suggestive, and quite at odds with his swaggery tone elsewhere. This place got him, in a big way.

This could, however, have had something to do with the growing unease of his boat's crew – a cargo of Gaels with a certain rural skittishness that began to intensify the closer to nightfall the shadows crept. With nothing to give scale to the scene, MacCulloch was confounded by the length of the loch. Although he estimated it to be no more than a few hundred metres in a valley of less than a mile (as opposed to the true scale of, respectively, a mile to over two), he noted white torrents at the head of the lake 'so remote they seemed not to move; they thundered as they fell, yet were inaudible.'

In order to assist with this distress of perspective, he dispatched his companions – for whom it is difficult not to hold a degree of sympathy – in a line towards the loch's end. MacCulloch, observing from a distance, noted that before they were halfway they were 'all invisible'.

Recalling the crew, the entire troupe set out to encircle the lake together. Perhaps in a nod to the 'Skye mile', MacCulloch noted that for half an hour they walked but seemed not to move. The vista ahead remained remote, grey and misty, the rocks around them unchanged, and only the view to the rear revealing that the entrance had been left far behind. 'The men began to think they were enchanted,' he reported.

My rough fellows, little given to metaphysical reasonings, did not well know whether to be frightened or astonished: they looked at each other, and at me, and around, and I found, in the course of the evening, that they considered the place as 'no canny'.

And then darkness approached. Wanting to 'witness the effect of night', MacCulloch elected to stay in the valley as twilight deepened despite rapidly losing the goodwill of his couriers. Finding them unwilling to risk themselves on such peculiar, enchanted ground, MacCulloch left them with the boat and set off alone as high as he could up what he refers to as the 'eastern hill' – which we can presume was Sgùrr na Stri. As the valley 'prolonged into the regions of endless night', MacCulloch found himself on mountainside surrounded by difficult ground, very much alone and very much in the dark.

Somehow he found his way back to the boat – given MacCulloch's less than intrepid mountaineering feats it's doubtful he was very far from it to begin with – only to find the crew had vanished. Understandably upset, MacCulloch called out for them, before resigning himself to simply sitting down and awaiting their return whilst listening to the 'universal silence' of the Coruisk night. And return the men did, having apparently set off in search of MacCulloch, fearing him lost. MacCulloch noted their somewhat exaggerated alarm, heightened when the fourth boatman arrived at some speed and in a state of considerable agitation. '"Ech," said he, as he came to his breath again, "this is an awfu-like place."' It was then the penny dropped.

'I had forgotten that the lake was considered the haunt of the Water Demons,' he wrote. 'The men piled into the rowing boat and set off for their vessel, anchored off shore,' while MacCulloch observed 'an unusual air of silence and mystery amongst the men . . . looking about at every moment, and then at each other, til as we gained the opener sea, their terrors seemed to disappear.'

We can't know if MacCulloch was making some of this up. Given the proliferation of vaguely similar stories that would later emerge, you suspect maybe not. It does seem that rural Highlanders were rather superstitious, not just influenced by folklore but haunted by it. So either the people of Skye were particularly susceptible to local legend or something about this place manifested a certain, shall we say, *impressionability* upon those who visited it. Alexander Smith put it rather well when he said in *A Summer in Skye*:

> The island is pervaded by a subtle spiritual atmosphere. It is as strange to the mind as it is to the eye . . . a smell of sea in the material air, and there is a ghostly something in the air of the imagination.

Is this 'no canny?' While Skye is drenched in folklore, it hardly needs to be said that Scotland in general likes a legend. The entire country trades on its natural stock as a place of haunting beauty, wild and noble, covered in fanciful landscapes that drip with northern whispers. Perhaps you haven't noticed that the animal on the country's royal coat of arms isn't a horse, but a unicorn – and it figures. While the world may have taken notice of this atmosphere post-Ossian, the lines of folklore go back as long as human history in the country itself. As far as Skye in particular goes, the occasionally spicy fusion of cultures from the Picts to the Gaels and the Norse – all earthy, myth-spinning peoples – led to a busily intertwined mongrel folklore quite unique to the place. This is the reason why on Skye there never seems to be a straight answer for anything concerning the origin of a word, the root of a particular belief or the naming of a place. It's also one of the reasons why legend and superstition seem to cling as tightly to the island as its much-romanticised mists.

Of the Cuillin, J. Hubert Walker wrote 'those oft repeated phrases such as there is a magic about the place, it is spell-binding and so on, keep on coming to mind when thinking of the Cuillin . . . but there is something unearthly, not of this world about them.' Norman Collie wrote more generally of the disquiet of mountain places:

> Sometimes when the winds are at rest, the mists come down and all is hidden in a garment of white stillness. The loneliness and silence is of another world. Strange thoughts wander through one's mind. The old mysterious tales of ghostly beings who haunt the wilds. There are places that one dreads, where one trembles and is afraid, one knows not why, and fears stand in the way.

The celebrated culture of Highland storytelling has long been associated with the endless winter nights within the crofts and black houses, where in the warmth amidst the cold, yarns would be spun and interwoven with tales from past generations. This was then concentrated by the atmosphere of its landscape, which seemed built to draw legend around it like a tailored cloak. As described in the well-titled *Old Skye Tales* by William Mackenzie, 'in the solemn stillness [and] deepening gloom . . . one cannot but have the expectancy that those legendary tales of the fireside may materialise.'

What is undeniable is that Skye's landscape, its isolation and its legends have been entwined for as long as living memory. The pagan balance between the earth, the elements, the heavens and the spirits who dwell between and amongst them has had a palpable effect on the people of Skye, who worked the land and treated it with the same courtesy as if it was a particularly revered neighbour, though with a palpable edge of respectful disquiet – particularly when it came to the edgeland places: the forest, the mountains and the sea. Consider this line in an old Gaelic prayer: 'Send God in his strength between us and the Sidhe, between us and the dread Hosts of the Air.'

Even centuries after the spread of Christianity throughout the isle, long before the mournful sound of Gaelic psalms filled the air, the practicality and earthiness of what we might today call paganism still percolated through many islanders' beliefs. Celestial bodies had a great influence on the island's people. The habit of *deasil*, or circling an object three times 'sunwise' – the direction in which the sun tracks the sky – to mimic its life-giving power extended to all aspects of life.

The moon, too, dictated certain customs. Peat cutting and stacking for fuel was not conducted during the fortnight of the moon cycle in June, in the belief that unless peat is stacked when the moon is waning it will give no light, no heat and will simply smoke. Similarly, animals would only be slaughtered under a new moon, due to the superstition that the meat would shrink in the pot if cooked during the waning weeks of the lunar cycle.

Skye was dotted with sacred wells, said to give water that carried a healing spell cast by the spirits who lived in them. Anyone wishing to derive benefit from the well and its water would circle it three times sunwise, drink from or bathe in the water, then leave a personal offering – money, a pin, or a scrap of clothing tied to a bush – perhaps ensuring a link between the infirm individual and the spirit in the well, and a conduit for its beneficial powers. The modern habit of tossing a coin in a well for good luck is likely to have its origins in such practices.

Other things were tossed into wells, too. One Skye story concerns an outlaw named John MacRaing, who robbed and killed a girl near a well beneath Blàbheinn, on the shore of Loch Slapin. MacRaing's son, horrified by the act, was then dispatched too, and – with curious brutality – decapitated, his head cast into the well. The water source in question is called Tobar Ceann, which means 'well of the head'. It is one of many so named across the Highlands, most of which have a similarly gruesome tale attached to them, which somewhat casts doubt on the MacRaing story's authenticity.

Skye's MacRaing does seem to have existed at some point, though; William MacKenzie mentions him in *Old Skye Tales*, in the context of the Bealach Mòr on the Trotternish peninsula being 'infested' with robbers until more robust justice on Skye compelled them to seek more secluded haunts. 'One of these, MacRaing, had made himself especially obnoxious,' he wrote, suggesting Carn nam Bodach, a cave near the Old Man of Storr, as being his 'lurking place'. MacKenzie then states that 'MacRaing disappeared, and later was heard of in the Coolins.' His ghost is said to haunt the range.

Such skulduggery aside, much of Skye's mythology relates to the domesticity that dominated day-to-day life such as chores, the keeping and milking of animals, the spinning of yarn, the harvesting of crops – wholesome enough stuff, though invariably with a black sting in the tale. The *Bean-nighe*, or washing woman, is a precursor of coming doom often seen washing linen in lonely streams or lochans, and beating it with a stone. She is described variously on different islands, but on Skye is said to take a small, withered form, the *paisde beag bronach* – literally, 'small, pitiful child'. If you saw her, death was near.

Superstitions often had an edge that reflected the occasional brutality of belief and the difficulty of subsisting on the island, both of which were amplified with the arrival of Christianity. Unbaptised children and suicides were routinely buried in secluded areas beyond the yard of the *kirk* (church) and away from seaward aspects; it was said no herring would be caught in waters that could be seen from the grave of someone who took their own life.

Specific landscape features also had their own magical properties and spiritual connotations. Trees were always particularly important: a wand of rowan placed above a byre or barn door was said to ward off witches and evil spirits, while a fire made of rowan wood was said to be three times more sacred than a fire made of other trees. A copse near Uig was said to be so hallowed nobody would cut so much as a twig from it, while the loch nearby was considered off limits for fishing. Certain plants possessed powers, too: St John's Wort for warding off the evil eye and unwanted enchantments (but only when accidentally found), figwort for ensuring a productive supply of milk when placed in the cowshed, and the last sheaf cut from the harvest when placed above the door of a household for bringing luck in the coming year – the so-called *Maighdean-Bhuana*, or 'corn maiden', believed to hold the life of the crop.

The *gruagach* was a mischievous brownie or nocturnal household spirit who would lurk around a croft and cause mischief or disquiet. Small boulders dotted around the island were said to represent the spirit and were named *gruagach* stones; milk was poured over them as an offering to keep the entity appeased and to ensure a good supply of the same from the livestock. Occasionally the *gruagach* was mischievous in a rather different way; a report from 1794 even credited one as being the father of a child born near Duntulm.

As was perhaps predictable, the further from the lit windows of the croft and its environs, the darker and scarier the superstitions concerning the landscape became. The legends of sea and mountain served to inspire dread, whether to keep children away from danger or to simply exercise the imagination upon an evocative and powerful feature of the landscape.

The sea of the Hebrides was the haunt of the 'blue men of the Minch' – said to be the devil and his henchmen, who fell from heaven into the frigid waters and spent their nights seeking boats to wreck and sailors to drown. The Blue Men could only be appeased by the sailors' skill in verse, evidence not only of the importance of song and poetry to the Gaels, but a suggestion that their life might depend on it.

Mountains were the darkest realms, the places without sheep or crops, and – certainly until the 19th century in the Cuillin – the places where no one ever trod. Even thereafter it was considered by many a questionable enterprise to go amongst them, especially at night.

The Cuillin, you could argue, spooks people out, even by day – or at least, certain days. J. Hubert Walker, in *On Hills of the North*, described a companion with whom he was making an ascent of Sgùrr nan Gillean:

> a man of great strength of mind and character, very sensitive to beauty…
> who nevertheless on looking down into a corrie below Sgùrr nan Gillean
> on a day when truly the atmosphere was oppressive and the Cuillin at
> their most forbidding, suddenly said: 'I can't stand this place, it is
> accursed.'

To Skye folk, monsters lurked in many recesses of the Cuillin. Apparitions, demons and fairies haunted the peaks, wailed on their winds, and dwelled within their waters and in their caves. However unpleasant the aforementioned outlaw MacRaing was, it's unclear when he went from being a malign fugitive in the Cuillin to a ghost haunting it, but why he did so is easy to fathom: the ridge is the perfect environment in which to imagine such a ghoul. Concerning other wild places, there's an ancient Skye story of a priest who was approached whilst travelling through a forest near Broadford after nightfall by a group of *Daoine Sithe*, who begged the priest to bless them so they might regain their souls. The priest condemned them as evil, and as he fled through the forest he began to hear a wailing that erupted in the valley around him and extended up the slopes of Beinn na Caillich. Later, consumed by guilt, the priest sought the little people again and again, but was answered only by the same wailing that only he could hear.

Then there's the story of the *luideag*, or 'ragwitch' – a female demon who assumed the form of a slovenly woman. The *luideag* was murderous, haunting Lochan Dubh nam Bhreac between Broadford and Sleat, terrorising travellers or snatching them from the road having gained their sympathy. Similarly, the *glaistig* was a hag or she-devil, once a woman of good repute until she was cursed. She's a common feature of Gaelic folklore, almost invariably described as a thin, grey woman with long yellow hair who haunted houses or the living places of cows or goats. Skye's *glaistig* was said to be tall and extremely slender, and pale like a white reflection, sometimes haunting the *gruagach* stones. The *glaistig* is associated with the inner corries of the Cuillin and other barren and lonely places, where she hides from people and only emerges at dusk. Her name is a marriage of *glas*, meaning grey, and *stig*, meaning a sneaking, crouching object. I challenge anyone to sleep easily in these mountains after hearing that.

The water demon in the frightened minds of John MacCulloch's Coruisk boatmen was the *each-uisge*, better known as the 'kelpie' – an ancient Highland monster thought to haunt rivers and lakes. Kelpies weren't peculiar to Skye, but it seems that this particular breed of terror had an affinity for the deep-cut corrie lochs of the hills. Said to resemble a horse – at least at its front end – but of gigantic proportions, the kelpies were devious, seductive creatures. They would tempt children onto their backs, whereupon their manes would clutch at the little hands, grasping them and preventing dismount, carrying the unfortunate cargo into the depths of their lake. Particularly disobedient horse foals were said to be the illicit offspring of kelpies, impossible to tame unless you were in the unlikely possession of a silver bridle. Others say the creatures would shape-shift into siren-like women, luring lustful locals close before revealing their true form and devouring them.

A loch on Sleat – Loch na Dùbhrachan – was once so haunted by rumours of a kelpie it was actually dredged. This kelpie was allegedly seen by a cattleman. 'The beast swam out with its head below water, putting little waves ashore,' a witness later recounted. 'You can be sure the people were terrified.' Locals became so afraid to walk past the loch after nightfall the laird, Lord MacDonald, dispatched a group of ghillies with a net to rake the lake bed and catch the creature, or else dispel concern of its existence. During the dredging – an event of such interest the local schoolchildren were granted a holiday to watch it – the net fouled an obstruction on the floor of the loch, causing spectators and dredgers alike to flee with 'the fear of death in them'. And this was in 1870! Though as Derek Cooper dryly notes in his 1970 miscellany of the island, 'if it strikes you as strange that the simple-minded folk of Skye should seriously waste their time in searching for a water-horse, pause and reflect ... less than a hundred miles east and a hundred years later, research teams are using all the resources of modern technology to find an equally mythical monster.' He refers, of course, to the famously evasive denizen of Loch Ness.

Rather presciently for anyone sleeping in a hole high in the Cuillin, Coruisk – somewhat predictably – has its own collection of nasty super-stitions concerning caves in particular. Coir' Uisg, the corrie above Coruisk and beneath the crags of the Druim nan Rahm, aptly translates as 'Corrie of the Water Cauldron', but it was once known as Coire-nan-Uraisg: 'Corrie of the Monster'. The 'urisk' in question was said to be a creature with the legs of a goat and the upper half of a man, with 'long hair, long teeth and claws'.

The poet Robert Buchanan visited the loch in the company of a guide named Hamish, who told him of another cave near the loch, where a man from Dunvegan had come across the darkest foe of all on its shores. 'It was whispered about that he sold himsel' to the De[v]il, at night, here by the loch,' Hamish recounted, 'and he didna deny it.' In return the man was shown the way to a cavern covered with strange marks 'like writing all o'er the walls', where at the entrance he came across an old pair of shoes, the handle of a plough and a set of human bones. Unperturbed, the man made the dark transaction and became rich and troubled.

Hamish also knew of another dark place, the Cave of the Ghost, where 'the taisch [ghost] o' a shepherd has been seen sitting in it cross-leggit, and branding a bluidy sheep.' Even the hardy-headed climber Willie Naismith makes reference to the 'cave of the ghost' in his 1890 article in the SMC journal, where he mentions its location at the head of a lonely corrie. There's a cave on a knoll above Loch Coruisk's western shore that could answer both stories with its name, and location: Meall na Cuilce, 'Hill of the Shepherd'.

'Branding a ghost sheep, ah,' said Matt, his voiced muffled by his sleeping bag, bivvy and whatever else he'd sealed himself off against the elements with. 'Well, good that he's got something to do anyway.'

Back in the Sgumain Cave, the moon eventually ascended into the cloud, and what had been an ethereal spotlight became a diffuse, platinum glow. Matt was long sunken into his sleeping bag, pulling his bivvy over his head and now just a long orange tube to my right, every fidget a rustle of nylon against rough rock.

Using the Velcro fasteners, I'd stodged together my bivvy bag over my head. I've never been fond of these things. No matter how many fancy fabric signs it sports – usually with optimistic arrows depicting airflow and respiratory names like 'Exchange' and 'Vapour' to reassure you that breathing in such coffin-like accommodation is not only possible, but positively wafty – something about sealing myself up in the consumer equivalent of a body bag fills me with claustrophobic dread. Propping a rolled fleece under my head, I shuffled into a comfortable position, every movement a cacophony of crackly layers, before letting out that long sigh that signals the end of fidgeting and the beginning of sleep.

Sounds were just the occasional drift of breeze lifting the end of the plastic sheet near the door, or the caw of a corvid down in one of the corries below. The dark darkened, and quiet filled the Sgumain Cave. I was warm. I was *almost* comfortable. It was nearly perfect. And then it began.

I say began, but of course it had been like that all along – I just hadn't noticed. With all the shifting and shuffling and the cooking and organising, my awareness of the cave's constant and copious dripping had been limited to the odd damp patch, a well-timed splot on an exposed patch of skin, or Matt's ominous grumbling about the night to come. I'd ignored most of it. But now, in the quietness of the cave, ignoring it suddenly seemed rather harder. The worst part wasn't that we were getting slowly soaked, which we were. It was the noise: that 'plick' of water on nylon, which was completely maddening and impossible to escape. In the silence the drips took on rhythms, slid in and out of each other's time signature, had sudden ebbs and flows, and were felt as well as heard. Trying to sleep was like trying to take a maths exam with someone tapping a pencil on your head. And as the cold began to take grip, I became wired to the sound.

I don't usually have trouble sleeping in the mountains. I could sleep stacked up with the brooms in a shed if I was tired enough, as long as I was relaxed. But I wasn't relaxed. Worry about the day tomorrow, about the opportunity to sleep ebbing away with the hours, about the gravitational sliding towards the mouth of the cave that wasn't enough to land me on the Sgumain scree slope but was enough to keep me just a little bit tense, about the stone under the third rib up on my left-hand side. I couldn't sleep. And increasingly, my tired mind blundered in and out of preoccupations of half-read stories and ancient beliefs.

As an aside, if the geological explanation of how the Cuillin was formed is a little prosaic in pace, you can always rely on Skye's mythology to offer an alternative. So here, 'when the world was new', we have the Cailleach Bheur, the 'hag of the ridges' – otherwise known as Winter. She came from the north, and would often use the Sea of the Hebrides to wash her clothes, then spread them out to dry on Skye. Enter Spring.

The Cailleach Bheur was holding Spring's true love hostage as a wash-maiden; Spring fought against her power but could not win. Spring then appealed for aid to the sun, who threw a spear of fire at the Cailleach Bheur while she walked the heather moor of south-west Skye. The spear struck the earth and caused a blister, six miles long and six miles wide, from which the Cuillin ridge grew in a hot mass of molten rock. 'For many, many months they glowed and smoked, and the Cailleach Bheur fled away and hid beneath the roots of a holly, and dared not return. Even now, her snow is useless against the fire hills.'

This retelling of the formation of the Cuillin, along with a neat explanation as to why snow rarely lingers upon the ridge, comes courtesy of the grand empress of Skye mythology, Otta Swire. Swire's idiosyncratic and atmospheric book *Skye: The Island and Its Legends* (1952) is a concentrated source of much of what makes this place, as described in her chosen, apocryphal epigraph, 'not a place, but an intoxication'.

Describing herself as 'half Skye blood', Swire's interest in the folklore of the island stemmed from childhood holidays, which eventually culminated in her moving to the island in 1946 and buying a house in Orbost, where she wrote what would become her most significant book. Wry and affectionate but full of dark undertones, Swire's Skye is a stew of magic and myth; a place outside time, where the present looks square into the eyes of the past – a concept anyone who has spent time on the island can't fail to recognise. It is telling that a book about Skye's *mythology* was described by the academic Ronald Black as 'the best book about Skye ever written.' And for sure, it is best read at night, with the wind keening and the fire alive.

And so, high on the flank of Sgùrr Sgumain, our night crept on. A slow, thick breathing from a few feet to my right told me that Matt was weathering this somewhat better than I was. Strange, vivid half-dreams drifted in and out of my head: someone coming into the cave dressed in a life vest; the sudden fear that the stove was about to explode; all wrapped by the setting of the Sgumain Cave. No malign presences entered my thoughts, or the cave. And for that, if nothing else, I suppose I should be grateful.

9

Summit

Imagine you're on Skye, the conditions are clear and for whatever reason you find yourself at a loose end. Admittedly, the last two are generally mutually exclusive, but bear with me. Wait until the sun is low then go to one of those places where the Cuillin forms a flat black screen, and try to name the big peaks. It's not easy. Mainly because we're not talking four or five very distinctive summits but fourteen, all of which change the cut of their jib against the sky depending on the angle from which you look. Then there are the many other smaller peaks of the ridge – some thirty-one in all – which at a distance are easily mistaken for each other.

You might expect this with any interestingly built object, but there is something about the Cuillin that feels almost Machiavellian in its efforts to confound. Pinnacles and summits that sit kilometres apart slide behind each other at a distance and combine to make unfamiliar silhouettes, and fleeting phantom peaks might only look a particular way at the end of one precise and remote line of sight. The only common quality all aspects truly share is that they always look hard, and they always look sharp; there is no soft side to the Cuillin. Someone we're about to get to know quite well wrote of this shapeshifting nature:

> And go wherever you may
> With a new and deep surprise
> The Coolin blue will fill your view
> And fix your gazing eyes.

Of the great peaks, Sgùrr nan Gillean is perhaps the easiest to spot. This is due to its position at the extreme north-eastern end of the ridge, its claymore-point shape and proud bulk. And, of course, when in view, those pinnacles. These ratchet out to form a staircase of teeth to the true summit, and give the ridge its most recognisable and distinctive eye-jag.

At the ridge's southern extreme, Gars-bheinn too is difficult to mis-identify, despite being the baby of the range in height terms at least. It has an elegance to it, the crescent of ridge slacked between it and its neighbour Sgùrr a'Choire Bhig giving the pair the look of devil-horns from certain angles. From Elgol, for instance, the mountain you remember is Gars-bheinn. But while from the south it dominates, from the north it's invisible, completely eclipsed by the rest of the ridge.

Of the peaks that remain, it perhaps sounds unimaginative to say that the one that I could always spot was the highest point on the ridge – but not *because* it was the highest point on the ridge. Sgùrr Alasdair's qualifica-tion in this respect is pretty meaningless, given it is only the highest by six metres and is separated from the lowest major peak in the range by less than a hundred. But the highest it is – higher than Blàbheinn, higher than the topmost inch of the Inaccessible Pinnacle, and higher even than the famous Sgùrr nan Gillean, the mountain most commonly presumed to be Skye's highest summit in the days before we knew better. Why could I name it? I can't say. I would be tempted to say it just had something about it.

Sgùrr Alasdair retained a sort of dark charisma that endured well beyond the days of the Cuillin's initial explorations. The pioneer climber Charles Pilkington wrote of it in 1891:

> Its name does not occur on any map – there is a mystery hanging around it like the mists which so often veil its precipices. The ordinary tourist ignores its existence. He may see its sharp peaks peering over the other ridges, but he fails to understand that they belong to some higher and more distant mountain.

The thing that worried me about Sgùrr Alasdair was its summit. One of the old local names for this peak above Coire Làgan was Sgùrr Biorach, which literally means 'Pointed Peak' – an interestingly specific christening in the context of the Cuillin ridge, where everything is pointed. It made me wonder what it was about this one that deserved to be singled out. Lots of descriptions referred to its top as being 'airy', 'compact', 'tiny' even – but these terms could mean vastly different things from person to person. It's only when someone pins a recognisable quantity to a summit that you get a true measure, but people rarely do, despite it being, to me at least, the immediate question that springs to mind when considering an ascent of a mountain. (As an aside, I once asked an Everest summiteer to describe the very highest point on the planet in relatable terms; his response, after a long pause, was that it was like standing on an upturned bathtub.)

When it came to Sgùrr Alasdair, for me it was a description in W. Kenneth Richmond's *Climber's Testament*, where he wrote of this summit that 'a point it undoubtedly is: no room for a doll's house.' Now, I don't know how big a doll's house was in 1950, but the footprint of the one in my house isn't of a size I'd comfortably stand on atop a summit with drops of a thousand feet all around. J. Hubert Walker – I'm not sure what it is with these mountain authors with their keenness to abbreviate their first name – described mounting his camera tripod on the summit and finding himself unable to walk around it. 'The top of Alasdair is very sharp indeed,' he wrote. 'There is barely room for two people to sit down.' For someone trying to negotiate the Cuillin and manage a keen fear of exposure at the same time, I don't mind saying that I didn't like the sound of this place one bit.

When it came to the very first person to experience this pedestal, with all the off-comer and rather scientific action in the Skye mountains up until that point, it's perhaps fitting that it was a *Sgiathanach*, a Skyeman – and a rather soulful one at that – in the company of another who would claim its first ascent. The year was 1873, and alongside a shepherd named Alexander MacRae was the man often referred to as 'the Sheriff', from whom the highest mountain on Skye, and the Hebrides, would eventually take its name.

It's likely the mountain didn't have a name at all when the man who would later be memorialised by it was born in 1827 in Husabost on the Duirnish peninsula in Skye's north-western edge. To address the obvious first of all, Alexander Nicolson may be his most recognised name – but it wasn't the name by which he was addressed on home ground. As a child he was known as Alick Husabost, but in the mother tongue he was Alasdair MacNeacail, which of course accounts for the mountain rightly bearing the name Sgùrr Alasdair (rather than Sgùrr Alexander). 'Mac' meant, effectively, 'son of' – and so, anglicised, MacNeacail becomes Nicol*son*.

To the young Nicolson – given this book is written in English we'll call him by his anglicised name – the Cuillin would have been remote, on the edge of his world. In his writings he describes seeing its peaks from Husabost 'with unspeakable awe and admiration', but it took a return to Skye in later life, after spending his formative years in Edinburgh, for his mountaineering urges to take form. Nicolson evidently meditated on the Cuillin whilst away, 'the great blue mass ... with profile so clean-cut and memorable as a historical face'. Arriving back on Skye in 1865, with adventurous intentions, he checked in at the Sligachan Hotel, where he engaged the son of Duncan MacIntyre – the first ascensionist of Sgùrr nan Gillean with Forbes in 1837 – as his guide.

In the period since the Forbes–MacIntyre ascent, interest in Skye's yet-to-be-explored mountains had hardly blossomed. Barring the inebriated exploits of Algernon Swinburne and John Nichol on Blàbheinn in 1857 (in an escapade that sounds like a boozy version of *The Inimitable Jeeves*, the pair claimed the first ascent of this outlier whilst the former was being unsuccessfully nursed to sobriety by the latter), the main action was a great many repeat ascents of Sgùrr nan Gillean. Aside from that, and a first off-comer ascent of Sgùrr na Stri by Charles Weld in 1859, by 1865 the Cuillin had seen little recorded exploration by outsiders for several decades, although it seems unlikely it escaped investigation.

There was at least enough interest in climbing Sgùrr nan Gillean for MacIntyre junior (his first name doesn't appear to be recorded) to be sufficiently introduced to the mountain by his father and to lead Nicolson to the top of Gillean one 'glorious' midsummer day in 1865. Following the same route blazed by Forbes and MacIntyre senior decades earlier, Nicolson and his guide admired the summit views of the Atlantic and the atmosphere of the 'awfully fine and mysterious' corries of Harta and Lota, and shouted enough to conclude that the peak carried the 'most wonderful echo'. An idea of Nicolson's exploratory nature comes in his description of the descent:

Wishing to return by a different way, as I always like to do, I proposed that we try the north-west ridge . . . my companion was quite willing, though he said it had never yet been done . . . being considered impracticable.

The pair descended a little way down the ridge, until reaching a cleft which, to their eyes, looked to be the only means of reaching the foot of the formidable cliff above Coire a' Bhasteir:

. . . down which the only mode of progression was crawling on our backs. During the last few yards of our vermicular descent we could not see where we were to stop, and great was my satisfaction when I found my heels resting at the foot of the precipice.

The strange adjective used in that description – 'vermicular', meaning 'worm-like' – would become a favourite for Nicolson when describing his later climbs. Upon reaching the foot of the chimney, he appraised it and, as they'd made its first descent, vowed to ascend the mountain this way at some point in the future. His mountaineering torch was lit.

At least two likenesses exist of Alexander Nicolson. The one most widely published is a head-and-shoulders photograph showing a square-faced, strong-featured man with a rakish Balmoral bonnet pulled onto a head of bear-like proportions. This is clean shaven but for a wiry, greying moustache. Either the photographer was exceptionally good at capturing the character of the man or his features deftly reflected his personality, but you somehow sense at once that the man is strong but languid; the knitted brow suggests a somewhat stern presence, but something in the eyes says he was warm-humoured with it.

'A man of the most kindly and genial nature, he made many social friends,' confirmed one account of the character who would become the first real mountaineer-laureate of the Cuillin, while another stated: 'His geniality and his exuberant humour made him a universal favourite.' So clearly, here was a popular man. Nicolson's charisma, conscious or otherwise, was apparent in his presentation as a larger-than-life Highland gentleman and a Skyeman through and through. Described as a 'colossal figure attired in a kilt', the second likeness is a full-length portrait depicting him resplendent in full Highland finery, including a velvet blazer, kilt, buckled brogues and a sporran of such flaxen luxuriance it almost reaches his feet.

Nicolson was undoubtedly enthusiastic and varied in his interests, though never especially successful at any of them. Professionally he was said to have had a 'lethargic constitution', yet the bewildering array of professional hats he wore throughout his career ranged from educational consultant and lawyer to editor of the Scottish *Daily Express* (later the *Caledonian Mercury*). Invariably referred to as Sheriff Alexander Nicolson, in recognition of his position as Sheriff-substitute, his realm was Kirkcudbright and Greenock, although he was a sort of learned omnipresence on the islands too, often lending his voice to legal tribulations and sitting in on local disputes.

Nicolson was a Gaelic scholar, and his enthusiasm for the language's survival was highly influential in encouraging its study in schools in the face of widespread suppression in the 19th century. He also produced a book of his poems, which were often set to music. These chirpy if occasionally mawkish verses 'dropped by him on his path through life in the most casual and fitful way', according to a friend, are often quoted in descriptions of Skye. It was Nicolson who wrote the lines reproduced earlier in this chapter, as well as passages such as:

> Let them sing of the sunny South
> Where the blue Aegean smiles,
> But give me the Scottish sea,
> That breaks round the Western Isles!
> Jerusalem, Athens and Rome,
> I would see them before I die;
> But I'd rather not see any of these three
> Than be exiled forever from Skye!

And the oft-remembered:

> But if you're a delicate man,
> And of wetting your skin are shy,

> I'd have you know, before you go,
> You had better not think of Skye!

Nicolson, in his roving position of relative privilege, was one of the few voices that spoke reverently of Skye's beauty in positive terms, as most contemporary writing about Skye was preoccupied either with the landscape's oppressiveness, as with the Romantics, or was a sorrow-filled lament for a lost homeland by those banished from it during the Clearances.

In producing some of the most celebrated pieces of writing about Skye, Nicolson challenged the long-peddled view of tourists that his home isle was a place of 'stern solemnity', to use a term of Walter Scott's, which was ever so politely chided by Nicolson in an influential piece published in *Good Words* magazine in 1875:

That sense of loneliness and sadness which oppressed the genial soul of the minstrel, accustomed to Lowland greenery, and delighting in the haunts and the converse of men, is not natural to the born mountaineer, to whom the silence of the corrie is not the less delightful that it is unbroken by any sound of human voice.

It was, he added, referring to English tourists:

most natural that they should imagine Skye to be the veritable Ultima Thule, a desolate and inaccessible region, 'placed far amid the melancholy main', where all the people wear tartan and kilts, and see second sights, and never see the *Daily Telegraph*.

This 1875 article on Skye – published when Nicolson was 48 and a kind of personal summary of his relationship with the island – is perhaps the finest factual account of the Cuillin and its place within the fabric of Skye, as well as being a testimony of its first bona fide mountaineer. Written by a self-confessed 'poor unscientific blockhead and child of the mist', it reads with an enthusiastic bounce as if penned yesterday. Johnson and Boswell might have drawn the eyes of the learned masses to Skye; Forbes brought the scientific 'curiosity men' to the Cuillin, whilst MacCulloch, Turner and

Scott spurred their artistic awakening. But Nicolson was about to bring the mountaineers. As Ben Humble would put it much later, 'he opened the door wide: he was the first mountaineer and explorer among the Cuillin.'

Before we return to the ridge, let's consider Nicolson as a mountaineer. His spirit was one of adventure for adventure's sake, a very modern attitude. Ironically he seemed blind to a peak's height and focused rather on its appearance, once remarking that while grandeur was a factor, 'outline and features are, as with human beings, even more important.' He was bold, varying his routes to and from summits to maintain interest, walked in all weathers in all seasons, but was anything but reckless on the hill, having an acute awareness of his own capabilities. He also possessed a phenomenal stamina in the mountains, rather at odds with the accusations of his 'lethargic constitution' when it came to professional matters.

Whatever the mountains threw at him served only to add to Nicolson's visceral pleasure in the occasion, whether observing 'the mountain side, where a hundred chasms and ravines the torrents come roaring down the glens, streaking their slopes as with threads of silver', enduring an unplanned night out on treacherous ground or undertaking what's believed to be the first winter ascent of Sgùrr nan Gillean, alone in February 1872.

'These are feelings not for common men,' he wrote of mountaineering,

> they are more spiritual than physical ... [and] there is none more inspiring than the sensation of standing on a great height, attained with difficulty, and with nothing higher around.

Nicolson was here referring to Sgùrr nan Gillean, which at the time had recently been demoted by the Ordnance Survey to 3,167 feet, 33 feet shy of a barometer measurement made by Forbes in 1845. Despite this loss of height, Nicolson wrote that 'the heights of the other principal peaks of the Coolin have not yet been determined ... [but] there can be no doubt, I think, that Scur-nan-Gillean is the highest.' He didn't know it yet, but Sgùrr nan Gillean wasn't the highest in the Cuillin. That accolade belonged to a peak that he'd not only made the first ascent of two years earlier, but one that would later bear his name. And whose reputedly very compact summit was one of the spires above the Sgumain Cave, where nearly 150 years later, some damp companions were attempting to pass a night that was dragging, damp and spent, into day.

It seemed to me I got no sleep at all. But this couldn't be quite true, as a cautious sunlight roused me from something. The light, reflecting off wet rock on the flanks of the peaks outside like a tableau of broken mirrors, filled the view outside the door. That view again – for all the wretchedness of the night, the memory of this I knew would make it worth it, although I now had the queasy feeling that there was no more sleep, no more comfort or reprieve, from what was coming. With luck, wonder was on the way today. And with or without it, terrors.

Matt was already awake, and I could see him layered up and cross-armed standing just outside the cave's mouth, the sun on his face and his breath in the air. The sky was white, the sun that watery light of dawn heralding a day that could go any which way from there. It was cold and I was damp. One side of my bivvy bag had fidgeted loose in the night, and water had found my sleeping bag and – apparently – run amok.

'Eurgh,' I said, and coughed onto the cave floor. It smelled of old rain.

'Morning,' Matt said, strolling in and extracting the stove from his equipment. 'Well, I think that's just about as wet a night as you can have without being out in the rain.'

I made another noise. I wouldn't have traded the night in the cave for anything, as experiences go. But there had been a cost – little sleep, and I felt absolutely wretched for it.

'How are you?'

'Fine,' I lied.

Matt sloshed some water into the stove and lit it. 'So, the forecast has changed. Probably shouldn't hang around too long. Would save a trip down the scree if we can get by with the water we have left for now,' he said. 'You still have a couple of litres?'

I looked at the pile of full plastic bottles at the back of the cave. 'Yes.'

We busied ourselves getting stirred and packed while the stove rolled a boil. Matt went off to re-stash the kit in his nearby hidey hole, and I made a breakfast consisting of a chocolate bar, a pot noodle and coffee. Dietary conventions are meaningless in the mountains – it takes less than twenty-four hours for them to slip as you revert to being a mere machine in need of fuel. Sugar, carbs, protein and water in whatever form, whenever needed. I sat, letting the warmth of the coffee seep into me, steam rising into gummy eyes.

By the time I was packing away the last of my gear the light was halfway across the floor of the cave. Then, abruptly, it switched off. The sun had climbed into cloud and, peering out, I saw the landscape had lost its lustre, the hitherto shimmery faces of the mountains outside now looking back with flat expressions. A noise: a cyclic swish-swish-swish of nylon. On the other side of the cave mouth Matt was wheeling his arms in their sockets, a frantic windmilling motion, chasing cold out of his muscles. His helmet and harness were on, metal hung from his waist and he had a coil of rope slung diagonally across his chest. There was an urgency in his manner. Turning back to my sack, I pushed the rest of my gear in, keeping my food bag near the top, and pulled out the harness Matt had given me back at the car. A looped sling, a belay plate and two karabiners hung off it. I looked at it and tried to remember what to do.

There are two types of climbing harnesses: those you step into, and those you wrap around your waist. You use the one you wrap around your waist in the Cuillin, because then you keep both feet on the ground. The ones you step into can make you trip, and trips can become falls. Matt told me that, and you can't knock his logic.

I wrapped the waist belt above my hips, over my jacket. A part of it dangled down behind me like a tail, which I pulled between my legs, then looked for a way of connecting it all together and saw none. Just the process of putting it on, feeling it, hearing that clink of metal, made my guts squirm. Harnesses mean safety, but they also mean danger. I'd climbed before, under supervision. A few times I'd even reached a point approaching confidence while wearing a harness, but that was a long time ago. Everything felt ill-fitting and strange. Not being the sort of things you want to twist together and hope for the best, I walked out of the cave to where Matt was fine-tuning his kit, holding the harness in my hands like a child with a busted toy. He directed me, in the practised manner of someone who'd done it a thousand times.

'I'd do it for you, but you need to know yourself,' he said. Cold hands worked unforgiving, tight straps and cold alloy buckles, until it was together. Then he said, 'Can you just get your hand in the gap between the harness and your waist? That's how tight it needs to be.' A pause. 'Your life depends on it.'

It felt odd. Not comfortable. Harnesses don't tend to feel right until they're under tension. Matt ran the end of his rope through the karabiner and tied it on. He yanked it lightly and I felt the harness go tight. That done, he stood straight, paused, and looked at me.

'Had something to eat? Feeling clear? At least a couple of hours' sleep?'

I nodded. I wasn't sure I'd had a couple of hours, but I knew what he was getting at.

'So. A nice bit of Grade 3 scrambling. Just along here there's a chimney. Then a little bit of slightly broken ground as we ascend, then some zig-zags,' his arm indicated rocky slopes unseen above, 'then we pop out, onto the summit of Skye.'

With the cave at our backs, we traversed out onto the path, which ran like tape across the top of the scree, the rock fragments underfoot sounding like broken pottery. Wet-black crags rose to the left in walls – followed along with the eye, these became the Cuillin ridge crest, but followed upwards, their outlines became tatters against the sky.

The rope ran slack between us; there was no danger here. Matt was holding a coil in his gloved hand. My boots skittered on the loose path, and I slowed down. Walking while tied on to a rope takes practice – and sometimes it instils jitter in a gait. But we weren't walking far enough to worry. We stopped where a crag met the scree, and there was an obvious cleft in the rock. Matt let out some of the rope and I saw him click into a slightly different gear. His movements became brisker, his manner stiffer. Things were getting more serious. 'If you feel the rope going tight it's not because I want you to speed up,' he said, then took hold of the rock and I watched him go.

If you're a gymnast, or of an age still acquainted with the nimbleness of youth, it's possible to be dignified when climbing. With sprightly spatial awareness and joints that move like well-oiled bearings you can make the act of negotiating a steep pitch of outdoor rock look almost elegant, in a hard-edged kind of way. Watch a Cuillin guide negotiate their turf and you immediately see that it isn't tough at all. It's easy. Your heart fills with confidence as you watch their limberings unhesitantly unfolding in front of you. It all looks so effortless that you stop watching where they're putting their hands and feet because quite clearly it just happens.

And then you try it yourself.

It's then you realise that for most of us, most of the time, climbing is not elegant. It's a fight – a heavy, hurtful struggle. Then add ten years of home comforts and the insidious solidification that comes when you're approaching 40, and you start to appreciate that you're not quite as sprightly as you thought you were. A moment to recognise this in stark relief – should you need one – is the first time you put on a bulky, heavy rucksack with a varnish of rain and try to haul everything, including 70 kilograms of yourself, in a direction quite at odds with gravity, up something resembling a very long, quite slippy and extremely broken ladder. Grown-up humans are quite heavy and unwieldy things, especially when carrying other heavy and unwieldy things. And it's rarely dignified to move such a combination of objects so ambitiously upwards.

The final confirmation comes when you hear the words, 'Lovely holds. All the way just here – no problem whatsoever. I love this hold here, it's particularly nice.' And as you look up and see a wry little smile cross the face of your guide you realise that this is, actually, the start of the hard stuff. The dangerous stuff.

Alexander Nicolson said of a guide he knew, Alexander MacRae, that he had a 'peculiar style of walk, a sort of amble, and seemed to glide up the hillside like a cloud'. I saw something like that in Matt. Like watching any specialist at work, it's fascinating to see a guide move over the Cuillin. I'd describe the way he moved as a kind of serene bearing – deliberately measured, with never too much pace to pant and, as a result, quite relentless. He walked like he weighed a couple of pounds, humming tunelessly as he went.

But now he was climbing, I saw something different. When climbing you have to use every bit of your body, all your strength, deploying corners and surfaces you never thought you'd use for anything at all, let alone adhesion. I watched him ascend the chimney with a purpose I'd not seen from him at any point thus far – almost like he'd just discovered friction and kicked into gear. He found a stance, regained his composure and looked down at me. 'OK, up you come.'

Using arms and knees on edges and ledges of murky-smelling, oil-black rock, I heaved up the chimney towards Matt, who was watching my progress splay-legged from above and gently taking in the rope as I came.

'Does this chimney have a name?'

'Ah ... Simon's Chimney.'

I took the excuse to stop, a leg on each wall of the chimney, and look up at Matt. 'Really?'

'No, I don't think it has a name.'

The gabbro of this enclosed crack scratched into my rucksack with a sound like ripping paper. You don't think 10 kilograms is that much until you try and haul it upwards, and mine wasn't even a particularly heavy bag; when I passed Matt his off the boat yesterday I thought it was going to pull me over the side. But once I was used to the extra bulk – and learned not to be thrown off balance by it – it was easy to move with. My boots gripped, my gloves protected my hands, I felt confident. When Matt said 'Okay?' I said yes, and I meant it. I felt like I was in contact with the mountain, it felt solid and amenable, and I could see where to go next. This wasn't a pioneering new route. I wasn't exploring. But this was new to me. And I *loved* it. I was climbing on the Cuillin ridge, approaching the highest point on Skye, after a night in a cave with the sea in my lungs and the thrill of height filling my body. Compared with most of the population at this hour on this particular late September morning – hell, any morning – I was mining gold.

The rope, however, I found a nuisance. They say, 'Climb as if there is no rope' – but that's hard. The chimney wasn't especially exposed; a very painful slide and perhaps a broken leg or two to finish might be the outcome of a bad slip, but it would take some awful judgement or lack of attention to achieve any kind of slip here. This wasn't the sort of exposed ground I disliked – I was happy as long as I had some rock either side to grab. But having a rope to keep shifting out of the way or keep below my arms was something I couldn't get used to. Not least because its interference reminded me it was there – which in turn reminded me why.

It did make me feel safer, but I could understand why it was that many of the early climbers chose not to use one. An enduring story is that climbers exposed to the infamously moist Skye weather shunned a rope due to its enthusiastic habit of absorbing rain. Ropes in the pioneers' days were made of hemp, which, while eminently durable, sucks up water with such efficiency it's used in nappies. Naturally when it came to rope, this resulted in a heavy, shrink-and-rot-prone piece of equipment that was more millstone than lifesaver.

This, with the tendency of early ropes to acquire insidious weaknesses with the slightest mishandling – weaknesses that only turned into breaks when someone mortally dependent upon the rope decided to test it with a fall, say – had the consequence of instilling a certain lack of confidence in their use. The Scottish climber Harold Raeburn described a near miss with a rope he'd loaned to a friend who evidently hadn't dried it with due care before returning it. 'I bent it sharply, when it at once broke half way through,' he wrote in his book *Mountaineering Art*. 'It proved to be thoroughly rotten, and unable to bear a strain of more than 50 pounds.' When the rope broke, Raeburn had been moments away from using it to descend a sea cliff.

The situation with ropes didn't really improve much right into the 20th century, up to which point they were more of a mountaineering placebo than anything to which you'd feel comfortable trusting your life. Some enterprising experiments by climber John Hart Bell in 1897 revealed that ropes of the time would break under falls vastly shorter than the wearer might have expected – some as little as 9 feet, for a falling weight of 11 stone. 'Probably many of us have had delusions as to the value of a rope hitched 20 or 30 feet below the leader,' Bell wrote, before making the additional unhappy observation that in such a case a falling body would have to absorb 660 *kilograms* of lacerating strain as a rope went tight against it – and that 'whether a man has any chance of standing such a jerk without serious injury is a question for the doctors'. It is therefore unsurprising that early climbing manuals are filled with stoic proclamations like 'Trust in the rock,' and the peerlessly solemn 'The leader must not fall.'

Today, however, take a look in any serious outdoors shop and the choice of ropes is bewildering. You won't find a piece of equipment that demonstrates the development of the sport quite so impressively whilst remaining so outwardly simple; it's a shame the terminology doesn't follow suit. In terms of mode of use, you can have 'twin ropes', which are one thing, and you can have 'half ropes' which are another – despite the latter also rather confusingly being known as 'double ropes'. Then you can have ropes that can be used as all three and are called 'triple rated', but evidently these aren't very durable, so you probably won't relax using them in any case. A 'dry' rope is a rope that is good in the wet; work that one out. You can buy ropes from 8.7mm to 11mm in diameter, and construction is generally a sheath-and-core system, which comprises a weave of polyamide fibres that are spun into twine. The twine is then twisted together to form a strand, or cable, several of which run together down the length of the rope to form the core, or 'kern', to use the German word indelibly attached to this design. This is then covered by a tight braid of yet more strands, which forms a protective sheath or 'mantle'. This *kernmantle* construction means most ropes these days are called 'dynamic', which basically means they stretch under load, making a fall a much more civilised, less rib-popping affair – not quite bungee jumping with an edge, but not far off.

And, of course, as we live in the 21st century, everything is regulated by safety standards. It all gets very complicated, involving sums, ratios and something called a 'fall factor', but all you need to know is that any decent rope sold these days must be capable of withstanding at least five pretty heavy falls before losing its dynamic properties. Signs of wear or damage to the mantle are easy to spot before the core is exposed, meaning you have two stages of safety – and as most ropes are now strong enough to lift a Range Rover before breaking, these safety margins are quite generous. In short, modern ropes are extraordinary pieces of engineering that make it unlikely that any accident, were you to be unlucky enough to have one, would be down to a snapped rope.

Matt would later inform me that the rope we were using was a fine example of how far this hallmark piece of climbing equipment has come on in the intervening century or so. His 'traverse rope' was 9.1mm in diameter and 40 metres long. 'That's enough for all the abseils with two clients. You could get away with 37 metres if it was just two of you. Basically ropes are about the balance between something light, because I have to carry it a lot, and something durable' – he tapped a jag of gabbro – 'because of this.'

In the past – and it applies now too – the Cuillin ridge undermined the basic conventions of using a rope in the mountains as the rock was simply too abrasive. The idea of 'hitching' – that is, the casual wrapping of a rope around handy pinnacles and edges in a way that would interrupt a fall – was common in the Alps, but on the ridge it had the downside of putting the rope in uncomfortable proximity to something that would happily slice through it with enough encouragement. Given that alpine travel typically involved one person roped to another with nothing connected to the mountain, the correct method of arresting a fall was sketchy at best. One school of thought, should you see the person connected to you by a length of rope suddenly take to the air and the slack between you start stiffening, was to fling yourself over the opposing ridgeline to counterbalance the weight and pray that the rope didn't find a sharp edge. More often than not – if you had time to think – it was a case of bracing, clutching and praying.

The cover of Ken Crocket's *Mountaineering in Scotland: The Early Years* illustrates the almost ludicrous optimism with which early climbs were conducted. Above Glen Coe, one F. S. Goggs sits in a brace position on a coil of rope whilst his companion – W. A. Morrison – investigates the corner of a vertical wall above and across from him, with oblivion beneath. Both have an old-fashioned rope knotted above their hips, the length between them running straight up then straight across – a kind of inverse 'L' – with its corner resting on a little nub of rock as big as the blade of a Stanley knife and probably about as sharp. The theory was, if the intrepid Mr Morrison took a slip, the reliable Mr Goggs would brace and the force of the fall would land in a sudden and concentrated manner onto a couple of square centimetres of slender rock. This rock – despite being, in terms of vindictive physics, the equivalent of hanging a wet sheep on a picture hook – would hopefully arrest the fall.

The optimistic outcome would be that Mr Morrison dangled for a while, they'd share a joke, a chuckle and, once recomposed, a pipe of tobacco (Mr Morrison's would have to be inserted into his mouth while he was upside down). Then the pair would say something chipper to each other and the climb would go on. I jest, of course – but it's hard not to when at least one of the protagonists in this historical scenario is wearing a *tie*, for god's sake. The pessimistic outcome, of course, would be that the rope snapped at the point of stress and Mr Morrison fell to a violent end far below, watched by his helpless ropemate, who then would probably smoke a pipe of tobacco and in all likelihood continue the climb. Hence the adage, 'the leader must not fall'.

Given these factors, the Cuillin gabbro's lacerating nature is likely to have contributed to a reluctance to use ropes in the early years. But more likely is that the confidence-giving grip of this rock rendered ropes unnecessary for the early Cuillin pioneers, who at this point were still exploring the summits of the ridge – rather than the minutiae of the harder, more vertically inclined rock routes on the crags. Many descriptions of the Cuillin carried implicit warnings that the rock was in fact not suitable for novices to learn climbing on because it was *too* grippy, thereby instilling a false sense of security in no way compatible with other mountains.

Alexander Nicolson was a case in point. He carried no rope, but did enjoy the occasional assistance of a pleasingly Scottish multi-functional piece of aid, about which he recorded much praise: '[There are] many uses to which a plaid can be turned, of which no other garment is susceptible,' he wrote.

> With the help of a belt, it can, in a few minutes, be made into a full dress for a man; it is the best and lightest of wraps by day, and serves for bedclothes at night; it can be used as a bag; it will serve as a sail for a boat; it is valuable as a rope in rock-scrambling; it can be turned into a curtain, an awning, a carpet, a cushion, a hammock. Its uses, in fact, are endless, and as a garment it has this superiority over every other, that 'there's room in't for twa'!

Plaid is the folded sheet of traditional Highland tartan – more of a blanket, really – such as the kind often seen wrapped around bagpipers. Nicolson's description of it being 'big enough for t'wa' suggests that he is describing the 'full' plaid which, for all its usefulness, must have been murderous to carry when dry, never mind when wet. Traditionally cut to be around twice the height of its wearer when unfolded, the plaid is made from woven wool, and therefore kept some warmth when saturated – but of course becoming weighty with it.

The idea of Alexander Nicolson's use of plaid as attire on the hill and as a kind of buccaneer-style rope conjures up a fine image indeed, seeming to belong to a quite different time. One amusing observation about Nicolson – regarding both the practicality of his attire and his general attitude in the hills – was that 'one night he paid the mountaineer's penalty of having to sleep out in his kilt, the mist having come down when he was near the summit of a very ticklish downward path.' Nicolson's response to this, inevitably, was a verse:

> Here wrapped in my plaid in the heather,
> I envy no monarch his bed,
> Come, dreams of the hills and the Highlands,
> And visit in slumber my head

Even in 1873, the thought of anyone exploring the Cuillin in a kilt seems out of time somehow – yet it was the late summer and early autumn of this year that would see Nicolson's most memorable *tour de force*. Were you to wither down Nicolson's decade of heady exploration on the ridge, it would be two days – two remarkable, separate expeditions – that would stand proud as his legacy, and would in a stroke double the number of summits that had felt the scratch of bootnails or indeed, the tickle of plaid. Or rather, two days, and most of a night.

At this point only a possible five peaks on the ridge itself had been recorded as being climbed – most of these at the northern end, only four with anything approaching certainty, and only two of what you might call the major peaks of the ridge. The certain four were Sgùrr nan Gillean by James Forbes and Duncan MacIntyre in 1836, Bruach na Frithe in 1845 (again by Forbes, for his mapping project) and the satellites of Sgùrr Thuilm and Sgùrr na h-Uamha by Admiralty surveyors – the former an outlier of Sgùrr a' Mhadaidh, the latter an underlier of Sgùrr nan Gillean.

The fifth other possible ascent of the era was that of Sgùrr a' Ghreadaidh by William Tribe in 1870. If it occured, this peak, a formidable objective in the central Cuillin, was the highest anyone had climbed on the ridge up until that point, its crenellated 973-metre top standing higher even than Sgùrr nan Gillean by nine metres – though of course at the time nobody knew that. The ascent was significant, given that Tribe was reputedly in the company of a certain 13-year-old ghillie named John MacKenzie. Despite an alleged ascent of Sgùrr nan Gillean by MacKenzie at the age of ten, the Sgùrr a' Ghreadaidh ascent is disputed – because, it seems, the union with William Tribe doesn't quite live up to its presumption.

Rather than the young ghillie being employed by a tourist or well-heeled visitor, Tribe was in fact only fifteen himself, which gives the episode the air of two youths at large rather than anything more formally intrepid. Usually referred to as William N. Tribe, it's interesting to note that a certain William W. Tribe, who was the right age to be the youth in question, became a noted rock climber in the Lake District and later returned to Skye with his wife to climb in the Cuillin. It seems a little too neat to be a coincidence, and if these two individuals were one and the same, it makes this unlikely first ascent all the more credible. It certainly shouldn't be discounted merely on the grounds of the protagonists' rascally age.

We have another glimpse of MacKenzie around this time, this one from the pen of author Robert Buchanan – the man who imparted the unpleasant legend of the devil in the Coruisk cave. On one excursion from Sligachan, Buchanan found himself in the company of a guide, recording in *The Hebrid Isles* (1871), 'a gloomy Gael of thirteen, as sturdy as a whin-bush, and about as communicative . . . uttering ever anon an eldritch whistle much like the doleful scream of the cerluw'. It's the first appearance of Skye's most famous ghillie-guide in mountaineering literature.

Other than Blàbheinn and Sgùrr na Stri, another peak that might also have seen feet was Gars-bheinn, which according to historian Stuart Pedlar was possibly climbed by the Admiralty Survey in 1857 – being accessible from the sea and a relatively easy ascent. You can see the thinking: it's a fine vantage point from which to survey the wriggly coast and its land-marks.

Often the only evidence of a climb was, literally, evidence – such was the urge to leave something on the top of the mountain to prove you'd been there. Graffiti, a message in a bottle, a cairn. But evidence of earlier ascents were perhaps less symbolic. Nicolson himself described finding a wooden stake on the summit of outlier Sgùrr Thuilm – one of two peaks possibly climbed by the Admiralty Survey – when he climbed it in August 1873. Nicolson came to this conclusion, given that Sgùrr Thuilm was one of the few of the Cuillin that had over the course of the years acquired a height: in this case, 2,884 feet.

The peaks clustered around Sgùrr nan Gillean were achievable from the good road and inn at Sligachan, and the path into the glen was by far the most known of the route into the Cuillin, upon which Blàbheinn, Sgùrr Hain and Sgùrr na Stri were natural objectives, so the idea that the Admiralty Survey also climbed Sgùrr na h-Uamha is entirely plausible. Nicolson, however, expressed a specific dislike for this path, describing it as the 'worst on Skye'. Gars-bheinn, moreover, would have been easily accessible directly by sea, or from Coruisk.

It's perhaps harder to understand why it took the adventurous Nicolson until 1873 to investigate the Cuillin above Glen Brittle, or 'Glean Breatal'. By this time the glen had become largely depopulated, save for a cluster of buildings near the loch, of which one was Glen Brittle House – soon to be well stamped by climbers. As late as 1948 Glen Brittle's road remained notorious, a 'rough, stony track', according to J. Hubert Walker in *On Hills of the North*, 'and though cars can and do use it, much time is taken over the journey'. Of Glen Brittle itself Walker wrote, 'without a car this village is useless as a base for the Cuillin, and almost so with one.'

Nevertheless Nicolson made it down to the glen in late August, where he said that he was 'told ... that another peak, a very beautiful one, which forms a prominent object from the house there, had never been ascended, and had foiled the Ordnance men. This naturally stirred my desire to attempt it.'

The peak, to Nicolson, would have appeared from Glen Brittle House as a pronounced pyramid to the high right of the tableau of the Cuillin that filled the view to the east. Here, partly masked behind the splay of Sgùrr Dearg's western flank, was a sight of the ridge's sharp innards, over which this mysterious, set-back summit held a dignified sway.

First he made a reconnaissance, walking up into Coire Làgan to the shore of the 'small dark loch' in wringing conditions. From it he caught 'out of the midst of driving mist, a single glimpse of ... one of the wildest objects

I ever saw'. From up in the corrie – where I had failed to see anything much at all the previous spring, and to which I owed a revisit – the views around you are sensational. Even in mist you can tell that rock rises all around you, purely by feel. From its shore, Sgùrr Alasdair rises in a near perpendicular pyramid of crags and buttresses, climbing to a summit invisible from the low, deep angle. It's but one of the many frowning summits that surround the corrie, separated by high passes and draped with long screes, every one of them unclimbed when Nicolson made his ascent into it.

The following morning, in the company of the shepherd Alexander MacRae – he of the cloudlike walk – Nicolson took the first steps of the most adventurous days the Cuillin had yet seen.

Alexander MacRae is an exceedingly overlooked character in the history of the Cuillin. Particularly given the relative fame of John MacKenzie, whose achievements were perhaps more prolific and certainly more reported, but in many ways no more ground-breaking.

Born in 1806, fifty-one years before MacKenzie, MacRae lived for a spell in Camasunary before settling on the Isle of Soay, where he worked Croft No. 1 in the shadow of the ridge, a kilometre across the sound. According to Norman Macdonald and Cailean Maclean in *The Great Book of Skye*, MacRae developed a 'national reputation for his knowledge of the Cuillin and was an advisor and guide to early climbers' – and this he undoubtedly was. To Nicolson he was a shepherd who was 'well acquainted with all the hills and passes and a first-rate climber,' which certainly seemed enough to justify his presence on Nicolson's historic excursions of August 1873.

Nicolson's recording of these days seems to have been limited to a breathless but elegant digest in his *Good Words* article in 1875 – later climbers would spend thousands of words describing much lesser achievements – which lends them a tantalising air, unspoken details swirling in the mists like the mountains he describes. Concerning the 'wild object' that had caught his eye and was the goal of the day, Nicolson said of MacRae that 'he, too, had never been up, and had never heard of any body having done it.' But first, they had other business.

Nicolson and MacRae climbed from Glen Brittle up Coire na Banachdich with the intention of first ascending Sgùrr na Banachdaich, of which there was also no recorded ascent. Nicolson – maybe considering the peak a lesser endeavour due to its fairly anonymous profile, or the fact that it had been dismissed by James Forbes as 'perhaps [being] accessible from the Glen Breatal side' whilst evidently not being worth the professor's trouble to attempt. Whichever may be the case, it would be Nicolson and MacRae who would definitively climb this peak first. Exactly which way they found their way up is unknown, but it evidently wasn't a chore. Nicolson notes the detail chirpily: 'a charming climb ... we found no difficulty in any part of ascent,' before discussing the name of the peak: 'There I discovered the meaning of that singular name, the Smallpox Peak, which I never could understand.'

I'd heard it mentioned that Sgùrr na Banachdaich meant 'Smallpox Peak' too. I'd assumed – and this is an unlikely scenario given that peaks were rarely given Gaelic names for a resemblance – the name came from the mountain's resemblance to a pustule. You can just about see it; its slightly rounded and scabby profile perhaps lends itself more to this unpleasant comparison than other peaks of the Cuillin, though not by much.

I asked Matt about this in the Sgumain Cave the night before, if only for the pleasure of using the word 'pustule' while he was stirring up his meal, and he added an interesting but rather darker offshoot to the theory, saying that another meaning of *Banachdaich* is 'dairy maid'. The rumour of immunity to cowpox amongst those who worked with bovines was commonplace for some forty years before Edward Jenner finally proved it in 1796, using cells from cowpox lesions to inoculate James Phipps with the first ever vaccine. The cells were gathered from the lesions of Sarah Nelms – who was a milkmaid. Interesting stuff, but why would they name a mountain after them?

Matt frowned. 'Well ... the corrie is called Coire na Banachdich. It might be that the peak is named after the corrie, rather than the other way around. Which isn't unknown.' He stirred his meal some more, then said, 'I've heard that when Glen Brittle was still populated and someone had smallpox, they were isolated up in the corrie to prevent the spread amongst the village. If you got better, you got better. Or you died. And who would you send up to nurse those suffering from smallpox?'

'A dairymaid immune to it.'

'Just a theory.' He stirred some more, then said, 'Brutal times.'

It was just a theory, but it was reasonable. Seton Gordon thought *Banach-daich* could translate either to 'dairy maid' or simply to 'pitted'. The other possibility is that the smallpox association was a red herring and that Sgùrr na Banachdaich was named for a dairy maid alone – the corrie beneath it was used to keep livestock, and the names of peaks and corries often reflected one another. Because corries were useful and peaks were not, it's likely the corrie was named first. Peter Drummond thinks this is probably the case, and wrote in *Scottish Hill Names* that the remains of shielings in Coire na Banachdich prove it.

The problem with this prosaic explanation is that it's likely that Nicolson – Gaelic scholar that he was – would probably have been able to deduce it. And if he hadn't, then shepherd MacRae, certainly as a farmer if not also as an expert on Cuillin nomenclature, surely would have. It's worth noting that MacRae by this point was a remarkable sixty-seven years old, and so presumably in possession of a tremendous amount of local knowledge.

Regardless, the meaning of the name was settled to Nicolson, at least, when he reached the summit with MacRae and noted that 'the surface of the rocks is marked by little red spots, caused by oxidation, whence no doubt the name.' The uncomfortable truth is, of course, that for someone to name the peak after the appearance of the rocks on its *summit*, means that someone else must have been there in times past to see them. This notwithstanding, the pair are credited with the first recorded ascent.

Proceeding south along the ridge, the next peak on MacRae and Nicolson's agenda that day was, remarkably, also a first ascent – and perhaps a much more significant one, as it put them in proximity to the most infamous feature of the entire Cuillin ridge:

We went on, down then up, to Sgur Dearg and made the acquaintance of that formidable horn ... it stands out a little from the main ridge, and is the termination of a precipice of some 1,200 feet that goes right down into the basin above Coiruisg.

The Inaccessible Pinnacle is the thing that sticks in the eye on Sgùrr Dearg and forms the true top, by seven metres or so, of what otherwise would be a rather broad and featureless mountaintop, but Nicolson preferred instead to rest his eyes and ambitions on the much more enticing view that was spread out before him. One writer has judged that Sgùrr Dearg minus the Inaccessible Pinnacle – a circumstance which will no doubt one distant day become a reality – would be 'the dullest of all the Cuillin summits', but its top is without doubt one of the great viewpoints of Scotland.

Sgùrr Alasdair dominates it, a long, tapering triangle, rising in ruckled, bony shoulders to an exceedingly sharp summit. This point is rent in two slightly on the left side, giving an uneven twin peak, like a beaked mouth, facing the sky and frozen mid-snap. A long, fluidic stain drips from the side of this mouth, pale against a spreading apron of scree plunging deep into the corrie. The corrie is Coire Làgan; the stained scree slope the infamously mobile slog known as the Great Stone Shoot. Almost waterfall-like, the Shoot is strangely serene amongst a catastrophe of ravaged crags, overhanging buttresses and a skyline bristling with spines and pinnacles. From this angle, there's a peculiar, rounded step on the slope to Sgùrr Alasdair's left shoulder, like the elbow of the folded wing of a bat – Sgùrr MhicCoinnich – and on the opposite side a subsidiary peak: Sgùrr Sgumain. The lower of the twin summit peaks is Sgùrr Thearlaich. It's a remarkable tableau, or as Nicolson put it so well from his vision the previous day, a 'wild object' indeed. It was his first clear sight of the summit that would later bear his name.

The panorama from Sgùrr Dearg could present Sgùrr Alasdair's most impressive angle – but it's debatable. As I had seen it from Sgùrr nan Eag the previous evening, the mountain's silhouette from the south is no less arresting. From there the Stone Shoot is broader, the gap between Alasdair's summit and the raggedy spike of Sgùrr Thearlaich more slot-like, no longer a mouth, but a claw. But from both angles it's extraordinary: naked rock, piled up in dramatic gothic lines, dark and commanding.

From Sgùrr Dearg Nicolson and MacRae proceeded along the ridge, though they soon found their way blocked by the impasse of the Coireachan Ruadha Crags and Sgùrr MhicCoinnich, a technical section of ridge that was probably beyond the two men that day. Surmounting the obstacle didn't seem an option, so the two descended via the screes into Coire Làgan. Crossing the high basin above the loch, they ascended the Great Stone Shoot – a notorious slog for modern mountaineers – in penance for skirting the difficulty of the crest. Nicolson described it with presumable understatement as 'stiff and warm'.

'Some judgement was required to find a way,' he wrote of the last section to Sgùrr Alasdair's summit, 'and still more when it came to circumventing the peak. We did it, however, without much difficulty: one or two places were somewhat trying, requiring good grip of hands and feet; but on the whole I have seen worse.' And with that, they were there.

A chasm had opened beneath us as we climbed out of the chimney. A long way down it, I could see a snake of corries leading down towards Coruisk. It was dizzying, but the footing was good, and before long I was comfortable enough to start enjoying and scaring myself just a bit. This was apparently the point, after all. I could sense the weather was breaking, possibly badly. But just for now I didn't want to think about it. Matt was here, he knew the ridge, could judge the weather and would say if we needed to change tack. You trust your guide.

Above Matt the chimney kinked a right, and as I came up beneath him a tickle of air on the back of my neck indicated that we were on the ridge once again. Soon the skyline began to lower towards us as Matt led the way up steep, broken ground, this way and that, up corners and steps; pathless, but secure. Cloud had begun to swirl around us, masking the space below my feet. Matt had stopped, and I found myself looking at his ankles and listening to my own breath. The rock had changed from gritty and black to smooth edges and blocky breaks, with tinges of green lichen. I knew what that meant.

'This is a basalt summit,' Matt said. I looked up, and he appeared as a black hole against a sky bright and filled with cloud vapour alive on the wind. 'It's been struck by lightning a lot. So it might be slippy, there might be some loose bits, so. . .' He stopped short of saying, 'Be careful,' as there really was no need.

He began to move again, and I followed before the rope went tight. And then very quickly the last block underfoot became the last block on the mountain. We stepped out onto the highest rocks of the Cuillin ridge, of Skye, and the Hebrides.

The clouds were thin and painfully bright. Behind them I could see the ghosts of mountains, shadows beyond the grey-white. There was no real view, just impressions of shapes: slender ridgelines, steep drops, the occasional glimpse of a summit, everything white and deep. It could have been three thousand feet high or twenty thousand feet – there was no visual anchor, just us, the summit, the cloud and its shadows. This mountaintop, 3,255 feet above the sea, was a weather-sharpened point in silhouette, hard-angled and solid, against empty air. The summit of Sgùrr Alasdair, as I had read, and feared – fell away briskly on all sides. Slip into a fall, and you'd die. But it wasn't a fearful moment. For the first time that morning, the air seemed motionless. And I was grateful to discover that there was in fact a secure place to stand, and a bit of rock to hold on to. Somewhere to just stop, and soak it in.

We were in a little dip, like a gap in a stone wall, between two outcrops. To the right, perhaps ten feet away, was a rough apex. One side was a sloping slab tattooed with white lichen and furry with moss.

Matt took out his water bottle, wandered slowly forward and stood on the platform. He took a long drink, replaced the lid, then placed the bullet-shaped bottle on the very top rocks. I didn't know if it was a conscious thing, but as he did it the mountain suddenly had an informal little summit marker – a shape that visually drew together the slopes of the rocks either side into a human-augmented point. Matt, his feet below but head above, stood there for a moment. Beyond him, far off in the distance, the sun burned through the cloud and lit the sea in bright gold lashes. The scene was completely *other* – one of those feelings of unreality you sometimes get in the mountains. I thought back to the times I'd seen Alasdair from afar. Then I looked at the mossy rock underfoot and the summit just there, and thought: *I'm on top of that.* It was a moment. We didn't speak.

And then, just as quickly, it faded. The invisible sun dimmed. The shadows of the mountains around and beneath lost their veil-like appearance and disappeared into the grey. Matt looked around, picked up his bottle, and the summit was once again a naked, unadorned top. His movements had lost their unhurried slack, and became purposeful and brisk.

'Time to go,' he said. The sky had darkened, as if somewhere a huge pair
of curtains had just been swept shut and – with frightening speed – bright
white became a heavy, cindery grey. In less than thirty seconds, we were on
a different mountain, on a different day.

How long Nicolson and MacRae spent on this summit is unclear, as in his
account of the climb Nicolson doesn't dwell on it long either. He also doesn't
mention the conditions, though his descriptions of the view – 'exceedingly
fine and varied' – suggest they were reasonable. But he does comment on
the unadorned state of the summit:

> Whether this peak was really ascended for the first time that day, I cannot
> say, but it seemed very like it. There was, at any rate, no sign on the top
> of any one having ever been on it before.

In the early days of recreational Cuillin climbing, bottles were left on
summits with a paper inside as a kind of informal log of those who'd made
it up there. As time went on these became more sophisticated – Matt
mentioned he'd found a log from the 1980s the previous week near the
summit of Sgùrr nan Gillean, sealed in a military waterproof container –
but the more typical act to record your passage was to build a small pyramid
of rocks on the highest point – a cairn, or 'stone man'. The absence of
human traces on Sgùrr Alasdair since it was carved out some 57 million
years ago until the late summer of 1873 would end with the visit of Nicolson
and MacRae. 'Of course, we thought it our duty to make up for that by
erecting a cairn,' Nicolson wrote, concluding with the rather ambitious-
sounding, '[thus] adding a few feet to the height of the peak.'

It would seem unlikely that building such a grand cairn was even possible
from the rocks the pair found around the summit, although many subsequent accounts noted the quantity of rubble on the summits and unclimbed
routes of the Cuillin. Evidently the peaks were a lot more stony before the
modest but clearly effective human traffic of climbers cleared the way.
Whether it was 'a few feet' high or not, Nicolson adds that later he was able
to admire the cairn from an adjoining peak, suggesting it must have been
hefty enough.

Obviously Nicolson and MacRae derived both pride and amusement from piling up a cairn on Sgùrr Alasdair, but marking the highest point of a very big rock with a pile of small rocks is a peculiar thing to do when you think about it. On the one hand you could see it as a harmless, simple record – a kind of geological leg-cock, something to prove to others that you'd got there, a common behaviour in cultures from the ancient Greeks to the Inuits of Alaska, hard-wired into us as a species. But you could also say it's human arrogance, the symbolic denial of something natural by ensuring that it's you who places the final full stop on it, as bad as slapping a sponsor's logo on the Great Barrier Reef or sticking a lighthouse on the moon. In these slightly more environmentally reverent times you could have a good chew on this idea.

Nowadays, aside from cairns, the most common feature you might expect to find on British mountain summits is an Ordnance Survey triangulation pillar. These were not intended to be summit markers – they're just generally found on summits as these tended to be the best viewpoints around for sighting other trig points; a further two had to be seen from each point to make triangulation, and therefore early maps, possible. As we have seen, the early surveyors didn't reach many of the Cuillin's supposedly impregnable summits, let alone do any meaningful surveying work there, which is why the early OS maps of the Cuillin were somewhat impressionistic.

Later, when the decades-long retriangulation of Great Britain began in 1934 and trig points started proliferating across the country's exposed and wild places – and elsewhere – the Cuillin ridge presented even more of a problem. Consider the practicalities and labour involved in climbing onto compact rocky summits, excavating into them and installing a few hundred kilograms of concrete, then conducting days of precise survey work, all in a tempestuous climate and on exposed ground, and it starts to make sense why almost all the summits of our steepest mountain range escaped having trig points installed on them, making them notably unadorned as British mountaintops go. The only one that didn't escape was Bruach na Frithe, whose pillar we'll come to later.

As well as summit ornaments, another thing the mountain Nicolson and MacRae had just climbed lacked was a name. The shepherd said he knew of none, but that the shorter peak on its western shoulder was called Sgùrr a' Sgumain. Nicolson expressed doubt at this, certain that this was surely a case of mistaken identity and that the name – meaning 'Stack Peak' – was misplaced, and intended for the higher mountain. It's a fair point. Why, after all, would you give a name to a lower peak but leave its grander neighbour without one – not to mention many of its smaller and less distinctive satellites? Despite also liking the name 'Sgur-a-Laghain', so that the corrie and the peak it overlooked were matched, Nicolson declined to give a name to the mountain that, ironically, would later bear his. 'I renounce the honour of bestowing a name on this lovely peak,' he wrote. This could have been modesty, but more likely because – given that he continued to refer to 'the perfectly symmetrical and beautiful ... Sgur-a-Sgumain' – he was convinced that the mountain already had a name.

Clearly this was a common misconception. While the first six-inch-to-the-mile Ordnance Survey sheet – surveyed in 1877 and published in 1882 – confirmed MacRae's assessment of the peak being nameless, the first one-inch map, surveyed the same year but published in 1885, depicted *over half a mile* of ridgeline beneath the luxuriantly arcing name of Sgùrr Sgumain. This suggests that either the mapmakers were aware of the ambiguity and were unwilling to specify precisely which peak bore the name or that they really didn't care all that much. Given the number of other errors on the map, the latter seems distinctly more likely.

In actual fact, the mountain *did* already have a name, or at least an informal one –Sgùrr Biorach, which means 'Sharp Peak'. While this was unknown to MacRae and doesn't seem to have made it onto any notable map, it was later known as such amongst local guides, including John MacKenzie. Sorley Maclean even recorded the name in verse, albeit not his finest:

> An Sgurra Biorach sgùrr as airde
> An Sgurra nan Gillean sgùrr an fhearr dhiubh
> An sgurra Sgitheanach thar chaich dhiubh.
> (The Sgùrr Biorach the highest sgùrr,
> but Sgùrr nan Gillean the best sgùrr,
> the sgùrr of Skye above the rest.)

Concerning original and misappropriated mountain names, John MacKenzie also insisted on referring to the Inaccessible Pinnacle by its local name of An Stac – a name that does appear on the current Ordnance Survey map but was at some point shifted to a smaller, lower pinnacle that lies immediately to its east, where it remains to this day.

It's tempting when considering these pioneering ascents – which would be prizes of almost unimaginable cachet to modern mountaineers – to think of Nicolson and his companions as being more luckily opportunistic than skilled. Here were British peaks that were apparently unclimbed and in some cases unattempted, all claimed by a Highland raconteur who just happened to have developed a taste for climbing mountains. But this argument is weakened when you consider his exploratory descent of Sgùrr nan Gillean's west ridge in 1865, and extinguished when you consider another expedition he made just days later.

Sgùrr Dubh, as it was called at the time, is perhaps the most formidable of the main Cuillin summits. Its name means 'Black Peak', and it's steep, sharp, confusing and difficult (today it's known as Sgùrr Dubh Mòr, 'Big Black Peak'). It sits slightly away from the main ridge, one of a trio of toothy summits – the Dubhs Ridge – linked by a lean crest rising in ragged steps from the Coruisk basin, with clamber-friendly slabs at its base but treacherous upper reaches.

Nicolson made its first ascent on 6 September 1873 in the company of an unnamed friend – most likely a geologist staying at Sligachan along with him and his friend from Edinburgh, John Veitch. No guide or ghillie is mentioned in Nicolson's account; by his rendering, this was a two-person expedition.

Having paid a visit to a pair of artists who had set up a 'curious habitation' on the banks of Loch Coruisk, the pair commenced their ascent from the rocks above Loch Scavaig at 4 p.m. With just three hours before sunset, this was ambitious – something Nicolson himself conceded when he wrote, almost apologetically, that 'it would have been extreme folly to have attempted such an excursion so late in the day, had not the barometer been at "set fair", and the night been that of the full moon.' The pair's plan evidently contained a whimsical element, with Nicolson keen to see Coruisk by moonlight. They would get their wish in a way that was perhaps more exciting than either expected.

Despite the optimistic forecast, Nicolson and his friend – perturbed by mists on the ridge above – made their approach using An Garbh-choire, the deep corrie between Gars-bheinn and Sgùrr Dubh. This was a wilderness of cindery boulders that was difficult to move through, and Nicolson describes being overtaken by a rain shower, the pair sheltering beneath a ledge, before proceeding, trusting the barometer reading that the summit above would clear. Striking towards it obliquely from the south, 'the last quarter of the ascent was very hard work . . . and not quite free from danger.'

They reached the top at 7 p.m., the climax of 'a very narrow, rocky ridge, but covered at the highest point with a thick bed of green, spongy moss'. With the sun dropping away, Nicolson noted the colour of the rock, 'very dark in hue, blacker than usual, whence the name of the peak'.

After a brief moment spent admiring the view, the pair considered their options:

We hoped to have twilight to last us to the bottom of the corrie on the other side. It did suffice to light us to the first floor, but no more, and even that we found no joke.

Nicolson's habit of describing each segment of the descent towards safety in 'floors', as in storeys of a house, is an interesting way to visualise the pair's progress as they made a hurried, haphazard descent of the mountain's north side. This was a bold choice, and while apparently normal behaviour for Nicolson – as seen from his descent on Sgùrr nan Gillean by the chimney that would later bear his name – it also suggests the pair considered their ascent route hairy enough not to attempt it in descent, especially given the late hour.

Steep and intricate, the descent was made entirely by sight, into the high-tucked Coire an Lochain, cupping its eponymous lake. This is a wild place indeed – and a daunting prospect when approached at the onset of darkness, without light. 'The descent was tremendously blocked with huge stones, and the tarn at the bottom of the corrie is surrounded with them,' Nicolson wrote. Reaching an impasse about halfway down, Nicolson's plaid came into useful play – as a rope.

My companion, being the lighter man, stood above, with his heels well set in the rock, holding the plaid, by which I let myself down the chasm. Having got footing, I rested my back against the rock, down which my lighter friend let himself slide till he rested on my shoulders.

This manoeuvre, described by Nicolson as 'a little piece of gymnastics', would have been incredibly taxing, not to mention frightening. We don't know how old his companion was, but Nicolson was the wrong side of forty-five – and to do such a move 'several times . . . over two or three distinct floors between the first and the last' during a descent of a few hundred metres to the sanctuary of the corrie was quite a feat. Nicolson describes this taking two and a half hours, from 8 to 10.30 p.m., in almost total darkness. The moon had risen at 9, but was hidden from view by the steeple-like peaks at the climbers' backs, throwing the corrie into which they were descending into deep shadow.

Once into this remote nook of the ridge, the moon still obscured but for a 'mild glory', the route down to Coruisk was no clearer:

Most of the way was among shelving ledges of rock, and in one place it seemed to me that there was no going further, for there was no apparent outlet from the environment of rocks except down a dark gulley . . . the thought of passing the night there was not pleasant.

Imagine how difficult it must have been to descend something so sheer without any source of light at all. While their eyes would have adjusted to the darkness – and human eyes can do this, to an impressive degree – the detail of their route must have been incredibly challenging to see, let alone negotiate safely. But sure enough, the pair managed to find their way down to the banks of Loch Coruisk.

'I certainly never in the same space of time went through so much severe bodily exercise as in that descent from Scur Dubh to Coiruisg,' Nicolson wrote.

My very finger-tops were skinned from contact with the rough-grained rock. But the difficulties of the descent were compensated for when we got, with thankful hearts, into the full flood of the moonlight on the last floor, the valley above Coiruisg.

Nicolson was in raptures. 'How the loch and the surrounding mountains looked at that hour I will not attempt to describe,' he says, before attempting just that. There was a silence deepened by the noise of distant streams, the great peaks bending round as if to listen, the water glittering. He could have stayed quite happily 'on the nice gravelly beach of one of the little creeks' until morning. But Nicolson and his companion, perhaps wary of causing alarm back at Sligachan, and probably craving food and comfort, set off back to the hotel.

The walk back to Sligachan from Coruisk is an undertaking on its own, let alone after a long, danger-filled day. Interestingly, Nicolson and his companion attempted to vault over the Druin nam Ramh ridge, the hurdle that divides Coruisk and Glen Sligachan, intending to use Harta Corrie as a short cut in much the way Charles Lesingham Smith and Duncan MacIntyre had done in 1835, but they found their way barred by a precipice and backtracked. By the time they arrived back at Sligachan at 3 a.m., the inn was in darkness and the door locked. Ringing at first gingerly then increasingly desperately, they were received by their hosts, who fed and watered them, and informed them that their 'geologist brother' had waited up 'un-dined' until midnight for their return. Nicolson describes how they then lay down on abraded joints and slept until Sunday noon.

Nicolson and his companion had been out for fifteen hours. Not long, considering they had covered something in the region of twenty-five miles over very rough ground, and made a first ascent and descent into the bargain. Although there was nothing particularly unusual for the time in terms of severity or achievement, there was something about the mindset at work on that day that raised the bar, that redefined what was possible in the Cuillin.

Ben Humble stated in *The Cuillin of Skye* (1952) that Nicolson's ascent (or rather descent) that day was a feat that rivalled Edward Whymper's fateful ascent of the Matterhorn in 1865, just eight years earlier. This comment has provoked much chortling from later writers, but they are possibly missing Humble's deeper meaning: it wasn't the miles, or necessarily the prize. It was Nicolson's attitude, his grit and his guts. He was fired up just by *being* there – and was tasting the thrill so many later generations would seek. 'Few climbers of today would venture the descent of

Sgùrr Dubh to Coir' an Lochan in darkness, and without a rope,' Humble wrote. 'His descent . . . was the finest thing done in climbing in Britain up until that time.' And even during his weary tramp back along Glen Sligachan, Nicolson was hungrily eyeing up Marsco and Blàbheinn, before accepting that the need for sleep and food was more pressing than even these moonlit peaks.

As far as the naming of Skye's highest mountain after his given name goes, whether or not Nicolson enjoyed it is a question worth asking. Despite the novelty – even then considerable – of naming mountains at all, let alone after a living person, it's possible he declined to name Sgùrr Alasdair himself either out of modesty or because he did indeed believe it was already called Sgur-a-Sgumain, or Sgùrr Biorach. But the peak's eventual name seems in every way as appropriate as any of the other Cuillin peaks subsequently named after mountaineers. Nicolson strenuously insisted that the names of the 'Coolins' shouldn't be mangled by mountaineers and should only be referred to by the name by which they were known to the people of Skye; he noted with what reads like bemusement in an article reprinted in the *Scottish Mountaineering Club Journal* in 1892 that climbers had taken to calling his 1865 descent route on Sgùrr nan Gillean 'Nicolson's Chimney'. But in a footnote in the same paper he makes a casual reference to 'Sgur Alasdair'. So it is perhaps hoped that despite his love for the island and its history, or perhaps because of it, he found some honour in this: the mightiest doff of the bonnet to the Cuillin's first great explorer. And, of course, he wasn't the only namesake on the summit that day in 1873 – let's not forget Alexander MacRae, whose Gaelic christening would also have been Alasdair. It was no more Nicolson's summit than his.

Nicolson stopped climbing in 1889. His final contribution to the Cuillin's history would come that year when he fulfilled the solemn promise he made after his first climb on the ridge in 1865: the first *ascent* of his own chimney on the west ridge of Sgùrr nan Gillean. It was the closing of a circle, and suggested that he at least wasn't beyond climbing over his own name.

At the time of his sudden death in 1893 – 'gone in a moment' at the breakfast table – Nicolson was vice president of the Scottish Mountaineering Club, formed four years earlier in Glasgow. Nicolson's membership was honorary, awarded to a talismanic figurehead by a club that was dedicated to continuing the exploratory work that he himself, in many respects, had initiated. His guide, Alexander MacRae, outlived him; he was still rowing himself to and from Soay into his late eighties, and died aged ninety-six in 1902.

Preparing to descend from the summit of Sgùrr Alasdair in deteriorating conditions, we tightened straps and zipped zips. Matt motioned for me to go first. Gingerly, I moved in a crouch over the topmost point of the mountain, placing my feet on the rock step to the right. I could sense the gulf either side – now filled with grey – as I passed over it. The rock was slick, and in the building wind I ended up sending my legs first in an undignified kind of slide: the Cuillin arse-shuffle.

As we left the summit the cloud tore from flat grey to a scudding, smoke-like strafe. For a second a view opened and I saw the mountains that lay deeper into the ridge, ramparts raised aloft and tilting below the tower on which we stood. Within it something caught my eye: a straight line amidst a chaotic buttress, diagonally slashing across the middle of a peak that had the profile of a clenched fist. My eye followed it, and then up to the right to another peak, where a black disc of rock raised itself unmistakeably from the summit. Stopping, I grasped in my pocket for my camera. Sunlight found the creases of the face, and for just long enough the whole thing looked like delicate, hammered gold behind a veil. Not wanting to take my eyes off it, I held my camera at chest height. Three shots, and then it was gone as a fresh wave of murk swept it from view.

I turned to tell Matt what I'd seen, but he didn't look in the mood to discuss the view – there was something in his face. We turned, facing down towards Coruisk, the way down involving moving off slabby rock with a few awkward steps. A small path soon appeared, weaving from one side of the crest to the other on the very apex of the ridge.

Then something happened that I didn't expect, and couldn't really believe. The wind eased for a minute or two, our straps and various pieces of flapping nylon settling still in the deafening quiet. This was followed, with spooky calmness, by the slow, silent fall of snow. A few flakes initially, then sheets of it, billowing silently around the summit like blown cotton. It was beautiful and strange and scary, all at the same time. I looked at the flakes on my black gloves, fat, loose-bound crystals that stuck for a second then spread. Around us the meandering snow suddenly shifted into a uniform direction and gained intensity. I wrestled my hood up over my helmet, squirming as the cold flakes caught in its folds slid down my back, and kept descending. After a few minutes the snow changed to hail, then sleet, then the sleet turned to rain and the rock became a slimy mirror. Still we kept moving down.

By the time we left the steep rock of the summit cone and reached a broad flattening, the weather had collapsed. Here we stopped to gather ourselves. To our right were the faintest outlines of an abyss, down into the murk of Coruisk, that scene so resplendent and dynamic the previous day now a different place altogether, built from shades of grey.

To our left was a chasm of scree. As the rain fell and the wind kicked up once more, I realised we were standing in the gap between the twin peaks of Sgùrr Alasdair and Sgùrr Thearlaich – that skyward-snapping mouth – at the top of the Great Stone Shoot. The Ordnance Survey map marks this 'Chute', as in slide. The first mountaineers called it 'Shoot', as in firing range. Both are apt.

Matt stood still, gathering in his rope and eyeing me sideways, one eye squeezed shut against the sideways rain. I could tell he had something to say.

'So . . . the next section. Coireachan Ruadha Crags.' He paused. 'A long section. Very exposed and slippy. Especially in this. The other option is a very exposed ledge running beneath that cuts up to the crest. And then beyond Banachdaich, some quite technical climbing.' He stopped fiddling with the rope. 'Not ideal.'

I breathed in and held it. 'Because of the weather?'

'The weather. The forecast. And we didn't have the best night. And also . . .' He hesitated, as if choosing the words carefully. 'I don't think you're going to like it.'

I exhaled. As he said it, I felt a weight lift – then immediately, another one drop in its place. Matt was right. He was my guide. You listen to your guide. He had made a call that was as much about me as it was about the weather – which was bad, and seemed set – or the time, which was creeping on. He had been watching, he had been making decisions – and now he had pronounced judgement. In this moment – the critical one, as all moments are in mountaineering – he was right. For now, at least, my traverse was over.

It had been a quick decision, which meant this felt right – but to me, still like failure. I unclipped the rope from my harness and Matt coiled it around his shoulders. The Great Stone Shoot lay below us, a waterfall of scree descending steeply beneath walls impossibly tall and black. So we began to move down it, the echoes of the plate-sized fragments ringing off the cliffs. Immediately as we moved, there was a smell. I had read about the smell of the Stone Shoot, released by the jostled concussion of thousands of suddenly mobile pieces of rock, disturbed and grinding as you make your way. Dust rising – like the mountain exhaling. Its breath smells like the air after fireworks.

Some accounts likened the Shoot's smell, not inappropriately, to cordite; Seton Gordon observed the 'curious smell given off by the moving rocks in friction'. Lesingham Smith said the smell of colliding rocks on his inaugural skirmish on the Druim nan Ramh reminded him of sulphur. Like touching those glacial scratches in the rock, it was an odd feeling to be connected to climbers of a century past by something as tangible as a smell.

Nicolson and MacRae travelled up this way on that 'stiff and warm' ascent of Sgùrr Alasdair. From above looking down, it appeared a monstrous prospect to climb, like tackling a downward-travelling escalator. What the Great Stone Shoot actually comprises is an eroded basalt dyke around four hundred metres in length. Once the dyke filled that slot-like gap between Sgùrr Thearlaich and Sgùrr Alasdair, a slot now gradually eating its way downwards and deepening, as if invisibly sawn by a taut wire dragged to and fro across the crest, with the scree its shavings. It's all pitched at such a steep angle it seems inconceivable, when you're in it, that the Shoot can hold anything at all. Your brain tells you that there should just be a huge mound of gravity-deposited debris at the bottom, like a pile of crumbs in the bottom of a toaster. Yet it finds the right incline to just sit, a collective of friction, rather than falling down.

Moments like this and you realise how much material these mountains must erode. My pervading feeling was one of guilt – for causing, by my steps, the movement of rock from restful repose. Each foot went in to the ankle; by the time we were halfway down we must have displaced thousands of kilograms of the stuff. The air was filled with dust and the tinkle of moving rock like pieces of china, a sound that continued and faded even when we paused to look about. Considering the traffic this route must get – which, while by Lake District or Snowdonian standards is nothing, by Skye standards is huge – the volume of the scree displaced must be phenomenal.

As we reached the bottom of the Great Stone Shoot, we dropped below the cloud and I could see the shapes of the mountains around us. Where the slope relented was a grassy basin, below which lay Coire Laígan, the little lake around which I'd walked in a soup-like mist the previous spring. Matt stopped by some boulders, and sat resting. I joined him, reflexively opening my rucksack in search of food, which I found in the form of damp shortbread, which I offered to Matt, and he took with an apprecia-tive 'mmm'. There, hatted by cloud, was that view I'd missed in spring. Descending from the high left, a massive rock face, a whole limb of mountain – Sròn na Cìche – dropping down out of cloud towards Glen Brittle. Further out, Loch Brittle and all the way to Canna. Visibility stopped with the indistinct shadow of this little island; but had it been clear, we might have seen a hint of the 'Long Isle' of Lewis and Harris that guards the horizon, the last of the Hebrides.

Now we were off the ridge, tiredness and disappointment seeped into me. As we sat in the rain, I noticed with idle interest that the slabs we were sitting on carried James Forbes's glacial scratches. I ran my glove over them, then pulled it off to feel the rock. I noticed that the material on the finger-tips of my gloves was bobbling and abraded. My eyes went to Matt's gardening gloves, and I noticed he was looking over, with a hesitant half-smile. During our brief but intense acquaintance I'd learned this probably meant he was about to say something.

'One day I came down the Shoot after a rough night on the ridge,' he said. 'The wind was battering us, it was pouring with rain, like this. So we bailed. I got here, and just lay down for a little sleep,' he smiled, 'and when I opened my eyes the first thing I saw was this beautiful blue sky above. And it stayed like that for five days.'

We were quiet for a second and then he said: 'You know, it's actually pretty unusual for a full traverse to be someone's first experience of the Cuillin. It happens. But not often.'

I looked at him. For some reason I'd assumed that was how most people experienced the Cuillin. 'Really?'

'Normally, people get to know it first. They do the peaks, find out what it's like, how it feels. What to expect. And then they come back and string it all together. If they want to see what that's like.' The rain was falling hard now. Matt didn't seem to notice.

'As a guide you learn the ridge in chunks, a day here, two days there, this peak, that valley. You make mistakes, you get lost – but you learn. And you end up knowing a place far better. If we'd pressed on, your clearest memory would have been of me telling you to put your foot here, grab that hold there, and telling you not to take pictures. And of probably being pretty gripped for quite a lot of the time.'

I listened. I think this was already the longest I'd heard him speak continuously.

'Sometimes, going straight in to the traverse is a bit like buying a house without seeing it,' he said. 'You've got to get in there, got to feel it. Fall in love with it a little bit first.'

We sat eating our damp shortbread and I thought about what he said. And all of a sudden, I saw it. I had been going about this all wrong. Doing the traverse meant I would experience less of the ridge, not more of it. The combination of speed, physical fortitude and skill – and the constant volatility of the weather – meant that failure was in no way unusual. The traverse was a challenge.

It was a different thing to what I was been looking for. I wasn't in this for an endurance test. For me, the advantages of *not* doing the Cuillin in one go far outweighed those of pushing myself to the limit and remembering very little about the experience other than exhaustion and fear. That didn't sound like the right thing to me. An account that summed this feeling up rather sharply was that of Ernest Maylard in an article in the *Scottish Mountaineering Club Journal*, 'A Day in the Cuchuillins'. Upon being confronted with Sgùrr nan Gillean at the end of a long day, he lamented that his party 'had lost much of the interest we should certainly have attached to it had it lain in our course earlier'. Which obviously makes total sense.

On a traverse, the route was set. The ridge was the boss. But it didn't have to be that way. Exploring the Cuillin ridge is a quite different thing to attempting a traverse. It's like the difference between racing around a vast museum with a stopwatch in your hand and browsing the exhibits at your own pace. Yes, you can prove you've got what it takes to negotiate sharp bends and slippy floors at a blistering clip, but have you actually *learned* anything? Can you remember any single thing with any kind of clarity?

I would later pick up J. Hubert Walker's *On Hills of the North*. He had the following to say on the matter:

> Naturally, I went with the intention if it was at all possible to tread every peak in the range and see the inside of every corrie … but not, be it said, in any circumstances, all at one go.

He went on to acknowledge the traverse as *possible* within twenty-four hours – this was 1948 – and that it was a grand physical undertaking, like riding a bike from London to Brighton:

> in all such cases the would-be 'record breaker' knows as much about the country he is passing through as a blind man. Time is the essence of the country he is moving through, not the exploit.

That's my perspective, anyway. And it's not like we'd fallen at the first hurdle. 'I'd say we had a pretty successful couple of days up there,' Matt said. 'We both survived.'

And hey – instead of walking away with the ridge done and dusted, I'd be unexpectedly leaving with the prospect of returning to spend more days up there. Which meant more days on Skye. And more days getting to know this place. The more I thought about it, free from the shackles of my original itinerary, the more sense it made. As Matt had told me, Skye and plans don't get on too well together.

The fact was, I wasn't going to make the traverse of the Cuillin ridge. Which meant that now I was free to get to know the ridge on my own terms. Alexander Nicolson said, 'A day on Skye is worth two elsewhere.' And honestly, I'd had *quite* the two days. I'd been dropped into Coruisk by boat, traversed a section of the ridge relatively few walked in eye-melting conditions, spent the night shivering in a cave, increased my Munro count by two (not that I cared about that) – and stood on the highest point of Skye in ethereal, calm cloud before getting battered by September snow. That was, by any measure, two pretty exceptional days on the ridge.

I'd come down with something else, too. Sitting with Matt in Coire Làgan, I pulled my camera out, powered it up, then, sheltering the screen with my hand, showed him the image I'd taken from the summit of Sgùrr Alasdair. 'Remember the picture I showed you in the café of the woodcut on the back of that mountain anthology?' I said. There was the sunlit flank in my photo, and across it that pale, steeply raked slash. Matt took the camera, wiped the raindrops from the screen, and nodded: 'Ah – Collie's Ledge.' He peered up towards the mountain the picture had been looking down on. 'Would have been exciting today. Maybe a bit too exciting.' He tapped the picture. 'You were close, though. You weren't there,' he pointed at the picture, before waving his finger in a twirl in the air, 'but you were *there*.'

I think in my head I'd imagined myself standing in the spot where the climber in that enigmatic woodcut had stood – perhaps peering around the corner to see what lay beyond. Fate had other ideas. But just by being up there, the highest ground in the labyrinth of the Cuillin, enveloped by that atmosphere and surrounded by the same landmarks in the image that had fired me up so long ago, had been enough for now.

Around us, inscribed in the walls and the peaks like a museum in stone, were the names of those who would spearhead the next phase of the Cuillin's exploration. Sgùrr MhicCoinnich. Sgùrr Thearlaich. Sgùrr Thormaid. Those names, in their Gaelic guise: MacKenzie. Charles. Norman. The only British mountains named after mountaineers. The Romantics had discovered the Cuillin's aura, the scientists had unpicked its origin and the first explorers had skinned their fingers on the rock. And far above us, lost in the cloud, was that infamous jag of rock with its goading name, the lightning rod for the first wave. The climbers were coming – and the Cuillin was about to enter its golden age of discovery.

10

Pinnacle

Sligachan
Autumn

From a gilded frame high in a corner of a lounge in the Sligachan Hotel, the gothic features of John Norman Collie appraise the room that bears his name. The expression on the face of the sharp-eyed, hawk-nosed mountaineer-scientist who haunts this inn – the place he died – is questioning, fixed somewhere above and to his right, as if on some distant objective. Were it directed at the viewer, it might be unsettling.

On this particular October morning, Collie was scrutinising a room of five men: four, silently watching one. Outside, rain was falling hard. Total rain, the kind that seemed to cover every surface to a rippling depth. You might drown if you walked out into it.

It was 10 a.m., but for some reason this felt desperately late. In the circular turret of Collie's Lounge on the side of the hotel facing the glen, Matt Barratt sat in a hunch, legs crossed at the knee, delicately sipping from a cup of Earl Grey. The peak of his grubby cap threw his face into shadow, except for when he lifted his head up to stare balefully out of the window.

Four faces – one of them mine – looked back at him with unblinking and almost identical expressions somewhere between expectation and resignation, and all on pins: an appropriate term if ever there was one. We must have sat there for an hour, largely in silent attention directed towards the man sitting at the window like a beatnik sage, sipping his tea. Then he moved a little. The four of us leaned forward, eyes wide. 'Some days on Skye,' he began, 'it's good to just have another cup of tea.'

Matt looked like he'd been awake for a long time. He also looked like he'd been fighting for some of it. A huge scab hung off his lower lip like a rosette – sunburn, I would later learn – and his eyes peeped deeply from a face carpeted in stubble, roofed with coils of hair hanging from beneath his cap. He oozed weariness. I asked if he was all right, to which he offered a particularly enigmatic reply, even by his standards.

'Struggled a little to get up today. I've been in the Congo.'

I wondered for a second if this was some Hebridean euphemism, then it struck me it might not be. 'In Africa?'

'That's the one.' He sipped his tea. 'Quite an interesting adventure.'

Quite indeed. It turned out that Matt had just returned from guiding Martin Fletcher, a sixty-one-year-old journalist from the *Financial Times*, up Mount Stanley, a 5,109-metre jostle of volcanic rock that stood half in Uganda and half in what I understood to be one of the most frightening places on the planet. Being Africa's third-highest peak, Mount Stanley was relatively established as a mountain climb. But most people ascended from the Ugandan side, where you start and finish your climb in safari huts and go to bed on goose-down pillows with little fear of guerrilla skirmishes, or kidnap at the sharp end of an AK-47. Very few climb it from the Congolese side, which is how Matt and Martin approached the mountain. 'Really quite an interesting adventure,' he said again, with a slow nod.

Much later, I'd look up Martin Fletcher's article to see exactly how interesting. There was a photo of Matt – wearing the same filthy cap, I noticed – in a fantastical jungle of lobelia and giant groundsel, with local porters, guides and an ever-present guard, oily assault rifle dangling diagonally across his chest. Fletcher doesn't hold back:

> I am lying prone and panting, on a steep glacier, scarcely 200m beneath the mist-shrouded summit of Africa's third-highest mountain. Wracked by indecision, trapped in a cold, harsh, black-and-white world thousands of metres above the lush green jungles of the equator. I am spent, more exhausted than I have ever been, incapable of more than a few steps at

a time without my wildly beating heart, oxygen-starved lungs and buckling legs forcing me to stop.

Scene set? He continues:

Matt Barratt, a mountaineer from the Isle of Skye to whom I'm roped, is pressing me to abandon my effort to reach the summit. Even if I succeed, he argues, I would lack the strength to get down again. 'You're playing with your life,' he warns. But Alexis Paluku, a Congolese guide, urges me to keep going. '*Courage,*' he exhorts in French. 'You're so close.'

The three of them made it to the top, down again and home alive, in case you were wondering, though not with much by way of margin for error. There was lightning. Some evasive manoeuvres, evidently. Enough of a close call to suggest's Matt's advice had been far from unreasonable.

The presence of similarly snaggly volcanic peaks aside, you might think it surprising for a Cuillin guide to be hauled away from Skye to get sweaty and scared in the Congo on a mountain five times higher than anything on his home isle. But then, in another way it's not that surprising. Cuillin guides have to deal with a level of danger and unpredictability of entirely another order to most guides in Scotland, and they know it. This isn't something enshrined in law, *per se* – crossing the Sound of Sleat doesn't necessitate the kicking in of any additional level of qualification to guide in the Cuillin – but everybody knows the mountains are different here. There is a different set of rules for climbing them, and guiding them. And now here was Matt, navigating another moment of indecision for another group of clients. Different place, similar dilemmas – albeit of a slightly different flavour. To go, or not to go. To climb, or not to climb. To live free of risk, or freely take the risk.

Making the correct decision is especially important when it comes to one particular summit; a summit that, beyond most others on the mainland and all others on the Cuillin ridge itself, will ensure a disproportionate amount of interest from people who would not be here for any other reason than to climb it – to *bag* it. This summit is, of course, the very top of Sgùrr Dearg: a narrow fin of rock projecting from the top of the summit of its parent peak like a raised and taunting middle finger. For those on a mission to climb the Munros, this summit presents a problem. In order to be a so-called 'compleater' of all 282 summits on this famous mountain list there's no avoiding it, despite the irony that the list's namesake, Sir Hugh Munro, inadvertently dodged it himself. Nobody round here calls it Sgùrr Dearg. Nor, it seems, the more intimidating and suggestively impossible name it has come to be known almost everywhere else. Round here they seem to just call it the 'Pinn'. And today was my turn to not dodge the Cuillin's infamous Inaccessible Pinnacle – and the decision rested on the man looking out of the window, staring at the rain, drinking another cup of tea.

Pore over enough mountaineering literature of a certain vintage and you realise it was never enough to describe something just as a piece of rock sticking up fifty metres out of the top of a mountain. Particularly around the turn of the 20th century, it was *de rigueur* to recruit something familiar to compare such a thing to in order to cause a ping of recognition amongst genteel lowlanders. This was especially true of the Inaccessible Pinnacle, the classic Cuillin 'mimetolith': something natural that looks like something else. Many of these comparisons betray the social position of those monkeying around the Cuillin at this time. Since being noticed, the pinnacle has been likened to a 'weird obelisk', 'a slate stuck vertically into the top of a wall', a 'chimney can', a 'wild beast's horn' and, my favourite, a 'comb, stuck in the middle of a hair brush, for convenience of packing', this last coined by Clinton Dent in the *Alpine Journal*.

Ashley Abraham, one of the Cumbrian brothers who photographed the pioneers of rock-climbing, had a fine time here in the first years of the 20th century and disparaged this tendency in *Rock-climbing in Skye*:

> at a distance such comparisons may be fairly apt. But at close quarters the pinnacle is a very fine object, and not for a moment to be likened to any domestic article.

Clearly uncomfortable with comparing it to dubious masonry or conveniently stowed hair-styling tools, Abraham decided instead to give the

Inaccessible Pinnacle a character. '[It] towers up above the adjacent rock in much the same way a strong personality dominates its more weak or plastic fellows.'

This it most certainly does. Even in photographs – which had been one of my preoccupations this past year, during which I had been unable to get to Skye – in form it is amorphous, changing drastically with even subtle revisions of position. At its most dramatic angle from the south-west, if you'll permit one more analogy, it perches on Sgùrr Dearg like the fin of a diving whale – with a long, languid side and a short, steep side. The top is a family of staggered boulders, ludicrously poised, like a cockerel's frill (sorry, two more analogies), as if the ridge wanted to continue but was sliced messily short. Beneath this precarious-looking top, the west ridge falls at a much steeper rake, in places near vertical, to join at an acute angle the ascending slopes of Sgùrr Dearg, which continues to its comparatively broad summit slabs. Most conquistadors of the In Pinn these days experience both of these sides – one in ascent, and one in descent.

Malcolm Slesser rather sourly described the Pinnacle as an 'absurd excrescence', but concedes that Sgùrr Dearg would be the 'least interesting peak in the Cuillin' without it, although this is surely nothing to do with the view. If pictures – and Seton Gordon's description in Chapter 8 – are to be believed, these slabs in clear weather provide a view of the Cuillin ridge that grabs you by both shoulders and shakes you.

While this side of the Pinnacle stirs the imagination, the view of its opposing end sets the nerves on edge. This is the comb-stuck-in-a-brush angle, though you'd be forgiven not making the immediate connection when faced with it. Looking nose-on to the east ridge – the side most people ascend – it looks steep, skinny, long and scary. Broadside, its southern side seen from a distance is a tall, brawny-looking disc buried in the mountain, a clear vertical fracture crawling up its crinkly skin a third of the way from the right. Look at it squarely from the northern side – difficult, unless you can fly – and it's bulbous, shapeless and rotten, like many north faces typically in shadow, and thus more prone to the gnawing action of frost and lichen. The same vertical crack runs up this side, prompting the disturbing thought that one day the In Pinn might become the Thin Pinn.

It's visible from afar at certain angles, too. From Sgùrr na Stri it's quite obvious, at 11 o'clock from the head of Loch Coruisk, up in the rafters of the ridge and quite pronounced, its top block a thorn spiking from the skyline. From here and other places on the ridge you see it in context, and precarious it most certainly looks.

If the pictures were to be believed, it looks different from every angle. But what is irrefutable is the whole thing is very narrow and its sides are very steep. And Sgùrr Dearg's position near one of the highest points on the crest of the Cuillin ridge is already exposed, before anyone starts suggesting clambering up an additional sticky-up bit of rock.

It's easy to appreciate – even from a remote desk covered with maps and books five hundred miles away – how the Inaccessible Pinnacle earned its name. And why, in those rather more utilitarian times, it was for a long while considered pointless to even attempt it. In 1873 Nicolson, passing by the peak with MacRae, described it as having a 'very peculiar and puzzling appearance', but nonetheless treated the problem of its fearsome topknot with a certain pragmatism, pronouncing that 'with rope and grappling irons it might be possible to overcome it … but the achievement seems hardly worth the trouble.'

As for that name, some writers note that in the days before the summits around it were trodden one by one and its apparent inaccessibility became a thing worth comment, it was called the 'Old Man of Skye' – in the manner of the Old Man of Storr, the photogenically weathered, skittle-shaped mono-lith beneath its namesake hill north of Portree that signals the start of the Trotternish peninsula.

Combs stuck in hairbrushes, horns, fins, slates, discs, cockerels, excres-cences, Old Men. But the description that really captures its character is both literal and impossible. It's also anonymous, and actually misappropri-ated – appearing in Ashley Abraham's *Rock-climbing in Skye* as a line he'd heard repeated by an old school friend to describe any kind of alpine arête. Abraham had remembered it when writing about Skye, and it's lingered ever since. Matt had enjoyed telling us this one in between cups of tea – either because it amused us, scared us, or both:

a razor-like edge with an overhanging and infinite drop on one side …
and a drop even longer and steeper on the other.

We'd all had a nervous chuckle at that. I was apprehensive, for sure: there were no other mountains quite like this one. Up close, I had no idea what this, the most infamous summit in the British Isles, was going to look like or feel like to take hold of. But when I noticed that Matt wasn't ordering any more tea, and was slowly sliding his waterproof jacket off the back of his chair and onto his shoulders, I knew that I was probably about to find out.

The rain stopped all of a sudden as we rounded the bend from Sligachan into Glen Brittle, the wipers grinding noisily on dry glass for a few swipes until Matt shut them off. As usual, everything elemental seemed on fast-forward; as the rain stopped, a huge tear of blue sky appeared above where a clearing of the horizon ahead indicated the sea, but the Cuillin remained a shadow behind stubborn-looking low cloud to the left. Matt drove his van down into the glen, the rear empty and creaking except for a plastic barrel filled with equipment that clinked ominously with every bump. We could feel something else too, tugging at the tall sides of the van: wind.

Matt leaned over the steering wheel, sharp eyes boomeranging from the road up to the ridge as we descended towards the fist of buildings that made up Glenbrittle itself. 'This weather . . . complicates things a bit with the In Pinn,' he said. I could tell from the tone of his voice the decision to press on had been, and was perhaps still, finely perched. 'It was worth waiting to see if the rain would stop. But you know . . . I don't think it's a day for hanging around up there.'

Behind us, the headlights of the car containing the rest of the group bounced up and down out of view as the road dipped and slinked. Therein lay perhaps the other reason Matt had to be wary. Illness had grounded his second guide, meaning that he was in charge of a larger group than was strictly ideal. From his point of view this meant he'd probably be climbing it twice with two groups. And for this the weather had to hold out long enough to allow not just one ascent, but two.

We reached Glenbrittle, parking up next to another van also liveried with the name of a guiding company. It was empty, and looking up into the glen I could see a few bright-coloured figures bobbing their way slowly upward, suggesting that we weren't the only group that had been holding out for a window.

I stepped out of the van with some reluctance. I often feel like this – I enjoy the drive, and when it comes to getting out, getting wet and getting walking, it's sometimes a wrench. I looked about as Matt busied himself sorting gear, emerging with a handful of harnesses and helmets. He passed me one of each, along with a karabiner and a belay device. Then the other car arrived and offloaded its eager cargo.

I hadn't met these guys until this morning. Since I'd last seen him, I'd asked Matt to keep an eye out for any groups I could join that were heading up into any of the bits of the Cuillin I hadn't done. He said he didn't think that would be a problem, as there were lots of those.

I'd said, 'Lots of bits of the Cuillin I hadn't done, or groups going up?' And he'd said, 'Yep.'

So the call came that a group of friends was coming up from Edinburgh to tick off some of the central Cuillin Munros, including the Pinnacle, and there was a space. I grabbed it.

So today I was the grateful guest of George, Chris and Kevin – three friends in their fifties who had spent most of a week on the island. George and Kevin were Scottish; Chris a Boston native whose rounded accent had been given further colour by years living in Ireland. 'I like to cycle, mainly,' Chris had said as we'd chatted earlier in the Sligachan. When the issue of the Inaccessible Pinnacle came up he said: 'It'll be my first Scottish mountain.' Noticing my surprise, he quickly added, 'but I'm not fazed. Not at all.'

There was an irony that Chris's first Scottish summit was set to be the one many leave for last – or at least leave until they feel they can do it without going to pieces. While holed up in the hotel earlier, expectation management triggered by the weather had reduced the day's objective to the Inaccessible Pinnacle, with the Munros of Sgùrr na Banachdaich and Sgùrr a' Ghreadaidh as add-ons if time in any way permitted. I was sorely hoping it did, but the way things were looking, climbing up anything at all would be a miracle today. So as the party left the roadside with Matt in the lead, there was very much a single key goal in mind: that sticky-up piece of history that lay up there in the rafters of the Cuillin ridge, somewhere in all that cloud, and getting closer with every step.

The path we were on rose slowly, which meant what came later would be steep indeed: you had to make the height up somehow, and we were heading for one of the loftiest points on the ridge. As we climbed, the sea rose into view on the right, filling the western horizon and cutting into the land with the great bite of Loch Brittle. The land beyond to the north was high basalt plateau skinned with a delicate felt of grass, the beginning of much more of the same running over the lava flows of northern Skye.

While I could say with qualification now that the Cuillin wasn't as mysterious as it once had been to me, I was far from *au fait* with its geography. This particular section, between Sgùrr Alasdair and Sgùrr na Banachdaich – one of the highest and most complex on the ridge – confounded me every time I tried to picture it. I couldn't work out which way round it all went, and how it linked together, or how you got from one bit to the other. More than anything I was curious how it would feel to be standing beneath the Inaccessible Pinnacle – I daren't be optimistic enough to imagine getting up it, or standing on top of it, not yet – on that much mythologised bit of the ridge. That's one thing that always gets me about mountains and other objects: they don't care how famous they get. They have no idea of their notoriety, how historic and significant they are. Whatever they are on a human level stops with the human – it doesn't transfer to the object. You can fear it, revere it, surmount it, get stuck on it, treat it badly or with disrespect, get killed by it. But whatever you do, the Inaccessible Pinnacle just stands silent, says nothing and goes right on being a piece of rock. Whatever you feel and whatever you do is right down to you.

At the back of the line behind George, I took out the folded map in my pocket and looked at it as we went, trying to reconcile the surroundings with its landmarks. We'd just passed a large gorge, ringed with vegetation and split by a fine waterfall, the Eas Mòr – one of countless that were named 'Big Waterfall' across the Highlands – which was engorged by the morning's rain. It was a grand sight, and we all stopped to take it in – Matt leaning on his walking pole, patiently watching us coo, as no doubt he did with every group he brought this way. And then we were off again, with gentle haste. Soon the ascent began to stiffen and we were walking into the embrace of the great coire of Sgùrr Dearg itself, looking up at the warren of crags on the right wall of the corrie. An opaque murk sat on top of the summits ahead upwards of a hard line at, I guessed, about 2,000 feet. One crag in particular stood proud of the wall where it met the cloud, like the eye of a needle: 'That's Window Buttress,' Matt said. 'See the way the light comes through it? We're going up alongside that onto the ridge. Little scramble up there.' He had everyone's attention now. 'Kind of a little preparatory exercise. Let's just say that if that doesn't go well, the In Pinn isn't going to happen.'

The rock was now bare underfoot – all vegetation had gone – and we were making speed up the west ridge of Sgùrr Dearg itself. Soon enough, Matt halted at the foot of a tilted wall of rock, a half-gully like a broken ladder to the left. A lesson. We listened.

'Concerning rocks,' he began. 'This,' he jabbed his pole into the stepped ground beneath his feet, 'is gabbro. This is basalt.' He moved his pole several inches higher to a rock of identical colour, but a blockier consistency. 'Basalt is stepped. If you see a rock with cracks all around it, it's probably basalt. One is grippy, and one isn't. I'm not going to tell you where to put your hands and feet, because I want you to look for yourself. It's really important.' Matt let this hang in the air for a second. He definitely had our attention: the four of us were looking at Matt as if he were explaining how to defuse a grenade.

'So I'm going to tell you to climb with your feet, to get your feet *up*. Don't trip. And make sure,' he paused, raising a hand in a catlike pose, 'that whatever your hands have hold of is actually a part of the mountain. If you don't, sooner or later something is going to come down on you or someone behind you. If that happens, the best word is "Rocks". Or "Below".'

The four of us murmured a chuckle. 'Reckon I could think of a better word.' Kevin grumbled in my ear.

With that, Matt began to ascend our preparatory exercise. It wasn't a hard scramble – just a few metres of hands on rock, but when it was our turn I could see him watching us, taking note of every grunt, every noise, every movement, every pause. When we all arrived at the top, he nodded his approval and, without a word, on we went.

Back when the Cuillin was first being explored, it was the Inaccessible Pinnacle's position that gave it novelty as an objective – the fact that it was on *top* of something, that it actually formed a high point. This was decidedly inconvenient to those committed to besting the heights of these mountains but who were unwilling to entertain unworthy trials in order to do so. At this moment in time – the early 1880s – climbing statuesque bits of rock for the sake of wilful difficulty, as opposed to their being a means to ascend something bigger, was still very much in its infancy. It was catching on in places like the Lake District and Snowdonia, where rock climbing (as opposed to summit hunting) was developing, due to the lack of virgin summits – or at least ways up them that offered a sufficiently adrenaline-simmering challenge. The first ascent of Pillar Rock, a tombstone-shaped outlier on the fell of the same name above Ennerdale in the English Lake District, had been the unofficial start line of an entire movement in 1826 when it was climbed – for apparently pointless, frivolous and therefore 'sporting' reasons – by a local shepherd named John Atkinson. Napes Needle, a finger of rock on the southern flank of Great Gable, wasn't climbed until sixty years later in 1886, and was done so with such athletic flair it's frequently cited as the 'birth' of rock climbing – a ludicrous claim when you consider what was happening on the Cuillin ridge by that point, however puritanically subtle the difference in motivation. But both Pillar Rock and Napes Needle were and remain outliers, vestigial nubs far beneath the summits of their parent peaks. The Inaccessible Pinnacle *was* the summit – therefore its relegation of status as a quirky triviality sat rather uncomfortably. This piece of rock was as covetable an ascent as anything else on the Cuillin ridge – if not more so.

The earliest literary reference to the Inaccessible Pinnacle comes in 1859 courtesy of Charles Weld, who in *Two Months in the Highlands* took brief time out from giving bad reviews of the island's hostelries – and just about everything else – to make some marvellously dread-dripped observations about the Cuillin. Most of these came during a guided excursion to (or some degree of ascent towards) the summit of 'Sgor-na-Strith' – Sgùrr na Stri – in a 'hurricane' to take advantage of the intimate view of the Cuillin above Coruisk. Weld's knowledge of the peaks is, to be generous, gappy – for which he gallantly blames his 'boy' guide: '[the] lad was useless, for though his life had been spent amongst the Cuchuillins as a shepherd, he was ignorant of all the names except those close to Sligachan'. Given the same boy had never ascended Sgùrr na Stri, Weld left 'the pony in charge' and ascended the hill alone. Had he achieved the summit, he'd have been the first off-comer to do so, probably. But regardless, he was confronted by the view of the Cuillin:

a wilderness of weird shapes, dark, solemn and awful ... sunshine occasionally illuminates their rugged crests ... but the darkness of eternal night dwells in their gorges.

Of the view, Weld goes on to indicate what was then thought to be the highest peak on Skye, the 'giant Sgor-na-Gillian' as being 'there' (again, specifics weren't really Weld's forte), then mentions another peak 'a little to the south ... laid down by the enterprising Captain Wood on the Admiralty chart as being 3,212 feet high, and *inaccessible*.' So, Weld wasn't the first to coin the phrase; he was actually quoting someone else who had made the observation, and a cartographer, no less. Weld seems to have had some sort of vested interest in 'the enterprising Captain Wood' – either that, or Captain Wood was really quite enterprising indeed, as soon after calming down following his ascent of Sgùrr na Stri, by coincidence Weld finds himself sharing a pony trap bound from Sligachan with none other than Captain Wood himself. Wood – whom it is presumed was in the employ of the British Hydrographic Office when compiling his map – duly gives valuable insight to Weld into the perils of creating what he calls 'the only authentic chart of the coasts of Skye'.

[Wood] told me that the survey of the shores of this storm-vexed island was a most arduous task, involving great time, labour and even danger. Frequently he had to wait for weeks to obtain peeks of the mountain peaks, in order to make his triangulations and often his surveying ship has been blown out of Sounds into places of great peril.

He goes on to note that such work off Skye was comparable to Arctic surveys and should be 'remunerated by double pay'.

Fortuitous meetings aside, Wood's chart is another one of those maps that offers a real window into the mind of the maker – and as such is a really interesting thing to look at. Being an Admiralty chart, it features only coastal and offshore detail, which swiftly fades to blank inland no more than a mile from the coast. This means that only the mountain summits of particular notability and navigational usefulness to the sailor were recorded – and in this, Wood's eye for a mountain object is as particular as it is peculiar.

The seaward bulwark of the Cuillin is there, a line of circles with spider-web shadings, along with a few embryonic names and spot heights. The name of Sgùrr Alasdair is absent, as this was prior to the Sheriff's ascent, but its earlier name of Sgùrr Biorach is nowhere to be seen either, despite its prominence surely being unmistakeable from the sea. Then, sure enough, as Weld indicated, is a pair of summits in close proximity: 'Sgor Dearag, 3,059 feet' and the 'Inaccessible Pk, 3,212 feet'.

Might Wood have been able to see the Inaccessible Pinnacle from where his survey ship roamed? Quite possibly – and the bulk of Sròn na Cìche *could* have eclipsed the view of its higher neighbour. But for Wood to be able to identify both its approximate height – though ambitiously mismatched versus its parent peak – and its status as 'Inaccessible' from his vantage is extraordinary. It's a shame we don't know more about him. Weld ends his observations about the In Pinn with a call to arms: 'Surely some bold member of the Alpine Club will scale this Skye peak ere long, and tell us it was but a stroll before breakfast.' It would be a while before such a member presented themselves. And a stroll before breakfast – then, as now – it was not.

High on Sgùrr Dearg the cloud was down, and all context lost. Whereas earlier we were on a mountainside with a horizon of sea, a view of where we'd come from and another to where we were going, now we were walking along a floating ledge of rock the colour of wet iron. The path widened to a slack, and here we came across another group, the bright colours of their clothing sharpening through the mist. Matt knew the leader, and they exchanged some good-natured abuse as they passed. Then one by one the four of us passed the four of them, four hellos, four smiling faces. Just the same as us – and up here for the same strange reason. A hundred metres or so beyond them, we too stopped. Matt took off his rucksack, then said, 'Time to put some gear on.'

Things were getting serious, and so was Matt. I watched his demeanour shift, felt the chill of lofty air and nerves as cloud danced around us to the chafe of jackets and the clink of metal. Matt pulled an intestine of steel and nylon from his rucksack: a rack of climbing nuts and slings he heaved on to his waist, and a length of rope which he began looping over his shoulder. His special gloves went on; he replaced his cap with a helmet. Then he turned to us and began running through a kind of Riot Act.

'Your. Life. Depends,' Matt said, talking to his harness, then looking up at us, 'on *this* strap being tight.' This was important. 'If you can get your hand in, it's tight enough. If you can make a fist, it isn't.'

The four of us had disgorged the harnesses from our bags and in unison looked down towards the same strap. Kevin's was on and he looked pleased with himself. Chris and George were fiddling with theirs. Worried not to look like a chump in front of people I might soon be tied to, I wrestled mine on but noticed with dismay that it was upside down. Attempting to hide this, I quickly unclipped and rectified it – *harnesses like belts on the Cuillin, not like underpants* – and once again felt that awkward, tightened feeling around my thighs and waist. Harnesses feel like fear to me.

Matt carried on. 'Gloves, hats, extra jackets – put them on if you want, and I suggest you do. If other groups are up there, we might be waiting around, so dress warm. And another thing' – he looked at me, I don't know why – 'if you want to look at your phone, stop and look at your phone. If you want to look at the view, stop and look at the view. Don't try to do either while you're walking.'

We continued a rising traverse on steepening ground. The rock echoed. Soon the world became monochrome. I was up on the ridge again, back up in the labyrinth – only this time it was different. This time I could see nothing but the rock and the smoke-cloud drifting across it.

Matt led us up a path cut like a slash across the buttress along which we were making slow progress. I could see him, red jacket; behind him Chris, black jacket; then Kevin, blue; in front of me George, navy. We were all just moving, not really talking, just making progress. Occasionally one of us turned back to check on another, or wait for an obstacle to be safely surmounted by all, but generally we just walked – over loose rock, around ledges, across small gullies. It was a weird sort of mobile huddle we were in; I could hear boots scratching rock and the synthetic swish of waterproof clothing. Down to the right there was a steep drop, interrupted by terraces; beneath that, at the limit of my vision, I saw a scree slope, wide and pale. Below all that in the murk was Coruisk, another world. Refocusing on Matt, I tried not to think about getting lost up here. In the cloud, everything looked the same and everything was steep.

Ahead, the black jacket moved unexpectedly; Chris had stumbled. Just for half a second, but Matt turned immediately and I heard his voice, sharp but not hard. I noticed the pace slowed after that, though this could have been down to the terrain steepening and becoming trickier. A little further on, Matt stopped and the line bunched together in front of a crack running through the path, interrupting it enough to warrant a pause. Matt crossed to the other side, then supervised the crossing of the rest of the group. I was standing at the back, unhappy with suddenly having to occupy myself without looking down at the drop on the right.

'Put your hand on the rock,' I heard Matt say to Chris. 'Left hand up, up, right, right, *there* – that's your hold.' How about that, I thought. To know one hold, one little lip of rock amongst hundreds of thousands on this route, the one hold that would enable passage across this obstacle. To know this place that intimately. I was impressed. One by one, we all went across. A few minutes later we were back in the wind, and I realised that we were crossing the ridge crest. The rain was intensifying, the cloud was thick and I wondered how exposed we were as we crossed over one by one. And then I saw Matt throw down his pack, indicating for the rest of us to do the same, and I realised where we were. We were just below the summit slabs of Sgùrr Dearg. And, tilting through the mist, there it was.

Twenty-one years after Charles Weld had thrown down the gauntlet to 'an intrepid member of the Alpine Club' to present themselves and scale the Inaccessible Pinnacle, one of them did. Or rather, two. Their story is the most extraordinary and exemplary, yet strangely sidelined, examples of the generation of alpinists who came to Skye in the late 19th century.

'The Alps of Switzerland are exhausted … the mountaineer must go farther afield if he wishes to see new country and climb fresh peaks. He must go to the Andes, the Caucasus, the Himalayas – or Skye.' So wrote Charles Pilkington, in a paper entitled 'The Black Coolins', read before the Alpine Club on 13 December 1887. Charles and his brother Lawrence are pivotal figures in the history of the Cuillin's exploration. And perhaps more significantly, they beautifully epitomise the class of privileged gentleman travellers who found their way to Skye – a class who, having cut their teeth in the Alps, found a playground of unexplored and largely unnamed mountains perfectly suited to their continental skill set almost right underneath their feet.

Charles and Lawrence were two of the five sons of Richard Pilkington, who with his brother William had founded the Lancashire glassmakers of the same name in 1826. After the Second World War, the same company would transform the world's skylines with the groundbreaking 'float-glass' method of production and make its owners unfathomably rich. In 1880 they were merely extremely rich. Enterprising industrialists themselves – Charles and Lawrence would become the proprietors of collieries and tile manufacturers – the Pilkingtons were members of the class of wealthy young Victorians of considerable means who, in the latter years of the 19th century, made the Alps their playground.

Theirs was a kind of adventurous Grand Tour of a type making a resurgence amongst the intellectual and landed classes of Victorian Britain. But unlike the previous century, the focus wasn't classicism, but alpinism – the conquest of the great mountaineering 'problems' of Switzerland, France and Italy. In this age, many of the major snow and rock scalps of the Alps were claimed by British mountaineers, although nearly always in the company of skilled local guides. These guides were almost certainly capable of making the ascents themselves, but in the manner of those accustomed to the presence of great mountains, much like the mountains of Skye, it appeared to take a paying visitor to justify the enterprise.

One look at the other achievements of these paying visitors, and you realise how much climbing was a game for the rich and the thoughtful: these people were influencers, intellectuals, societal game-changers. Leslie Stephen (Bietschhorn and Schreckhorn first ascent) was a celebrated writer and the father of Virginia Woolf; Charles Barrington was an entrepreneur who made the first ever climb of the Eiger to prove he could, then promptly hung up his boots, choosing instead to invest in a racehorse that won the Grand National; John Tyndall (Weisshorn) was a physicist who would determine what made the sky blue, define the greenhouse effect and enter a lengthy squabble about glaciation with James Forbes; William Mathews (Monte Viso) was a botanist who suggested the formation of the Alpine Club. And then there was Whymper (Matterhorn) – a wood engraver, inventor, explorer, and a man who was simply the most forcefully ambitious mountaineer of his day.

Even amongst this company, Charles and Lawrence Pilkington were not typical. They were born into this mountaineering generation – perhaps the first generation to hit a youthful stride in a still youthful pursuit – and they started hard. Lawrence had climbed Pillar Rock in the Lake District in 1869 at fourteen with his brother, who was nineteen. Their first trip to the French Alps was in 1872, and they frequently returned during the following years. Despite their privileged origins, they were pioneering in their approach to their alpinism, increasingly doing without the help of local guides and striking off on their own – part intrepid, part pragmatic, mostly puritanical. Local knowledge was useful in places, but more for those to whom mountaineering was a secondary motivation, such as tourists, scientists and have-a-go conquistadors like Charles Barrington.

The Pilkingtons, perhaps as a bi-product of their wealth, were part of the first real generation of mountain climbers for whom ascents and frivolous adventure were the sole motivation, rather than a pleasing by-product of some worthier justification. Their 1878 season saw the brothers make the first independent ascents of the Barre des Écrins and La Meije – landmark climbs that ushered in the controversial but self-reliant era of 'guideless' climbing in the Alps. At this the Pilkingtons would continue to set the standard, with similar expeditions up the Finsteraarhorn and Wetterhorn, and – in the company of Eustace Hulton – the first guideless ascents of Piz Kesch, Piz Rozeg and Monte Disgrazia. In amongst these continental escapades, the Pilkingtons found themselves on Skye.

Charles had made his first trip to Skye in 1870 with his older brother Alfred, recording the visit in the Sligachan Hotel guest book – the same year that saw entries by Alexander Nicolson and one John Thom of Liverpool, who would have the distinction of being the first person to die in a climbing accident on the Cuillin; don't worry, we'll get to him.

If the lure of Skye was unclimbed ground, the reward the Pilkingtons found was certainly rich and – if you look at Charles's extraordinary 1887 paper, *The Black Coolins*, which reads like a digest of his time on the island – you get the sense that they knew it. If there was ever an account that wrote mountaineering history with almost every seemingly off-the-cuff sentence, it was this – remarkable, given that as Charles indicates early on, the loose collective of the Pilkingtons and their alpinist contemporaries Horace Walker, Eustace Hulton and James Heelis only made 'four short visits' to Skye. A picture that hangs in the Sligachan today portrays the brothers and Hulton posed in near-caricature: the brothers, sternly bearded and dressed almost identically in the alpine uniforms of felt trilbies, plus fours and stiff-looking wool suits, sitting either side of Eustace Hulton, who appears to be receiving a drink from Lawrence into a cup he holds. It's posed, of course, and oddly theatrical – but a closer look shows scratches on their alpenstocks, wrinkles in their hats, scuffs on their boots and wear on their faces. They look like visiting gold prospectors from California.

And you couldn't call the Pilkingtons single-minded in their pursuit of Skye's mountains; as with many others, the potential of the Cuillin took some time to assert itself. Their first visit was made with angling in mind; 'dried up streams and blue sky' was what they found. 'We tried to catch impossible fish, but failing, contented ourselves with crossing a humble pass or so,' wrote Charles.

The second visit was to shoot – or at least scope out the potential of a moor for such. 'The traces of grouse on the particular part of the island we visited being scarcer than the traces of ancient glacial action [a strange joke, presumably feeding off the scientific zeitgeist and intended to suggest the region was 'not hilly'], we did not take the shooting, but went on to Sligachan.'

Sligachan, it seems, suited them just right. Late on the afternoon of their arrival, the Pilkingtons set out for Sgùrr nan Gillean, rising behind the inn with that notorious illusion of achievability, with the intention of climbing it before supper. In his paper Charles concedes there was some arrogance involved in the enterprise: 'Two of us were members of the [Alpine] club, and thought little of Skye hills, so we went straight at the N.W. face of the mountain.'

The group failed, and – after spotting a weakness in the west ridge – decided to postpone and regroup on the ascent the following day. It was a shock to the ego for these continental veterans to return to Sligachan scalpless. 'I must say, we felt rather small – as an elder brother, who was not an Alpine climber, was one of the party,' Charles wrote.

The following day – imbued with 'a much greater respect for the mountain' – the Pilkingtons climbed Sgùrr nan Gillean. Extolling the precipitous nature of the summit, 'a jump from which in any direction would relieve you of your next annual subscription to the [Alpine] Club', Charles describes the view of the mountain as 'very beautiful'. He adds, however, a reference to a climb made on Blàbheinn in the fog two days later, where he witnessed something that made me think of my own snatched view of Sgùrr nan Gillean from Sgùrr Hain:

> By degrees the cloud curled back, showing a sea of mist over the valley below, whilst high away to the left a small black pinnacle soared up into the sky. It was blotted out for a moment only to return again with another, and while we gazed, Sgùrr nan Gillean with all his pinnacles bathed in the morning sun, appeared majestically above the mist.

Perhaps it was this vision – clearly a common lure, and much expressed in the years that followed, right up to your humble author – that truly seduced him to the Cuillin; but it would be a different pinnacle for which he and his brother would earn themselves the range's most enduring accolade.

Writing in 1887, however, Charles makes little fuss about it.

> The Old Man of Skye, as the highest point of Sgùrr Dearg is named, this needle, usually called the Inaccessible Pinnacle, is the Matterhorn of Skye … it deserved its name of Inaccessible till 1880, when my brother and I climbed it by its easy edge. As the mountain on which it stands also shoots steeply away on either side, the eye seems to plunge immediately to Glen Coruisk, 2,500ft below, giving an extra feeling of insecurity to anyone clinging to the narrow east ridge … on which he may be seated astride.

Of that first ascent, Charles remembers the whole slab vibrating with the blow of falling rocks, which he had 'levered out of the crest above … stones, loose but still part of the natural rock, and often the whole of the edge, which by the way is only six inches to a foot wide in many places'. It would be tempting to think of this as an embellishment had this strange observation not been echoed by his brother Lawrence, writing in 1939 – nearly sixty years after the climb, and two years before his death. His brief

account, wilted down to its most memorable constituents by over half a
century, is also brief and to the point, but fascinating.

> I shall always remember that as the noisiest climb I ever had ... there
> was a foot or more of loose rock that had been shattered by the lightning
> and frost of ages. This formed the edge of the pinnacle and had to be
> thrown down as we climbed up. The noise was appalling; the very rock
> of the pinnacle itself seemed to vibrate with indignation at our rude
> onslaught.

In 1892, Walter Brunskill commented that 'to those who first climbed
this edge, the difficulty must have been considerably greater than now, as
it is very rotten, and bears the unmistakeable evidence of having been thoroughly cleaned.' It's hard to imagine the pinnacle vibrating under rockfall,
or anything else short of an earthquake – get up to it, and this is no maypole.
It's a hell of a big thing. Physically big, but psychologically bigger.

I stood in the rain at the foot of the Inaccessible Pinnacle's east edge, that
'easy edge', looking up at it, trembling a little. True, I was overawed by its
history, its odd and discomfiting form, its dizzying position – but I think
I was basically just very scared. In the part of your brain where your reflexive
fear lives, self preservation – for no other reason than continued existence
– is hard-wired into you. And everything about the Inaccessible Pinnacle
was in those wires, and tinkering.

The conditions had deteriorated further, and the top of the Pinnacle was
lost both to the angle and to cloud. Things had all happened very quickly,
in a squally rain that made you hunker down into waterproof clothes, with
the ridge now a warren of tall, slanted shadows seen through a curtain of
mist. There were drops around us, there had to be, but I didn't see any. This,
I thought, was all right.

Matt had verbally manhandled the four of us down from just beneath
the summit slabs of Sgùrr Dearg to the Pinnacle's base. I noticed a large
crack big enough to crawl beneath in the join between it and the rest of the
mountain. Then there was a rise to a kind of rough podium, onto which
we clambered and waited. I had no camera, no phone, no notebook –

everything had been stowed up on the ridge with the rest of the group's sacks. This wasn't how I'd expected it to be. Hasty, windswept, wet – and summarily mobilised, with little time to think about it. But at least we hadn't aborted. Not yet, anyway.

I was trying to see the way up. The Pinnacle's long south-facing wall, the one we'd just walked beneath, looked near-vertical; but the Pinnacle's east ridge, above us and clearly the way up from here, was pitched forward at a slightly – *slightly* – more accommodating angle.

Matt was moving quickly around its base, uncoiling the rope he'd been carrying on his shoulders. There was something in his face. 'So we're all going to go up together. This weather's not for hanging around in. More chance this way.'

Seconds later, the rope was being fixed firmly onto our harnesses. I was last, and Matt tied the rope off with a fat knot at my waist. I felt the familiar, rough tug of the harness garrotting the tops of my thighs and felt sick. In front of me was Kevin, then George, then Chris. Matt walked down the line again, double-checking the rope. 'I'm keeping you close together,' he said, but didn't say why – and I didn't wonder, not then. 'Don't forget there's someone behind you. There will be a point where I will tie you on to a piece of the mountain,' he added. He used that phrase a lot – a *piece of the mountain*. Perhaps this was his way of suggesting security, mountains being the most solid and immovable object of all.

He reached his hand up to the Pinnacle's first hold, on the stepped sides of a crack running below and to the left of the ridge – not where I expected him to go – but now he was moving I could trace a logical route above him towards the crest of the east ridge. I watched him moving stiffly and roughly, testing the rock, hefting himself up, the rack of silvery gear round his waist clinking and swaying like a gunslinger's belt. The four of us watched.

The east ridge of the Inaccessible Pinnacle is tackled in two pitches of around thirty metres each. In plain language, this means that a single length of rope isn't long enough to see you safely to the top – you need two sections, or 'pitches', in order to do it. The leader fixes removable protection on his ascent, then brings the rest of the party up on a tight rope after he has secured himself to the rock at the top of each pitch.

At some point Matt must have stopped and shouted to the first man

– Chris – to 'climb when ready'. I don't remember. At this point I was breathing quickly, listening to a world muffled through a hood, a helmet and a hat, and trying to slow my heart rate down, as if what was about to happen wasn't about to happen.

Only it was, and quickly. There was a yank at my waist and then we were moving. *Climb as if there is no rope*, that old adage, wasn't exactly possible – this was more a collective shuffle upwards, a kind of damp, vertical chain gang, what must from a distance have looked like a length of Christmas lights strung out over a cliff. My hands gripped the Pinnacle, the leather of my gloves smearing over the rock, which was sharp-edged but slippy. Another yank. Another. There was no time to sit and think about what was happening – we were all roped together, so we had to move together, which meant I had to focus right in front of myself and repeat without thinking, otherwise I'd be dragged off my feet, and nobody wants to be dragged off their feet on a rock climb. I decided then to simply watch the rope – the few feet of orange and black rope, like a snake, its fine knits like scales. I watched it go tight, watched it go slack, tried to keep it somewhere in between. This worked as a good distraction, a way to stay focused on simply moving upwards, with the ascent becoming just an objective, rather than a terrifying pinnacle of rock sticking out of the top of a terrifying pile of rock.

The first section wasn't challenging, made up of heavily fractured, blocky rock in a shapeless sprawl, polished by the passage of countless feet, but so cracked and jointed that holds were plentiful and the way broad and inviting enough. These joints then tapered, finding direction and form. What we were climbing up wasn't an edge, but a crack, a nice way to climb as you had a little wall to your right to shield you from the drop on that side, and something to wedge your hands and feet into. I allowed myself a glimmer of optimism that perhaps it was all like this; that the 'infinite' exposure the Pinnacle was so famous for was perhaps something theoretical rather than actual. But as we moved upwards, teasing gusts of wind from the right suggested the edges were drawing together into a crest. It had to happen at some point. And it was happening now.

A fin of rock to the right: then a big step over it, crossing over from the left lee of the Pinnacle onto the crest. There was no more crack, no more hiding place. I watched Kevin go over the fin, then saw his body stiffen and take on that jerky, hesitant gait of someone distracted by something fearful. As he proceeded, I saw the rope go tight on the rock and felt it start to tug. When the rope goes tight you have to move, unless you want to call a halt to the whole party. No time for thinking. No time for panicking. No time for finding a solid hold, either. You just need to watch, then move and hope you're all right. Which, when every bit of the rock looks like it could come off in your hand, is quite some hope.

Above, the Pinnacle steepened. It now had a near-vertical feeling, but it was probably nowhere near. The difficult movement wasn't hard if you discounted the synchronised daisy-chain arrangement, but I kept getting flashes of photographs I had seen of this thing and my own visions of it, and imagining myself shimmying up it. I tried to push them out, tried to focus purely on the rock right in front of my eyes, jigsawed with black cracks, and nothing more. Then I looked down – it was an accident – and caught the line of the Pinnacle between my legs, saw the continuing sightlines down into the corries on either side, saw its long, angled shape, buried into the mountainside like a javelin. I pictured myself halfway up it. And then my legs went. 'Oh.' *Shit*.

Something was happening up above, as the rope went slack. Matt was tying us on to the mountain. So that was the end of the first pitch; halfway. I pressed my forehead to the rock and breathed deeply, trying to quell fear rising inside. The wind was kicking up a little and I tried to squeeze into the cracks between the rock, wet-smelling, doodled with white marks where crampons had scratched, a little bit of calm, a place to pretend just for a moment that I wasn't here.

At least it was cloudy. The curses of clear weather were, perhaps, worse. In May – the betting person's month for fine conditions on Skye – the afternoon sun slides to a lethal angle right in the sightline of ascent, discomfiting the climber and making the upward view a mixture of dazzling light and deep, detail-swallowing shadow, like trying to find your way up an uneven staircase while someone blinds you with a torch. Then, of course, there was the ever-visible exposure. From where I was lying, prone against the rock, my eyes wandering over one side of the crest while my body remained slightly but firmly on the other, I could appreciate that the Pinnacle's two sides were starkly different to each other, yet oddly deceitful in severity. The left side – the south – was sheer and smooth in layered slabs, loose rock clustered in the cracks where a new layer began, running at a steep angle down to the base, where a ledge and a path interrupted any very long fall below the Coireachan Ruadha Crags, and eventually Coruisk. A fall before a certain height, you could probably survive. The right side was bulbous and knotty, less blocky – but beyond its initially more comely nature, this one didn't stop. It was swiftly bare of holds, and then there was a sheer, endless fall. Nobody could survive that. I remembered what Matt had said, half in jest, several times now: 'If you fall, try to fall to the left.'

Things were moving again. The rope began to gather from my feet and I started to move before it went tight. The Pinnacle had become very steep – much steeper than before. I was now in full contact with the rock, slithering up it, past a little flattening – probably the point where Matt split the pitches – then up onto the crest, which was now narrowing substantially, fractured into rung-like blocks, like climbing the edge of a twisted cog.

I had a moment where I couldn't decide on my next move; my attention had been focused on Kevin's boots, then suddenly the rope went tight, I felt the yank on my waist and I was suddenly stretching uncomfortably, my feet scrabbling frantically for an upward step.

'I don't have a hold! *Wait!*' I heard my shout go up the line, and it stopped.

Don't think, just move. But what if it was a bad move? I could slip and fall, pulling everyone else off their feet, a sudden shock-load on the rope. This all now felt wrong to me. I looked up. Kevin's slick nylon trousers, boots shiny with rain and muck, so close to my nose I could smell them, were eye-level. *They* all seemed calm. Was I the only one having this turmoil? I had the sudden urge to detach myself from the rope – a bad idea, and not just for me. I looked down at the knot in my harness and realised that even if I wanted to, I couldn't. I couldn't untie a loaded knot and I had no knife. *I had no knife.* This hit me oddly hard, triggering a mad chain of thoughts in my head. Why didn't I have a knife? What if I needed to get off the rope? Then a bit more rational. Why *would* you have a knife? What would you do with it if you did, you daft shit? Who and where do you think you are? Listen to the guide, play the game and everything will be fine. You're just panicking. Stop panicking.

'You all right, Simon?' It was Kevin.

'Fine.' Just panicking.

Our eyes met and he must have seen something.

'Sure?'

'Sure, I'm fine.' I wonder what would happen if I wasn't.

Kevin began to move. I heard a laugh from somewhere up above, and this seemed to steady me. Nobody would be laughing if things were out of control. Things were fine. Just a little panic. We moved again. The crest sharpened. No longer a twisted cog, the ridge was now like a blade. The cloud to the right billowed, then opened, but I kept my eyes fixed on the rock right in front of me. No drop that way. No exposure. Just this little bit of rock right in front of my nose and that rope – tight, slack, tight, slack.

The crest became thinner still. The drop to the left was no longer survivable; it was sheer on both sides now. On their own, the moves weren't difficult. If you were six feet from the ground this would be easy, you'd skip along it. The mist hid most of what would trip you psychologically so things were fine. I took hold of one polished block-edge and it moved, but that was OK – there was another just above it. I felt the twinge of cramp in my leg – tension mixed with adrenaline, probably – and sensed my anxiety rising again. Then there was a little lift, a bit to clamber over, then here was a novelty: a descent. Just a step, but here was a slab, and coils of rope and a stop. We were at the top – the very top – of a lightning rod of mountaineering. We were up.

Few other details are given about the first ascent of the Inaccessible Pinnacle. Charles Pilkington's 1887 paper is muddled, jumping back and forth in time, and actually refers to three Pilkington ascents of the Pinnacle – the first ascent in 1880, a second in 1883 by Lawrence, Horace Walker and Eustace Hulton, then a third in 1887 with James Heelis, in which they tackled its much more difficult west ridge – first climbed by Stocker and Parker the previous year. In their company on at least this occasion – and possibly all three – was 'the ghillie from Sligachan', John MacKenzie.

Given the Pilkingtons' propensity for guideless climbing in the Alps, it's interesting that John MacKenzie would become such a fixture of their ascents on Skye. Much of his work for them was as a 'handy man' – Charles's term – and he was clearly considered a fixer of sorts, able to manage logistics, carry photographic equipment and indicate which peaks had or hadn't been climbed, rather than being a facilitator of ascent.

In other similar arrangements, this didn't always go well. Take the case of the accomplished alpinist Professor William Angus Knight, who in 1873 enlisted the services of Angus MacPherson on an intrepid ascent of Sgùrr nan Gillean. Knight evidently found his local sage reduced to a clammy wreck at the prospect of ascending one of the pinnacles that gave this peak its dash. While ascending this subsidiary top, which would later bear his name – Knight's Peak – the professor had to bribe his guide to accompany him, doubling the sum before the final push from the col. As Ben Humble wrote in *The Cuillin of Skye*, MacPherson, 'like certain early guides in the Alps, knew one route up one peak. That was enough; he had no desire to venture into the unknown.'

This is perhaps a little unfair on MacPherson. Firstly, Knight was fond of climbing without ropes, which as a pursuit is a rather grave ask of any companion not used to unjustifiable risk. Secondly, MacPherson was probably one of the more overlooked figures of the Cuillin's shadowy early years. He was the principal guide at Sligachan and active between the years 1854 and 1887, straddling arguably the most pioneering period of exploratory climbing on the ridge – and was reputedly instrumental in introducing John MacKenzie to the role that would define his life. Again, this casts a shadow on the fame of MacKenzie as the first true guide of the Cuillin. As pithily deduced by Norman Macdonald in Vol. 3 of *The Great Book of Skye*, MacPherson, who accompanied Alexander Nicolson on at least one ascent, was active in the mountains in the 1860s 'not only [in a period when guiding was well] established at Sligachan... but a gradation had developed allowing for a 'principal' guide.'

Anyhow, back to MacKenzie and the Pilkingtons. At this point in his career, much like most of the 'guides' at work in the Cuillin, MacKenzie's technical skills were outgunned by those of his clients. He was, in effect, the student. Photographs of the man in his prime show a hollow-cheeked, wary-eyed individual, awkward in front of a camera and usually looking at it askance. Ashley Abraham, who took a number of these images, made MacKenzie something of a celebrity in life from his account in the influential

Rock-climbing in Skye, and certainly laid groundwork of sorts for the reputation that followed:

> [He was] a good and careful rock climber ... it is a great delight to sit with him on top of some grim tower and question him on the topography of the surrounding peaks. The Coolin are to him an open book, every page of which he knows by heart. When in his company one feels that his predominating qualities are his love for the mountains, his genial and kindly nature, his unremitting care, and a fine sturdy independence of spirit.

When MacKenzie first began taking tourists into the shadow of the ridge he probably had very little English: he was a Gaelic speaker first and foremost, and as Sheriff G. D. Valentine noted, 'The turns of his phrases showed in what language his thoughts had been moulded.' Quizzed once about the notorious 'short' side of the Inaccessible Pinnacle, he replied, probably due to misinterpretation but *possibly* humour: 'I know it is impossible. I've been up it ma'sel!'

Precisely when MacKenzie did climb the Inaccessible Pinnacle is uncertain. He had reputedly been present for the Pilkingtons' first ascent in 1880 and was offered the chance to accompany them on it. He declined, saying he would wait for another day. Charles Pilkington mentions that the next successful attempt on the Pinnacle was the following year, when a 'shepherd got up ... having first taken off his shoes'. It's thought that this was MacKenzie, solo. He's also thought to have climbed the shorter but harder side of the Pinnacle before the Pilkingtons, in the company of R. C. Broomfield in 1886, although it seems that this wasn't known to the Pilkingtons when they made their ascent a year later, suggesting that either the Skyeman was coy about what he divulged or the Pilkingtons didn't ask.

Either way, in 1887 MacKenzie had been enlisted on the Pilkington outing to carry James Heelis's camera. Charles refers to MacKenzie as the group's 'guide, photographer and friend' – though strangely he uses inverted commas, suggesting this is perhaps how MacKenzie referred to himself. On the 1887 ascent of the western face of the Pinnacle, Charles recalls an eager response from MacKenzie when asked if he would like them to 'take him up' too. 'Oh yes,' was his ready reply.

Off went his boots and we tied him on to the rope. I believe his great anxiety at the time had been that we might send him round with the luggage to the other side and not give him the chance of a climb.

Descending by the east ridge, thus completing a traverse of the Pinnacle, Charles remarks that the way was 'easier now ... for on the first ascent very great care and labour were required to pull out stones ... often forming the whole of the edge.'

What's curious is that the one thing nobody seemed to agree on during this period of prolific description – and later – is perhaps the most crucial of all. Here's Walter Brunskill, writing of the Pinnacle in the *Scottish Mountaineering Club Journal* in 1892:

It is a survival of the fittest of the range, being a hard slab of trap which has, more successfully than the rest of the mountain, withstood the weathering action of the elements.

Then here's Ashley Abraham, in 1904:

It may be taken as survival of the fittest ... for it has withstood the storms, frost and sun of ages past ... a hard mass of gabbro which at one time was bedded between two 'dykes' of basalt and diabase ... weathered away by the action of the elements and left standing this unique pinnacle.

Plenty of similarities in these descriptions, indeed – but one crucial difference. Brunskill says 'trap', which was common shorthand for basalt; Abraham says 'gabbro'. The pattern continues through various descriptions made at various times. J. Hubert Walker in the extensive geological appendix of *On Hills of the North* quite confidently describes it as an 'isolated thin slab of gabbro, left standing where two dykes either side had worn away'. The Scottish Mountaineering Club's *Skye Scrambles* also lists it as gabbro, as does Malcolm Slesser's SMC guide, *The Island of Skye*. But *Hostile Habitats: Scotland's Mountain Environment*, the standard text for students of the mountain landscape of Scotland, lists the Pinnacle as being a particularly good example of a basalt dyke, which, given Matt's descriptions of the difference between gabbro and basalt, seems accurate. The ascent was blocky and stepped, surrounded by fractures, slippy and – as attested by the Pilkingtons – loose in places.

Isn't it a bit odd that nobody can really decide what the thing's made of? This might seem pedantic, but given the marked differences of adhesion between gabbro and basalt, and the degree of attention this was given by would-be assailants, you'd have thought this would be clear from the outset. Basalt becomes treacherously slippy when wet; gabbro retains its friction. From the accounts I'd read, the Pinnacle was either a slab of gabbro that once had dykes of basalt either side of it, or a dyke of basalt stood aloft after the gabbro either side had collapsed. I asked Matt what he thought.

'It's basalt. The bits that matter, anyway.'

'How do you know?'

He looked at me. 'Because it feels like basalt. And it looks like basalt. And it breaks like basalt.'

I crouched with my head resting against the summit blocks of the Inaccessible Pinnacle, my eyes focusing on the tiny denticles of rock in front of my nose, smelling the rain and the lichen. These are the 'Bolster Stones' – a lion's claw of rocks, arranged in size order with the biggest to the end, which actually form a continuation of the ridge crest.

The truth in Alexander Nicolson's throwaway comment about the Inaccessible Pinnacle 'hardly being worth the trouble' to ascend is perhaps most apparent from its top, which, even on a claggy day like today, offered enough of an immediate view to demonstrate what he was getting at. Stand on the top of the Pinnacle, look towards the summit of Sgùrr Dearg, a few dozen metres over the void to the west, and you're standing proud of it by a mere seven metres. The 'trouble' can these days be precisely quantified – in the British rock-grading system the east ridge is the easiest grade of all, a 'Moderate'.

Looking across to Sgùrr Dearg from the top of the Pinnacle is, however, oddly comforting. It looks close – almost near enough to jump – and it's easy to ignore the nasty void in between. It's here where the four of us were sitting in a line, while Matt began to rig the abseil. What surprised me most was how green it was – the ledge was covered with a springy, tight-coiled moss, as were some of the cracks in the Bolster Stones, along with the black organic slime that often builds in damp rock crevices.

'Boys, you're going to have to get a lot more friendly than that,' Matt said. Looking back and forth awkwardly, the four of us pressed ourselves together with the scratch and shuffle of nylon and boots or rock. 'Little bit more. Come on, don't be shy.' Scratch, shuffle. We were now more or less sitting in each other's laps. That was OK. You get to know people pretty quick in the mountains.

Then – for a moment – activity ceased, the wind dropped and everything went quiet. I could hear Kevin's breathing in front of me. A clink from far below, the echo-bent shout of a voice. The rain was still falling, and I was beginning to shake a little with the cold, but the pause was enough to just enjoy being there – to forget the worry, to forget the abseil that was coming, to not think about anything other than just being at the very top of this tilting, spire-like piece of rock, itself on the top of a very precipitous mountain. It was a good moment and – maybe or maybe not influenced by the fact we were practically giving each other a cuddle – I think we all felt it.

I was expecting someone to say something profound. But in a slightly wild tone of voice Kevin said, '*What* the hell am I doing up here?'

I suppose that was fairly profound. He was fine, but as it turned out Kevin didn't much like the idea of the abseil. Neither, as soon became clear, did Chris. Oddly, the abseil was the only part of the climb I was happy with, as it was the thing I was in the least control of. Maybe that said something about our confidence levels, with me being resolutely on the bottom rung. I think Kevin was having a moment of context during that little pocket of reflection, but it was soon hustled away without fuss as the time to move had come. At the top of the western drop I could see Matt's back and hear him running through the drill to Chris, whose attentively inclined head I could see over Matt's shoulder. Matt's words were muffled, but I could hear him emphasising something, probably talking about the potential for death or terrible injury in the moments that followed. Matt stepped back and sat against the rock, and we saw Chris, rope tensioned against his weight, right hand poised to lower himself, beginning to lean back over the void, his skin the colour of paper, his eyes on stalks.

'Tell my wife I loved her.' His joke couldn't disguise the wobble in his voice. We'd all had our little wobble at different stages – me on the way up, Kevin on the top, Chris on the abseil – all except George, who'd been quiet throughout. I guess it was just the different ways we reacted to things like this.

One by one we went down. As George started to descend I saw Chris making his way up the slope to the summit of Sgùrr Dearg beyond, with a lope that spoke of adrenaline-battered knees. Then George joined him, as Kevin started his abseil. Then it was my turn, and I found myself next to Matt on the edge of the In Pinn's summit. We shared a glance, mine presumably wild, his weary but focused – and I looked down at the ganglion of ropes and slings around his stance. I also noticed something gleaming around the bottom of the biggest, most precarious-looking Bolster Stone. I bent down and peered. It was a chain, slung round the base of the stone. Matt's gear was clipped to it via two chunky steel karabiners. Through the karabiners were his ropes, on the end of the rope was Kevin, and in a minute, me.

'Who checks the chain?' I asked.

Matt looked at me for a long moment, then said, 'We all do.'

Kevin landed at the base of the pillar and let out a whoop that was coloured by the queer angles of the rock. For a moment I was off the rope as Matt attached another to my waist. He threw the lowering line down behind me, and I heard it whip to the ground below. 'Lean back,' he said. 'You're in control.'

I nodded. Soon I was backing out along the stepped slabs to the edge. Abseiling is a peculiar, unnatural feeling. You control the rate of your speed with the rate at which you allow the rope through your belay device at your waist with your right hand, while your left hand grips the rope above you. At first you're fighting an array of instincts. Fail to feed the rope through at a pace that matches the movement of your feet and you end up losing your footing; grip the rope too hard with your right hand and it can't run through. And if you don't lean back fully into the abseil with all your weight and all your trust – so your body makes a right angle with the rock face – your movement is unnatural and off-kilter, and you're liable to end up spinning like clock hands and planting your face in the rock.

So there is the moment, and I felt it now, when you truly put your life in someone's hands. A relative stranger, to whom you are trusting absolutely everything; everything you were, everything you are, everything you could ever be. There are many moments in life when this imminent threat to mortality is effectively the case; surgery, stepping on a plane, eating seafood, watching *Mrs Brown's Boys* – but for some reason, hanging on a rope with a chasm below you, and looking into the eyes of your guide as they watch you lean back into their charge over a drop, is particularly powerful.

The edges of the Pinnacle were disappearing in the mist, and even the splintery ground below, which I caught glimpses of through my splayed legs as I found my stance, was softening as wisps of cloud curled their way over the ridge. Through the rain I looked up and I saw Matt nod. I leaned back, felt the harness creak, felt the tension creep into the ropes, then the reassuring feeling of everything going tight – and holding. My feet started to move backwards over easy-angled, broken ground, down to the lip. I looked up at Matt again – now just a shape and a pair of boot grips above – raised my left hand to free the rope and went over. For a second or two I was mid-air, allowing the rope frantically through my left hand and trying to keep up with my right, before bringing it back beneath me to slow the rate as my boots found the rock again. I started to breathe. Found a rhythm. Half a dozen movements later and my boots touched the ground, and I felt my weight transfer from the rope to the mountain.

A few seconds and I'd unclipped. 'I'm off.' And that was that.

The ascent of the Inaccessible Pinnacle in 1880 by the Pilkingtons shifted the nature of climbing on the Cuillin. In the years that followed, a gradual revolution began to take place. To quote climber Peter Bicknell's nifty classification of the ridge's climbing evolution, this was the transition between the 'easy way' period and the 'gully' period.

By 1887 almost all of the major Cuillin peaks had been climbed – several of the last few by the Pilkingtons themselves. Charles, his brother and their companions pioneered routes with seeming ease, making first ascents, absorbing the knowledge of local sages and tourists alike to find their way to the tops of untrodden summits, often naming them after friends. One of Charles's great footnotes concerns the speculative christening of the peaks around the head of Coire Làgan in 1887, or to use the Gaelic as they did, Coire Labain.

We would suggest the name of Sgùrr Labain for the sharp N. Peak. We jokingly called the nameless peak at the head of the corrie 'Pic MacKenzie' after our gillie, who went up with us, and we hear that it has since been known as Sgùrr Mhic Coinuich [sic], the Gaelic equivalent.

In an interesting echo of Alexander Nicolson's similarly modest deferral, the sharp northern peak, however, was not named Sgùrr Labain as Charles suggested; it was, some time later, named Sgùrr Thearlaich – 'Charles's Peak'.

The Pilkingtons were possibly amongst the last to enjoy such a free, fruitful time. Their Cuillin, and Skye, were at a watershed, and change was coming. As Ian R. Mitchell states in *Scotland's Mountains Before the Mountaineers*, by the late 1880s the Cuillin was 'receiving as many ascents in an average week as it had in the previous half century'. In many respects, it was Charles's 1887 paper – significantly, the first article on Skye climbing to appear in the *Alpine Journal* – that shone light onto the Cuillin and conjured up a vivid image of this virgin Hebridean curiosity, with its strange and incongruous mountains reminiscent of the Alps.

Lawrence Pilkington's climbing career would not outlive the decade; in 1884, whilst making the first exploration of Piers Gill on the slopes of Scafell Pike in the Lake District, a rockfall crushed his hip and crippled him for life. He remained a spectator, writing many poems about the mountains that had so enthralled him. One such verse reads:

> Oh, for the hills of Skye,
> With storm-wracked cliffs on high,
> Where sunset's streaming fire,
> Drapes Sgùrr nan Gillean's spire;
> Where climbers gladly greet
> Rock safe for hands and feet,
> On which dear life to trust
> However fierce the gust
> Oh, for the hills of Skye
> Dark Cuillin hills of Skye.

Lawrence Pilkington died in 1941. Charles, meanwhile, would become something of a cheerleader for the Cuillin. In the wake of his interest-triggering paper, he led parties of world-class mountaineers into their heights, including in 1890 William Slingsby, Clinton Dent, Geoffrey Hastings and Horace Walker – a collection of Alpine Club members who were between them tackling unclimbed peaks in ranges all around the world. In the same year he climbed with his wife up the Inaccessible Pinnacle, giving Mabel Pilkington the distinction of being the first woman to reach the true summit of Sgùrr Dearg. Also in 1890 he would, like James Forbes before him – and in answer to the criticism made of the Ordnance Survey – produce his own map of the Cuillin. Drawn in disciplined pencil, it showed the main crest of the ridge and its spurs as an angular narrow strip of white.

It records the names in Gaelic, makes the first formal cartographical mention of 'Sgùrr Alaisdair' and modestly reduces the Inaccessible Pinnacle to a nameless dot below the main summit of Sgùrr Dearg. It names Sgùrr MhicCoinnich but doesn't name Sgùrr Thearlaich, referring simply to the satellite of Skye's highest point as the 'NE Peak'. And as is any cartographer's prerogative – like James Forbes with his glacial scratches – he inscribes places of personal interest: Brittle House, the paths between the glens, the tops of each buck of the ridge, and, of course, the Sligachan Hotel. Again, such a personal interpretation, but one that was applauded as just the job by many of his peers; the Alpine Club sold the map to interested parties for a modest fee. And in the coming years, there were plenty who were interested.

Matt, heavy lifting behind him, became more animated as we descended. The evening light was gilding the sea, throwing little puddles of sunlight onto the strait between Skye and South Uist, the latter a bulky shape anchored on the north-western horizon. It had gone from feeling grim, to becoming spectacular. No weather; just conditions.

Where the cloud allowed them to emerge, Matt began to point out landmarks. Loch Brittle, the peninsula of Rubha an Dùnain, onward to the other Hebrides. For charity, he once rowed out to St Kilda on a boat he and some friends restored, he told us. In his economical way, he described it as if sailing across a sort of parallel existential plane, like sailing to the rock at the edge of the world. A wild time was had, he said with a grin. Then his gaze turned towards Soay, the little island drifting off the western coast of Skye, nebulous and loch-holed, like a spill of wine on the sea.

Matt pointed his stick towards the island. 'That's the island Gavin Maxwell used to own.'

'The naturalist guy?' someone said. I remembered saying the same thing when Matt had pointed out Soay on the ridge from Gars-bheinn the previous year, and saw the same frown in response – but come to think of it, he'd never explained why. 'I'd call him something else,' he now said.

This might come as a surprise to those who associate Gavin Maxwell as the benevolent friend to an orphaned otter in the *Ring of Bright Water* trilogy, but his first book *A Harpoon at Venture* – set on Soay, in the shadow of the Cuillin – was an altogether darker and more peculiar work. In it Maxwell's image disintegrates into something very far from a man in the thrall of nature in all its forms, and more an agent of its destruction. His target was the oceanic equivalent of a buffalo – the gigantically placid, filter-feeding basking shark. His aim was wealth, or at least a living, having returned from the war and bought Soay in 1944 on a flight of idealistic fancy, intending to set up a factory for harvesting the liver oil of the giant shark. His weaponry was a fishing boat, a crew and an array of borderline psychotic methods of dispatch: harpooning, dragging, drowning, beheading and in one passage, machine-gunning. The whole reads like a prolonging of the bloodshed, brutality and gore of war by other, stranger means.

And don't be fooled by the idea of 'shark hunting' as being some macho struggle with a mortal foe, as implied by the companion book written by Maxwell's rascally harpoonist muscle-man Joseph 'Tex' Geddes, entitled *Hebridean Sharker*. These are no toothy, streamlined predators; basking sharks are about as nimble as a shipping container. Easily spotted by their meandering dorsal fins, this wasn't hunting: it was slaughter.

Regardless of this – much like Hemingway and H. W. Tilman, whose prose had been similarly numbed by war and shot through with equally regressive attitudes towards the dispatching of large and now rare quarry – Maxwell was a fine writer. His evocations of the Hebrides make *A Harpoon at Venture* grim but atmospheric reading.

Maxwell's Cuillin was:

a great splintered ridge ... from everywhere on the island the Cuillin seemed towering and imminent, three thousand foot of bitter black rock rising stark and hostile out of the sea.

He was sensitive to the deeper, human-seeded moods of the landscape, too; he described Rum, omnipresent across the sound, as:

a strange place ... eerie and haunted if ever a Hebridean Island was. It is all mountains, dark and savage as the Cuillins themselves; but they seem to have a different soul, something older and more brooding, almost evil.

Read that, then look at Rum and try not to shiver.

As an island, Soay certainly possessed its own magic, drawing the eyes of mountaineers on the southern ridge for decades with its dark mystique. 'Seen from Gars-bheinn it seems so riddled with lochans that it ought by rights to sink. In fact it is a jewel,' wrote Malcolm Slesser of the island. And it was on this 'jewel', within sight of these austere mountains, that Maxwell would carve his own surreal brand of horror. Maxwell turned the hillside behind the 'factory' on Soay into an awful charnel-yard of cartilaginous spinal columns, flensed fins and other decomposing body parts from count-less sharks flung across an area as big as a football pitch. The focus on death, its methods and its aftermath, is uncomfortably excessive – and the black and white imagery in the book repulsive; sharks hung, skinned, beheaded, dismembered, spilled over gangways, their vacant, big-eyed faces gaping in death. Some have suggested the book is an allegory of war, of the carnage on the beaches of Normandy, of the mindless slaughter and aban-donment of humanity and compassion between nations. If it is, it's a costly one. Perhaps this is evidenced by a man seemingly untroubled by the dichotomy of having a deep devotion to one species – as clear in his compas-sionate account of rearing the Sandaig otters of 1960 – whilst laying waste to another. And on this level, the book is fascinating. Certainly for the man to be remembered and honoured as a conservationist, it's a peculiar and dark chapter to ignore.

Whether deserved or not, Maxwell would atone for Soay in later life. His was reputedly an unhappy one of concealed homosexuality, which in an old age plagued by illness would drive away those who loved him. His famous otter Mijbil was accidentally lost while on a walk with the woman described as his 'great love', the poet Kathleen Raine – with the beloved animal casually clubbed to death by a road worker. His house at Sandaig, overlooking the Sound of Sleat, burned down in 1968. Maxwell died a year later of lung cancer at Eilean Bàn, the lighthouse near Kyleakin, between Skye and the mainland. The tiny island today supports a pillar of the Skye Bridge and a museum dedicated to his life.

On the subject of interesting individuals, Tex Geddes – Maxwell's Quint, if you like – was a man of fanciful origin and reputation who in later life would become something of a local celebrity. Many of those who knew him on Skye presumed him of Australian extraction, while Geddes himself attributed his nickname to a First Nation American with whom he had served in the Commando corps. He died in 1998, and an obituary recorded his early years:

> an accomplished knife-thrower and bayonet fencer, a boxer, a former rum-runner in Newfoundland, an orphaned lumberjack 'tree monkey' whose father had been blown up while dynamiting a log jam, and who had been expelled from school at the age of 12 as 'unmanageable'

– a vivid vision of a man who would later inherit Soay and act as its laird until his death. One of Geddes's last controversies was in 1995, when he advised a fellow Hebridean landowner Marlin Eckhard Maruma, the German-born professor who had recently bought the neighbouring island of Eigg, what would befall him if he abused the rights of the island's eighty tenants. If Maruma was expecting sympathetic and sage pointers from a fellow laird he was perhaps over-ambitious; Geddes threatened to eat him.

The five of us sat on the shoulder of Sgùrr Dearg, in the serene afterglow of adrenaline, watching the day lift and the sun drop. We had just slayed something too. Our own bit of shark hunting. No harpoons and lines, just walking poles and ropes. War, killing sharks, mountaineering, danger, death – what is it about humans and their risks, these substitutes for existential peril?

After the Inaccessible Pinnacle was first climbed, other seemingly impregnable obstacles of the Cuillin began to fall to a new breed of technically adept, alpine climber who came to Skye to slay their own monsters. The impossible had been proven assailable: the Pilkingtons had spread the word and set the scene, and with that the climbers came swarming.

The ascent that drew much of this together rather neatly came in 1886, when A. H. Stocker and A. G. Parker made an audacious ascent of the (unofficial) fourth pinnacle of Sgùrr nan Gillean – known as Knight's Peak, after Professor Knight. Watching from below was a young scientist who – like the Pilkingtons a decade earlier – had come with his brother to Skye to fish and had been thwarted. Taking a wander from Sligachan up Coire a' Bhasteir in the shadow of Sgùrr nan Gillean, he had looked up and seen Stocker and Parker

climbing on the rock face of one of the pinnacles ... hundreds of feet above me, on what seemed to be rocks as steep as the walls of a house. In those days I knew nothing about climbing, and it seemed to me perfectly marvellous that human beings should be able to do these things.

After questioning the two climbers, he telegraphed for a climbing rope, and with his brother Harry, attempted and failed on Sgùrr nan Gillean twice on consecutive days, before snagging the elbow of a guide at Sligachan for advice as to the best way to tackle it. This meeting would spark a friendship that would last half a century – and would, much later, inspire a pair of statues. The guide was the twenty-nine-year-old John MacKenzie, the scientist a lean twenty-seven-year-old chemist named John Norman Collie.

By the following year, MacKenzie had a mountain named after him and Collie was back on Skye, enlisting his services. Together, the two would begin the partnership that became the most famous in the Cuillin's exploration, leaving their story indelibly inscribed on its maps, its rocks and its history.

11

Edge

I'd driven back to Portnalong to the Taigh Ailean Hotel and, after piling all my wet gear into the boot of my car, made straight for the bar. The next morning I drove in stormy sunlight into Glen Brittle and sat just off the road, to look up at the ridge. Here, if you step back as if admiring a painting, you can get a broader view of the Cuillin's spiky middle ground, the section between Sgùrr Dearg over to the right, its flanks like draped wings, and Bidein Druim nan Ramh to the left. A line of corries bites into the ridge, the crest fretted and darting and high, its summits a succession of abrasively named *sgùrrs*: Banachdaich, Thormaid, Ghreadaidh, Madaidh, Fheadain. Forbidding, and for now to me, forbidden. Cloud was clipping across the tops and by noon the rain was falling in industrial cascades. I had that vaguely sore feeling in both body and mind, the feeling that today the mountains were best seen from below.

On a map the middle of the Cuillin ridge is a cartographic stipple, a *terra incognita* when it comes to distinctive landmarks – a big slice of nasty, zig-zagging ridge crest. For walkers it's hard on the head, legs and stomach: the most technical part of the ridge. There are no photogenic pinnacles, but there are big drops, awkward passes and devious impasses. It's the cruel interlude that, from a traverse perspective, strips out the unqualified, who by the time they've overcome the Coireachan Ruadha Crags, succeeded on the In Pinn and topped out on Sgùrr na Banachdaich, are hitting adrenaline fatigue. Speaking as just one of these, I'm happy to conclude that this section is, in many ways, the climbers' domain – less about the crest, more the faces either

side. You know that because it's one of the few parts of the Cuillin, with the
exception of Sgùrr nan Gillean, that's more famous for features seen from
the roadside than from its heights. This place is all about the verticals, its
walls and cracks. And one catches the eye more than any: it's probably the
most photographed feature in the Cuillin, yet it's never named in the pictures
you see. But to the early rock climbers, it was the most perfect exponent of
the shift from the airy summits to the chewy midriff.

In the years after the Pilkingtons' first ascent of the Inaccessible Pinnacle,
the number of virgin summits on the ridge was dwindling to the hardest,
sharpest and least desirable objectives. There were still a few peaks to be
had, but what there was in abundance – dripping and opulent from every
conceivable aspect and angle – were rock climbs. Climbing on the mainland
was gathering apace, and the reputation of Skye and the Cuillin, thanks in
no small measure to the writings of Charles Pilkington and rumours of the
extraordinary gabbro with its supernatural grip, was reaching a select band
eager for ever-harder objectives.

Out went the explorers with their plaid and whimsically romantic intentions; in came the climbers with their ropes, hobnailed boots and flinty eyes
that ran appraisingly over gullies, cracks and walls, who talked in a new,
strange language. Theirs was a mindset calibrated differently, their ambition
preoccupied with the way, rather than the destination. Mountaineers gain
their reward on a summit; for climbers, it's the physicality of the journey
and the quality of a pitch, regardless of what lies at the top. And with such
a copiously cragged labyrinth of rock up for grabs, the Cuillin ridge became
a swarming-place for Britain's most promising rock athletes keen to see just
what they could do.

It's hard to describe the next period of Cuillin exploration without
sounding like you're emptying a magazine of Scotland's finest climbers onto
the ridge, all of whom blasted their own bullet hole of history onto it. But
that's essentially what happened.

One of the most purposeful climbers to step into the breach was William
Naismith. He had made a visit to Skye in April 1880, and after an impressively careful ascent of Sgùrr nan Gillean in the company of two friends
(and significantly, no guide), he left his name in a bottle at the top and

navigated down using a self-built system of cairns. Before the weekend was out he'd climbed Bruach na Frithe and Blàbheinn, and made the first ascent of the north top of Bidein Druim nan Ramh, one spire of the pincer-like spike that crowns this central point of the ridge. It was a convoluted outing as the group got completely disorientated, the Cuillin map at the time being so vague that Naismith actually thought he'd climbed Sgùrr a' Mhadaidh, and believed so for years afterwards.

Cuillin cartography would not improve until the decade was over, with Charles Pilkington's 1890 map outstripping even the first OS one-inch map in 1885 for accuracy. Naismith's acuity got better too. Following a long apprenticeship in the Alps and on the mainland – and a remark made in a letter Naismith sent to the *Glasgow Herald* in 1889, in which his complaint about the lack of information exchange between climbers was met with some encouraging replies – he became a founding member of the Scottish Mountaineering Club (SMC). This collective of alpinists and pioneering climbers, with their meets and journal, their songs and rivalries, led some of the most daring Scottish routes ever attempted.

While it's tempting to think that climbing was then a fashionable pastime, most of the activity was undertaken by a very small group of extremely intrepid individuals. Ken Crocket in his definitive *History of Scottish Mountaineering* estimates that in the years leading up to 1900 there were fewer than twenty-five experienced individuals – that is to say, those who had climbed in the Alps and were now investigating objectives closer to home – active in Scotland. The *Scottish Mountaineering Club Journal* was full of their lamentations, evocations and discoveries, their shared experience of wilfully dangerous and gleefully pointless rock climbing creating a genuine sense of camaraderie. A popular club song was the instantly infamous ode to discomfort, 'Oh, My Big Hobnailers' (1893), with its chorus:

> Oh, my big hobnailers! Oh my bog hobnailers!
> How they speak of a mountain peak,
> And lengthy stride o'er moorland wide!
> Oh, my big hobnailers! Oh, my big hobnailers!
> Memories raise of joyous days
> Upon the mountain side!

That's not to say that before the formation of the SMC the show-offs hadn't already staked their claim on the Cuillin. In 1886, *Wunderkind* of the Lake District Walter Parry Haskett-Smith ascended the Inaccessible Pinnacle, had a two-minute rest at the top, and then descended in a total of twelve minutes. Proof positive, surely, that no matter how hard won a first ascent, there's always a smart-arse-in-waiting keen to go one better – a trend that continues on the Cuillin, and indeed in mountaineering in general, to this day. The year 1886 was clearly a significant one for climbing on Skye, as amongst the stew of climbers loading off the boat was the reedy silhouette of John Norman Collie.

You'll have to excuse the following digression, but Collie was a singularly fascinating individual. Born in Alderley Edge, near Manchester, in 1859, he was christened John after his father but always known by his middle name – shortened further by his family to 'Nor'. His childhood was gently privileged, with both his mother and father bequeathed textile empires: his father cotton, his mother silk. John senior rented an estate in Deeside, and much of Collie's youth was spent outdoors, climbing trees and local hills, investigating birds' nests, and generally doing the rough-and-tumble things children like to do when given the opportunity. In an event that would become significant in later life, at some point a toy pistol exploded in his hand, burying a piece of lead in it.

Collie was given a good education, but one largely away from his family in boarding schools. When he was in his late teens, the family hit hard times – he often had to beg relatives for money to feed himself. He decided to study chemistry, and made what would become characteristically swift progress, eventually becoming Professor Emeritus in Organic Chemistry at University College London.

His observational capacity and insight were fuelled by a natural instinct for experimentation, and appreciation of an interesting result. His lectures were either coveted or dreaded, depending on the receptiveness of the student to his digressions and eccentricities. One student remarked, 'There always appeared to be something intriguing beyond the horizon of what he was saying.'

But Collie would rightly become a celebrated scientist, and as with many of his Cuillin peers – from understanding glaciers to driving a car with a windscreen made of Pilkington glass – his legacy lives on in the most unexpected of domestic scenarios. If you've ever loaded colour film into a camera, been guided into a premises by a neon light, or broken a bone and needed an X-ray, you owe a debt to Collie. Which when you think about it is really a rather remarkable record for one person to boast, given that these three things are not exactly snuggly bedfellows.

Despite this, or perhaps because of it, Collie appears to have been a man of permanent distraction. 'In my days as a young student he gave me what he called the education of a gentleman,' wrote one pupil, E. C. C. Baly. He continued:

> At a series of dinners in his rooms in Camden Grove he discoursed at length on the beauty of early printing and incunabula, the perfection of Chinese porcelain, the glories of Chinese lacquers, the grace of Japanese carving, and the knowledge and appreciation of vintage clarets. One evening his great friend, the late Sir Herbert Jackson, was present and he remarked, 'Collie, it seems to me that you are a chemist only in your spare time.'

Christine Mill wrote an excellent biography of Collie called *A Life in Two Worlds*, which ostensibly his was. But read about how he applied himself to each, and you can see the two mingle, like vapour. 'Beauty, wherever he found it, made a strong appeal to him ... one realises the delight he experienced in crystalline form,' wrote one admirer of Collie. In another passage, he was said to be 'no specialist – anything which savoured of narrowness was repugnant to his nature, but he was a true philosopher'. He was also an expert glassblower, and would enthral his students by making his own apparatus and specimen bottles.

The resulting applications of his work with neon were at the time credited to William Ramsay, Professor of Chemistry at University College London, though all of Collie's peers apparently suspected the acclaim should lie with him. It appears to have been a sore point: Collie once remarked that if 'anyone ever happens to write an obituary of me, I want two things said – I first discovered neon, and I took the first X-ray photographs'.

Regarding the latter, Collie had asked his colleague A. W. Porter to take an X-ray photograph of his right hand, having blown his own glass ray tube for the purpose. Weeks earlier in November 1895, Wilhelm Röntgen had discovered X-rays in Germany. By February 1896 Collie was X-ray photographing snakes, fish, lizards – and his own anatomy, using this newly discovered miracle. There were the bones, the shadow of his muscles and – clearly visible like a wisp of smoke – those fragments of lead from the exploding pistol of his childhood. Some time later, a young actress was sent to Collie with a sewing injury – a needle entirely embedded in her thumb. Its position and size were revealed in an X-ray photograph captured by Collie, the first such image for surgical purposes ever taken.

One of the more outlandish theories about Norman Collie is that he was the inspiration for Sherlock Holmes. This seems to have stemmed from an illustration in *The Strand* magazine, in which an artist had rendered Holmes in a manner physically very close to Collie, but the idea is sadly and easily refuted. In Sir Arthur Conan Doyle's own memoir, *Memories and Adventures*, he identifies his principal inspiration as being an Edinburgh surgeon named Joseph Bell, whose tendency to make diagnoses and deductions based on the briefest of observations inspired those of literature's most idiosyncratic detective.

There were, however, similarities. Collie was described by various sources as being 'tall, with long limbs allowing for a good reach to a high rock hold', a man who was 'lean and erect', his features 'long and pointed with sombre eyes', a 'serious look … and hair that hung lank and greying', easily conversant with Holmes as described in *A Study in Scarlet*. Both were committed smokers – one of Collie's students wryly noted the only time he smoked cigarettes was when he was filling his pipe. These similarities extended to Holmes's creator too. Collie shared Conan Doyle's interest in the occult – a slide of Collie shows the professor relaxing in his Gower Street flat surrounded by all manner of peculiar mystical objects, stroking an ornate oriental dragon with an unsettlingly attentive expression. To this end, it is also telling that Collie was intrigued by the young Aleister Crowley, a promising climber in the 1890s whom Collie befriended and mentored when the teenager visited Sligachan with his mother. Crowley took an interest in chemistry, and the two climbed together on several occasions – a winter ascent of Pinnacle Ridge on Sgùrr nan Gillean, or so it's said – with Collie later nominating the man who'd later become the infamous 'Great Beast' for membership to the Alpine Club.

Collie, like Conan Doyle, had an interest in ghosts; his tenures of Glen Brittle House in the company of artist Colin Phillip were said to feature 'nightly ghost stories', and it was Collie who gave birth to the *Am Fear Liath Mòr*, the 'Big Grey Man' of Ben MacDui, a fearful tale of a presence encountered some years earlier on the mountain in question, imparted during a Cairngorm Club dinner in 1925. For those interested, a curious little book called *Between the Sunset and the Sea* contains the full story of this fable.

Like Collie, Doyle was an adventurer as well as a scientist, with both men being born in the same year. Yet, while it is conceivable that Doyle and Collie's paths crossed, all of this is unlikely to be anything more than coincidence, given their similarity in age. Holmes's crotchety character was fully formed well before Collie's idiosyncrasies matured into eccentricity. What is irrefutable, however coincidental, is that both Collie and Doyle had life-defining events befall them at the age of twenty-seven in 1886: Doyle, the writing of the first Sherlock Holmes story, and Collie, the first steps he took on Skye.

Collie's entry into the world of distinguished adventure was not entirely unprecedented in his family. Thanks to the intrepid exploits of Alexander Collie, his paternal great-uncle, there was a species of Mexican magpie (*Calacitta colliei*) bearing the family name, as well as a river and town in Western Australia. On the other side of the family, one of his early benefactors when the family fell on hard times was Stephen Winkworth, his maternal uncle, a keen alpinist and an acquaintance of Cuillin pioneer James Forbes. Another uncle, on his father's side, was married to Flora MacNeill, a descendant of Flora MacDonald, who had aided Bonnie Prince Charlie's escape across the wilds of Skye. Small world, no?

The Australian town of Collie even has a monument to its namesake, so the Sligachan sculpture would only be the second permanent tribute to a Collie (albeit almost certainly the most expensive). By the time the living Norman Collie would hang up his boots, he would have a mountain in Canada named after his last name, a peak in the Cuillin named after his first (Sgùrr Thormaid), and be remembered in the names of countless gullies and routes, as well as in a step and a ledge – not to mention apparently having the blessing to name scores of landmarks including, it is rumoured, Sgùrr Alasdair. How such things are awarded seems to be the right combination of interest, aptitude and a pioneering spirit at just the right time.

So in perhaps the most absolute sense, the Cuillin ridge got Collie. It *really* got him, and it never let him go. Which makes it so frustrating that nobody really knows much about his actual climbing in the Cuillin. We know he did a lot of it, and with a lot of people – but his unwillingness to record his own exploits or keep any kind of journal gave him the dual honour of being at once the most famous and the most mysterious of the Cuillin pioneers.

The problem with his combination of charisma, an unwillingness to record his movements and his enduring presence around Sligachan, is that Collie became mythologised. This eccentric professor of chemistry, who decoded the mountains like the formula for some new compound, solving their mysteries with his brilliant brain, always surrounded by reverential tourists, fellow lovers of exotic ephemera and elegant ladies, seems to have been both everywhere and nowhere on the Cuillin for the duration of its headiest decades.

Collie makes a great contrast with Henry Chichester Hart. Hart – who you must surely remember as the discoverer of Britain's only alpine rock-cress, and the deducer of Sgùrr Alasdair as the highest peak of Skye – perhaps holds the crown for being the least-known interesting person in the Cuillin's mountaineering history. He was also one of its most unjustly eclipsed, most notably (though probably unwittingly) by Norman Collie. Essentially this was because Hart wasn't nearly as popular as Collie, for reasons we'll get to.

Like Collie, Hart was a polymath and a rather brilliant one. Born in Dublin, his wealthy background ensured he had the means to get deeply lost in any warren of academia he wished, so he chose a few. He was devoutly religious and saw his nature studies as complementary to his faith; one lent 'a new force or additional beauty' to the other, he once wrote, and his many and varied interests produced such works as *The Animals Mentioned in the Bible* and *On the Botany of Sinai and South Palestine*. Hart was naturalist-in-residence on HMS *Discovery*, which between 1875 and 1876 made an unsuccessful attempt to reach the North Pole, during which Hart amassed a considerable haul of arctic flora. He was also a notable Shakespearean scholar, editing seven plays for the Arden series.

But far from being an intrepid but bookish botanist with a fondness for whimsy and literature, on and off the mountains Hart was a beast. And where Collie was modest and retiring, Hart was considered a sociopath, belligerently competitive – and cocky as hell.

With a formidable moustache and mutton chops beneath an oily mop of hair – like those old caricatures of gentleman pugilists – Hart stood well over six foot tall, with a competitive streak that ran perilously close to antagonistic. Fellow naturalist R. L. Praeger warmly described him as 'somewhat dictatorial, impatient [and] difficult to handle', and he was by no means reluctant to back his own abilities in the hills.

In 1886 – before his Cuillin exploits – Hart bet fellow naturalist R. B. Barrington fifty guineas that he could walk from Dublin to the summit of Lugnaquilla and back in the space of twenty-four hours, a distance of seventy-five miles and on rugged hills for most of the way; he made it with ten minutes to spare. He beat two parties up the Weisshorn and the Dent Blanche in Switzerland for a wager in 1889, even though he gave both an hour's head start. Then in Egypt, Hart describes his pleasure at eluding his Bedouin guides to tear off into unclimbed gullies and onto ledges and, in one case, a rather illustrious sacred structure. 'I succeeded in dodging them and ascending the second and dangerous pyramid without their troublesome escort, and, what was to them inexcusably unsafe,' he wrote of the 'pyramid Arabs' on his unauthorised climb of one of the country's most iconic monuments. 'They ceased to meddle when they saw that they couldn't control.' So there you have the measure of the man.

Some of the more colourful comments written in the Sligachan Hotel Climber's Book come courtesy of Hart, whose scorn for using ropes on any of his ascents led him to openly and perhaps rather rashly poke fun at those who did, as if the act of preserving one's life was worthy of the highest ridicule. In Hart's sights was the risky target of Charles Pilkington, who found to his consternation that someone had cheerfully scrawled beneath one of his careful and meticulous accounts the words, 'Ropes all the time!' To which Charles replied, 'This remark is heartless and need not have been added by Mr H. C. Hart.'

A later comment by Hart concerning one of his days in the Cuillin – in which he highlighted his own rope-free escapades – was itself answered anonymously with the slightly excessive, 'A rope with a noose at the end and a long drop would have suited this idiot.' Given this, perhaps it's *not* so extraordinary that Hart isn't particularly famous in the annals of Cuillin climbers, despite really having every right to be.

For starters, it's everywhere written that it was Collie's measurements with his aneroid barometer that crowned Sgùrr Alasdair as the highest peak in the Cuillin. As recounted in Christine Mill's biography of Collie, the ascent of Sgùrr Alasdair is one of the few ascents of Collie's that we have an approximate date for: 1888. Collie and MacKenzie had just climbed the Inaccessible Pinnacle by its west ridge, whereupon Collie noted the summit of Sgùrr Alasdair 'looked higher', a suspicion he felt the impulse to confirm at once, which he did.

Hart had pipped him to the conclusion, however, not only recording his result but publishing it. He stated in the 1887 *Journal of Botany* – hardly the *Alpine Journal*, but still – alongside his discovery of the rock-cress, that he'd measured Sgùrr Alasdair and deduced it was the highest (albeit without other supporting measurements) a whole year before Collie even climbed it. Collie's *Scottish Mountaineering Club Journal* paper of 1893 – entitled 'On the Heights of some of the Black Cuchullins in Skye' – shows the workings for his deduction, and doesn't mention Hart at all. Though given the diligence with which Collie applied himself to the task, we can forgive him that; the professor could at least compare his measurements with the others in the range to make his conclusions more than simply a hunch. Amusingly, in an 1892 paper, even 'Alasdair' himself, Alexander Nicolson, noted with the deepest pride that Collie merely confirmed his own aneroid measurement of Sgùrr Alasdair, which was made even earlier than Hart, in 1874. The difference was that like many, Nicolson had always considered Sgùrr nan Gillean to be higher. But Ben Humble in *The Cuillin of Skye* writes that Collie was the first to measure it – and so the accolade stuck.

It gets worse, I'm afraid. One thing I was slightly dismayed to learn was that Collie also wasn't the first to tread on the thing that most famously takes his name and, for me, started this whole fascination: Collie's Ledge. Who was? Guess what.

In July 1887 a certain Mr Henry Chichester Hart engaged the services of a certain John MacKenzie, during which time the two men made probably the most sustained attack on the Cuillin ridge yet seen over such a short period of time. This included the meaty first ascent of Am Bàsteir, the summit that stands with angled attitude at the northern end of the ridge, off which splinters the eye-grabbing jag of rock known as the Bàsteir Tooth. Even amidst the context of the Cuillin, this was a mountaineers' peak through and through – and it's a great shame Hart didn't record his impressions of the enterprise. Collie climbed it a year later.

Hart's most impressive achievement is the 'round' of Coire Làgan, in which he traversed the Inaccessible Pinnacle (unroped, of course) from the harder west ridge to the east ridge, before continuing to Sgùrr Thearlaich and Sgùrr Alasdair, but bypassing the section between Sgùrr MhicCoinnich's summit and the col beyond – electing instead to take the ribbon of path across the terrace that would later be known as Collie's Ledge. And wrongly, it would seem.

It's this terrace, running beneath the summit of Sgùrr MhicCoinnich, which many of the few mountaineers in the know now call 'Hart's Ledge' – though whether rightly seems to be a point of some dispute, in a kind of affection versus justice argument. Given that MacKenzie was present on both occasions, it would perhaps be fairer if the ledge bore *his* name, were the mountain across which the ledge runs not already named Sgùrr Mhic-Coinnich: MacKenzie's Peak.

MacKenzie is himself often drawn into misappropriation, appointed to an involvement in events and situations in which he had no part, purely because people seem to think he should have been there. It's commonly written that MacKenzie was present on Alexander Nicolson's plaid-assisted ascent of the Dubhs, for instance, but he wasn't. This was instead an unnamed friend. As relayed to me by historian and Cuillin chronicler Stuart Pedlar, there's no evidence other than vague assertions that Nico and Cuillin chronicler and MacKenzie ever climbed together.

Speaking of MacKenzie, it's also occasionally claimed that Collie 'taught' him how to climb. In Collie's obituary in the *Alpine Journal*, the normally reliable Geoffrey Winthrop Young claimed that 'MacKenzie [was] the only authentic local guide ever produced in our islands, whom

Collie himself had trained'. A wee bit flippant, since MacKenzie had been exploring the Cuillin for years by the time Norman Collie crossed his path, and indeed had been an advisor to Collie's first ever mountaineering exploit on Sgùrr nan Gillean after his double failure on the peak. Collie's acquisition of technical competency, plus his international experience, no doubt gave the practically minded Skye guide plenty of opportunity to absorb new skills and information brought back by his companion, and Collie's eye and talent undoubtedly complemented MacKenzie's natural guile. But 'trained'? Rather sends the wrong message, don't you think? In reality, it was a partnership with mutual benefits. As Sheriff Valentine wrote of the pair, 'Collie appears to have been the innovator, the man who saw the possibilities, while on more than one occasion MacKenzie was the actual leader on the climb.'

Collie and MacKenzie were, however, fine hooks off which to hang the legendary exploration of the Cuillin because they embodied its spirit so well – and thus they became more than the sum of their individual achievements. The Beatles didn't invent Merseybeat, but they're synonymous with it and mythologised for popularising it – so it goes for Collie, MacKenzie and the exploration of the Cuillin ridge. The story is more convenient than the reality, so why not? But what was the reality? Was Collie as good as his legacy would suggest?

It's tricky to say. As mentioned, Collie left little detail of his climbing, much to the exasperation of fellow climbers and those whose business it was to record important ascents. 'It would only be a very bald narrative,' Collie once wrote to William Douglas – then editor of the *Scottish Mountaineering Club Journal* – who was one of many who would gently press the steadfastly reticent professor for more detail on his endeavours in the interests of future study, if nothing else. 'We went up a snow slope, then we went up a rock, then we went up some snow and ice then some ice and snow and finally got to the top.' As Christine Mill puts it, 'The idea of recording routes in sufficient detail to enable other parties to follow exactly the same lines, stripping mountains of their mystery and depriving others of the chance to explore for themselves, was against his principles.'

So while other mountaineers concerned themselves with their 'bald narratives', what Collie did was be a scientist. He spotted a gap that needed filling with knowledge. Conducted fieldwork. Did his research. Examined the terrain, compared it, contrasted it, built up a picture of its nature, tested it, then gave an exacting conclusion. In a sentence, he firmed up the map of the Cuillin with the detail it needed.

Collie's SMC paper of 1899, 'On the Heights of some of the Black Cuchullins', is a great example of this. In the abstract, Collie lamented the fact there was no map containing anything in the way of reliable heights for the range. He mentions Charles Pilkington's map as being an improvement on that of the Ordnance Survey, which it was – but both maps failed to give heights for most of the major peaks. And so Collie made it his mission over six years to measure, compare, analyse and scrutinise the results of aneroid barometer measurements made across the Cuillin in a variety of weathers. Regardless of what we've already said about Hart discovering Sgùrr Alasdair's true significance, Collie's findings were comprehensive and fastidious enough to be called the first serious measurement of Cuillin heights: essentially the definition of a job not done quickly, but done well.

Much, you could say, like the slowly developing map of the Cuillin itself. It had been started by Forbes, improved by Charles Pilkington, numerically stiffened by Collie and finally rubber stamped by the geologist Alfred Harker, who – with the assistance of John MacKenzie – spent six years making a map from field bases at Sligachan and Glenbrittle. His work finally yielded a map in 1898 that stands as relatively accurate to this day, largely thanks to Collie's work on the ridge. It was so precisely observed that the Ordnance Survey used his results to augment its own maps.

So however much we might nitpick about what Collie did or didn't pioneer, he was perhaps – and this is fitting, considering the Sherlock Holmes comparison – the Cuillin's great interrogator. He might not have been the first to make certain deductions, or blaze certain trails, but Collie was a painstaking surveyor and a fine inquisitor – there's no doubt that his were the most thorough observations made of the Cuillin at the time, and quite possibly since. Read his 'Heights' paper, and it invites an endearing vision of the scientist breezing up all manner of precarious objectives in search of a measurement. Sixty separate spot heights were published, of which only eight had been measured previously by the Ordnance Survey.

These were of most of the main features of the ridge, from the top of the Bàsteir Tooth to the summit of the In Pinn and the pinnacles of Sgùrr nan Gillean.

It's not heaving with excitement, mind. But Collie's lean article, written like a scientific paper – forensic, intelligently reasoned and trustworthy – held in its largely numerical insights the most extensive single record of exploration in the Cuillin ever given by one person. Throughout its length it contains no direct narrative, no anecdote or flights into whimsy outside of the nuts and bolts of how he came by his conclusions – apart from a little set of tips for the would-be Cuillin climber, written like experimental best practices.

Many, including Alexander Nicolson, probably made plenty of theories off the back of a whim, from what they saw or witnessed. To be proven right in a suspicion by Collie's investigations would be a high compliment indeed – as Nicolson noted concerning his own namesake peak in 1892. It would have been nice to have Hart's thoughts on this matter, but – given his colourful outbursts elsewhere, rather sadly – none seem to be recorded. While Collie awaits his sculpture, Hart will have to make do with an alpine rock-cress, his significant but little talked-about first ascent of Am Bàsteir, and the occasional tribute of a ledge on Sgùrr MhicCoinnich.

As for Collie, apart from being the Cuillin's grand inquisitor, what firsts *did* he have to his name? According to Ben Humble:

> [the] pioneers naturally took the easy way to the summit of the unclimbed peaks. Collie led the exploration of the secondary routes by gullies, cracks and chimneys, and obvious lines of weakness on the face of the crags.

In short, Collie represents the moment when we see the exploration of the Cuillin pivoting from mountaineering towards climbing – 'gaunt gullies, huge rock slabs set at the most awe-inspiring angles, great cracks and towers are met with in all directions', as he himself would write.

From scraping around, certain exploits do rise to the surface of what was clearly a very committed campaign on the ridge. Collie is known to have made the first ascent of the Bàsteir Tooth in 1889; a gully on Sgùrr nan Gillean in 1890; a climb on Sgùrr Alasdair's north-west face, 'Collie's Climb', in 1896; the south-east ridge of Sgùrr a' Ghreadaidh, 'Collie's Route', in the same year, as well as a face of the first pinnacle of Sgùrr nan Gillean; the Window Buttress on Sgùrr Dearg, also in 1896; and a few more in a similar vein. Often these were with MacKenzie, but not always; sometimes they were with forceful peers such as Naismith, or Hastings, or Slingsby. Occasionally, he was alone.

In 1896 he made the first ascent of the last unclimbed peak in Britain. This was the north top of Sgùrr Coire an Lochan, an anonymous spike deep in the Cuillin's inner citadel, in a north-to-south traverse with MacKenzie, Naismith and Howell. This ascent's symbolism far outweighed its standard as a mountaineering achievement: the last peak of the Cuillin climbed sixty years after James Forbes's ascent of Sgùrr nan Gillean.

But as far as first ascents go, a few faces, a couple of jags of rock, some variations – fine achievements all, but no more noteworthy than Naismith, Hart, the Pilkingtons or even Nicolson – and certainly not MacKenzie. Not a *huge* amount upon which to build a legend. Especially since we've already seen that the famous Collie's Ledge wasn't actually named after its pioneer. So what's the big deal about Collie, you might ask? He did have a peak on the Cuillin ridge named after him, after all – albeit a slightly apologetic, indistinct lump, perhaps in ironic vengeance for a passage he wrote stating 'the individuality of the Coolin is not seen in their summits, which are often almost ugly.'

To answer this – much like Collie offered the 'two things' he'd like said in his obituary concerning his works of physics – I would offer three headlines to Collie's contribution to the history of Skye's black ridge. They're not his only contributions, of course. But they are perhaps the most demonstrative, and, particularly when coupled with his interesting character and occupation, give a little more justification for, say, casting him expensively in bronze. MacKenzie, too. They span his forty years of climbing, and beyond. I'll let you know when we get to them.

Meanwhile, though, one ascent epitomises the kind of activity in the Cuillin that was proliferating in the final years of the 19th century. Such was the surge in interest in Skye during this period that W. Brown wrote, in an essay that reads very much like a eulogy for this last bastion of unclimbed peaks in the land, that:

there comes a time ... even in the richest centres, when the search for new climbs has to be conducted through a microscope. The Alps reached that stage long ago ... the best instance in point are the mountains round Wastdale. This minute form of the sport has not hitherto been necessary in Scotland. But the historian of the future will no doubt record the fact that it began in Skye in the summer of 1896.

We're not going to get into the nitty gritty of the climbing development of the Cuillin. It all gets very technical and – I truly am sorry to say this – slightly pedantic. Climbing is different, you see.

Climbing talks in numbers, grades and that strange, arcane language of difficulty: 'diff' for difficult, but denoting something relatively easy; then 'severe', 'hard severe', VS, HVS, E5, VHS, UHF, DDT. I don't understand any of it. I admire those who do it, and appreciate the impulse – certainly in terms of its theatre of action. But taking the most difficult line, actually *seeking out* difficulty as opposed to merely choosing an exhilarating way to the top, and we start dealing with something that engages a rather different gear.

The fact that some mountain walkers dabble in climbing and some climbers dabble in mountain walking is by the by; there are plenty of participants in both that never participate in the other. It may sound strange, but it's true. A lot of climbers detest walking anywhere, even to get to a crag. And a lot of walkers don't understand climbing, and care even less to read about it.

Rock climbs are rarely very distinctive to those who don't know what they're looking for: a corner, a wall, a buttress. The really big ones – a face, a spiky pinnacle, an overhang – are impressive features, but often the route needs to be pointed out to be appreciated. The really remarkable routes are the ones that are self-evident at first glance: the way they look is the way they go.

Looking at it through this lens, that of the mountain enthusiast whose eyes go to the strongest and most striking features of a range, one particular climb perhaps exemplifies the idea rather well: a difficult rock climb, which also happens to be one of the most photographed features of the Cuillin. This climb goes only one way, and it's a long way. Drive into Glen Brittle like I did on this particular morning, or visit the Fairy Pools, and it's impossible to miss – the remarkable slash that bisects Sgùrr an Fheadain, turning this elegant, triangular peak into a dramatic cloven hoof: Waterpipe Gully.

Waterpipe Gully is astonishing to look at. At once distinctive, darkly interesting and impressively ballistic – around four hundred metres in length – it's immediately obvious in any journey through Glen Brittle. It's also aesthetically perfect: near vertical in parts, its status as a natural conduit for water draining off the Cuillin making it as tricky to climb as it is suited to its name. The presence of actual mountaintops to ascend on the ridge meant it took a while for the gully to become an objective worth considering, but when it did it heralded the age of difficulty of which Collie would be a key exponent.

Collie had in fact named Waterpipe Gully as a side-effect of naming the mountain it bisects: Sgùrr an Fheadain, or 'Peak of the Waterpipe'. He and William Wickham King had attempted the gully in 1891 and managed to climb the lower section, but for unknown reasons decided to abort the ascent, despite ideal conditions.

The first complete ascent of the gully demonstrates very nicely the mood of the time and the new age of harder objectives, because it had it all: competition, controversy, the presence of little-known off-comers slaying a much-mythologised objective, and a whiff of one-upmanship that still characterises the sport today.

This ascent was made on 9 September 1895 by an industrialist named Joseph Kelsall and a chemist named Arthur Hallitt. The key to the controversy that followed was their very modest entry in the Sligachan Hotel's Climber's Book, as close to a bible as there is for such preoccupations on Skye, being the critical record for much of the activity on the Cuillin. The entry recorded the climb as 'affording constant, interesting and sometimes difficult climbing'. Ben Humble, in *The Cuillin of Skye*, notes that later climbers would regard the gully as 'without equal in the British Isles, with no less than twenty-five pitches, some of them monstrous'. This naturally cast doubt on the veracity of the account of its first ascent by two climbers nobody had heard of, and – much in the way of online message boards these days – soon prompted a barbed and sarcastic riposte in the Good Book itself.

'It is possible that Messrs Kelsall and Hallitt are two of the most eminent and admirable climbers living,' went the first response to their entry, which also levelled the charge that the aforementioned duo had committed a 'gross misrepresentation of the actual character of the climbing'. And so started an argument as to severity, conditions, competence, reliability – a kind of battle of written opinion concerning said difficulty of a crack up a mountain face, and the question of whether its difficulty had been described with sufficient accuracy. Hallitt and Kelsall would quip in response that the entry read as a 'striking tribute to the abilities of the writers as carpers and sneering sceptics than as climbers'.

There then followed a series of ascents of the gully that underlined the accuracy of their initial entry, culminating with Collie's climb of the entire route on 8 September 1896. His note: 'not specially difficult to one accustomed to gullies'. In many senses, this was climbing of the age in a box.

We come then, to Collie's first great legacy to the Cuillin's history, and probably the most remarkable – and the most *Collie* – of all, combining many of the man's skills, from his keenness of observation and powers of deduction, to his handiness as a photographer and his commitment to an idea. He and MacKenzie had been developing routes on the face of Sgùrr a' Mhadaidh, the Velcro-like Dubhs slabs above Coruisk and the ridges of Sgùrr Alasdair for years – but in 1899 Collie found something truly unexpected. Newly bewitched by the southern end of the ridge above Glenbrittle, Collie, Charles Bruce and a Gurkha named Harkabir Thapa were high in Coire Làgan. They were later than expected, having lost time rescuing sheep that were stranded and starving on the corrie's ledges. The great rock face that formed the south wrap of Coire Làgan, still untouched by climbers and still unnamed, unrolled to the west. And up there upon it, Collie spotted something spilling across in the late, side-angled sun. A shadow. Something was causing it, but Collie couldn't see what. So he photographed it, intending to return and investigate at a future date.

Collie's image of this shadow takes some decoding – the detail in the lantern slide is monochrome and indistinct, as you might expect in a faraway image of a rock face made while Queen Victoria was still on the throne. But once you spot what Collie was seeing, it's impossible to miss: a large black cast, the shape of a face in profile, darkening the right side of the frame, with no obvious source. The gabbro of Sròn na Cìche, as the cliff would come to be known, is busy – fractured into cobwebs, pummelled by time. Rock flattens to the eye, and you could hide anything in there, provided it was the same colour and texture. What Collie had discovered was an optical illusion. Something was standing proud of the face; something huge. It was just impossible to see head on, unless someone shone a light on it sideways and threw its shadow across the flat cliff, like a kind of geological sundial. You would have to be standing at a certain place at a certain time of day to see it – yet it was still testimony to the virgin nature of this cliff that nobody had spotted it sooner.

It took him seven years to get around to exploring it, though, during which time he climbed in Lofoten, Norway – those sharp, spire-like mountains off the north-west coast that are so reminiscent of the ridge in looks, so much so that Frank Smythe described them as the Cuillin's 'only counterparts.' He also explored the Canadian Rockies, where he had earlier discovered the Columbia Icefield and made several first ascents following expeditions through thickety wilderness. Then in 1906, Collie was back on Skye, chasing his shadow. In the intervening years nobody else had investigated either the photographic anomaly, or the cliff on which it stood. Based at Glen Brittle House with Colin Phillip, Collie – with a day to spare before MacKenzie arrived from Sligachan – walked alone up into Coire Làgan for a closer look. His suspicion had been that that shadow had been thrown by a rock column of some sort, as it could really be nothing else. But the object he found was far more interesting than he expected. 'I soon saw that the rock was a very real and interesting tower, quite removed from the great rock face, standing out in a most imposing way over the corrie below,' he wrote. 'From the top of the precipice to the bottom is at least 1,000 feet, perpendicular in many places.'

He tried to climb it but backed off, opting instead to wait for MacKenzie to arrive. The following day the two had a 'climb full of excitement, for one never knew what was around the next corner' – a series of gullies, some peculiar manoeuvres and finally a 'queer traverse unlike any traverse I had ever seen', with a switchback extending out like a pitched roof to a platform atop a boss of rock the shape of an inverted comma, poised above the corrie below.

Collie had found what would become the last undiscovered rock icon of Skye, a kind of weird crow's nest, hefted out of the cliff like the craned neck and upturned head of some ancient rock-reptile peering out of its den. But its tendency to look different from every viewpoint, from angular to bulbous, from accessible to terrifyingly out on a limb, was fascinating. MacKenzie – ever pithy – came up with a simple description. He called it A' Chioch, or the Cioch, which means, for want of a more dignified translation, 'boob'. Collie had the honour of naming the cliff itself, which he called Sròn na Cìche, or 'Nose of the Breast' – an odd anatomical mixture, although 'sròn' was a common Gaelic term for a sweeping cliff or ridge.

Collie, despite his now worldly marinade, was enraptured by the find. And for the two men to find such an interesting object – a piece of rock you would assume was visible from miles around – after nearly two decades of thorough investigation of the Cuillin, who could blame him?

'After that everyone at Glen Brittle had to climb it,' he wrote. 'I believe that during that July and August John and I made the first ten ascents of the Cioch.' His slide collection confirms this cosmopolitan recruitment; the owners of the first feet to stand on the Cioch's impressive prow wore impressive bonnets, flowing dresses and smart tweed suits. What a time.

In the years since, the Cioch has become famous as a movie set piece – the only scene in *Highlander* that everyone remembers, for instance – has loaned its image and name to a brand of locally made outdoor clothing, and become infamous as the scene of several deaths. Not from falls, but from rocks rolling and falling around it.

Matt, when I asked him about it, called it a 'very agreeable place to have lunch. On a nice day.'

'Is the fame deserved?'

'Oh, it's deserved.' Matt was a man of few words, but you knew when he approved of something.

I had one more appointment today. And fittingly enough, Waterpipe Gully had everything to do with it. The image of Sgùrr an Fheadain – that dark, cloven hoof – that I remembered being drawn into the most was in the village back along the road. Starkly black, on a canvas, hanging on a wall.

In the cluttered room above the Old Inn in Carbost I stood looking out of the window at a world of water. There was Loch Harport, there was the jetty at the end of the pub's garden, and there was the rain. What weak light made it through the deluge was grey, filling the corners with shadow. Elsewhere in the room was the paraphernalia of a sound system, records, a bit of overflow from the pub. And paintings. Lots of paintings. Some were scattered round on walls, old work kept for sentimentality or display, extravagant and coloured – faces, figures, abstracts. Others, on the side of the room where I was lingering with a stoop in my back and searching eyes to the wall, were stark black and white canvasses. Some were big, some small. Some formed triptychs. Some were only half finished, but captured a moment. All of them portrayed sections of the Cuillin ridge. In the corner was an easel with some paints, a pot with a splay of brushes, and a few canvasses that had seen recent tinkering.

Behind me, on the brown leather sofa in what was effectively a living room, bent forward to the table and indifferently rolling a cigarette, was Ali Niven. The artist cum pub manager was wearing the same gilet he'd been wearing when I met him collecting glasses downstairs last winter. Back then, his gaze had drifted to the pictures he had drawn of the ridge, and there had been something in his eyes. I'd been itching to ask him what.

Ali caught me looking at a picture, an unfinished piece about the size of a coffee table. The inking was incredibly stark. He pointed, using the roll-up between his fingers. 'If it's a really heavy, hard day I'll just go straight in with the thickest black I've got. The Indian ink pens I'm using, the chisel edges are about an inch thick. Make a mark with one of those, you're committed. That one,' he said, putting the cigarette in his mouth and finishing his sentence out of its corner, 'was looking down on Coruisk from Sgùrr na Stri ... I've been there twice. That's as far as I got the second time when it started to rain.'

I turned back to the picture, then back to face him. 'You lug the canvas in with you?'

'Oh yeah, I just bag them up and get to a spot. None of these are from photographs. I did go through a phase of cutting a load of little canvas blocks up and carrying them around in my bag with a load of pens. And any time I stopped, or saw something, it would be just "*chuk chuk chuk ...*" – he made some slashing motions with his hand – 'just recording, recording,

recording. Then putting that one away until the light changes, then doing another one.' He lit his cigarette and leaned back on the couch. 'So I'd have these triptychs of exactly the same view and yet they'd all be slightly different, just ten minutes apart.'

I asked him how many he'd done. He shook his head, and said hundreds. I asked him why he did them.

'Just to get back to *looking*. When I came to Skye, I'd see what other artists are doing, and it was all the same. They weren't looking. They were making pretty pictures for the sake of sales. I did that sort of thing in the past, but I grew sick of it pretty damn quick. You'd be dealing with agents, or galleries, and they'd say, "We'll have another four of those blue ones, please."' He made a face. 'But this ...' – he indicated the canvasses around us – 'I enjoy it. It's a release. A reason to have a little expedition somewhere.'

I looked back at the canvasses on the easel. The starkness was total. Black on white. Shaded shadow, crags and buttresses scrawling in amoeba-like patterns and forms that, however impressionistic, were recognisable. Bàsteir Tooth, Waterpipe Gully, Sgùrr MhicCoinnich. This was a man's mind – a place, his sight of a moment – spilled out. This was what Ali saw when he saw the ridge. This was Ali's map.

'The ridge is about shapes and silhouettes. Like the Bàsteir Tooth.' He pointed to his picture of it. 'I missed the chance to climb that. It looks alien, to the point of how did this rock end up looking like that, sort of shaped and bent over, you know? It's prehistoric, the Cuillin. *Pre*-prehistoric. It's got limbs and spines and arms, that kind of brutality.' Then he said, 'It's thrown me off it twice.'

'Really?'

He nodded as he pulled on his cigarette. 'Once on the Dubh slabs. Dislocated my thumb, popped one of my tendons. Sliding down it in the wet, just scrambling to get a grab, got these fingers in.' He lifted his fingers like a scout salute. 'It just flipped my whole body right round and I heard this *chuk*, horrendous.'

He shook his head. 'Other time was coming down the Stone Chute in the winter, coming down a bit too quick. It was just completely frozen, and I jumped down onto this bit of shale, and I just went straight off – must have fallen fifteen feet. Luckily I had a helmet on.'

I could hear the muffled jostle and clink of the pub downstairs as I looked out at the rain. Carbost, blessedly, isn't a big place. There was a shop and an antiquated petrol pump, neither of which looked like they had been operational for years, but both of which were – fortunately, considering how far both were from the next available of each. There was the Oyster Shed. There was the Talisker Distillery. And there was the Old Inn. The Old Inn is really the only place in Carbost guaranteed to be open and dispensing food, drink and a conversation – and as a result it almost always has an underlying beat to it. The sessions of live music in here were notorious, its low roof reverberating with the sound of fiddle and snare played by some of the liveliest musicians in the Hebrides – an ember of *craic* in the dark. The Cuillin ridge is broadside from Carbost, a glowering battlement, appearing much bigger and higher from here than from Sligachan. In Carbost everybody knew everywhere and everybody. And everybody knew Ali.

As far as Skye stories go, Ali's was unlikely enough. He was a successful graphic artist in Edinburgh. Then, suddenly, Skye got him. Or rather the Cuillin did. 'I was getting bored doing the commercial thing. So I sold my van, bought a car and some climbing gear, got a job running the hostel down in Glenbrittle.' A bit of a pay cut, he chuckled as he tapped his cigarette on his ashtray, his voice a rumble. 'Working down there ... I just sort of fell in love with the ridge. I could be on it in forty minutes from the front door. I asked if I could do maintenance in the hostel over winter, if I could live there. So I had a season, isolated down there with all the storms. It was mental. And I just thought, hell with it – I'll just stay on Skye for a while. That was eight years ago.'

Forty-ish, with a shaved head and handy build, Ali's easy manner suggested unflappability, with a touch of world-weary nihilism. The sort of guy who, were you to set his room extravagantly ablaze and leap cackling from the window, you could well imagine remaining with his feet up finishing his drink before he got up to sort it out – which he would prob-ably do without breaking a sweat. He was known in Carbost for being the man who accomplished the seemingly impossible: keeping the Old Inn walking the tightrope between being a civilised pub and a miniature temple of Hebridean anarchy. It could easily be one or the other: under Ali, it was a happy balance of both. And behind the guy behind the bar, there was the guy I was talking to this afternoon; someone who had painted the Cuillin like nobody else. Again and again.

'The thing is,' he continued, squinting and pointing a finger at his work, 'you're taking away the colour, but not the light. And the light does so much with the ridge. It could be winter, and flat light. Or summer, and it's so bright it all merges together and it's like felt. Get down Slig glen as early as you can and sit up on the bank, and watch the sun coming up over the other side of Coruisk, it just ripples all the way along the ridge, and the whole thing lights up.' He pointed out the window at the rain. 'Sometimes you can see Glamaig from here in the morning. It can be all gloom, and suddenly there's this beacon of gold and red, boom – it's there for three or four minutes, and then it's gone. I think that's what this island has got to offer. If you dress appropriately, every day's a winner on Skye.'

Laughter from the pub downstairs. It was filling up. Tourists. I asked him if he'd seen a change while he'd been here, and he nodded. 'It's kind of unrecognisable. When I turned up eight years ago the Fairy Pools were just a set of pools the locals called the Fairly Pools. You'd see maybe a car there at the weekend. I think 125,000 cars went down there last year. But walk half an hour from them, you lose all the people and it gets special again.'

The power of the Cuillin to compel those it gets – be it visitors to Skye or its denizens, the former often becoming the latter – is quite remarkable. Any place can inspire art. But the range of emotions this ridge of mountains triggers occupies a spectrum of light and dark as kaleidoscopic as the conditions that wash over it. Anger, joy, turmoil, despair, majesty, eeriness, a bearer of mythology, vehicle of adventure or catalyst of terror – to those sensitive to its power, the ridge acts as a kind of Rorschach inkblot, a scratching post for any underlying emotion, which is then spilled out into verse, music, story, painting, photography. The landscape speaks, and the people translate it into whatever language they hear. Joy, wonder, beauty – and darkness. I saw darkness in those pictures. The black and the white of Ali's images were the perfect contrast: the brightest bright and the darkest dark. And, unseen, everything in between.

I asked Ali whether he thought the Cuillin was a dark place. He thought about that. 'It's a brutal place. I remember being on Alasdair once and the cloud came in. I didn't even see it. I was fannying about, and before I knew it I turned round and it was just going . . .' He made a rising motion with his hands, accompanied by a hiss through his teeth. 'And I was like, right . . . focus, focus, focus.' By the time I got my shit together, visibility was gone. I was disorientated, even though I knew exactly where I was . . . and my balls went. I wrapped myself up, got myself some hot drink, and sat it out. Five and half hours. It lifted about fifteen minutes before sunset.'

'Did you know the route down?' I asked.

He nodded. 'Only been up there maybe ten or twelve times before, though. The guides have been up there like six hundred times before, and they know every rock. You hear Tony downstairs.' He pointed at the floor, down to the bar, where a retired guide regularly sat. 'I might know certain places, but when you're talking with people who know the ridge, they'll talk about certain *stones*. Rest places I've never heard of, springs, all of these little specific points.'

He thought for a moment. 'Most people around here know someone who has died on that ridge. I've lost three personal friends in the mountains, people I've known since I've been here. One was a guide, they couldn't find him for six days. Then, a friend up in Trotternish who got hypothermia. Then a couple of other guys, one of them survived . . . His wife was here with me, like, for three days as they searched for him. His brother didn't make it.'

We let the rain fill the silence. Ali started rolling another cigarette. 'Did you ever see that little image I did of Sgùrr an Fheadain? Waterpipe Gully?' he asked. I said yes, and I did, of course: the dark, frantic triangle that I'd first spotted hanging in the pub. 'I was angry at the time. It was pissing rain, and I was just determined, saying, "I'm going to *finish you* . . ."' he chuckled. 'That picture was overworked to a point. But it's so dark, it's ominous, you get lost in the corrie, and that would be you gone, swallowed by the mountain. I was feeling a bit dark at the time.'

It was time to go. I finished my drink and took another look at the paintings, then back to the rain. I thought about asking if I could buy one, but I was either afraid I couldn't afford one, or afraid I'd offend him, so I didn't. I asked him what his plans were. He was going to Australia for a few weeks.

'Always fancied swimming with a great white shark,' he said.

'Cage diving?' I said.

He looked at me and frowned. 'Ah, no, fuck the *cage*.'

You've got to accept the danger. True enough.

12
Tower

Something Matt had said to me about Skye on the day I met him had hung in my ears ever since. He'd described the island as being a 'frontier'. I'd taken this to mean the island had a sort of knockabout charm, where people dress in battered clothes, don't grumble about the cold and might look sideways at you if you asked for a salad. But I was now beginning to realise 'frontier' meant something rather different.

While we're off the mountain let's consider Skye for a moment. Not the island – the place. When it comes to the residents, no two Skye stories are the same, but spend enough time here and you do start to see patterns emerging.

First of all, there are those who you might describe as the born-again artisans: off-comer creative types who came to Skye to live a life that leapt from the well-ploughed tracks of A Sensible Career. Skye has no shortage of these. The briefest of glances at its history would certainly support the idea that Skye, with its singular flamboyance of scenery, has good cause to be seen as an eccentric, arty-farty outpost of Scotland, a place that has attracted travellers, essayists, artists and explorers in search of atmosphere and whose gasps and coos have echoed around Coruisk, the Cuillin and the cafes of Portree, drawing ever more of the same kind of person to it to do the same kind of thing. It's a wilder, flintier-skinned version of the Lake District, which is another place that over time has nurtured a reputation as a lightning rod for your more intrepid type of artiste. Walk into any gift shop in Portree, poke around any of the croft-turned-galleries around

Carbost or let your eyes wander around the walls of any cafe just about anywhere on the island, and you'll see that it has cultivated its own brand of bohemian craft. Skye is immeasurably the richer for it.

This admittedly does run the gauntlet of quality, from the covetably gorgeous (vivid cyanotype artworks, driftwood sculptures, exquisitely detailed hand-drawn maps) to the tatty but cheerful (Fairy Pools fridge magnets, bow ties for your cat in a Skye tartan of your choice) to the deeply questionable ('earthy' jumpers made of wool painstakingly combed off some goat-like creature, costing £400 and after one wash becoming 'earthy' flannels). This is, of course, expected of a place so keenly fed by tourism; but on Skye, artistry as industry seems to be in the water. Creative people continue to gravitate to Skye as if drawn in by invisible threads, and this gives the place a pleasingly electric and eccentric air that cannot fail to bewitch.

As I spent more and more time on Skye, I was, however, beginning to see that this wasn't what Matt was getting at when he described the island as a 'frontier'. There's a magnetism running through this island that cuts far deeper than simple arts and crafts. And once that gets into your bones, it's very difficult to get it out. The place takes a piece of you, and it plays with it. Tempts you with strange adventure; seduces you with the cosiness of long nights in inns, hunched against the cold, filled with firelight and folklore and music and whisky; whispers at you through the wind-hiss of the grass; hypnotises you with its lightplay, its moods and textures; traps you with its isolation. If you need any convincing of this, simply consider – out of all the people you meet up here – the number whose Skye stories begin at the point when they came up here for a summer and, in spirit at least, never left.

You find people who came here for the mountains, for the island air, for the far-cast nature of it all, perhaps those who decided to start a business or open a studio, to live 'the good life' and all that stuff that basically describes a person who has woken up to find their life suffocated by the superficial. The nicknames the 'English Isle' and 'MacLondon-on-Sea' pop up around about now, but they're not worth believing; most of the people you'd be tempted to put in that particular idealistic box don't last a Skye winter. Those that do were meant to.

Someone I knew, a music journalist-turned-author named Paul Rees – who once lived in the same English town I now call home – had made the move not long before. He'd jacked in a career spent flying around the world with the likes of Bruce Springsteen and Paul McCartney to move his family to Skye and build a house from scratch, open a B&B retreat and take an evening spot presenting a show on a local radio station called – of course – Cuillin FM. The station had then been in a shed in a field, and on his first shift most of the equipment was out of action due to storm damage. He told me this one evening when we had a drink in his not-quite-finished house on the dark hillside in Fiscavaig, above Portnalong, during which I sat across the table from a man positively oozing glee.

'It's just . . . epic,' he said, with a head shake and an atypical lapse in eloquence. He then described his day-to-day life of odd jobs here and there, dawn jogs to distant bays, his kids adapting to a routine unfettered by the neurosis of middle England, and a community where everyone mucks in and helps out doing, well, whatever. 'I feel like I've come on holiday forever,' he said. And he meant it.

That was one Skye story. And it wasn't unusual, at all. Were you asked to describe the uniqueness of the Skye condition – it sounds negative when put like that, but I can't think of another way of describing it – simply calling it an offshore retreat for thrill-seekers and the artistically sensitive doesn't really cut it. This was a real place, with real problems – but also a place full of people who came here to find something nowhere else could give them. A place they could connect with, reflect in, and find themselves reflected back. A place where, simply, they could live as they wanted to live.

Native Skye folk – *Sgiathanach* – have always been different. Caught in the middle between the remote Outer Hebrides and the mainland, Skye's mindset has mirrored its neither-here-nor-there geography by cultivating an identity it has fiercely defended – and which has doubtless lured many to its shores. And in many ways, the island's adrift-but-accessible position and unique genetic mingling have produced a population that is as robust as it is individual. Botanist James Robertson, who among other things holds the first recorded ascent of Ben Nevis to his name (though it's almost certain the Gaels beat him to it), remarked of Skye in 1768 that 'perhaps there is no part of the inhabitable globe where so few bodily imperfections are to

be seen,' describing his hosts as 'musical, hospitable ... and [they] drink a
lot of spirits'. An astonishing chapter in Archibald Geikie's *The Scenery of
Scotland* – a geological textbook, remember – is entitled 'Influence of the
Physical Features of Scotland upon the People'. Of this he says:

> Though not obtrusive, it is real and close, and amid other more potent
> influences has never ceased to play its part in the moulding of national
> character and progress.

He goes on to dissect the character of the Scottish Highland Gael,
contrasting it with that of his Irish counterpart, describing the former as being:

> neither merry nor witty, like his cousin across the Irish Channel ... yet
> he is courteous, dutiful, persevering; a courageous foe, an unwavering
> ally, whether serving in the ranks or leading his comrades where dangers
> are thickest ... he stands among the mountains face-to-face with nature
> in her wilder moods.

Geikie's broader point is that the landscape has sculpted not just the
fortitude but the character of those who dwell in it – and this is if anything
more concentrated on Skye than anywhere else on the west coast.

Then, of course, there were the Clearances. Devastating to the cultural
history of the island, in a few short decades this despicable feudal experiment removed a thousand years of ancestry in a stroke. In the years following
Culloden, Highlander culture had been watered down to almost extinction
– wearing of plaid was outlawed; Gaelic was being replaced by English. But
to call the Clearances the final, ultimate punishment of the Jacobite uprising
and the expulsion of the Highlander from Scotland would be wrong; those
who were evicted from their lands weren't militias seeking power, they were
farming folk cruelly caught in a changing of the economic winds.

While the legacy is complex and still being atoned for, the initial motivation for the Clearances was depressingly simple: landowners coming to
the collective realisation that replacing subsisting, crofting tenants – most
of whom had worked the land for generations – with heads of grazing sheep
might make them more money. A flexing of de facto power, via decisions

made in the wood-panelled rooms of estate houses, would have chilling ramifications for the Gaelic-speaking folk who worked the land. Technically tenants on owned land, the almost inconceivable idea that their lairds would exercise their feudal powers was greeted with horror, chaos and, in some cases, resistance.

And then, alas, came retribution. Villages were burned, the frail and elderly carried out on their beds and cast into the muck, families summarily loaded into disease-ridden ships that sailed across the Atlantic to Newfoundland, Nova Scotia (literally, New Scotland) or to Australia, often with some tweedy landlord attempting saintly magnanimity by *paying their fares* – though this only in the lucky cases. Many died on the way. Families were split up, if not on the ships, then in the detention quarantines where they frequently ended up on the other side of the ocean. And if they survived the voyage and the quarantines, they had to rebuild their lives in a place far from *their* place. One writer quotes a House of Commons report that in one year, of 106,000 emigrants from Ireland and Scotland, a total of 17,300 died – '6,100 on the voyage, 4,100 on arrival, 5,200 in the hospitals and 1,900 in the towns to which they repaired'.

According to John Prebble's account in *The Highland Clearances*, Skye was divided into several packets of land – seven in total – governed by a group of landlords, many of whom were erstwhile clan leaders, principally MacDonalds and MacLeods, whose agents acted with ruthless efficiency.

The sorts of numbers we are dealing with are chilling, showing just how different Skye is today than it once was – that is to say, how much emptier. Prebble states that between 1840 and 1880 the factors of Skye would 'serve 1,740 writs of removal . . .' and that all those involved, 'whether they were removed or not, had to pay 10 shillings for the cost of the summonses against them'.

Not all emigrations were evictions: 100,000 acres bought in North Carolina by Lord MacDonald saw a surge in Skye dwellers departing for America to work it, with 370 leaving in 1771. A boom in coastal kelp farming saw the island's population peak at 23,000 in 1841. But emigration, including forced evictions, continued throughout the 19th century. One figure puts the total number of people evicted from Skye between 1840 and 1883 at a staggering 34,000, though with some conjecture. Notable villages emptied and left to ruin were Boreraig, Tungdale and Suisnish, where evidence remains of dwellings to this day. Archibald Geikie, in *Scottish Reminiscences*, recalls being present in 1852 when Suisnish, on the shore of Loch Slapin opposite Blàbheinn, was cleared under the hand of the notorious MacDonald factor Ballingall. This man had a tendency to destroy houses in front of their former residents to prevent any thoughts of remaining. 'One afternoon, as I was returning from my ramble, a strange wailing sound reached my ears at intervals on the breeze from the west.' He describes the 'lamentation becoming loud and long', and seeing a 'motley procession' along the road, and the minister standing by the church to bid the people farewell. Closer to, he saw:

> old men and women, too feeble to walk, who were placed in carts; the younger members of the community on foot were carrying their bundles of clothes and household effects, while the children, with looks of alarm, walked alongside … everyone was in tears … it seemed as if they could not tear themselves away. When they set forth once more, a cry of grief went up to heaven.

Of Suisnish he comments, 'Not a soul is to be seen there now … but the greener patches of field and the crumbling walls mark where an active and happy community once lived.' That was written in 1902. Today Suisnish is precisely the same: empty. This period was a truly astonishing lapse of human decency, and one that should never be forgotten.

Amongst the more enduring verses from the period, 'The Canadian Boat Song' is the lament of generations, of those separated from the shores that were their own and who were now grappling with an old identity in new, unfamiliar lands. It was said to have been sung in Gaelic by exiled Highlanders paddling canoes upriver in Ottawa, as they gradually and sadly became Canadians.

> From the lone shieling of the misty island
> Mountains divide us, and the waste of seas
> Yet still the blood is strong, the heart is Highland,
> And we in dreams behold the Hebrides.

> Fair these broad meads – these hoary woods are grand;
> But we are exiles from our fathers' land.

If you wanted a more contemporary example of the Clearances' longer legacy, consider the lines in The Proclaimers' song 'Letter from America' (1987):

> I've looked at the ocean
> Tried hard to imagine
> The way you felt the day you sailed
> From Wester Ross to Nova Scotia

Followed by the refrain:

> Lochaber no more, Sutherland no more
> Lewis no more, Skye no more

Back on Skye, the peninsula of Rubha an Dùnain – which you might recall saw continuous habitation from the Neolithic and throughout the rule of the Vikings and the Lords of the Isles – finally fell vacant in 1861, when the last of the MacAskills gave up the farm. Most of the family had long since decamped for the Carolinas. It has been vacant ever since, except for – somehow perversely – the odd errant sheep. By 1900 the population of the island had fallen to 13,800. By 1968 it had dropped to 6,700. According to the last census in 2011, it stood at a tentative 10,008. Let nobody say that modern Skye is crowded with residents. It is not.

A curious, recent twist on the feudal mindset came in 2000, when the 29th Chief of Clan MacLeod decided that the roof of Dunvegan Castle was reaching an unacceptable state of disrepair. With reports that his guests were having to put up umbrellas in the bedrooms, he decided to fund the repair by selling off a piece of his property. Soon after, the Cuillin ridge appeared on the market for £10 million.

The reaction was, predictably but fortunately, immediate – with conservation bodies, politicians and Skye locals accusing the chief of cheapening a priceless natural asset. Calum MacDonald, Labour MP for the Western

Isles, described the sale of the Cuillin as 'ridiculous, but at such a price obscene. MacLeod should hang his head in shame for trying to exploit what God has given the people of Skye.'

The pariah of the matter – John MacLeod – responded rather nobly, considering. Quoted in *The Scotsman*, he said the decision had caused him 'intense inner grief', adding that people were 'whingeing and whining as if I'm going to pocket 10 million quid and run off to Bermuda to drink Martinis.'

Some questioned whether MacLeod even legally owned the Cuillin, let alone had the right to sell it – stipulating that the papers, such as they were, dated from 1611 and were vague at best. In the eyes of some, these may even have confused the Cuillin with the rather more modest and more local MacLeod's Tables, across Loch Dunvegan.

Then there was the matter of quantifying the *worth* of something like the Cuillin ridge – in legal terms just land, albeit a rather spectacular and sizeable chunk of it. £10 million: the black ridge, a historic mountain range for the price once paid for a 1982 Porsche 956. Then there were some who suggested it was too much; a sale of the area around and including Ben Nevis to the John Muir Trust in 2000 for £450,000 suggested the range should be valued at around £2.4 million, or £107 an acre – though this assessment was probably in the interests of realistically securing it for the purposes of preservation. Eventually, the John Muir Trust would buy Strathaird, including Blàbheinn, the Red Hills and the eastern side of Glen Sligachan, which it manages as a wild land preserve to this day.

The sale of the Cuillin itself did not happen – despite, as the matter descended into ever-more complex squabbles, there being no real legal reason for it not to. Failing to find a buyer, and desperate to restore the crumbling castle, talk moved to gifting the mountains to Scotland in return for government funds, which in the event came to nothing. MacLeod died in 2007 and the matter passed to his son Hugh – who found other ways of raising funds for the roof. The MacLeods technically own the Cuillin to this day, so all in all the affair was a rather circular argument, calling into question historic land ownership, the right to sell it, the concept of land-scape value – and, if nothing else, gave us all many good reasons never to own a castle.

Any study of the character and breadth of Skye's ever-changing ranks of interesting folk begins and ends with *The Great Book of Skye*, a remarkable recent trilogy of volumes that serves as the island's most extensive testimony. As you might expect, the authors are two locals: a photographer and broadcaster named Cailean Maclean – nephew of Skye poet Sorley Maclean – and a Skye-born professor of Gaelic studies named Norman Macdonald.

I met Norman for a coffee in the inn at Sligachan one rainy afternoon. A tall, kindly man of around sixty, he delivered words delicately in a rich accent. His father had been one of the Portnalong croft settlers who had come to Skye from Harris in 1926, and had met John MacKenzie. Norman was born and raised here; remarkably, of all the people I'd met and who knew Skye intimately, I couldn't think of anyone so far who could say that.

We chatted and looked out of the window at a bus disgorging smiling Chinese tourists, all of whom were running into the bar and shaking off raincoats. 'When buses used to stop out here, instead of people rushing upstairs to get a phone signal or turn on the TV, they would throw their rucksacks down and pile onto the Sligachan Bridge there, to look up at the mountains,' he said, before looking to me and frowning. 'I think . . . the tourist is very different now. In the 60s, 70s, the people who came on holiday to Skye were ordinary people, climbers, working-class people. They came because it was cheaper than going to the Alps. Now, you've got to be reasonably well off just to get here. You used to get a bed and breakfast on Skye for £4.' He nodded at my cup. 'Your coffee probably cost about that.'

Norman taught at Sabhal Mòr Ostaig on the Sleat peninsula, known everywhere on Skye as the Gaelic College. He had returned to Skye in the 1990s after spending twenty years in Nova Scotia, where his three children were born. 'A few wee traverses of my own,' he said with a chuckle. I asked him if he'd wanted to leave when he was younger. He thought about this, then said, 'When I was going through high school here,' he said, 'nothing else was considered *except* leaving Skye. Where it's different now, is that by and large, if people want to go on to higher education they still have to leave . . . but there's a far more keen awareness that one can actually come back and do something useful.'

Norman had spent the first years of his life in Drynoch, between Portnalong and Sligachan, where he could see almost the whole of the main ridge. 'You couldn't be here without being aware of this remarkable backdrop to your life. When I was a teenager, I would try and expound the philosophy that my entire personality had been shaped by the Cuillin. I couldn't explain it too well, so I stopped doing that.' He laughed deeply, then frowned a little. 'Back then you know, it was always *Sgùrr nan* Gillean. Now, it's just Gillean. The Inaccessible Pinnacle was *always* the Inaccessible Pinnacle. I'd never heard the term "In Pinn" until about fifteen years ago.' He leaned forward over his coffee at this with an expression of dismay. 'Nobody knows what it's *called* now.' I was suddenly glad, with my swaggery new status of having climbed it, that I hadn't called it 'the Pinn' – or indeed, suggested we meet at the 'Slig'.

The *Great Book* project was Norman and Cailean's painstaking act of protection for as many of Skye's stories as they could unearth. These books carried in their pages the collective memory of the island: maps, cuttings, landscape photographs, tables, sheet music, poetry and cartoons – all relating to people who had passed through Skye's history, left their mark, then passed into the great beyond. Knowledge from a generation now gone, or at least one fast disappearing. You can't search by subject; you find your insights by starting with the people. In many ways, that's the way it should be.

Norman explained that his life growing up was shaped by his neighbours and parents talking about the past. 'What is now loosely called the Gaelic culture: stories, songs, folklore. And that came to me orally, in a very subconscious way. Nobody ever said, "Sit down, I'll teach you a song or tell you about someone who lived here a hundred years ago." You were just very conscious of being part of something that extended back . . .' He took a sip of coffee, then said, delicately as if creeping around a subject strewn with pins: 'That's where I'd be different to someone coming to live here from outside. Their idea of home here would be very different to mine.'

Skye's history has, nevertheless, been defined by its off-comers, and its emigrants – a cycle of transience that mirrors the weather systems that strafe across the island. A frontier, indeed, where all kinds of treasures are washed ashore, from all corners of society. To illustrate this, you need only consider the peculiar tale of the Leopard Man of Skye.

Were you loitering around Loch na Bèiste between 1988 and 2008, perhaps cruising by on one of the tourist boats that pass that way, you might have caught a glimpse of a bald man tattooed from head to toe with leopard spots and wearing nothing more than a gold thong, waving at you from the shore. Had you snagged the arm of a local and enquired who on earth you were looking at, they might have said something like, 'Ah, that'd be Tom,' adding, as if it somehow explained the whole thing, 'the most tattooed senior citizen in the world.'

'Tom' was Tom Wooldridge, a Surrey-born former Special Forces soldier who, upon finding it difficult to settle back into society after his military career, renounced what you might call 'normal' life in favour of a derelict croft on one of the most remote points of eastern Skye – a place only accessible by foot or boat. At some point he changed his name to Tom Leppard and underwent the presumably excruciating and costly (£5,500) process of covering his entire body with tattooed spots, including his eyelids and all over his skull. His motives were, rather surprisingly, avaricious – 'I knew if I got the biggest of something and lived in a strange way people might pay me,' he said in 2001. Leppard was until 2006 the most tattooed man of any age in the world – and retained the title of world's most tattooed senior citizen until his death. But if money did come his way, it didn't filter through into his lifestyle, nor did it appear to taint the outlook his simple life on Skye had given him. Tom was a common sight in nearby Kyleakin, or across the mainland on Kyle of Lochalsh, where he would make a three-mile canoe crossing once a week to collect his pension and pick up supplies. He lived largely on beans and ratatouille cooked on a camp stove, washed down with white wine. His accommodation had an earthen floor and a roof of plastic sheeting and tin, no furniture and a stack of non-fiction books, mainly about the Indian colonial wars and historical biographies. Passing walkers, the few that there were, would be treated to a beer or glass of rum. A committed Catholic, he prayed for three hours every day. He found the winters impossible to get used to. And, largely, that was life for the Leopard Man of Skye.

'I have everything I need here,' he told the *Guardian*. 'I was lonely in the city. I'm never lonely here, and I'm never bored.'

Tom Leppard's life took a bizarre and sinister turn in 1997 when a young German woman called Manuela Ruda took an interest in his life and paid him four visits, later entering into a correspondence with him. In 2002, along with her husband Daniel, she was convicted of stabbing to death a man named Frank Hackert in the town of Witten, Germany, in a gruesome and ritualistic murder she claimed was ordered by the devil. During her trial, Ruda claimed she'd been taught to worship the devil and drink blood during her time on Skye. Leppard, understandably, was horrified. In 2008, at the age of seventy-three, he gave up the croft and moved to a small house in Broadford, claiming he was becoming too old for 'that kind of life'. He later entered a care home near Inverness, where he died in 2016.

I was reading all about Tom Leppard in the breakfast room of the Taigh Ailean, watching the grey waters of Loch Harport out of the window, when Katie Heron steamed in with a plate of eggs and toast and placed it in front of me. 'So then, tell me where you're going today. Tell me it's somewhere interesting.' She sat down next to me and placed her fingers against the arms of her glasses. 'This island is gorgeous. It's *gorgeous*. But I have two lovely American guests staying with me this week and, god bless them, I know that when they walk through that door in five minutes and I ask them the same question, they'll say they're going to go to the Fairy Pools, then to Neist Point, and then possibly stop off at the distillery on the way back.' She took a deep breath. 'And they should. They *should* go to those places. But they're leaving *tomorrow*. And everyone goes to the same places. This is a place to *be*, not to tick off. I have guests who come for two weeks every year. They still haven't seen everything.'

'I've never been to the Fairy Pools,' I said. 'Are they nice?'

She cocked her head incredulously. 'They are *lovely*. Of course they are. But oh my god, they're not the only thing here. And they get so busy. The roadside along Glen Brittle is just swamped with cars sliding around in the mud as there isn't any space to park. Then you read all this about Skye being "full" in the news. It's just a few places. The rest of it is practically empty.'

The source of my host's raw nerve on the subject – one shared by many locals, I gathered – was that in August the BBC website had run a story entitled 'Is Skye reaching the limit for tourists?' in which the writer had suggested the island was 'bursting at the seams'. The pick-up would become impressive, culminating in US news network CNN listing Skye as one of its 'places to avoid' in 2018. All of which was understandably not welcomed by the local tourism industry – particularly those whose seams were quite a long way from bursting during the less busy times of year. The thrust of the story was that the island's infrastructure of narrow roads and lack of sprawling parking facilities were putting the place under pressure from 'drive-through tourism.' Quoting Police Scotland, the article stated 'unless people planned ahead they might end up spending the night in their car.'

It's worth pointing out that this is not a new problem. Concerning Skye in particular, the limited amount of accommodation on the island has been a well-voiced refrain for – quite literally – centuries. As far back as 1875, Alexander Nicolson lamented:

> If people will come, by all means let them do so . . . I think it but fair to let the public know that they had better not come all together in the month of August. Those of them who have any partiality for sleeping in beds, rather than on tables and sofas, and who like the amenity of a basin-stand to themselves in the morning, cannot be certain in that month of these modest luxuries.

Of course, in those days Skye was very much an island in the true sense, as in a place where one could find oneself marooned.

Like Venice, that other bewitching island of allure, tourism on Skye is very far from new – and nor are the arguments surrounding its ability to cope with it. The island's entire history has been defined by influx and exodus, usually with a disagreement of some sort in between. The island's resting population of just under 10,000 permanent residents – less than the average British market town – swells to a rather portlier 60,000 during peak season. Therein lies the problem.

'I mean, honestly,' Katie continued. 'Isn't it reasonable that people might pick up the phone and actually *book* somewhere first in high season? Isn't that normal behaviour?' She flapped her hands around her head as if clearing a smell, then poured a coffee. 'So where *are* you going?'

Today, I too was doing the tourist thing – or the closest thing to it the Cuillin had to offer. With a day spare and the opportunity, I was sneaking ahead a little along the traverse into the thick of the ridge's middle, to do something I'd been quietly hankering after: an ascent up onto the ridge by myself. So I explained to Katie that I was aiming to climb up what is generally considered the most accessible of the Cuillin ridge peaks, and the only one that could be described as a walk. I could use the word 'easy', but I won't; in the same way that the rise in Skye's temperature above 25°C for a few days a year doesn't classify it as generally 'balmy', the relative ease of a mountain on a luxuriously dry day, without wind, snow or mist, doesn't make it 'easy'. Given inclement conditions, anything over a certain height could be lethal.

This one was a single, accommodating eagle's-nest summit at the end of one slender balustrade of easy-going ground, and surrounded on all sides by steep drops, magnetically treacherous rock and spurs that were only briefly amenable. Its status as the 'walker's' Cuillin potentially placed less experienced mountain-goers hugger-mugger with much riskier ground, which – given a tickle of mist or a momentary lapse of concentration – it wouldn't take much to blunder into. To anyone who didn't have a grasp on what they were doing, it sounded like jumping for a cushion in the middle of a bed of nails. Once you got there, though – what a position. What a view! Surely that was worth the stretch. Or at least, that was the impression I had of Bruach na Frithe.

'Come again?' Katie asked.

'Bruach na Frithe'. Suddenly self-conscious, I attempted it again, without the edges. 'Bruar na free'.

'Ah, I know it.' Anticipating my next question, she shook her head. 'I haven't been up it. Generally I only walk where Fritz can walk. I think the Cuillin ridge is perhaps a little beyond him.' We shared a solemn nod. Fritz was a sausage dog.

'Although,' she continued, 'if you're going from Glen Brittle, which I presume you are, you do know you'll have to park in with the Fairy Pools lot? So maybe you'll get to see what all the fuss is about after all.'

Her two other guests emerged from the stairs, and she went over with coffee to take their order and enquire of their plans. Through the tinkling of plates I heard a deep American voice slowly and thoughtfully intone the words 'Fairy Pools' and 'Neist Point'. Then the woman asked if the distillery was worth going to. 'Absolutely,' Katie replied. Order in hand, she threw me an inscrutable half-glance and disappeared into the kitchen, humming softly.

*

Where the road into Glen Brittle stops approaching the Cuillin ridge and turns to run alongside it down-glen, the crowds and cars started. It was still fairly early – about 9.30 – but already gangs of people were emptying from minibuses, jacketing up outside open car boots and fine-tuning parking along a road barely wide enough to take a single moving car, let alone dozens of vacant stationary ones too. In fairness, it was a brief melee – after a hundred metres or so the cars stopped, and the glen was once again serene – but it was enough to make me appreciate Katie's point. The Fairy Pools were clearly the place to be on Skye.

I was very excited. I'd been looking forward to climbing up to Bruach na Frithe ever since I started investigating the Cuillin. It was interesting to me, because of the way it juxtaposed the achievable, in the middle of something that was decidedly less so. True to the Cuillin's refusal to fall into line with the rest of the British mountains, here was another reverse of convention: usually it was the difficult bits that were in the minority. The odd few feet of clambery summit rock aside – Helm Crag in the Lake District, and The Cobbler above Loch Long being notable examples – almost every hill and mountain in the British Isles has an easyish way to the top of it. A dozen or so don't, and they're all in the Cuillin.

Of course, we're going by the guidebooks. There are actually many places where you can get up onto the Cuillin ridge without too much trouble. There's a bounty of lines of weakness, passes, sketchy scree runs and even spurs which you can navigate to reach an airy point on the ridge without too much distress. The thing is, you'd have to find your own way up. You won't find most in guidebooks. And as such, to those used to driving on roads, camping at campsites, walking on paths and generally conforming – as most tend to – to well-worn furrows of travel, such a prospect edges too far into uncharted territory. But could a normal mountain walker do it?

Seton Gordon wrote in 1929:

> there is still an impression that the Cuillin are a field for rock climbers … this is not so. Personally I have never climbed on a rope, yet without any difficulty I have climbed Bruach na Frithe, Sgùrr na Banachdaich, Sgùrr nan Eag and Gars-bheinn.

Having now ascended the latter two without technical equipment or excessive peril I'd be inclined to agree – though being expertly guided through the maze of the Cuillin is in many respects as valuable to safety as being tied to it.

Bruach na Frithe was evidently the exception. To the normal, experienced mountain walker – in whose ranks I firmly count myself – here was a mountain peak, a Munro, if you covet such things, in the very teeth of the Black Cuillin that required no additional equipment, no double-galvanised head for heights and critically, no guide. It was no dumpling either, but a proud and high pagoda – at 958 metres (3,143 feet), just 35 metres shy of the highest point on the island. It stood right between the middle and the northern ends of the ridge, bridging the summit-studded central section of Bidein Druim nan Ramh and Sgùrr an Fheadhain, and the spiky final tail-flick of Am Bàsteir and Sgùrr nan Gillean. There was nothing conciliatory about it. It just so happened there was an amenable line of weakness to the top well tramped by normal hillwalkers. Given its position, the view from the summit had to be sensational.

Another thing that made today different was that I was on my own. No Matt this time, nobody at all – I had to look after myself. I was very used to walking alone in the mountains, but the Cuillin was different. This gave me a fizz of excitement and apprehension as I gathered still-damp gear into my rucksack from the car boot. You know it's going to be an interesting day when you get those feelings. It's what it's all about – trying something new, giving yourself a bit of a stretch, heading into exciting territory. You *might* be up there to scare yourself – though after the Inaccessible Pinnacle my conviction in this assurance from Matt was shakier than my knees had been. My damp clothing was also the reminder I needed to toss my emergency shelter into the backpack as I pulled it onto my back, locked up, and set off back up the spindly Glen Brittle road, passing parked car after parked car, and joining the jostling queue of macs, trainers and jeans bound for the famously lovely Fairy Pools.

My intention here isn't to be unkind – I'm a tourist too – but when in close proximity with so many in an environment that's far from user-friendly and purpose-built, it can be quite something to observe. There is clearly the potential for friction in the zones where mountains and mainstream tourism meet. And the proximity of the Cuillin ridge to some of the busier places of interest make it inevitable that on occasion the latter might overstep into the former.

The Fairy Pools is the ultimate case in point. Look at the incident pages on the Skye Mountain Rescue Team's website, and there's little doubt about the location of one of the island's premier accident blackspots, particularly when summer kicks in. This was in some ways a good thing, as it meant most of the mishaps weren't generally of a serious nature. But it was also depressing as the majority were a result of visitors to the pools behaving, how shall we say, as if they were under the umbrella of safeguards found in more synthetic locations. The Fairy Pools – essentially a collection of natural stepped rock pools and waterfalls at the end of a well-built path – don't present themselves as being desperately hazardous to anyone who can judge when something might be slippy. The problem is, so ingrained is the expectation that such things are rigged and softened, some people who go there simply don't realise they're expected to look after *themselves*.

This being these days, all you have to do to confirm this is to take a look at the weird window onto the mind of the modern traveller that is Tripadvisor. Here you will find proof positive that a small but vocal percentage of the visitors to the Fairy Pools – aside from the usual moaning about parking and crowds and midges, which, let's face it, we're expecting by now – really don't seem to grasp the fact that they're visiting a free beauty spot at the foot of a mountain range, and that a certain amount of self-reliance might be in order.

'The pathway to the pools harks back to rough roman roads strewn with jutting out stones and rocks presenting a trip hazard ... the stepping stones over the small streams again present danger. My wife fell,' reads one, before citing the whole affair as an 'embarrassment to Scotland'. Another reports 'the pools are just a series of muddy holes, crumbling banks and unimaginative [!] water trickles ...' then adds, 'My wife was particularly upset by the visit.'

There are more. 'No loos!' one says. 'False advertising!' another cries. And, alas, many more tales of people running in terror back to their cars because it was 'starting to rain', and further distress at witnessing 'nearly naked' people jumping into the pools for a swim. One review came under what one suspects is a sadly accurate headline: 'used to be beautiful, now ruined by tourism.'

Which is the problem. Something can be wonderful to you, but once it becomes wonderful for everyone, expectation starts to kick in. And if you're one of the people who believe the Fairy Pools – lest we forget, an entirely wild and nature-crafted feature – should have wardens, toilets, barriers and dramatic lighting, you might well also be one of the people who forgets to be careful and expects to be safe. Thus, the Fairy Pools have quite understandably racked up a formidable casualty record. And when that happens, somebody has to come and sort things out.

'A young adult jumped across the top of the pools, slipped and fell 20 feet into the water, knocking himself unconscious on the way down. Rapidly and very luckily extracted from the pools by some divers who were present in wetsuits,' reads one incident report on the Skye Mountain Rescue website. 'Adult fell into a pool whilst trying to get a better photo,' reads another. 'An 11-year-old female was swimming at the Fairy Pools, and when jumping in broke her leg.' And so on. I noticed two of these call-outs were on the same day, mobilising eight members of the Skye Mountain Rescue team twice within a few hours.

The teams would never criticise the people they rescue – that just isn't the done thing, and god bless them for that – but remember, these people are *volunteers*. They stand by on call, in all weathers, day or night, 365 days a year, to go out in the filthiest conditions onto dangerous ground to help out total strangers, possibly witnessing scenes of utter horror – and all for no material reward. These are just normal folks, who work in cafes, schools, hospitals, pubs. They're saints, and never once should anyone ever take them for granted.

Which brings us back to the Fairy Pools, and that point where mountains and tourism collide. Thank goodness, you might think, that it's only the tourist spots like the Fairy Pools being an attraction – albeit a natural, rugged one – that warrant a page on Tripadvisor. Thank goodness that actual mountains are a different quantity, and exempt from such subjective 'reviews'. But you'd be wrong. Mountains, too, are popping up on the site, and while most are described helpfully, and some are successfully played for laughs – presumably – some posts suggest a worrying attitude shift. How long will it be, I wonder, before you have to fill out paperwork before heading out into the backcountry? Answer questions about your experience or choice of kit? When the mountains are full of signs warning you to be careful of this rock or that gully?

This might sound extreme but by goodness it's possible. You could argue that there is little difference between grumbling Victorian tourists expecting Coruisk to conjure up the drama of Turner or the majesty of Scott and writing about the magnificent misery of Skye in hardback books, and the ranting of disgruntled, Instagram-primed tourists on Tripadvisor. But thankfully – and I say this hoping dearly this observation is still relevant in years to come – going into the mountains is still, as it always has been, self-accountable. You do so at your own risk. Long may this be so – because if we lose that, we lose something terribly important. And with that, may I ask you to very carefully step off the path to the Fairy Pools and come with me as we leave the tourists behind and once more head into the black ridge?

The speed at which I found myself alone – after being so comprehensively crowded out – was startling, if not exactly unexpected. The Fairy Pools, unseen up ahead, were in most cases the only reason these folks had come into Glen Brittle; they might enjoy the demonic cloven hoof of Sgùrr an Fheadain above the pools – or not enjoy it – before turning back to the car and probably going to Neist Point and the distillery at Talisker, then calling it a day and perhaps writing a Tripadvisor review. Ascending east up a muddy path, I kept an eye on the long line of brightly coloured macs and umbrellas and white shoes as they shrank ever smaller, and their frailty against the great rock walls they were beetling into became ever more stark. Eventually I lost sight of them altogether.

The weather was in that Hebridean halfway place that could go one way or the other then back again within minutes if it wanted. I'd packed a bag with waterproofs and a cap, and after taking them on and off again twice, I put them on and left them on.

You get used to seeing a variety of different weathers in the same view on Skye. Over there, basking in sunshine, were Portree and the Storr, with

a bay of attractive blue and a sea horizon of fluffy white clouds. A slight
head-turn towards Sligachan revealed a bank of ash-coloured clouds over
Raasay, which looked overcast and gloomy. Back west down the glen was a
world of brightly lit cloud and diffused mist – the rain. And up above me
to the right, the ridge was holding steady between all three: a skyline of
grey rock against grey cloud, neither raining hard nor riotously glorious. I
was happy with that.

It felt good to be alone, to move at my own pace. While the occasional
but always engaging piece of commentary from someone such as Matt was
welcome, sometimes it was nice to just discover things of interest by yourself, and enjoy the mystery around you. The route climbed up to the Bealach
a' Mhàim, where a large cairn marked the pass between Glen Brittle in the
west and Coire na Circe – the open, stream-coursed runout down to
Sligachan – in the east. It's a real junction, a join between two sides of the
island. It also marks the point where the two choices of ascent onto Bruach
na Frithe present themselves: the north-west ridge, and the secretive valley
of Fionn Choire.

I stopped at the cairn to take in the view – it's remarkable how much of
the island you can see from here – and to decide which of my two route
options looked the best, when a young woman in hiking gear came huffing
up from the Sligachan side.

'Hey, do you have a map?' she asked without preamble in a New Zealand
accent.

I said that I did, and she took it with a slightly irritable fluster.

'Where are you going?' I asked.

'Don't know,' she said, with an inflection that sounded like a question.
She was looking hard at the map, as if trying to locate a particular spot.
'Thought I'd go look at Glen Brittle. Is that Glen Brittle?' She pointed over
my shoulder, and I nodded.

'Is there anything there?'

'The Fairy Pools, which looks busy. The glen is beautiful.'

She looked at me then back at the map and frowned. 'But is there anything
there? I need to be back down in Sligachan in a couple of hours and I just
wanted to go for a walk.' She then looked at me as if she'd just spotted a
concealed motive. 'Where are *you* going?'

Suddenly protective of being solitary, I indicated the ridge, climbing into shadow to the right, in what I hoped was an intimidating manner. 'Up there.'

She followed my gaze then looked back at me and sniffed. 'Really? Looks like *Lord of the Rings* to me.'

She returned her attention to my map, thankfully dismissing this idea. 'Anyway, so I think I'll just go a little further. Thanks.' She handed me my map and huffed off. As she went, I noticed another walker coming up from the direction she was descending. This place was clearly quite the passing point. Leaning on walking poles and moving slowly but doggedly, he was easily in his sixties, and American. He was wearing a US Navy cap and a khaki gilet emblazoned with the insignia of an Alaskan fishing cruise.

I nodded hello, he said a pleasant 'Hi', stopped to catch his breath, then looked up from behind apparently opaque aviator sunglasses and said in a deep wheeze, 'Hey, if you're still here when my wife gets here can you tell her I went this way?' He indicated the way down towards Sligachan.

I couldn't believe this. 'I don't think I will be, but ... doesn't she know?' I looked behind him towards Glen Brittle. Other than the figure of my New Zealand friend disappearing down into the valley there was nobody I could see at all. I turned to suggest perhaps he should hang on, given that the area didn't have a good track record when it came to wives, but he was already off, waving dismissively with a sticked hand. 'She'll be fine, just fine. Have a good day, now.'

I looked again back down towards Glen Brittle. New Zealand had now disappeared from view; there was nobody else. Suddenly anxious to get somewhere with less social responsibility, I turned up towards the splayed mouth of Fionn Choire and headed once again up into the Cuillin ridge.

Above me the glass-fragment skyline of the ridge was tipping back and losing its look of impregnability, like a storybook dragon throwing down its tail for you to hop up onto its back. Even on the hardest mountains in the land this does usually happen; things seldom look as hard up close as they do from afar. And it was interesting to explore a bit of the ridge that was at least thus far behaving like what you might term a normal British mountain.

Being ridge-bound, climbing to a peak of the Cuillin isn't really like climbing a mountain for its own sake – something free-standing, something with a shape, a silhouette, 360 degrees. On the ridge, summits presented themselves as bucking obstacles as you walked across, but approach the ridge broadside and you have to consider them somewhat differently. Your choice of spur, valley or direct approach was less defined, and the mountains inevitably and rather pleasingly assumed more of a solitary identity, requiring individual consideration to ascend. That's another advantage to exploring the ridge outside of a traverse itinerary. You might not have the bragging rights, but you do see more of the place.

I chose Fionn Choire rather than the north-west ridge for a couple of reasons. First, after my adventure on the Inaccessible Pinnacle I felt entitled to something a bit more sedate, however briefly. Climbing spurs to reach summits was fun, but rather like climbing a wall to reach an upstairs window. A corrie approach was like walking in through the door and taking the stairs. Besides, the spur looked damn steep, in a relentless rather than thrilling way. And I'd heard quite a lot about Fionn Choire and was keen to see what it was like. As I turned in to the ridge, crossing small, happy streams as I walked into the embrace of the corrie, I felt the air change. A kind of shift in electricity. The breeze slackened to an ebb, then vanished completely. The frequency of sound shifted from open and soft to claustro-phobic and clinky, every footstep giving off a metallic ring before fading to a deep, cavernous silence. I heard a raven pronk high above, and counted to two before the sound stopped echoing. And just like that, I was in a different world.

A common translation of this place means 'fine corrie', with the sugges-tion that the large, north-west-facing scoop somehow feels more verdant and less oppressive than other Cuillin corries. 'Fine' is a relative concept, for sure; anyone expecting to turn into Fionn Choire expecting cool woods, butterflies and leaping bunnies is sure to leave briskly, and disappointed. But even with this expectation safely managed, I still found the corrie rather more austere than its name insinuated. Another interpretation of the word *fionn* is 'pale' or 'white' and I wondered if it instead referred to the screes that skirted the buttresses ahead. Halfway up there was a large flattening with a cairn in the centre, a good place to stand and take in the skyline of the ridge above. It encircled the corrie with a rim of long-edged jags, like the base of a broken bottle. This flattening had a thin cover of green turf riveted with boulders small and large, but to call it comely would be exces-sive. It wasn't overtly hostile at least, which I suppose counts for something.

I could see ahead on the skyline a peculiar bristle, like an upturned claw, that seemed to be retreating into the skyline the closer I walked – a reminder that some of the Cuillin's most distinctive features lay at this end of the ridge, and I was likely to get an eyeful if the weather held. I was tremen-dously excited and – with conditions amenable for the moment – wasted no time dithering.

Soon the rock steepened and its features began to swell to mountain proportions; streams became gulches, then gullies, at first water-filled, then dry and steep-sided, built of cinder-grey rock with white-bleached patches. The way steepened more, and the path – such as it was – became indistinct amongst sharp blocks and pockets of scree. It was impossible to tell how close to cresting the ridge I was by looking, but the buttresses leaning in on me soon loomed nearer, what little vegetation there had been was gone and my watch altimeter read 750 metres. I was getting close.

In the course of my intermittent adventures on the ridge I was still working through my big pile of books about the Cuillin. I'd begun this literary traverse chronologically, but had given that up at around 1817, and had instead been dipping in and out according to whim. The latest of my finds was the naturalist Seton Gordon's *Highways and Byways of the West Highlands*. Gordon spent the last fifty years of his ninety-year life living at Upper Duntulm, near Kilmuir in the far north of the island, until his death in 1977. His appraisal of Fionn Choire – offered with the casual confidence of a local – carried an enticing lure:

> The highest spring in the Cuillin is near the head of the Fionn Coire of Bruach na Frithe, and is encircled by a delightful rock garden, where the white flowers of the starry saxifrage and the mauve blossoms of northern rock cress cover the ground and the emerald moss.

Doesn't that sound magical? He goes on:

> The waters of this well are crystal clear and are ice-cool even on the hottest summer day. This little oasis is surrounded by scree and stern rocks, and is all the more beautiful on that account.

This was something I wanted very much to find. To be able to locate and drink that water and observe the modicum of life clustered around it would be a wonderful thing to do, I thought. The trouble was, reading about it in a 1935 book, picturing it in your head, then actually reconciling both of these with what you find on the ground are three very different things. As a result, I ended up standing near the head of Fionn Choire acutely aware that finding this little oasis was probably going to be harder than I'd imagined. Suddenly Gordon's description, which over a pint or three in Portnalong the previous night I'd considered quite adequately detailed (in my imagination, this place was going to look like a kind of Cuillin Las Vegas appearing out of a desert of rock), suddenly seemed woefully vague. And perhaps unwilling to cheapen his lovely prose with specifics, Gordon gave no indication of its altitude, its size or its position relative to the peaks above.

All around me was a huge bowl of grey-brown, splintery rock, whorled with lichen and deep, black-bottomed scratches where water might once have flowed. Nothing else. I tried to follow the line of a stream called the Allt an Fhionn-choire to where it disappeared, then consulted the map, which rather optimistically showed a cluster of tiny lochans near the 700-metre contour. I tracked back and forth, up and down, for maybe half an hour. Either I had missed it, or it was no longer here, but I was suddenly very glad I hadn't staked the day's water supply on finding it. A little disappointed, but chivvied on by the prospect of the summit, I gave up and pressed on.

Ironically, given my failure to find much life in the corrie, what I first noticed when I crested the ridge at the Bealach nan Lice around half an hour later – literally the first thing that caught my eyes as the ground drew level with them – was a large spider, moving over a lichenated rock with angular, delicate legs. I don't know how I spotted it, particularly given what else was in the view and about to monopolise my gaze, but there it was: a damn spider. A brown-black, sinister critter with long limbs and dark associations. It seemed quite fitting. But the spider didn't hold my attention for long.

If there's a place in the British mountains that visually knocks you sideways as hard as the Bealach nan Lice, I don't know of it. In part this is because it happens so quickly – you see nothing for ages but busted-up grey rock. Then suddenly you break out onto the ridge, and it hits you. It hits you so hard it makes you gasp.

Bealach nan Lice means 'Pass of the Ledge of Flat Stone', and it's apt. You don't feel threatened here, despite standing on the very crest of the Cuillin ridge, right in the thick of the thing. It's a meeting place. Here, where Fionn Choire breaks onto the ridge, Coire a' Bhàsteir races up to meet it from the north-east, and Lota Corrie does the same from the south-east. It's one of those places where Skye's geographical jigsaw falls into place; down there, down past spire-sentried gates, I saw a peep of the prow of Blàbheinn beyond the steep scree of Lota Corrie, the tapering headland to Elgol, and – closer – the humps of Sgùrr Hain and Sgùrr na Stri. Cama-sunary was down there too, where I'd spent that lonely winter night, and Captain Maryon's monument lay somewhere on that ridgeline. I was now up amongst the barbs and darkness I'd spied so fleetingly from that weather-battered vantage point. I was now in that view.

For corries to meet here from so many directions suggests a ridgeline just as complex. Bruach na Frithe's summit marks the point where the crest of the Cuillin ridge makes an elbow change of aspect, from north to east. Then, at the Bealach nan Lice where I was now standing, the ridge splits into a terminal, spectacularly splayed claw – the fearsome finishing limbs of the monster. And my goodness, what a finale. From here you can go north to Sgùrr a Bhàsteir, west to Bruach na Frithe, or east to the last great prize: Sgùrr nan Gillean. Only you can't go east. There's something in the way. And really, regardless of all that other stuff, it's the only thing you've been looking at since you got here.

It's a tower. From here it sticks out of the ridge like the end of a black-grey railway sleeper that's rotted raw, then been burned – all spidery fissures and glassy concavities – looking like it would crumble if you touched it. And it's *big*. It looms at you. It's usually impossible to estimate the scale of most things in the Cuillin – not their absolute height, but the relative size of the individual obstacles as you hit them – given the absence of anything human to help you do so. But as I stood there on the Bealach nan Lice I saw, far below on a ribbon of path through the scree right beneath where the obstacle broke out into buttresses, a line of three or four red jackets proceeding down the slope, looking impossibly tiny. I stared and – with calipered fingers – tried to make an approximation of how many of them, standing on each other's shoulders, it would take to surmount this tower. I lost count at thirty, and this was around halfway up. So say sixty people at five foot eight or so – hey, not all mountaineers are giants – meant this thing was just shy of 340 feet, or just over 100 metres in entirety, and the shape of a bombed-out version of that elegant tower in London with the dreadful name: the Gherkin. But this tower is a summit, with a scary name. Its name is Am Bàsteir: 'The Executioner'.

What a tableau. I stared at it with a kind of amazed horror. Amazed that there it was, almost within touching distance, and I could just look at it; horror, in that in the not too distant future I was going to be climbing up and across that thing. My eyes moved over it, looking for possible routes – and finding none. But that was for another day. Time was creeping on, and there was no sense in worrying about something that wasn't on my radar this afternoon. And with that I turned away from one of the trickiest Munros on the ridge and began the final ascent towards the one I'd come to climb.

It's probably around now I should introduce the man whose name I keep mentioning. As you'll have gathered by this stage, pinning down the heights of the Cuillin summits was no easy task – not least because the Ordnance Survey couldn't get up most of them, despite its best efforts. Not that the maps it produced would have been any less maddening if it had, given the complexity of the ridge at a practical scale. For the early mountaineers this complexity was at worst an irritation, at best a curiosity – the latter so ably demonstrated by Norman Collie. But the man for whom all of this was the most vexing was the same man with whose name the loftiest Scottish summits would become quite literally synonymous: Sir Hugh Thomas Munro.

Interestingly, given the associations that would define his legacy, Munro was English by birth. His father, Sir Campbell Munro, was 3rd Baronet of Lindertis, and Hugh, the eldest of nine children, was born in London in 1856. His formative hillwalking was as a teenager in the German Alps, which was then followed by a career of considerable mileage working as a courier, first for an irregular cavalry corps during the Basuto War, then as a king's messenger of dispatches for the Foreign Office. His work took him all over the world, but his ancestry always drew him back to Scotland, where he eventually settled to manage the family estate near Kirriemuir, Angus.

Munro's story – and his notoriety in relation to the Cuillin, and the Inaccessible Pinnacle in particular – has been the subject of a little misinterpretation over the years. Munro was a founding member of the Scottish Mountaineering Club in 1889, and would become its president. But he will always be best known for logging and publishing the first studiously compiled list of Scottish mountains with summits that exceeded 3,000 feet in height – a legacy that, to history at least, has perhaps rather unfairly typecast Munro in the role of the pedantic book-keeper rather than any sort of devil-may-care ropeslinger. This quest was not entirely self-driven, as he was commissioned by the editor of the *Scottish Mountaineering Club Journal* to make the list in 1889. But Munro's tendency for compulsive note-taking and his notoriety as a collector of specimens, from fossils to souvenirs, along with a natural doggedness, made him a canny choice.

It's hard for us, in these days of satellite navigation systems, watches that watch us and excellent mapping, to appreciate just how daunting this task was for Munro. Back then scarcely anyone knew, and far fewer really cared, about the specifics and quantities of Scottish mountain heights. A number of basic guides existed, but these were mainly for the benefit of estate owners and deer stalkers (Collie was still some years off his own landmark paper on the especially problematic patch of the Cuillin). Munro's list, however, was purely for mountaineers, and armed with the one- and six-inch-to-the-mile Ordnance Survey maps of the time, he began his highly systematic task, pretty soon realising he was in for a far lengthier journey than he'd imagined.

On its publication in the *Scottish Mountaineering Club Journal* in September 1891, *Munro's Tables*, as the list would become universally (and rather dryly) known, was greeted with delighted surprise – or if not delighted, then certainly bemused. It was thought that there were fewer than thirty mountains that broke 3,000 feet in Scotland, which suggests how little attention had been paid to the subject up until that point. There were in fact nearly ten times that number: 283, by Munro's first reckoning. Today, the total stands at 282 summits, though it has contracted and expanded many times since the list was first published.

How can that be, you might rightly ask? Despite his supposedly pedantic attention to detail, Munro never overburdened his list with the triviality of specifics beyond that 3,000-foot criterion. A separate summit was all he said, and what qualified a summit as separate was simply down to his own opinion. In the accompanying notes to the *Tables*, Munro wrote:

> The decision as to what are to be considered distinct and separate Mountains, and what may be considered Tops ['lesser' ground that hits the 3,000ft benchmark], although arrived at after careful consideration, cannot be finally insisted on.

As a consequence, people continue to argue over what is and what isn't a Munro, many armed with high-tech altimeters and surveying equipment to comprehensively and technologically trample over Munro's hard-won but rather more subjective conclusions. You might consider this distasteful, but Munro himself was forever tinkering with his own list right up until his death, and would probably be flattered for people to still be arguing about it over a century later. And goodness knows they do, from the practical considerations all the way to the point of philosophical rupture. One hilarious article in the *Scottish Mountaineering Club Journal* in 1981 – entitled 'Theoretical Munroology: The Metaphysical Approach' – begins thus:

> Counting a set of semi-magical entities such as the Munros is a metaphysical problem, as an arithmetical solution cannot be arrived at without destroying the magic.

The writer, sadly anonymous, then quotes an obscure Celtic parable concerning the Magic Pigs of Cruachu that 'were impossible to count ... were never completely counted ... and if anyone tried to count them they would go to another land.' This was then followed by 'the Statistical Approach':

> In recent years it has become apparent that Munros go up and down and have lateral movement... the summit tracing a sub-circular path over the years perhaps linked in some way with the erratic wanderings of the

magnetic pole. Those near the boundary of 3,000ft are constantly
entering and leaving the tables.

Would Munro himself have approved of such jesting? In his obituary for
the *Scottish Mountaineering Club Journal*, J. A. Parker lamented the fact that
Munro would now be 'little more than a name for any mountain in Scotland
exceeding 3,000ft', an accolade many of us would consider quite adequate
a legacy. But what of the man? Munro is typically pictured stone-faced, with
a beard and hooded eyes beneath an ever-present Balmoral bonnet, often
wearing a Highland rig and carrying, rather intriguingly, a small bag made
of black cloth that he was reputedly never seen without. Speculation as to
its contents generally suggested a compass, aneroid barometer, measuring
pole, thermometer and a map.

His personality was perhaps at odds with his severe image and potentially
mind-numbing mountaineering vocation. Munro apparently returned from
quite outlandish places in order to attend the club's meets. At these,
according its members, he took great delight in making 'racy comments',
and being imbued with a 'strange mixture of courtesy and pugnacity'. He
was certainly committed; between 1895 and 1913 he went to thirty-one of
the club's thirty-four meets.

The story goes that Munro failed to climb all but one of his compiled
list of 3,000-foot peaks, and that another enterprising hill-bagger, the
Reverend Archibald Eneas (A. E.) Robertson, beat him to it. The truth is,
although Munro failed to climb the Inaccessible Pinnacle (and he's known
to have attempted it several times, the last in September 1915), even if he'd
reached the top, it wouldn't have taken him any further towards completing
his list of Munro summits, as the Inaccessible Pinnacle wasn't on it. Munro
listed it as a 'top', which meant it exceeded 3,000 feet but not with enough
singularity to merit it being a separate summit. Given the Pinnacle was
attached to Sgùrr Dearg, Munro deferred the status to the parent peak, and
it was only a subsequent posthumous revision of his list in 1921 that saw
the hierarchy reversed, and the Pinnacle enshrined as the 'summit'.

Regardless, the Inaccessible Pinnacle, its Munro status and Sir Hugh's
climbing ambitions are a moot point, as he clearly wanted to climb it anyway.
And besides, the list that he never quite finished included all the Munro

tops as well as the summits, of which he climbed 535 out of 538. Along with the Inaccessible Pinnacle, the other two Munros that he never climbed were the summit of Carn an Fhidhleir in the Grampians and the 'top' of Càrn Cloich-Mhuilinn in the Cairngorms – the latter supposedly so leisurely Munro was saving it for his dotage. Sadly, this never came. A dose of the flu contracted in a French canteen during the post-war pandemic of 1919 spirited the baronet away at the premature age of 63.

The Reverend A. E. Robertson is generally considered the first person to complete – or 'compleat', to employ the idiosyncratic spelling – Munro's list. Robertson climbed his first 3,000-foot mountain in 1889, two years before Munro published his list. A decade later, Robertson began a committed campaign – impressive for its time – to 'bag' the remaining summits, using the developing rail network and his bicycle to link the mountains as briskly and efficiently as possible. But Robertson was only climbing the 'true' Munro summits, missing out the tops, and between 1898 and 1899 managed to climb 147 of those remaining, having racked up a hundred in the years previous. The last he climbed was Meall Dearg in 1901, on the fearsome Aonach Eagach ridge above Glen Coe, in so doing becoming – certainly according to him – the first to climb the 283 summits on Munro's list. It's said that Robertson kissed the cairn, then kissed his wife.

Lord Moncrieff, who was also present, presumably escaped the reverend's lips, but probably helped drink the huge bottle of Ayala champagne the group made short work of on the summit. Kissing, it would seem, was something of a preoccupation for Robertson; when asked by a friend that immortal mountain-related question of 'why', followed by the observation that 'no-one has ever kissed every lamp post in Princes Street, and why should anyone want to?' his riposte was that for many years he had very much 'wanted to kiss every summit that finds its place in the historic Tables'.

Robertson's claim hasn't got past the doubters, as a question mark hangs over his ascent of Ben Wyvis. An entry in Robertson's hillwalking diaries – written sometime after the events they describe – reads:

I did B[en] Wyvis, taking train to Auchtemeed from Tain. I followed the usual way up but near the top it came on heavy rain and as I did not want to get soaked I turned.

There's no record of him having gone back to bag (or, indeed, kiss) it, but that doesn't mean he didn't. And yes, Robertson did make it up the Inaccessible Pinnacle, too, in 1908 – over a decade before it became a Munro. Incidentally, if he didn't get to the summit of Ben Wyvis, the title of the first compleater would fall to yet another resplendently initialled clergyman, one A. R. G. Burn, who finished his round in 1923.

In terms of highlights on his campaign, Robertson listed the Cuillin as 'first and foremost ... the best climbing hills, presuming you are prepared to seek out difficulties'. He rounded off his review of his decade-long preoccupation with a playful swipe that one suspects wasn't entirely a joke:

> And to the silly people who ask me: 'what will you do now since you
> have no more worlds to conquer?' I can only say, 'I am going to climb
> them all over again.'

Robertson's threat has been fulfilled again and again by foot-following disciples in the years since. The pastime of climbing all the Munros – once nicknamed by a commentator as 'Munrosis: the Scottish Disease' – is rampant and spreading, with over 6,000 now having endured it and survived. The tendency for compleaters to start again and work back through the 282 mountains is fairly common too – which you might think a little odd, given the geographically slightly exclusive nature of the list and the fact that it's essentially going over old ground. The record stands at fifteen rounds, by Scottish mountain guide Steven Fallon. At worst, this suggests that 'bagging' breeds a kind of benign, semi-institutionalised mindset. At best, it's just a great reason to be out in some beautiful hills in nice places in all different weathers. As an answer to the inescapable 'why' question, that's really as good an answer as any.

There are eleven Munros on the Cuillin ridge. I should say 'currently', but it seems unlikely the number will change. It's taken me until now to bring up the issue of Munros as I don't really go for lists; they have their place as a way of organising experiences, but in my opinion, defining a mountain's value purely on the basis of its height is awfully narrow-minded. If there's a mountain that looks worth climbing, climb it.

Bruach na Frithe certainly fits the bill. It rises up on sweeping limbs, and from ground level and at distance it's the only summit on the ridge that has what appears to be a flat top – a very proud, accommodating little platform amidst the barbs.

From my position on the Bealach nan Lice it lay about three hundred metres along a gently angled, scrambly and narrowish balustrade – which doesn't sound like much, but it was one of the finest three hundred metres I've ever walked in the mountains. Which is to say, ever walked anywhere.

The weather was fidgety, but fantastically so. From the corrie it looked like there wasn't very much going on up here, but there was. Cloud was coursing over the ridge, trading the parts in view and the parts obscured every second. It was like being inside a revolving door – but only the world moved, not me. One minute I was on a ridgeline between two oceans of cloud, the next the oceans of cloud became dark, threatening drops and I could no longer see the ridge ahead. Then everything sucked in, and all I was really sure of was the ground beneath my feet and a couple of metres around it. Blink, change.

The final stretch to Bruach na Frithe's top was sentried by the knuckle of Sgùrr a' Fionn Choire, a fist of rock that I traversed on its nearest side, examining the gabbro – brown and very lichenated here – at close quarters as I went. Then the way broadened into a skywalk, moving out of the claustrophobic towers that leer above the bealach and giving some perspective. It was amazing to stroll along, to ridge-wander, to just take it all in. There was even a slight change in the shade and consistency of the ground I was walking on – dammit if there wasn't a bit of a path up here. Over to the south-east, Blàbheinn was elongated and showed its full, magnificent length, with the sea beyond a bright white. And the rest of the ridge, a layered chicane of peaks, top after top, the afternoon sun picking out the high, blackened summits of the southern Cuillin across the horizon as a line of busted-up triangles.

What was most arresting, though, was the view back to where I'd come from. As you move away from it, the tower of Am Bàsteir begins to taper and sweep, to lose its brutality and gain a sort of elegance. You'll remember earlier I compared it to the Gherkin – well, at this point it starts to lean, angled out at a weird tilt. Beyond it, the west ridge of Sgùrr nan Gillean rises to a stubby summit, and Sgùrr a' Fionn Choire begins to develop a silhouette of its own. With the three of them in one view, it was like looking along a colonnade of strange sculptures, the peaks jostling against each other to get a peep between strafes of cloud and bursts of sun. It's totally unique.

As I stood and gazed at the view, a little figure popped up right on the summit of Am Bàsteir. It was soon joined by another; a guide and a client, perhaps. The two of them stood side by side, forming a miniature gunsight on the summit of 'The Executioner', again giving me a chance to grasp its scale.

For some reason, as I watched the two little figures on the summit – the one first climbed by Henry Chichester Hart and John MacKenzie – I was struck by something. Looking at something in silhouette means time disappears. Robbed of detail, or the paraphernalia of the present, I could well have been looking at two people from another era: Hart and MacKenzie themselves, maybe.

Then, a short salvo – a few seconds, no more – of rain crackled against my right side and I remembered where I was and what I was supposed to be doing. Turning, and relieved to see the way ahead still clear of cloud, I took the remaining steps to the summit of Bruach na Frithe.

Ordnance Survey trig pillar S9744 was completed on 3 May 1958 at a cost of £18 2s 7d. It is approximately four feet tall, weighs around 330 kilograms, is rather cracked and is of the type known as a 'Vanessa' pillar – which, I was rather disappointed to discover, was for reasons no more interesting than a mispronunciation of Vanesta, the company that made the moulds for its concrete. Vanessas are exclusively Scottish. Appearing during the latter stage of the secondary triangulation of Great Britain when the survey had reached the Highlands, they were cheap, simple to move around and easily erected in inhospitable places. Their lack of aesthetic finesse was because these pillars were sited where few would encounter them, the Ordnance Survey seeking – as stated in *The History of the Retriangulation of Great Britain, 1935–1962* – to 'reduce the risk of criticism from the more sensitive element of the population to an acceptable level'. Which, as a statement, has rather a lot of interesting stuff loaded into it, don't you think?

I include these details not to suggest that trig points are uninteresting as objects, but to underline why Vanessa pillar S9744 is particularly interesting amongst them. This is because the brown tube sticking out of the top of Bruach na Frithe is the only trig of any kind on the Cuillin ridge. As I covered the last few paces to the summit and caught the familiar, comfortingly regular, ugly-but-acceptable-given-the-connotation sight of the pillar, it was odd to think that of all the Cuillin summits, it was this one that was selected. Odd but not inexplicable. Aside from the happy practical situation of Bruach na Frithe being the easiest to reach with trig-building kit and the most generally accommodating, trig stations are primarily selected for triangulation purposes, as mentioned earlier. But it did seem sort of cruel, if inevitable, that the one peak you could walk up on the Cuillin ridge was doomed to wear the furniture of a 'normal' mountain.

The trig isn't the only man-made thing on the summit, however. A semicircle of stones has been clumped together here and is doubtlessly used as a bivouac by climbers desperate to find human-feeling shelter when daylight runs away from the ridge – to keep the primeval at bay with a little glimmer of civilisation, a bit like leaving a nightlight on in a quiet, strange house.

As I reached the summit and put my hand on the trig, the mountain fell away to the north into drops and ridges, a swirl of fine, briskly swirling cloud wreathing the top. My heart beat hard and fast in my chest – I was exhilarated to be here. A modest achievement as far as mountaineering goes, but being alone on top of the Cuillin ridge for the first time did feel like a significant moment for me. It even made me a little cocky.

For a moment I put aside the Cuillin's reputation for fast-changing conditions and navigational deviousness, and pressed on excitedly a little way past the summit, turning south along the ridge as if making a play for the 860-metre summit of Sgùrr na Bàirnich. I daresay I might have made it, too – but as the ground began to descend steeply on a sharpening crest I realised that this was perhaps not the cleverest plan, that I was being lured into this by sudden confidence, and all it would take was a slip. So I stopped and stood, looked over at the view across the ridge, then slowly retraced my steps up to the trig point. The pillar looked comically brittle in comparison with its burly surroundings – like a match stuck in a haystack.

While the weather held, I didn't want to rush off. I pulled on an extra jacket, slumped into the lee of the shelter and yanked my hood over my head. I could stay here all night if I wanted, if that was the right decision. Which is just the thing about walking on your own – the onus is entirely on you. You've got to find your way alone and you've got to make decisions without anyone else's input. If I stood up and the mist had thickened, I was going to have to make the route decisions necessary to get myself down, which sent a flutter of worry up my back. Bruach na Frithe, its rocks full of iron – that brown-reddish colour – was documented as one of the least reliable summits of the Cuillin on which to obtain an accurate compass bearing. This brought with it a thrilling unease. Yes, I'd walked up, and yes, if I played my cards right I could walk down just as easily. But I couldn't shake off the feeling that I was creeping around up here with a very thin margin of error on terrain that could throw me off it at any point. I felt like a mountain voyeur.

Throughout my pile of books there are many references to this peak, often refererring to its appropriately comely name – 'Slope of the Wild Mountainous Land' (or 'Deer Forest'). The name is a strange one; *Bruach* is a word rarely applied to a mountain, meaning 'bank' or 'slope'. It's unusual for a hill – let alone a mountain, and a relatively high one at that – to hang its name on this word.

What is clear from these old references is that against this summit, the two Cuillin tribes split: there are more upwardly mobile walkers than down-wardly interested climbers, it seems. The climbing guides snobbishly scorn Bruach na Frithe; descriptions are generally brief, as there's little of interest on it for the rock climber. 'One of the best view-points on the range, and is the hill most easily ascended by tourists,' reads the clipped description in Malcolm Slesser's guide, before conceding that 'for the inexperienced, it cannot be stressed too strongly the difficulties of route-finding off Bruach na Frithe in low mist are considerable.'

Give the climber something easy to consider, it seems, and they lose interest rather quickly. Give the tourist (and I use the term cautiously) something straightforward to ascend in mountaineering country, however, and they do appreciate it. 'The Black Cuillin are not for ordinary mortals ... many of the summits can be reached but only by desperate scrambling,' wrote one of these, continuing:

> There is one summit, however, that can be attained by red-blooded fell-walkers and, by great good fortune, happens to be a magnificent belvedere for appraising the surroundings. It has a comprehensive view of the ridge and spectacular views of the fangs and pinnacles characteristic of this unique range.

The writer of this, remarkably, was Alfred Wainwright – well, we've mentioned Munro in this chapter, so why not? – who despite being very much a Lake District institution, did wander north of the border when on holiday (indeed, it was the *only* place he wandered when on holiday) from writing his distinctively illustrated guides to the Lakeland fells. Although without doubt adventurous, Wainwright was timid when it came to heights; much like Munro failed to climb the Inaccessible Pinnacle, for different reasons Wainwright famously declined to climb the very top rocks of diminutive Helm Crag above Grasmere, for instance. He did, however, manage to scale the far more monstrous Sgùrr nan Gillean, albeit on his second attempt, the first forcing him to turn back through fear of his 'imminent demise'.

Wainwright was deeply affected and impressed by what he termed the 'mystic spires' of the Cuillin. 'Compelling, and repelling... The Black Cuillin are the stuff of which ambitions are made. And dreams. And nightmares.' His book *Wainwright in Scotland* (1988) is light on his famous sketches in favour of biscuit-tin photography, but the section on Skye is commendably filled with his own illustrations of the Cuillin, oddly similar to his Lakeland drawings, though grander and more savage. Most of these were drawn from the Bealach nan Lice or the summit of Bruach na Frithe and faithfully capture the fearsome form of the place in his gritty black and white style. The thing missing from the images – and yet the one thing that really gives the place its soul – is the weather. Wainwright's illustrations feature no cloud, no snow-boned ridgelines, no mists creeping in at the edges. They show only the rock.

I stayed on the summit as long as I dared, which was probably an hour or so. There was some comfort in knowing that if I stayed just here, I was safe – and for a while I shut my eyes, enjoying the calm of the little wall-shelter, focusing on the sounds of the wind rattling around the corries below, the sightlessness of shut-eye, and that way just being here keens your other senses. I felt the stones digging into my back and neck, heard the loud scratch of my boots on the grit when I moved them, sensed the air washing against the tip of my nose, sticking out from my hood like a beak from a burrow. For a moment I did toy with the idea of staying up here, of breaking out my warm layer, tipping myself back in the shelter and watching the stars come out. Not having much food didn't bother me; little water bothered me more, and I had visions of Katie Heron and Fritz the sausage dog emerging from the mist with a mountain rescue team in tow at some deathly hour and scolding me for making her lose sleep.

I shivered hard, an indication that I should probably get moving, stood up and stamped my feet. It was remarkably cold. But then, I was nearly a thousand metres above the sea I could see all around me; it was several degrees colder up here than in the valley. As the light started to dim, I turned and, with some relief, saw that the way down to the bealach remained clear, sparing the need for any troublesome navigation decisions. My eyes went up to the top of Am Bàsteir, now black in shadow, scanning for the two climbers. They were probably long down, on their way to Sligachan. I hadn't seen anyone else but them up here. Which, considering I was on the 'walker's' Cuillin on a relatively fine day, was surprising.

I reached the Bealach nan Lice a few minutes later, and decided to push on past it a little way, just to see the shapes of the peaks change. Up on the crest of the ridge things did change appearance drastically with even slight changes of position, and my eyes were once again fixed on the colossal tower of Am Bàsteir. As I moved along the ridge on the other side of the bealach and I began to see it side on, though, something happened to it. It started to split. Am Bàsteir has two parts: the summit itself, that big, ruinous form. And something altogether more striking.

Look at the ridge from a distance – from Sligachan or upper Glen Brittle, or from Blàbheinn or Sgùrr na Stri, or from over the water on the mainland – and your eye is hooked by a strange, leaning spike just beyond the summit of Sgùrr nan Gillean. The pinnacles of Gillean are impressive enough, for sure, but this thing is *different*. It juts out, like the head of a striking snake. From Sligachan it gives the view a visual discordance that distinguishes it from being just another mountain view and lends the whole range a sinister, gothic dash. First ascended by Norman Collie and John MacKenzie in 1889, I'd wondered about it for years, and now here it was: the Bàsteir Tooth. From close quarters it looked even more impressive – a blade of rock some thirty metres tall, elegantly lethal-looking. Its shape reminded me of the bow iron of a Venetian gondola, forged to symbolise various parts of the city's geography. The Tooth is the Cuillin's own sculptural symbol, its fetish, whose dramatic shape epitomises everything that's so pleasingly discordant about these mountains.

In my eagerness to see more of the Tooth I realised I was ascending towards the top of something. A glance at my map suggested that this was Sgùrr a' Bhàsteir, a little-considered northern spur off the main ridge. I could bag *this*, I thought. As I half walked, half scramble-walked, Sgùrr nan Gillean began to unfurl to my right.

Sorry to go on, but it's a hell of a sight, all of this. The Bàsteir Tooth, Am Bàsteir itself, then the great climax: Sgùrr nan Gillean, and its three remarkable pinnacles, along with Knight's Peak. Up close it's a wonder of mountain architecture, all rough-ribbed steeples and scree fans. But its *presence* is what really gets you. As I walked, a burst of late sun from the west hit the back of the peak and threw a massive shadow down into Glen Sligachan, a triangle of darkness extending over miles of brown, stream-riddled land and almost reaching the hotel. What a sight, and I didn't even really notice getting to the unadorned summit of Sgùrr a' Bhàsteir. I'd climbed another top on the ridge, and Bruach na Frithe to boot, and was very happy about that. But today hadn't been about list-ticking – it had been about just being up here. Exploring the Cuillin, being alone amidst them, proving to myself I could enjoy these mountains on my terms. It was a bit of a walk back to the car, but I was looking forward to it. No worries lay ahead, and soon I'd be back in Portnalong, to a hot dinner, cold drinks and a warm bed.

The shadows lengthened and I watched their weird, land-crumpled shapes of pinnacles advance across the island like grasping claws. It would seem that if you're on Skye, somehow – sooner or later – either you reach out and touch the ridge, or the ridge reaches out and touches you. I stood for one last moment amongst it all, then retraced my way back to the bealach and began my descent. Back into the land of people, company, warmth, stories. I was leaving Skye tomorrow for a while, and was looking forward to my last evening. Life was good. And I had no idea that the next time I would leave Skye, it would be in quite different circumstances.

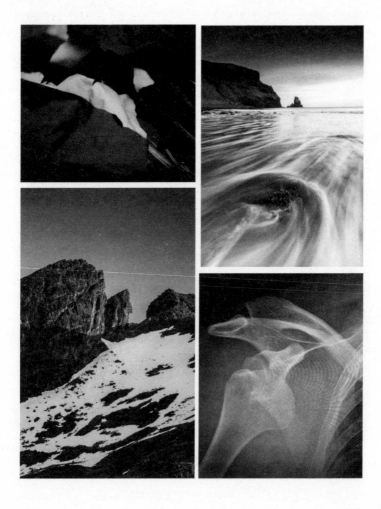

13

Executioner

Here's an awful story you're probably going to wish you'd never heard. It comes courtesy of a retired Scottish mountain rescue team member who, over a cup of tea, was telling me that whilst out on a walk with a friend many years ago, he took a moment at a rest stop to fold down the turn-ups of his trousers. In the crease there had gathered a dried, crumbly dust, which he shook out onto the path.

As they sat, enjoying the air and the rest, his friend idly enquired why he turned up his trousers in the first place, given the likelihood of them gathering dust like that. The mountain rescue chap looked at his trousers, then remarked that they were the same pair he'd used on a particularly 'bad shout' – parlance for 'rescue' – that week.

Recounting the story to me, he continued: 'And I said to him, "That's not dust – it's brains."' He chuckled at the memory, as if recalling a particularly amusing vocational quirk. 'Bodies, gore, you know – you get used to it.' After which he took a cheerful bite of his biscuit, and I felt the urge to vomit.

In much the same way that you can't conquer a mountain, you also can't really be killed by one. Unless you're unlucky enough to fall foul of what climbers call 'objective' danger – something that lands on you, knocks you off or buries you – mountains are passive things and can't be provoked. They don't *try* to hurt you. People hurt themselves against them, and you can't really hold the mountain to account. So when people have accidents, although tragic, most of the time these are due to the fact that, from an anthropological point of view, they probably shouldn't have been there in the first place.

You hear about them, accidents. The statistics. But you're not put off by them. Because, to echo the common refrain uttered by so many, accidents in the mountains are something remote, something in every way removed from *your* own activities, *your* own judgements. Bad weather. Equipment failure. Shit luck. They were the unfortunate ones, you think. And so you sympathise, you rationalise, committing little details to memory as cautionary tales, perhaps. Then you move on, because you have to, and, most importantly, because accidents are things that happen to other people. They never happen to you.

Real life had resumed back home, and it was seven months before I could get back to Skye. It was May, and I'd set aside a week to hook up with Matt once again, to explore the middle stretches of the ridge before heading for its northern end to climb that spectacular final sequence: Am Bàsteir – 'The Executioner', with its dramatic, unmistakeable Tooth – and the climax of Sgùrr nan Gillean. It seemed fitting that these barbed, catch-eye summits were left until last. The first peaks of the ridge I saw from a distance, the first to intimidate and captivate, and the last to put beneath my boots. However modest, it seemed the right way to close my own personal Cuillin circle.

Along this time was my friend Kingsley Singleton, a photographer who'd expressed an interest in coming to Skye to indulge in a little healthy exercise after a winter of cardiovascular hibernation – and with the intention, as you might expect, of taking some pictures. The island's storm-lit and otherworldly landscapes have always been a magnet for photographers, and on a visit some years ago Kingsley was duly captivated – though a wall of cloud and rain meant he hadn't seen the ridge for the two days he was there, and that clearly wouldn't do. Tall, dry-humoured and adaptable, he was good company for a trip where you really didn't know what would happen from one day to the next.

As had become apparent on the drive up the previous night, given how much we'd discussed back pain and the fact that our outdoor gear felt strangely tight all of a sudden, neither of us was getting any younger, so it was decided that a bit of stiff walking and some elemental jousting were just what we needed. We'd pencilled in a repeat ascent of Bruach na Frithe to warm up, then Kingsley would head off to explore on his own while I tackled the bits of the ridge I'd missed. I was excited, indecently so. And every glance at the forecast seemed to gild my keenness with suggestions of benign winds, dry clouds and – whisper it – *sun*.

Breaking the journey at an inn near the Scottish border, we spent the following day linking glens through the Highlands in a drive I'd come to love, and thoroughly enjoyed sharing. Reaching Skye for a fiery sunset, we pitched camp at Sligachan. The Cuillin corries were still mottled with snow above the campsite. While the weather was benevolent, there was still a chill in the air suggesting that the hard, very late winter that had only just departed had perhaps left some of its luggage behind. We'd repaired without the briefest delay to the bar.

The next morning dawned drizzly, so instead of revisiting Bruach na Frithe as planned, we stayed low, exploring the corries beneath Am Bàsteir up to the cloud base, and walking into Glen Sligachan as far as the Bloody Stone at the gateway to Harta Corrie. The ground was winter-brown and the shadow of the ridge, wearing a thin carapace of snow, bled pale through the cloud.

It was desolate. The few walkers we met were either nibbling off sections of the Skye Trail, a low-level circuitous tour of the island, or just nipping out for a constitutional gasp between showers. Nobody was climbing up onto the ridge. Not today.

As the day progressed conditions improved enough for me to feel vaguely optimistic. Determined not to waste rainless daylight (spend any significant time on Skye and you learn to do this very quickly), we decided to chance our luck for a sunset from Coire Làgan. It seemed unlikely the cloud would lift, but fortune rewards the persistent – and if tomorrow's forecast was even vaguely right, the weather would have to break at some point. At the least it would be a nice walk into an interesting place.

Passing through Glen Brittle – where a few intrepid souls in trainers, skinny jeans and furry parkas were struggling down to the Fairy Pools – we pressed on to the campsite, then began the walk up into the corrie, up in its little nook beneath Sgùrr Alasdair.

By the time we got there we were completely in the cloud. There once again was the lochan, so devoid of context it might as well have been disappearing eerily off into infinity. I'd learned a few things about Coire Làgan since my first visit. I'd learned that every spring a local man symbolically breaks the ice of the loch with a swim. And that in 2017 a concert was held in the corrie, organised by Matt's co-guide and music aficionado John Smith. That lanterns had been placed around the lochan, and a classical singer had sung an old Gaelic song with cello and violin accompaniment to an audience of seventy-five people, and to the mountains and the mist. What that must have been like!

We looped the lochan, and I showed Kingsley the distinctive glacial boulder scars, and told him all about James Forbes and the formulation of his theory of glaciation on Skye. He found this fascinating, or at least I assume he did, given that he stayed studiously silent the entire time and seemed so eager to explore more of the corrie that he began to inch further and further ahead of me until I had to shout to get his attention.

By the time it was approaching 7 o'clock the cloud seemed thicker than ever, and we agreed that dinner and several beers were preferable to hanging about for a sunset that was unlikely to set any cameras alight. So we started to descend.

Kingsley – perhaps eager to track down some more glacial scarring for us to discuss – took the lead, and before long was fading into the cloud ahead. As I reached one of the concave boulders where the neck of the corrie steepened, somewhere deep in my pocket, I felt my phone vibrate.

I had been out of signal most of the afternoon, and the vibration stirred that very modern irritation you get in these times of constant contact – that somehow something awful or wonderful or potentially costly had happened in the brief sliver of time you'd been off-grid. Given I had a guide booked for tomorrow and various other vaguely time-sensitive things that might need attending to in an emergency, and there was no guarantee I would be back in signal for at least a couple more hours, I decided to have a look. Remembering Matt's maxim – 'Don't try to do two things at once' – I shouted for Kingsley to hang on, and took out my phone. The message was junk, some insurance circular, but I took the opportunity of a breather to send Matt a message reconfirming timings for tomorrow, message home and check my voicemail.

Wandering absent-mindedly to where a boulder offered an airy view below, I noticed Kingsley moving down the path. Shouting to alert him that I'd stopped, and bringing the handset up to my ear, I scuffed the floor and looked out at the cloud hanging heavy on the surrounding spurs, waiting for the phone to connect. I took another step, just one small step to the left. And then everything went wrong.

I really don't know how it happened. As my left foot made contact with the rock, it catapulted from beneath me as if it had just met black ice or a discarded skateboard. My leg swung up bolt straight with my hip with enough momentum for my right leg to pivot away from the ground, and for a split-second I was airborne. My phone flew out of my hand as if fired from it.

As my body tipped, I automatically flung my right arm back. My hand hit the rock obliquely, and as my weight impacted, my arm went rigid and I felt something snap in my right shoulder: a fibrous crack, the sound and feeling of an electric shock spreading across my chest, then a sick-chill as a bomb of pain spread out of my arm. I landed insecurely on my back, hard, and immediately began to slide. There was momentum in it. Pain turned to panic as I realised I was moving towards the drop in front of me and wasn't going to stop. I rolled over my slack arm, shrieked in pain, then felt the strange sway in my guts as I pitched over the edge of the boulder, saw the drop that was coming – and the fall I couldn't stop.

In a career spent walking in the mountains you do sometimes wonder what you would do if you fell. I lost a friend to a mountain fall, so it's unavoidable, however uncomfortable, that the thought wanders into my consciousness from time to time. Would I scream? Would I go down with a kind of stoic acceptance, or pointlessly flail and shriek, full of anger or fear?

Nobody wants to find out. Of course, if you had the luxury of time to consider such a thing, eventually your feelings might stop being about yourself and instead focus on those you were going to let down because of this selfishly dangerous activity, and you'd think that the best way to go would be meekly, with quiet, unwitnessed embarrassment. And hopefully, speed. But nobody does that. When it happens, thinking goes out of the window and is replaced by instinct, reflex and panic.

I screamed. I couldn't help it. In my head a couple of horrible, short squeals – once, when my arm hit the deck, then again as I started to fall, felt the hard scratch of the gabbro biting through my pack and my trousers as I reconnected with the rock, racing frighteningly swiftly beneath me. I felt my jacket tear with a sound like parting Velcro and saw what was coming: a messy, narrow landing of rocks.

A single thought: *legs down. Don't tip forward. Because your arm is bust. So keep your legs down.* And in the last second of a total of about five, three words that still make me feel sick: *Here it comes.*

I slammed into the ground at the foot of the boulders, hard on my back. My pack compressed beneath me, and seemed to pitch me onto my side, like a rebounding tyre. I felt the air leave my lungs and I gasped for breath with a loud croak – I'd been winded, hard, a feeling I hadn't felt since child-hood. I saw my glasses skitter and land nearby. For a split second everything was quiet as I gasped for breath. Then a cascade of little white bits of fluff began descending around me like delicate snowfall. It took a moment, then I realised my down vest, which I'd been wearing over my jacket for warmth, had shredded and spilled its contents on the way down.

Then I caught my breath. I was alive. I was conscious. My first thought was that adrenaline was somehow masking the worst of it, that I was actu-ally dead or something, and my brain just hadn't realised. Almost reflexively I leaped up and staggered a few steps, clutching my right arm to me, my ears abuzz with a high-pitched whine, a sick fear in my gut. My legs worked. My back worked. I could move my neck. Then – like someone turning the volume up on a muted stereo – the pain began to hit, at first in the back-ground, then deafeningly. I pulled my right arm rigid to my body and fell into a crouch. I yelled for Kingsley. The first shout was meek, like a shout in a dream from sleep-slack lungs – I couldn't gather enough air to push out the word, and it echoed thinly around the rocks. I gasped again, then again, and finally my voice rang out, loud. 'Kingsley. Help.' Nothing. '*King-sley.*' I heard an affirmative noise from down below – he'd heard me. The ringing in my ears subsided and slowly I took stock.

I'd fallen about fifty feet. A steep diagonal of boulders in the middle was where I must have bounced – a loss of momentum that could have saved my life, but I was hurt in a way I knew was quite serious. My right shoulder was dislocated. The humeral head, that thickening at the top of the arm bone, had broken out of the socket and was now in spasm, bone grinding against tendon and nerve, straining to get back in. Only the angles didn't work; the shapes were out of line and couldn't slide home. Like a spring-loaded bayonet, the bone had to be twisted and angled, out and across, for it to snap back. Contrary to what Hollywood might have you believe about door frames and brute force, relocation of a traumatically dislocated shoulder is not a manoeuvre for amateurs at ground level – let alone up here. It's extremely painful. There are nerves and veins and things that could be trapped or nicked by any chipped bone, leading to anything from irreparable damage to fairly immediate death. Mess about with it and you risk turning a bad and very painful injury into a life-threatening emergency. And you don't want an emergency in a place like this. The instinct is to keep still, and clench.

I knew all of this because I'd dislocated my shoulder before, years ago, after a hard slip in a sports hall, and I knew what it felt like. That disabling, crushing pain of displaced bone and over-wrenched muscle that makes you feel like the whole side of your body has collapsed and you just want to freeze in any position that doesn't make you screech. This was going to be OK. All I needed was someone to put it back in, and the pain would lessen enough for me to be able to move about, to function again. To get down. Before, I'd been in a city and it had been bad enough. Now I was halfway up the Cuillin ridge.

And all of a sudden it occurred to me that it might not be OK. There was another pain in there, a sharper, deeper pain down my arm. I prayed it wasn't fractures. I touched the back of my arm and squeezed the skin through my torn jacket. I couldn't feel it. A wave of fear: nerve damage. Something snapped, trapped, severed? I felt around again, moved my fingers, pinched the ends. I *could* feel that. Otherwise, other than probable bruises and maybe a nasty graze where my clothes had torn against my back, I seemed OK.

Suddenly Kingsley appeared over the boulders in front of me. His expression changed from quizzical to slightly shocked.

'Oh, I thought you were having me on. I heard you shout. But ... What happened?'

'I fell. I've dislocated my shoulder.'

He looked up at the top of the boulder. 'Fell from up there? Well . . .' He shrugged in a conciliatory way, 'it definitely could have been worse.' Gamely, he started to fuss. He loosened my rucksack strap and helped me to slide it off my shoulder. I yelped with pain as I moved my arm up to let it free, and immediately returned to a crouch, clutching it to my body.

'Do you think you can stand?'

I looked up at him. I was starting to chitter with cold, or shock. 'Let's try.'

He bent over to help me and I tried to shuffle myself onto my feet. As I pushed up, the pain sliced into my right side again and I slumped back down, stars flashing against clamped eyelids. I could taste something in there, metallic, nasty.

He waited for a second, then said, 'Do you think if you just rested for a while the pain will pass?'

'Not until someone puts it back in. It'll get worse if anything.'

'Do you want me to try?' he said. 'I mean, I've got no idea how. But happy to have a go.'

'No. No, thank you.' From what I remembered, just getting me to relax enough to let a doctor do it required heavy drugs, a lot of pain and a hospital. The thought of letting a pal figure out how to do it here on a mountainside didn't appeal.

Kingsley's expression changed a little. 'Are you going to be able to get down?'

I looked behind. Up above, out of sight, was the head of the corrie where just ten minutes and a whole other set of rules earlier we'd been discussing where we were going to go for dinner. It was three kilometres down to the car, down a steep, rock-choked valley. Nothing as a distance, normally. But right then, to me, it felt like a thousand. I couldn't even stand. I tried again to get up, and again the pain hit and I gave in to it. I slumped back, panting. The cloud covering the top of the buttress of Sròn na Cìche above us was starting to turn a weak bronze. Soon it was going to start getting dark. My thoughts turned to my pack. We had stuff, but only for a quick jaunt before dinner. I had an extra jacket. A hat and some gloves. But this was for a gentle walk into a corrie; neither of us expected this. We didn't have enough for a night out, nothing in the way of painkillers and we'd eaten our meagre food. And I was shaking. Light-headed. Breathing quickly and sharply. Shock, maybe. In short, a situation that could easily get worse before it got better. Stupid. But these things don't happen to you, do they?

'Do you have a signal on your phone?'

He pulled it from his pocket. 'No.'

'Mine's over there somewhere, I think. Probably broken.'

He rooted around amongst the rocks and found it, and raised his eyebrows. 'Case is cracked, but phone intact,' before adding brightly, 'You have a signal, too.'

I hesitated, as if a few seconds of pause would improve things. The clouds were climbing down from the summits above us. Dark was creeping up from the valley as light was leaving the sky. I didn't want to do this. I'd never done this before. But honestly – who was I kidding?

'Call 999. Ask for Skye Mountain Rescue.'

It took ten tries. Each time a switchboard operator would pick up, then connect us to the local police, as was the protocol. Often a different voice each time. Then, just as some critical piece of information was being relayed, the signal would die. At first frustrated, then slightly desperate, Kingsley tried opening the call with the location – 'Just beneath Lochan Coire Làgan above Glenbrittle' – in the hope they'd build the scenario piecemeal. When the tenth call died mid-sentence, Kingsley swore at the phone.

'Do you think they're coming?' I asked.

'Christ knows. Surely we must have given them everything they need.' He sat down next to me and patted my knee. 'Don't worry. Let's talk about something else. How about *The Empire Strikes Back*? It's thirty-eight years old this year, you know.'

Right then, through the pain, I hated myself. Hated that I couldn't push through it, and be like all those people who had crawled off lethal, ice-covered mountains with broken legs and pneumonia. Here I was in a damn rock-filled dip on Skye, and I was properly stuck. I could imagine the alert going out to the mountain rescue team. The volunteers. They might be settling down for family dinners. Putting children to bed. Starting a shift at work. And now they had to jack it all in to trek up into the Cuillin to rescue me, an idiot who clearly hadn't been paying enough attention to what he was doing.

Unless they weren't. Maybe they hadn't joined up the dots. Maybe they thought we were hoax callers. Kingsley had quite a posh voice – although he hadn't meant it, his request for mountain rescue had been delivered in the tones of a man calling in an air strike in 1943. Maybe they weren't coming. Maybe nothing was happening.

Kingsley seemed to have had the same thought. 'Do you think I should call them again?'

I hesitated, then nodded. I'd only ever called 999 once before in my life; now we'd called it ten times in ten minutes. But this time the connection stayed steady and the operator on the other end remembered us. Kingsley put him on speaker. It was a strange relief to hear another voice.

'The mountain rescue team is gathering in Glenbrittle. There's a helicopter on its way.'

Helicopter? I started to shake my head. 'I don't need a helicopter. I just need someone who can put my shoulder back in.'

Kingsley held the phone over to me. A calm Scottish voice said, 'You should take the helicopter. It will get you down a lot quicker. You've had a fall.'

'But I could walk down if they just did something. Just gave me something.'

'You'll need an X-ray. There could be complications. The team will assess you.'

I started to protest, but gave up. What a complete balls-up this was turning into.

'What would really help is some accurate coordinates,' the voice said. 'We only have a rough location at the moment. And it's getting dark.'

I motioned for the phone. 'I've got an app. I can give you a grid reference.'

Kingsley passed the phone over and I fumbled with it. As usual in situations of need, the thing that was needed refused to work properly, the screen twitching indecisively, refusing to display a map I knew was on there. The area where a grid reference would usually be was conspicuously blank. Swearing, I indicated to Kingsley that there was a paper map in the top pocket of my rucksack. Kingsley pulled it out, a Harvey sheet, and unfolded it. The focus helped distract me from the pain as I scrolled along the bottom axis of the map, then climbed the edge, reading off the approximate grid reference, checking it twice. To my relief I heard an affirmative. They had the location.

'Received word ETA of team is forty minutes with you. Stay warm.' The call rang off.

I was crushed. Forty minutes! Forty minutes' more pain. Forty minutes further into darkness. I don't mean to sound like I was grumbling at this, as I really wasn't. It was miraculous that these saintly people would give up their time and energy to assist complete strangers, abandoning whatever it was they were doing to walk halfway up a mountain in the dark. More so, considering they weren't getting paid and didn't have to do it at all. But I was worried about the helicopter. The way the clouds were drifting down the mountain and the nature of the ground around me, god knows how the thing was going to get close enough to make the rescue in any way less hazardous than the injury itself. And a helicopter just seemed an awful lot of trouble.

But when you're in pain – and I *was* in pain – your mind craves time-scales, these measures of further endurance, like buoys to cling to on a choppy sea.

By contrast, Kingsley seemed to have just had several tonnes taken off his shoulders. He sat down next to me and patted my knee again, this time more brightly. 'They're coming. That's the important thing.' He pulled out a silver hip flask. 'Want some whisky? Cheapest I could find. It's excellent.'

I did. I wanted to down the whole thing. 'I don't know if this shaking thing is cold, or shock, or what.' My words were sliding into each other and I was now trembling constantly.

Kingsley draped his spare layer over me, pulled mine out of the bag and draped that over too before jamming his hat onto my head. It helped, but not much. 'Just hang in. They're coming. But, you know, it might get to the point where I'll have to cuddle you.'

He offered me the hip flask. 'Can I have some water first?' My mouth was dry. That stale taste still, too.

He nodded and pulled out his bottle. I took an awkward, deep swig and immediately started to cough, nerves and bone jarring together as I did. Bad idea.

'Do you have any of that gum left?'

He pulled out a packet of chewing gum and shoved a piece into my mouth. It helped.

Then he stood up and looked about, as if realising where he was for the first time. The light was fading, and with it the cloud was changing, from a pervading wispiness to a hard line at around 2,000 feet. All around us the buttresses were climbing into it. He stood for a long moment, taking it in.

'It's quite . . .' He paused, as if forming thoughts. 'I mean, I can see why. Under different circumstances, it would be . . .' His voiced trailed off. I watched him look around in weary wonder, hands on hips, as night started to settle on the Cuillin, cloud rising in a thin mist from Glen Brittle, underlining the dark peaks above us. Apart from the dark, it's the last really clear memory of the evening I have.

Some time after that we heard the deep beat of helicopter rotors in the distance. For a long time they stayed muffled, then Kingsley said, 'I can see it.'

Over the skyline, against the silver of Loch Brittle, we saw the lights of a helicopter rise into view below, then start to hunt around this way and that at the head of the corrie. Kingsley rooted around in my pack for a head torch, turned it on and began to signal in broad sweeps. The helicopter was about a kilometre away; in the failing light they should have seen us, but the aircraft was still fidgeting around, the rotors echoing like a tribal dirge off the towering walls of rock around us. I was relieved to hear it at first, but I didn't like the sound that the mountains reflected back, that deep, thudding bass, bouncing off the buttresses like thick, nasty laughter. Then it became obvious something was wrong.

'They can't land,' Kingsley said. Suddenly the helicpoter held still for a few moments. And then, with relief in his voice, he said, 'Someone's coming.'

We waited, too long it felt, then over the rocks ahead a head torch popped out, beneath which was a man wearing a helmet, a red waterproof and carrying a hefty box. Kingsley started talking at a gallop.

The man held up his hands. 'Gents, just need to catch my breath for a wee second.'

And then he leaned in to me, inclining his head to look into my face closely, as if examining a keyhole, and said, 'I'm Andy. Can you tell me your name?'

Things get a little hazy from here, I'm afraid. Cold, shock perhaps, the fatigue of pain, the numbness of inactivity. It's night now. I'm sitting, backside like wood after hours on sharp nubs of rock. Practised hands work down the ridge of my spine one nobble at a time, around my ribs, then to my neck. Gingerly around my shoulder. Click your teeth together, Andy says. Follow my finger. Squeeze my hand. Push against me. He takes my temperature and tells me I'm not hypothermic, which is a relief, but in early shock, which isn't. He removes his jacket and places it over me.

Then he's on the radio. He finishes off his appraisal with the words, 'No claret.' *No blood*. They don't like to use that word. I ask him if he can put my shoulder back in. He says no, there are nerves and veins and things. I'll need an X-ray. There could be complications. Then he leans into my ear and he says what I was waiting to hear, or near enough. 'I'm going to give you some drugs now, Simon.' This was it: diamorphine. Relief. I remember nodding the OK to cut off what was left of my jacket, seeing clear plastic tubes in the light of a headlight, a bottle, a syringe. Feeling the sharp jab of a needle in the top of my hand. Then again. Then in my inside elbow. Then again. My veins are too deep, he says. He can't get the needle in. 'So it's pills until we can get you to hospital.' Relief dashed.

Then suddenly more people. Bright jackets. Head torches. The scrawk of radios. The mountain rescue team arriving. A few introductions, conducted over the top of me like I'm watching from a hole. It's now pitch black – my world is in this huddled, busy few feet of coloured nylon and lamp-lit rock. And pain. Still pain. Someone's palm extends, containing six pills: two red buttons of ibuprofen, two white bullets of paracetamol, two tiny white fullstops of codeine. All go down. I cough again, but not as bad.

Someone puts a heavy foam blanket over me, a casualty blanket, and I feel the warmth seeping in. Then someone hands me an Entonox line and a bite valve, and I jab it into my mouth and breathe deep. Gas and air. I breathe deep and fast, too deep, too fast, and my little cave starts to spin.

Then Andy's head is in the cave again and he says, 'OK, Simon – you've got a choice now. You can wait for a stretcher. Or we can strap you up, let the painkillers kick in, put someone on each side of you, then try and walk you to the helicopter. It'll hurt, but you'll get there a lot quicker.'

'I'm sorry,' I say.

'Don't be sorry,' someone says back. Someone else jokingly says, 'It's nice to actually have a proper injury to deal with. Not for you, though.'

'I'm supposed to be doing the ridge tomorrow,' I say heavily.

I hear a chuckle, and someone else says, 'Well, guess what. But you know, you're not dead and you don't have a broken neck. You're lucky.'

I raise my head and look at the lights of the helicopter, down there in the dark. I don't like either choice but it's no choice. I'm tired. The pain is wearing. It's been hours now. I can't remember the last time I saw Kingsley, but he must be here somewhere. The Entonox line wedged in my mouth, I nod. 'I'll walk.' I'll try.

The news is good to everyone and they start to mobilise, first strapping my arm to my body where I sit. Then it's time to try to stand. Hands underneath my backside, they ease me up and I scream again as my shoulder grates. My body feels bruised and stiff, like I've been sitting there for days. I've actually been there just under five hours.

The pain subsides a little, then I start to walk, as quickly as I can bear. I'm being held on both sides by people trying to ease my way. Follow those boots in front, they say. It's steep. The strange feeling of people talking to each other about you, but not to you. The awful feeling that this is all because of you. I slip a couple of times down steps I don't see and yell in pain. I walk, I don't know how long. I hear someone say, 'Casualty is walking, ETA ten minutes.' The helicopter engine begins to sharpen to my ears. I smell the fumes. The noise builds, then it's deafening. They lead me to the door, then they turn me round so I'm facing away from it, lift me up by the waistbelt, lift my legs, swing me in. Pain clangs around my right side again. But it's softening. Either I'm becoming numb to it or the painkillers are helping.

Then I'm off the rock and into a dry, clean, darkly amber space full of lights and panels. It smells warm. They strap me onto a side seat and I slump forward. The rotors ramp up, and Andy leans in to me, puts the blanket over my head and taps my knee. 'Well done.' A few people shout best wishes, I say a thank you and another sorry. The ground rumbles, the engine pitch lifts, and we shudder up.

*

The first person known to have died in a climbing accident in the Cuillin ridge was a man named John Thom. His was the first whose death was climbing-related and documented, I should have said; there were other deaths before him, if not on the ridge itself then certainly in Skye's mountains. Glamaig, the steep, bare pyramid of granite and scree lying to the east of Sligachan and the highest of the Red Hills, still bears the local name Sgùrr Mhairi, 'Mary's Peak', and is said to have been named for a woman who died on the mountain while searching for a lost cow – although the manner of her passing is unrecorded. There are several mountains in the Highlands with similarly wistful tales attached to them, quite possibly with good reason – but what on earth a cow would be doing on Glamaig is a question worth asking.

John Thom's unenviable position in the history of Skye is recorded in the Sligachan Hotel's visitors' book of 1870, in which he had earlier signed his name alongside a remarkable collection of pioneers, including Alexander Nicolson, and Charles and Alfred Pilkington on an early visit. A thirty-year-old Liverpudlian – the son of a vicar – Thom was an alpinist who, on the morning of 2 September 1870, had left Sligachan with a climbing companion to climb Sgùrr nan Gillean. The pair got lost, returned to the inn, then set off again later that same day. His companion turned back mid-way on the ascent, leaving Thom to proceed alone towards the summit. He was evidently successful – a card bearing his name was found in a bottle there – but neither Thom nor his wary companion returned to Sligachan that evening.

No alarm was raised, as it was thought they had probably found rustic digs on the other side of the ridge. But the return of his climbing partner the following morning to Sligachan confirmed that Thom was missing, and a search was raised. On 4 September his body was found at the foot of a steep rock wall just north-west of the summit with, as reported by *The Scotsman* a few days later, a 'deep cut over his forehead' and 'another on the side of his head, showing that he must have met his death by a fall from a cliff'. This apparently occurred just as he began his descent. Thom's grave in Portree Old Cemetery crisply states the manner of his death: 'killed by a fall while descending Suir-n-Gillean'.

Thom's death in the Cuillin prompted newspaper stories in *The Scotsman* and the *Liverpool Post* – and marked the first time this emerging, adventurous destination was brought to national attention as a place where it might be wise to exercise caution.

What's remarkable about this is that the next recorded Cuillin fatality wasn't for another thirty years. Again, the scene was Sgùrr nan Gillean, where – on 16 August 1901 – Alexander Whincup, a solicitor from Aberdeen and a member of the Cairngorm Club, was leading a climb near Nicolson's Chimney. Having disappeared around a corner, he shouted for assistance with a foothold to his companion – one James Fraser – who later described hearing a loud shriek and seeing his friend in mid-air to his left, falling with 'such violence onto the scree plateau that he was precipitated over a steep rock face and fell to the great scree slope below – a distance not less than 200 feet'.

Fraser hurried down and found Whincup unresponsive and severely injured, before hastening back to Sligachan for help. This materialised as a team of six, including, by lucky but ultimately futile fortune, a doctor who happened to be staying at the inn. They reached Whincup's body in the early evening, whereupon he was pronounced dead. A strange footnote to his death was the coroner's verdict, which contained the unexpected observation that his fall was most likely due not to a misjudgement or slip, but a seizure. As recorded later in the *Climber's Club Journal*, Whincup's 'constitutional tendency to such seizures . . . was quite unknown to his climbing companion'.

For nobody that we know of to die on the Cuillin ridge between 1870 and 1901 – over three highly active decades of exploration, the scaling of unclimbed peaks, the forging of new climbing routes and the explosion of interest – is quite remarkable. Remember, these are – and always were – the steepest and most hazard-shod mountains in the land, despite climbers such as Harold Raeburn, one of the founders of the Scottish Mountaineering Club and quite the coffin nail in terms of durability (he once climbed a new 140-metre Moderate grade rock climb on the north face of Ben Nevis in eighteen minutes), describing most of the climbs on the Cuillin ridge as 'ridiculously easy . . . the gabbro of the Cuillin is *too* good, it makes one discontented with one's power on smoother rocks.' What Raeburn made of the basalt hasn't been recorded.

Were you a climber perched right at the top of the ability spectrum you might grasp his point given ideal conditions, but it does of course fall down when you factor ice, mist, wind, rain, magnetic anomalies and normal human beings into the equation. Indeed, one of the conclusions you could draw from this is that because the peaks of the Cuillin were so frightening an objective to behold, those who didn't have at least rudimentary mountain skills were likely to stay off them, thus markedly reducing the chances of mishaps occurring due to elementary mistakes.

But we know from the litany of starchy dispatches from Skye and images of groups of bemused tourists photographed in precarious outcrops that the range *was* travelled by amateurs – though usually in the company of a knowledgeable host such as Norman Collie, or a local guide like John MacKenzie, or both. That these early sages of the Cuillin were so strikingly good at their vocation as to never lose a companion is – given how prolific they were at escorting them into the Cuillin – impressive, even when you consider that mountain deaths of any kind across Highland country were still extremely rare.

That's not to say there wasn't the odd near miss. While MacKenzie was reported to have never put a foot wrong or lost a client, he struggled at times with his rudimentary shepherd's boots to keep up with the ever-advancing endurance of his charges. On rock climbs he frequently removed them and climbed in socks, echoing the 'fowlers' of St Kilda, who frequently climbed barefoot. It was only after an ascent of Blàbheinn that left his footwear next to useless that Collie ordered some bespoke mountaineering boots for him.

Collie, meanwhile, was infamous for taking anyone who showed even a passing interest up into the heights of the Cuillin. His slide collection is filled with images of ladies in voluminous dresses and bonnets in intrepid places, and there are many photos of Collie surrounded by the children of friends and relatives whom he spent time with in, for instance, Glen Brittle – so it seems inevitable that many of these were introduced to his favourite objectives, such as the Cioch.

Collie also pops up in many accounts by others – my favourite being that of one A. Ernest Maylard, who wrote a paper entitled 'A Day in the Cuchuillins' after spending said period in the company of Norman Collie and John MacKenzie. Near the end of a resplendently verbose account of derring-do on the northern end of the ridge, attention turns in exquisite detail to the effect the day had on his clothing:

> To speak of 'breech-splitting strides' is only to modestly suggest a 'line' in the direction of cleavage ... but when it is remembered that much of one's progress is, for obvious mechanical reasons, upon as broad a surface as possible, the nature of the lesion likely to ensue is not difficult to conjecture. I regret to say that not one of us left the Cuchullins without irreparable damage to our knickerbockers.

Collie was a cautious climber – there are no recorded incidents of anything untoward occurring on any of his outings – but then this being Collie there were no records at all, save for those left by others. Geoffrey Winthrop Young wrote of Collie that 'he is never known to have made a mislead or false step, and on more than one occasion his skill and nerve saved a party or individual from disaster.' An illustration, undated but probably from the 1890s, shows a string of three cartoon climbers – amongst them a lady in flowing attire and hat, and an extremely portly chap in bewildered repose – dangling perilously on a rope, whilst the lead climber, a clear caricature of Collie, holds them all, the rope hitched around a pinnacle of rock. The caption reads: 'Sgurr Allister. The professor saving his party.'

Had the professor *not* saved his party, it is likely that a procession of locals – postmen, shepherds and ghillies – would have set out in search of the lost group. These volunteers would be clinging to hope, but galvanising themselves for whatever horror they might find. And so it was across Britain's mountain areas for many, many years. In some respects, that's how it still is.

The precise moment that mountain rescue ceased to be conscientious but rag-tag bands of locals, and became conscientious, rag-tag bands of locals under the banner of 'Mountain Rescue' is unclear. But the drive for an organisation that drew together best practice when it came to assisting stranded and injured walkers and climbers began in the late 1940s, when a series of incidents made it obvious such a thing was becoming very necessary. It followed decades of unofficial participation by ad hoc bands of locals, initially often helping stricken quarry workers, farmers or road-builders who had come to misfortune in their line of work and needed to be transported down the mountain with haste.

During the war years of the early 1940s, this increasingly incorporated the recovery of the dozens of air crews that were lost when their planes – reconnaissance craft, bombers, postal planes, transports – went down in the mountains. There had been a steady increase in recreational walkers and climbers since the end of the First World War, and the expansion of the activity from the gentried classes to the working masses – comprising those for whom being outdoors was a snatched and blessed relief from the grind of daily life, rather than a leisured game of skill for those with the time to perfect it. This inevitably led to a rapid increase in people requiring some sort of assistance in the mountains.

Being a mountain casualty in those days must have been a particularly gruelling business. Presuming you were lucky enough to survive whatever bad luck had befallen you, there was then the problem of rallying assistance from whatever remote settlement was likely to offer it in the days long before mobile phones. The next problem would be retrieving you in your broken state from terrain that was challenging enough to get into even when able-bodied.

Take the case of the spectacularly unlucky Edgar Pryor, who in 1928 was knocked forty feet off the Long Climb at Laddow Crags in the Peak District by a climber falling from a pitch above. Landing hard in a gully, Pryor fractured his skull and broke his femur. With only the most basic first aid on hand, initially he was swaddled with blankets and hot water bottles by relays of runners descending from the distant roadhead. A stretcher was fashioned from a rucksack and the wood from a path sign, but poor Pryor was manhandled for some four hours down rough terrain to reach an ambulance, itself severely overstretched on the narrow country lanes. There followed a journey of another ninety minutes to Manchester Royal Infirmary – whereupon the attending surgeon, a man named Wilson Hey, deemed the patient in such a severe state of shock that a blood transfusion was needed before he could even consider operating on his much-jostled limb. 'The absence of morphia [morphine] with the transport had done more damage to the limb than the mountain,' concluded Hey, shortly before he amputated Pryor's leg.

The challenge of careful transportation of casualties over difficult ground was a scenario repeated again and again. If you've ever carried a stretcher over even gentle ground, you'll know it's not an easy thing to do: you can't really see very much of your feet or where you're putting them, and the manoeuvring has to be done as a team to stop your casualty from pitching around and potentially tipping off – all a little too thrilling for someone who has recently survived a mountain fall and probably isn't in the mood for further peril. Throw in poor conditions, darkness and slippery, sometimes icy ground, and the retrieval of an injured climber from a mountainside becomes a difficult and very dangerous task. By 1932 this specific issue was vexing enough for the English mountain societies of the Rucksack Club (of which Pryor had been a member) and the Fell and Rock Climbing Club to form the specific-sounding Joint Stretcher Committee. This aimed to identify a suitably practical conveyance – eventually decided to be the sleigh-like but far from perfect Thomas stretcher – acquire a number of them, and place them in key mountain blackspot areas, along with iodine, bandages, splints, stove and an eiderdown. This stashing practice continues in principle to this day, particularly in more popular rock-climbing areas of the Lake District. Here you can still find casket-like chests emblazoned with the bold words 'Stretcher Box' – incongruous and sobering reminders to all who venture into these places.

Mountain Rescue as an organisation was still a long way off at this point. With incidents increasing and the stretcher issue attended to if not exactly solved, in 1936 attention turned to the formation of a new co-operative between groups with an interest in the outdoors – such as the newly formed Youth Hostel Associations and the Ramblers Associations, as well as university outdoor organisations. This would become the First Aid Committee of Mountaineering Clubs, and it was agreed that 2 per cent of the organisations' take would go into a central fund for the provision of equipment, and that all accidents would be reported to the committee. It was the first formalised body dedicated specifically to the care and avoidance of mountain casualties.

It was around this time that Wilson Hey, the surgeon keen on strong pain relief who amputated Edgar Pryor's leg, re-enters the frame. The name of this extraordinary man deserves to be better known amongst mountaineering circles. You may think I'm keen to press this point as from a narrative point of view I'm still stuck in a turbulent helicopter with my arm hanging out of its socket; but regardless, let's consider why.

Described as a man of cheerful and strong personality but quiet manner, Hey had served as a doctor on the front line in France during the First World War. He was decorated for his deft patching up of the wounded there – an experience you can imagine brought him close to all manner of catastrophic and deeply urgent injury.

Returning to his post at Manchester Royal Infirmary in 1919, like many others he took up hillwalking soon after and was soon to be found enthusiastically exploring his home ranges, as well as the Alps. The mountain landscape affected him – it could 'produce in us every emotion that possesses the heart of man', he once wrote – and he was rumoured to have spent his coffee breaks hanging from outside windows of the infirmary by the window-sill in the hope of strengthening his climbing grip. He was soon active in the establishment of mountaineering clubs, founding Manchester University's, and was swiftly elected as president of the Rucksack Club.

In this role, Hey was at the centre of the First Aid Committee of Mountaineering Clubs, and a vocal advocate for the formation of organised mountain rescue – particularly following the incident of Pryor and his mangled leg in 1928. In 1939 the First Aid Committee of Mountaineering Clubs became the Mountain Rescue Committee, and Hey took the chair – a position he would hold for seventeen years. He pressed for the introduction of those enduring mountain rescue posts across the hills and stressed the urgent need for treatment of a casualty immediately post-incident, with his impassioned belief that morphine – 'morphia' – was critically important. He lobbied for its provision in the posts likely to need it, his pleas reaching as far as the Home Office. 'Morphia reduces suffering, and suffering produces shock, and prolonged shock causes death' was his refrain. But nobody in power was listening.

What Hey then did went a step further than simple lobbying. Gambling his position, reputation and occupation by taking a stand on what he believed in – like Benny Rothman and the access campaigners of the Kinder trespass of 1932 – Hey broke the law. As there was little positive movement on morphine from government, Hey decided to use his influence as a surgeon to personally supply the drug – unlicensed, and at his own expense – to mountain rescue posts. The practice was exposed in 1949 after Hey failed to justify his suspiciously robust stock of morphine to an inspector and was summoned to explain himself. When ordered to cease, Hey politely told the authorities to go to hell – adding, 'If you will not give your permission to supply morphine, please take legal proceedings against me.' This was, alas, the eventual result – and after a high-profile court case, Hey was fined £10 (£350 today), which he refused to pay.

Hey was hoping for a jail sentence to give publicity to the case, but clearly misjudged the esteem in which he was held. His fine was quickly paid in full by the Rucksack Club, with an array of other supporters – including the Scottish Mountaineering Club – offering to do the same. This is surely one of the few times a person has actually been *annoyed* at being spared jail – and by the actions of the very organisations he was trying to help.

The affair did eventually reach Hey's desired outcome. He received considerable support from institutions such as the Royal College of Surgeons and a number of sympathetic politicians, and in 1950 the law was amended to allow rescue volunteers to carry and administer morphine without fear of reprisal. In addition, the government agreed to supply three-quarter-grain ampules to each post – with six to the accident black spots of Glen Coe in the Highlands and Ogwen in North Wales. Just a few years earlier in England's Lake District, Coniston and Keswick had seen the formation of the first civilian mountain rescue teams. And to this day, every team has a member who's trained in the administration of morphine – a direct result of Hey's stand.

Hey, however, never fully recovered professionally. With the able assistance of local newspapers, who gleefully dragged his name through the dirt with headlines like 'Surgeon on a Drugs Charge', his practice suffered. By the time the full facts were known and the legacy of his actions secure, he was near the end not only of his career but his life, dying at the age of seventy-three in January 1956. He is now seen as *the* key figure in the establishment of a unified, organised and medically capable mountain rescue. And thanks in no small way to Wilson Hey, people who fall in the mountains have a far better chance of things getting better, not worse.

*

In the low, warm thrum of the helicopter I feel a pat on my knee. Here's Andy again, his head a white orb against the red of the helicopter's cabin. He has more bad news. 'We can't land at Broadford, the cloud's too low. We're taking you to Stornoway, about another twenty minutes.'

It takes a while for my befuddled head to process this. 'Stornoway? On Lewis?'

'That's the one.'

Lewis was a whole other, more far-flung island. 'But how will I get back?'

'Don't worry about that, pal. Let's just get you there and get you seen to.'

The helicopter touches down in Stornoway just before midnight. Having been lulled into a stupor by the noise, the gentle motions and my new-found warmth, my shoulder pain had dimmed a little. Now, with the jerky movements, it's back. Transferred to a stretcher – jolt, *bang*, scream, 'Sorry, pal,' pain and more pain – I'm rolled over bumps on the tarmac, then Andy pats my knee again and he's gone. I'm in an ambulance, amidst half conversations with chipper medics and more bumps as it pulls into a hospital. Then I'm being wheeled along shiny taupe corridors and into a room with a big light and monitors on wheels. There's a nurse, who asks my name and date of birth. Two men are in the room, my T-shirt is eased off and they're looking at my shoulder. I hear talk about X-rays, painkillers. Morphine, ketamine, water buffers. I feel the jab again in my arm – activity, fiddling – then a stillness and a push into my vein. Then a warm, spreading feeling across my chest. Apathy, an unclenching, finally, comfortably, numb.

I look down at my shoulder with dopey interest, the novelty of seeing it oddly squared-off, the clavicle projecting to a right angle, my arm dropped beneath, too low. Then I'm on the move, into the dark, tomb-like X-ray room, slipping in and out of woozy sleep as they position the plate this way, then that way, then this. No fractures, someone says, back in that bright room. Then it's time to 'reduce' it, to relocate it, the bit that nobody likes but everybody wants, the bit where they wind your arm back, and wait for the moment it slides again into its socket. The bit you have to be relaxed for. I was. Too relaxed, it seems. They try to put it in. They can't. Then they discuss, and try again. And this time it slots in. I feel the buzz of a nerve twanging free, and I have my arm back. Relief, again.

I'm left to doze for a few minutes. Then a nurse comes in, tells me it's four in the morning, that I'm probably exhausted and there's a family room with a cot where I can go and lie down for a few hours. She helps me up and I shuffle in a drooly stoop to the room and slide onto the bed. She places a plastic bag containing my scissored effects next to it, along with a cup of water.

'What happened?' she asks at one point.

'I fell off a mountain.'

'Ooo. You were lucky,' she says.

I knew this. But I'd screwed everything up. I had to call people. I had to let Matt know I wasn't going to materialise at Sligachan in a few hours for a now quite impressive raft of reasons. More pressingly, I had to tell Kingsley which one of my rucksack's seventy-four pockets contained the car keys. And somehow most importantly, I had to figure out a tactful way to tell my wife I'd had an accident. Then it would be the small matter of determining how the hell I was going to get back to Skye from this distant island in the Outer Hebrides with nothing to my name but a plastic Co-op bag containing a torn jacket, a burst gilet and a hat that wasn't mine. But right now, all I want to do is sleep. And for three blank, blissful hours, that's what I do.

With the end of the Second World War, and in the years of austerity that followed, low-cost activities like hillwalking and camping saw another surge in popularity. The abundance of rugged army surplus kit, the establishment of the first British national parks in 1951 and the ascent of Mount Everest in 1953 brought the outdoors into everyone's lives, and it didn't take long to catch hold. And as more people began to head for the hills, more of them began to have accidents. Local mountain rescue teams began to pop up at the end of the 1940s, with the Keswick and Coniston teams the first to become official in 1947, and more in the years that followed – Kendal (1953), Kirkby Stephen (1952), Glossop (1957), Central Beacons (1959).

North of the border, individual civilian teams were slower to form, but due to the number of incidents involving aircraft over Scottish ground during the war, mountain rescue already existed under the umbrella of the RAF at bases across the Highlands – notably RAF Leuchars, Wick, Lossiemouth and West Freugh. It's been argued that the rather looser arrangement with locals being roped in to Scottish rescues worked well enough in Scotland, reducing the need to formalise the duty – despite the teams' equipment being rudimentary, to say the least. Most volunteers were local shepherds with no gear except sticks, heavy boots, lanterns and tenacity. With the popularity of climbing soaring, and rescues tending to be required when conditions were at their most hazardous and inclement, this was a situation that needed to change.

Between 1962 and 1965 mountain rescue teams really started to develop in earnest. Over a quarter of the 113 teams still in operation today formed in this short space of time – most likely due to the greater economic freedom and increase in leisure time that these years brought. In addition, the end of National Service and the proliferation of motor vehicles meant that there was suddenly a large number of people with time on their hands and the ability to explore new places.

Back on Skye, it was also during this period that some of the most pivotal figures in what you might call the Cuillin's final great phase of exploration would emerge – and the final great challenges of the British Isles would fall. People like Ben Humble, W. H. Murray, Gwen Moffat and Hamish MacInnes would begin to change people's perception of the Cuillin, through their climbs, their writings and their scrapes. But we'll come back to that.

Skye's mountain rescue team officially formed in 1962 – a year after Glencoe's, and the year before the Cairngorms team. In many ways it was merely a formality. Throughout the 1950s a volunteer team had been led by Portree postman and shinty enthusiast 'Jonacks' MacKenzie – who, along with a team of ghillies, shepherds, the necessarily present constable and increasing assistance from RAF air support, managed the rising numbers of incidents between them, and did so rather well.

What the legitimising of mountain rescue teams did, however, was create an uneasy levelling post across the country. And Skye's team has always been a little on the edge of this. Like everything else here, rescuing people called for slightly special measures. In the same way that the Southern Uplands called for tenacity in remote country and the Cairngorms needed crack navigation under at times heavy snow, Skye – being off-shore and home to much more scary terrain than the mainland – presented a call-out patch with a far greater degree of immediate danger for its members. An

incident at the very close of 1962 would highlight this in the most dramatic
way possible. It remains the worst single mountain incident in Skye's history.

But enough disaster for now! I was alive, and I woke from my brief night's
sleep – little more than a long blink, it seemed – with a headache, amongst
many other things. I could hear tinkling, and saw the nurse who had deposited me in here not all that long ago. A kindly lady of late middle years, she
opened the curtains to a world smeared with rain.

'Good morning. So I checked the timetable for you,' she was saying.
'There's a ferry leaving from Tarbert this morning at 11.30. It's the only way
you're going to get to Skye today, especially with this forecast. If you were
to go to Ullapool, it's far easier . . .'

I screwed my eyes shut and tried to sit up. 'I can't go to Ullapool. My
car and my friend are on Skye.' She bustled about a bit more, this time
slightly more disapprovingly.

'Well, if you get your skates on I'll give you a lift to the bus station. My
shift is just about to end and it's on my way. You'll get a ticket to Tarbert
there.'

I looked at the plastic bag containing the things I was wheeled in with.
A sliced-up waterproof jacket, Kingsley's hat, that gilet. Nothing that would
repel anything more than a meteorological sneeze. I had spares in the car.
Spares of spares. Crisp waterproofs and warm jackets. But here on Lewis,
they were useless – separated from me by most of two islands and a wind-
wracked channel of water. I was evidently about to get wet.

The wind was darting and filled with cold spray as I emerged into the
white air of Stornoway, my arm trussed in a navy sling. I accompanied my
saintly new friend to her car, and she dropped me out on a corner in the
town centre. Opposite was the bus station and the sea. Hunkering down
and weaving across the road – as if this somehow would help me not get
wet – I reached the door, and discovered it didn't open for another twenty
minutes. Glumly, I turned, pressed my back to the wall and looked out at
the town.

Under other circumstances I might have been excited to be here. I'd
always thought of Stornoway as a pleasingly far-cast sort of place, where
lighthouses winked on storm-shattered headlands and the bars were all

filled with hard punters in fisherman's jumpers drinking rum. It may well
have been too – but 8 o'clock on a very wet Monday morning evidently
wasn't the most atmospheric time to experience the town, as it just looked
back at me with a pale-stoned, gritty expression.

Stornoway is the largest settlement in the Hebrides, though this is of
course a relative term. With just over 8,000 inhabitants, population-wise
it's about in line with Alnwick, Northumberland, or Cromer, Norfolk – both
of which you'd file under 'charmingly compact' rather than 'teeming and
sprawling'. But the difference is that rather than being a rural backwater,
the light and bite in the air remind you that as far as Britain goes, Stornoway
– nestled on the lee side of the last bit of westbound land before the wild
North Atlantic – is the final stop before Newfoundland.

A few other similarly scrappy-looking people had joined me at the bus
terminal, and at 9 a.m. a lady shuffled up, wordlessly looked at us and
unlocked the door. Half an hour later I was in a warm, largely empty coach
doing my best to study the landscape out of a window almost opaque with
rain. I could see the water-wobbled shapes of hillsides, then long stretches
where the view beyond the window was simply a horizontal line, with green
below and white above.

From what I could tell in my still slightly drug-woozed state, the coach
was occupied by an interesting mixture of locals and foreign backpackers.
Every now and again on the journey south the bus would stop at some
barren outpost – a farm gate with a rusting tractor nearby, or a long track
leading off the road with no building in sight but a sign saying something
like 'An Guirdil Farm – log's for sale' or 'Leurbost 2km', whereupon an old
lady carrying a bag sagging with weighty essentials or a young backpacker
glowing with limber keenness would alight and strike off into the rain to
god knows where. I'd watch them leave and wonder how long they'd be
walking before they got to where they were going. But it's the way of the
Hebrides. And it's a thing to appreciate.

Stornoway is on Lewis, and Tarbert is on Harris. If the prospect of a bit
of island-hopping before breakfast in order to catch the lone boat out of
here sounds unappealing, what a lot of people don't know is that Lewis
and Harris are joined, and actually comprise a single island rather than
two separate Hebrides. Lewis is clearly the dominant partner, resembling a

huge Christmas tree aligned to the north, with Harris for the most part its fragile, vestigial stump – although Harris is by far the more mountainous of the two. Where one becomes the other is not at all clear geographically. Harris technically begins when the island narrows slightly between the deep-probing waterways of Loch Reasort and Loch Shiphoirt, some way to the north of the very obvious separation at Tarbert, which is the place – were I tasked with the responsibility of dividing one island into two with appropriate proportioning of geography – one might logically make the divide.

Tarbert appeared to be a port with a distillery attached to it. Walking from the bus to the ticket office took minutes, and a ticket to Uig on Skye was easy to secure. Then there was the matter of caffeine, which, as directed by the chirpy ticket clerk, lay in quantity in the distillery. With an hour until sailing, I struck off for this through steadily increasing rain past ranks of waiting cars on the ferry slipway, whose drivers might remember the sight of a man walking by with his right arm in a sling, carrying a Tesco bag and wearing, solely by the hood, a waterproof jacket flayed into strips like a kind of ragged cloak. The coffee shop was well appointed and friendly, and I bought a large cafetiere of coffee and a chocolate brownie, both of which made me feel considerably better.

After this came another destitute shuffle through the rain back to the hulking Caledonian MacBrayne ferry, into which I installed myself and waited for the off. Soon after, with a deep hum, the boat slid out of Stornoway and began its choppy crossing of the Minch.

I didn't have a seatmate, though if I'd had one they might have spared me – by way of self-conscious proximity – the phone call to my dear and distant wife, which was not something I'd been looking forward to. Along with a hold-fire text to Matt and a status update to Kingsley, I'd sent her a brief but non-panic-inducing text very late the previous evening, something along the lines of 'I'm OK.' But given the vagaries of phone signals in the mountains – something which, like all of those who have anything to do with people who have anything to do with climbing in remote places, Rachel has had to deal with over the years – that could have been a mere check-in after a period out of signal. Rather, that is, than a reassurance following an accident. The call connected and I heard the usual breakfast bustle, the sing-song voice of my son in the background, and then my wife, who came into the conversation in the practical but bright tone of someone in no way aware that something untoward had occurred.

For a second I thought of not telling her, of not having the conversation at all. Of hunkering down for the next few days, letting the bruises fade, disposing of the sling, then going home as if nothing had happened. Of sparing myself the pall of a nasty accident sure to fall over every future trip to the hills. But, of course, I couldn't. I told her, heard then answered the salvo of questions, attempted to calm the alarm, then tried to reassure the upset. Then I listened to the long silence, trying not to focus on the fact I had brought bad news into my family's morning.

At last she said, 'I'm so sorry.' She paused, then said softly, 'You could have died. What would I have told the children?'

I closed my eyes. This was, really, the worst thing you could do to someone left at home. I could hear my daughter in the background asking what was going on, then the neutered, explanatory exchange, then the next voice I heard was hers, in that admonishing four-year-old falsetto, repeating back to me the words I'd said to her more than once: 'Daddy – you need to look where you're going. You could hurt yourself.'

That did it. I held on enough to finish the conversation, then, as my daughter happily went back to her day five hundred miles away, on the ferry between Lewis and Skye I quietly cried my eyes out.

Shadows flitted beneath the cloud ahead, and Skye's low north port began to materialise out of them – a line of lights in the morning murk. My arrival wasn't going to be accompanied by an undercurrent of possibility, or excitement. It was the first time I'd approached Skye knowing that I wouldn't be climbing something.

Waiting on the quayside at Uig was Kingsley, his tall frame a yellow punctuation mark in the drizzle. He was hunched against the rain, dressed just as he had been the previous evening, arms jammed in pockets, plastic bag hung in the crook of an elbow. I'd lost sight of him when the rescue team had arrived, and – to my shame – had assumed he'd gone down with them and back to the car. He must have found the keys. It was good to see him, and he actually looked glad to see me.

'You don't look too bad, considering,' he said. 'I'd hug you but I don't want to injure you further. I've got you a jacket in here.' He indicated his plastic bag.

I pointed to mine. 'I've got your hat in here.'

'Well, that's the important thing.' He nodded in the direction of the low-rise, drizzle-misted town. 'Come on, I'm freezing.' We walked back down the quay.

'Well, *I* had a dreadful night,' he said, as we climbed back into the car. 'I walked down with the team to the base in Glenbrittle and it really was pretty dark after the helicopter went. We had a chat and a cup of tea, by which time it was the early hours and I just curled up in the car. I say curled up, as I really couldn't figure out how to slide the seat back...'

I shut the door and, with difficulty, strapped myself in.

'...I think I broke my spine,' he continued. 'Luckily, I found a load of spare clothes in the boot so I wasn't cold. Ended up in Portree at some cafe. They sold a cake made out of Coca-Cola. Is that a Skye thing?' He paused for a long moment, then said, 'So, without wanting to add anything to your plate . . . what the fuck are we supposed to do now?'

I didn't know. I just knew I couldn't face thirteen hours in the car just yet. 'I think I need a day or two to just not move. Do you mind?'

'Sounds great. Could do with a good meal, though. And drink. Lots of it, and soon.'

'I know a place,' I said, as we headed south, then turned towards Portnalong.

For the next two days I slept. Perhaps it was the adrenaline, or the cold, or the long wait in pain, but I was oddly exhausted. Katie Heron, given a miraculous late availability, put Kingsley and me in one of the Taigh Ailean's outside rooms, in a little annexe facing the loch, and we liked it immensely – the bright light and sea air knocking me into a healthy but painful slumber for long hours. I had no interest in the mountains; probably my own way of dealing with the fact I couldn't get up into them even if I wanted to. Matt had fixed himself up with another client, who enjoyed two days of almost perfect weather on the ridge, which depressed me further, but Kingsley kept me chipper – along with Johnny's cooking and large quantities of Skye Ale. We watched tourists come in and go out, and heard them talk about going to see the Fairy Pools and Neist Point and perhaps calling in at the Talisker

Distillery on the way back, we smiled and chatted and watched Katie send them on their way with the same degree of enthusiasm that she always did. On the morning of the second day two young Swedish backpackers announced their intention to scramble to the summit of Sgùrr na Banachdaich, and I saw Katie click into mother-hen mode. By the end of breakfast she'd made them list their car model, colour, intended parking location, route, and the colour of their jackets and rucksacks. They didn't ask why.

What was remarkable and truly heartening about all of this was that none of it had to happen at all. I'll say it here as simply as I can: if you come a cropper in the mountains, *it is nobody's job to come and get you.* Mountain rescue teams are, and have always been, volunteers. And the hoteliers who keep watch – like those at Sligachan and Glenbrittle a hundred years ago, right up to Katie and those like her now – are something so intrinsically part of what makes this place, like most other mountain places, so special. In the mountain places, people look out for you, whoever you are. They have to. Because they get it, and they care. It's a grim but beautiful thing. And despite the pain, and the embarrassment, and the guilt – and whatever would come next – it made me fall in love with this island a little bit more.

On the last evening Kingsley and I drove out to Talisker Bay, a U-shaped inlet with a dramatic sea stack to the left and a fibrous waterfall cutting the cliffs in a pale streak to the right. In typical Skye style the name 'Talisker' is ambiguous, but it almost certainly refers to its geology – either from the Scottish Gaelic *talamh sgeir*, meaning 'land of the cliff' or the Norse *t-hallr skjaer*, which means 'sloping rock'. The bay faced west, away from the Cuillin and towards the sunset. We drove out of Portnalong over bare moorland, then walked past a fistful of houses, the grandest of which used to be the home of the MacLeod clan chief. Its walls were white, its windows blazing in the dusk. We then took a track to the beach. The sky was a deepening, flawless blue, and above us corvids and petrels cawed around roosts on a clifftop lit by the last of the sun.

We reached the beach, stony but mercifully pristine, punctuated only by the occasional piece of driftwood big enough to sit on or by a blackened rings of stones where others who had sat there before us had lit a fire. Kingsley took some pictures, I sat and watched the sun drop slowly into a bath of reedy mist on the horizon. It was intensely pretty; the end of everything, seemingly.

Samuel Johnson visited Talisker, and had something typically ambivalent to say about its sequestered nature and its discordance with his genteel tastes:

> Talisker is the place beyond all that I have seen, from which the gay and the jovial seem utterly excluded; and where the hermit might expect to grow old in meditation, without possibility of disturbance or interruption. It is situated very near the sea, but upon a coast where no vessel lands but when it is driven by a tempest on the rocks.

While presumably uncharitable in its context, I found Johnson's words quite fitting. I was bewitched by the place.

As the sky deepened, the sun dropped and the tide began to recede, a few other people gradually appeared from nowhere and joined us. Wordlessly, they all just sat around on widely spaced bits of wood, not talking to us or each other. And from our places, we just watched the sun go down. Then, one by one, everyone got up and started to wander back to wherever they'd come from. A woman wrapped in a cable-knit shawl, with wild hair and a nose-ring, gave us a little wave as she left. We waved back, then returned our gaze to the sea. We stayed until the tide was just a line in the distance, its sound a breath, stars starting to pierce the navy above. Then in the dark, we got up to go.

It was perfect. Indescribably peaceful. I imagined what it must be like to be here every day, to own this experience, night after night, through all seasons. A half stumble on the rocks and the realisation I had an arm bound up in a sling made me suddenly skittish on my feet. We were going home tomorrow. I couldn't wait to see my wife, my kids. And for the first time in a while, I didn't know when I'd be back. But as we left the sea and slowly wandered up the wooded lane, listening to night sounds emerge beneath a sky glowing brilliantly above, I said to Kingsley: 'It would be incredible up on the ridge right now.' And as I said it, I knew it wouldn't be long.

PART THREE

DESCENT

Beware the Jabberwock, my son!
The jaws that bite, the claws that catch!
'Jabberwocky', Lewis Carroll, 1871

14

Shadow

There's a darkness to wild places, and some people seek it out. They remove themselves from modern civilisation, inserting themselves elsewhere instead, into an old, fearful existence of simplicity, of shelter sought, of survival gained with effort. A state of living away from what we've been moving towards as a species for thousands of years. This human rewilding is usually undertaken by choice, and often forsakes comfort, sometimes briefly, occasionally entirely. Your poets and painters grasping for theatrical, demon-haunted landscapes. Your climbers and mountaineers desperate for an antidote to the dull, antiseptic boredom of societal success. Your frontier-fleers, your leopard men, desperate for somewhere, and something. What is it about the wild shadow, the threat of a dangerous place, that's so life affirming, so damn exciting?

There are and continue to be many instances of those walking, climbing, craving the outdoors to fortify a troubled mind – to escape, as George Borrow put it, the 'horrors'. But why people escape *to* the horrors, those landscapes devoid of comfort, often most captivating under an ashy pall, is a question worth asking. It's the sublime, the rapture of terror, of horror, that inspired the Romantics, something that transcends, defies, all conventional measures of beauty but as such becomes fascinating and absorbing. If this isn't you, you'll wonder what I mean. But if you've ever been drawn to the moorlands of the Brontës, the bleak Dartmoor heaths of Du Maurier, sought the thrill of a thunderstorm high in Snowdonia, the remoteness of a particular bothy that – even better – has some awful ghost story attached to it, then, brothers and sisters, it's you. It's you if your nerves twitch and your heart quickens and your excitement builds at the mention of things that in every rational sense shouldn't appeal at all. Have you ever wondered why?

Like so many before me, when I saw the profile of the Cuillin of Skye I was repelled and intrigued at the same time. Felt the stirrings of something inside that told me that this place, this fearsome place, would *give* me something. Would *bring* me something in return for its dangers and its rigours. A place that, if I could weather its challenges, would make me more of the person I am, somehow. Like Cuchuillin, I would walk the Bridge of the Cliff, raise the watermark of my own limits, and come home able to brave the struggles of normal life with the swagger of a gladiator. Or something.

But there's more to it than that. Mountaineering lures the sane into a world of false logic and peculiar motive. It tempts people to gamble all they have in pursuit of the frivolous. Snarling a smile at you as it creeps ever closer, it manipulates your judgement. Answers are lacking here; we all have our own reasons. But no matter what happens to you in these places, it rarely lessens your desire for them. They run through you like bone. You can fight the mountain impulse if you like. But really, all you need to do is survive it.

The bad dreams began a few weeks after I returned from Skye. I want to tell you they were the sort of dreams you see in films, dreams from which some poor haunted person wakes, sits bolt upright, panting and shiny with sweat, and their concerned spouse comfortingly says, 'What's wrong, hon?' But they weren't like that at all. I'd feel myself plunging, feel the pull in my guts, see the ground racing from beneath me, then I'd wake with a compressed moan and feel as if I was going to vomit. And then I couldn't sleep.

Bad dreams are normal after any kind of accident, I was told, particularly if injury is sustained or a much worse outcome narrowly avoided – which seemed to be my own preoccupation. The event kicks around in the short-term memory, often emerging at unwelcome moments. Intrusive thoughts, the symptoms are called, and they often waltz hand in hand with inexplicable and enduring feelings of guilt or shame. Emotion and memory are intertwined, apparently, and until the memory of the event transfers between one bit of the brain to the other, from short-term into long-term memory, and settles down, the person is likely to be a little fragile and unpredictable. Or so I'd read. When things like this happen, though, it does raise questions: that tedious old question of *why*, usually asked by people who don't get it, who aren't suffering from even a mild case of the mountain fixation.

Climbing a mountain in the 21st century is any number of things: a resetting of priorities, a reacquisition of proper decision-making, a removal of yourself from attention-span-decimating technology and a reminder of how it feels to be a creature of nature – alive, alert and saturated with the subtle narcotic that is the great outdoors. And that is a powerful, powerful drug. Overcoming obstacles, revelling in the basics and enjoying a world of little victories: it's all a kind of primal euphoria. And once this makes its bed in your life, your life is forever less when it goes. And go it often does, one way or the other, either through age, change in circumstance, the loss of the one with whom you used to share the mountains and can't now face enjoying them without – or an erosion of the memory of times past. That feeling of vitality, or perspective, of simple times in astonishing places.

Some people choose mountains – and mountains alone. They overindulge themselves. Surrender themselves completely to the adventure, fill their lives with it, attack ever-more challenging objectives. And then, as their bodies and memories fail and mountain climbing becomes harder, a vacuum takes hold. A void, where once there was a thrill to be pursued at the cost of much else. Friedrich Nietzsche wrote about this, in *Beyond Good and Evil*, in a notorious passage that's been applied to everything from drug abuse to genocide, and endlessly pondered by those who live with a finger to their chin. Taken at face value – an amusing idea with Nietzsche – it could just as equally have been informed by his prolific mountain wandering. 'Whoever fights monsters should see to it that in the process he does not become a monster,' he wrote. 'When you look long into an abyss, the abyss also looks into you.'

Here's where this fascination stumbles towards rockier ground: when you factor in danger, overconfidence and obsession. Things that you do that you know threaten your life. You might get lucky, but you might also get hurt and come close to losing it all. Or rather, the people important to you come close to losing you. At worst, you'll be dead; you won't care. But the mountains might have also taken away a husband, a father, someone who didn't need to have departed just then, and whose decision to do something risky in the mountains affected the lives of people who were actually quite happy with you being around. Needed you to do simple, important things. Who wanted you to help them through life, to be there for them, teach them practical lessons or give them the occasional hug. Who needed you just like you, now, needed them. This could be true for an array of situations, but I'll pick this one, as it's mine. Become a parent and you come to realise one thing very quickly. Suddenly, it's no longer OK to just die.

Mountaineering has no shortage of people who follow an ultimately selfish impulse. People who disappear for months on end to chase summits, gamble with their lives, push themselves further than they should, and who occasionally die for their trouble – often leaving loved ones behind who try to figure out why any of this was necessary. You could argue rationally that any passion is ostensibly pointless. It's their choice: there is of course the argument that it enriches your life, and provides a balance that makes you better, which I strongly believe it does. But this becomes harder to defend when it ends it. Then, it comes down to the palpable toll it takes on those around you. You see this articulated sometimes in obituaries to those who succumb to their hazardous pastimes, featuring that tragic, grasping rationalisation: 'the only comfort is, they died doing what they loved.'

It's weird, that line. And very sad. They *lived* doing what they loved. It isn't a comfort they *died* doing it. It's a disaster. I wouldn't ever criticise someone else's feelings on this matter, and don't get me wrong – I *love* the mountains. I go to the mountains to live. But they're the last place I'd want to die.

I suspect some climbers live in a kind of adrenaline-blinkered denial of this, with their apparent confidence reaching a zenith as the margins of error grow ever thinner. William Naismith's peculiar but absorbing article in the *Scottish Mountaineering Club Journal* of 1909 entitled 'Courage in Climbing' contains some fascinating observations about the nature of fear and the ways in which climbers deal with it:

It has been said that fear is itself more fatal and injurious than the circumstances which evoke it. Some [climbers] become unusually cheerful or loquacious, or take the opportunity to deliver a short discourse on the geology of a district. Others become silent, or a trifle irritable. While one climber smokes 'like a limekiln', another keeps his pipe in his mouth and allows it to go out.

Concerning courage, he offers some sensible advice. Time of day, evidently, is a factor in bravery. Naismith adds that most climbers find themselves more 'impervious to "thrills" in the afternoon than in the early morning … as the climber is hardened'. After the slightest chiding of those who take unnecessary risks when unroped – 'a peculiar zest for some queer people' – his closing message is simple, and interesting:

Once embarked on a climb, if unbidden thoughts seek to enter … refuse to harbour a suggestion of danger. Elaborate efforts to steer clear of all risk may have a contrary effect.

This is absolutely right, I think. You aren't safe up there. And any presumption that you are puts you in harm's way. Total commitment, physically and mentally, is what's needed. *You've got to accept the danger. Otherwise, you'll be terrified.* But confidence is a dangerous thing. Become habituated to risk, and your life increasingly turns into a numbers game, where those margins of error become sickeningly thin.

Perhaps the ultimate example of total commitment is Alex Honnold's rope-free, or *free solo*, ascent of El Capitan, a 3,000-foot vertical rock face soaring out of California's Yosemite valley. Honnold practised the route he chose up this face for years – every move calculated, every pinkie-sized hold worked like a chess piece, the whole wall analysed and thought out like a long, strategic game. Rehearsed, climbed, re-climbed, returned to, until the day in 2018 when the ropes came off. He had controlled as much as he could, and it paid off; he made the climb in less than four hours, nail-shreddingly documented in the film *Free Solo*. A bird bursting from any of the cracks, a sudden gust of wind, an ill-timed sneeze – that would have been it. Zero margin for error. When you free solo, as Honnold himself pithily noted,

'You're either perfect or you're dead.' The flipside to this is, of course, caution. The moment of hesitation before commitment, which should you heed it, might save your life.

Regarding the Cuillin, amongst my own much less sensational set of variables, I was hesitating now. Hesitating over whether to ignore the nasty, nervous feeling that had made me suddenly skittish, or to be sensible and thoughtful, and to park any further mountain endeavours until enough time had passed for the bad memories to lose their edge. I didn't then know that returning or not to Skye's black ridge might not be my choice at all.

In the months after my accident my shoulder didn't get better. It was clear from the worrying slips and slides and grinds I could feel inside my joint that something was wrong. A CT scan revealed I had something called a Hills–Sachs lesion – a chipping of the bone at the top of the humeral head of my right arm. 'It's like a little gateway out of your socket,' my consultant told me. He said that I needed surgery, something complicated called a Latarjet procedure. I thought this sounded pleasingly sleek, perhaps involving lasers, but no: they would saw some bone off my shoulder blade, graft it to my shoulder socket, detach my bicep, rehook it onto another bit of bone, tighten everything up, then hope for the best. The best was a stable shoulder, but with reduced movement, possible arthritis – and a long time of not doing anything much more strenuous than tapping a keyboard.

'What if I left it?' I asked.

The consultant bobbed his head thoughtfully, but his answer was unequivocal. 'It'll keep dislocating. And each dislocation makes the next more likely, and could chip off more bone.'

I felt a weight settle in my gut. 'Can I do anything in the meantime?'

'Physio. That'll strengthen the muscles but won't help the bone. And it will be vulnerable. Any position where you can't see your elbow.' He thought for a minute. 'Or you make any unexpected movements. Or a load of weight suddenly goes onto your arm.'

'So I can't climb?'

He looked at me over his glasses and frowned, as if my question suggested I hadn't been listening. 'I can't tell you not to. But I can't advise it. Climbing is what got you here.'

'Falling is what got me here.'

'Either way, you're where you are.' He shifted on his seat a little irritably. Then, extending his arms, he mapped out an area in front of him roughly between his chin and his waist, as if describing to someone the ideal positioning of a tie. 'This is your safe zone. Keep your arms in this area. No reaching. No loading. And no sudden movements.'

I looked at him, and he shrugged and said, 'Look, I love the mountains too. I get it. You need to weigh up your mental health with your physical health. In the end it's just a case of managing the risk.'

I walked out of there feeling depressed. I remembered looking forward to the Cuillin ridge as a kind of exclamation mark at the end of my British mountain ambitions. But never once had it occurred to me that the exclamation mark might turn into a premature full stop. Not going to the mountains on my own terms was one thing, but it was quite another to not even be *able* to go, through fear of my body letting me down in some painful and unexpected way. My nerves had let me down plenty of times, but not my body. This was a new feeling, and I didn't like it one bit. It seemed my options were either an operation to rearrange the muscles and screw in a piece of bone, followed by a long lay-up; or continuing my journey along the ridge with a pop-happy shoulder. Neither appealed. But for the time being at least, as far as Skye was concerned, I was grounded.

By 1911 climbers' eyes had moved from the summits of the ridge to the midriff, and they were soon gnawing earnestly on the meat they found there – the ribs, the creases, the upper limbs. The Cuillin's great cliffs were being explored and climbed by some of the rising stars, but one tantalising objective on the crest remained: the Great Traverse.

I mentioned earlier that amongst much else, Norman Collie left three particularly telling legacies from his mountaineering career on Skye. One was the discovery of the Cioch, and now here was a second. In 1891 Collie, William Wickham King and John MacKenzie found a way to cross the steep-sided notch between Sgùrr Dubh an Da Bheinn and Sgùrr Thearlaich, better known as the Thearlaich Dubh or TD Gap, the principal barrier to anyone wishing to traverse the ridge and stubbornly adhere to its crest. There isn't much of a story, at least not one we know; they just managed to figure out the manoeuvring of its steep sides, through a mixture of clever ropework and deduction.

It's interesting that mountaineers made sure they'd thought hard about the difficulties and intricacies of the sections before even attempting the full traverse of the ridge. By this, to recap, we mean travelling from one end of the ridge to the other, uninterrupted and preferably in a single day. That nobody seems to have at least *tried* something a bit more leisurely first – perhaps a two- or three-day attempt – maybe says something about the mindset of the climbers of the time.

The theory that moving quickly and unencumbered might make a quick-and-dirty dash possible was discussed by many – particularly when, in 1905, the Lakeland walker A. W. Wakefield managed 23,500 feet of vertical ascent on the Lake District's highest and roughest fells in a mere twenty-two hours. Despite the difference in the technicality of the ground, the traverse of the Cuillin ridge had only around half that amount of vertical ascent and considerably less distance, at around fifteen miles all-in. Wakefield's achievement raised eyebrows and – particularly around Glenbrittle and Sligachan – hopes.

It was a fruitful time for exploring the limits of human endurance. The rise of 'gigantism' events in cycling (the first Tour de France, 1,509 miles in six days, took place in 1903) mirrored the tests that explorers of both the poles and the highest mountains of the greater ranges were setting themselves. In 1906 the philosopher William James gave a talk entitled 'The Energies of Men', in which he called for the further study of what he called the 'topography of the limits of human power', claiming that 'in exceptional cases we may find, beyond the very extremity of fatigue-distress, amounts of ease and power that we never dreamed ourselves to own.' But while philosophers debated the theoretical issues, mountaineers on Skye were thinking of the ridge traverse in rather more practical terms.

Following Collie and party's unlocking of the TD gap, there were two further obstacles to be overcome, like niggling knots in a line of rope, for the crest to be smoothly followed. One was the prow of Sgùrr MhicCoinnich above Coire Làgan, finally cracked on 8 August 1896 by three Williams of the Scottish Mountaineering Club: King, Naismith and Douglas. A week later, on 15 August, Naismith and A. M. Mackay made the first ascent of the Bàsteir Tooth from the Bealach nan Lice side, thus straightening out the trajectory for an assault directly along the crest and meaning that the Cuillin end-to-end traverse – from Gars-bheinn to Sgùrr nan Gillean – had become, by piecemeal problem solving, theoretically possible. But the need for speed on dangerous, complicated ground seemed to rule it out as folly. So who would rise to the challenge?

The climber and photographer Ashley Abraham offered the following description of any would-be traverser:

> He would need to have exceptional physique and staying power, to be a quick, skilful and neat rock climber (particularly neat . . . otherwise his hands would be torn to pieces), to possess an intimate knowledge of the entire range and familiarity with the various different sections, while perfect weather, a light rope and carefully arranged commissariat would be necessary.

Timing systems were suggested, locations to cache food and drink, and of course, the direction of the traverse. South to north was generally considered the most sensible, as the downclimbs were thought easier in this direction than they would be in ascent from the other. In general it just *seemed* more aesthetically pleasing – a thing of elegance and beauty rather than bloody-minded difficulty, like stroking a dog along the lie of its fur, rather than against it. Daylight would be critical, as were calm conditions, so June – when night lasts only a few hours, darkness is never total and the weather is often reasonable – seemed the appropriate month.

In terms of potential conquistadors, nobody really knows how many were gearing up for the first attempt. Ken Crocket suggests in *Mountaineering in Scotland* that aspirants 'withheld their interest, so as not to encourage potential rivals', which isn't that hard to understand. Despite being one of the first to suggest the possibility of the traverse, Collie was beginning to look more lingeringly at his fishing rods by this point, his most physical days in the Cuillin largely behind him. One who'd made his intentions known was Geoffrey Winthrop Young, a mountaineer-poet of a deeply philosophical bent who was fascinated by the Cuillin. His mental fortitude was considerable and his seasons in the Alps made him technically capable, but just before his rumoured attempt his climbing partner A. M. Mackay broke a leg on the Isle of Arran, while Winthrop Young would later lose one of his in the First World War. Another slightly unlikely name in the mix was the writer and politician John Buchan, author of *The Thirty-Nine Steps*, who was also bewitched by the ridge. But it wasn't a floridly named mountaineer-poet or a soon-to-be-famous novelist who would first complete the traverse.

I'd like to introduce here something called 'nominative determinism'. You know what this is; it's where someone's surname fits with their job – Mr Cleaver the butcher, Mrs Bunn the baker, Mr Yank the dentist, and so on. Although it seems a little silly to suggest that people seek out certain professions based on their name, studies suggest that they sometimes do. Apparently it's all about a thing called implicit egotism, which essentially means you are drawn to things you unconsciously associate with yourself.

In the mountain world there are a few uncanny examples of people whose names fit what they do just a little too well. A runner specialising in record-breaking speed traverses of sharp aretes named Sarah Ridgeway; an endurance fell-racer named Ricky Lightfoot; a rock climber and guidebook writer called Chris Craggs. We're about to meet someone famous for lofty exploits on the pointy Cuillin named E. W. Steeple. The man responsible for accomplishing some of the most gruelling Scottish climbs of the time and advancing the technical grade of the sport? One William Tough. And also – this is my favourite – a former president of the Alpine Club, remembered as an outspoken critic of over-rapid speed climbing between the wars, whose general refrain was that everyone should just slow down and take things in a little more. His name? E. L. Strutt.

So it's pleasing that the sleek duo who would make the first continuous traverse of the Cuillin ridge, from Gars-bheinn to Sgùrr nan Gillean in a single day, were appropriately named for the job. The date was 10 June 1911, and their names were Shadbolt and McLaren.

Leslie Shadbolt and Alastair Campbell McLaren were a formidable partnership who had first come to Skye in 1906. Developing their skills with routes on the mainland – where they both left an array of eponymous chimneys across the Highlands – by 1911 they were ushered into the Scottish Mountaineering Club with enthusiasm, after Shadbolt was observed by Willie Ling casually making a fine variation to Collie's route on the Cioch. They would roundly reward Ling's endorsement four days later when, in Shadbolt's words, 'the time had come to translate the dreams of the winter fireside into accomplished action.'

Conditions on the day were discouraging, with mist wreathing the highest summits of the ridge. But nevertheless, the pair launched into their attempt with one rucksack, considerable vim and a bit of profitable bickering, covering the distance between Glen Brittle and the summit of Gars-bheinn in just over two hours. Thirty-one-year-old McLaren was a stickler for meticulous timekeeping, and Shadbolt – twenty-eight at the time – remarked later that an argument about their pace was settled in 'McLaren's favour within the first ten yards', which evidently put a stop to the former's habit of sleepwalking for the first few hours of the day. 'Though averse to speed on the road as a rule, [McLaren] was today eaten up with a lust for it,' he wrote in his account of the traverse in the *Scottish Mountaineering Club Journal*.

Their gain in time was set back a little when mist descended on the Dubhs, making them wonder whether or not they were off route until a cairn put them right; McLaren noted a time of one minute to rope up for the TD Gap, before timing their progress across it – much to Shadbolt's irritation. The pair bested Sgùrr Alasdair and braved 'aggravatingly numerous obstacles' to the base of the Inaccessible Pinnacle, which they reached at a remarkable 10.55 a.m., two and a half hours ahead of schedule – and a whisker under seven hours after setting off from Glen Brittle.

Here, Shadbolt was finally allowed to slow down. The Inaccessible Pinnacle was 'treated with great respect ... and its history, geological formation and beauty fully discussed'. Discussion completed, Pinnacle climbed and weather now perfectly clear, the pair celebrated in the only way climbers of their time seemed to know: 'pipes were lit.' From then on, with the time pressure eased and the chance of success a real possibility, the day shifted tone from frenetic to rather more fun.

Perhaps surprisingly, neither Shadbolt nor McLaren were experts on the ridge. They'd done sections of it before, but there was still a good deal of it that was new to them. They expressed surprise at encountering Caisteal a' Garbh-coire above Loch Coir' a' Ghrunnda, and weren't sure whether or not they should climb it or 'turn it' in order to stay true to the traverse. But in the section between Sgùrr na Banachdaich and Sgùrr a' Mhadaidh – the formidable middle section of the ridge – timekeeping and record-chasing were set aside in favour of the simplicity and purity of the endeavour. Shadbolt later wrote:

> One experienced to the full the delight of striding along narrow ridges almost unhindered by problems as to the best route … and able to enjoy to the full the aesthetic side of mountaineering . . . only reached with sustained physical effort to the limit of one's powers.

By the time they reached Bidein Druim nan Ramh, despite having a 'few drops of water' in reserve, they were parched. The only topic of conversation was the pool they'd heard lay close to the foot of Sgùrr a' Fionn Choire – possibly Seton Gordon's fabled spring – but before they got to it they were faced with a section of unexpected difficulty, its narrow ledges requiring them to edge towards the Coruisk drop. The next part afforded quicker progress, with Bruach na Frithe and Sgùrr a' Fionn Choire bagged with five minutes in between. The pool was found, and presumably emptied. Then the pair set about the business of climbing the Bàsteir Tooth, via Naismith's Route – using shoulders for aid. McLaren was apparently as fresh as when he had started; Shadbolt was impressed with the quality of the climb, and its challenge at this late stage of the route.

Reaching the summit of Sgùrr nan Gillean at 6.25 p.m., what should have been a triumphant coast down to Sligachan was replaced by a last-minute bit of pioneering, with the pair traversing across plates of gabbro between – presumably – the south ridge and the south-east ridge in order to quicken the descent. They reached the inn just shy of seventeen hours after leaving Glenbrittle, with a 'ridge time' (Gars-bheinn to Sgùrr nan Gillean) of twelve hours and eighteen minutes. By the time they reached Sligachan, they had 'thrilled again to all the delights and doubts' of what would become a historic day for British mountaineering.

The traverse of the Cuillin had been done. After Shadbolt and McLaren had proved it possible – as is often the case with such things with a competitive dimension – it was now simply a case of whether *you* could do it, and if so, could you do it quicker, more gruellingly or more peculiarly than the last person to do it. Despite this, Shadbolt and McLaren remained the Cuillin's first and only traversers for nine years. One reason was probably that climbers – to use the term in its true sense – were more interested in developing first ascents on the many tens of square kilometres of virgin rock faces beneath the Cuillin's crest, and had little desire to follow the footsteps of others, not least on a long outing fraught with logistical issues, physical exertion and elemental luck. The lure to be first on a climb elsewhere in the Cuillin was far more of a draw than being second, or third, or tenth on a mountaineering expedition, however hallowed. Another reason was, of course, the First World War – which would not only slow the flow of climbers making it to Skye but would rob the Cuillin, and elsewhere, of a generation of explorers.

That in mind, with its perfect storm of technical and physical challenge unmatched in Britain, by 1920 the traverse again came onto the radar of a new kind of climber-mountaineers, their eyes collectively fixed on the final great objective: the peaks of the Himalaya, and one in particular.

The world of high-altitude summit hunting had not enjoyed the best of success to start with. The first attempt on an 8,000-metre peak, one of the fourteen highest mountains in the world, had ended in tragedy in 1895 when Albert Mummery, a gifted but reputedly reckless British climber, and two Gurkhas were buried by an avalanche whilst trying to navigate the Rakhiot face of Nanga Parbat, in what's now Pakistan. Their bodies were never found, and while mystery surrounds the exact nature of their death, the fact they were trying to climb a mountain nearly twice as high as those in the Alps in a similar fast-and-loose style is thought to have contributed to their fate. Altitude sickness, little understood at the time, had already left two of the expedition's most skilled climbers out of action by the time Mummery made his fatal attempt. One was a Yorkshire businessman and skilled rock climber named Geoffrey Hastings; the other was Norman Collie.

Undeterred by Mummery's fate, and perhaps encouraged by another Skye enthusiast in a certain George Mallory, the Cuillin became the sharpening stick for many of the climbers bound for mystical, faraway objectives – Mount Everest most of all.

To this end, some impressive names pop up on the list of those who next did the Cuillin traverse. The second party, in 1920, was actually largely a solo affair. Theodore Howard 'T. H.' Somervell – four years before setting altitude records in the Himalaya and becoming one of the last to see Mallory and Andrew Irvine alive on Everest in 1924 – was the second to traverse the ridge, as an end-stop to a climbing holiday with his brother. With the latter leaving early, Somervell teamed up with a Fell and Rock Climbing Club member named Graham Wilson. They left Glenbrittle at 7 a.m., but as the day grew hot and windless, thirst took hold. Wilson threw in the towel on Sgùrr na Banachdaich, but Somervell continued on alone, his lack of water increasingly – but clearly not *too* – excruciating. He made it to Sligachan in fourteen and a quarter hours, and maintained that with a pound of raisins and a full water bottle he could have bettered the time by an hour.

The first north–south traverse was made in 1924 by B. R. Goodfellow and F. Yates. Arguably the harder direction – with the trickier climbs coming at the end of the day rather than the start, the final sting being the more difficult side of the TD Gap taken in ascent rather than descent – the pair managed seventeen hours. This was perhaps made more impressive by the presence of thick mist for the entire day.

Also in 1924, Frank Smythe and J. H. B. Bell made a traverse of the main ridge. Bell was a legendary figure in British climbing, whilst his protégé Smythe was well on the way to a career as an explorer in the Himalayas, as well as being a prolific author. Cautious of the desiccated dispatches of those who preceded them, Smythe and Bell took a length of tube with which to siphon water from pools. In the interests of keeping weight to a minimum, Smythe wore nimble rubber shoes, which barely survived the outing. Occasionally misty, and with a descent interrupted by 'refreshing bathes and losing each other', their time from Glenbrittle to Sligachan was a little over sixteen hours, door to door. In 1935 Bell would become the first person to do the traverse twice. Smythe would later climb high in the Himalaya, attempting both Kangchenjunga and Everest in the 1930s – the latter no fewer than three times – and in 1931 made the successful ascent of Kamet, which at 7,756 metres was the highest mountain climbed in the world at the time. Smythe described the Cuillin as 'the only range of genuine mountains in Britain'. And here was a man who truly knew what that meant.

One campaign that should be recognised for the sheer boldness of its approach was instigated by a group of climbers calling themselves the Pinnacle Club, in the spring of 1924. The idea was that the ridge shouldn't be viewed as a linear expedition but a circular one – a return to origin, or a job not done until the starting threshold is re-crossed on return, if you like. The threshold in question was that of a shelter near where the Coruisk Hut now stands. The peaks of the ridge lean around this place like faces peering at a bug, so it makes sense; not only could it justify an entertaining approach from Elgol by boat, but it would remain a 'mountain journey' for its duration, with nothing approaching civilisation at any point or either end, save for a rudimentary hut in one of Britain's wildest places. The Cuillin horseshoe, if you like.

The first party to scout the ridge to formulate this idea was in 1924, and saw it benighted in torrid weather. Spending the night on a rocky ledge 'near Bidein', its leader – M. M. Barker – later wrote that they crossed the Cuillin, but never actually saw them:

> That was our first round with the Coolins, and they won hands down. They wreaked their will on us that night, and wove strange enchantments from which we shall never recover.

In 1925 an assault team – Barker again, with C. D. Frankland and H. V. Hughes – made a base in the hut near Coruisk, cached food at the base of the Inaccessible Pinnacle, then set off at 5.30 the following morning into mist and a wind so strong they were forced to remain on the lee side of the crest. They made it as far as the Inaccessible Pinnacle, then called a halt in worsening conditions, before failing to find a safe way off due to the compass being affected by the notorious magnetic anomalies. A long retreat back along the ridge and a descent placed them back at the start, seventeen hours and just shy of half a ridge later. One climber was moving so raggedly, they left a trail of 'bloody marks, like a paper chase.'

In August 1926, Pinnacle Club members made another attempt on the horseshoe, with Barker and Frankland remaining from the previous team. From their start in Coruisk over Gars-bheinn, they were battered by every kind of condition from mist to hail, to brilliant sunshine and rainbows – but finally stood on the summit of Sgùrr na h-Uamha beneath Sgùrr nan

Gillean, 'the whole landscape clear, and Lochan Dubha and the Scavaig River crimson in the sunset glow'.

They'd left at 5 a.m. and returned to the hut long after dark, at 1 a.m. – a trip of twenty hours. Successfully back at the starting point, in a single day, with the ridge in between: at over eighteen miles, and with 10,000 feet of ascent, it was the longest and toughest Cuillin expedition yet attempted. It was also – stunningly – attempted faithfully along the entire crest, and without a rope.

A noteworthy point here is that the Pinnacle Club was composed of people who, up until that point, held little influence in the world of serious mountaineering – and were viewed by some in the mainstream climbing world with a sneer. The Pinnacle Club was, and remains, a climbing club for women.

History has not distinguished itself, it must be said, in its treatment of female climbers – and this is perhaps more true for the Cuillin than elsewhere. Even some of the most respected records of the time adopt a detectable shift in tone when discussing what was certainly then considered a peculiar and ill-advised activity for a lady – and a tone approaching near delight when their endeavours failed. Depressingly, when writing of their achievements some female climbers disguised their first names with initials, to blend in with their male contemporaries and thus be judged without the distraction of their gender.

The final horseshoe milestone, it must be said, was accomplished by a mixed team, of which only half was female – Mabel 'M.M.' Barker, accompanied by Claud Deane 'C.D.' Frankland – despite having Gertrude Walmsley and Edith Davies in support. Ben Humble noted in *The Cuillin of Skye* that the escapade revealed 'a very high standard of climbing and endurance on the part of the female member of the party' – without acknowledging that this was actually a heck of an achievement for either gender. 'We were the first of any sort,' the ever-witty Barker wrote of the challenge in the 1926 *Fell and Rock Climbing Club Journal*.

The Pinnacle Club returned to the Cuillin in 1927 for an all-female traverse in the traditional style, from Glenbrittle to Sligachan. This was an ill-fated twenty-one-hour epic that was binned at Sgùrr a' Mhadhaidh – roughly halfway. A year later, the 'Pinnacles', as they were nicknamed, tried again, this time being met with scorching heat. Another epic: thirty and a half hours, with little or no water over rocks painfully hot to touch. Reaching Bruach na Frithe at 9 p.m., they stopped for a half-bivouac, setting off again at 2.30 a.m. and reaching Sligachan at 9 that same morning. They were sufficiently recovered by the afternoon to walk back to Glenbrittle across the Bealach a' Mhàim.

Even in the 19th century, women climbers were by no means unusual. Collie in particular was known for taking female tourists onto the ridge, and his slide collection held by the Alpine Club depicts many ladies, skirts and motoring veils billowing, on such redoubtable objectives as the Inaccessible Pinnacle and the Cioch. But in the main they were sisters, wives or acquaintances of the male climbers of the day. From a climbing standpoint, they were frequently aligned anecdotally with easier options and often mentioned in the same breath as children.

These accounts were of course largely written by men, and some of the reports of female achievements of the time read uncomfortably today. Some over-applauded with an air of wonder and disbelief, as you might clap a child who had just grasped a crayon. Male accounts of climbing adventures in the Cuillin tended to look outward, focusing on the difficulty of the rock, the other great challenges and the stoicism of the climber within that brotherhood of the rope – almost as if recording any sort of physical frailty at all was a sin. Read accounts of female ascents of the time (written by males, of course) and suddenly we're in a world of feelings, of lying down, of not even having put on woollies yet, of 'parched throats despite a good supply of oranges', of huddling together, of feeling cold and of unanimous decisions to 'give up the struggle'. Fellow climbers weren't partners or companions, they were 'accomplices'. Was it sexist? Without getting too revisionist, it was certainly chauvinistic.

Norman Collie, as an old man, was quizzed by a young climber named Bill Wood about the difficulty of Window Buttress and replied, 'I can't remember anything about it except that I've taken hundreds of women and children up it' – all Wood needed to know concerning difficulty, it seems. But these individuals were, of course, beginners or tourists. Women *climbers* were rarer – and these exceptions to the rule had to work extra hard to be taken seriously. Hence the establishment of the Pinnacle Club in 1921, and before that the Ladies Alpine Club (1907) and the Ladies Scottish Climbing Club (1908). These gave female climbers an environment that wasn't overly male-oriented, albeit by default deepening the existing segregation.

Climbing was – and some would argue still is – very macho, a pastime invented by men, for men, so men could be men, with other men. There have been many exceptions: Lucy Walker, Lily Bristow and Lizzie Le Blond are the usual names mentioned when discussing female climbers of the 19th and early 20th century, although they're more famous today for being female than for the climbs they were involved in, or the films they made, or the characters they inspired. But the truth was that the women who were climbing were about as far from delicate or incompetent as could be.

Ida Fitzgerald Dalton is a case in point. In 1897, whilst holidaying with her family at Sligachan, the twenty-six-year-old enlisted John MacKenzie for expeditions into the Cuillin, and knocked off big sections of the ridge with impressive gusto. On 6 August she climbed Sgùrr nan Gillean by the south-east ridge, descended via the west ridge, then climbed the Bàsteir Tooth. Two days later, with MacKenzie and his brother Murdo, she climbed the Inaccessible Pinnacle in rain and mist. This evidently wasn't enough to dissuade her from more climbing before the week was up – and whilst we don't know what or where, she returned to Skye for the following two summers. Little else is known about her climbing, sadly, though according to historian Stuart Pedlar, she was apparently in correspondence with MacKenzie as late as 1931, just two years before his death.

It's been suggested that it's Dalton who's depicted in the illustration of a 'Woman Climber in Skye' published in *The Graphic* in 1898 – and reproduced in Ben Humble's *The Cuillin of Skye* – which shows a woman in a flowing dress, a Balmoral bonnet and brandishing a stick, gazing with a determined expression out of the frame. She has a small pocket stitched into her dress, but other than that she is indifferently dressed for the mountains and even appears to be wearing heels. What's funny is the chap next to her in the drawing. He's dressed in plus fours and a blazer cut for action, and stands with an indignant air, his arms folded, looking at the woman as if to ask, 'Where the hell do you think *you're* going?' This may have been a total accident on the part of the artist, but it's impossible to ignore once you see it and is, one suspects, typical of some contemporary attitudes. A similar illustration, also published in *The Graphic*, shows a woman dreamily gazing at a mountain range, with a local guide and tourist regarding the woman. The sketch's caption is the vaguely seedy:

Tourist: 'Can she climb, Donald?'
Guide: 'Ou aye, she's been all over the Inaccessible Pinnacles, sir!'

On occasion, the map can give clues to some of the hidden characters of the past. The Cuillin is said to be the only British mountain range named after men, but the two ascenders of the Stac na Nighinn – 'the Ladies' Pinnacle' – a sketchy climb on Sgùrr Sgumain, were Mrs. C. B. Phillip and Miss Cecil Prothero in June 1908. C.B. was actually Mary Louisa, the wife of Colin B. Phillip, the artist and climbing confidant of Norman Collie – and by the conventions of the time is apparently stripped of her own identity in favour of her husband's initials. But the intrepid Miss Prothero also pops up in the *Scottish Mountaineering Club Journal* in the same week, and is on record as guiding one Hugh T. Munro over Sgùrr MhicCoinnich, and then a few days later Sgùrr na Banachdaich, and over the mountain 'now sometimes called Sgùrr Thormaid', in reference to Norman Collie's given name in Gaelic. Prothero guided Munro in both instances.

Another formidable character frequently found on Skye in the years around 1920 was Dorothy Pilley, a woman whose presence evidently struck fear into the heart of the manageress of the Sligachan Hotel on account of her scandalously appearing in the dining room wearing her 'climbing breeches'. A feminist to the bone, Pilley would later help found the Pinnacle Club, and as president was responsible for much of its success. Hers was a dual existence: in one life a Cambridge academic married to celebrated literary critic I. A. Richards (she is often referred to as Dorothy Pilley Richards), in the other a formidable Alpine climber who put up several first ascents – including the north-north-west ridge of the Dent Blanche with her husband – at a time when only the most exacting major routes remained for the taking. Like other mountain-loving Cambridge alumni such as Geoffrey Winthrop Young and George Mallory, both Ivor and Dorothy compensated for their lack of mountain stimulus by climbing the university's rooftops, an illegal night-time activity still reputedly practised today.

Pilley drew her climbing experiences together in the excellent *Climbing Days* (1935). Of her time on Skye, Pilley wrote with an admirable sensibility, and she was acquainted with the obstacles women climbers faced – many of them not made of rock:

> The *Alpine Journal* wavered between incredulity and stern disapproval, announcing the first woman's lead of the Grépon with a hesitant 'it is reported,' and declaring that 'Few ladies, even in these days, are capable of mountaineering unaccompanied.'

Of her own relationship with the mountains, she wrote:

> something in the fall of the slopes, or the grasp of the vegetation, the tint of the rocks, the tension of the summit-lines, would tell me – though what exactly it was might beat all efforts at analysis. Can a lover explain just what is different from all others in his beloved?

An insightful account of a female adventurer on Skye describing events from the 1920s came courtesy of Elizabeth Knowlton, a powerhouse U.S. East Coast mountaineer writing in the *American Alpine Journal*. As the only female member of the 1932 German–American Nanga Parbat expedition, Knowlton was one of the first female climbers to reach high altitudes in the Himalaya. The *Portland Press Herald* described her presence on the expedition as 'a painter, who will "mother" the expedition'; actually, she lived in a tent for a month at 20,000 feet on one of the world's most dangerous mountains filing dispatches for the *New York Times*.

On Skye, she described arriving in Glenbrittle to find the village's well-seasoned accommodation – Glenbrittle House, Agnes Chisholm's post office and Mary Campbell's cottage – at one-in, one-out capacity. Mary Campbell she described as 'completely unhelpful'; despite having two rooms and only one lodger, she had turned her spare room into a sitting room and refused to compromise the arrangement, and so turned the 'tired and hungry' Knowlton away. At Agnes Chisholm's she received the opposite response, with the hostess promptly giving her sitting room over to her guest. 'The rights of other guests had short shrift with Mrs.

Chisholm, when it was the needs of a "climber" that were in question,'
she wrote.

The next day she tackled a route on Sròn na Cìche in the company of
Ernest Wood-Johnson, an English climber. As they tied on, there followed
what was possibly one of the more peculiar exchanges between a male and
female climber. I paraphrase here, but it presumably went something like
this:

> Wood-Johnson: 'I say, Miss Knowlton, would it be all right if I called
>   you George?'
> Knowlton: 'For why, may I ask?'
> Wood-Johnson: 'Miss Knowlton seems a little formal, don't you think?'
> Knowlton: 'Indeed, but my name is Elizabeth.'
> Wood-Johnson: 'But my younger brother is called George, and I usually
>   climb with him, you see. Be a sport, won't you?'

Knowlton conceded, and as she appeared to have taken it as a compliment, Wood-Johnson continued to call her George for the rest of the climb.
The rain was incessant, halfway up the mist rolled in and the pair became
lost. Holds were scarce, progress slow and they veered wildly off route,
eventually pioneering a new climb up a chimney blocked by a slippery basalt
overhang, emerging at the top as the storm clouds rolled back, revealing,
according to 'George':

> [a] sunset of bright gold, under a band of ink-blue clouds ... the crowd
> of sharp Coolin peaks clustering black against [it], and just below our
> feet the dark rolling moors and the first appearing lights of Glen Brittle.

They hastened back, and Mrs Chisholm – true to form – miraculously
had a hot meal waiting. It was 11.30 p.m.

Perhaps the most telling and simultaneously disheartening instance of
conditioned sexism came about when the first guidebook for scrambles in
the Cuillin – that's to say *scrambles*, not rock climbs – was published by the
Scottish Mountaineering Club in 1980. Entitled *Black Cuillin ridge: Scramblers'
Guide*, it was met with slightly sniffy criticism from some quarters, with the

magazine *Climber* suggesting that it was not particularly adventurous. The author, S. P. Bull, was later quoted as saying that the book came about as there 'was a need for a guide which would serve as an introduction for the non-rock climber'. A perfectly acceptable motive for a book that a slightly less rope-keen audience would find engaging. The book remains little known, however, and although popular amongst those who appreciate its considerable virtues as a key for the mortal wishing to unlock the Cuillin, was never accorded the praise it was due. The images were fantastic, the copy lucid and the subject matter sorely welcome.

But what's significant here is that S. P. Bull – ostensibly just another one of those mountaineers who liked to style themselves with initials – was disguising something behind those letters: the 'SP' stood for Shirley Patricia. Shirley 'Bunny' Bull, a charismatic lover of fast cars, an excellent photographer and a Pinnacle Club member, for whatever reason remains concealed as the author of this fine book. Was it a commercial decision? It doesn't sound like it was Bunny's. 'I was very chuffed to have it published by the S.M.C. – and written by a woman! – when one thinks of that chauvinistic male preserve,' she later wrote. Gender doesn't matter out there, of course. The mountains don't care, so why should anyone else? But even so, it seems rather a shame that in order to be taken seriously in this field, some felt it was something they needed to hide. As an aside, one former occasional resident of Glen Brittle was Gwen Moffat – an extraordinarily gifted climber who hot-footed it wherever the work was – from mountain rescue, to working ranges like the Cuillin as Britain's first professional female mountain guide. The year she qualified: 1953. She once said: 'The best things about climbing? Unlimited space. I know where I am in mountains.'

As Ben Humble noted, apparently without irony, in *The Cuillin of Skye* after 1924, 'women having done the traverse, men lost interest.' Climbs would continue to be developed on the ridge, and ever-more difficult routes undertaken. Some exceptional mountaineers would alight on Skye, recording their names in the guest books and occasionally on the rock faces themselves. George Mallory, tragic immortal of Everest, read history at Cambridge where he studied Boswell's *Journal of a Tour to the Hebrides.* His interest in the island was piqued and he became a regular visitor in the years before, during and after the First World War, often climbing with Leslie Shadbolt and most notably leading the first ascent of 'Mallory's Slab and Groove' on Sròn na Cìche in July 1918.

It wasn't until 1932 that interest in the traverse was rekindled, when Peter Bicknell set a speed record on the ridge of eleven hours and fifty-seven minutes. Then, as if the Great Traverse and the Cuillin Horseshoe weren't hard enough, came the 'Greater Traverse' – more of a circuit, really – encompassing the ridge, plus Blàbheinn and Clach Glas, the rim of gabbro that overlooks the main ridge from the east, and a part of the Black Cuillin in spirit, if not physical attachment. The Greater Traverse was first considered by Howard Somervell following his successful crossing of the main ridge, but it took until 1939 for Ian Charleson and W. E. Forde to accomplish it, with a system of camps, caches and meticulous timings. They reached Blàbheinn twenty hours after setting out from Gars-bheinn. In order to ensure they didn't accidentally fall asleep during rest stops, they carried with them a full-sized alarm clock.

It's all very impressive. But is it just me, or does spending your hard-won moments in this magnificent landscape with one eye on the time take the fun out of it a little? By now, of course, we're dealing with an ever-thinning end of the wedge. Like so many challenges of its type, as records go, in just over a century the traverse has gone from the seemingly impossible, to the gruelling but possible, to the eminently possible, to the realm of infinitely finer shavings off a sprint. At the time of writing, the fastest known traverse of the ridge stands at an almost inconceivably swift two hours and fifty-nine minutes, by someone – and here's another one of those names – called Finlay Wild. Someone has even ridden a bike across some of its scariest bits: the Dunvegan-born Danny MacAskill, whose nerve-shreddingly shot short film *The Ridge* has racked up – again, at the time of writing – a staggering 75 million views on YouTube. All of which, I might add, threw my own increasingly painful dealings with the ridge into ever sharper relief.

With the pleasantly absorbing distractions of family life, my bad dreams began to lessen, then disappear. The black ridge was once again something unfamiliar and distant – but now with a slightly nasty, treacherous edge. Perhaps because of my temporary inability to do anything about it, the Cuillin nudged and rankled me, like rucks in a mattress sheet, an unreachable itch. I remembered a guy in his fifties Kingsley and I had met in Sligachan on our previous visit, who had told us he'd been 'trying' to do the Cuillin for twenty years. That haunted, hungry look. Perhaps that was me twenty years from now. That unfulfilled ambition, those unmade memories.

It didn't disappear, though. That fretted outline, the cloud-marred spires, the smells and the light. A distant place of wild angles, frills and steeps and jags and barbs, something seen in every break of glass, or wind-sheared cloud, or raked skyline. Far away, on the edge of unreality, and full of dangers.

My preoccupation hit home when I was reading a story about Lewis Carroll and came across 'Jabberwocky' – the unsettling poem from *Through the Looking-Glass, and What Alice Found There*. Written in 1871, just as the trickier peaks of the Cuillin ridge were beginning to feel their first exploratory footfalls, it tells the story, in slippery and sinister gibberish, of the killing of a creature called the Jabberwock. It's a childhood spook story, conjuring up thoughts of strange, black monsters in the dark. 'Jabberwocky' is a work of atmospheric genius. It's incomprehensible, by and large, and yet by that same token so malleable that the mind can transform it into almost whatever it wishes, a kind of poetic Rorschach inkblot: vivid, and totally unique.

My interpretation was instant. The fantastical scene is sketched in the first stanza, a sequestered world with strange names and singular features:

> 'Twas brillig, and the slithy toves
> Did gyre and gimble in the wabe;
> All mimsy were the borogoves,
> And the mome raths outgrabe.

Here was Skye; its shifting tides, mists, boiling clouds, its light and rock. Then there was the thing in it. The thing itself, Carroll's 'manxome foe':

> 'Beware the Jabberwock, my son!
> The jaws that bite, the claws that catch!'

This clawed, toothed, dark and fearful thing *had* bitten me. Caught me. Got me, as predicted. But Carroll's Jabberwock was slain; I couldn't slay the Cuillin. It's not a human's place to slay a mountain: that's rule number one. 'Tis not the mountain we conquer but ourselves, and all that.

I didn't want to walk away, but then I didn't want to commit the deadliest sin of the mountain climber: that nasty mix of will, ego and bloody-mindedness that answers the siren call of a summit every time, until the bastard thing finally gets you and does you in. I'd had the smallest taste of the latter, and as much as I wanted to tuck the experience into a zipped pocket and leave it there, part of me couldn't help but wonder that perhaps this was a bit of a warning shot.

After my accident, the ridge sat at home with my family like a spiky shadow. Things were different now. No trip to the mountains would ever be casually dismissed. Always now, that little thought, creeping into frame. Anyone who spends time with anyone who spends time in mountains can't say it's never crossed their minds that at some point they might get a phone call they don't want to get. But then, you never think it's going to happen to you. Until it does.

I still didn't have a date for my operation. But after a couple of months of physio, I was starting to feel the first brushes of something which – in good light – might have been confidence. In the end it was Rachel who raised it.

'So are you planning on going back to Skye?'

'Well,' I said, as breezily as I could, 'if I can.'

'When?' Something in her voice.

'September, maybe. If, you know, I can.'

There was a pause. I could see she was trying hard to be supportive – balancing my peculiar needs with her own personal concern.

'I don't think you should do anything on your own.'

I considered raising the point that technically everything I'd done on my own had gone without a hitch and in that respect Kingsley had not exactly been a lucky charm, but who was I kidding? If I'd been on my own things would have been a hell of a lot worse.

'OK.'

'Please be careful.' She looked at me hard, her eyes finishing the sentence for her. 'Your guide's good?'

'He is.'

She nodded. Even before this, she had always worried.

By the late 1920s and early 1930s, things were shifting on Skye. The Depression, and the emergence of a new class of mountain adventurer, increased the natural schism emerging between Sligachan and Glenbrittle. There wasn't a rivalry between the two places, not exactly – more a kind of natural parting of ways and means. On the northern side of the ridge, the Sligachan Hotel was still where you'd find china and fresh linen and hot baths, for those who had the money to pay for them. Glenbrittle was its more kick-about counterpart at the ridge's southern end, where every summer a mini city of tents and spare-room hostelries, formal and informal, catered for the increasing numbers of scrappy young working-class climbers who were prepared to slum it in more rudimentary lodgings for a crack at the Cuillin's meatier end. The lack of tempting luxury in valley digs meant the climbers had less to hurry back for. Days were getting longer, routes harder and objectives more ambitious.

The road to Glenbrittle was too poor and the demand – while growing – was never great enough to make the village anything more than a backwater, which bred a particular intimacy and familiarity amongst those who stayed here. Everyone knew Agnes Chisholm's post office, where the postmistress would put climbers up in the adjacent annexe; also well known was Mary Campbell's Cuillin Cottage – once cruelly described as a 'howff' – where climbers slept in recess beds in the walls of the living room. A telling picture from the period shows E. W. Steeple and A. H. Doughty propped up in these, framed by doilies and frilly bits of linen, stoically smoking pipes and reading hardback books amidst a chaos of china, as if berthed in a chintz submarine.

There was also the MacRae barn, Glenbrittle House and the campsite. All the climbers of the time would speak of these establishments with the greatest of reverence, as if describing the house of a particularly dear aunt or a childhood holiday home – and all soon had their own Climber's Books. It's amazing what a warm welcome and hot meal does for your appreciation of a place following a long and sometimes dangerous day on the hill, and Glenbrittle in the first decades of the 20th century most certainly provided these.

Those who couldn't stay at either Sligachan or Glenbrittle might camp up in the corries. Early adopters of this practice were Steeple and Guy Barlow, who would place tents high up in Coire Làgan or Coruisk from which to mount assaults on the surrounding cliffs without the inconvenience of a walk-in every morning.

The toughest would make do with cracks under rocks and became sort of mountain hobos – leading to the pursuit of 'howffs', in the truest sense. Howffs are natural shelters – little caves, hollows, lean-tos – and their utilisation was an idea that had spread up from the hills outside Glasgow, from where people were increasingly venturing further north.

The formation of local clubs gave focus to groups of unemployed young men from industrially failing areas, most notably Clydeside in Glasgow, which had been hit hard during the Depression. This new breed of more steely, working-class versions of the well-to-do Scottish Mountaineering Club type occasionally took on a class-war mindset, but generally they were reverential and curious. On Skye the younger generation took inspiration from the literature left by the early Cuillin pioneers, and delighted in the moments when they bumped into those from an earlier era. Those from the older guard – the Raeburns, the Naismiths, the Inglis-Clarks – who were still active on the island sometimes came down the glen to partake of the hospitality and *craic* in a wilder, edgier shadow of the Cuillin than Sligachan. And there are a few notable examples where the paths of the generations crossed.

By the 1920s Collie and MacKenzie had become common fixtures around Sligachan, and occasionally Glenbrittle. The playwright St John Ervine visited Skye on holiday several times and wrote of:

> the stimulating sight [of] Collie and his friend and gillie, John MacKenzie, pacing up and down in front of Sligachan, two old men, one a distinguished scholar, the other a simple peasant, smoking their pipes and seldom speaking because their intimacy was such that it needed no words.

Despite their trips to the mountains becoming increasingly occasional, as the years passed they did do more than just pace – mostly fishing and

grouse shooting. Deer stalking was off the cards for Collie, who claimed
the animal was 'too high up the scale' to kill. In the evenings they were a
kind of novelty for tourists, and a thrill for the climbers who came to Skye
and knew their names.

Through the history of the black ridge you spot these encounters
between figures of different generations that feel, with hindsight, like the
passing of a torch – the end of one period and the dawn of another. Ben
Humble, on his first visit to Skye in 1929, unknowingly encountered John
MacKenzie, his day's catch in hand, by chance whilst seeking a bed for the
night. 'Here was an old man, yet walked easily, and his eyes were clear...'
he wrote later, before describing MacKenzie's appearance: 'a grand white
beard and an ancient suit of plus fours, heavy boots, a deer stalker's cap'.
Humble and his friend were invited in, sat around the fire and noted the
odd presence of a stack of *Alpine Journals* in the corner of his simple two-
room croft house. The young men caught the old man's attention when
they mentioned the Cuillin.

> Obviously he knew them well, for, instead of talking of danger and diffi-
> culty as most folk would have done, he said that Sgùrr Alasdair, the
> highest of them all, was 'just a walk, just a walk'. There seemed to be
> nothing about the Cuillin which he did not know.

On Humble's return to Glasgow he visited the library and suddenly
realised whom they'd had fallen in with that night. The trout MacKenzie
had been carrying was caught that day, in Loch Fada, with Collie. Pictures
of MacKenzie around this time show him precisely as Humble describes:
dressed in purposeful tweed, with an alpine hat pulled low over a white
beard, a dark slot for his eyes.

In his later life, as he grew out of his more exploratory endeavours in
the mountains and became more reflective, Collie's expression of his
feelings about the island turned ever more elegiac. He considered *Dreams*,
a meditation on landscape and memory, the best thing he'd ever written.
Beautiful, complex and nostalgic, it's difficult not to agree. Here's a passage
about the Highlands:

A land with as many changing moods as the white mists on the mountains, or the fleecy clouds weaving strange pageants athwart the azure sky. A land now glad with the soft kisses of the sunshine, now sad with the gloom of dark clouds and the memories of times gone by. A land of mystery, a land of the Heart's Desire.

Collie was growing old. Although still climbing into his sixties, his final trip to Canada in 1911 marked the end of serious expeditioning. In the following years he was increasingly busy, holding ever-more distinguished positions in both chemistry and mountaineering circles – his most cherished being as president of the Alpine Club, to which he was elected in 1919. Dorothy Pilley saw him at around this time, 'surrounded for us with the halo of the early mountaineering greats . . . we exchanged a few words which I wish [I] could remember.' Collie began to paint scenes of the Canadian Rockies and Skye, often in the company and under the guidance of Colin Phillip, with whom he rented Glen Brittle House every summer until 1915. Fittingly, given his chemical preoccupations with vibrant gases, colour was Collie's speciality on the canvas. The two would hold an open house for guests, tell ghost stories and occasionally revisit old climbs. MacKenzie was usually there. Then in 1919 he wrote a piece to be read before the Alpine Club entitled simply 'The Island of Skye'.

It's interesting to read the account of someone's life and times written from a distance, to see what rises to the surface, what emerges with relief from memory, like peaks on a ridgeline. By now Collie had made all his mountain discoveries. He had journeyed into the Himalaya, attempted Nanga Parbat and endured the loss of Mummery; climbed in Norway and the Alps, and hacked his way through the Canadian Rockies; throughout the Highlands and the Lake District there were routes and features bearing his name. The First World War had ended and taken with it many of the young climbers who were once frequent visitors to Skye. His mountain life was all under his boots and now it was time, in a way, to choose his favourite photographs to put on a shelf.

Collie picks his first sighting of Stocker and Parker on Sgùrr nan Gillean, and his meeting with MacKenzie, a warm tribute to the man who was at that time still a frequent companion. He talks of the long day when they climbed Sgùrr Dearg, then measured Alasdair, arriving back to Sligachan in the dark; about the bridging of the TD Gap and the unlocking of the ridge; and about the Cioch, and the marvellous fortune of the great unclimbed cliff of Sròn na Cìche. But what speaks loudest is Collie's wonder: his delight at simply being there, amidst glorious, glorious colour. The 'deep blue waters'; the 'delicate azure' of the sky; the 'rich colour of the grasses and the heather'; the 'clean brilliant tints that clothe the Skye moors in late autumn', so much more brilliant that the mainland; the 'delicate summer hues of amber yellows and gorgeous oranges and velvety browns'. And then there was the ridge and the dark purple of its corries, as if hung with antler felt. For Collie, the black ridge – the austere, sinister Cuillin – was riotous, a patchwork, 'a wonderful feast of colour'.

How nice that Collie's first significant writing about Skye was about numbers and measurements and exactitude, and his last was, really, all about colour. The Cuillin ridge was his laboratory. Exploring it, his experiment. And here, spilled onto the pages of the *Alpine Journal*, in wonderful hues like the noble gases that so entranced him, were his memories amongst them – in which the mountains and adventure and curiosity had become his life's choice. In *Dreams* he speaks of memory as a gift given by the gods, who 'have relented, and are … giving back some of the gold that they robbed from us in the days of long ago, when we troubled not that the years were slipping silently beneath our feet'. Now, at the end of his life, those memories – all that gold – were what he had left, along with a frustration about age and of the friends who had left him. A line in a letter from his Canadian guide Fred Stephens contained the unhappy words, 'I know Doctor you are far too old for any of that strenuous mountain climbing; isn't it Hell to get old when one don't want it.'

In 1933 John MacKenzie died. It seems to have been sudden; like Nicolson, gone 'in a moment', or at least swiftly enough to take Collie completely by surprise. MacKenzie was seventy-six, but astounded everyone with his spry and seemingly indefatigable energy well into elderly life, 'as fresh as a youth in his prime' even in his sixties, according to Sheriff Valentine. The loss was devastating to Collie. He wrote MacKenzie's obituary for the *Scottish Mountaineering Club Journal*, perhaps less hyperbolic than his earlier tributes, perhaps speaking of a sadness still numb. 'Those who knew him will remember him as the perfect gentleman,' he wrote, 'one who never offended by word or deed. There was only one John, simple minded, most lovable, and without guile. There is no one who can take his place.' Hugh Welsh would later write interestingly of Collie that 'John was more than a friend to him; one would almost think he was his other self.'

After MacKenzie's death, the seventy-four-year-old Collie walked alone to the summit of Am Bàsteir. It was believed to be the mountain on which the two had first climbed together. Unlike the callous attitude often exhibited by mountaineers, Collie was a sensitive man deeply affected by death. Whatever memories must have overcome him on that slender summit can only be imagined; it must have been deeply sad to look on the mountains, unchanged, speaking so much but saying nothing. The human equivalent might be imagined as growing older while a partner, or friend, or spouse didn't – that feeling of one life speeding away, while another remains just as you remembered it when you wore a younger person's clothes – rendering the change in yourself so much more real as a result. He would have been able to see the beginnings of his climbing career: the routes from Sligachan, all the peaks he'd climbed with MacKenzie, the peak that bore his own name, and those of his friends, the landmarks of his climbing life, from this island to some of the wildest places in the world. In a way, comforting: in another, cruel. When Collie returned to Sligachan he announced it was his last climb.

Collie's final years were marked by increasingly long periods on Skye in a kind of welcome but lonesome exile. Travel was difficult, and although still robust and agile, he was by now an old man and increasingly misanthropic. For ease, his haunt was mostly in Sligachan and its environs. A vestibule in a corner of the inn, near where Collie's Lounge is now, was then known as Collie's Corner – where its namesake would sit chewing his pipe and gazing out of the window. Very occasionally he would 'unbend' and engage (or not) with one of the many climbers to whom he had become something of a local dignitary – a sort of Hebridean *lama*, Sligachan his Dharamshala-upon-Sea.

'I often wondered what he thought of as he gazed out with far-reaching and listening eyes,' wrote the climber Hugh Welsh. 'Sometimes when spoken to, he seemed to return from a great distance.' Campbell Steven, author of

The Story of Scotland's Hills, described once meeting the elderly Collie at
Sligachan but found communication almost impossible due to the old man's
deafness. When war was declared in 1939 Collie was in residence, and it
effectively confined him to the island for the last four years of his life.
Unable, or unwilling, to make the journey to his house in London, he spent
much of his remaining energies writing worried letters home fretting over
the treasures he had amassed there and had now deserted amidst the falling
bombs of the Luftwaffe. Much of Gower Street was bombed, but Collie's
property and its contents remained intact.

The war threw a new, vaguely suspicious light on Collie's scientific background – particularly amongst young people. Derek Cooper wrote of his
childhood summer spent on Skye in 1939 in the shadow of the coming
conflict, and of hearing stories of a strange scientist who spent his days
walking the moors:

> He was, said the gossip in Portree, the world's leading expert in poison
> gases and had come to stay at Sligachan Inn while he worked out an
> even more deadly formulae in his mad, brilliant brain.

Sligachan's strange scientist's mood was as fickle as the Skye weather
beyond the window, and many descriptions depict him as a kind of wary
sheepdog. 'Collie was not communicative until he knew you,' wrote St John
Ervine. 'Then his conversation was rich and ample . . . but he could be
devastating to presumptuous people.' In the early 1930s, when Geoffrey
Winthrop Young introduced Collie to German climber Willy Merkl, eager
to discuss his upcoming expedition to a mountain the old man knew all
too well, he could not stomach the encounter. Recoiling when presented
with the young climber's neatly printed card – 'Leader of the Nanga Parbat
Expedition' – the crestfallen Merkl was ushered from the room, leaving
Collie, allegedly, 'muttering about the optical illusions presented by the first
character of the Chinese alphabet'. Winthrop Young described the encounter
as 'blond and bluff young modernist, efficient and hustling' meeting a
'supersensitive Wandering Scholar-artist out of the Middle Ages, with something of a werewolf lurking in his half-smile . . . the gap of time and
temperament proved unbridgeable.' Merkl wouldn't return from Nanga

Parbat. In echoes of Mummery – and, by this time, Mallory – in 1934, nine others would die there with him.

However unapproachable he seems to have been in those final years in Sligachan, a common term used of Collie was modesty, sometimes to the point of farce. The chemist E. C. C. Baly enjoyably recounted an occasion at Sligachan when a traveller began leafing through an album of photographs of the Cuillin, close to where Collie was sitting, casually enquiring as he did if the ancient, perpetually smoking resident had ever been mountaineering. Collie responded 'through the stem of his pipe' that he had done some. Upon being asked if he had climbed one particular peak in a picture, he replied with a solemn nod. The exchange had continued in a similar vein, to the same result, page after page, until the book was exhausted – the traveller increasingly incredulous, Collie consistently monosyllabic. In exasperation, the man pointed to the most extreme-looking peak in the book he could find and asked the same question. Upon receiving another nod, he exclaimed hotly: 'What are you, a steeple-jack?' Collie made no attempt to support his claims but merely continued smoking his pipe.

Amidst the remote echo of bombs and gunfire, there comes a final record of Collie's Sligachan haunt – and while it's been told many times, this book simply wouldn't be complete without it. On the continent, the Second World War was in full, murderous swing. Skye was difficult to access from the mainland, but those who found themselves training in the Highlands – pilots mainly – often sought peace and rest when off-duty, availing themselves of the clean air as a healthy balm away from the hot, oily onslaught of combat.

Let's put ourselves there. It's March 1940, and here we find two such young men, Noel Agazarian and Richard Hillary, on leave for four days, who have made their way on impulse to Skye on the ferry and draw up outside the Sligachan Hotel, where they are welcomed. Twenty-one-year-old Hillary, an Australian-born Spitfire pilot, wrote a book during the war called *The Last Enemy*, in which he described the hotel:

> From every window was the same view, grey mountains rising in austere beauty, their peaks hidden everywhere in a white mist, and everywhere the feeling of stillness ... turning now into night. I shivered. Skye was a world that one would either love or hate.

Hillary shares this sentiment with the landlord; who agrees, before adding that 'only mountaineers or fools would climb those peaks.' Hillary and Agazarian rest at Sligachan; they smell the odour of the ground after rain and the pine fire in their room, and are content. 'For these are the odours of nostalgia, spring mist and wood smoke, and never the scent of a woman or food.'

The two are alone at Sligachan – except for one other guest:

One old man, who had returned there to die. His hair was white but his face and bearing were still those of a mountaineer, though he must have been a great age. He never spoke, but appeared regularly at meals to take his place at a table tight-pressed against the window, alone with his wine and his memories.

The next morning dawns clear, and the two young men climb Bruach na Frithe, at first leisurely, then in greater haste, competing with each other for the summit.

With feet and hands we forced our way up … Once I slipped and dropped back several feet, cutting open my hand. Noel did not stop … I would not have forgiven him if he had.

Bursting with muscle fatigue and blinded by mist, Hillary feels the wind on his face and knows he's near the top. Agazarian beats him by two seconds, and the pair collapse on their backs.

The black wet rock cold against us, the deep mist against our faces, the sweat as it trickled in our eyes, the air in deep gulps within our lungs. The war was far away and life was very good.

They start to descend, the inn a mere speck in the distant mouth of the glen. Reaching the impasse of a stream, they take it in turns to strip and cross, Hillary falling in and soaking both their clothes. The March air is cold, but the brisk pace dries them, and by the time they reach Sligachan their only need is hunger. Over dinner the landlord hears the story of their novel descent and utters only, 'Humph'. And then Hillary writes, 'But the old man at the window turned and smiled at us. I think he approved.'

This is really the final glimpse we have of Norman Collie the mountaineer: a conspiratorial look, thrown across the room at two strangers. Strangers he would otherwise have ignored, were it not for a few caught words that spoke of misadventure and magnificence in the mountains.

However contrasting the images of elderly Collie and youthful Hillary, they would die just a few months apart. Hillary flew during the Battle of Britain, and in September 1940 – six months after his Skye interlude – was shot down by a Messerschmitt over the North Sea. In a miraculously lucky escape, he passed out but fell from his aircraft as it plunged to destruction, regaining consciousness just soon enough to deploy his parachute. He was terribly burned, but after several operations of painstaking reconstructive surgery, begged to be allowed to fly again. It was an act of gallantry that would achingly anger fate; during a training exercise in January 1943 his plane crashed over Berwickshire, killing him and his navigator.

Collie died on 1 November 1942 in his bed at Sligachan, at the age of eighty-three. His sickness had been mercifully brief; in the autumn of the previous year, whilst fishing in one of the Storr lochs, he'd stumbled into the water, the drenching giving him a deep cold and delivering a blow to his health that started a decline he couldn't halt. Following his fall, Collie wrote letters to friends telling them of his pain, which the doctor ascribed to neuritis, lumbago and sciatica. Having outlived many of his friends and contemporaries, Collie spent much of his remaining months alone, seeing only those who had become familiar faces to him on Skye, including his great friend G. H. Lee. There is an irony here: the man who came to the island nearly sixty years earlier to indulge in the innocuous pastime of fishing and found the dangerous game of mountaineering was spared by the mountains and finally fell foul of fishing. Skye was his place, and it was to Skye he gave himself.

Obituaries from the worlds of chemistry and mountaineering ran to great length and complexity, all giving a measure of a curious man of manifold interests, and one who loved Skye more than them all. Winthrop Young perhaps wrote the most perceptive – and backhanded – tribute to the man who had become his friend:

Most of us, as the years pass, find our once exclusive devotion to mountains becomes divided – at least, between them and more human ties.
Of all the wholehearted mountaineers I have known, Collie alone
remained to the end wholly and passionately devoted to the mountain
world. His old age and death may seem to have been, in the result, solitary... [but] he died surrounded by the unageing beauty of his principal
devotion.

This devotion was Collie's final contribution to the Cuillin's lore, the
reason people remember him as the one this place 'got' most of all. He was
buried in Skye earth, end to end with the grave of John MacKenzie behind
the church at Struan – finally at one with the island that had enraptured
him so deeply and captured him so completely.

15

Treasure

I

There's an old folk story attached to the Cuillin that's recorded in Otta Swire's *Skye: The Island and Its Legends*. The passage reads thus:

> In the Cuchuillins ... though exactly where must not be said, is a cave of gold. Unlike all other treasure caves, there are no barriers here between men and untold wealth. No magic word is required. No fearful monster guards the entrance. He who finds the cave may take as much gold as he needs and return as often as he desires more, but each time he enters the cave, and each time he uses the gold, he will become a little more evil and a little more evil, until he loses his soul. That is the price.

Now I was off the ridge, doing my physiotherapy and waiting for a hopefully far-off date for my operation, I'd gone back to bingeing on my now teetering pile of books about Skye before I returned in the autumn – self-medication for not being able to be there physically. I'd read Swire's book twice over the years but had completely missed the story about the evil cave of treasure. By odd coincidence, in the same week I was reading this and about Collie's memory 'gold', I was directed to a relatively obscure graphic novel that carried as its frontispiece a reference to this very legend in Swire's book, before hanging its hat almost entirely upon it. It was written by the best-selling fantasy author Neil Gaiman, and entitled *The Truth Is a Cave in the Black Mountains*.

I'd come across plenty of descriptions of Skye's outright otherworldliness – all those drama-dripping attempts to depict the island as something a misty step to the left of the normal. But here was a book that knowingly crossed the line into unreality. In it was Skye – always referred to as 'The Misty Isle' in the story, but effectively acknowledged as Skye by Gaiman in the author notes – with the Cuillin as a place free from the restrictions of mere metaphor, and set loose to be what it seems straining at its existential membrane to be: fantastical. And in all its strangeness, it captured this place better than so many straighter accounts that struggled to articulate not just the way it is to the eye, but the way it plays with the soul.

In its 'journey of travel and darkness', Gaiman's book is driven by familiar motifs – a quest, a guide, a goal – but becomes a collage of the many shades of Skye through the lens of fantasy. Here we have a diminutive traveller who enlists the services of a sinewy, red-haired guide with wolf-like features named MacInnes. An island that's sometimes there, sometimes not, depending on the mists and the intention of the traveller. A both literal and allegorical reward – 'the gold' – fraught with peril, heavy with dilemma and sacrifice.

By the time the narrative's moral conundrum rises to dominate proceedings, the impression you have of the island has taken possession of you. It's an extraordinarily unique evocation of Skye – and a wonderful surprise to me at a time when I thought I'd read most forms of literature on the island.

Even from afar, Skye always seemed to me a place where unreality and reality taunted each other. Many others have felt this way too. One of the most beloved love letters to Skye is in many ways a fantasy too. Alexander Smith's *A Summer in Skye* is a prose-poem in which the author's impressions of the island are expressed in a stew of locations, characters and scenes. It's filled with a haunting, strange melancholy, a mythology and seductiveness that perfectly capture the peculiar lure of this place. Written in 1864, Smith was also an off-comer – from Kilmarnock – and the book is a distillation of seven summers, not just one. It's beautiful, probably the most lyrical book ever written about the island. And it's powerful because it coalesces fact and legend, populating its stage with peculiar characters with ambiguous local names, bringing the past and present together so that they breathe

the same living air. 'In Skye I am free of my century,' Smith wrote. 'The present wheels away into silence and remoteness.' It's the only one of his books remembered today.

Skye's latter-day fame has been as a reliably nightmarish set piece, particularly the spired, unreal-seeming Storr and Quiraing, which also keep landscape photographers in thrall, and the island has lent its atmosphere to everything from science-fiction blockbusters to video games. This power to compel those it 'gets' – be they visitors to Skye or its denizens, the former often becoming the latter – is quite remarkable. Any place can inspire art. But sometimes the emotions this island, this ridge of mountains provokes, span a range of tones as extreme as the weather that washes over the place. Anger, joy, turmoil, despair, majesty, eeriness, a bearer of mythology, vehicle of adventure or catalyst of terror – to those sensitive to its power, Skye acts as a spur for whatever underlying emotion is then spilled out into verse, story, painting, photograph. The landscape speaks, then people translate this into whatever language they hear.

And one of those languages – an important one – is music. On a windy afternoon the previous autumn I'd briefly met up at the Sligachan Hotel with Donald Livingstone, a musician who plays and teaches all across the Hebrides, and lives just outside Broadford. His surname has earned him an inevitable nickname, to the degree that his actual name sometimes means little. I told Matt I was meeting him, and he looked at me blankly. I had to physically describe him, state his profession and remind Matt he'd guided him up the Inaccessible Pinnacle the previous year as well as met him on several social occasions before the penny had dropped.

'Oh, you mean Doc.'

A neat, solid man in his mid-forties with a rumbling Glaswegian accent, Doc had initially moved up to Skye to work in the hotel business. Then – after a stint driving a 'bank van', a kind of mobile cashpoint for the elderly or isolated to get their pension money – he fell into music, and he's been swimming in it ever since. 'I just wanted mountains and sea. I didn't care what I was doing,' he told me. 'Nobody cares what you do here. Which is good, because you end up doing a bit of everything anyway.'

I'd listened to his recently released CD, *Sleeping with Your Boots On*, which for me captured something of the textures of the island – the air and light

– in its sounds. Skye had gotten Doc, I knew that much from listening to his music, from reading his tracklisting – 'Westerly Seas', 'Wayfaring Songs', 'Cuillin Skies' – and looking at the cover of the album, a painting of a sleeping man beneath a window lit by a lighthouse, of boats on a sea, a high headland beyond.

'A lot of that album is based on how I feel about this place,' he said. 'When I'm out in the hills I get the beat, the rhythm of the walking . . . I've always got a tune in my head. It's a great place to rehearse.'

Doc moved to Skye in 1997 just after the bridge opened, and he witnessed the island shift from being an isolated place where nobody locked their doors to somewhere in the grip of change. 'Back then folk were just getting used to the civilisation of being able to drive to get their shopping, drive to Inverness. Before, it was a big ordeal. You might have to get the ferries overnight, they might be cancelled because of the weather,' he said. 'In winter, the pub became a real focus point. The bridge changed that. Things became less isolated.'

The island's transformation during the 20th century was remarkable. Derek Cooper, who wrote the affectionate but admirably unsentimental memoir *Hebridean Connection* about his youth on Skye in the 1940s and 50s, painted a picture of an island caught between past and present through the eyes of a person yearning for the future. Cooper's Skye was a place where kitchens smelled of paraffin and tea leaves, damp oilskins and fish, where brown water ran out of the taps and where curses were Gaelic in delivery and holy in nature: '*A Chruthaidheachd!*' ('Oh, Creation'!) and '*O Shiorruidh!*' ('Speak of the devil!'). Flora MacDonald was a folk hero, Bonnie Prince Charlie an ingrate for fleeing without gratitude.

Cooper described the winter as Skye's 'darker face' – a season when there wasn't much laughter about and drink reared its head. Catholicism had encouraged preservation of the Gaelic ways, but Presbyterianism – the 'Hebridean preoccupation with Sin' – quashed cultural quirks with 'evangelical thundering and the threat of eternal damnation'. Sunday was a good day to be buried: 'everyone was already in the right outfit and frame of mind.' And, of course, the Sabbath was dry, except to tourists. Many locals therefore took to touring around the island themselves, visiting remote hostelries to get a drink – an open secret, but a loophole to which most publicans turned a blind eye. The only caveat was that the drink had to be served with food, so the minimum requirement – cheese and sandwiches – was always placed 'in amongst the drams'.

'If you go to Lewis now you get more of an idea of how Skye used to be in some ways,' Doc told me. 'Luckily a lot of the kids have Gaelic now, so the music and the culture are keeping on like that here. But the old characters who are there, the old characteristics . . . they won't be replaced. I know people who are my age and above whose parents have Gaelic, whose kids have Gaelic, but they don't.'

I'd heard this said quite a lot. The Gaelic College – Sabhal Mòr Ostaig, near Armadale – had been established by entrepreneur Ian Noble in 1973, and was widely credited with preventing the Gaelic culture on Skye from sinking out of relevance following a period when it was in danger of doing just that. Indeed, following the forced exodus of the Clearances many held that the transplanted culture became stronger in Canada than in its homeland. Norman Collie observed it in 1899:

> This vague shadowy land of the Gael in which he sees beauty everywhere is now almost a thing of the past . . . The beautiful Blessings, Invocations, Charms, and old songs are being forgotten. Still, however, a few folk remain in whom the old spirit lives. An aged crofter who could say – 'Every morning I take my bonnet off to the beauty of the world,' or the old woman, throwing sticks into the sea – ''Tis sorrows I am throwing away,' they have the knowledge.

Many continue to blame the arrival of Presbyterianism for quashing the 'gregarious love of life' from the Highlands and Islands. Historian William MacKay wrote that it had 'to a great extent destroyed the songs and tales which were the wonderfully pure intellectual pastime of our fathers', suppressing the 'innocent customs . . . merriment and good fellowship out of the souls of its people [and] planting an unhealthy gloominess and dread entirely foreign to the nature of the Celt'.

It seemed that because of religion, landlords and the education system, the old ways hardly stood a chance. I asked Doc why he thought Gaelic culture was so rich in storytelling. 'The dark nights. People talked more,' he said. 'People were illiterate here for a long time. Some right up to the early 20th century. Everything was passed by word, it was all story.' He continued: 'The songs are still there but you need the language to keep the stories and the music going. And places like this.'

At that point a large number of people entered the bar: heavy, bearded men in tweeds, walkers in bright nylon, maybe a guide or two, all with hair slicked by the rain and expressions of great relief for being there. It was a bad day to be out. It made the inside better.

'The last big storm, there was a lock-in at the place I worked in Broadford,' Doc said. 'This hurricane wind was coming in, and I was driving down from Sconser. It was getting dark and I could feel the storm behind the car. I stopped at the pub, and there'd been a power cut. There were candles in there, fire, a fiddler playing, you could hear the storm outside, you're locked in, you're safe . . . the *craic* was tremendous.'

He went on to describe his local village hall, where there was a folk club a couple of nights a week. 'It's lovely at the night-times when you can hear the wind, and you know the building's an old building and it's had music in it for a long, long time. There's another building down at the Gaelic college, which has probably had *ceilidhs* in it for generations, and when you're in there singing or playing, you can almost feel everything coming out of the walls. And the hills are like that as well. That immediate attachment with history, that depth, up there in the Cuillin.' He pointed right towards the ridge through the wall. 'Because you know how old the mountains are, how long the people have been here. You can just feel it. It rises around you.' He paused. 'You know?' I did. And as history and my pile of books had proven, others knew too.

Skye's most decorated bard, Sorley Maclean, used the Cuillin itself to symbolise feelings of loss and longing, amongst much else. Maclean – or Somhairle MacGill-Eain – fought in the Second World War at the Battle of El Alamein, and in addition to a slew of honorary positions at prestigious universities around Scotland was awarded the title of *Filidh*, a Gaelic term for a poet on the cusp of transcendence, at the Gaelic College on Skye. He chose to call his longest, most complex and ultimately most tortuously laboured poem 'A' Chuilthionn (The Cuillin)'. Written in 1939, the ridge becomes a sink, a kind of evocation in rock for the bloodshed of battle, the

Clearances, the struggle of the Skye people – and of people everywhere –
against oppression, the range intrinsically bolted to the moods and trials
of those living around it, conversant with a world about to plunge into the
darkest conflict it has ever known. It's long for a poem, appearing in gathering forms over the course of fifty years and reaching 1,600 lines in one
incarnation. Its most famous passage runs:

> Beyond the lochs of the blood of the children of men,
> beyond the frailty of the plain and the labour of the mountain,
> beyond poverty, consumption, fever, agony,
> beyond hardship, wrong, tyranny, distress,
> beyond misery, despair, hatred, treachery,
> beyond guilt and defilement; watchful,
> heroic, the Cuillin is seen
> rising on the other side of sorrow.

Another modern poem of simpler, darker desperations is by Andrew
Young, this time up on the ridge, amongst its echoes and shadows, and
fears:

> Each step a cataract of stones
> So that I rise and sink at once,
> Slowly up the ridge I creep;
> And as through drifting smoke
> Of mist grey-black as a hoodie-crow
> The ghostly boulders come and go
> And two hoarse ravens croak
> That hopped with flapping wings by a dead sheep,
> All is so hideous that I know
> It would not kill me though I fell
> A thousand feet below;
> On you, Black Cuillin, I am now in hell.

But the literature of Skye isn't all dark rumination. Ben Humble, the
young man who fortuitously fell in with John MacKenzie that day, would

return to Skye both during and after the war, and would write probably the best book about the ridge – *The Cuillin of Skye* – in 1952. The front and endpapers of the book carry an extraordinary rendering by artist Arthur R. Griffith depicting the Cuillin in black, scratching lines that makes it look like it's built from curled bark, savage and dramatic. Because Griffith has omitted names of any kind, as well as contours or any other interference that detracts from the purity of the rock, the ridge looks strangely naked, as if it has just been made, as if humans had nothing to do with it.

Humble's book also contains many images of the Skye climbers of the time, of which one in particular stands out: W. H. Murray.

Murray and Humble were in some respects the spiritual heirs to Nicolson and Collie – the philosophical prose-poet and the idiosyncratic man of science. Both Murray and Humble left legacies to the Cuillin in books and photographs that are more notable than their mountaineering on or below the ridge – this was the 1930s, and the Cuillin was now 'under the microscope', to use a common term, as far as new climbs went. But the attitude had, again, shifted. From the curiosity of the early days, to superstition, to science, to horrified wonder, to the pursuit of a goal in the relentless quest to be 'first', the years between the wars brought a new emotion up into the rafters of the ridge: escape.

There are several curious parallels between Humble and Collie. Like Collie, who was steeped in the fields of physics and particularly X-rays, Humble too was a scientist and a lover of numbers – a dentist specialising, uncannily, in radiology. Born in Dumbarton in 1904, his first visit to Skye was in 1929 in a cattle-class cabin on the antiquated steamer *Glencoe*. Humble's was the quintessential experience of Skye between the wars: the island remained challenging to reach and still relatively free of the trappings of tourism, yet full of diversion and adventure for those awake to its potential. He slept in Agnes Chisholm's Glenbrittle homestead where he touched George Mallory's signature in her guest book. He was plagued by midges, walked through rain on the Trotternish peninsula, and, following his serendipitous meeting with MacKenzie, climbed Sgùrr Alasdair on the ageing guide's advice – triggering a fascination with the Cuillin that would never leave him. Like Collie, Humble was an exacting photographer and an articulate writer, producing three books about the island. The first was an account of his 1929 summer, *Tramping in Skye* (1933), followed by *The Songs of Skye* a year later. Then, in 1952 he wrote his black ridge epitaph: *The Cuillin of Skye*.

According to his nephew Roy Humble – who later wrote a biography of his uncle entitled *The Voice of the Hills* – 'Ben's whole life turned on that 1929 holiday to Skye.' Humble wasn't the best climber; although he was 'competent and never came off', as one partner commented, he had issues with balance, having slowly become deaf from the time of his schooldays. Communication was also therefore understandably difficult, with complicated exchanges requiring the use of a notebook. This fostered a determined mindset; grasping at the hope of recovery, Humble never learned to lipread, and he spent a term at dental college carving his name on a desk out of sheer boredom being unable hear a word the lecturer was saying. He couldn't hear his own voice either, and this gave him a distinctive delivery often suffixed with a long 'aaaaah', which many observers remarked was particularly expressive and unique.

Humble's deafness understandably meant he had a slightly abrupt and distant persona; Collie enjoyed a similar reputation in his dotage at the Sligachan Hotel, also on account of deafness, though his was age-related. Both were prone to playfulness – Collie was well known for his ghost stories and the skilful withholding of information for his own amusement, and one associate once described Humble as 'an imp of mischief'. While Collie's haunt was Sligachan, Humble was, for want of a better term, a humbler guest, choosing to camp or bed down wherever was close to the mountains, particularly at Glenbrittle. He was well known for his love of the howff, or natural shelter, where he would forgo comfort for the sensory proximity of nature's night. 'The inside of a tent is always the same,' he once said, but 'each howff is different, each has its own charm, each its own memories.' A tea room was even named after him in Portree in recognition of his contribution to tourism in Skye. Humble recalled visiting it after the tribute had been made, and upon finishing his tea 'was presented with the bill in the usual way'.

Superficial similarities aside, more significant was the fact that like Collie, Humble fell into the embrace of the Cuillin and found himself seduced by it in the most profound and lasting way. He devoted much of his life and himself to the mountains – receiving an MBE for his statistical services to mountain rescue in 1971. Humble maintained throughout his life, and in the first paragraph of *The Cuillin of Skye*, that the Cuillin had 'no equal in all the world', repeating it to the man who accompanied him on many of his adventures in those mountains, when presenting him with a copy of the book. The man would later write of Humble: 'I knew from his voice that he meant it.'

This was William Hutchinson 'W. H.' Murray, one of the most extraordinary mountain characters of any age. Born in Liverpool in 1913, and perhaps more poetically inclined than Humble, Murray was a romantic and a mystic who saw mountain climbing as a way that would lead him, in the words of his biographer Robin Lloyd-Jones, to 'inner purification . . . and oneness with Truth and Beauty'.

The intricacies of Murray's philosophies require a book in themselves, and would develop rather more following the Second World War – but even as a youngster he had no interest in competitive mountaineering. Murray instead found kinship with Ben Humble, whom he met in 1935. Both men loved to write and to climb, relishing the visceral quality of the mountains, and both gave considerable amounts of time in later life to mountain rescue.

Their friendship led to one of the iconic photographs of the Cuillin. At around 8 o'clock in the late sunlight of a June evening in 1936, Murray walked onto the slab of the Cioch, that striking protuberance from Sròn na Cìche, as the light was beginning to deepen. Humble, further up the ridge, began to take pictures. As sunset approached, a rising mist began to creep up into Coire Làgan, creating a blanket of serenity beneath the pinnacle, upon which the figure of Murray stood in a contemplative stance, creating a perfect silhouette.

It was a grand moment, albeit hard won. Standing on Collie's 'great discovery,' Murray lingered a long time on the Cioch, unable to communicate with the photographer, who was waiting for the perfect shot. 'I found his photography a sore trial of my patience,' Murray would write of Humble and his camera. 'He was so keen, his eye so constantly given to the endless search for dramatic stances, unusual lighting, right composition, revealing effects, that hours would seem to go by while we dilly-dallied.' Despite a 'trying hour', Murray described the picture as 'true to the Cuillin at their best'.

Soon after, war was declared. Humble made educational films for Britain's effort, his deafness ruling him out of active service. Murray was conscripted into the Argyll and Sutherland Highlanders, and was shipped out to the Middle East. In 1942, during the campaign in the Western Desert, Murray's regiment was pinned down by a German Panzer division. Upon destroying everything in his pockets that might be of use to the enemy – compass, identity card – he came across an address book which, he noted, contained mostly the names of mountaineers. 'I had the sudden realisation of what they had given me over the years, all that I'd learned from mountains and men,' Murray would write.

That night, battle raged. Tanks glowed red with the batter of shells, and many soldiers died. Murray was captured and found himself confronted by a German commander pointing a machine-pistol at him. Murray held his breath. The man lowered his gun. 'Are you not feeling the cold?' he remarked, of his meagre fatigues. Murray responded that it was as 'cold as a mountain top'. The tank commander then exclaimed, 'You climb mountains?' and the war suddenly seemed the only difference between these two desert-grounded, war-struck and homesick young men.

The German put his gun away, gave Murray a coat, and the two shared food and a beer, talking of 'the Alps, Scotland, rock and ice'. Murray said to the man, 'Mountains give us some good things. Friends worth having, battles worth fighting, beauty worth seeing.' The man responded: 'We call it Leben. It means, "to be alive".'

Murray was transferred to a string of prisoner-of-war camps, first in Chieti, Italy, then Czechoslovakia and Germany,where – amongst worsening conditions – he retreated in his mind to the cold and vital slopes of the Cuillin, in words and verse:

> Coming down late
> I race against dark;
> Trip over stars,
> Catch at the moon,
> Plunge in its beams
> My eyes held
> While my feet
> Set the mountain running.

During his incarceration Murray would write two drafts of a book, both
on toilet paper. The first was discovered held closely on his person, and was
confiscated by suspicious Gestapo interrogators. The second survived the
war, and would become one of the finest books ever written about the British
mountains: the inauspiciously titled *Mountaineering in Scotland*. It opens with
a chapter entitled 'Twenty-Four Hours on the Cuillin' – written about his
holiday there with Ben Humble in 1936. This is the first paragraph:

> It was ten o'clock at night, in Glen Brittle. The June sun had left our little
> cluster of tents, which nestled behind a screen of golden broom between
> the Atlantic and the Cuillin. Eastward, the peaks were written along the
> sky in a high, stiff hand. High above us, the brown precipice of Sron na
> Ciche, which reacts, chameleon-like, to every subtle change of atmos-
> phere, was dyed a bright blood-red in the setting sun.

It was during one of these snatched days in June 1936 that Humble
captured that photo of Murray on the Cioch. Taken before the war and
published after, here was an image burning through the trauma of conflict:
a hard silhouette between sunset and sea. It was the emotion of the time,
the new attitude that flowed in the words and pictures these two men left
behind them, and indeed held on to them for dear life through the darkest
hours of humanity; Murray's from the hell of a POW camp, Humble's from
a soundless world where images and feeling meant everything. 'There is a
voice that the deaf can hear as clearly as any other person,' he wrote. 'The
voice of the hills.' Here, high in the Cuillin, sung by that voice to both men,
was *joy*. Escape. A place where the need to discover and pioneer gave way
to the honest, life-affirming *joy* of simply being. Being in that place, where
whatever horror that lay beneath the swirling clouds – back in the real
world, back in the complicated world – meant nothing. Lay unseen, beneath.
To be there. *Leben*. To be alive.

It's easy to become lost in the mythologised stories of people who
are no longer with us. Ben Humble died in 1977 in his seventies; Murray
in 1996 in his eighties. They left us great stories, well told; but left us
they have.

As I prepared to go back to Skye, I began to grow despondent that times were indeed changing and that a lot of what I'd been reading about had gone forever. Those who had made these pioneering firsts, who linked back to those who knew those who had known Humble, Collie, MacKenzie, Hart, Nicolson, Forbes, MacIntyre – that Cuillin-hewn stratigraphy of pioneers – all eroded away, with only their names left standing in the mountains. I found myself wishing I could bump into someone from another time myself; have one of those fortuitous meetings with someone who had been there, someone who had felt the thrill of a true 'first' on the ridge in a way that I never would, or could. A hand I could shake, that had shaken that of Humble, say, who had in turn shaken MacKenzie's, whose hands had shaken Collie's, and Naismith's, the Pilkingtons', Nicolson's even – whose hands had been the first to touch the rocks on the Cuillin's most famous reaches. But that time was over. The generations had shifted into history, along with everyone who'd been there. Climbing accidents, illness, old age. Those who were there in the thick of it, who knew others who were in the thick of it, were all gone. All except one.

II
Glen Coe, West Highlands

A rainstorm has passed. The afternoon air has that gleam as I ease the car into a spacious driveway just beyond the neck of Glencoe village. As I get out of the car and stretch sore muscles, there's a movement in the workshop to the right. It turns into a lean figure, moving stiffly with a stoop, but with purpose, up the gravel. Here is a very tall, very old man – nearly ninety – but one who has that bearing, like they say, of a mountaineer. A man who had seen more of life, and a lot more of death, than most of us. He wears a red fleece and a pale cloth cap, and walks up to me and holds out a hand as gnarled as a birch branch. As I shake it, I make my own link to the Cuillin's history. Everyone in mountaineering knows this man's name, but around here and across the Highlands, everyone knows him simply as Hamish.

From his birth in Glasgow in 1930, his falling-in with the infamous Creag Dhu climbing club who used tenacity forged in the clinker-and-grit of the Glasgow shipyards to batter their way through the snow and rock of the Highlands, to the largest expeditions ever mounted amidst the world's greater ranges, Hamish MacInnes was there. Hamish the engineer invented the first all-metal ice axe, and the stretcher that made mountain rescue practical on challenging ground. Hamish the safety man, who ensured the well-being of movie stars in the mountains. The lives of Sean Connery, Robert De Niro and Clint Eastwood have all hung on the end of his rope. Hamish the author: twenty-six books. The mountain rescue pioneer: he founded the Glen Coe team and the Search and Rescue Dogs Association, and has an honorary OBE and doctorate to his name for it. The Cuillin climber – with more first ascents to his name on the ridge than anyone. You could argue that nobody alive has more mountain under their boots than Hamish MacInnes. And there's no single person to whom more survivors of mountain accidents owe their lives.

They call him 'the Fox of Glencoe' not because of his once red hair – Neil Gaiman's 'MacInnes', the wizened guide in his strange tale of the Black Mountains, also fits this description – but because he always had a habit of escaping whatever scrape he found himself in. He's been avalanched five times. Declared dead three times. Been embedded in big international expeditions, explorations and adventures too numerous to list and sometimes too madcap to believe. We'll pick two at random: the audacious ridge traverse of Shkhelda in the Caucasus, reached in a Mini, and tackled on a diet of Complan and caviar. And his notably crackpot attempt on the then unclimbed summit of Mount Everest in 1953, a fast-and-loose, highly illegal two-man affair with John Cunningham, that aimed to magpie the supplies of a previous expedition. A rival, more authorised team with porters and yaks and support teams and eight tonnes of equipment beat the two Scots to it. Their lead climbers: Tenzing Norgay and Edmund Hillary. If they hadn't, you suspect Hamish might just have made it.

But it was on the Cuillin that he made the history that I wanted to hear about. On Skye his climbing record is unmatched. He has reputedly put up the most first ascents on the Cuillin – 28 in total. The names of the routes vary from the dramatic ('The Crack of Double Doom,' 'Depravity', 'Vulcan Wall', 'Odysseus'), the mystically sinister ('Styx', 'Prometheus', 'Creep'), to the painfully anatomical ('Prolapsis'), the functional ('Access Gully', 'Route One', 'Central Pillar'), to the amusing ('Grand Diedre', 'Penitentiary Grooves').

These are, of course, all rock climbs, things with hand-jams and belays and grades. But two polarising experiences that define Hamish MacInnes's Skye story are also pivotal in the Cuillin's history – two events, within three years of each other, both over half a century ago. One, the final great first: the winter traverse of the Cuillin ridge, the ultimate British expedition, and the last of the Cuillin's to yield. Bright, white, happy and glorious. And the other: a central role in the aftermath of its biggest disaster.

I was just a little worried that he might not remember all of this himself. Hamish's friend and neighbour Rob Taylor, an American fellow climber, warned me before coming that recent years in Hamish's life had been less swashbuckling, if no less visceral. Hamish had nearly died, he said. But that had been only the start of his nightmare.

Two years ago, a urinary infection had spread and sent him into a spiral of confused illness. A collapse outside his home led to him being hospitalised, then sectioned – with Hamish believed to be in the grip of dementia, and a danger to himself. It was, Hamish says, an illegal diagnosis. The eighty-six-year-old, whose relatives mainly live far away, disappeared into the healthcare system and was eventually deposited in a psychiatric hospital. To friends, he simply vanished; one day he just wasn't there. In a fog of illness and medication he lost his memory. His weight plummeted from fourteen to eight stone and by the time he was tracked down he was dying. Their intervention and a slow, painful rehabilitation led, in all appearances, to a miraculous recovery. Back here in his idyll-like Glen Coe home his handshake is firm, his eyes bright. He's still gaunt, his words flinched out through a pain in his jaw, but he's cheerful, courteous and in every respect back from whatever death he had come close to in recent months.

I follow Hamish into the house. Through the doorway I catch the faint smell of whisky, then enter the bright, open living room, where an armchair stands before open bay doors, beyond which lies the most extraordinary Highland view. The outdoors breathe into the room, and into every sense. The mountains of Glen Coe stand steeply on either side, reflected in a group of small, landscaped lakes just beyond the balcony. It's a like a cross between a Japanese garden and a northern wilderness: one man's personal paradise, its backdrop the mountains where he has lived and worked for over half a century as a cornerstone of Scottish mountain rescue.

'Will you have a cup of tea? Got lots of biscuits,' he says, his voice a bright sing-song that whistles on the 's'. He sits in an easy chair, we drink tea and conversation gradually turns to the island a hundred miles to the north-west.

'You know, my mother was from Skye,' he says. 'Camastianavaig, just round the coast from Portree. That peninsula, where you can walk along the coast to Sligachan. I first went when I was four. Took the boat from Glasgow, straight to the island.' Then he adds, just a touch slower, 'That doesn't happen any more.'

The remarkable thing about Hamish's recent salvation is that it was his own past that ended up rebuilding his present. His own memories – recorded in books, on film and in thousands of photographs – of places, of people, of mountains he could once read like faces.

'I've been reading back over my life and times, you know. I couldn't remember anything. Now I can remember the Cuillin like it was yesterday. Not just the ridge, which is amazing, but the situation. I've got almost a hundred per cent memory recall now.' He was quiet for a minute. 'And I've got some terrible memories of Skye.'

It began with a fleeting sight, a blur of motion, from the mouth of Coire Làgan. It was early afternoon on New Year's Day 1963, and Hamish was taking the air outside Cuillin Cottage in Glenbrittle, where he was visiting friends for Hogmanay. He had just finished pruning some of the surrounding trees, when looking up towards the snow-silvered Cuillin he noticed a man running very quickly down the path from Coire Làgan. When he arrived, Hamish caught the smell of blood on the man – 'That stale smell, which one who works with corpses doesn't forget and recognises instantly,' he would later write.

The man told him there had been an accident on the Dubhs Ridge: two dead, a third in a bad way. The party was part of a bigger group, seven men and seven women, from two university mountaineering clubs who had walked in to the Coruisk Hut to celebrate Hogmanay. With the ridge in rare winter condition, three of the more experienced members had left the evening before to traverse the Dubhs, the spur of spires that intersects the main ridge close to the TD Gap. It was an impulsive move; no one had a head torch and one man lacked crampons – essential equipment on the hard ice of the slopes. It would seem the lesson was learned the cruellest way: a slip, a sudden jerk on primitive rope, and one had pulled all three into the plunge of An Garbh-choire like coins down a well, landing in a broken pile in one of the most remote points on the island.

The man who arrived smelling of blood in the garden of Cuillin Cottage was George Wallace. After a sleepless night, at dawn on New Year's Day he'd set off from Coruisk with four others – Robert Russell, Colin Stead, Cammy MacLeay and Alan Laird – to search for the missing. The group split into two, one retracing the Dubhs route, and the other climbing onto the ridge crest near the TD Gap, with neither group losing sight of the other. A misheard shout from the former to the latter raised the spectre of hope – they were found and were safe! – briefly. Then came the discovery of an ice axe lying in the snow, then a glove, then sliding crampon marks, then spots of blood in the snow. These led a hundred metres down a snow-packed gully into An Garbh-choire, to the by now inevitable find at the end of it. Inevitable or not, it was still a shock.

The three who had fallen were John Roycroft, Tom Reid and John Methven. They were young: twenty-eight, twenty-three and nineteen. Roycroft was dead, face down on the step, his crampons wrenched off by the fall. Reid appeared to have survived the impact enough to have moved up to a sitting position against the rock with his arms folded, but he, too, was dead. Methven had been the one without crampons, and he was still alive, mumbling and moving his head, but in too terrible a state to move. The three were still roped together.

It was decided that Wallace, with good knowledge of the ridge, would cross to Glenbrittle to raise the alarm. Russell set off for Coruisk to fetch blankets and shelter, while Stead remained with Methven, awaiting the arrival of MacLeay and Laird. By the time Wallace reached Hamish it was mid-afternoon. With no formal rescue team yet on Skye, Hamish put out a call for help to the entire West Highlands.

The logistics were chilling. Hamish had been involved in rescues over the Christmas period, and was exhausted. The rest of the mountain rescue contingent of the West Highlands were celebrating Hogmanay and were miles away – not to mention hungover, or still drunk – as were most ferry pilots who could convey them to the island. Added to this was the remoteness of Coruisk, where the rest of the party were located, and the fact that the Cuillin ridge was enjoying one of its rare periods of full winter cover: both the cause of the accident and the principal challenge in its rescue. The ridge, forming a barrier between Glen Brittle and Coruisk, made communication between the two groups not only difficult but time-consuming and hazardous to achieve. This still being a world of landlines, poor roads and primitive rescue equipment, it was a reedy call for help in a dark, cold and vast country. And yet, inbound to Glenbrittle on treacherously icy roads, the response came.

Nobody below knew that high on the ridge, the complexion of the situation had changed. After surviving the night on the ledge, while Colin Stead helplessly watched, at 2 p.m. John Methven had quietly succumbed to his injuries. Rescue had become recovery. 'I remember that time vividly,' Stead would later write. 'I sat shattered and lonely. It was my first experience with death.' The other group arrived to the sound of Stead's whistle. And together they returned to the hut to break the news to the rest of the party.

There was no way of communicating this to the scrambling parties down in the valley: the distances, the weather and the difficulty of crossing the ridge to pass on word made it impossible. By midnight three separate groups had arrived: an RAF team from Fort William, a team of mountaineers who had piled into a sliding Mini Cooper to rush over from Kintail, and Hamish's group on the ground in Glenbrittle. Torchlights blinked on the ridges; a cutting east wind made it uncomfortably cold, and a series of missed rendez-vous made confusion rife – on ground that threatened to throw the rescuers off with every step.

Eventually Hamish's party judged that nothing more could be gained before daybreak, and made the exhausting journey along the coast to the Coruisk hut. They arrived at 2 a.m., where they joined the remainder of the tragic group, who were processing the news that three of their party were dead. Concerned for the well-being of any would-be rescuers heading onto the ridge that night, from the other side of the ridge, MacLeay and Stead – evidently men of considerable fortitude – set off to Glenbrittle along the coast path, reaching the valley just as the RAF team were about to set off.

Hamish, meanwhile, passed the remainder of the night in the Coruisk hut, preparing for a dawn push to recover the bodies from the ridge. The atmosphere in the remote building was dreadful, one of haunted grief – monosyllabic conversations, screams from sleep, numb shock and exhaustion, and the sounds of a windstorm moving in over the sea. Minute by minute, the team waited for morning.

The most hazardous hours were yet to come. The RAF team arrived at 11 a.m. the following day in *The Western Isles*, a fishing-turned-passenger boat from Glenbrittle, organised by team leader John Hinde. Attention then turned to the recovery of the frozen bodies from one of the most inaccessible corries in Scotland.

Hamish would later write, 'For the thirty-five of us on that evacuation it was a living hell.' Crampons scratched on icy rock, bodies were lowered precariously on ropes and slipped around in cumbersome stretchers, which themselves became jammed in chimneys and trapped between rocks that didn't want to give them up. For the rescuers, who by now also numbered some Junior Mountaineering Club of Scotland boys, it was ghoulish, treacherous work: 2,300 vertical feet of slabs, ice and boulders. At one point a body slid off the stretcher and headbutted one of the rescuers, whose response was – in his own words – to 'shit bricks ... I thought he'd come to life.' When the bodies were finally deposited at the Coruisk hut, frozen and shrouded, one of the holidaying walkers caught sight and fainted.

The 1963 New Year rescue on Skye remains the longest and most gruelling ever attempted in Scotland. It was the perfect storm of geography, conditions, timing, physical challenge and communication difficulties, straddled across the most dangerous ridge in the country. And, of course, it demonstrated just how badly things can go wrong – how terribly a recreational, celebratory holiday can become a tragedy of the most awful kind with a series of bad decisions and a single slip. But the most extraordinary thing about the rescue was not the tragic outcome – which it's likely no rescue could have prevented – but the response. The will, against all the odds, to try to help. And when that failed, the risk undertaken to mount a recovery. Of how far the tenacity and will of those who put themselves into harm's way to rescue the injured (or, perhaps even more admirably, recover the dead) can stretch. And also, just how numb it seems necessary to become if you make that journey into the darkest side of mountaineering.

On *The Western Isles*, bucking in the storm with three dead climbers strapped to the deck, rum began to flow. Someone started to sing, and before long the words of the folk song 'The Titanic' filled the boat as it left the embrace of the Cuillin for Elgol:

> The lifeboats they set sail
> Across the dark and stormy sea
> And the band struck up
> With 'Hail my lord to thee'
> Little children sobbed and sighed as the waves went o'er the
>   side,
> It was sad when the great ship went down.

One of the RAF rescuers, Ian 'Spike' Sykes, recorded the ordeal in his book *In the Shadow of Ben Nevis*. 'It may seem callous,' he wrote, 'but rescuers have a way of making light of death. Not through any disrespect . . . [but] a release from a very grim situation. If we took the thing too seriously we would never be able to do the job.'

I asked Hamish what he remembered of the Skye New Year rescue. He nodded slowly and, for the first time, heavily. 'All of it. It was a real epic. I was five nights without sleep. The thing is,' he said, 'I have to talk about then and now. Then, there were no radios and no good gear. When I formed the Glencoe team in 1961, these blokes were shepherds.' He pointed a finger out of the open window, down the glen. 'The Eliotts, the local farmers. They were going out to help people in wellies or shepherds' boots. No ice axes, just a crook. No headlamps, just an old paraffin storm lantern, you know? That's why, when I got here, I thought, this is ridiculous – we've got to get some help, get a proper team formed, as climbing is escalating. And the danger is . . .' He paused, as if this was perhaps something rarely considered. '. . . on a rescue, rescuers have to go out in conditions you wouldn't normally go out in. So it can be very dangerous.'

Mountain rescue has been Hamish's life. Hamish's choice. His books give an affectionate but matter-of-fact snatch of a time of change, with death simply a part of life in the mountains – albeit one battled against with spirit. In one book, *Call Out*, there's a series of black and white photos from the 1970s. Most consist of the usual gritty fare of people bundled into warm-weather gear amongst black rocks, detail lost to print-grain, snow merging with white sky. It looks cold and grim. There are a few portraits of some of the team members mentioned, some smiling, some squinting against the Highland weather, a landscape or two, and a few images snatched from between hips and knees during rescues. And one that's rather different. It's a photo of a dead body.

I'm not a voyeur of such things. I'm squeamish and can't even handle the bodies of birds that have flown into the house wall or mice caught by the neighbour's cat. Some find images of frozen corpses, left where they died on Mount Everest in their down-suit coffins, grimly interesting and – because these people, these souls, took a gamble with their lives and paid the price – somehow acceptable to ogle. But you rarely see images of mountain accidents here in Britain. And for that reason, or possibly others, I couldn't stop looking at the image in Hamish's book.

It's not gruesome. The figure – a man of middle-age, maybe – lies flat in a bed of rocks, crumpled into the shape of the ground, but not unnaturally. His left arm is thrown above him and loosely clenched, his right arm rests on his stomach. He's dressed in the clothes he put on to keep him warm, to keep him safe, clothes he would have expected to remove that evening, perhaps in a pub, in the room where he left the rest of his things. His head is thrown back, mouth slightly agape, his features anonymous slits in a carapace of black blood. Other than this last detail, he could be asleep. But something even about the way he lies there tells you he's not. Even without the brief caption – 'A fatality' – you know. The man is not asleep. He's dead.

I didn't find it traumatic to look at. Just very, very sad. Nor did I find it an incongruous addition. As I'd been told before, bodies were bodies, part of the proceedings in these hard, unforgiving places. Part of mountain rescue life. In a way, a book on mountain rescue could be considered remiss not to feature the result of a 'bad shout' – like a book on surgery without any glistening visuals. Bodies weren't something that could be ignored, something that could be avoided, despite everybody trying.

I noticed in reading accounts of the New Year disaster on Skye that as soon as the men were dead, they lost their names and their gender, and became objects. The *bodies*. The *dead*. Perhaps this was a way of dealing with the awful reality, to objectify them. I ask Hamish about this, and the tone of his voice softens. 'M-huh,' he says. 'You get so used to death.' His voice falters. 'Except when a kid gets killed. You don't get used to that.'

A silence grows in the room. I'm keen to break it and steer the ship out of potential darker territory, out and away from all this gloom, perhaps to Hamish's other piece of Cuillin history. It was three years later, in January 1965. And the black ridge was bright white.

Winter in the Cuillin – as I'd experienced myself – can be rough, grey, cold and wet. The ridge rarely holds snow for long, and when it does it's even rarer for what is Britain's most alpine ridge to clutch on to it for long enough for it to solidify into what you might call 'condition' – that is to say stable, consolidated and complete coverage. The scientific reasons would be the ridge's coastal position and the wind; if you prefer something more romantic, it's that ancient fires still burn in the mountains, melting the snow that clings to them.

The first winter ascents of the main peaks had been long claimed, colourfully enough by three Eton schoolmasters – T. Cunningham Porter, A. Benson and H. T. W. Tatham – who between them managed to ascend most of the big names of the range in opportunistic assaults over five consecutive winters in the late 19th century. A full winter traverse was quite another matter, however. Here were all the complexities of the summer traverse with the added vagaries of winter conditions.

With a keen eye on this final prize, in the settled cold of early 1965 Hamish made a call to Tom Patey, an Ullapool doctor, and announced he was leaving for Skye to 'take a look' at the ridge, and he'd see him at Sligachan later that night. Patey had looked at his clock and seen that it was already 10 p.m. 'Who else,' Patey would later write, 'but Hamish MacInnes would phone at this hour with such a preposterous suggestion?' The answer to 'who else?' was probably Patey himself. He was a doctor, but also something of a hellraiser in the climbing world. Hamish tells me that Patey would often hear of a party in North Wales on a Friday, grab his 'squeeze box' (he was an accomplished accordion player) and drive ten hours through the night from Ullapool, enjoy himself, then reverse the procedure – returning in time for his Monday morning surgery.

As it happened, the plan proposed in that particular late-night phone call didn't come to fruition; Hamish ploughed into a snowdrift on the way to Skye and was forced back to Glen Coe – but the idea was planted, and on 31 January a team of four was assembled, ready to wait for the snow that would qualify the outing as being a 'winter traverse'. This was a thorny subject, as when could a ridge famed for not holding snow be classified as being, to use mountaineering parlance, 'in condition?'

'Tom said that the best time to do the ridge is when there's no snow at all on the lower ground – but you look up and the Cuillin themselves are plastered,' Hamish tells me. 'And because of the extra altitude, at night it freezes and you get this wonderful névé – excellent for climbing on.'

Patey's article on the first winter traverse of the Cuillin is very funny. Some of it may be true, too. The complicating factors of cold, questionable snow tenacity and witheringly short days meant a single-day traverse was out of the question, which meant a night out. Patey and fellow climber Brian Robertson were recovering from a late and spirited night at a ceilidh, whereas MacInnes and his companion Dave Crabbe were fit and primed after an early night. The bickering was good-natured but near constant. Patey had the idea of carrying rucksacks up to Sgùrr na Banachdaich with overnight gear beforehand to save weight, but Hamish said that he thought that was cheating. In the end an ethical compromise was reached, with rucksacks packed with the heaviest bivouac gear left at the summit of that central, relatively comely summit.

Despite Robertson stopping every half-mile to be sick, and Crabbe breaking a crampon – a serious problem, meaning he could climb only with one full foot and a heel – the first part of the north–south traverse from Sgùrr nan Gillean went rapidly, the team moving in two groups of two. A snagged abseil on the Bàsteir Tooth meant Hamish needed to rig another nearby, which Patey thought unwise with the length of rope he had to hand. 'I happened to measure this pitch last summer,' Hamish replied, adding that he knew the pitch was exactly 135 feet. Patey wrote: 'MacInnes has such an impressive array of facts and figures at his fingertips that one occasionally doubts their authenticity.'

Sitting in his living room, Hamish chuckles and nods. 'I was guiding a lot at the time. I made a mental note of the length of every abseil. Because it's critical to know absolutely everything, and how long it may take. I think by then Tom must have tried it about five times.' He smiles. 'But I'd tried it much more than that.'

There then followed the long middle section of the ridge traverse linking north and south, between Bidein Druim nan Ramh and Sgùrr a' Mhadaidh. The névé was iron-hard, filling the gaps in the ledges into a perfect knife edge. They walked unroped, with both Patey and Hamish of the opinion that a coil of rope in your hand was far more hindrance than help – and if you weren't happy walking that section unroped in winter, you probably shouldn't be up there at all. 'It was pure white, and azure blue. You could see all the islands. Just beautiful walking, perfect conditions.' He chuckles darkly. 'Tom had a good way of describing that section: he said in places that if you slipped there, you might not die.'

They reached Sgùrr na Banachdaich and cut snow ledges, anchored themselves in and watched the quiet darkness of night settle around them. They named the lighthouses, saw the lights of Glenbrittle beckon, enjoyed the vantage point, then settled down for sleep on what was, then at least, more the white ridge than black.

They awoke, stiff with the chilly damp of condensation, to mist and snow falling. The stove didn't fire and they set off late, climbing 'with the agility of four knights in full armour'. Eschewing the responsible tactic of stowing their rucksacks neatly for later collection, Patey flung his off the ridge as hard as he could into Glen Brittle, with Robertson following suit. Miserable and tired, they carried on to the first obstacle of the day: the Inaccessible Pinnacle. The rock 'plated from top to bottom with black ice', Patey made an ascent of the long side free-solo – a remarkably brave decision, though an inadvertent one, having committed himself to it whilst testing the rock. Ropes were fixed and the others followed, and they continued, over Sgùrr MhicCoinnich, over Sgùrr Alasdair. And then to the last obstacle: the TD Gap.

Here was a problem. 'It needed only a few seconds' inspection to confirm that its ascent under present conditions would be exceptionally "thin" . . . an evil veneer of ice obscured every wrinkle in the wall,' Patey wrote. Reluctant to abort the traverse or to skirt the difficulty, Hamish recalled another reconnaissance he'd made the year before and suggested a peculiar plan: slinging a piece of rope over the gap and attempting to snag a spike of rock he remembered was there. His very first throw landed the rope on the spike, which he then 'persuaded to lie behind it'.

Patey asked, 'How do you know the rope is safe?'

'I don't,' Hamish replied.

'Well, how are we supposed to find out if you can't tell us?'

'Try climbing up it.'

You get a flavour of the enterprise. However flippant, this was the crucial roll of the dice – the 'Moment of Truth, that was the difference between success and utter disaster'. Patey went first. The rope held. They had cracked the last problem.

In the warmth of the afternoon sun, they walked the final, joyous mile from Sgùrr nan Eag to Gars-bheinn – their final mile of the white ridge, my first on the black – then glissaded 2,000 feet down into Glen Brittle, the Atlantic filling their eyes. 'There are many ultimates in mountaineering, and every generation finds its own Last Problem,' Patey wrote. 'Yet I feel confident that the winter traverse of the Main Ridge will always retain its place as the greatest single adventure in British mountaineering.' He then praises Dave Crabbe and Brian Robertson for making the achievement with 'half a crampon and half a stomach, respectively, thereby revealing – to use Hamish's own phraseology – a determination that is truly Scots'.

It's difficult not to feel the joy in Patey's writing, despite the dangerous world it chronicled. Patey would be killed five years later, on a sea stack off the coast of Sutherland. Hamish tells me he has lost forty friends in the mountains. His oldest climbing partner, Chris Bonington, had lost a similar number. 'And not forty collectively – individually,' he says.

With two such strongly contrasting experiences on Skye, I wonder which left Hamish with the more abiding impression: the light or the dark. Was the Cuillin to him a frightening place?

'Not in the least. It's a very special place.' He thinks for a moment. 'You know, I don't consider the hard bits of climbing there as the highlights of Skye. Just walking along the ridge . . . seeing right out to St Kilda, just to be *there*.' Then, unexpectedly, his voice fills with emotion. 'It seemed a fantastic privilege. It's just being in that environment, you know? If you want to know my good and bad for the Cuillin, there it is. The good is walking that ridge crest, on that lovely winter névé. And the bad, the maelstrom of that rescue. And all the things about it.'

We chat some more. Those generational links. Hamish knew Ben Humble, who met John MacKenzie. I ask him what Humble was like. 'A lovely bloke. A very good photographer. You've seen that shot he took on the Cioch? With Bill Murray? Do you know how long he made him stand there to get that shot?' I nod and smile. There's that other name from the Cuillin's history: W.H. Murray. Someone else Hamish knew well. 'You know Bill, he spent some time in a monastery, and he meditated all his life. And he definitely had a psychic streak. I'd sum him up in two words: he listened. He would be just back from his trips to the Himalayas and whatnot, these very interesting places, yet he was only interested in what *you* were doing. He did a lot for me, Bill.'

I mention Murray's autobiography, published posthumously, entitled *The Evidence of Things Not Seen*. Hamish wrote the foreword. Before his death in 1995 after heart surgery, Murray had written its final words. 'The past was a good age to live in ... looking back over a wide landscape, cloud shadows racing over the mountain sun, wind. I know that I have known beauty.' He finished with a verse:

> All the day's light was ours...
>
> So slight were we
> Who walked the edge
>
> So brief our hold
> Who had the world beneath our feet.

Hamish's eyes fill again, and suddenly he gets up and leaves the room with a brief "Scuse me.' And suddenly I wonder if this is a good idea. To me these were names in a book, pieces of history. To Hamish they were people, friends, memories. People long departed, like his own times of activity, also gone. People around him who had fallen away, while he had endured. Maybe he doesn't want me reigniting these feelings.

He re-emerges, dabbing his nose with a tissue, sits in an easy chair, then hands me a stack of papers with some of his first ascents, which he has been compiling to help with his memory recall. 'In the early days, we didn't record anything. I said it would be a good thing if people didn't record the routes. If we had just gone and found the pleasure of the routes ourselves, why would we want to deprive others of doing the same thing?' I nodded, thinking suddenly of Collie. Hamish was older now than Collie ever got. Beyond the door, the sun was shining on the hills of Glen Coe.

It's time to go, and I thank him. He shakes my hand and smiles warmly, wishes me luck and means it. I leave him standing on his terrace in the pale sun, his arms spread on the rail, looking up at the mountains. Hamish MacInnes, who lost his memory of a life in the mountains and has now found it again, reconnecting the trails of his life. That's important to him. Memories are important, when a person can no longer live the life they once lived. It gives them an identity, reminds them of who they were, what their life has been. Memories are a comfort, in many ways. When your life is given to the mountains, sooner or later memories become all that's left.

I watch for a moment, then leave Hamish with his. I still have a journey ahead. I drive back through Glencoe village. To the left, nine hours down the road, is home. I take a right, and – for the last time, for a while – turn for Skye.

16

End

Sligachan, Skye

At a little before 9 a.m. I stood in the cold car park of the Sligachan Hotel, waiting for Matt Barratt. After leaving Glen Coe, the weather had collapsed into wind and rain, and then swift darkness. Driving soon became a fight with the steering wheel, and weary from a long day already, I'd given in and with two hours' drive remaining decided to look for somewhere to stop for the night.

There is nothing more romantic in principle but dispiriting in execution than driving through the Highlands in search of a bed. I'd always loved the idea of stopping at some convenient coaching inn or deep-tucked guesthouse with a crackling fire, beds piled high with sixty blankets, a well-stocked bar and a kindly old host who cooked a mean fried breakfast. But this was – even on a stormy night in September – not to be. Every hotel that loomed up through the rain-smeared windscreen had 'No Vacancy' pinned up, or, if I stopped and went in, a receptionist who seemed taken aback that I was even seriously asking about a room. I phoned ahead to the much-mythologised Cluanie Inn, almost pointlessly distant just a few miles from the Skye bridge, to ask if they had anything, only to be quoted a figure equal to my trip's food budget for their sole vacant single room.

I'd resigned myself to sleeping in the car when, as I was passing through Spean Bridge, I spotted a modest-looking hotel with a 'Vacancies' sign upside down in the window. The hostess was friendly, the bar still open and the price a third of the next cheapest I'd found. The room had a heater with melted control knobs, a toxic-looking kettle and a bed about the size of a bath towel, but it was a room, and as I lay there listening to the Highland night batter the window, I couldn't have been happier.

The next morning the road ahead looked a little calmer. I covered the remaining miles to Skye through a rosy dawn over roads littered with wind-blown debris. The day gradually flattened to grey, then claggy rain and mist, as I drove on along now familiar roads. By the time I saw the island it was a shadow across the span of the bridge ahead.

I'd wondered how it would feel to be coming back to Skye. The drama of the drive yesterday had distracted me from thinking about the circum-stances in which my last visit had ended, and now, as I drove through damp, misty hillsides starting to catch fire with autumnal colour, I felt a lightness in my mood. I was happy to be going back. I stopped at the same coffee stops, recognised the same views, spied the same pair of boots draped on an overhead telephone line – touchstones of familiarity, and an affection that had taken hold over the last few years of returning here again and again.

But as I passed Balmacara, on the blustery shores of Loch Alsh, all of a sudden this felt like my first trip, three winters ago – the same cold, the same murk, the same gnawing uncertainty – and plenty of new ones, to go with the now persistent ache in my shoulder. These mountains were more than capable of earning your trust, then stabbing you in the back. But I didn't linger on this idea. Not least because I had an appointment with the sharpest one of all, and it didn't seem like a good start to be late. Least of all because its pinnacled summit, ragged and riding high, was looking at me from across the water.

Some parts of the Cuillin are coy from afar, rewarding only the intrepid with a glimpse, and only then if they're lucky – the murky infamy of Coruisk, the sequestered heights of Lota Corrie, the wilderness of crags, ledges, summits and breathless views that breaks onto you at the top of the Great Stone Shoot.

Others are less known to the casual observer, but picked out by the knowing eye: the Inaccessible Pinnacle from all its angles; the muscular pyramid of Sgùrr Alasdair and its status as Skye's highest ground; the shapes thrown by the Bàsteir Tooth and the jawbone of Am Bàsteir from which it juts.

But when it comes to the peak that encapsulates fame and flamboyance, married to a shifty complexity and a brutal appearance, there really is only one mountain that can step convincingly up to the plate. It's the sign-off, the savage flourish at the end of the ridge's tail that gives every sighting of the Cuillin that unmistakeable visual sting. It serves as the ridge's compass, its weathervane, its proof of place. When people started to climb these mountains, this was the first prize they wanted – the peak that, in an instant, hooked upturned eyes and fired ambitions. Of the big Skye peaks it's the one we can be certain was climbed first, under the feet of James Forbes and Duncan MacIntyre; it was Nicolson and Collie's first peak and countless others' only peak.

Ashley Abraham described the mountain with pugilistic reverence:

> One cannot fail be struck by its arresting presence, nor help feeling proud that there belongs to our homeland such a fine mountain as this. For mountain it is, in the most exacting sense ... there is no way of reaching its summit without actual hand-to-hand climbing.

For me, it was the first thing that caught my gaze – and sparked my incredulity all those years ago from across the sea. That weird dichotomy, the sight of it scaring me off Skye's mountains for years, yet strangely hypnotising me, stirring my curiosity. In many respects, it started this journey. And today, I was finally going to climb it.

Sgùrr nan Gillean is a confusing mountain to look at. It's so black, it swallows detail like an abyss. Its most striking feature when viewed broadside from the east or west – the four warted spikes climbing in perfectly stepped fashion that make up the Pinnacle Ridge – are invisible from Sligachan, which is the mountain's most viewed and consequently most famous perspective, despite also being the mountain's most uninteresting angle. Stand in the car park of the inn and look up at the elegant but most definitely singular point of the summit, and any reasonable observer might think that the pinnacles are hidden away somewhere behind the cone of the summit, like a line of children hiding behind a parent. But in fact the four pinnacles are lined up *in front* of it – staring you right in the face – but so well camouflaged you can't see them. Take the road into Glen Drynoch and cast an eye up to the left as you go and you will see the pinnacles peep, then creep, then start to stagger out into the formidable profile so recognisable from afar like the uncoiling tail of a monster: spiky, dark and lethal.

This visually shifty nature isn't reserved only for Pinnacle Ridge. Sgùrr nan Gillean hides other peaks in its shadows, too. Looking back on my photographs from our boat ride across Loch Scavaig, in one – an otherwise unremarkable shot of Sgùrr na Stri, with Sgùrr nan Gillean rising in silhouette to the left – I noticed a strange but huge triangular shadow catching an edging of light in the void of darkness beneath Gillean's summit. It was a shadow within a shadow. It looked so peculiar I dismissed it as the influence of stray light or flare or whatever. But later I noticed it was caught in a second image from a slightly different angle and I looked on the map. There it was, sure enough: a 736-metre stab of gabbro, which, if it were detached and standing anywhere else, would be a well-known landmark. I'd looked at this view a hundred times by now and never noticed it. 'Sgùrr na h-Uamha,' Matt said with a nod when I'd shown him later. 'Technically the true end of the Cuillin ridge.'

I didn't know if Sgùrr na h-Uamha was on the agenda for today. In truth, it had taken months of physio just to get to the point when I could sensibly walk on a mountain again – and I didn't even know if my nerve would break before the summit of Sgùrr nan Gillean, let alone anything more ambitious. But I wanted to try. I had unfinished business on the Cuillin, and while Sgùrr nan Gillean was nowhere near close to the final balance, it was at least a healthy and symbolic payment – emotionally, at least.

When I had raised the issue of my injury with Matt he'd been surprisingly candid, and, ultimately, filled me with confidence. 'I once took a guy up the Inaccessible Pinnacle who had phocomelia. From thalidomide. He was climbing with his teeth. Literally. I think we'll survive.'

Speaking of Matt, I hadn't been waiting long in the car park when two Volkswagen vans pulled in. Matt emerged from one and sidled over to shake my hand. It was good to see him. He even looked like he'd had a haircut.

'No hat?'

'Having a wash.' He appraised me a little more sharply. 'So ... how are you? Shoulder?'

I updated him. He looked at me, nodding. Not doubt, just concern. As if calculating the variables. 'OK.'

The noise of a sliding door closing on the second van and a handy-looking woman dressed in well-seasoned mountain gear jumped out and said hello. She looked familiar. I didn't know why.

'This is Gill,' Matt said. 'A friend. She's learning the ridge so is keen to come along, if that's all right?'

I nodded. 'Of course.'

'Plus, Gill's in mountain rescue, so ...' I caught a suppressed smile in his voice as he busied himself in the back of the van.

Gill looked questioningly at me, so I relayed the story of the previous May, as Matt finished packing up. As it turned out, she looked familiar because she'd been part of the team who'd come up into Coire Làgan to get me. I felt embarrassed.

'Och, don't worry about it. It's what we do. It's good to see you back out,' she said. 'From what I remember, we were delighted with you. You walked for a way.'

'Probably screaming my head off.'

'We don't mind the screamers.'

Changing the subject, I asked Gill what she thought was special about climbing in the Cuillin.

'All of it! But most of all I'd have to say,' she said, before folding her hands primly in front of her and inclining her head towards my feet with a sympathetic expression, 'the grippiness of the rock.'

I laughed. I hadn't gone near those boots since.

Matt joined us, extending his single walking pole and adjusting his pack. He handed me the blue helmet and harness, and nodded at my pack. 'Plenty of food? Waterproofs? Warm jacket?' I nodded, and together we walked out of the car park into Glen Sligachan. This was probably the most travelled route in the Cuillin – the ghillie's route, the tourist's route, the mountaineer's route – the way from the Sligachan Hotel to the mountain that has more history to its name than any other in the range.

The route over the moor was clear, a ribbon of well-tramped path leading through grass on the autumn turn. A bridge was crossed over water of beautiful clarity, holding a tint of tropical blue even in the monochrome conditions. Pale stones, rounded by the constant flow and jostle, lined its edge. Then, as the ground beneath us began to escalate in ramps of russet and green, we paused, the crackle of rain on nylon filling the silence.

The glen was open now and I could see the feet of Marsco, a fine-looking free-standing peak on the opposite side of the River Sligachan and its glacially flattened valley. We caught our breath, adjusted clothing, then there was a brief discussion about the route.

'So,' said Matt, asking me his usual question, 'what do you want to get out of today?'

Survival, I thought. 'I'd be happy with the summit. Any which way.'

Matt nodded steadily. 'We can do that if you want. Or there is the mountaineering route. A traverse of the peak.'

'What's that like?'

'More interesting.' Something in his look. 'A different side to the mountain. More of an experience.'

'OK.' Now I was here, the sky the colour of dark iron, the mountain darker still, I was nervous. More nervous than I cared to admit. 'How's the exposure?'

Matt bobbed his head. 'Maybe just the one bit where you'd need to not look that way,' he waved an arm to his right, 'if you really don't want to see the height.' He looked about at the thick air above. 'Might not be a problem you'll have today.'

I looked uncertainly at Gill. 'I'm up for whatever,' she said gamely. 'Always good to take opportunities.'

There was a pause, the three of us shared a look, then Matt clicked into gear. 'I think we'll see how we go. Then make some choices. Could be grim up there. Could be very grim.'

The weather was already what I'd call grim. Cloud sat on the pinnacles above. As we approached and the mountain gathered its shape, that very familiar view from Sligachan began to twist and deepen and fill the way ahead – and the whole look of the landscape began to change. Rock layered upon rock, and we climbed beneath huge boulders and over braids of water, the whole lot scarred with scree. Spotting a line of travel through this bewildering detail was almost impossible. Even with a map, amongst this labyrinth I'd have no clue which way to go.

The ridge feels very different here. Sgùrr nan Gillean's outer curl faces to the north, and the approach is from that direction. In this, for the Cuillin, it's unique. Its start is more civilised and more open, with the conviviality of a car park, the hotel and the crowds, making the strange contrast of the landscape closing in around and above you all the more striking. It was probably because of the weather, the fact that I couldn't see the sky beyond the clag, but under the sway of the northern crags of the mountain I didn't like it. It felt menacing, a place of walls, of massive, oppressive claustrophobia. See a person move towards the mountain and they keep moving into the scene, smaller and smaller, until the scale moves from the looming to the overbearing to the intimidating. Every step sent an echo rattling off the rock above and around it. I remembered reading about that 'hard-headed' companion of J. Hubert Walker, and the words he uttered on Sgùrr nan Gillean: 'I can't stand this place, it is accursed.'

We stopped to pile on waterproof clothing and I heard the familiar clink of metal climbing gear being hoisted out of Matt's rucksack. I was cold and nervous. Perhaps this showed. Matt had stopped and was adjusting his gloves, his gaze resting lightly on me as he did so. And then he said, 'When was the last time you were on a mountain, Simon?' He'd tried to put a skip into the question, but I stiffened a little. The last time I was on a real mountain, I'd left it in a helicopter.

'Well . . . I went for a walk on Saddleworth Moor a couple of months back. There were rocks there.'

Matt nodded thoughtfully. He was contemplating. I felt the nudge of paranoia.

'Why?'

His nod became a bemused headshake and he smiled a little. 'No, no reason. Just good to know these things.'

The Pinnacle Ridge must have towered above us, but we couldn't see it. Up there in the murk I could sense shadow, and the oddly disquieting weight of history. Get in amongst Sgùrr nan Gillean, and a lot of the

Cuillin's past looks down on you. Collie catching sight of Stocker and Parker high above in those rafters, a sight that jolted his mountain heart-beat to life. Those Ordnance Survey surveyors who were foiled by the west ridge. John Thom, the first to be killed on the mountain, and the first recorded fatality in the Cuillin. So much of the Cuillin's mystique stems from this peak. It's ironic, this: there are some – many, even – who pass by Sligachan with the incidental thought that the view of Sgùrr nan Gillean from there is the entire Cuillin ridge. Those who get to know the ridge as a whole, they realise how little of the ridge that view reveals. And then eventually even they come full circle, and come to understand that so much of the character and presence of the Cuillin as a whole is indeed rammed into this one, temple-like mountain.

Beneath the towers of the invisible Pinnacle Ridge, Matt paused and looked at the sky. 'We'll see how the top looks, but we'll aim for the mountaineering route. Which begins with the badly named Tourist Route,' he said. 'That way you cross the whole peak. A traverse of Gillean.'

As we moved across the lower limbs of the mountain we crossed the tops of rock-choked corries. We were climbing, over rock and into cloud. From ahead I heard the *crockle* of piled debris being scattered with intent. Matt was hefting his stick into a cairn, breaking up the rock, guiding the collapsing stones with his foot.

'Why do you knock them down?'

'Confuses people. Disturbs the rocks, and people think they mean something.' He trailed off with a head-shake, his face a knot of frowns. 'That cairn there,' he said, pointing his stick down to where the ridge met the corrie path, at a modest pyramid of stones that – other than having more of an air of permanence, maybe – looked identical to the one he'd just removed, 'is the only one we don't destroy.'

Cairns are one of those strange opinion flashpoints in the outdoor world, principally as there's no way of telling what they signify, who built them, and if they're markers, or memorials, or something else. Consider those moments where you're in your car on a slip-road, your eyes go to the wing mirror to check for oncoming traffic before you pull onto the carriageway, and you see a truck barrelling towards you at great speed. They flash their lights, forcing you to rather briskly consider, 'Now then, does that mean, "I see you, pull out" or does it mean, "See *me*, *don't* pull out?"' In the mountains, those are cairns: ambiguous kindness-or-kill moments that would make life safer if they simply didn't exist, due to the likelihood of misinterpretation. See a little pile of stones somewhere and it could be a reassuring direction, or it could be a warning.

Even Samuel Johnson was bemused by cairns, in his unfulfilled consideration of an ascent of Beinn na Caillich, across from us now over Glen Sligachan:

> A cairne is a large heap of stones upon the grave of one eminent for dignity of birth . . . it is said that by digging, an urn is always found under these cairnes. They must therefore have been piled by a people whose custom was to burn the dead.

As well as being a memorial, they were also a signal of first presence on a summit (an old name for a cairn in the time of the pioneers was 'stone man') or an indication of topmost progress on a climb, or a cautionary note of some sort. At some point, cairns shifted from being generally indicators of where *not* to go to being indicators of where *to* go, but with no means of knowing which. Following his historic Cuillin traverse with Alasdair McLaren, Leslie Shadbolt wrote of this ambiguity on the ridge leading to Bruach na Frithe, noticing a conspicuous cairn 'on the edge of a forty-foot overhang, presumably erected by some climber to commemorate the fact that he did not fall over this deceptive place; or, possibly, is merely a negative cairn marking the way not to go'.

Naismith used a system of cairns to guidelessly navigate up and down this very mountain in 1880, and Collie, while never one to record climbs in any formal manner, enjoyed a certain notoriety for leaving a breadcrumb trail of these little rock hills – often to the consternation of those who came across them. Such was the chagrin of Buckle and Barlow, who in 1906 believed they were about to claim the first ascent of Cioch Gully, but were surprised to encounter a cairn beyond the crux of the route. Later, at the Sligachan Hotel, the pair approached Collie in the lounge and attempted to extract an explanation, but finding the professor in one of his moods backed off and the subject wasn't raised. Collie and MacKenzie had in fact climbed the route but declined to record it, other than in stone. As recalled by Geoffrey Winthrop Young, in later life Collie

> might now and again chuckle grimly over accounts of 'new' climbs on Scottish cliffs, and remark with the familiar saturnine sidelift of his lip, 'They'll find a little cairn there when they get up.'

I could understand why Matt wanted them toppled – lost walkers led to accidents, or call-outs for the local volunteer teams, of which Gill was one. Though from what I'd observed, there was never a bad word said about a call-out, or a rescue. As she and many others had said, it was just what they did.

We stopped for a rest. 'Quite a playground you've got,' I said to Gill.

'There's a lot here,' she nodded, before adding with a good-natured chide, 'It's not a playground, though. It's a real place. It's important people remember that. Like this.' She picked up the brown end of a cigarette butt from within two luxuriantly mossed rocks. 'Nice bit of plastic in there, to be up here for a thousand years or so. Sometimes you find treasure. This,' she said, putting it into the side pocket of her rucksack, where she had collected several other objects of litter, 'is trash. And it needs to come down. Nobody else is going to do it.'

Soon we were on the move again, and I watched Gill go up the ridge with the sure-footedness of someone who hops along precipitous edges very regularly. She took it like a balance bar. Occasionally Matt said something, and I heard her response. Sometimes it would be about kit. Shoes, mainly – about any particular new model they'd tried out, that might perform well or with tenacity on the gabbro. Matt had already told me that most footwear doesn't last long with hard use on the Cuillin gabbro. Gill was trying out a new pair, which to me looked like the sort of thing I might wear to go jogging in, if I went jogging. Matt also wore low shoes instead of boots, a choice evidently arrived at through years of hard testing. The benchmark for Matt was one summer. If your shoes lasted one summer, that was good going.

Other times I caught snatches of Skye domesticity in their conversation. Comings and goings, mutual pals in sickness and health, adventures planned or undertaken. Good spots for climbing. Pools that had been particularly good for swimming this year. A beach where a plastic clean-up was imminent. A good place to have a canoe paddle repaired, or an alternative place to have a bike seen to, seeing as the guy who usually saw to bikes had broken his arm playing shinty. An otter that had been through a vegetable patch. What a wonderful place this was.

Often, it would be about the route. Again, I'm paraphrasing here but the exchanges were things like:

Gill: 'Would you go left or right just now?'

Matt: 'What do you think?'

Gill: 'Well, I know the right is slippier but the rock on the left always seems a bit looser. Especially that one hold.'

Matt: 'You can bypass that hold. So there's no right or wrong way.'

Gill: 'But there's a righter way and a wronger way.'

Matt: 'So go the way you think is righter. It's left, though.'

This particular exchange ended with Matt waiting for me on a widening of a ledge, and pointing upwards. 'Follow Gill.' I moved past him, as he added, ' . . . unless she goes the wrong way. In which case, don't.'

I've said it before, but the level of knowledge – the almost reflex awareness of every rock, the familiarity of spaces and dimensions and distances – was amazing. It's what working the same patch earns you: you get to know it like your own.

But I also came to realise this place wasn't unchanging, just evolving with each day. Ageing slower than us, but ageing all the same. More than once Matt pointed out little things he'd noticed: a certain wearing of a place, a change in the boulder cover. Once, when moving between a gap, he said with a slight wistfulness in his voice, 'These rocks – they're getting further apart. Little by little.' Gill pointed out a boulder that was split in two, the bare face of the shearing a pale grey, like sandpaper, the weathered covering of the rock black and worn smooth. 'I remember this breaking. Last spring.'

It was on Sgùrr nan Gillean that a rather more significant collapse took place – of the gendarme, a French term for 'policeman', but also an alpine term for a sentry-like pillar of rock, particularly one stubbornly blocking your way. The gendarme here had foiled many who'd attempted the West Ridge, calling for scary edging around it or bold surmounting. Back in the

day, the obstacle presented a problem over which a pipe was smoked; so
said Naismith, when he and William Douglas first caught sight of it one
stormy evening. 'The passage ... promised to be sensational, if possible at
all,' he wrote later in the *Scottish Mountaineering Club Journal*.

> We camped in full view of the difficulty, discussed it leisurely ... made
> fun of it and finally strode over it without much difficulty. On arriving
> at the *policeman* ... we climbed him until we could put our arms around
> his neck, and so swing ourselves around him, and drop to the ridge at
> his back.

Later, when the route became an established one, a famous photo opportunity was to place a daring climber atop it. It cannot be overstated how
strong the nerves said subject must have possessed to manage composure
in such a position. But in early 1987 the gendarme fell, making the ridge
more accessible from that direction, if rather less photogenic and initially
very unstable. A warning note in the *Fylde Mountaineering Club Newsletter* of
July 1987 carried news of the 'disintegration': 'Technically the traverse is
easier now. But those rocks certainly wobble!' Yikes.

We were climbing fast now. The cloud was creeping below us, as well
as above. Ahead of us in the murk was a dip in the skyline – the moment
when we'd crest the ridgeline, where the route found its direction onward
up onto the south-east ridge and we'd reach the top of an interminable
climb and saw what lay on the other side. In the Cuillin these moments
tended to be rather more revelatory than most. I could feel wind falling
down from the slack. Expecting to be hit by gusts, I braced as the rock
dipped and the sky opened out. But then the unexpected happened.
Instead of increasing, the wind dropped. And instead of seeing a wall of
flat grey to the east beneath a low blanket of cloud, here was a landscape
of supernaturally bright clarity. Here at close quarters was the huge shark
fin of Sgùrr na h-Uamha, that mysterious peak whose shadow I'd spotted
in the photograph, Matt's 'true end' of the Cuillin ridge. It looked close
enough to touch. From the sea looking back, this hidden peak disappeared,
black against black. From here it was a peak in its own right, freed from
being flattened against its parent mountain, standing proud against a

landscape that seemed equal parts water and rock. Patches of the corries were shimmering deep olive where the sun caught heather, which at this distance looked like velvet ripped in its upper reaches by rock bursting out. The rest was a monochrome negative: molten silver of water against mountain, black except where cut by streams and pools, which shimmered in the shadow like flung jewels. Despite most of the ridge hiding under strafing cloud moving in a north-easterly clip across the ridge, it was almost painfully bright. Over the sea, the sun was shining somewhere. Sgùrr nan Gillean stood, seemingly in perpetual shadow, with its own private mantle of cloud.

The place does *feel* dark. Even the typically optimistic Alexander Nicolson namechecked the mountain in the bright and bouncy *Isle of Skye: An Edinburgh Summer Song* in a verse that rings as black as night:

> The Matterhorn's good for a fall,
> If climbing you have no skill in,
> But a place as good to make ravens' food
> You can find upon Scoor-nan-Gillean.

At this point, it's worth re-examining the unfortunate tale of John Thom, whose place in the Cuillin's history, you may recall, was as the first recorded death in the range whilst attempting to descend Sgùrr nan Gillean in the dark on 2 September 1870. His fame devolved from tragic to strange, when riddles began to appear in guest books as far afield as the Alps, like an odd footprint of the proliferation of the Cuillin's clientele. These riddles were seemingly using the thirty-year-old Liverpudlian's death as a kind of cautionary scapegoat, the likely result when the foolhardy take to the hills – any hills – unaccompanied. An anonymous entry in the Bar Hotel, in Switzerland's Kandersteg, read:

> Welcome, John Thom! As through the list I look
> I hail thy writing in the Strangers' Book
> Good omen brings it of avoided dangers,
> Through endless time may thou and I be strangers.

While the Sligachan guest book carried the rather less eloquent:

> Don't attempt the grim old Cuillin without a guide:
> John Thom did this: the same day he died
> The hills have secrets that no tourist knows:
> He risks his life who solitary goes.

Nicolson, too, adopted a slightly chiding tone in *Good Words* regarding Thom's incident when he mentioned the 'fine young Englishman' who ascended Sgùrr nan Gillean without a guide, was misled by mist, and then felt the wrath of the 'insulted spirit of the mountain'. Nicolson wrote, 'Let no one despise [Sgùrr nan Gillean] as an easy performance; if he does, he may find cause to repent.'

The 1960 *Alpine Journal* contained an interesting article entitled 'John Thom: Mountaineer', examining the truth of the man so many mocked as unwary. Thom was no tourist; by 1869 he had climbed thirty peaks in the Alps, including Mont Blanc, Monte Rosa and the Jungfrau. In 1868 he would also have attempted the Matterhorn in the company of Peter Bohren, the guide who led the first ascent of the Eiger, had it not been for bad weather. In 1869 this was no mean record. Yet despite this, Thom was blackballed, or 'ploughed', for membership to the Alpine Club no fewer than three times, despite fitting the experience criteria quite commendably, his last rejection coming the year before his death. No reason has been recorded, and while the club at the time was undoubtedly cliquey, and well-to-do Victorians could be sniffy towards those in what might be called 'lower industries' (Thom was a cotton broker), there were sufficient members similar to Thom to suggest this shouldn't be a deal-breaker.

Possible reasons were that Thom was considered reckless and not especially good at navigation. Although he had diced with bad weather in the Alps, it was always with guides. But a number of accounts of Thom's Lake District adventures did show a tendency to make blunders when visibility was poor. The ones we know of — and I'll spare you the details — were the classic small errors in direction left uncorrected, which compounded into major ones. The confusing nature of British mountain terrain, the indistinct shapes of the land, the wont of the weather to supply cruel and unusual challenges: these are all qualities that Skye administers more swiftly and in a greater concentration than anywhere else in Britain. This seems to have been the case for Thom's final outing on Sgùrr nan Gillean. The separation from his partner, the descent of mist and darkness, a wrong turn on the summit – which even on a good map looks like a daddylonglegs of spindly ridges meeting at a tiny node of a summit – a fall, a search, the inevitable discovery. Nicolson noted that Thom was found 'at the foot of a sloping precipice not far from the summit . . . his back against the rock, his neck broken and one of his legs, his paletot [coat] drawn behind him, covered with fragments of the rock'.

There is certainly a case for Thom being a man of ill-considered decisions on the mountain, but there's also a case for him being simply unlucky. Whichever you believe, as the mountain and the ridge it is attached to continue to prove, there are the British mountains, there are the Alps – and then there is the Cuillin ridge. Difficulty is subjective. Difference is not.

Up on the ridge skyline I could see Matt in his red jacket, hood up, hunched against the now strafing wind. The strap on his backpack was flapping outwards, a kind of ancillary windsock. Above him the ridge sliced upward, shadowy and cloud-softened, its skyline barb-edged.

Matt was putting his gloves on. 'Think I'm going to put you on a rope,' he said, but didn't explain why. I looked past him to where the ridge narrowed into the cloud. I knew he was being cautious, but I didn't argue. I noticed as he uncoiled his rope that he'd replaced his bright orange builders' gloves with new red models.

'Upgraded your gloves?' I asked.

He nodded. 'Ninja Flex. *Deluxe*,' he said dramatically, then frowned. 'Very good but they cost a bit more. £4.'

I looked at the gloves. They had a neoprene top and abrasive-surfaced rubber fingers and palm, perfect for sharp-edged concrete and bricks, rain, cold and hard labour. Perfect for the Cuillin.

The ridge was raking up, not perilously steep, but narrowing, losing its enclosed feel – less a chimney, more an apex. I didn't know what came ahead. I looked at the rock. It was a pale grey, pinned with lichen rosettes and almost cheerful, the colour of wood ash. Rock seems to brighten closer up, and I'd somehow expected Gillean's gabbro to be darker. Matt handed me the rope. I clipped on. He took it in and slung the coils over his shoulder.

'So, same as usual. If it's tight, it doesn't mean I want you to go faster. Watch your feet.'

'Fall to the left?'

He smiled. 'Maybe just don't fall.'

As Matt adjusted himself on the ledge, Gill appeared next to me. She wasn't on a rope.

'Matt says you're learning the ridge?' I said.

She nodded eagerly. 'I've done it before, a few times. Just not loads and loads of times. And never the whole thing in one go.' She cocked her head up towards Matt. 'I'll never know it like him.'

I nodded. 'He's pretty good.'

'That's a given,' she said. 'But he cares if you have a good day too. That's what you need in a Cuillin guide, in weather like this.'

Matt was up above us, humming, then looked down. He had that look on his face. 'So. This bit just here. No trouble at all. Lovely hold here, and here,' he said, indicating them. 'No reason to worry even slightly.'

Gill leaned in and said: 'You know when he says something like that it means there's a hard bit.'

I nodded. 'I'm beginning to learn that.'

Gill went ahead, and soon she was up beyond Matt. Making to follow, I reached up with my right arm and pulled on the rock. And as I did, a buzz travelled down it and I felt a familiar, sickening pinch in my shoulder – like something being moved that shouldn't. Immediately I retreated back down to the ledge, eyes wide.

'Hang on,' I shouted up. The buzzing had stopped but it still felt wrong in there. Gingerly turning my arm to the left, I felt something slide home inside my shoulder. I looked up and saw Matt eyeing me with concern.

'OK?'

'Yeah. Something happened there. Seems all right now.'

He looked down and nodded, still frowning. 'Sure?'

I nodded. I knew what I'd done. I'd forgotten. I'd reached, and loaded. Gone outside the safe zone, exactly what I needed to not do. Not up here, anyway. And I'd done it without a thought, on the easiest move in the world.

It was sobering – a depressing moment. Confirmation that just now, I had to be very careful. Until I got it fixed. But I wasn't turning around now. Easing up the ridge and gingerly leveraging myself up with both arms held close, I made my way up.

Matt stood a couple of metres ahead, the pair of us linked by a slack length of rope. The ridge seemed almost level now. As we'd been climbing, the mist had shifted from pale grey to translucent, a delicate blue seeping into it.

'The summit is literally in sight,' Matt said, and I looked past him and saw a cairn resolving through the cloud, a little pile of rocks, perched right at the apex we were moving towards. I felt a surge of relief.

But I knew that this final section of the ridge also held the route's biggest fright. Alfred Wainwright had turned around here to avoid an 'imminent demise'; some friends of mine had done the same.

And here it was: the final obstacle. The bad step, the *mauvais pas*, that every ridge seems to feature at some point. Like the jump atop Tryfan – just a little too far for a pair of legs to stretch in safety, or tilted just a little too temptingly over a nasty drop. The choice. Just a few feet of blocky corners. Matt kept the rope tight. I focused in on the rock, keeping my face inward to it. This was no doubt the bit Matt had mentioned, the place to not look if heights were a worry. I felt like a fraud; the terror was the point, apparently. But today the terror of the drop was hidden by the thin, quickly diluting murk. Not for the first time, I was grateful for it. In Pinn aside, the weather had been a good friend all along the hairier bits of my Cuillin endeavour. And if what was happening continued, on the last few upward steps, it might just be about to become my *best* friend.

The cairn ahead was almost gleaming, caught by delicate sunlight clawing its way through the cloud. It was brightening. We were moving out of the clouds – or the clouds were moving off the summit. My heart was beating hard, and this time not because of nerves.

We reached the cairn, the height of my hip, in a murk that hid every aspect of the view but for some strange shapes close by, lit by an invisible sun, burning through. Another ridge led up from the left, topped by precarious, blocky fingers of rock. I recognised the signature from old pictures; down there was where the gendarme used to be.

The summit of Sgùrr nan Gillean was a pile of sturdy rocks sitting on a tilted slab that dropped over the south face of the mountain. The topmost rock was upholstered with a wig of green moss, as was a good deal of the summit. I remembered Alexander Nicolson's description: 'The crown of the peak ... you find a tolerable carpeting of moss, coarse grass, and lichen, by no means unpleasant to lie on.' Odd to inhabit such a small square of history, occupied by so many more, right here, through the years. Nicolson found an eagle's feather on the summit, with which he made a quill to write the above words, and many more, about Sgùrr nan Gillean.

He then went on to describe the echo from the peak, particularly strange given the belief at the time of it being the highest. 'It is undoubtedly a very solemn place to be in,' he wrote, 'and the slight suggestion of danger gives it an awful charm.'

The danger was avoided with faith. 'Thy foot, He'll not let slide,' he told himself, despite acknowledging the comforting chemistry of the gabbro under it. He accepted the science that drew Forbes up into this place, but Nicolson was a religious man. Like many before him, he believed the mountains were helped into their existence by a 'paternal mind'. I looked, and saw geology – fiery birth, agonising rise – together with the myths people had draped upon them and the shades of wonder they saw reflected back. And, of course, the joy in just being here. The mountain faith, if you will.

Matt shook my hand. 'Congratulations,' he said. And as he did, the view began to sharpen. The mist thinned. Very quickly, wondrous sights began to emerge. Perhaps we would get just a glimpse. But it became sharper, sharper, sharper – then, just seconds after we arrived on the topmost ground of Sgùrr nan Gillean, the summit tore clear of cloud and the whole world appeared.

Space opened up at our feet and into the distance. Yawning space. We went from standing on a pedestal amidst murk without any context, to being on a hoisted plinth amidst nothing but clarity, and thousands of feet of rock and space and water and air. You spend enough time in mist and your eyes become accustomed to groping for sight. When visibility suddenly improves, it's an almost overwhelming sensory reawakening, like flicking a light on after a night in the dark. You might have only been in the murk for a few hours, but you still can't believe that the world is *this* sharp, has *this* depth and crispness. And what you see is astonishing. From here, you can see almost the whole of Skye.

It was calm and the sun was out, so we put our bags down. Matt and Gill sat. Sgùrr nan Gillean's summit is small. It's not frighteningly small, though; there was space for the three of us, and the three of us again, without a squeeze. But you don't need to move your feet to see every angle of the view from here. I tried to form a word or two but ended up just making a noise. Gill said: 'It's a different day.' Matt stood on the edge of the summit looking out towards Sligachan.

The view moved around us. Parts of it appeared and disappeared. There were the buildings of the Sligachan Hotel, the bite of the loch, other remote buildings, their white walls picked out by the sun. The mountains of Glamaig and Marsco, far below across the glen, their forms now revealed – Glamaig more complex than the triangular pile it is from Sligachan, from where most see it, Marsco complicated, fluted, steep-sided. The Isle of Raasay, with its distinctive thimble summit. Between us and all of it, three thousand feet to a ruffled blanket of brown moor, cut by lines natural and human – streams, roads. The shadows of clouds moved across it, cruising puddles of darkness. This summit felt so very, very high above it all.

Beyond it was the mainland. I saw impressions of the mountains of Wester Ross – Applecross, Torridon – across to Knoydart. Places from which I had looked this way, and seen the unmistakeable barbs of this very mountain, caught the signature of the ridge, its compass, and wondered – however idly, then – what it would be like to climb it. And now here I was. My own Cuillin circle, closed.

I turned around, to the ridge. There it all was. Sgùrr Dearg and the In Pinn, Sgùrr Alasdair, hulking black silhouettes against the luminous sea. I could see Loch Scavaig, the scything line of the Druim nan Ramh spur, this whole place, its entire history, in one turn of the head. Beneath the knuckled profile of Sgùrr na Stri I could see Sgùrr Hain. In all that shadow was Captain Maryon's monument, from where I'd snatched a glimpse of Sgùrr nan Gillean through the murk. Nothing between us but a few miles of empty space filled with aeons of mountain building, millennia of history, and the most spectacular mountains in the land. And for me, a few years spent in the thrall of this ridge.

Gill and Matt had just been sitting on the mossy summit, watching the view in silence. Matt mumbled something and pointed. Cloud was rising up from the Bàsteir gorge like steam, slowly obscuring the depths close at hand with a soft, grey pall. Gill stood up and walked to the edge, holding her hands aloft, the sun catching her back. 'There we go. Just faint, though.' She stepped back and motioned for me to take her place. I stood and looked over the edge, down onto the cloud. It was there for three seconds, maybe five: then cloud moved behind me, obscured the sun, and it was gone. The Brocken Spectre – the mountain ghost. A human shadow, projected onto the cloud below, into oblivion, surrounded by a halo of beautiful rainbow colour. A silhouette – a person, anonymous, a human shape from any time. But always you. You can't experience a Brocken Spectre vicariously, they say. You have to see your own. A fleeting moment. And hard to forget.

Perhaps it was this. Perhaps it was because the weather had given us this extraordinary break, just as we had reached the top. I'd climbed hundreds of mountains; I don't know why this one meant more. But it did, because as I stood there, watching the cloud rise around the mountains, drifting up until their tops floated above them, black rock and pale vapour, I felt a souring in my throat and that sting in my eyes. I don't get emotional on mountaintops. I get emotional at the birth of a child, the death of a friend, something in music that compels a memory. But for some reason, on the summit of Sgùrr nan Gillean, I felt it. I think it was the realisation that I was nearing the end of something – and this was the moment that I wanted to take away with me.

Of course, the summit of a mountain is only halfway, and we were far from down. Before too long the cloud took the view again – and we took the hint. Matt gave Gill the nod to lead down a ridge that descended into the mist like the blade of a circular saw. I took off my gloves and felt the scratch of the gabbro and the damp of the moss, of flaking lichen like dead skin. It started to rain again, thick, stodgy drops, just a degree or so from sleet. Ahead, the ridge looked like it was running off into oblivion, but each step yielded more downward rungs on its ever-steepening way. Then something unusual: a square aperture, the size of a playhouse door. It looked like it had been created when a rock had fallen onto two others, to create a kind of portal. I watched as Gill climbed through it, then I followed.

Eventually we could go no further, at a spike of rock ringed with two pieces of rope. Gill had stopped and was peering over the edge. I stayed warily back. Matt arrived next to me and said to Gill, 'Rope?'

She was on her knees, examining it. One primary, one back-up. 'Mantle's coming away,' she reported, 'but core's intact. Back-up looks fine.'

Matt nodded and checked it, glove off, fingers probing. Who checks the rope? *We all do.*

Soon his own rope was uncoiling off his shoulder and I heard that unsettling sound of clinking again. Then Matt adopted his 'light' voice again.

'When was the last time you abseiled, Simon?'

'With you, on the In Pinn.'

'Oh! Grand.' I couldn't tell if he was being sarcastic or happily surprised. 'You remember how to do it?'

'Think so. This arm up, this arm on the brake.'

'Other way round, but yes. Watch your shoulder. Stay here with Gill.'

Then he disappeared out of sight, and I heard the scratching of rubber and nylon on rough rock, and watched, hypnotised, as the rope tensioned and slackened rhythmically against the rock. And then the rope ceased its elastic seizure and I heard a rock-ringy voice from below. 'OK, Simon, down you come.'

Abseiling is, and apologies if I have mentioned this before, a cascade of emotions: dread, horror, a feeling of profoundly unnatural posture, followed by gradual relief, then – typically in the second or so before you reach the bottom – a cautious feeling of fun. Underpinning it all is trust: complete trust in the equipment, the rock, the conditions, your own abilities and, critically, the person who has set it all up and is more than likely gazing up at you from the foot of the abseil. That moment when you feel the air change as the drop opens beneath as you lean right back – the most committing position, the most unnatural one, but perversely the only one that allows efficient movement – you are absolutely on the redline of everything. If anything goes wrong with any part of the equation, you're in serious, serious shit.

Initially hesitant, struggling for grip on the shadowed, slimy rock, I took a deep breath, leaned back, and began to walk down the rock. The rope felt stretchy, the harness's squeeze around my hips reassuring. I thought for a second what it would feel like for the tension in the rope to suddenly go, and to plummet, then immediately pushed the thought away. This was too special for fear to ruin.

There was an overhang in the middle – my feet scrabbled around, maintaining traction somehow. As I went, I remembered to look away from the rock, out to the view. The ridge was holding cloud and rain, but below a hard line of cloud, out there the sea was blue, the landscape rich with sunshine. Someone on the west coast might spy some of Gillean's spikes, see its black, fluted triangle. They wouldn't see me abseiling down from it. But away on that distant, spiky eye-hook of a peak, that was exactly what I was doing.

The abseil was about thirty feet. Soon – dare I say too soon? – I was standing next to Matt, waiting for Gill to descend. She came down with practised speed, and Matt was promptly unthreading the rope and re-coiling it around his shoulder. We descended further along the ridge, Gill indicating upwards where a tiny needle-eye of sky appeared on the skyline, and I realised it was the hole we had crawled through, up aloft in the spires, strangely precipitous-looking in a way it hadn't felt when we were there. Mountains have a habit of doing that.

Gillean dipped to a bealach and the slender, dark disc of Am Bàsteir rose ahead, its scorched profile softened by the cloud, black with damp. There it was, right there. Another summit towards linking the chain. Joining the dots. Maybe we should carry on, I thought, momentarily confident – momentarily tempted. There was another summit. Another mountain. Another memory.

As if sensing this, Matt turned and squinted up at me. 'Feels like we had a pretty lucky time up there. But we could go on . . .' He waggled his head contemplatively to finish his sentence.

Further up the slope, Gill was pulling another jacket out from her bag and removing her harness. I looked up at Am Bàsteir, 'The Executioner'. Cloud was again rising over the peak, its top protruding far above like the bow of a sinking ship. Then it was gone. In a few minutes, it would probably be back again. Then a few minutes after that, gone. Maybe for a minute. Maybe for a week.

I felt an urge, for sure. But I also felt that I'd got what I came for and that maybe enough luck had been pushed just for now.

'No, that's OK,' I said. 'Another time.'

Matt nodded. 'You'll be back. And they'll always be here. So they say.'

He stood for a moment more, taking in the view down the Bàsteir gorge, the wild pinnacles of Sgùrr nan Gillean above us, the shadow of the deep valley below – terrifying, elemental, beautiful. Would I be back? With all this left, just try and stop me.

'We're good for today, then?' Matt said.

'We're good.'

'You're happy?'

I smiled. 'Very.'

'Good.' He nodded crisply. 'That's why I'm here.'

Gill rejoined us and with a wordless acknowlegement we began the descent towards Sligachan – out of the wild spires of the ridge, back to civilisation. Above, the black ridge stood silent. Said nothing.

Tonight I was staying at the Sligachan Hotel. I'd decided I needed to spend at least one night at this ember of comfort so inextricably linked to the ridge. My first instinct had been to seek out the room that Collie had died in, but that seemed a bit too macabre. As a compromise, I rang ahead and asked for the cheapest room they had.

I'd said cheerio to Gill, thanked her again for helping rescue me, then wished Matt a final goodbye.

He finished loading his stuff up, then gripped my hand in the squally wind. 'You take care of that shoulder. No more accidents.' He smiled. 'And bring the family next time. Make them some memories.' Then he was back in his van and gone, and I was alone in the car park.

As I turned, I noticed with a start the curved window of Collie's Lounge, mirroring the mountains that were perfectly gathered in it. The shape of the glass meant that in the reflection the mountains looked unnaturally steep, spire-like, a vision of exaggerated reality reminiscent of those savagely romanticised peaks in paintings of old. From the other side, looking out, they would just appear normal, as they really were. I stared at this reflection for several moments, then walked up to the entrance and fell heavily into the arms of the hotel.

The Slig, as those in a hurry call it, is a fine and stately place of rambling corridors, heavy drapes and thick walls against the weather. Negotiating the warrens of its corridors is made more rewarding by a series of displays in which memorabilia from the glory days of climbing are displayed rather splendidly in cases, with descriptions more comprehensive than in some museums. After checking in, I was directed to a small, slightly draughty room with simple furnishings and – blessedly – a bath. I was very happy. I had a long soak, then wandered into the hotel's Seamus's Bar, where I ate a large meal and proceeded to sample the hotel's selection of beers.

Later, the room filled. Tired walkers, a large table of tourists led by kilted guides passing around flights of whisky, a few locals and a ceilidh band all began putting down roots for the evening. Steadily, the volume cranked up and the atmosphere took on a beat.

Later, I wandered into the deserted, curtained-off Collie's Lounge, where candles burned in the windows, lighting thick marbles of rain on that curved black glass. The mountains were invisible behind the dark, but they were there.

I don't think I was supposed to be in there. I sat in the easy chair beneath Arthur Trevethin Nowell's portrait of Collie, who was still gazing sternly and slightly askance into the room, and listened to the wind dancing outside the building and the muffled noise of the bar.

Collie wasn't the first of the Cuillin explorers, nor necessarily the greatest. He was a good climber, but probably not the best. I liked Collie's story because it epitomised the strange lure of this place, for better or worse. He became absorbed by Skye and its mountains, remaining with them until his solemn end right here in this hotel, a man willingly giving in to the isolating power of wild places, and, at the end, retreating into his past within them. As he wrote:

> Many are the memories one can bring back from the mountains, some of peace and some of stern fights with the elements, but they are all memories of freedom. The restraint of ordinary life no longer holds us down, we are in touch with nature, the sky, the winds, the water, and the earth . . . surely these ancient elements of life can teach us secrets that a more protected existence hides from us.

Sitting beneath his picture, I suddenly realised I could do something that – until now – I couldn't do. Something that I became convinced I *should* do. On rain-smeared notebook paper with a black marker pen, beneath Collie's querying gaze, I sketched out my own map of the Cuillin. My own way of seeing the ridge. My own interpretation of its impression on my mind.

It was a mess – devoid of artistry of any kind and inaccurate to the last detail – but as faithful a testament to my own relationship with the ridge as any. My very own Skye story. And this one was about to end. I folded the map up, stowed it away, and, with a salute to Collie, made my way out of his lounge and back to the bar.

I had a few more drinks. Well, why not? Things became a thrash of furry light and sounds, the band a frenzy of activity, English intermingled with Gaelic. A collective rise in volume, in atmosphere, in revelry. I stamped happily along from my seat, like a bystander at a party, alone but not lonely. Scribbled unintelligible notes in my notebook, deposited an uncertain, possibly large amount of money into the bar-top mountain rescue box, went and scrutinised the Collie and MacKenzie sculpture miniature once again, possibly even holding a conversation with it. I'd had a few drinks. And again, why not?

Eventually I shuffled off to my room as the band played their last song, in soaring Gaelic. Just a voice and a fiddle, sung to the walls, the rafters, the memories and the ghosts.

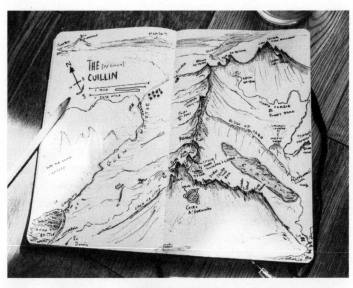

Last Look

I awoke to rain, cloud, a sore shoulder and a headache.

I had to make one final stop. It didn't feel especially desirable, but it did feel necessary – a kind of pilgrimage. I ate a hot breakfast looking out at the rain, paid my bill, dragged my bags of kit to the car, then turned uphill towards Struan, where Skye's north-western peninsulas reach inland.

The small graveyard behind the Free Presbyterian Church on the shores of Loch Harport is unsigned – the kirk a boxy, grey-washed building end-on to the road. I had to ask directions. It's really only identifiable by windows that, rather chillingly, feature white skeletons bowing in a vaguely ecclesiastical manner.

Swinging open a gate, I made my way round the back. Here were a couple of dozen graves, all of them poorly tended, some tilted at surprising angles. A fenced mausoleum burst comically with overgrowth, a messy centrepiece to a yard containing names that numbered several MacLeods, several Campbells. A stream ran to the right, climbing into a tight valley, above which houses stood and buzzards circled. And there at the end, facing away from the loch, away from the church, lie John MacKenzie and Norman Collie.

The weather was squally as I walked around the little yard, feeling slightly depressed. I was expecting some grand plot beneath the mountains, occasionally lit by crepuscular rays, a place where these two great stalwarts of the ridge could rest within sight of it. There is a graveyard near Carbost, adjacent to the ruins of an old church; the ridge rolls out before it, Loch Harport laps against it and the sun shines on it. It's a beautiful spot. In it lie locals, climbers, mountain rescue team members. So to find Collie and MacKenzie elsewhere, facing away from the Cuillin towards a gulch – I don't know why, but it was a surprise.

Collie's grave is the more remarkable at a distance. His height is marked out on the ground using stones that looked – and felt with my hands, still raw from the ridge – to be gabbro. His headstone is almost conspicuously unremarkable: in copperplate on faded brass it reads simply:

John Norman Collie

FRS

1859–1942

MacKenzie gets a more expressive plaque, on a lichen-whitened piece of basalt that once was a cross, but now, after the best part of a century in Skye air, has assumed the broken shape of an upturned boot.

To the memory of

John MacKenzie

Cuillin Guide

Died 20 July 1933

Aged 76

Something else struck me. All the descriptions – all of them, without fail – of the graves of Collie and MacKenzie describe them as being beside each other, but they are not. They are end to end, one slightly uphill. Not Collie watching over MacKenzie, but MacKenzie watching Collie. This was contrary to the proposed sculpture, back at Sligachan, where Collie stands behind MacKenzie, towering watchfully above. This probably doesn't mean anything, any of it. But I thought it was interesting.

Well, what can I say? This book opened with a search for a grave of sorts, albeit to one not even vaguely remembered in anything other than stone and landscape. It occurred to me that in all that time, I still hadn't found out anything meaningful about Captain Maryon, about the man who had his own little peak crafted in his memory, in the royal box overlooking the most atmospherically evocative mountain range of all. The mountains that had witnessed everything – all of this – stood silently above, saying nothing. Maybe there wasn't anything to find. But there was a lot to be understood, I think. About someone who came here, to this place – looking for something. A place that inspired, bewitched and tolerated people, elevated people, took them to ecstasy and fired their imaginations. Challenged them. Haunted them. *Got* them. It took people away, in more ways than one; consumed them, willingly or otherwise. Maryon was one. Perhaps so was Collie – and also, to varying degrees, were many of the people whose paths I'd crossed or whose stories I'd read.

And now here I was, standing in a graveyard on a cindery Skye day, shivering in wind-buoyed rain, much like I had been that day on Sgùrr Hain, a few years and most of a mountain range ago. Everything just ends up pointing at the sky, like these graves, like Maryon's monument. All else is just memory, kept by the mountains in their voiceless stone.

I walked back to the car. On my hunt for Maryon, I'd come here looking for the marker to his death, but I didn't want to leave the island straight after visiting another one. In the end, being in the mountains had to me always been about feeling alive. And Skye's black ridge, despite all its inherent darkness, meant life to me, too. So I drove back to Broadford and made the right turn for Elgol.

It was a long drive but a beautiful one, and it felt good to be returning there. After Portnalong, it was the place I'd been to most on Skye, and the place where, to me, this adventure had begun. I arrived at the harbour, parked the car and walked over to the slipway. The red RIB was just on its way out into waves chopped into white horses. Seagulls wheeled around in a lively wind, and the air had the tang of salt and seaweed. It smelled fantastic. And there was the ridge, softened by cloud, impassive, spectacular. The boat might be carrying people out to it. People who were going up there, tonight.

In so many ways it had all gone wrong. I didn't really expect my adventure in the Cuillin to be anything more than a ragged, symbolic crown placed on years of exploring and revering the British mountains. I certainly didn't expect to fall in love with the ridge, or its island, in a way I knew I was never going to shake off. Or would ever want to.

The thing I really didn't see coming was the odd feeling that fell upon me with the realisation that, after today, I wouldn't have a specific reason to return to a place that – for better or worse – had kept a bit of me for itself, scratched off on the sharp rock, caught on it, captured by it.

And the more you get to know the Cuillin, the more you realise you've got left to know. Samuel Johnson wrote of the Skye Highlanders: 'The inquirer . . . knows less as he hears more.' I felt like that about the ridge.

But that was OK. I'd be back one day and it would be there, standing silent, saying nothing. Just as it has been for those who came before, and whoever comes next.

It's this that makes the Cuillin so maddeningly fascinating. That seductive, frightening magic that draws you in and doesn't ever let you go. It's not a place to rush. In many respects, it isn't even a place; it's a geographical marinade. It takes time and deep immersion to really start to absorb it. How much do you give in to it? That's your choice.

My choice was home. I was going back to my wife and my kids, and I couldn't wait. I turned from the ridge, climbed into the car and drove back towards Broadford, the bridge, the mainland, and all the rest. And as its spires crept further and further back in my mirrors, I knew that – like all mountains, and all those wild places we are richer for knowing – it would always be there, the spiky shadow in the corner of the room that keeps you looking, keeps you curious, keeps you scared. And keeps you coming back. Because true to something I was told way back at the beginning of this strange journey, the Cuillin *had* got me. One way, and the other.

Ahead on the singletrack, there was something in the road – the Highland cattle again. I smiled, braked gently and gradually eased into their space. Slowly they shuffled to their feet and, eventually, moved. Maybe they recognised me. I hoped so.

Acknowledgements

This book very nearly didn't happen. Thank you to everyone who helped me or encouraged me in whatever small way, whether you're named below or not.

To my Cuillin guide Matt Barratt of Skye Adventure, for being honest, dependable, accommodating and – true to reputation – good. To Katie and Johnny Heron at the Taigh Ailean in Portnalong, purveyors of the finest steak pie on Skye and the friendliest welcome, for running the best place to feel like a local on Skye's wild fringe.

For sharing their Skye stories: Alasdair Niven, Donald Livingstone, and Paul and Denise Rees. And to Rob Taylor and the late Hamish MacInnes, for a remarkable few hours of storytelling under the storeys and stories of Glen Coe. Hamish died at the age of 91 in December 2020, propped in his easy chair, in front of his magnificent panorama of those magnificent mountains. Considering the many ways the end could have been, it was probably as it should have been, in the end.

For having my back: Kingsley Singleton for, amongst many other things, sitting with me for five hours on a mountainside and stopping the fear from weedling in; to the saintly people of Skye Mountain Rescue, who came and helped me down; and to the staff of the Western Isles Hospital in Stornoway, who put me back together again. I implore anyone who goes to Skye and sees a mountain rescue tin to stick a quid or three in it – because it was me, and one day it might be you, and these people do not get paid for coming to get you. To see those lights coming up the mountain in the dark is a moment I won't forget any time soon. Thank you so much, and – once again – sorry for the trouble.

For much-needed encouragement along the way, even with the odd word of little-considered consequence: Lyle Brotherton, Tom Bailey, Matthew Swaine and my old mountain pal James Provost.

The oracles: I would like to thank Professor Norman Macdonald, whose stunning books on Skye – co-authored by Cailean Maclean – are a window onto the history of a place unlike any other, and whose insight on that rainy afternoon at Sligachan was a privilege. And to Rob Johnson, for helpful comments on an early read, and being a generally splendid fellow concerning all things mountaineering, Snowdonia, and Skye.

The sources: thanks to Ken Crocket, Iain R. Mitchell, David Craig and the late Campbell Steven, Ben Humble and Otta Swire for producing the best and most readable works committed to print on the history of the Scottish hills. Your books – all detailed in the Bibliography – were an indispensable source of research and collectively brought to life some of the characters who so captivated me in the making of this book. Also thank you to Stuart Pedlar, whose knowledge of the Cuillin's history is peerlessly detailed and whose help was greatly appreciated; your manuscript *Across Uncharted Space* is surely destined to be the great mystical text of the Cuillin.

I am also indebted to Dr Simon Wellings for providing geological insights; Kathleen Dickson at the British Film Institute for tracking down footage of John MacKenzie; Nigel Buckley at the Alpine Club for providing an excellent scan of Charles Pilkington's map of the Cuillin; the staff of the Scottish Mountaineering Club for unearthing old reports from their journal; Gill Houlsby, for assisting my research with some great detective work; Jill Croskell of the Pinnacle Club; and D&M Books in West Yorkshire for doing me a hot deal on a rare book.

Thank you to Myles Archibald of William Collins, for his faith and godlike patience; to Mark Bolland, for sensitive and insightful work on the edit; and to Hazel Eriksson for dilligently shepherding it to print.

For immeasurable support in all years: my parents and my family, having the faith and confidence to let me set off and have my own scuffles with the world. Particularly you, Mum – for giving me the words to write with in every form.

Most importantly, thank you to my wife Rachel for patience, kindness and support throughout difficult times. To my children Evelyn and Eliott, for being my best adventure and proudest achievement, and for keeping me smiling every day. It goes without saying that the most important part of me will always belong to the three of you – but I'll say it anyway.

And to Skye itself. You are a remarkable and eccentric place of the most extraordinary light, and extraordinary darkness. Five years isn't long enough. Forty wouldn't be enough. Thank you for the ride. Stay wild, stay dangerous. And stay there – because I'll be back.

Bibliography

Abraham, Ashley, *Rock Climbing in Skye*, 1908

Baker, Ernest A., *The Highlands with Rope and Rucksack*, 1933

Bell, J. H. B., *A Progress in Mountaineering*, 1950

Benson, Claude E., *British Mountaineering*, 1909

Boswell, James, *The Journal of a Tour to the Hebrides*, 1785

Brooker, W. D. (ed.), *A Century of Scottish Mountaineering*, 1988

Bryson, Bill, *A Short History of Nearly Everything*, 2004

Buchan, John, *Mr Standfast*, 1919

Buchanan, Robert, *The Hebrid Isles*, 1871

Bull, Shirley P., *The Black Cuillin Ridge Scrambler's Guide*, 1986

Burke, Edmund, *A Philosophical Enquiry into the Origin of Our Ideas of the Sublime and Beautiful*, 1757

Cameron, Alexander, *History and Traditions of the Isle of Skye*, 1871

Campbell, John Gregorson, *Superstitions of the Highlands and Islands of Scotland (Collected Entirely from Oral Sources)*, 1900

Carroll, Lewis, *Jabberwocky*, 1871

Collie, J. Norman, *From the Himalayas to Skye*, 2003

Collie, J. Norman, *Climbing on the Himalaya and Other Mountain Ranges*, 1902

Cooper, Derek, *Skye*, 1970

Cooper, Derek, *Hebridean Connection*, 1977

Craig, David, *Native Stones*, 1987

Crocket, Ken, *Mountaineering in Scotland: Vol 1 – The Early Years*, 2015

Crocket, Ken, *Mountaineering in Scotland: Vol 2 – Years of Change*, 2017

Crumley, Jim, *The Heart of Skye*, 1994

Cumming, C. F., *In the Hebrides*, 1881

Drummond, Peter, *Scottish Hill Names*, 1991

Forbes, Alexander Robert, *Place-Names of Skye and Adjacent Islands*, 1923

Gaiman, Neil, *The Truth Is a Cave in the Black Mountains*, 2014

Geike, Archibald, *The Scenery of Scotland*, 1865

Geike, Archibald, *Scottish Reminiscences*, 1904

Gordon, Seton, *The Charm of Skye: The Winged Isle*, 1934

Gordon, Seton, *Highways and Byways in the West Highlands*, 1935

Harker, Alfred, *Tertiary Igneous Rocks of Skye*, 1904

Hawkes, Jacquetta, *A Land*, 1951

Humble, Ben, *The Cuillin of Skye*, 1952

Humble, Ben, *Tramping on Skye*, 1933

Hutton, James, *Theory of the Earth, Volumes I–III*, 1788–1899

Ingram, Simon, *Between the Sunset and the Sea*, 2015

Johnson, Samuel, *A Journey to the Western Islands of Scotland*, 1775

Kenny, Anthony, *Mountains: An Anthology*, 1991

Lauden, Rachel, *From Mineralogy to Geology: The Foundations of Science
    1650–1830*, 1987

Lesingham Smith, C., *Excursions through the Highlands and Islands of Scotland
    in 1835 and 1836*, 1837

Lloyd-Jones, Robin, *The Sunlit Summit: The Life of W. H. Murray*, 2013

MacCulloch, J. A., *The Misty Isle of Skye*, 1905

MacCulloch, John, *The Highlands and Western Isles of Scotland, Vols I–IV*,
    1824

Macdonald, Norman and Maclean, Cailean, *The Great Book of Skye, Volume
    1*, 2014

Macdonald, Norman and Maclean, Cailean, *The Great Book of Skye, Volume
    2*, 2016

Macdonald, Norman and Maclean, Cailean, *The Great Book of Skye, Volume
    3*, 2018

Macfarlane, Walter, *Macfarlane's Geographical Collections, Vol. II*, 1906

MacGregor, Alasdair Alpin, *Over the Sea to Skye*, 1924

MacGregor, Alasdair Alpin, *The Enchanted Isles*, 1967

MacInnes, Hamish, *Call Out*, 1973

Mackenzie, William, *Old Skye Tales*, 1930

Maclean, Allan Campbell, *The Hill of the Red Fox*, 1955

Maclean, Sorley, *An Cuilithionn – 1939 and Unpublished Poems*, 2011

Manley, Gordon, *Climate and the British Scene*, 1952

Martin, Martin, *A Description of the Western Islands of Scotland*, 1703

Maxwell, Gavin, *Harpoon at a Venture*, 1952

McKirdy, A. & Crofts, R., *Scotland: The Creation of its Natural Landscape*, 2010

Mill, Christine, *Norman Collie: A Life in Two Worlds*, 1987

Mitchell, Ian R, *Scotland's Mountains Before the Mountaineers*, 2004

Morton, H. V., *In Search of Scotland*, 1929

Murray, W. H., *The Hebrides*, 1966

Murray, W. H., *Mountaineering in Scotland*, 1947

Murray, W. H., *Undiscovered Scotland*, 1951

Murray, W. H., *The Evidence of Things Not Seen*, 2002

Playfair, John, *Biographical Account of James Hutton*, 1805

Poucher, W. H., *The Magic of Skye*, 1949

Prebble, John, *The Highland Clearances*, 1963

Raeburn, Harold, *Mountaineering Art*, 1920

Richmond, W. Kenneth, *Climber's Testament*, 1950

Slesser, Malcolm, *The Island of Skye*, 1970

Smith, Alexander, *A Summer in Skye*, 1865

Smythe, Frank, *Mountains in Colour*, 1949

Stainforth, Gordon, *The Cuillin: Great Mountain Ridge of Skye*, 1994

Steven, Campbell, *The Story of Scotland's Hills*, 1975

Steven, Campbell, *Island Hills*, 1955

Swire, Otta, *Skye: The Island and its Legends*, 1952

Sykes, Ian, *In the Shadow of Ben Nevis*, 2016

Taylor, William C., *The Snows of Yesteryear*, 1979

Upton, Brian, *Volcanoes and the Making of Scotland*, 2004

Wainwright, Alfred, *Wainwright in Scotland*, 1988

Walker, J. Hubert, *On Hills of the North*, 1948

Weld, C. R., *Two Months in the Highlands, Orcadia, and Skye*, 1860

Winthrop Young, Geoffrey, *Mountain Craft*, 1920

Wordsworth, W. & Coleridge, S. T., *Lyrical Ballads*, 1798
Young, Andrew, *Selected Poems*, 1998

Other sources

I would like to acknowledge these invaluable repositories of information: *The Fell and Rock Climbing Club Journal*, *The New York Times*, The Pinnacle Club, The Alpine Club, The American Alpine Club, The British Geological Society, *The Guardian*, *The Times*, *The Holocene Journal*, The Scottish Mountaineering Club, The Royal Society, Ordnance Survey, Imperial College London, The British Mountaineering Council, *Trail Magazine*, Electric Scotland, JSTOR, *The Geological Conservation Review*, The British Library, The National Library of Scotland, Harvard University Library, The Botanical Society of Britain and Ireland, Scottish Natural Heritage, The John Muir Trust, The Met Office, *Good Words Magazine*, and *National Geographic*.

Index

Note: FA denotes first ascent

Abraham, Ashley, 324–5, 326, 511
  on Cuillin traverse, 451
  Rock-climbing in Skye, 302, 304
Addison, Joseph, 25, 148
Admiralty Survey, 275, 276
Agassiz, Louis, 130–1
Agazarian, Noel, 475, 476
Alba, Kingdom of, 116
Alexander III, King of Scotland, 119
Allt an Fhionn-choire, 390
Allt Coire Làgan, 98
Allt na Buaile Duibhe, 98, 110
Alpine Club, 225, 311, 313, 314, 332, 345, 452, 459, 471, 522
Alpine Journal, 79, 174, 302, 349, 470
  first Skye article (Pilkington), 331
  'John Thom: Mountaineer', 522
  'On the Heights of some of the Black Cuchullins in Skye' (Collie), 348, 351–2
Alps, 131, 223, 289, 314, 354, 392, 461
  Cuillin comparison, 128, 134–5, 178–9, 180
  Hart in, 347
  Pilkingtons in, 313, 315
  Thom in, 522
altitude sickness, 455
Am Bàsteir, 76, 77, 192, 391–2, 398–9, 403–4, 408, 510, 530

Collie's last climb, 473
  Hart/MacKenzie (FA 1887), 349, 352
  see also Bàsteir Tooth
Am Fear Liath Mòr (Big Grey Man), 345
American Alpine Journal, 462
American Civil War, 147
An Caisteal, 77, 242
An Corran, 63, 109–10
An Cruachan, 98
An Cuilthionn/An Cuiltheann, 98, 101, 103
  see also Cuillin
An Dorus Mòr (Bealach Coire na Banachdich), 76, 196
An Garbh-choire, 287, 497
An Guirdil, 433
An Stac, 286; *see also* Inaccessible Pinnacle
An t-Eilean Sgitheanach, 13
Annapurna, 207
Anne, Queen, 145
Appalachians, 59
Applecross, 23, 110, 185, 527
Arabis alpina (alpine rock-cress), 222–3, 225–6, 389
Ardnamurchan Peninsula, 64
Argyll and Sutherland Highlanders, 491
Arran, 38, 51, 53, 64, 195, 452
Atkinson, John, 309
Atlantic Ocean

formation, 57, 64–5
mid-ocean ridge, 59–60, 65
see also seafloor spreading
Atwater, Tanya, 62
Avalonia, 58

Baker, Ernest A., 73
The Highlands with a Rope and Rucksack, 242
Baly, E. C. C., 343, 475
Baltica, 58
Barker, Mabel 'M.M.', 457–8
Barlow, Guy, 469, 517
Barratt, Matt (guide)
first meeting with author, 182, 183, 184–7
guides author on Great Traverse, 209–18,
220, 223–5, 226–30, 234–5, 236–8,
267–70, 281–3, 291–5, 296–7
guides author on Inaccessible Pinnacle,
305–8, 311–13, 318–23, 327–30
guides author on Sgùrr nan Gillean,
512–16, 518–19, 520–1, 523–31
Mount Stanley expedition, 300–1
Barrington, Charles, 314, 315
Barrington, R. B., 347
basalt, 51, 74, 133, 281
columns, 66
cone sheets, 84–5
dykes, 83–4, 85, 293, 326–7
flood, 64–5, 307
shield volcanoes, 67
soil 66, 221
vs gabbro, 68, 72, 209, 218, 308, 327
Bàsteir Tooth, 76, 81, 360, 404
Collie/MacKenzie (FA 1889), 352, 404
McLaren/Shadbolt (Naismith's Route,
1911), 454
Naismith/Mackay (Naismith's Route, FA
1896), 450–1
Basuto War, 392
Bealach a' Garbh-choire, 228
Bealach a' Mhàim, 386, 459
Bealach Coire na Banachdich, 76, 196
Bealach Mòr, 249
Bealach nan Lice, 390–1, 398, 402, 403
Bean-nighe (washing woman), 249

Beinn na Caillich, 151, 234, 517
Pennant (FA 1772), 193
Bell, J. H. B., 85, 456
Bell, John Hart, 270
Bell, Joseph, 344
Ben Cleat
author's night on, 41–3, 55–6, 71
view of Cuillin, 71, 74–6, 80, 241
Ben Nevis, 131, 190, 369, 374, 422, 500
Tower Ridge, 178
Ben Wyvis, 396–7
Benbecula, 146, 152
Benmore Hill, Rum, 105
Benson, A., 502
beryllium dating, 139
Between the Sunset and the Sea (Ingram), 345
Bicknell, Peter, 38, 330, 465
Bidein Druim nan Ramh, 76, 77, 339, 382, 454,
504
Naismith (north top, FA 1880), 341
Big Grey Man, 345
Blàbheinn, 40, 84, 100, 216, 220, 275, 276, 341,
374, 423, 465
naming, 222
Swinburne/Nichol (1857), 260
view of Cuillin from, 317, 403–4
see also Clach Glas
Blackstones Bank, 64
Blaeu, Joan: *Atlas of Scotland*, 13, 14, 99–100
Blair, Hugh, 156
Blaven, 40, *see also* Blàbheinn
Bloody Stone (Harta Corrie), 121, 189, 409
Blue Men of the Minch, 250
Bohren, Peter, 522
Bolster Stones (Inaccessible Pinnacle), 327–8,
329
Bonington, Chris, 505
Boreaig, 372–3
Borrow, George, 443
Boswell, James, 150–1, 154, 263
Journal of a Tour to the Hebrides, 464
Boulton, Sir Harold, 147
Bowles, Tho, 13
Brecon Beacons, 26, 430
Bristow, Lily, 460

British Admiralty, 105
British Film Institute, London, 169
British Hydrographic Office, 310
British Tertiary Volcanic Province, 67
Broadford, 11, 28, 241, 251, 378, 429, 483, 486
broch (*dun*), 111
Brocken Spectre, 528
Bronze Age, 111
Brotherton, Lyle, 31
Brown, W., 353–4
Browne, James, 162–3
Bruach na Frithe, 76, 77, 165, 341, 380, 381, 382,
      409, 454, 459, 476, 517
   author's ascent, 385–92, 397–401, 402–5
   Forbes (FA 1845), 274
   naming, 401
   trig pillar, 284, 399–400
Bruce, Charles, 356
Brude, King of the Picts, 114
Brunskill, Walter, 318, 326
Bryson, Bill: *A Short History of Nearly Everything*,
      54
Buchan, John, 452
Mr Standfast, 73
Buchanan, Robert, 252
The Hebrid Isles, 275
Buckland, William, 131
Buffon, Comte de, 47
Bull, S. P. (Shirley 'Bunny'): *Black Cuillin Ridge:
      Scramblers' Guide*, 463–4
Burke, Betty, 146
Burn, A. R. G., 397
Burney, Fanny, 149

Cadair Idris, 242
Cailleach Bheur ('hag of the ridges'), 254–5
Cairngorm Club, 345, 422
Cairngorm Mountain Rescue, 431
Cairngorms, 57, 138, 152, 236, 396
cairns, 283–4, 341, 516–18
   ambiguity, 516–17
   burial, 111
Caisteal a' Garbh-coire, 229, 453–4
Caledonides (mountain range), 58–9
Camasunary Bay, 80, 212

bothy, 15–19
   naming, 16
   walk from Elgol, 15
Cambridge University, 61, 188, 461, 461, 464
Campbell, Mary, 242, 462, 468
   'The Canadian Boat Song', 372
Canna, 111, 215, 294
Carbost, 29, 84, 96, 361, 367, 535
   Old Inn, 29–31, 358–9, 361
   Oyster Shed, 29, 30, 361
   view of Cuillin, 82, 361
Carn nam Bodach, 249
Carroll, Lewis, 441
   'Jabberwocky', 466–7
Catastrophism, 47–50, 130
Catholicism, 113, 145, 249, 484
Celts, 116, 162, 485
   and Gaels, 115–16
   gods, 243
Cesarotti, Melchiorre, 157
Charleson, Ian, 465
Charles I, King, 144
Charlie, Bonnie Prince, 144, 145–7, 151, 345, 484
Chisholm, Agnes, 242, 462–3, 468, 488
Christianity, 113–15, 116, 248
Cioch, 423, 449, 459, 472, 490, 492, 506
   Collie discovers, 356–7, 449
   Collie/MacKenzie (FA 1906), 357–8
   Gully, 517
cirques, 128; *see also* corries
Clach Ard (Tall Stone), 112
Clach Glas, 100, 222, 465
clans, 29–30, 119–22, 144, 148, 373
Clearances, *see* Highland Clearances
climate change, 128
Climber (magazine), 464
climbing gear
   crampons, 321, 496–7, 499, 503
   footwear, 518
   gloves, 210, 213, 294, 523
   harness, 266–7, 312
   ice axe, 494, 497
   ropes, 269–72
climbing, rock, *see* rock climbing
Cluanie Inn, 509

Cnoc Carnach, 83

Cobbler, The, 381

Cockburn, Henry Thomas, Lord
  on Loch Coruisk, 26, 219
  on Skye, 11–12

Coir a' Ghrunnda, 228, 241; see also Loch Coir'
  a' Ghrunnda

Coir' Uisg, 252–3

Coire a' Bhasteir, 261, 336, 391

Coire a' Chruidh, 215

Coire Labain, 330

Coire Làgan, 101, 241, 276–7, 280, 281, 330, 356,
  357, 469, 496
  author in, 98, 125, 128–9, 135–6, 139–41,
    165–6, 169, 297, 409–11
  author's accident/rescue, 411–20, 429–30,
    434–5, 513
  round (Hart, 1887), 349
  see also Lochan Coire Làgan

Coire na Banachdich, 76, 196, 277–9

Coire na Creiche, 87, 121, 226

Coireachan Ruadha Crags, 75, 280, 292, 322,
  339

Colby, Col Thomas, 191–2

Collie (Australian town), 345

Collie, Alexander, 345

Collie, John Norman
  Alpine Club president, 471
  Bàsteir Tooth (FA 1888), 352, 404
  and cairns, 517–18
  character, 342, 343, 344, 346, 347, 350, 473,
    474, 475
  Cioch discovery 356–7, 449
  Cioch (FA 1906), 357–8
  and Crowley, 344–5
  Dreams, 470–1, 472
  final years/death, 470, 473–8, 489
  on Gaelic culture/Clearances, 485
  grave, 535–6
  guide, 180, 423–4, 459, 461
  in Himalayas, 455
  and Humble, 488, 489
  Humble on, 352
  Inaccessible Pinnacle, 348
  'The Island of Skye', 471–2
  last climb, 473
  and MacKenzie, 172–3, 180, 337, 349–50,
    353, 423–4, 469–70, 471–3, 517–18
  on mountains, 247, 532
  namesakes, 345–6, 352–3, 471, 473
  'On the Heights of some of the Black
    Cuchullins in Skye', 348, 351–2
  portrait (Sligachan Hotel), 299, 532
  scientist, 342–4, 351, 474
  Sgùrr a' Ghreadaidh ('Collie's Route', FA
    1896), 353
  Sgùrr Alasdair, 348, 352–3, 424
  Sgùrr nan Gillean, 344–5, 350
  Sherlock Holmes comparison, 344, 345
  at Sligachan Hotel, 469, 473–4, 475,
    476–7, 489, 517
  statue (Sligachan), 172–3, 345, 536
  TD Gap (first crossing, 1891), 449–50
  Winthrop Young on, 424, 474, 477–8, 518

Collie's Ledge, 23, 75, 297, 348–9, 353

Columba, St, 113–15, 116

Columbia Icefield, 357

cone sheets, 84–5

continental drift, 58; see also seafloor spreading

Cooper, Derek, 252, 474

corries, 93, 121, 125–6, 128–9, 130
  formation, 137
  see also individual Coires

Corry, 11

Coruisk Memorial Hut, 214, 457, 496, 498, 499
  see also Loch Coruisk

Crabbe, Dave, 503, 505

Craig, David: Native Stones, 171

Creag Dhu climbing club, 493

Creationism, 47, 48, 131

Crocket, Ken
  History of Scottish Mountaineering, 341
  Mountaineering in Scotland: The Early Years,
    272, 451

crofts, 86, 250

Crowley, Aleister, 344–5

Crumley, Jim: The Heart of Skye, 13

Cú Chulainn (Cuchullin/Cuthulinn/Cúchu-
  lainn) (Irish warrior), 160, 233–4

Cuillin

character, 23, 82–3, 482, 483
  colour, 72–4
  darkness/dread, 11, 24, 26, 31, 95, 219,
      238, 244, 250, 252–3, 310, 362–3,
      443, 487, 515, 521
  desolation/sterility, 11–12, 26, 218–19
  lure of, 26–7, 31–2, 175, 482–3, 537–8
  at nightfall, 235–6, 241, 245
  shapeshifting, 257
  steepness, 83, 85–6
  vs Alps, 134–5, 178–9, 180
  vs Lake District, 26, 38, 236, 367
  vs Rum, 104–5
  in winter, 502
etymology
  of mountains, 24, 76–7, 105, 297; see
      also under individual mountains
  of range, 98–105, 118, 234
flora/fauna
  birds, 220–1
  flora, 101, 219, 220, 221–3, 225–6,
      249, 389
  mammals, 220, 222; see also Highland
      cattle
for sale, 373–4
geology/geological history, 43–7, 55–7,
    62–8, 72–3, 82–4, 98
  glaciation, 126–35, 136–9, 140–1, 514
  see also corries
Great Traverse, 24, 27, 28, 174, 179, 181,
    296
  author's attempt, 209–18, 220, 223–5,
      226–30, 234–5, 236–8, 267–70,
      281–3, 291–5, 296–7; see also under
      Sgumain Cave
  author's attempt, preparation, 32, 87,
      186–7, 203–7, 208–9
  distance, 235
  Goodfellow/Yates (north to south,
      1924), 456
  Greater Traverse, 465
  in a day, 235–6, 296
  MacInnes/Patey (winter, 1965), 502–5
  McLaren/Shadbolt (first, 1911), 452–5,
      517
  major obstacles, 449–51
  Pinnacle Club (horseshoe attempts,
      1925/6), 457–8
  records, 38, 465
  Smythe/Bell (1924), 456
  Somervell (second, 1920), 455–6
in literature and art
  Buchan, 73
  Cockburn, 26
  Forbes, 165
  Harker, 83
  Kershaw (artist), 22–3
  MacCulloch, 71, 175, 244
  MacGregor, 77–8, 81
  MacInnes, 506–7
  Maclean (A' Chuilthionn), 486–7
  Morton, 100–1
  Murray, 492
  Nivan (artist), 30–1, 359–63
  Pilkington (poem), 331
  Poucher, 81
  Richmond, 23
  Scott (The Lord of the Isles), 25, 160,
      161, 218
  Shadbolt, 454
  Smith, 73–4
  Smythe, 456
  statues (Collie/MacKenzie), 172–3,
      345, 536
  Swire, 481
  Turner (Loch Coruisk), 161, 220
  Wainwright, 402
  Weld, 310
  Young (poem), 487
maps, see maps
mountaineering and guiding
  access, 87
  caves/howffs, 242–3, 469, 489; see also
      Sgumain Cave
  compasses and magnetism, 28, 62,
      177, 401, 457
  first explorations of ridge, 187–92
  first fatalities, 421–2
  first tourist on ridge (1834), 188–91
  gear, see climbing gear

guide, author chooses, 181–3, 184–7
guide, first, see MacIntyre, Duncan
guide, first female, see Moffatt, Gwen
guides/guiding, 177–8, 179–81, 193,
    194, 268
  hazards, 27–8, 95, 176–7
  Munros, 397
  navigation, 28, 236
  need for guide/rope, 28, 177, 522
  severity, 173–6
  water sources/difficulties, 179, 228,
    389, 454, 456
  see also individual mountains
views from
    Ben Cleat, 71, 74–6, 80, 241
    Carbost, 82, 361
    Drynoch, 83
    Elgol, 209–10, 258
    Glen Brittle, 339, 403
    Portnalong, 87
    Redpoint, 24
    Rum, 104
    Sligachan, 80–1, 403–4
Cuillin Coffee Co, 97
Cuillin Cottage, 242, 468, 496, 497
Cuillin FM, 369
Culloden, Battle of, 145–6, 147, 157, 370
Cumming, C. F. Gordon: In the Hebrides, 89–90
Cunningham, John, 494
Cuvier, Georges, 47–9
cwms, 129; see also corries

Daily Express (Scottish), 262
Daily Telegraph, 263
Dal Riata (kingdom), 113, 114, 115, 117, 119
Dalton, Ida Fitzgerald, 460
Daniell, William, 161
Dante, 25
Daoine Sithe (Spirit of the Hills), 243, 251
Dark Ages, 112
Dartmoor, 443
Davie, James, 50
Davies, Edith, 458
Deane, Claude, 458
Deccan Traps, 65

Demon Shower (waterfall), 97–8, 122–3, 125
Dent, Clinton, 302, 332
Depression, 468, 469
Dickens, Charles: Household Words, 90
Dietz, Robert, 60
dinosaurs, 49, 59, 62–3, 131
Discovery, HMS, 346
Donan, St, 115
Doughty, A. H., 468
Douglas, William, 350, 450, 520
Doyle, Sir Arthur Conan, 344–5
    Memories and Adventures, 344
Druim nan Ramh, 76, 77, 85, 103, 190, 293, 339,
    341, 382, 454, 504, 527
Drummond, Peter, 279
    Scottish Hill Names, 101
Drynoch, 512
    view of Cuillin, 83
Dubh Ridge, 75, 77, 237, 251, 360
    1963 accident, 496–500, 502
Duirnish Peninsula, 39, 66, 259
Dun Caan, Raasay, 151
Duntulm, 13, 111, 250
Dunvegan, 39, 66, 111, 252, 465
    Castle, 373, 374
dykes, 83–4, 85, 293, 326–7

Earth
    asthenosphere, 64
    crust, 52, 57, 60, 61, 64
    early theories of, 46–50
    magnetism, 61–2
    mantle, 60, 64, 65, 67
Eas Mòr, 306
Eckhard, Marlin, 335
Edinburgh, 50, 54, 134, 145, 150, 154, 260, 344,
    361
Edinburgh Philosophical Journal, 132
Edinburgh University, 132, 152
Eigg, 113, 215, 335
Eilean Bàn, 335
El Alamein, Battle of, 486
El Capitan, 447
Elgol, 15, 39, 87, 146, 189, 457, 537
    view of Cuillin, 209–10, 258

Emer, 233
English Civil War, 144
Ensmark, Jens, 130
Eriskay, Outer Hebrides, 145
Erse, 152
Ervine, St John, 469, 474
Everest, Mount, 430, 455, 456, 494, 501
Executioner, The, see Am Bàsteir
extinctions, 48

Fairy Pools, 84, 355, 362, 368, 378, 380, 381,
    382–5, 386, 409, 436
Fallon, Steven, 397
Faroes, 65
Fell and Rock Climbing Club, 426, 456, 458
Fenian Cycle, 153
Fergus the Great, King of Dal Riata, 113
figwort, 249
Fingal (Fhionn mac Cumhaill), 102, 152–4, 156
    see also Ossianic poems
Fingal's Cave, 66
Finnian of Clonard, 113
Fionn Coire, 386, 387, 388–9
Fionn mac Cumhaill (Finn MacCool), 153
    see also Fingal
First Aid Committee of Mountaineering Clubs,
    426, 427
First World War, 86, 425, 427, 452, 455, 464,
    471
Fiscavaig, 369
Flat Stone, 391
Fletcher, Martin, 300
Forbes, James David, 132–3, 141, 160, 164, 263,
    278, 345
    Cuillin map, 194, 197, 332, 351
    glaciation theory, 134–5, 314, 410
    Sgùrr nan Gillean (FA 1836), 164–5, 175,
        187, 188, 194, 260, 274, 511
    Sgùrr nan Gillean height measurement,
        264
Forbes, Sir William, 132
Forde, W. E., 465
Forlani, Paolo, 13
Fort William, 92, 498
fossil fuels, 48

fossils, 44, 45, 48, 49, 54, 59, 63, 393
fowlers/fowling, 193, 194, 423
Frankland, Claude Deane 'C.D.', 457–8
Fraser, James, 422
Free Presbyterian Church, Loch Harport, 535
Free Solo (film), 447
Fylde Mountaineering Club Newsletter, 520

gabbro, 43, 74, 133, 225, 227, 269, 326, 357, 398,
    518, 523, 528
    formation, 68
    friction/grip, 72, 86, 134, 136, 165, 175,
        204, 209, 273, 340, 422, 513, 526
    magma core, 98, 127
    resistance to weathering/strength, 83, 85
    screes, 86
    vs basalt, 68, 72, 209, 218, 308, 327
Gaelic
    Cuillin naming, 99, 100, 101, 102, 103
    culture, 158, 376, 484–6
    Erse, 152
    folklore/mythology, 94–5, 158, 248,
        249–53, 254–5; see also Ossianic
        poems
    Irish, 100, 101, 103, 116, 152
    language, 148, 152, 262, 325, 370, 485
    mountain names, see under individual
        mountains
    place names, 103, 109, 118, 437
    proverb, 194
    prayer, 248
    Scots, 14, 100, 101, 103, 116, 437
    Skye naming, 12, 13
Gaelic College (Sabhal Mòr Ostaig), 375, 485,
    486
Gaels, 115, 116, 117–19
    and Celts, 115–16
    Irish vs Scottish, 370
Gaiman, Neil: The Truth Is a Cave in the Black
    Mountains, 481–2, 494
Gars-bheinn, 75, 77, 87, 212, 214–15, 216–17,
    227, 258, 275, 276, 287, 334
gear, see climbing gear
Geddes, Joseph 'Tex', 335
    Hebridean Sharker, 333

Geikie, Sir Archibald, 55, 104, 137
  Highland Reminiscences, 164, 372
  The Scenery of Scotland, 158, 370
Geological Society of Edinburgh, 54
George I, King, 145
Giant's Causeway, 66
glaistig (hag/she-devil), 251
Glamaig, 100, 104, 143, 362, 421, 527
Glasgow Herald, 341
Glasgow, 114, 291, 469, 493, 496
Glen Almain, 158
Glen Breatal, 278
Glen Brittle, 76, 82, 87, 88, 141, 196, 278, 385, 386
  geological dividing line, 98
  road, 96, 276, 378, 381, 382
  view of Cuillin, 339, 403
  view of Waterpipe Gully, 354–5
  see also Fairy Pools
Glenbrittle (settlement), 87–8, 96, 242, 305
  campsite, 96–7, 468, 492
  Cuillin Cottage, 468, 496
  MacRae barn, 468
  vs Sligachan, 468
Glenbrittle House, 276, 332, 357, 462, 468, 471
Glen Coe, 73, 158, 178, 396, 503
Glencoe (settlement) 493
Glencoe Mountain Rescue, 428, 431, 494, 500
Glencoe (steamer), 488
Glen Coruisk, 317; *see also* Loch Coruisk
Glen Drynoch, 512
Glen Roy (parallel roads), 131
Glen Sligachan, 76, 81, 121, 172, 188, 190, 289, 374, 404, 409, 513; *see also* Sligachan Hotel
Glorious Revolution, 145
gneiss, *see* Lewisian gneiss
Goethe, J. W. von, 49, 148, 157
Goggs, F. S., 272
Good Words (magazine), 263, 277, 522
Goodfellow, B. R., 456
Gordon, Seton, 279, 293, 303, 381, 454
  botanist, 101, 221–2
  The Charm of Skye, 94, 196, 243–4
  on Cuillin, 177, 196, 381, 389

Highways and Byways of the West Highlands, 389
  night on Sgùrr Dearg, 243–4
Grand Tour, 80, 129, 148, 314
granite, 51, 53
  plutons, 68
  weathering *vs* gabbro, 83
Great Book of Skye, The (Maclean/Macdonald), 153, 277, 293, 324, 374–5, 376
Great Stone Shoot, 86, 244, 280, 292, 293–4, 360
Greenland, 45, 58, 65, 226
Greece, Ancient, 156
Grenier, Katherine Haldane: *Tourism and Identity in Scotland*, 162, 219
Griffith, Arthur R., 488
gruagach (a spirit), 250
Guardian, 92, 377
Gulf Stream, 91
Gunn, Robert, 114
Gurkhas, 356, 455
guyots, 59, 60

Hackert, Frank, 377
Haco (Haakon IV Haakonsson), King of Norway, 119
Hadrian's Wall, 57
Hall, Sir John, 50, 51
Hallitt, Arthur, 355
Hallstatt, Austria, 116
Harker, Alfred, 137
Hess, Harry Hammond: 'History of Ocean Basins', 59–60
Harker, Alfred, 83, 137
  Cuillin map (1898), 351
  'The Tertiary Igneous Rocks of Skye', 73
Harris, 14, 29, 38, 86, 195, 294, 375, 433–4
Hart, Henry Chichester
  in Alps, 347
  Am Bàsteir (FA 1887), 349, 352, 399
  character, 347
  Coire Làgan round (1887), 349
  'Hart's' ledge, 349, 352; *see also* Collie's Ledge
  naturalist, 225–6, 346–7, 352

scorn for ropes, 347–8
Sgùrr Alasdair height measurement, 226,
    348
Harta Corrie, 289
    Bloody Stone, 121, 189, 409
Haskett-Smith, Walter Parry, 342
Hastings, Geoffrey, 332, 353, 455
Hawkes, Jacquetta: *A Land*, 46–7, 56–7
Hebrides, 94, 111, 114, 115, 116, 117, 118, 119, 120,
    148, 159
    see also individual islands
Heelis, James, 315, 323, 325
Heron, Johnny, 28–30
Heron, Katie, 28–9, 79, 378, 436
Hey, Wilson, 425, 426–8
Highland cattle, 40–1, 211, 538
Highland Clearances, 122, 263, 370–3, 485, 486
Hillary, Edmund, 169, 494
Hillary, Richard, 475–7
    The Last Enemy, 475
Hinde, John, 499
Holmes, Sherlock, 344, 345, 351
Honnold, Alex, 447
Horner, Leonard, 54
Hostile Habitats: Scotland's Mountain Environment
    (Wrightham/Kempe), 326–7
howffs/caves, 242–3, 469, 489; *see also* Sgumain
    Cave
Hulton, Eustace, 315–16, 323
Humble, Ben, 24, 431, 487–90
    and Collie, 488, 489
    on Collie, 352
    The Cuillin of Skye, 72–3, 146, 242–3,
        289–90, 324, 355, 458, 460, 464,
        487–8, 489, 490
    encounters MacKenzie, 470
    on Nicolson, 264
    photographer, 488, 490–1, 492, 506
    The Songs of Skye, 489
    Tramping in Skye, 488
Humble, Roy: *The Voice of the Hills*, 489
Hume, David, 156
Husabost, Alick, 260
Hutchinson, William, 490
Hutton, James, 50, 52–3, 54–5, 58

'Hutton's Unconformity', 51
    'Theory of the Earth', 52–4
    Theory of the Earth, 54, 55
    tour of Scotland, 50–1

Iapetus
    Ocean, 57, 58
    Suture, 57
Ice Age, 126–35, 136–9, 140–1, 514
Iceland, 64–5, 66
    Skjalbreiður, 67
Inaccessible Pinnacle, 75, 181, 216, 280, 402,
    512
    ascent/descent, author, 305–8, 311–13,
        318–23, 327–30
    Collie/MacKenzie (1888), 348
    Dalton/MacKenzie (1897), 460
    descriptions of, 302–4
    east ridge, 303, 326, 327, 349
    first literary reference, 309, 310, 311
    geology, 326–7
    Hart (solo traverse, 1887), 349
    Haskett-Smith (1886), 342
    height measurement, 311
    MacInnes/Patey (winter, 1965), 504
    McLaren/Shadbolt (1911), 453
    and Munro, 301–2, 395–6
    naming, 286, 302, 310, 376
    Pilkingtons (FA 1880), 313, 317–18, 323,
        325, 330, 332, 340
    Pilkingtons/MacKenzie (traverse, 1887),
        325–6
    west ridge, 323, 325, 348, 349
Inse Gall ('Islands of the Foreigners'), 118
Iona, 13, 113, 114
Irish Gaelic, 12, 100, 101–2, 103, 152
Irish mythology, 153; *see also* Cú Chulainn
Irish Scoti, 112–13
Iron Age, 109, 111–12
Irvine, Andrew, 456
Islay, 13

Jackson, Sir Herbert, 343
Jacobites, 145–6, 148, 370
James II, King, 145, 183

James, William: 'The Energies of Men', 450
Jefferson, Thomas, 157
Jenner, Edward, 278
John, St, 249, 469, 474
John Muir Trust, 374
Johnson, Dr Samuel, 148–52, 159, 192, 263, 517, 538
   Journey to the Western Isles of Scotland, 155
   and Macpherson, 154–5
   on Talisker, 438
   Tour of the Hebrides, 193
Joint Stretcher Committee, 426
Journal of Botany, 225
Junior Mountaineering Club of Scotland, 499
Jurassic period, 63, 66

kelp farming, 371
kelpies (*each-uisge*), 251–2
Kelsall, Joseph, 355–6
Kershaw, Paul L., 23
Keswick, 92
Kikiktaksoak Island, 92
Kildare, County, 102
Kilmuir, 146, 389
Kilt Rock, Staffin, 66
King, William Wickham, 355, 449–50
Kingsburgh House, 146
Kirwan, Richard, 53–4
Knight, Prof. William Angus, 324, 336
Knowlton, Elizabeth, 462–3
Kruse, Arne, 12, 118
Kyleakin, 13, 119, 335, 377
Kyle of Lochalsh, 37, 38–9

laccoliths, 84
Laddow Crags, 425
Ladies Alpine Club, 460
Ladies Scottish Climbing Club, 460
Laird, Alan, 497
Lake District, 23, 27, 57, 178, 471
   early rock climbing, 275, 309
   Helm Crag, 381, 402
   mountain rescue, 426, 428
   Pilkingtons in, 315, 331
   Thom in, 522

   vs Cuillin, 26, 38, 236, 367
   Wakefield in, 450
Largs, Battle of, 119
Largs festival, 119
Laudan, Rachel: *From Mineralogy to Geology: The Foundations of Modern Science*, 54
Laurentia, 45, 58
Le Blond, Lizzie, 460
Leabhar Dearg (the Red Book), 153–4
Leclerc, Georges-Louis, 47
Leppard, Tom (Leopard Man), 376–8
Lesingham Smith, Charles, 187–91, 193, 194, 293
   Excursions Through the Highlands and Isles of Scotland, 187–8, 191
   first tourist on ridge (1834), 188–91
Lewis, 14, 86, 92, 195, 429, 433–4, 485
Lewisian gneiss, 44, 62, 65, 72
limestone, 49, 66
Ling, Willie, 452–3
'Little Ice Age', 138
Liverpool Post, 422
Livingstone, Donald: *Sleeping with Your Boots On*, 483–4
Lloyd, Robin, 490
Loch Alsh, 510
Loch Bracadale, 14, 39
Loch Brittle, 88, 98, 110, 122, 294, 307, 332, 418
Loch Cill Chriosd, 40
Loch Coir' a' Ghrunnda, 222, 234, 236, 238, 453
Loch Coruisk, 25–6, 75, 76, 89, 137, 189, 215–16, 253, 286, 288, 303
   Cockburn on, 26, 219
   MacCulloch discovers, 160–1, 244–6
   Scott on, 25, 161, 216
   Turner painting, 161, 220
   Victorian tourists, 162, 219
Loch Coulin, 102
Loch Dunvegan, 39, 374
Loch Eishort, 39, 118
Loch Eynort, 39, 98
Loch Fada, 470
Loch Harport, 28, 29, 39, 82, 86, 359, 535
Loch Leven, 35

Loch Long, 381
Loch na Bèiste, 376
Loch na Dùbhrachan, 252
Loch Ness, 115, 252
Loch Reasort, 434
Loch Scavaig, 15, 39, 80, 160–1, 162, 188, 286, 512, 527
Loch Shiphoirt, 434
Loch Slapin, 39, 40, 248, 372
Loch Sligachan, 81
Loch Snizort, 38, 39
Lochan Coire Làgan, 139, 140, 410, 415
Lochan Dubh nam Bhreac, 251, 458
Lochan na h-Àirde, 116, 120
Lofoten, Norway, 357
Lota Corrie, 121, 391, 510
Louisa, Mary (Mrs. C. B. Phillip), 461
luideag ('ragwitch'), 251

MacAskill, Danny: *The Ridge*, 465
MacCulloch, Dr John A., 133–4, 162–3, 175, 193, 263–4
    on Cuillin, 71, 175, 244–5
    Description of the Western Isles of Scotland, 133
    discovers Loch Coruisk, 160–1, 244–6
    geological map, 133
    The Misty Isle of Skye, 71, 90
MacDonald, Angus Mor (Aonghus Mór mac Domhnaill), 120
MacDonald, Calum, 373
MacDonald, Flora, 146–7, 151, 345, 484
MacDonald, Lord, 371
Macdonald, Norman, 153, 277, 324, 375–6
MacFarlane, Robert, 14
MacGregor, Alasdair Alpin, 74, 81, 91, 176
    Over the Sea to Skye, 77–8, 176
MacKay, A. M., 452
    Bàsteir Tooth (Naismith's Route, FA 1896), 450–1
MacKay, William, 485
MacKenzie, 'Jonacks', 431
MacKenzie, John (guide), 171–2, 275, 285, 286, 323–5, 348, 375, 423, 460
    Abraham on, 325
    Am Bàsteir (FA 1887), 349, 352, 399

Cioch (FA 1906), 357–8
    and Collie, 172–3, 180, 337, 349–50, 353, 423–4, 449–50, 469–70, 471–3, 517–18
    grave, 535–6
    Humble on, 470
    MacKenzie's Peak, 331, 336
    Sgùrr Alastair (FA 1873), 258, 276–8, 280–1, 283–4, 293
    statue (Sligachan), 172–3, 345, 536
    TD Gap (first crossing, 1891), 449–50
    Winthrop Young on, 349–50
Mackenzie, Murdoch, 194–5
Mackenzie, William: *Old Skye Tales*, 247, 249
MacKinnon, Lachlan, 163
MacInnes, Hamish, 470, 493–5
    Call Out, 501
    on Cuillin, 505–6
    Cuillin FAs, 494, 506
    Great Traverse (winter, 1965), 502–5
    1963 Skye rescue, 496–500, 502
MacIntyre, Duncan (guide), 164–5, 189–91, 194, 511
McLaren, Alastair Campbell: Great Traverse (first, 1911), 452–5, 517
Maclean, Cailean, 153, 277, 375, 376
Maclean, Sorley, 14, 21–2, 32, 285, 375
    A' Chuilthionn (The Cuillin), 486–7
MacLeod, John, 373–4
MacLeod's Tables, 39, 66
MacNeacail, Alasdair, 260
    see also Nicolson, Alexander
MacNeill, Flora, 345
Macpherson, Alexander, 153
MacPherson, Angus (guide), 324
Macpherson, James
    and Johnson, 154–5
    and Ossianic poems, 152–4, 156–60, 163, 188
MacRae, Alexander (guide), 277, 290, 291
    Sgùrr Alasdair (FA 1873), 259, 276–8, 280–1, 283–4, 293
    Sgùrr Dearg (FA 1873), 279–80, 304
    Sgùrr na Banachdaich (FA 1873), 277–8, 279
    walking style, 268, 277

MacRaing, John, 248–9, 251
Mallaig, 23, 31, 35, 37
    Armadale crossing, 35–6, 37
Mallory, George, 169, 455, 456, 461, 475, 488
'Mallory's Slab and Groove', 464–5
Manchester Royal Infirmary, 425, 427
Manchester University, 427
maps
    Blaeu (1654), 99–100
    Forbes (1846), 194, 197, 332, 351
    geological, 45–6, 133
    Harker (1898), 351
    MacKenzie (1755), 194–5
    Ordnance Survey, see Ordnance Survey
    Pilkington (1890), 332, 341
    Regno di Scotia (c. 1560), 12–13
    Scotiae tabula, 13
    Wood's Admiralty chart, 310–11
Marsco, 104, 121, 290, 514, 527
Martin, Martin, 94, 193
    A Description of the Western Isles of Scotland,
        144
Maruma, Marlin Eckhard, 335
Maryon, Cpt. Arthur James, 20–1, 32, 41, 121,
    176, 391, 527, 536, 537
monument, 19–20, 21, 25
Mathews, William, 314
Matterhorn, 289, 314, 522
Matthews, Drummond, 61, 62
Maxwell, Gavin, 224, 333–5
    A Harpoon at Venture, 333–4
Maylard, A. Ernest: 'A Day in the Cuchuillins',
    295–6, 423–4
Meall Dearg, 84, 396
Merkl, Willy, 474–5
Mesolithic period, 109–10
Methven, John, 497, 498
midges, 93, 123, 166, 242, 383, 488
mid-ocean ridges, 59–60, 62
Mill, Christine: A Life in Two Worlds, 343, 348
Minginish, 118
Mitchell, Ian R.: Scotland's Mountains Before the
    Mountaineers, 192, 331
Moffatt, Gwen, 431, 464
Moncrieff, Lord, 396

Monro, Dean, 193
Monro, Donald, 143
Mont Blanc, 522
Monte Disgrazia, 315
Morley, Lawrence, 62
Moro, Anton, 49
morphine, 419, 425, 427–8
Morrison, W. A., 272–3
Morton, H. V.: In Search of Scotland, 89
mountain rescue, 31, 76, 88, 214
    Call Out (MacInnes), 501
    early (pre-Second World War), 424–6,
        500
    First Aid Committee of Mountaineering
        Clubs, 426, 427
    and Hey, 425, 426–8
    and Humble, 489–90
    Mountain Rescue Committee, 427
    post-Second World War, 428, 430–1
    and RAF, 430, 431, 498–500
    Search and Rescue Dogs Association, 494
    stretchers, 426, 494
    as volunteers, 437, 533
    see also Skye Mountain Rescue
mountaineering/mountaineers
    accidents, 407–8, 421–2, 425, 444–5; see
        also mountain rescue
    clubs, 469; see also individual clubs
    and fear/courage, 446–8
    first climbers, 192, 193–4
    gallows humour, 207–8, 407
    guiding, 177–8, 179–81, 193, 194, 268,
        464
    high-altitude, 207, 208, 455, 456, 462
    motives, 444, 445–6
    objective danger, 40, 407
    pivots to rock climbing in Cuillin, 353
    risks, 207, 208, 447, 449
    vs rock climbing, 170–1, 340
    women in, 459–64; see also Pinnacle Club
    see also under Cuillin
Muir, John, 139, 374
Mull, 13, 64, 113, 114, 195
Mummery, Albert, 455, 475
Mungo, St, 114

Munro, Donald, 13–14
Munro, Sir Campbell, 392
Munro, Sir Hugh Thomas, 302, 392–3, 395–6, 461
Munro's Tables, 216, 301–2, 393–4
Munro bagging, 301–2, 396–7
Murray, W. H., 431, 488, 490, 506
    The Islands of Western Scotland, 83
    Mountaineering in Scotland, 492
    in Second World War, 491–2

Naismith, William, 102, 253, 353
    Bàsteir Tooth (Naismith's Route, FA 1896), 450–1
    Bidein Druim nan Ramh (FA 1880), 341
    'Courage in Climbing', 446–7
    letter to *Glasgow Herald*, 341
    Sgùrr nan Gillean (1880), 340–1, 517, 519–20
Nanga Parbat, 455, 462, 471, 474–5
Napoleonic Wars, 157
nappes, 131
national parks, 430
National Scenic Areas, 222
National Service, 431
Necker, Louis Albert, 197
Neist Point, 378, 380, 385, 436
Nelms, Sarah, 278
Neptunism, 49
Newton, Isaac, 48
Niall, King, 113
Nichol, John, 260
Nicolson, Alexander, 259–60, 315, 324, 327, 331, 348, 349, 352, 421
    character/personality, 261–2, 526
    on Cuillin naming, 102
    Humble on, 264
    Good Words articles, 263, 277, 522, 523
    on Inaccessible Pinnacle, 304
    Isle of Skye: An Edinburgh Summer Song, 521
    on MacRae, 268
    mountaineer, 264
    'Nicolson's Chimney' (FA 1889), 290
    Sgùrr Alasdair (FA 1873), 258, 276–8, 280–1, 283–4, 293

Sgùrr Alastair, naming, 259–60, 284–5, 290, 346
Sgùrr Dearg (FA 1873), 279–80, 304
Sgùrr Dubh Mòr (FA 1873), 286–90, 349
Sgùrr na Banachdaich (FA 1873), 277–8, 279
Sgùrr nan Gillean (1865), 260–1, 511, 526
Sgùrr nan Gillean (winter, 1872), 264
    on Skye, 16, 262–3, 297, 379
    on Thom's accident, 522, 523
    use of plaid, 273–4, 287–8, 349
    vice president of SMC, 291
Nietzsche, Friedrich: *Beyond Good and Evil*, 445
Ninian, St, 114
Nithdale, Dumfries, 131
Nivan, Alastair (Ali), 30–1, 32, 359–60, 361–4
Noble, Ian, 485
nominative determinism, 452
Norgay, Tenzing, 494
Norman Conquest, 102
Norman, John, 299, 336, 342, 536
Norse, 99, 100, 153, 247
    place names, 38, 103, 118, 437
    rule, 12, 117–120
    Rum mountain names, 105
    Syke naming, 12
    see also Vikings
North America, 45, 57, 58, 127
North Atlantic Drift, 91
North Atlantic Igneous Province, 64–5
North Carolina, 147, 371
North Sea, 117, 477
Northern Ireland, 64, 66, 152, 153
Norway, 103, 117, 119, 130, 357, 471
Nova Scotia, 371, 373, 375

Old Man of Storr, 39, 66, 249, 304, 483
Old Testament, 47
Ordnance Gazetteer of Scotland, 11
Ordnance Survey, 216, 332, 393
    demotes Sgùrr nan Gillean, 264, 275
    one-inch Cuillin map (1885), 195–6, 285, 341
    map names, 76, 100, 104, 286, 292
    Skye survey (1819), 191–2, 193–4, 351, 392, 516

six-inch map (1882), 285
triangulation pillars, 284, 399–400
Ortelius, Abraham, 13
Ossianic poems, 152–4, 156–60, 163, 188
'Ossian's Cave', 158

paganism, 115, 247–8, 249
Pangaea, 58, 64
Panthalassa, 58
Parker, A. G.
    Inaccessible Pinnacle (west ridge, FA
        1886), 323
    Knight's Peak (1886), 336, 471, 516
Parker, J. A., 395
Parnassus, Mount, 242
Patey, Tom: Great Traverse (winter, 1965), 502–5
Pedlar, Stuart, 275, 349, 460
Pennant, Thomas, 99, 159, 218, 234
    Beinn na Caillich (FA 1772), 193
Perth, Treaty of, 119, 120
Phillip, Colin, 101, 345, 357, 471
Phipps, James, 278
Pictland, 112
Picts, 112, 113, 114–15, 116, 247
Pilkington, Charles, 95, 197, 258, 313–15, 332,
        347, 351
    Alpine Journal paper, 331
    in Alps/Lake District, 315
    The Black Coolins, 315
    Cuillin map, 332, 341
    Inaccessible Pinnacle (FA 1880), 313,
        317–18, 323, 325, 330, 332, 340
Pilkington, Lawrence, 313–15, 331–2, 421
    Cuillin poem, 331
    Inaccessible Pinnacle, see under Pilkington,
        Charles
Pilkington, Mabel, 332
Pilkington, Richard, 314
Pilley, Dorothy, 461, 471
    Climbing Days, 472
Pinnacle Club, 457, 458–60, 461, 464
Piton de la Fournaise, Réunion, 67
plaid
    outlawed, 148, 370
    use of, 273–4, 287–8, 349

Playfair, John, 51–2, 54
Pleistocene, 127
plucking, 137–8
Plutonism, 49–50
Pont, Timothy, 13, 14, 99, 143–4
Pope, Alexander: An Essay on Man, 48
Porter, A. W., 343–4
Porter, T. Cunningham, 502
Portland Press Herald, 462
Portnalong, 28, 29, 86
Portree, 66, 146, 151, 183, 197
    cafés/tearooms, 182, 183, 367, 436, 489
    Macpherson in, 153–4
    Old Cemetery, 20, 421
Poucher, W. A., 175–6
    The Magic of Skye, 81
Praeger, R. L., 347
Prebble, John: The Highland Clearances, 371
Presbyterianism, 484, 485, 535
Proclaimers, The: 'Letter from America', 373
Prothero, Miss Cecil, 461
Provost, James, 204–5
Pryor, Edgar, 425, 426
Ptolemy, 12

Quiraing, 40, 66, 483

Raasay, 24, 147, 151, 386, 527
Raeburn, Harold, 422
    Mountaineering Art, 270
Raeburn, Sir Henry, 54
RAF, 430, 431, 498–500
Raine, Kathleen, 335
Ramblers Associations, 426
Ramsay, William, 343
ravens, 220–1
Ravenna Cosmography, 12–13
Red Cuillin/Hills, 39, 68, 83, 100, 104, 374, 421;
    see also individual mountains
Redpoint, 24
Rees, Paul, 368–9
Regno di Scotia (map), 12–13
Reid, Tom, 497
Rhodes, Matthew, 410
Richmond, W. Kenneth: Climber's Testament, 23, 259

Robertson, Brian, 503, 505
Robertson, James, 369
Robertson, Rev. Archibald Eneas (A. E.), 395, 396–7
rock climbing, 186, 266, 267–9, 354
    climber appearance, 183–4
    clubs, see individual clubs
    early, 275, 308–9; see also fowlers/fowling
    and fear/courage, 446–8
    first ascents, 455
    grades, 354
    motives, 444, 445–6
    pivots from mountaineering in Cuillin, 353
    speed, 452
    vs mountaineering, 170–1, 340
    see also mountaineering
rock-cress, alpine (Arabis alpina), 222–3, 225–6, 389
Rockies, Canadian, 357, 471
Roman Empire, 112, 116
Romantics, the, 23, 25, 148, 263, 297, 443
Röntgen, Wilhelm, 343
Rothman, Benny, 427
Royal College of Surgeons, 428
Royal Engineers, 16
Royal Society of Edinburgh, 132, 134, 197
Roycroft, John, 497
Rubha an Dùnain, 110–11, 113, 116, 120, 122, 223, 332, 373
    Lochan na h-Àirde, 116, 120
Rubha Hunish, 40
Rucksack Club, 426, 427, 428
Ruda, Manuela, 377–8
Rum, 23, 38, 64, 111, 195, 215, 334
    Norse mountain naming, 105
    similarity to Skye Cuillin, 104–5
Russell, Robert, 497

Sabhal Mòr Ostaig (Gaelic College), 375, 485, 486
St John's Wort, 249
St Kilda, 193, 332, 423, 505
sandstone, 49, 52, 62, 66
Scandinavian Caledonides, 58–9

Scavaig, River, 458
Scotiae tabula (map), 13
Scotland: The Creation of Its Natural Landscape (McKirdy/Crofts), 45
Scotsman, The, 374, 421
Scott, Sir Walter, 32, 162, 263, 264
    The Lord of the Isles, 25, 160, 161, 218
Scottish Enlightenment, 47
Scottish Mountaineering Club (SMC), 291, 341–2, 393, 395, 422, 428, 469
    Black Cuillin Ridge: Scramblers' Guide, 463–4
    The Island of Skye, 14, 176–7, 326
    'Oh, My Big Hobnailers', 341
    Skye Scrambles, 326
Scottish Mountaineering Club Journal, 79, 174, 290, 295, 326, 350, 393, 394–5, 422, 446, 453, 458, 461, 472, 520
seafloor spreading, 60–2
Second World War, 20, 59, 314, 430, 474, 475, 486, 490, 491–2
Senchus Mór, 94
Serf, St, 114
Seymour, Lord John Webb, 54
Sgumain Cave, 237, 242
    author's bivouac, 238–41, 253–4, 255, 265–6
Sgùrr a' Bhàsteir, 404
Sgùrr a' Choire Bhig, 75, 77, 217, 221, 225, 258
Sgùrr a' Fionn Choire, 77, 398, 454
Sgùrr a' Ghreadaidh, 76, 85, 196, 242
    'Collie's Route', 353
    naming, 77
    Tribe (1870), 274–5
Sgùrr a' Mhadaidh, 76, 77, 196, 274, 341, 356, 454, 504
Sgùrr a' Sgumain, 285, 290
    see also Sgùrr Alasdair
Sgùrr Alasdair, 75, 77, 234, 362–3, 488
    Collie's ascents, 348, 352–3
    height measurements, 226, 348
    MacKenzie on, 470
    naming, 259–60, 284–5, 290, 346
    Nicolson/MacKenzie (FA 1873), 259, 276–8, 280–1, 283–4, 293
    Pilkington on, 258

summit, 258–9, 282, 283, 291
see also Great Stone Shoot
Sgùrr an Fheadain, 31, 339, 385
  Waterpipe Gully, 84, 355–6, 358, 360, 363
Sgùrr Biorach, 258–9, 285, 290
  see also Sgùrr Alasdair
Sgùrr Coire an Lochan: Collie/MacKenzie (FA 1896), 353
Sgùrr Dearg, 75, 85, 196, 222, 301, 303, 327, 329, 332, 395, 472, 527
  author's ascent, 306–8, 311–13
  cave, 242
  Gordon's night on, 243–4
  height measurement, 311
  naming, 77
  Nicolson/MacRae (FA 1873), 279–80, 304
  view from, 243–4, 280
  Window Buttress, 308, 353, 459
  see also Inaccessible Pinnacle
Sgùrr Dubh an Da Bheinn, 75, 77, 237, 449
  see also Thearlaich Dubh gap
Sgùrr Dubh Beag, 75
Sgùrr Dubh Mòr, 75, 290
  naming 286
  Nicolson (FA 1873), 286–90, 349
Sgùrr Hain, 9, 19–20, 25, 41, 100, 276, 317, 527, 537
Sgùrr Mhairi, 421
  see also Glamaig
Sgùrr MhicChoinnich, 75, 280, 297, 332, 461
  naming, 77, 331, 349
  prow (FA 1896), 450
  see also Collie's Ledge
Sgùrr na Banachdaich, 76, 196, 243, 306, 307, 381, 437, 454, 456, 461, 504
  naming, 77, 278–9
  Nicolson/MacRae (FA 1873), 277–8, 279
Sgùrr na h-Uamha, 77, 274, 457, 512, 520
Sgùrr na Stri, 9, 41, 84, 85, 100, 121, 212, 245, 275, 276, 359, 391, 403, 527
  view from, 303–4
  Weld (FA 1859), 260, 309–10
Sgùrr nan Eag, 75, 216, 217, 225, 226, 227–8, 238, 241, 280, 381, 505
  naming, 77, 227

Sgùrr nan Gillean, 76, 87, 172, 250, 258, 295, 331, 348, 471
  Abraham on, 511
  author's traverse, 512–16, 518–19, 520–1, 523–31
  Collie, 344–5, 350, 352, 353
  Collie/Crowley (winter), 344–5
  Dalton/MacKenzie (1897), 460
  Forbes/MacIntyre (FA 1836), 164–5, 175, 188, 260, 274
  height demoted, 264, 275
  Knight/MacPherson (Knight's Peak, FA 1873), 324
  Naismith (1880), 340–1
  naming, 77, 285, 376
  Nicolson (1865), 260–1, 511, 526
  Nicolson (winter, 1872), 264
  Nicolson ('Nicolson's Chimney', FA 1889), 290
  Ordnance Survey attempt (Colby), 191–2
  Pilkingtons, 316–17
  Pinnacle Ridge, 81, 511–12
  Stocker/Parker (Knight's Peak, 1886), 336, 471, 516
  summit, 525–6
  Thoms's death on, 421–2, 516, 521–3
  view from Sligachan, 80–1, 403
  west-ridge, 286, 290, 316, 398, 460, 516
  west-ridge, gendarme, 191, 192, 519–20
Sgùrr Sgumain, 229, 234, 236, 255, 280, 285
Stac na Nighinn, 461
Trap Staircase, 85
Sgùrr Thearlaich, 75, 197, 237, 280, 297, 332, 349
  naming, 77, 197, 297, 331
  see also Great Stone Shoot; TD Gap
Sgùrr Thormaid, 76, 77, 297, 339, 345, 461
Sgùrr Thuilm, 274, 276
Shadbolt, Leslie, 464
  Great Traverse (first, 1911), 452–5, 517
shark hunting, 333
Shkhelda, Caucasus, 494
Siccar Point, 51
Singleton, Kingsley, 408
Skiannach, Ellan, 14
Skye

accommodation, early, 16, 241–2, 379, 462–3
arts and crafts, 367–8
character, 9–10, 31, 73; *see also under* Cuillin
Christianity, 113–15, 116, 248
Clearances, 371–2, 373; *see also* Highland Clearances
folklore/mythology, 10, 94–5, 158, 248, 249–53, 254–5, 481–2; *see also* Ossianic poems
geographical form, 11, 12, 13–14, 38–40
geology/geological history, 43–7, 55–7, 62–8, 72–3, 82–4, 98; *see also* basalt; gabbro; Lewisian gneiss
immigrants/off-comers, 29, 367, 368–9, 376–7
'Isle of Mist', 12, 90, 160
landscape and people, 370, 483
in literature, 78–80
    Cockburn, 11–12
    early descriptions, 143–4
    Hawkes, 56–7
    Maclean (poem), 14
    Nicolson, 16, 262–3, 297, 379
    Scott (poem), 25, 161
    see also under Cuillin
maps, *see* maps
mountain rescue, *see* Skye Mountain Rescue
music, 483–4, 486, 533
naming, 12, 13–14
natives (*Sgiathanach*), 12, 259, 369–70
Norse rule, 12, 117–20
paganism, 115, 247–8, 249
place names, 16, 38, 103, 109, 118, 437
population, 373
prehistory, 109–11
pronunciation, 99
tourism, early, 11, 132, 148, 161–2, 163, 241–2, 385
tourism, modern, 368, 378–9, 382–5
weather/conditions, 12, 88–96, 144, 166, 184
see also Cuillin
Skye Adventure, 182, 185

Skye Bridge, 10, 37, 335, 484
Skye Mountain Rescue 383, 384, 407, 415, 431–2
    author's rescue (Coire Làgan), 415–20, 429–30, 513
    1963 rescue, 496–500, 502
Skye Trail, 17, 409
Siccar Point, 51
sills, 84
Sleat, 13, 38, 39, 44, 62, 252
Slesser, Malcolm, 14, 176–7, 237, 303, 326, 334, 401
Sligachan Bridge, 375
Sligachan Hotel, 21, 87, 171, 242, 260, 375, 461
    author's stay, 531–3
    Climber's Book, 347–8, 355
    Collie at, 469, 473–4, 475, 476–7, 489, 517
    Collie's Lounge, 299, 473, 531, 532–3
    Collie/MacKenzie statues, 172–3, 345, 536
    Collie's portrait, 299, 532
    Pilkingtons picture, 316
    view of Cuillin, 80–1, 403–4
    visitors' book, 315, 421, 521–2
    vs Glenbrittle, 468
Sligachan, River, 514
Slingsby, William, 332, 353
Smith, Alexander, 117, 246
    A Summer in Skye, 73–4, 482–3
Smith, John, 185, 410
Smythe, Frank, 173, 357, 456, 531
Snizort, River, 115
Soay, 110, 121, 223, 224, 277, 291, 333, 334, 335
Somervell, Theodore Howard 'T. H.', 456, 465
Sound of Sleat, 35, 55, 119, 301, 335
Southern Uplands, 57, 431
Special Protection Area, 222
Sròn na Cìche, 294, 311, 357, 414, 463, 472, 490, 492
    Mallory's Slab and Groove, 464–5
    naming, 358
    see also Cioch
Staffin
    dinosaur prints, 63, 66
    Kilt Rock, 66
Stainforth, Gordon: *The Cuillin: Great Mountain Ridge of Skye*, 95

Stead, Colin, 497, 498
Steeple, E. W., 452, 468, 469
Stephen, Leslie, 314
Stephen, Neil, 92
Stephens, Fred, 472
Steven, Campbell: *The Story of Scotland's Hills*, 473–4
Stocker, A. H.
    Inaccessible Pinnacle (west ridge, FA 1886), 323
    Knight's Peak (1886), 336, 471, 516
Stone Age
    Middle (Mesolithic), 109–10, 111
    New (Neolithic), 109, 111
    'stone doctors', 163–4
Stornoway, Lewis, 429, 432–3
Strabo, 120
Strand, The, (magazine), 344
Strathaird peninsula, 39, 44, 374
striations, glacial (striae), 140–1, 294
Strutt, E. L., 452
Stuart, James, 145
Suisnish, 371–2
Sutton, Sarah, 185
Swinburne, Algernon, 260
Swire, Otta: *Skye: The Island and Its Legends*, 12, 255, 481
Switzerland, 16, 130, 313, 314, 347
Sykes, Ian 'Spike': *In the Shadow of Ben Nevis*, 500
Sykes, Lynn, 62

tacksmen, 119–20
Taigh Ailean Hotel, Portnalong, 28–9, 78–9, 169, 182, 339, 378, 436–7
Talisker Bay, 437–8
    Johnson on, 438
    naming, 38, 437
Talisker Distillery, 29, 361, 385, 436–7
Tarbert, Lewis, 432, 433, 434
Tatham, H. T. W., 502
Taylor, Rob, 495
TD Gap (Sgùrr Thearlaich/Sgùrr Dubh), 237–8, 453, 456, 472, 496, 497, 504–5
    Collie/MacKenzie (first crossing, 1891), 449–50

tectonics, plate, 62
    see also seafloor spreading
Tennyson, Alfred, Lord, 7, 161
Terray, Lionel, 204
Thapa, Harkabir (Gurka), 356
Tharp, Marie, 62
Thearlaich-Dubh gap, *see* TD Gap
theology, 47, 54
Thom, John, 315
    in Alps/Lake District, 522
    death on Sgùrr nan Gillean, 421–2, 516, 521–3
Thulean plateau, 65
Tinney, Steve, 172
    'The Titanic' (song), 500
Tobar Ceann (water source), 248
Toravaig, 118
Torridon, 23, 102, 527
Torridonian sandstone, 62
Torrin, 40, 87
trap landscapes, 65–6
trees, sacred, 249
Trevethin, Arthur, 532
Tribe, William W., 274–5
Tripadvisor, 383–4, 385
Trotternish, 38, 39–40, 83, 118, 144, 249, 304, 363, 488
    geology/landslides, 66
Tryfan, North Wales, 203–5
    Adam and Eve, 203–4, 205
Tungdale, 372–3
Turner, J. M.W.: *Loch Coruisk*, 161, 220
tweed, 'famous Port-na-Skye', 86
Tyers, Thomas: *Biographical Sketch of Samuel Johnson*, 149–50
Tyndall, John, 314

Uig, 249, 435
Uist, 92, 146, 147
Ulster Cycle, 234
Uniformitarianism, 52, 130
University College, London, 342, 343
Upton, Brian: *Volcanoes and the Making of Scotland*, 67
Ussher, Archbishop James, 47

Valentine, Sheriff G. D., 325, 350, 472
Vaternish, 38
Veitch, John, 286
Vesuvius, Mount,132
Victoria, Queen, 158, 356
Vikings, 103, 117–20
Vine, Frederick, 61, 62
volcanism, 44, 53, 57, 63–7, 83–5, 126
    shield/strato, 67
Voltaire, 148, 158
Vulcanism, 49

Wainwright, Alfred, 401–2, 525
    Wainwright in Scotland, 402
Wakefield, A. W., 450
Wales, North, 27, 178, 428; see also Tryfan
Walker, Horace, 315, 323, 332
Walker, J. Hubert, 197, 247, 259, 515
    On Hills of the North, 72, 90, 208, 250,
    276, 296, 326
Walker, Lucy, 460
Wallace, George, 497
Walmsley, Gertrude, 458
Waternish
    Head, 13
    Peninsula, 39
Waterpipe Gully, see Sgùrr an Fheadain
weathering, 56, 68, 85–6, 125, 127
    basalt vs gabbro, 83, 85
    plucking, 137–8
    smooth vs rough, 83
Webb, John, 54
Weisshorn, 314, 347
Weld, Charles, 16, 241, 260, 313
    on Cuillin, 43, 219

on Inaccessible Pinnacle, 310, 311
Sgùrr na Stri (FA 1859), 260, 309–10
Two Months in the Highlands, 309–10
Wellings, Simon, 137, 138, 139
Welsh, Hugh, 473
Werner, Abraham Gottlob, 49, 53
Wernerians, 53
Wester Ross, 62, 527
Western Isles, The (boat), 499, 500
Westminster Abbey, 159
Whincup, Alexander, 422
Whymper, Edward, 289, 319
Wild, Finlay, 465
wild places, lure of, 443–4
Wilson, Graham, 456
Winkworth, Stephen, 345
Winthrop Young, Geoffrey
    on Collie, 424, 474, 477–8, 518
    on MacKenzie, 349–50
    roof climbing, 461
    traverse attempt, 451–2
witchcraft, 138, 144
Wood-Johnson, Ernest, 463
Wood, Bill, 459
Wood, Captain, 310–11
Woodridge, Tom, see Leppard, Tom
Woolf, Virginia, 314
Wordsworth, William: Lyrical Ballads, 158

Xenotopia, 14, 24
X-rays, 344

Yates, F., 456
Young, Andrew, 487
Youth Hostel Association, 426